THE DEATH MARCHES

THE DEATH MARCHES

THE FINAL PHASE OF NAZI GENOCIDE

DANIEL BLATMAN

Translated from the Hebrew by Chaya Galai

THE BELKNAP PRESS OF
HARVARD UNIVERSITY PRESS
Cambridge, Massachusetts, and London, England   2011

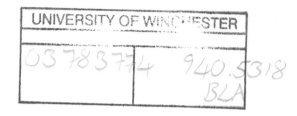
Copyright © 2011 by the President and Fellows of Harvard College
All rights reserved
Printed in the United States of America

Originally published as *Les Marches de la mort*
© *Librairie Arthème Fayard, 2009*

The translation of the epigraph from George Bataille on p. xi is by Robert Hurley.
Translation copyright © 1991 Robert Hurley. Reprinted by permission of City
Lights Books.

Library of Congress Cataloging-in-Publication Data

Blatman, Daniel, 1953–
    The death marches: the final phase of Nazi genocide / Daniel Blatman;
    translated from the Hebrew by Chaya Galai.
        p.   cm.
    "Originally published as Les Marches de la mort."
    Includes bibliographical references and index.
    ISBN 978-0-674-05049-5 (alk. paper)
    1. Death marches.   2. Holocaust, Jewish (1939–1945)
    3. World War, 1939–1945—Prisoners and prisons, German.
    4. World War, 1939–1945—Concentration camps.   I. Title.
D804.7.D43B528   2011
940.53'1846—dc22   2010015234

To Renée

Contents

Abbreviations

AEL	Arbeitserziehungslager	*Labor education camps*
BDM	Bund deutscher Mädel	*German Girls Alliance*
CO	Commanding officer	
DAF	Deutsche Arbeitsfront	*German Labor Front*
DDR	Deutsche Demokratische Republik *German Democratic Republic*	
DESt	Deutsche Erd und Steinwerke *German Earth and Stone Works Company*	
EMW	Elektromechanische Werke GmbH	
HASAG	Hugo Schneider Aktiengesellschaft-Metalwarenfabrik AG	
HQ	Headquarters	
HSSPF	Höherer SS- und Polizeiführer *Supreme SS and Police Commander*	
IKL	Inspektion der Konzentrationslager *Inspectorate of Concentration Camps*	
JDC	Joint Distribution Committee	
KdS	Kommander der Sicherheitspolizei und des SD *Commander, SIPO and SD*	
KPD	Kommunistische Partei Deutschlands *German Communist Party*	
Kripo	Kriminalpolizei	*Criminal Police*
LKA	Landeskriminalamt	*State Criminal Police*
NCO	Noncommissioned officer	
NSFO	Nationalsozialistische Führungoffiziers *Nazi political indoctrination officer*	

NSV	Nationalsozialistische Volkswohlfahrt *National Socialist People's Welfare*
OdF	Opfern des Faschismus *Victims of fascism*
Orpo	Ordnungspolizei *Order Police*
POW	Prisoner of war
RAD	Reichsarbeitsdienst *Reich Labor Service*
RAF	Royal Air Force
RSHA	Reichssicherheitshauptamt *Central Office for Security of the Reich*
RVK	Reichsverteidigungskommissar *Commissar for Defense of the Reich*
SA	Sturmabteilung *Storm Battalions*
SD	Sicherheitsdienst *Security Service*
SED	Sozialistische Einheitspartei Deutschlands *Socialist Unity Party of Germany*
SIPO	Sicherheitspolizei *Security Police*
SMT	Sowjetisches Militärtribunal *Soviet military tribunals*
SPD	Sozialdemokratische Partei Deutschlands *Social-Democratic Party*
SS	Schutzstaffel *Protective Squadrons*
Stasi	Staatssicherheisdienst *East German secret police*
UNRRA	United Nations Relief and Rehabilitation Administration
VuWHA	Verwaltungs und Wirtschafshauptampt *Administration and Business Main Office*
WVHA	SS-Wirtschafts- und Verwaltungshauptamt *Central Office for Economics and Administration*

I reached the limits of exhaustion, my strength abandoned me. The cold had the impossible, senselessly strained cruelty of a battle. Too far to return; would it be long before I fell? I would remain inert and the snow, which the wind was blowing, would cover me. I would soon die once fallen. Unless I arrived first at the castle . . . (Now I laughed at them, at those people of the castle: they would do what they pleased with me . . .) In the end I was weak, incredibly so, advancing more and more slowly, lifting my feet from the snow only with great difficulty, in the state of an animal that froths, fights to the end, but is reduced, in the darkness, to a miserable death.

George Bataille, *The Impossible*

Introduction

In January 1945, Nazi records showed that there were some 714,000 prisoners in the concentration camp network. It may quite safely be assumed that the actual number was much higher because even those who were responsible for and operated *l'univers concentrationnaire* (as David Rousset, a survivor of the Nazi camps, denoted it in his books by that name) were unable to gauge its vast dimensions with absolute accuracy. This figure does not take into account the unknown number of prisoners who were incarcerated in other sections of the Nazi oppression machine: forced laborers in private concerns, prisoners of war (POWs), and inmates of camps that were not part of the concentration camp system. The inhabitants of this world were dispersed in hundreds of camps, large and small, over the length and breadth of the disintegrating Nazi empire, from the Rhine in the west to the shores of the Vistula in the east, from the Baltic shore in the north to the Danube in the south. The inmates of the concentration camp world constituted a unique microcosm of the victims of Nazi terror. They included all the nationalities in Europe and some peoples who had strayed there from countries that were not even under Nazi control or that were fighting Germany. Among them were Uzbeks, Armenians, Georgians, Ukrainians, Russians, Poles, Lithuanians, and Letts. There were Serbs, Albanians, Greeks, Rumanians, Italians, and nationals of France, Spain, Belgium, Holland, and Norway, as well as Americans, Britons, Turks, and Arabs. There were Germans, Austrians, and Gypsies, and at that time there were also very many Jews. The camp population included Christians and Muslims, homosexuals, Jehovah's Witnesses, men and women, the old and the young, and even children. Each and every one of them had been persecuted and imprisoned on racial, political, religious, or social grounds. Four months later, when the clamor of war in Europe had died down and the Third Reich had departed from the stage of history, at least 250,000 of these prisoners were no longer among the living: many others did not survive for long after the liberation because of their desperate physical condition. This was a ghastly coup de grâce even by the criteria of Nazi genocide activities: more than 35 percent of the camp prisoners perished in Nazism's last murderous eruption during the death marches.

In the extensive literature on Nazi genocide, this last chapter of the Holocaust has been overlooked. The facts are known today only along general lines. In the past few decades, with the expansion of commemorative projects and the establishment of memorial centers in the Nazi concentration camp sites in Poland, Germany, and Austria, a number of studies have been devoted to the last journeys of prisoners from specific camps. Collections of testimonies, documents, maps, and photographs have appeared, and booklets, albums, and books have been published. These publications document and describe what happened along the routes of suffering and death. On the initiative of administrators of memorial sites and survivors of the death marches in the region, or local inhabitants who witnessed the horrors, monuments were erected after the war at sites where mass graves were uncovered. Today teachers, students, and visitors can follow the death march routes and learn what happened along them. But the explanation for this historical phenomenon—how hundreds of thousands of prisoners were force-marched for months at a time through the length and breadth of the collapsing Third Reich and how they were gradually liquidated, whether before departure, during the march, or after arriving at their destinations—has remained vague and incomplete, and is sometimes marred by apologetic and disturbing explanations.

By the time the war entered its last months, Nazi genocide activities were already an open and well-known fact. However, the press of the free world and the Hebrew-language press in Palestine published few references to the final stage, which began in summer–fall 1944 and lasted until Germany's capitulation in May 1945. In the last months of the war the British press paid scant attention to the concentration camps in general and to the evacuation and murder of prisoners in particular. If the evacuation of prisoners from camps in the East was reported, it was almost always in reference to Allied POWs, whose fate evoked much greater interest than did that of the concentration camp prisoners.[1]

The U.S. press also failed to cover the evacuations and the liquidation of prisoners along the retreat routes. In January 1945 it published only a handful of reports on the liberation of Auschwitz and made no mention whatsoever of the evacuation of inmates. It was only in April 1945, particularly after U.S. forces reached the camps and discovered the atrocities that had been perpetrated there, that more items began to appear on happenings in the camps before their liberation. The photographs of piles of bullet-torn, charred, and twisted corpses, and of the walking skeletons who had somehow survived, appeared in the U.S. press and reached the general public.[2] However, this information did not necessarily generate new insight into the period of the death marches, and the term "death march" itself did not appear in the newspapers. The horrors uncovered, sometimes depicted by liberated prisoners, contributed more to Western public opinion's understanding of the character and countenance of Nazism than to its recognition of the scope of the genocide perpetrated by the Nazis in the last few months of the war.

The few reports in the Western press seem to have reflected the impressions gained by Allied Army and intelligence bodies. The intelligence bodies collected information on what had occurred along the retreat routes from Poland westward. A considerable amount of data relating to the evacuation of Allied POWs from camps in the East in the face of the Soviet advance was dispatched to London and Washington in January–February 1945. The joint British-U.S. headquarters devoted a number of discussions to the possibility of achieving some kind of agreement with the Germans that would avert the evacuation of the POW camps and leave the prisoners in place until the Soviet Red Army arrived. However, according to most evaluations, there was no real chance of such an agreement because the Germans never made concessions to the Allies without demanding significant compensation. This was particularly true where POWs were involved, since they served as a protective cover against aerial bombings of evacuation convoys.[3] The Allied military leaders were also concerned about the plight of millions of German civilians, who were abandoning their homes, fleeing for their lives, and roaming the highways for fear of the Red Army. The Allied military commands, and especially the Americans, were perturbed by this problem because they estimated that they would be forced to tackle it in the near future, after Germany's surrender. But of the fate of hundreds of thousands of prisoners trudging along the roads and being murdered at the roadside, not a word was written. Nor do we know of any serious discussions of this problem.[4]

The Hebrew-language press in pre-state Palestine devoted little space to this chapter. In February 1945 several newspapers, most prominently *Hatzofeh*, the organ of the National Religious Party, reported the Nazi decision to exterminate the last of the Jews remaining in Polish camps before retreating. These items were based on information received from Germany and on rumors and fears in the West, and they related mainly to Auschwitz and Stutthof. As a rule, the term "death march" was not used, even on the rare occasions when the phenomenon itself was described. *Davar,* the daily of the Histadrut (General Federation of Labor), reported "death processions," and *Haaretz,* in its November 1944 report on the murder of Jews from Budapest deported to the Austrian-Hungarian border area to build fortifications against the Russian advance, wrote that the prisoners had "wandered on foot." Several weeks after the liberation of Auschwitz, *Haaretz* reported that camp inmates had been evacuated and transported by rail to Berlin before the Red Army arrived. In April 1945 several items were again devoted to German plans to liquidate the last of the Jews in the camps before the liberation. As is now well known, no such operative plan ever existed, although the mood in several camps was such that mass murder of prisoners was contemplated, and hence the wave of rumors arose. Concomitantly with these rumors, there were reports that concentration camp inmates had been stranded on trains and liberated by the Allied forces.[5]

Here we see one possible explanation of the circumstances that obscured the fact that the death march period was a unique chapter in the annals of Nazi genocide. The few reports in the Hebrew press in 1945 portrayed the death marches and the liberation of the camps as the last stage in the "Final Solution" of the Jewish question. Predictably, these fragmentary reports of killings or rumors of plans to liquidate camp inmates in the last few months of the war were associated directly with the previous flow of information about the extermination of millions of Jews in death camps and murder sites. No particular note was taken of the fact that, toward the end of the war, because of unique constraints and developments, the camp prisoners were a heterogeneous and complex group of victims, and the Jews were only one component of this group, albeit a large one. Even some years after the war, this fact was not given sufficient consideration and did not become the starting point for study of the period of the death marches.

Moreover, at the Nuremberg trials, references to the concluding months of the war and the evacuation of the camps did not promote understanding of the period of the death marches and the nature of the killings perpetrated at the time. As we now know, for a number of reasons the trial did not focus directly on the Nazi Final Solution or on the unparalleled nature and characteristics of Nazi genocide. If these issues were discussed, they were considered, as a rule, in the context of crimes against humanity, which lay at the core of the legal discourse at Nuremberg, and then only when the defendants were interrogated about persecution in Germany or the question of anti-Semitism.[6] The subject of the concentration camp evacuations was raised mainly during the trial of Ernst Kaltenbrunner, Reinhard Heydrich's successor as head of the Reichssicherheitshauptamt (Central Office for Security of the Reich—RSHA), and was then confined to the administrative aspects. The tribunal tried to ascertain who had been responsible for the directives and decisions that were implemented during the evacuation of the camps, and who devised the satanic schemes whereby prisoners in several concentration camps were to be liquidated by explosives, poison, or aerial bombing before the liberating armies arrived. Even in 1946, when the Allied occupying powers tried war criminals who had served in the concentration camps, the death marches were scarcely mentioned in the context of genocide. The Americans tried the criminals from Dachau, Flossenbürg, Mauthausen, Buchenwald, and Mittelbau-Dora; the British tried perpetrators from Bergen-Belsen and Ravensbrück; and the Soviets brought the Sachsenhausen murderers to trial. Whenever the evacuations were mentioned, the prosecution almost always tried to clarify who bore responsibility for creating the chaotic situation in the course of which thousands of inmates had perished. Naturally enough, the defendants, particularly if the camp commandant was among them, tried to shift responsibility to others.

Oswald Pohl, who headed the SS-Wirtschafts- und Verwaltungshauptamt (Central Office for Economics and Administration—WVHA—of the SS (Schutzstaffel—Protective Squadrons) for several years, was directly responsible for the concentration camp system during the liquidation stage. But even at Pohl's trial, focus was on the administrative responsibilities and the command hierarchy. Pohl disclaimed responsibility for the catastrophic evacuation conditions and for the murder of prisoners and tried to shelter behind his authority in such areas as economic management of the SS. He tried to shift blame for the camps in general and the evacuations in particular upward to Heinrich Himmler, chief of the German police and the SS, or downward to the head of the Inspectorate of Concentration Camps (Inspektion der Konzentrationslager—IKL), Richard Glücks.

It is doubtful whether the legal system that tried Nazi criminals in the postwar years could have dealt with the death marches from any angle other than clarification of responsibility for the orders to evacuate or preparations for that evacuation. All the legal discussions and the records they exposed were of inestimable importance for understanding the system and its functioning during the last months of the war, but they did not trace the fate of the prisoners after the evacuation of the camps. We must seek elsewhere for the answer to the question of what occurred in the convoys as they deteriorated into protracted death marches, the identities and motives of the murderers and the victims, and the reaction of Polish, German, or Austrian civilian populations to the advent of hundreds of thousands of evacuees. Needless to say, the same is true of the attempt to understand the reactions and coping methods of the prisoners themselves during the death marches.

On the other hand, in later trials and legal investigations conducted in the Deutsche Demokratische Republik (German Democratic Republic—DDR) or in Austria, the phenomenon of liquidations during the evacuations and death marches was discussed. Hundreds of inquiries regarding the murder and abuse of evacuated prisoners were conducted in the last four decades of the twentieth century. Testimonies were recorded, witnesses were interrogated, and reports on mass graves discovered along the evacuation routes were examined scrupulously. This abundant documentary material is important for several reasons. It enables us to look closely at local incidents of murder of prisoners or, in several cases, at incidents of mass slaughter during the death marches. It is of vital significance, particularly in the case of the nameless murderers, those who escorted columns of evacuated prisoners, but it is, by its very nature, of limited use for comprehension of a wider range of issues.

Without the testimony of the survivors, it is impossible to fathom a major part of what occurred during the death marches. It is interesting to note that in the first projects that collated testimonies—for example, those collected from camp survivors in Budapest in 1945 or the testimonies recorded by the American-Jewish psychiatrist David Boder in 1946 during his tour of Europe—the interviewees talked about this period. Over the years, tens of thousands of testimonies of Jewish and non-Jewish survivors relating to the evacuations and death marches have been added. This vast reserve of documentary material, collected by many sources and stored in archives all over the world, fills out the picture of the death marches from an angle that other sources do not cover.

In view of the abundance of documentary material it is even more surprising that the final stage of Nazi genocide has been merged into the overall extermination policy of previous years or into the state of chaos that prevailed in Germany in the last months of the war. However, several attempts have been made to deal with the phenomenon and the period in general separately and methodically.

From the mid-1960s, three striking historiographic projects attempted to examine the death marches from a comprehensive perspective. About a year after the war, the United Nations Relief and Rehabilitation Administration (UNRRA) Central Tracing Bureau published a three-part documentary compilation of great import, containing summaries, sketches of routes, and estimates of the number of victims murdered on some 110 death marches. While the information in these summaries is partial and the data are not necessarily precise, the very fact that information was collected by an international body indicates that the horrors of the camp evacuations were not unknown and had not been forgotten. On the basis of these facts, two Czech researchers published a book in the mid-1960s about the death marches, a pioneering work that stood almost alone for many years.[7] This book, however, is limited to statistical summaries and to description of the evacuation routes and does not tackle the larger questions of the period. An additional study was conducted in the late 1980s by the Polish researcher Zygmunt Zonik, who published a book on the evacuation of the camps. Zonik, himself a former inmate of a Nazi concentration camp, surveyed the legal examinations of the camp evacuations in Germany and Poland. He provided his readers with a valuable summary of the decision-making processes in the camp system on the eve of the evacuation and showed the various routes along which the convoys of prisoners marched westward and eastward.[8] But he tells us almost nothing about the murderers and the victims or about the social and political infrastructure within which massacres occurred in the final stages of the war.

In the past 15 years, research on the Nazi concentration camps has greatly expanded. The general monographs, quite a few of them written by researchers who had themselves been inmates of the camps they described and who sometimes included their personal narratives in the analysis, were succeeded by studies by a young generation of scholars, in particular Germans. Wide-ranging books about a series of concentration camps have gradually begun to appear, based on extensive archival documentation from diverse sources. But even in these important studies, the last chapter—the annals of the evacuations and the death marches—has been overshadowed by the other atrocities inflicted on the prisoners. Generally speaking, this period has been treated as an epilogue to the history of the camp rather than as a major part of its history, which is of course true from the chronological aspect. The exceptions are Auschwitz, Ravensbrück, and Mittelbau-Dora, each the subject of a monograph that focuses solely on the evacuation and liberation of the camp.[9] All these valuable studies view the death marches from a different, more or less wider angle, but do not extend their discussion beyond the specific camp. All, without exception, perpetuated an important methodological fact whose origins can be discerned in the postwar concentration camp trials: namely, discussion of the death marches and evacuations as part and parcel of the history of the Nazi concentration camps. In books and at scholarly gatherings in the past decade that have attempted to cast new, comprehensive light on the concentration camps and their place in the Nazi regime, the final chapter is always devoted to the evacuations.[10] The connection drawn between the death marches and the final closing of the camp gates behind the prisoners and camp guards hampered study of this historical phenomenon from a different angle: namely, its association, marked by both similarities and differences, with the Nazi genocide activity that began in 1941 and ended with Germany's surrender.

The scholar who made a pioneering attempt to conduct such an inquiry in the mid-1990s was Daniel Goldhagen. He devotes two chapters of his controversial book to the death marches,[11] and perceives them as a component in the range of murder techniques adopted by the Nazis in implementing their Final Solution policy. He claims that the Nazis employed death marches against the Jews as a liquidation technique from the beginning of the German occupation of Poland. Indeed, in more than one case the German occupation authorities transferred Jews from one place to another as part of their policy of mobilization and deportation of the population within the resettlement programs and demographic engineering project devised by Himmler and the SS command in 1939–1941. Hundreds of Jews perished in December 1939 in one of the deadliest incidents, when they were deported from Chełm and Hrubieszów to territories under Soviet control.

However, it is precisely this horrific event that highlights the difference between the deportations of the early war years and the period of the death marches toward the end of the war. On December 1, 1939, some 2,000 Jewish men were ordered to assemble in the central square of Chełm, and that afternoon a group of SS men began to march them toward the Soviet border. The wives of the deportees, who wanted to join them, were driven back by force by the Germans. The death march lasted all day and that night, and toward morning the column reached Hrubieszów. According to the testimony of survivors, between 200 and 800 Jews were murdered in the course of the march. Another 2,000 Jewish men assembled in Hrusieszów on December 2, on orders from the Germans, and joined the group from Chełm. The death march continued for another two days, and on December 4 the survivors were forced to cross the River Bug while Soviet soldiers on the far bank fired at them to prevent them from entering Soviet-controlled territory. The Jews who crossed the river were rounded up by the Russian soldiers, who then drove them back forcibly to the German-ruled area.[12]

The death march of the Jews of Chełm and Hrubieszów was more closely connected to the period of stabilization of the border between the Soviet and German-controlled areas, and cannot, in any respect, be linked to the murder of Jews in the following years. Local Germans feared that a wide-scale Jewish presence in the towns and villages in the Lublin area of the German-Soviet border posed a threat because of their sympathy and support for the Red Army, as often occurred when Soviet troops occupied towns in eastern Poland. The fact that only the men were deported and the women were left behind confirms the assumption that this move was not part of a liquidation scheme but was rather the savage application of a political and military decision. But since the objects were Jews, there was no special reason to refrain from killing those who tried to escape or collapsed by the wayside. As we know, tens of thousands of Jews were deported to the Generalgouvernement (the general government of occupied Poland) in the early years of the occupation of Poland from territories that had been annexed to the Reich, as well as from dozens of towns and villages in other parts of Poland. These deportations were carried out in a brutal and an inflexible manner, and there were countless cases of abuse and of looting of the deportees' property. Although there were also incidents of murder, no planned mass slaughter took place.[13] Any interpretation of this period as the prologue to the official extermination policy, or as a series of impulsive and spontaneous acts on the part of certain Germans in remote locations who were yearning to liquidate Jews, is somewhat far-fetched.

As a second period, Goldhagen proposes 1941–1944, the period when the extermination of the Jews was proceeding apace. But he refrains from citing examples and evidence of liquidation of Jews during the years of the Final Solution by what he denotes "the institution of the march." This period was characterized by the murder of other, non-Jewish victims by the technique of force-marching them hundreds of miles and murdering those who collapsed or were unable to endure the hardships of the march. First and foremost among these were hundreds of thousands of Soviet POWs who were taken captive by the Germans in late 1941 and early 1942.[14] Jews were not generally marched to their deaths in the peak years of the Final Solution; they were murdered close to home or were transported by train from the stations in their hometowns or ghettos to murder sites chosen for the purpose.

The last few months of the war, when the Third Reich was in the throes of its final decline, marked the third period of exploitation of this extermination technique. It was no longer possible to employ the previous techniques, mostly because the constraints of the war mandated the need to withdraw from the concentration and death camps. Killing in the course of evacuation was now the sole extermination technique. The Germans no longer had full control of the timetable of murder, since it was the advance of the victorious forces rather than Nazi initiative that dictated events. There were three subperiods within this period: the first began in summer 1944 with the commencement of the retreats and evacuations from eastern Poland and the Baltic states; the second was launched in January 1945 with the evacuation of the large camps in Poland; and the third began in March 1945 with the onset of the evacuations carried out on German soil and continued until the final surrender. This is indeed the accepted classification among researchers with regard to the stages in camp evacuation.[15]

However, the history of the concentration camps does not necessarily coincide with that of the Final Solution. The historiography of the camp evacuations beginning in summer 1944 does not enlighten us as to the murderous motivation of the killers and the bureaucratic apparatus that activated the extermination. It only serves to elucidate the last chapter in the annals of the concentration camps in Nazi Germany, which operated from 1933 to the evacuations in 1945. The death marches cannot be explained as the ultimate act of ideologically motivated murder within the framework of the Final Solution, on the basis of the evacuation stages that were determined mainly by administrative, economic, and above all military constraints.

The main problem, however, which calls for precise analysis and evaluation of the final stages of Nazi genocide, is not related to periodization. It stems to a considerable degree from the fact that the victims were no longer divided along such clear lines as before. The victims of the final stage were no longer solely Jews and, in many cases, not even mainly Jews—hence the difficulty in positioning this period within the framework of the Final Solution. Any approach that views this period as a stage in the extermination process not only creates a flawed historical explanation, but also undermines our perception of the Jews as a large and unique group of victims in the final stages of the extermination because it downplays the fact that the circle of victims had now expanded to include other nationalities. Also impeded is our ability to probe the motivation and circumstances of the liquidation, the various groups of murderers, the political circumstances in which it occurred, and the social infrastructure that supported it. Any attempt to explain the death marches solely from the perspective of the various stages of the Final Solution inevitably leads to selective choice of the events to be examined.

The present book, therefore, views the death marches not only as part of the history of the concentration camps or as the concluding chapter of the Final Solution, but mainly as the last period of Nazi genocidal activity. It takes as wide a view as possible of the period. Consequently, the treatment of the death marches is not confined to the marches of concentration camp inmates but it also examines several death marches of other prisoners. However, the central role of concentration camp inmates cannot be ignored because, in the final analysis, they accounted for the majority of the victims. Hence there is a need to understand the attitude of the Nazi terror machine toward the concentration camp prisoners in the last stages of the war, as well as the motives both of those who hindered the murderous activity and those who promoted it.

The term "death march" itself is devoid of political or ideological meaning. The liquidation of a defenseless population during their transfer from place to place in what is defined as a death march was not, of course, invented by the Nazis. Two striking cases of genocide in the early twentieth century—that of the Herero tribe in Namibia by the German Imperial Army in 1904 and that of the Armenians by the Turks during World War I—were perpetrated by this method. Murders during evacuations and deportations also occurred, as noted, during the first years of World War II, and the victims were Jews, Soviet POWs, or other population groups. But in all the periods of Nazi genocide before summer–fall 1944, the death march was only one of many terror or liquidation techniques employed by the murderers, and usually not even the most common one.

Unlike previous studies, this book analyzes the death marches of the end of the war not as a murder technique that served a political or local security need, but as a separate chapter in the annals of Nazi genocide activity, with its own unique characteristics. My basic premise is that, in this period, almost all and certainly most of the previous characteristics of Nazi genocide underwent change: namely, the political and social infrastructure within which it occurred, the identity of the killers, the supervisory apparatus and bureaucratic administration, the liquidation techniques, the choice of liquidation sites, and, above all, the ideological categorization of the victims.

I have not attempted to provide a detailed description of all the death marches in areas under Nazi control from summer–fall 1944 to the end of the war. This task would be beyond the capacities of an individual researcher, for there were thousands of routes, some stretching across Europe for thousands of miles and others only several dozen miles long. There is almost no extant information in many cases. The means of evacuation were varied: some prisoners were transported by rail, by truck, or on horse-drawn wagons, others proceeded on foot, and most marches were combinations of two or three methods. The motorized or pedestrian convoys joined up with other evacuation marches that set out from nearby camps, split up, dispersed, and met up again with others, all this in accordance with the conditions that prevailed along the routes. Any attempt to impose cartographic order on the multi-headed Hydra was condemned to failure. I have chosen to present as wide and representative a range of death marches and evacuation routes as possible, wherever a reasonable amount of documentation was available. Together, they provide an accurate and a representative picture, as I see it, of this cruel and complex historical period.

To the same extent, the attempt to arrive at the precise number of victims of this concluding chapter of Nazi genocide cannot end in well-founded conclusions. Generally speaking, any attempt to determine the number of those who perished or were murdered in the concentration camp network, even if we exclude those liquidated in the special extermination camps and installations of the Final Solution, must be considered problematic. Cautious estimates set the number of prisoners who died in the camps between

1933 and 1945 at 1.1 million out of the 1.65 million who passed through their gates—in other words some 66 percent.[16] For the period under discussion in this study, the data are even more indeterminate. Record keeping of the entry of prisoners into the system, their transfer from camp to camp, and lists of deaths and executions was generally lax in the last year of the war. It is even more difficult to estimate how many victims were murdered during the evacuations. Any such venture leads to an impasse or confronts us with implausible discrepancies. Even in cases where the number of prisoners who set out from an evacuated camp was recorded, by the time the convoy reached the destination camp, its composition had changed completely. Many prisoners were murdered or died during the evacuation, while others were added when two or three columns were combined. The figures noted in the files of the destination camps in spring 1945 were far from accurate, and the vast numbers of prisoners who arrived from the East, together with the prevailing disorder, precluded any possibility of accurate recording.

Data on the number of prisoners liquidated along the way was obtained from two sources. The first was the testimony of the survivors of the death march or the estimates provided by those who accompanied the convoy. The second source was the mass graves and sites of murder uncovered by the local population or by commissions of inquiry established after the war for purposes of identifying the victims buried in those graves. The figures cited by either the survivors or the murderers cannot of course serve as the basis for accurate numerical evaluation, and countless burial sites will remain unmarked forever. It is obvious that combining data on several death marches will affect calculations of the percentage of victims, which can range from 30 to 50 percent of the total number of prisoners.[17] The same is true even with regard to some of the marches examined in this book, where the existing data can be considered reliable. On several death marches the proportion of prisoners murdered was as high as 80 percent, on others 20 percent or less. The total number of victims naturally varies from case to case. With all the necessary caution, I found no evidence to justify a different evaluation from that which estimates the number of victims of the death march of the concentration camp prisoners at 35 percent, namely, approximately 250,000 out of the total number of prisoners in the system at the beginning of 1945. If one also takes into account the victims of the last massacre of camp inmates or prisoners in other coercive frameworks, the number will of course be higher, but then the measured target population must be altered. In any event, this finding only serves to highlight the unparalleled murderous brutality of the last period of Nazi genocide: at least one quarter of the victims of the concentration camp system, which operated for some 12 years, perished in the last five months of its existence.

That being said, it is clear that the precise number of victims of this final stage will remain unknown.

This study is composed of two parts. The first is devoted to the political and systemic history of the period of the death marches. Its six chapters examine how the concentration camp system, detention facilities, and labor camps reached the evacuation stage and how the evacuations turned into lethal death marches. The chapters deal with events in chronological order, from summer 1944 to spring 1945, with emphasis on the military, social, and political circumstances of the period. Special attention is devoted to the central theme of this entire study—the identity of the murderers, characterization of the victims by their killers, and the reaction of the prisoners to the events.

The second part studies the death marches from the angle accepted for more than two decades in historical research in general, including the study of Nazi genocide, namely, social history viewed "from below." At the heart of these four chapters is a study of German society at a time when most of the last stage of Nazi genocide was being perpetrated on the doorsteps of the local population. This part deals extensively with several massacres of prisoners that occurred in civilian settlements in Germany in spring 1945, and in particular the central, dramatic incident that was, to a large degree, representative of the entire phenomenon: the massacre in Gardelegen in April 1945. The aim of this microhistorical examination is to comprehend what happened in the world of ordinary citizens, their insights into the period in which they lived, their attitudes and reactions to what was being perpetrated before their eyes. The heart of the discussion is examination of the period and the outpouring of murderous brutality that characterized it from the viewpoint of those who witnessed it and occasionally joined in. However, this particular event in Gardelegen was far from being over in 1945. For many years, this small town in north-central Germany, which was part of the DDR until 1990, continued to wrestle with the issue of memory and commemoration and the question of how to confront its painful history.

As we know, the history of everyday life *(Alltagsgeschichte)* generally requires long-term scrutiny of the society under investigation. This is not the case here, since the period of the death marches was brief and replete with crises. Questions have often been raised as to the patterns of life and survival of German society under the Nazi dictatorship. Did the majority continue to live a normative and normal life at the time? The period under study in this book was marked by the close encounter of German society with the genocide instigated by the Nazi regime. This fact leads us to ask: Is it possible to identify normalcy and normative patterns in German society during the collapse of the Third Reich?

The assumption that the Nazi dictatorship did not utterly destroy the patterns of life, the social interactions, and the community and family ties of a society that continued to live its everyday life is controverted by the disintegration of that society toward the end of the war. The death marches occurred at a time when a dictatorship, which for years had pursued a violent and murderous policy of persecution and extermination on racial, political, and social grounds toward enemies both at home and abroad, was reaching its end. Examination of the modes of reaction and coping of the establishment, both the individual and the social system that were involved, in those final months of the genocide activity, in countless circles of life and involvement patterns, is the core of this book.

PART ONE

The System Disintegrates

CHAPTER ONE

The Concentration Camps, 1933–1944

In 1945 Eugen Kogon, a former prisoner at Buchenwald, published a pioneering study that attempted to tackle the world of the concentration camps, which he called *Der SS-Staat* (The SS-State). As early as the first months after the liberation, Kogon defined the centrality of the concentration camp world in the annals of the Third Reich and its underlying aims:

> Their main purpose was the elimination of every trace of potential opposition to Nazi rule. Segregation, debasement, humiliation, extermination—those were the effective forms of the terror. Any concept of justice was put aside. Better to put ten innocents behind barbed wire than to let one real enemy escape.[1]

When the Allied forces reached the Nazi concentration camps at the end of World War II, and information and photographs were released from Dachau, Bergen-Belsen, and Buchenwald, Western public opinion was stunned. Information on the appalling situation in the camps had already been circulated during the war, and the liberation of Majdanek and Auschwitz by the Red Army in 1944 and 1945 had revealed to the West what had been perpetrated there. Yet, the depth and extent of the atrocities committed in the final months of the war, as exposed in the liberated camps in Germany, had previously been unknown. The piles of corpses, the skeleton-thin survivors, the sick and the dying, the stinking, densely crammed barracks—all these were beyond imagination. The scenes photographed by American and British soldiers and by the war correspondents who accompanied the troops in Germany appeared in the newspapers and in cinema newsreels. The information was also displayed intensively to the German civilian population as part of the policy of "showing them what happened," which was adopted by the American and British occupation authorities.[2]

The perception of the concentration camp system as the symbol of criminality and as the ultimate representation of the iniquitous nature of the Nazi regime—as confirmed by the shocking visualization of atrocity and death—helps explain why, for a considerable period, the camps were not a focus of historical research. This avoidance also stemmed from the fact that the descriptions of the appalling acts committed within them raised the question: what, apart from the totality of the abomination, was there to investigate? Postwar historians, particularly in Germany, showed no interest in this subject. Suppression, forced labor, and death in concentration camps were extraneous to what was considered to be of scholarly value, according to accepted historical tradition. Hence, for many years, the history of the concentration camps was written not by professional historians but by former prisoners. While still imprisoned in the camps, these prisoners felt that their story must be told to the world and that it was incumbent on them to tell it. The first reports and memoirs of survivors appeared during the war and immediately afterward. Several of them evoked widespread public interest; others sank into oblivion.[3] Some of them contain, in addition to a personal narrative, a partial theoretical analysis of the concentration camp world from the viewpoint of the ideology, bureaucracy, economics, and politics of the Third Reich. This is true of Eugen Kogon's book about his lengthy imprisonment in Buchenwald, and of a study of a similar nature published in 1946 by Benedikt Kautsky, who was also a Buchenwald inmate.[4] Kogon and Kautsky were prominent members of the underground in Buchenwald, and the issue of resistance naturally played an important part in their books. Another example is the book by Erwin Gostner, a former inmate of Dachau, Mauthausen, and Gusen, which also appeared a year after the war and tells the story of his experiences in those camps. He too combines his personal story with a wider description of the camp and its functioning.[5] In a book about his two years in Buchenwald and Neuengamme, David Rousset, a Trotskyite activist in France before the war, tried to understand the characteristics of the society that existed there and their relevance to the totalitarian regime.[6] As the years went by, thousands of volumes, anthologies, and memorial albums written by camp survivors were published in a number of languages.

In Israel the first book of this type, containing the testimony of Jewish prisoners from Auschwitz, appeared in 1957. It gave a narrative description of the lives of the survivors, most of them members of the Jewish resistance movement in the camp. The personal narratives of this book are blended with preliminary historical analysis of the place of the Jews in the Nazis' main concentration and death camps. The main author and editor of this volume was Israel Gutman, later a doyen of Holocaust historiography, who was active in the Jewish resistance in the camp.[7] Despite the specific angle of this book, which depicts the unique fate of Jewish prisoners, its similarity to works by non-Jewish prisoners is greater than its dissimilarity. Like all such works that appeared in the first postwar decade, it focused mainly on direct revelation of the inner world of the camp prisoners. It discussed the prison society, and the internal hierarchy, the forced labor, the starvation, the struggle for survival and for preservation of humanity, and it dwelled on the constant presence of death.

One of the first attempts to formulate a theory of the concentration camp world from the starting point of the attributes of the terror practiced by the totalitarian regime was made by Hannah Arendt several years after the war. Since research on the subject had scarcely begun, she based her study mainly on the writings of survivors such as Rousset and Kogon. Arendt perceives the concentration camp as one of the most consistent institutions of totalitarian rule and identifies a number of characteristics of the camp system: isolation, negation of identity, detachment from the past, absence of the profit component and of rational economic management of the labor system, eradication of the juridical person, and murder of the moral person. However, Arendt asserts, the survivors' descriptions of a chaotic system of death and terror marked by appalling inefficiency should not mislead us. While the overt unavailing cynicism of the camps is plainly evident, in practice they, more than any other state institution, constituted a highly logical mechanism for perpetuating the power of the regime.[8]

Intensive historical research on the camps did not begin until the mid-1980s. Ulrich Herbert, Karin Orth, and Christoph Dieckmann believe that this long delay occurred because of the disturbing discrepancy between the constant presence of the concentration camps in political and public discourse in Germany and the actual availability of information about them. The prisoners' generation was dying out, and those members of the young generation who undertook to keep memories alive concentrated on investigating and examining the impact of the Nazi dictatorship on the places where they lived. The shift to local and social research on the Nazi period and the move away from analysis of its general political aspects led a new generation of researchers to study the subcamps of the larger concentration camps, to which almost no attention had previously been devoted. This research gave a first glimpse of the central role of the concentration camps in the armaments industry, the links between senior economic concerns and the SS, and the vital importance of slave labor for the economy of Nazi Germany.[9]

In 1993 the sociologist Wolfgang Sofsky published his book *Die Ordnung des Terrors: Das Konzentrationslager.*[10] For the first time a scholar was offering an explanation for the construction and operation of a system whose purpose was murderous oppression, based on and functioning by means of terror, which Sofsky calls *absolute Macht* (absolute power). The objective of his study, he wrote, was to create a "thick description" *(dichte Beschreibung)* of the brutal world of the concentration camps. In methodological terms, he states, "thick descriptions" are diagnoses of meaning. They do not provide lists of facts but rather interpretations of activities and situations—not reports but explanations of structures and processes.[11]

According to Sofsky, the concentration camps created a form of power and authority whose social components differed in essence from any of the accepted forms of power. Absolute power in no way resembles the power that is wielded by a tyrannical emissary, a dictatorial regime, or any other entity that employs political aggression. It is a force that extends its authority over its victims only after they are no longer capable of resisting, and its aim is not to break resistance. It is a force whose violence is free of restraints and limitations, and it is reinforced by the organizational system that operates it. Absolute power, says Sofsky, begins at the point where the terror of tyranny or dictatorship ends. Its objective is not to enforce total obedience or blind toeing of the line but to create a universe of total uncertainty.[12] Starting from this premise and relying widely on the testimony and memories of prisoners, Sofsky describes and elucidates a series of situations from life in the concentration camps: deportation, arrival at the camp, feeding and starvation, labor, torture, punishment, the activities of prisoner functionaries, the conduct of the guards, and so on. What emerges from Sofsky's book is a harsh, disquieting, and extraordinarily profound description. He does not deal with a specific camp but rather with the history of the concentration camps within a timeless and placeless sociological structure,[13] at the core of which lies the existential experience of those housed in them, prisoners and staff. Yet, despite the fact that the basic components of this system, which Sofsky diagnosed so perceptively, were present throughout its existence, one cannot survey the history of the camp system as a totality. It underwent changes over the years until the final stage of its existence during the evacuations and death marches.

The Years of Formation and Consolidation, 1933–1939

In the first stage of the Nazi regime, approximately up to summer 1934, various detention camps and centers sprang up throughout Germany.[14] These 90 or so camps and installations,[15] where political opponents of the regime were detained, were organized by the SA (Sturmabteilung—Storm Battalions), the local police, or the SS (Schutzstaffel—Protective Squadrons). By summer

1933 more than 26,000 individuals had been imprisoned in these detention centers, which were located in remote chateaus, abandoned army camps, or prisons.[16] This initial stage of Nazi rule was marked by an uncompromising struggle against all those perceived as political foes, and tens of thousands were incarcerated in those early camps. This phenomenon was by no means unique to the Nazi regime; it has characterized the early consolidation stages of various totalitarian regimes, such as the Soviet Union, especially when the Stalinist dictatorship began to gain momentum in the late 1920s. But in contrast to the Nazi camps, in the Soviet Union the establishment of the vast prison network was accompanied by economic calculations.[17] The Nazi camps, on the other hand, served to promote the racial state to which the new order aspired. From the outset, Jews who were imprisoned in these camps were the target of particularly violent and brutal treatment.[18]

The man who was given full authority by Heinrich Himmler to build and shape this terror system was Theodor Eicke. It was Eicke who established the concentration camp network and recruited and trained the manpower that managed and operated it. To a large extent, the Nazi concentration camp, and in particular its ideology, was his creation.

Eicke was born in 1892 in Alsace into a working-class family. He was forced to leave school at an early age because of his poor scholastic record. He was only 17 when he joined the army in 1913, fought in World War I, and won two medals for bravery. Like many extreme right activists in Weimar Germany, he could not find a niche for himself after the war. The trauma of defeat and his sense of humiliation, which persisted throughout the 1920s, impelled him to join the Nazi Party in 1928. Two years later he joined the SS, and that organization became his path to a professional career and the place where he could give vent to his political views. Himmler, who regarded him as one of his closest associates and trusted him implicitly, appointed him commander of an SS unit in 1931. In this position, two of Eicke's character traits came into play: independence and unwillingness to accept outside authority. He often clashed with party functionaries because of his refusal to accept their authority over the SS, which he considered an elite unit, exempt from following the procedures of the parliamentary regime under which the party operated. The SS, he believed, owed loyalty solely to the revolutionary concept, to the Führer, and to the supreme commander of the organization, Himmler.[19]

In late June 1933 Himmler appointed Eicke commandant of the first concentration camp he set up, located at Dachau in Bavaria. Only three months earlier the first group of 96 prisoners had been brought to an abandoned factory structure close to this small Bavarian town.[20] This camp was one of the series of concentration camps that sprouted in the period of savage political terror after the Nazi rise to power. The guards assigned there were members of the SS, mainly from Munich. They were familiar with the use of terror and violence toward political enemies, and regarded as such the prisoners placed in their charge in the new detention center. The first camp commandant, Hilmar Wäckerle, failed to prevent the growing number of deaths resulting from the guards' abuse and brutality. The stories of what occurred in Dachau leaked out and excited a wave of public protest, mainly in Bavaria. Himmler could not permit himself scandals of this type in those first months of the Nazi Party's supreme effort to stabilize its rule. Eicke's mission was to impose order in the new camp and to stabilize it.[21]

Eicke was not only a veteran Nazi and a fervent believer. He was also an excellent administrator and a man of action, and the bureaucratic aspects of his efficient management, for which he was careful to obtain constant official authorization, were reflected in a document he sent Himmler on October 1, 1933. In this document he discussed the pretexts for punishment of Dachau prisoners, the forms this punishment took, and the behavioral code for the camp personnel. Punctiliously, he listed the types of felonies to be punished by imprisonment and the number of days of detention for each type. He detailed the rules of conduct binding prisoners and the punishments to be inflicted for infringement. In a number of cases the punishment was to be augmented by 25 lashes. The rules also covered felonies for which the punishment was death. Eicke's document also granted the camp commandants wide scope for action, based on strict adherence to clearly defined rules rather than arbitrary instructions as before, all this in order to deal with those classified as enemies of the state *(Staatsfeinde)*. The uniform model Eicke devised and developed in Dachau became the model for future concentration camps. The provisional detention facilities, run arbitrarily by SA thugs, were replaced gradually by Eicke's model: an organized system, run according to explicit rules. These rules included directives as to the work, rest, and meal schedules for the guards, the composition of the meals, the rigid daily schedule of the prisoners, as well as instructions on the structure of the camp and its functional internal division and the number of bunks in each wooden hut.[22]

The personnel recruited into the camp system underwent a selection process, were accorded special attention by Eicke, and were regarded from the outset as an elite unit. They saw themselves not just as jailers and prison guards but, above all, as soldiers in the service of the nation and the race. As far as they were concerned, the camp was a vitally important security installation rather than a prison. The prisoners were not simply criminals to them but political and ideological enemies. Rudolf Höß, later commandant of Auschwitz, who was assigned to Dachau in 1934 for his first training period, described in his memoirs the new meaning his life took on when he was able, once again, to become a soldier in the service of the nation. The fact that the enemy he faced differed from the adversary he had encountered on the World War I battlefields was of merely marginal significance to him. Like Höß, almost all those who later made up the senior command and administration of the Waffen-SS (the military force of the SS) and the concentration camp system, received their training in Eicke's Dachau.[23]

Das Modell Dachau, which Eicke designed, was adopted by Himmler in summer 1934 when it was decided to establish the Inspektion der Konzentrationslager—(Inspectorate of Concentration Camps—IKL) and to place Eicke at its head.[24] The IKL was a typical German bureaucratic system, characterized by modern rational modes of operation, which took into consideration operative outlay, expenditure per prisoner, the cost of building maintenance, guarding, and the like. It was a typical example of a modern bureaucratic network operating an extensive terror network in the service of the political needs of a ruling ideology.[25] The IKL was a small administrative unit[26] and was directly answerable to Himmler. Its modus operandi was later adapted to facilitate its natural integration into the economic and administration system of the SS.

Eicke and the IKL apparatus organized and built up the concentration camp system between 1934 and 1936. However, the IKL was not established solely in order to formulate uniform and lucid standards of functioning for political detention centers directed against enemies of the state. Its main purpose was to remove handling of these prisoners from the traditional legal frameworks that dealt with felons, namely, the local police and the law courts, and to entrust it to the SS. By 1936 the traditional supervisory and judicial authorities wielded almost no influence over what occurred in the concentration camps. In any event, at that time the number of prisoners was still relatively low; in 1934/1935 it was less than 4,000.[27]

The year 1936 was the turning point in the development of the concentration camp system. New camps were set up, new objectives were added, and the composition of the prison population was changed. The regime had succeeded, in a relatively short time, in almost completely eradicating the activity of its opponents, so that now the conditions were ripe for waging a struggle against those elements in society that were undermining the healthy foundations of the nation. Classification of enemies of the state and society was problematic because the Nazis had never formulated a comprehensive definition of the term "political enemy" or criteria distinguishing such enemies from racially inferior and antisocial elements or habitual criminals. Jews, for example, were first and foremost a racial threat, but they were also perceived as dangerous political enemies because of their strong influence within the communist movement and on the political life of the Western democracies. Political prisoners, especially communists, were described in party propaganda as criminals threatening the integrity of the community, the harmony of the family cell, and the immunity of the social organism. Habitual criminals were often treated as a racial threat because of the danger that their offspring would follow in their footsteps. They were also perceived as a political threat who, for reasons of expediency and out of criminal calculations, participated in violent revolutionary action. The common denominator of all these groups was their classification as "community aliens" and a threat to the social order.[28]

Various government bodies in Germany, notably the ministries of Justice, Economics, and the Interior as well as the security authorities, were involved in the administration of the camps and the prison population through the internal camp structure. Five departments (Abteilungen) dealt with matters such as SS personnel, prisoners, guard personnel, labor, and internal administration. Of particular importance was the Political Department (Abteilung II— Politische Abteilung), which was, in effect, a branch of the Gestapo in the camps. It supervised the prisoners who arrived at the camp, recorded the circumstances that had brought them there, conducted inquiries against prisoners when requested by the Gestapo or the Kripo (Kriminalpolizei—Criminal Police), and supervised executions in the camps. This was an outside unit that was not, in practice, under the camp command's jurisdiction, but was (from 1939) subordinate to the RSHA.[29]

The criminal code of the Third Reich was extended between 1936 and 1939 through the introduction of new definitions and criteria, which turned various groups of social misfits into enemies who were to be totally removed from society. To the political criminals, whose only crime was their ideological resistance to Nazism, who had been persecuted almost from the day that Hitler came to power, were now added new categories. Jehovah's Witnesses were classified in 1933 as "enemies of the state" because of their nonconformist religious conduct and their refusal to adopt the new customs of the state—the Nazi salute and the oath of allegiance to the Führer—which ran counter to their own religious oaths. Also included in the new legal definition of dangerous criminals, namely, habitual offenders and irredeemable criminal personalities, were sex offenders and homosexuals.[30]

In 1936 all these newly defined criminals, who were convicted in accordance with the amended German legal code, were sent to concentration camps. Most of them never reached the camps. Some 120,000 of them were placed in solitary confinement in punitive installations within prisons that, as a rule, were guarded and operated by the SA or the local police. Only about 4,700 of the new offenders reached concentration camps. The prison installations where they were held were not necessarily better than the concentration camps, and the conditions were rigorous. Even at the end of 1938, when the concentration camp system had grown and expanded, it still housed only about 13,000 inmates convicted of various social crimes, as against 101,000 prisoners in other installations. The mass transfer from prison installations to concentration camps would not occur until the first half of 1943.[31]

The transfer of these prisoners to the concentration camp system, albeit in limited numbers in the mid-1930s, was of great import to the SS. Himmler, supported by Hitler, made every effort to increase the number of new criminals in this category being sent to concentration camps,[32] with two objectives in mind. The first was ideological: to set them apart from the healthy section of the German people. This objective was to be accomplished in order to boost the nation's racial vigor through sociobiological selection, which would separate the wheat from the chaff. Only concentration camps could fulfill this task, Himmler believed. The second objective was economic.

In summer 1936 a new concentration camp, Sachsenhausen, was established at Oranienburg north of Berlin. A prison installation and an SA camp already existed on the site, and hundreds of prisoners had been detained there in the months of unbridled terror in 1933–1934.[33] The first 50 prisoners reached the new camp in June 1936, and another 200 at the end of July.[34] The IKL regarded it as a new type of concentration camp, the first to be established on the basis of the infrastructure developed and the experience accumulated since the establishment of the office in 1934. The camp was also located close to a population center, in this case a town, and in 1938 the IKL was transferred from Dachau to Oranienburg. Because of the presence of an administrative center close to the camp, Oranienburg-Sachsenhausen became the new training center for concentration camp commandants. Rudolf Höß spent his last training period there before being dispatched in 1940 to Auschwitz to set up a camp there. Only at Oranienburg, he later wrote, did he learn how the concentration camp system operated from within and how it functioned in practice.[35]

In Sachenhausen and its subcamp, Neuengamme, established in 1938 near Hamburg (which became an independent camp in 1940), the attitude toward the issue of prisoners' labor began to change. This was the start of a lengthy evolving process that, toward the end of the war, was to transform the concentration camp system into a giant reservoir of slaves. Through their labor—labor that would kill tens of thousands of them—this workforce maintained a large part of the munitions industry and the war economy of the Third Reich.

Maintaining the connection between the slave labor of the concentration camps and the functioning of a rational economic system was by no means a simple task. It could only be implemented through adoption, both ideologically and operatively, of economic principles that served as functional substitutes for the conventional capitalist economy. The theoretical basis of the economic approach espoused by National Socialism had been laid in the 1920s. The individual who exerted the strongest influence on its formulation and integration into the party's ideology was Gottfried Feder, a party member since 1920 and one of its main theoreticians in its formative years. It was he who devised the economic formula of "creative capital versus parasitic capital" *(schaffendes gegen raffendes Kapital)*. Creative capital, as he saw it, promoted employment, social dynamism, and technological progress. Parasitic capital was that which was preoccupied with the narrow needs of the stratum of interest holders. Feder's theory was corroborated by other writers in the 1930s, who fostered a National Socialist model of ideal economics and technology. This model emphasized that only technological modernism based on racial superiority and force of will could withstand the titanic might of capitalist materialism and its total control by Jews. The combination of national capital, technology, and progressive bureaucracy with racial purity served as the foundation of the new economics that was to shatter the power of capitalist-Jewish materialism.[36]

The SS, more than any other Nazi organization, took the theoretical basis of the new economics very seriously. Himmler, from the early days of the party's rule, envisaged the SS as the force propelling the Nazi ideal and the catalyst of the revolution that would integrate racial superiority and modernism into the German economy and society. According to this approach, the economy was bound, first and foremost, to serve the needs of the state and the *Volk* (the people), not those of commercial concerns and the free market. Creation of a modern national economy and a racially pure nation were tasks too formidable to be left to the proponents of the free market and the capitalist economy.[37] Years later, when Germany was immersed in a bloody battle for survival, Dr. Leo Volk, one of the SS's economic specialists, explained what had led the organization to enter the sphere of economic activity in the 1930s:

Why does the SS engage in business? The era of liberal economic system demanded the precedence of the economy and then of the State. . . . National Socialism maintains this point of view. *The State gives orders to the economy; the State does not exist for the economy; but the economy exists for the benefit of the State.* The activities of the Allies, which brought about the present World War confirmed the rightness of principles of National Socialist economic leadership, which introduced an economy controlled by the State as early as 1933. The economy had to face problems which under all circumstances had to be solved in case war should break out. It was during this time that the economic enterprises of the SS were developed.[38]

Oswald Pohl was the man Himmler recruited to build up the economy of the SS. Born in 1892, Pohl joined the navy after completing his studies in 1912; during World War I he served mainly in the Baltic Sea. After the war he became associated with the Volkisch (populist) right-wing circles, was active in the Freikorps (post–World War I paramilitary organizations), and in 1925 joined the Nazi Party and the SA. In 1933 he met Himmler and became one of the SS chief's closest associates. In 1939 Himmler established the Verwaltungs und Wirtschaftshauptamt (Administration and Business Main Office—VuWHA) and appointed Pohl its head, a position that effectively rendered Pohl the individual with the greatest influence in the SS after Himmler. The system Pohl headed, which was reorganized in 1942 in light of the war situation, was largely a prototype and an ideal of the new Nazi economic bureaucracy. Pohl and the henchmen he recruited considered themselves above all to be modern administrators in charge of a system that must be conducted along progressive lines, according to the rules of rational management, cost calculations, and profitability. All these should serve the new social order, the needs of the nation, and its political ideology. Most of the members of this small group of young men (Pohl was the oldest), had degrees in engineering, economics, or law. Many of them were from upper middle-class families, sons of physicians, lawyers, or senior civil servants. Pohl, a careerist motivated by ideology *(ideologisch motivierter Karrierist)*, as Jan-Erik Schulte described him,[39] was the paradigm of this group: a veteran party member, a fervent and dedicated Nazi, as well as an organizer, and a professional in the spheres of economics and administration.

At this time the SS set up workshops and factories at Sachsenhausen and Neuengamme that manufactured bricks, roof tiles, or other construction materials. For the prisoners this was grueling labor, carried out under intolerable conditions. They worked in clay pits and next to primitive kilns without the proper machinery, and so productivity was low. This production line was of dubious worth and could scarcely be considered a model for modern industry. The bulk of the production in the camps at the time served the needs of monumental construction projects throughout Germany and was unconnected to the munitions industry. In 1937–1939, when Hitler brought his full weight to bear in order to promote the megalomaniac building schemes he envisaged in Berlin and elsewhere in Germany, the German economy was barely capable of supplying one quarter of the required building materials. Albert Speer, the architect responsible for realizing this vision, who was later appointed the Reich's Minister for Weapons, Munitions and Armament, was among the instigators of the exploitation of concentration camp prisoners in the building material production industry.[40] This was the background for establishing the Deutsche Erd und Steinwerke (German Earth and Stone Works Company—DESt) in April 1938. The DESt soon became the main employer of concentration camp inmates. Its enterprises were located close to Mauthausen and, after war broke out, also at Groß-Rosen and Natzweiler-Struthof.[41]

The concentration camps' first involvement in economic projects, namely, in supplying manpower for building material production, also marked the beginning of a dispute that would accompany the issue of prisoners' labor until 1942–1943. This dispute was bound up with the power struggles between two senior members of the SS, Theodor Eicke and Oswald Pohl. But above all it was a controversy about the character and aims of the concentration camps in the Nazi state and the treatment of their inmates.

Eicke attributed little importance to the economic aspects of slave labor. He regarded labor mainly as a means of exerting authority over the enemies of the party and the state. As he saw it, forced labor should serve the aim of breaking the spirit of political resistance and subduing its supporters. In the early years of the camps, up to 1936, there was widespread opposition to employing prisoners on productive work. They were considered a negative and unreliable human element, incapable of living productive lives. The principles of productivity and rational management were of no interest whatsoever to the camp personnel. Eicke's men, the senior officers and the camp guards, were concerned almost solely with security needs and matters of discipline and the smooth operation of the terror apparatus they managed. They generally left issues of labor to the kapos in charge of the prisoners.[42]

The camp world of Eicke and the men of his SS-Totenkopfverbände (Death's Head Unit) was a brutal one, with rigid schedules and savage punishments. It was self-contained and isolated from society, and this was true not only for the inmates but also for those who guarded them. It was a manifestly ideological system whose commandants and senior officers regarded themselves as warriors in the forefront of National Socialism's main battle, performing tasks that constituted a supreme historical mission. Inflexibility, group comradeship, and a sense of belonging to an elite order characterized this system.[43] Its responsibilities did not include running an orderly bureaucracy, calculations of input and outlay, organized follow-ups, or economic considerations. Rather, its core was the operation and administration of ideologically oriented terror. Such a framework could not function as a rational and effective bureaucracy even if it kept its files and data in good order.[44] For the Konzentrationslager-SS (camp-SS), the prisoners were dangerous enemies, a racially inferior rabble, parasites and corrupters of the social order and morals, whose right to live was in question from the outset. Their exploitation as a valuable economic asset was irrelevant.

The grueling working conditions in the camps, such as Mauthausen, which was established in 1938 after the annexation of Austria, resulted in rising death rates. The low productivity rate of the factories that operated inside the camps indicates that attention to the prisoners' labor was not the main priority of the camp command. During the years when Pohl and Speer sought to exploit the prisoners in construction projects, the mortality rate soared. In 1940 it topped 20 to 30 percent in some camps.[45] Suppression and liquidation of enemy groups remained the prime aim of the camps. The weight of political and ideological considerations in managing the prisoners' labor did not change appreciably until Pohl was granted full responsibility for the concentration camps in 1942.

What did change in the camps, however, in the last prewar years was the composition of the camp population. The Gestapo, which began to be significantly involved in dispatching people to camps, was sending increasing numbers of prisoners convicted under the new criminal laws. These prisoners had been classified as shirkers, antisocial elements, or habitual criminals. On July 1, 1938, only 26 percent of the 7,723 prisoners in Buchenwald were political prisoners. Of these, 59 percent were classified as shirkers, 14 percent as habitual offenders, and 5 percent were Jehovah's Witnesses.[46] After war broke out, the system grew dramatically. By 1942 six camps had been established or had altered status: Stutthof,[47] Auschwitz, Neuengamme, Natzweiler-Struthof, Groß-Rosen, and Majdanek. This expansion brought with it a natural increase in the number of prisoners and a reevaluation of the system's needs and aims. It was also accompanied by changes in the structure of the IKL.

In summer 1938 the veteran members of Eicke's SS-Totenkopfverbände began to leave the camps. These guards, Eicke's loyal henchmen, on whom the Nazi terror system rested, were reassigned to combat units and participated in the fighting in Poland and later in France. Their replacements came from the SS. In the same period, Eicke also left the IKL and, in November 1939, moved on to command a Waffen-SS division that he soon transformed into a crack and elite fighting unit. Replacing him as supervisor of camps was Richard Glücks, a senior IKL officer at Oranienburg.[48]

The Camps and the Vision of a Racial Empire, 1939–1941

After September 1939, Himmler's appointment as Reichskommissar für die Festigung deutschen Volkstums (Reich Commissar for the Strengthening of Germandom) marked the turning point in the revolutionary plan for German settlement in the East. This project involved demographic engineering and future repositioning of hundreds of thousands of human beings within the Slavic settlements of eastern Europe. German farmers from the Baltic states, Rumania, and the Ukraine were to be settled in territories annexed to the Reich after the division of Poland, and millions of Poles and Jews were to be deported from these places to the Generalgouvernement established in Poland.[49] The development of this racial-colonial settlement empire called for building unprecedented projects and manpower reserves. The construction of new towns based on modern technological principles, the planning of up-to-date agriculture for German settlement projects, the establishment of a wide industrial and economic infrastructure—all these required hundreds of thousands of laborers. Oswald Pohl was placed in charge of administering the system that was designed to bring the future German racial empire into existence. The new concentration camps were intended to supply the necessary manpower.[50]

Alongside these plans was the emergence of various security issues and the need to introduce a suppressive apparatus in occupied Poland. Auschwitz was established to solve the Nazis' security problems in the occupied territories while implementing their future imperialist schemes. The goals that Himmler and Heydrich set for Poland included the liquidation of the Polish intelligentsia, political activists, spiritual leaders, and senior bureaucracy. All these elements were to be liquidated or sent to concentration camps. During the wave of terror that engulfed Poland in the first months of the occupation, whose main victims were Jews and Poles, thousands of Poles[51] were dispatched to camps in Germany or imprisoned in provisional camps in Poland. But toward the end of 1939 and in early 1940, these camps, some of them run by the army, began to close down as the period of military government came to an end in Poland. The situation in Silesia and in western Poland, which had been annexed to the Reich, was the most urgent. Tens of thousands of Poles were arrested there after the German forces entered, and the provisional prison installations no longer sufficed to meet needs.[52]

At the end of 1939 Glücks received instructions from Himmler to examine the suitability of several prison installations and prison camps in the Reich and occupied territories in Poland for conversion into new concentration camps. Six such sites were examined, including the old Polish military installation at Auschwitz and the camp established by the Sicherheitsdienst—SD (Security Service) at Stutthof, not far from Danzig, in September 1939, which served the terror apparatus in operations directed against the regional Polish and Jewish populations.[53] In a report he sent Himmler in February 1940, Glücks estimated that Auschwitz could be a suitable site, following fundamental alterations and the construction of an appropriate infrastructure. The IKL commander rejected all the other installations, including Stutthof.[54]

Glücks's report indicates how unaware he was of the new role Himmler was planning to assign to the concentration camp system. A narrow-minded bureaucrat, who operated from his office in Oranienburg, Glücks explained to the SS commander that the places he had examined lacked plumbing installations or running water, and in some places the buildings were unsuitable. In general, he reported, various properties were owned by private individuals or by the state. Himmler, for his part, envisaged millions of Poles and Jews being driven eastward beyond the areas of German settlement; his construction and expansion schemes were spread over 124,000 square miles (200,000 square kilometers), with hundreds of thousands of forced laborers implementing the plan. This new order in the East, with its economic and racial aspects, represented the very essence of the Nazi revolution as Himmler conceived it.[55]

It was, of course, Himmler's vision that dictated the course of events. The number of prisoners began to rise rapidly after war broke out, and it soon doubled. In August 1939 there were 21,000 prisoners in concentration camps; two and a half years later, in early 1942, the number was 70,000 to 80,000. According to a report by Pohl, several camps underwent dramatic expansion. In Dachau in 1939 there were 4,000 prisoners, and by early 1942 the number had risen to 8,000: Sachsenhausen grew from 6,500 to 10,000 inmates; Flossenbürg, from 1,500 to 4,700; and Ravensbrück, from 2,500 to 7,500. In other camps, mainly those set up after the outbreak of war, none of which were included in Pohl's report, the process was even more dramatic. In May 1940, Auschwitz had 758 prisoners and by May 1942 more than 14,000. In Majdanek, the number increased in the first half of 1942 from 2,000 to around 10,000.[56]

The composition of the prison population by nationality also changed after the war began. Widespread arrests, directed mainly against political activists in the occupied countries, brought various nationalities—Polish, French, Czech, Yugoslav, Dutch, Belgian, and others—from all over Europe to the camp system. In 1942 various nationalities from the Soviet Union also began to arrive. Whereas the German prisoners had been almost the sole national group in the camps until 1939, they gradually became the minority.[57]

This system, whose main purpose was terror and the elimination of enemies, found it difficult to change its modes of operation and to convert itself into a framework for exploiting cheap manpower, all in the name of establishing a great empire in the East. Pohl and his henchmen understood clearly that if they wanted to improve labor efficiency and thereby achieve the Reich's economic and political goals, they would have to appoint their own people to run the camps. To this end, a special bureau, I/5, was established in

1940 in Section 1 of Pohl's organization, whose task was the placement and management of prisoner manpower. Officers from I/5 were posted to the camps in order to act together with the camp command and administer labor.[58] However, administrative planning carried out from an office desk in Oranienburg was unable to revolutionize a system that had been operating for seven years in a given fashion. This was particularly true because the people in charge, namely, the camp commandants, had been trained in Eicke's school, in Dachau or in Oranienburg-Sachsenhausen.

For example, in July 1941 a total of 2,000 prisoners were transferred from Dachau to Buchenwald. They arrived in poor physical condition, many of them sick, infirm, or suffering from diseases. Buchenwald's chief physician, Dr. Waldemar Hoven, reported that the arrival of so many debilitated prisoners had not only totally precluded any possibilities of providing local medical treatment, but was endangering the rest of the prison population, then numbering about 6,500.

> In conclusion it can be said concerning the state of health of the Dachau prisoners, that not a single prisoner is fully fit for labor duty and, that also in the near future only a very small percentage will be fully fit for labor duty. It may be in the interest of the entire camp, especially also for the members of the camp complement, to keep the Dachau prisoners for the time being isolated.[59]

In a letter he appended to the report, the officer assigned to Buchenwald by I/5 noted that the transfer of these prisoners had given rise to disorder in the management of manpower in the camp. It had also created an evident risk to the health of the guards and the camp staff, as well as endangering the work capacity of the healthy prisoners.[60]

This situation is indicative of that in all the camps at the time. Glücks, who was in charge of the camps, almost never interfered because he did not want to undermine the standing of the commandants. This veteran group of camp-SS was a focus of power that could not easily be disbanded. In Buchenwald, which was run by one of the toughest and most notorious commandants, Karl-Otto Koch, Bureau I/5 personnel had almost no say in policy-making in the camp. Koch totally ignored the issue of prisoners' labor. He and his wife, Ilsa, continued to administer the sadistic terror regime in Buchenwald without any outside interference.[61]

The Economic Needs and the Practice of Murder, 1941–1944

The organizational patterns of the labor system in the concentration camps were formulated along general lines in the second half of 1941 and early 1942, despite the difficulties raised by various elements in the system. But the effort to introduce regulated and calculated administration of the labor force had immediate consequences because of the decision to rid the system of anyone unable to provide economic benefit. Such was the aim of Sonderbehandlung 14f13, the "special treatment" campaign that led to the murder of debilitated or infirm prisoners who were unable to continue working. This classification was solely administrative. According to the IKL's records, files marked 14f related to the death of prisoners. For example, 14f7 was the notation for natural death, 14f8 was the administrative classification of prisoners who committed suicide, 14f14 indicated prisoners condemned to death, and 14f13 indicated those earmarked for liquidation as part of the euthanasia scheme that was introduced in 1939. The system was expanded in spring 1941 to encompass sick or physically disabled concentration camp inmates. As in other cases in which the Nazi's classified groups of victims, the category was expanded for ideological reasons and included prisoners who were considered dangerous and Jewish prisoners who had been in the camps in 1941. Where the Jewish prisoners were concerned, the physicians who assessed physical ability often did not trouble to examine them. It was enough to note that the subject was a hostile element.[62]

According to Michael Thad Allen, it is not entirely clear whether Wilhelm Burböck, who headed Bureau I/5, collaborated with this murder campaign or whether it was conducted entirely on Glücks and the IKL's initiative. It is patently clear, however, that the camp commandants, exploiting the pressure exerted by Pohl and Burböck's men for improvement of labor efficiency and rational use of manpower, murdered thousands of infirm prisoners who constituted a burden on the system. The camp administrators were all too willing to take part in this project inasmuch as it accorded with their basic outlook regarding the prisoners and the pointlessness of keeping them alive. These two elements in the SS—the camp personnel and the IKL on one hand and Pohl's economic and administrative experts on the other—were supported by the medical staff in carrying out the killings.[63]

One of the physicians who engaged in "medical diagnostics" was Friedrich Mennecke, who received his medical degree in 1934 and joined the Nazi Party and the SS in 1932. In the period during which he conducted the lethal selections of camp prisoners, he sent his wife a series of letters, written in the lighthearted style of a loving husband. These letters record his daily schedule, his work, and his spare-time activities. On November 27, 1941, for example, he wrote:

At 1:30 P.M. we began the examinations again, but Ribbentrop's speech began and we stopped to listen to it. He said a lot of good things, did you hear the speech? After that we did examinations until around 4:00; I did 105 pats.,

Müller 78 pats., so that in the end our first installment of 183 forms was completed. The second portion followed, a total of 1,200 Jews, none of whom are even examined; it is enough to take the reason for arrest (often very comprehensive!) from the file and enter it on the form. Thus it is purely theoretical work, which will certainly occupy our time until Monday, maybe even longer. For second portion (Jews), we did the following: 17 for me, 15 for Müller. At exactly 5:00 p.m. we "threw in the towel" and went to dinner: a cold plate of salami (nine large slices), butter, bread, and a helping of coffee! Cost: .80 marks without coupons!! At 5:30 we were driven back to Weimar.[64]

Prisoners were liquidated in a number of camps. At Groß-Rosen, the commandant reported to the IKL on the liquidation projects there in January 1942. A total of 293 prisoners of various nationalities were selected; about 70 of them were taken from the revier (sick bay), 104 from the camp blocks, and another 119 were Jews. In all, between 10,000 and 20,000 prisoners were murdered in these selections in the concentration camps before the criteria for selecting candidates for murder became stricter in mid-1943.[65]

The IKL carefully studied reports from the camps about selective liquidation and were apparently not particularly satisfied with the efficiency of the examinations. Their inspection revealed that in some cases prisoners capable of being sent back to work were liquidated.[66] The selections may be described at least as negligent; in most cases assessing the prisoner's ability to return to work was secondary to ideological considerations. In April 1943 an effort was made to impose some kind of order on this project. The decision was apparently taken by Himmler himself and transmitted through Glücks to the camp commandants. In his missive, Glücks wrote that only mentally disturbed prisoners or those with dangerous diseases or disabilities should be selected for special 14f13 treatment. As for the others, the sick, disabled, and feeble, their ability to continue working even if from their sickbeds should be checked. Only those who were not even of minimal value should be liquidated.[67]

The impression is that the camp commandants were only too happy to exploit the extensive opportunities granted them by the genocide apparatus that began to operate with full force in late 1941. They wanted to exterminate as many as possible sick and defective prisoners, enemies of the state and Jews. The impetus for rational administration of the labor force provided the economic pretext, but in practice had almost no importance. The concentration camps, sites of terror, violence, and death from the outset, fitted in well in late 1941 with the Nazis' genocide plan.

In early 1942 Pohl's office was reorganized as the SS-Wirtschafts- und Verwaltungshauptamt (SS Central Office for Economics and Administration—

WVHA). The main reason for the bureaucratic reorganization was the new situation on the Soviet front and the assumption that the imminent victory would mean new tasks and challenges for the SS in the areas of economics, construction, and settlement in the East.[68] A significant step taken as part of these changes was Himmler's decision to transfer the IKL, which had been an independent authority since its establishment, to Pohl's jurisdiction.

The labor shortage became a crisis in the second half of 1942, when demands were becoming greater and more urgent. There had been 39.4 million German workers in May 1939, but the number dropped to 35.5 million in May 1942.[69] As a result, Hitler ordered the establishment of a special office for recruitment and assignment of manpower for industry within the framework of the Four Year Plan Office and appointed Fritz Sauckel, Gauleiter (party district leader) of Thuringia, as Generalbevollmächtigter für den Arbeitseinsatz (General Plenipotentiary for Labor Deployment). The mission of this authority was to transfer as much manpower as possible from the occupied countries to meet the needs of the German munitions industry. Between April and December 1942, 1.4 million laborers were recruited and transferred to Germany from the occupied territories in eastern and western Europe, almost all of whom were posted to industry. In the East, this mission was often carried out by violent methods. Young men of working age were seized and transported by rail to industrial centers in the Reich, which were in dire need of workers. In the Reichskommissariat (Reich civil administration) Ukraine, more than 350,000 laborers registered voluntarily or were recruited forcibly in 1942. Violent manhunts for recruitment of laborers took place in both urban and rural areas.[70]

After the war Pohl claimed that he held several conversations with Himmler in late February and early March 1942 regarding the concentration camps. Himmler told him about Sauckel's appointment and said that the problem of manpower for the wider war effort had become a central issue that the SS would have to tackle. Himmler, unwilling to have the SS miss this opportunity, said that the camp inmates were a manpower resource that was totally under his control. He told Pohl that his office had the experience and ability to transform the camps into a source of labor for industry; hence he needed to take responsibility for supervising the camps. Pohl claimed that he had tried to persuade Himmler that the RSHA should be the body in charge of the prisoners, but Himmler insisted that it was no longer a political or security problem but an economic issue. Once the war had been won, the question would be reexamined, and perhaps then it would be possible to place the camps under the RSHA's jurisdiction.[71]

Because the system that Pohl took over functioned differently, however, it was impossible to obtain large numbers of prisoners by a simple stroke of the pen. Himmler hoped to be able to transfer to the camps some of the hundreds of thousands of Soviet POWs who had fallen into German hands in the first months of the war in the Soviet Union, but they did not arrive in the anticipated numbers. The army objected to the transfer of more than 350,000 POWs to concentration camps. By early 1942 it had become clear that two-thirds of them had perished in the first months of the war in mass liquidations in the POW camps where they were starved to death or in the course of lengthy death marches to their places of detention.[72] Of more than 3.5 million Soviet POWs taken by the Germans at the beginning of the war, only some 1.2 million were alive in early February 1942.[73] In his predicament, Himmler turned to the most available source of slave labor: the Jews. On January 26, 1942, six days after the Wannsee Conference that dealt with the steps to be taken for the liquidation of all Europe's Jews, he transmitted the following order to Glücks:

> As no more Russian prisoners of war are expected in the near future, I shall send to the camps a large number of Jews and Jewesses who will be sent out of Germany. Make the necessary arrangements for reception of 100,000 male Jews and up to 50,000 Jewesses into the concentration camps during the next 4 weeks. The concentration camps will have to deal with major economic problems and tasks in the next weeks. SS-Gruppenführer Pohl will inform you of particulars.[74]

From the end of 1941, the killings in the concentration camps converged with the Nazis' Final Solution of the Jewish question. The decision, approved by the Führer, to render the Reich "free of Jews," was assimilated by Himmler into his plan for rapid expansion of the available manpower pool in the concentration camps. Heydrich and his SD staff believed that the Jews deported from Germany should suffer a different fate; they should be transported eastward, there to share the fate of the Jews of the occupied countries, namely, immediate liquidation.[75] But in January 1942, Himmler outlined the parameters for managing the Final Solution until the end of the war: the murder of Jews was a central goal, but, when necessary, urgent and changing economic constraints were to be taken into consideration. The concentration camps, which had served as sites for the selective murder of sick, injured, and disabled prisoners since 1941, were now to be integrated into the Nazi genocide plan and the task of exterminating the Jews. However, the timing would be determined in light of a wide range of calculations.

Pohl, who took over responsibility for the camps in spring 1942, sent Himmler a report on the situation in the camps at that time. After surveying the increase in the number of camp inmates in the old Reich and Austria, he clearly described the tasks that faced the camps.

The war has brought a marked change in the structure of the concentration camps and has changed their duties with regard to the employment of the prisoners. The custody of prisoners for the sole reason of security, education, or prevention is no longer the main consideration. The economic situation has now become the most important factor. The mobilization of all prisoners' labor [forces], for purpose of the war now (increased production of armament), and for purposes of construction in the forthcoming peace, comes to the foreground more and more.[76]

It is questionable whether the concentration camp system for which Pohl was now responsible was equipped to handle a large slave labor resource, administered according to efficient economic criteria. The administrative manpower in the camps was limited, and the existing infrastructure was not able to immediately absorb hundreds of thousands of prisoners. In early 1942, 5,884 SS personnel were employed in the camps together with 511 outside workers, namely, German nationals who were employed in clerical and office work. In several camps there was a noticeable shortage of manpower, which the commandants often complained about. For example, in Ravensbrück, the camp for women, there were only 92 SS staff and 235 outside workers. In Dachau, Buchenwald, and Sachsenhausen, the SS manpower quota was 256, and there was almost no other staff. In the new camps in Poland, the SS manpower quota was larger: in Lublin (Majdanek) there were 423 SS men and 2 outside workers, and Auschwitz had some 2,000 guards and SS troops, with an auxiliary staff of 116.[77] In July 1942 this staff administered 98,000 inmates and in August 115,000.[78]

This unplanned increase in the number of prisoners, which was implemented hurriedly and inefficiently, had an immediate impact on living conditions in the camps and caused a steep rise in the mortality rate. In July 1942, 8.5 percent of the prisoners (8,329) died, in August the number rose to 12,217 (10.6 percent), and in September it dropped to 11,206 (10.2 percent). By the end of 1943 the number of camp inmates had declined, and in December of that year they numbered 88,000 as against 115,000 just 18 months previously. Pohl cited several reasons for this drop: disruptions in the food supply, the camp commandants' decision to ignore the order to permit prisoners to keep the warm garments they had brought with them to the camp, and various administrative hitches. Himmler expressed his appreciation for Pohl's efforts, in his first year of office, to convert the camps into a smoothly functioning framework and to enhance efficiency. However, Himmler too appeared to consider that an annual prisoner death rate of 10 percent was unalterable, and perhaps also that no change was required.[79]

Another problem related to the camp commandants. Concurrently with the report he sent Himmler in April 1942, Pohl dispatched explicit instructions to the camp commandants advising them that they bore exclusive responsibility for existing and future SS industrial concerns. He tried to convert the senior camp administrators from commanders of prison installations based on terror and punishment into managers capable of taking responsibility for a system employing thousands of productive forced laborers. Pohl freed them of responsibility for the labor schedule and emphasized that there was no specified limit to the number of working hours, leaving the matter to their discretion. However, such changes required a much more substantial reorganization of the entire camp system.[80]

In summer 1942 Pohl introduced sweeping changes in the senior command of the concentration camps. Several of the men he valued were left in place: Fritz Ziereis at Mauthausen, Herman Pister at Buchenwald, and Rudolf Höß at Auschwitz. At the same time, he made a series of appointments that stabilized the camp commands until the end of the war. Several commandants were transferred to other camps: Martin-Gottfried Weiß from Neuengamme to Dachau, Egon Zill from Natzweiler-Struthof to Flossenbürg, Max Pauly from Stutthof to Neuengamme, and Max Koegel from Ravensbrück to Majdanek. There were several new appointments: Fritz Suhren was sent to command Ravensbrück, Josef Kramer was appointed commandant of Natzweiler-Struthof, Wilhelm Gideon became commandant of Groß-Rosen but was replaced in fall 1943 by Johannes Hassebroek, Paul Werner Hoppe was given command of Stutthof, and Anton Kaindl was assigned to command Sachsenhausen. All the new commandants were senior SS men who had once served in the camp system. Pohl understood that only men who had been trained within this unique system were capable of doing the job, but he made sure that the new commandants were qualified to follow the new direction he planned for the system. Most were relatively young men with an administrative-economic orientation that accorded with his own outlook. For the first time since the concentration camp system was established, Eicke's henchmen were no longer the decisive factor in its administration.[81]

In fall 1942, when a military resolution was imminent at Stalingrad on the eastern front, understandings were reached with Albert Speer's ministry regarding absorbing prisoners into military production frameworks. Pohl, Speer, and senior members of the WVHA and the Ministry of Armaments met on September 15 and agreed that the manpower reserves in the concentration camps should be made available exclusively to the armaments industry. In a report Pohl sent Himmler on this meeting, he argued that in order to achieve this aim:

We (the SS. [D.B].) must waive one of our basic demands. We can no longer insist that all production be confined within the borders of our concentration camp. As long as we were dealing with crumbs—as you yourself, Reichsführer, correctly defined the scope of our work so far—we could make this demand. If we want to take control of a closed armaments concern with 10,000 or 15,000 prisoners in the near future, it is not possible to locate this labor "intra muro." As Reichsminister Speer so rightly said, this labor must be located in an open area. Then we need to erect an electric fence around the place; then we can supply the necessary number of prisoners and the project can function as the workplace of the SS armaments industry. . . . Reichsminister Speer anticipated the immediate recruitment of 50,000 Jews who are fit for work there.[82]

This agreement was of vital importance: it laid the foundations for the transfer in the last two years of the war of tens of thousands of camp prisoners to the armaments industry and to private industrial concerns producing for that industry. It also created the basis for the development of a vast network of subcamps, constructed over a wide radius, sometimes hundreds of miles from the main camp, adjacent to the sites where the prisoners slaved. This was a dramatic change: instead of a closed central camp that isolated criminals and dangerous elements from society, it created a wide-ranging presence of groups of prisoners, sometimes in isolated and insufficiently protected areas, in the midst of civilian populations, in settlements or factories, working alongside ordinary civilians. Speer dealt with this issue at one of his meetings with Hitler at the end of September 1942 and obtained his approval of the plan.[83]

The vast labor source in the concentration camps and the accompanying subcamp system was built up mainly in the last two years of the war. The fate of hundreds of thousands of concentration camp inmates in the final stages of the war and their chance of living to see the day of liberation became a function of the ability to transfer them rapidly to places where their labor could continue to be exploited. This upheaval transformed thousands of antisocial, political, criminal, and other prisoners into an economic resource of vital importance for the war effort.

Two WVHA officers played a crucial role in this upheaval. The first was Dr. Hans Kammler, one of the most prominent of the administrators recruited by Pohl. He was a typical well-educated, efficient, and intelligent German technocrat, who placed his talents and abilities at the disposal of the Nazi ideology. Born in 1901 to a military family, he was educated at the best schools and graduated as an engineer. In 1934 he published a book through the Berlin Technical University in which he presented his views on the best way to combine modern technology, efficient bureaucracy, and rationality based on the precise collation of data for decision makers, industrial planning, and the supremacy of the Aryan race.

In June 1941 Kammler joined Pohl's office, taking a central position in the organization's economic-administrative system. In February 1942 he was placed in charge of the construction projects in Pohl's office as commander of Amtsgruppe (departmental group) C. He took a wide-ranging view of his task and in no way confined himself to purely economic matters. In August 1942 he joined Himmler on a tour of Poland and the Ukraine, which included the main extermination sites where the Final Solution was proceeding at full force. On August 8, 1942, he visited the Bełżec death camp together with Odilo Globocnik, commander of the SS and the police in the Lublin district. Kammler's staff administered the intensive construction at Auschwitz in 1942 and the extermination system in the camp. His activities in the concentration camp network encompassed two areas that were to become indivisibly connected, namely, labor and extermination. The dialectical connection between them stemmed largely from his approach. This combination of functions reached its fullest application in 1943 when Kammler was placed in charge of the armaments and secret weapon system in the Harz Mountains in central Germany and the establishment of the Mittelbau-Dora camp network.[84]

Gerhard Maurer was the second individual who had a major impact on the change in exploitation of prisoner labor. He became part of the concentration camp supervision system in 1942 following the organizational changes in the WVHA. He headed Office D-II and was responsible for placement and movement of prisoners (Arbeitseinsatz der Häftlinge) in the important labor sites.

Maurer was only 34 years old when placed at the head of D-II. Like Pohl, he had an advanced degree in administration and economics; he had joined the Nazi Party in 1930 and the SS a year later. In 1933 he left a lucrative position in order to work for a Nazi publishing house. After joining the camp supervision network, Maurer became the most influential individual in the office, and almost no fundamental decision was taken there that did not bear his personal stamp. He introduced new methods of administration and supervision of the prison manpower and management of camp labor. Maurer demanded accurate information on the number of prisoners and the active labor sites and initiated new agreements with various elements in the economy and industry regarding the exploitation of prisoners in production systems. The most important change he instituted was the introduction of medical teams into the camps to determine whether prisoners were fit for work. The medical teams were intended to serve as a counterbalance to the camp command's decision affecting the fate of prisoners. The criteria were to be entirely professional rather than arbitrary.[85]

The transfer of concentration camp prisoners to the armaments industry and private industrial concerns was initiated in December 1942 in the following way. Maurer received all the data transmitted by the camp commandants on the number of prisoners capable of productive labor. Requests for manpower from various firms were submitted to D-II or directly to the camp command. It was the camp commandant's responsibility to examine whether the applicant was capable of supplying the prisoners' basic needs: housing, food, clothing, and medical treatment. He reported to Maurer, who personally examined the subject and then checked with Speer's office as to how essential the specific concern's products were for the war economy. Once a week Pohl, Maurer, and Glücks met to discuss new applications. Pohl was the supreme authority who approved the transfer of prisoners to the applicant. Glücks and Maurer then implemented the decision.[86]

In the second half of 1944 the method of assigning prisoners to armaments factories changed, and Speer's office again began to play a more central role in the process. Speer concentrated all the requests for manpower and passed them on to Maurer's office. Then the request was checked with the manpower administration in specific camps, and their ability to supply the workers was examined. These changes were made in order to simplify and accelerate the process. Speer's decision now carried greater weight.[87]

The transfer of prisoners from camp to camp, and their transportation by freight car under inhuman conditions over hundreds, even thousands, of miles in answer to labor needs became almost an everyday event from the end of 1942. However, despite all the efforts of the decision makers and authors of the new policy, Himmler, Pohl, and Speer, even they could not instantly convert the camp system into a new and different modus operandi. For example, at the end of October 1942, 499 prisoners were dispatched from Dachau and 186 from Ravensbrück to Auschwitz to meet the manpower requirements of the I. G. Farben Works, located in Buna-Monowitz. Their condition was reported by Department IIIa in the camp, which was responsible for assigning prisoners to work assignments:

> The 499 prisoners transferred from Dachau are in very bad physical condition and none of them is suitable for work in the Buna plant. Barely a third of them can be employed in other work and these only after two-week recovery time. 50 of the arrivals could be employed in their profession; 162 have no profession, and 267 of the transferees are farm workers. 186 prisoners transferred from Ravensbrück were in a better physical condition than those from Dachau;

128 of them are employed in their professions and only 58 of them have no profession.[88]

The death rate among prisoners continued to be high at the end of 1942, and it seemed that if it was not checked, there would be no prospect of transforming these prison and murder installations into workplaces capable of attracting private firms and major industries. As a result, in 1942 the camp industries accounted for a negligible proportion of the armaments industry: to be precise, 0.0002 percent.[89] Glücks, most probably on instructions from Pohl, issued a directive on December 28, 1942, to all camp physicians and commandants. He wrote that, according to the data in his possession (he did not note what period they covered but it was apparently up to 1942), out of 136,000 prisoners in the camps, 70,000 had perished. With such a high mortality rate, it would be impossible to select the required number of prisoners, as Himmler had instructed. The camp physicians were charged with central responsibility for significantly reducing the death rate. Glücks emphasized that, in order to carry out his job properly, a camp physician should not be overly inflexible but should be concerned with preserving manpower and raising productivity in the camp. Physicians were now required, more so than in the past, to attend to the nutrition and working conditions of the prisoners and to do whatever possible to reduce the mortality rate.[90]

The result of the effort invested, in particular by Maurer and his staff, was a statistical drop in prisoner mortality in the concentration camps; the monthly rate dropped from 8 to 10 percent in 1942 to 2 to 3 percent at the end of 1943. These figures are deceptive, however, due to the constant rise in the number of new prisoners in the camps, the absolute number of prisoners who perished did not decline drastically.[91] From early 1943 the number of inmates rose steeply. In May of that year there were 203,000, in August 224,000, and by August 1944 the number had ballooned to 524,286. On January 1, 1945, there were 706,650 concentration camp inmates, and the last available figures, relating to January 15, 1945, refer to 714,211 prisoners.[92]

Between October and December 1942 there were between 83,000 and 88,000 prisoners, and the average monthly mortality rate was 8,500. In February–March 1943 close to 12,000 of the 150,000 prisoners perished monthly. Only in summer 1943, when the number of prisoners had reached 200,000, did a significant decline occur in the mortality rate, but even then more than 5,500 were dying each month. This "optimistic" picture altered drastically in the last year of the war, when the camps became sites of slow death and of deliberate murder of tens of thousands of prisoners.[93]

This increase in the number of prisoners was accompanied by the sprouting of hundreds of subcamps. In late 1942 there were only a handful of such camps: 2 at Neuengamme, 7 at Mauthausen, 6 at Buchenwald, and 9 at Auschwitz. Toward the end of 1943 there were 9 at Neuengamme, 17 at Mauthausen, 20 at Buchenwald, and 15 at Auschwitz. By June 1944 Neuengamme had 51 subcamps, Mauthausen 24, Buchenwald 20, and Auschwitz 30. The number of subcamps continued to increase even in the last few months of the war, and in early 1945 some of the camps operated up to 100 subcamps, covering large areas where thousands of prisoners were housed and worked. In some cases subcamps spawned subcamps of their own. In June 1944 the concentration camp system included 341 subcamps, and according to several estimates, in the last months of the war the figure rose to 900–1,200 throughout the concentration camp system.[94]

These camps were often located within a radius of dozens and even hundreds of miles from the main camp. They were established in rural areas and sometimes in the heart of towns and close to factories; they were a vast source of income for the WVHA. Private industry paid the SS 3 to 4 marks daily for each prisoner, and in 1944, as the demand rose and the supply dwindled, payment rose to 4 to 6 marks daily. The payment for women prisoners was 3 to 4 marks daily. Although the concentration camps were able to offer private industry no more than 10 percent of the hundreds of thousands of inmates of the camps in 1942–1944, they still provided a sizeable income.[95]

From late 1943 there was an urgent need for manpower for the armaments industry, especially for military aviation production. From the summer of that year airfields, energy production centers, and aviation industry factories were the prime target of Allied bombers. Speer's Ministry of Armaments sought various ways to locate this vital production network as far as possible outside the range of British and American aircraft.[96] In light of the worsening military situation in late 1943 and the evident superiority of the Royal Air Force (RAF) and the U.S. Air Force over the Luftwaffe, the issue of aircraft and armaments production became crucial. Hitler and senior figures in the German military command believed that the key to halting the decline and changing the course of the war lay in the development of new fighter planes and sophisticated rocket weapons.[97] By 1944 the military aircraft industry would become the main employer of concentration camp prisoners.

In late 1941 the Heinkel-Werke Aviation Works began to exploit Sachsenhausen inmates. By early 1944 some 90,000 prisoners had become part of the construction and production network of the aviation industry, and the intention was to add another 100,000. The great majority of prisoners were not engaged in producing weapons. They worked for the SS, DESt, or Organization Todt (a large economic and military engineering concern that supported the Nazi regime), and in special construction detachments for which Hans Kammler was responsible, and on construction of the physical infrastructure of the giant production enterprises that manufactured aircraft, flying bombs, rockets, and other equipment. Such enterprises were set up in almost all the concentration camps and their subcamps: Auschwitz, Groß-Rosen, Buchenwald, Dachau, Flossenbürg, Mauthausen, Neuengamme, Natzweiler-Struthof, Sachsenhausen, and the camps that operated in the Reichskommissariat Ostland.[98] Pohl estimated after the war that, in early 1945, approximately 230,000 of the 799,000 concentration camp prisoners were connected in one way or another with the armaments industry. Some 170,000 of them were "construction prisoners" *(Bauhäftlinge);* namely, they were employed in strenuous infrastructure and construction work and were under the responsibility of Kammler's office.[99] The heart of this giant project, which included tens of thousands of slave laborers engaged in digging tunnels and building subterranean factories for production of aircraft and sophisticated weapons, was Mittelbau-Dora.

Extermination through Labor

When the issue of *Vernichtung durch Arbeit* (extermination through labor) during World War II is examined, it may sometimes seem that the SS personnel in Pohl's office who were responsible for the labor and economic system worked according to an orderly and coherent plan. However, in the last year of the war, the SS was faced with a serious policy question: the ratio between economic and ideological considerations and the dialogue between them. The conditions that prevailed at the gigantic and complex economic project constructed at Mittelbau-Dora, and the many victims it claimed, indicate that these two calculations were interwoven and that it was impossible to decide which was the more crucial.[100]

The Mittelbau-Dora network was closely involved in the German effort to promote the development of rocket weaponry, whose planning had begun in 1939. The armaments and aircraft production authorities began to treat the matter seriously only after the Stalingrad catastrophe. In August 1943 Hitler decided that the rocket project should be conducted underground. A special committee, which included Speer's representatives and Kammler's engineers, decided on the Harz Mountains in central Germany as the appropriate production site for the new weapons. Himmler took full responsibility for creating the required infrastructure. The individual who implemented the decision and was behind the recruitment and management of tens of thousands of slave laborers who excavated subterranean tunnels at the site was Hans Kammler.[101]

On August 28, 1943, the first group of 107 prisoners arrived from Buchenwald to prepare the infrastructure for the great building project. By the end of September 1943, there were more than 3,000 prisoners at Mittelbau-Dora, which was then a subcamp of Buchenwald. By the end of the year, the number had risen to more than 10,000. When it became an independent concentration camp in November 1944, there were more than 14,000 prisoners in the main camp and more than 19,000 in a series of subcamps and external kommandos.[102] According to the records of the camp physicians, some 3,000 prisoners perished at Mittelbau-Dora up to March 1944. Another 3,000, who were no longer fit for work, were evacuated from the camp on special transports to Majdanek (i.e., sent to their deaths). Hence, between early September 1943 and March 1944, the first six months of Mittelbau-Dora's existence, 6,000 of the 17,000 prisoners who arrived in the camp perished. A 30 percent mortality rate was unheard of at the time in any concentration camp.[103]

The grim working conditions—the damp, the dust, and soot in the subterranean tunnels—all these played havoc with the health of the prisoners and were the main cause of death.[104] In the absence of basic safety conditions, work accidents were common. "By accident I was injured in the head by the fall of a rock from the roof of the tunnel while I was working . . . several days before I had been hurt when my right foot was crushed between two wagons," wrote one of the French prisoners.[105] The long working day, consisting of about 12 hours of hard labor, the meager rations, and the inadequate clothing also contributed to the high rate of disease and death.[106] The cold weather, which began in early fall, was a particularly harsh adversary. One of the prisoners described the conditions in September 1944:

> We reached Dora and it was bitterly cold. There, underground, it was cold and there was a draught . . . there were piles of bodies. We weren't moved when we saw the dead, poor things. What did people do? If they saw a better shirt than they had, they stripped it off and took it for themselves. It's no disgrace to say it, it happened.[107]

What occurred in Mittelbau-Dora, as in other concentration camps in the last year of the war, cannot be explained solely through the prism of the policy of extermination through labor. It was not a case of adopting new murder methods to expedite the familiar genocide process, which had been under way since 1941. This was a new, different process. In contrast to the past, this new type of extermination was calculated and planned in terms of economics, cost, production, and output; extermination and exploitation (*Vernichtungs und Ausbeutungsprozess,* as Jens-Christian Wagner denotes them)[108] were tightly interlinked and inseparable. The extermination of prisoners was not the main objective of the concentration camps, several of which, like Mittelbau-Dora, Auschwitz, or Mauthausen, became giant centers of slave labor. Fitness for work was the decisive criterion, which determined the sharp borderline between life and death; prisoners who collapsed were often killed in the workplace. According to this selective extermination method, the victims were not chosen according to political or racial criteria, as were most of the victims of Nazi genocide, but instead on the basis of their physical condition.[109] Hans Kammler summed up this trend succinctly in an order to his men when the Mittelbau-Dora production enterprise was set up in 1944: "*Kümmern Sie sich nicht um die menschlichen Opfer. Die Arbeiten müssen vorankommen, und das in moglichst kurzer Zeit.*" (Do not be considerate of the human victims. The work must be completed in the shortest possible time.)[110]

This was a new stage in the Nazi genocide, and its main perpetrators came from an economic and administrative background. It combined total exploitation of the prisoners' work capacity with meticulous liquidation of those who were no longer fit for labor. It began with the changes in the concentration camp system in the first half of 1942 and reached maturity in late 1943 with the transition to a state of total warfare. The SS's unceasing efforts to transfer more and more prisoners to the concentration camps in order to proceed apace with building and industrialization brought into the camps vast numbers of prisoners who were perceived from the outset as undeserving of long-term survival: Jews, Poles, Russians, Ukrainians, French resistance fighters, and Yugoslav and Italian communists. They made up the bulk of the prisoners who were incarcerated in concentration camps in the last 18 months of the war. The process that transformed the camps into a giant national pool of slave laborers classified as enemies of the race, political foes, and enemies of society was reflected, for example, in the agreement between Himmler and the Ministry of Justice for the general transfer of certain categories of prisoners from the judicial system to the concentration camps.

In September 1942 the Nazi minister of justice, Otto Thierack, met with Himmler, and the two agreed on the transfer to the SS of Jewish, Gypsy, Russian, and Ukrainian prisoners from state punitive installations where they were serving sentences meted out by courts of law. These prisoners were to be transferred en masse without classification of any kind. The same rule was applied to Poles who had been sentenced to more than three years' imprisonment. Thierack was convinced that, at a time when the extermination of enemies of the Reich was proceeding at full speed and the Final Solution of the Jewish problem was underway throughout the territories occupied by Nazi Germany, only those capable of returning to society and being rehabilitated as worthwhile citizens should be left in state prisons. Inveterate criminals, Jews, Slavs, and Gypsies were not included in this category, and hence the camp system should deal with them. As a result of the understanding between Himmler and Thierack, the state handed over to the SS more than 17,000 prisoners between November 1942 and summer 1943.[111]

This was only one group out of the tens of thousands of prisoners–slave laborers who flooded into the camps in the last two years of their existence. The rapid increase in the inmate population led to amendments of the procedures for registration and follow-up of the arrivals. In spring 1944 Glücks informed his camp commandants that there was no longer any need to list by name prisoners from the eastern territories who were deported to the camps. It was enough to count and register them on arrival. This being so, there was also no need to report the number of deaths or any other data concerning them before they became mere numbers in an army of slaves.[112] This dehumanization paved the way for the effort to ease the administrative nightmare posed to the system by the population explosion. The demands of the armaments industry led to tactical retreat even from the effort to realize the vision of the racial empire. The most striking evidence of this retreat was the decision to transfer tens of thousands of Jewish prisoners in summer 1944 from Auschwitz to hundreds of subcamps established in that period throughout the Reich.

Before summer 1944 there had been relatively few Jewish prisoners in the old established concentration camps in the old Reich or Austria. Nor were the Jews one of the larger national groups in the camps established in occupied Poland after the outbreak of war. They were a larger presence in the labor camps, established by the army, administrative authorities of the Generalgouvernement, and private concerns in Poland and the Baltic states. In certain periods they constituted the majority of prisoners there.[113]

In mid-May 1944, after obtaining Hitler's consent, Himmler sent a letter to Pohl with instructions to arrange for the transfer of Jewish men from Hungary to the labor camps of the armaments industry and Organization Todt concerns. According to this letter, Hitler had approved the transfer of 200,000 Hungarian Jews to the Reich for these purposes. Himmler also spoke openly of this step in a speech to SS officers on June 21, 1944. He emphasized the extent to which this decision had called for compromise on his part, and he added that in no way did the dispatch of 200,000 Jewish males to concentration camps mean that their wives and children were to be left alive, since these children, when they became adults, would endanger the lives of the German population. He went on to stress that under no circumstances would situations arise whereby these Jews came into contact with citizens of the Reich.[114] From the second half of May 1944, trains left Auschwitz carrying thousands of Jews from Hungary to concentration camps in Germany. On May 23, 1,000 Jews were conveyed to Buchenwald, followed by another 2,000 on June 5. On June 6, 2,000 Jews were sent to Mauthausen, and on June 11 another 2,000 followed. On June 11, 1,000 Jews were transported to Buchenwald, and on June 17, 1,500 were sent to Mauthausen. On July 1, 2,000 Jewish women were sent to Buchenwald, and on July 14 another 2,000 were sent to Stutthof. On July 15, 2,500 Jewish men were dispatched to Buchenwald, and on June 30, 530 women were sent there.[115] The transfer of Hungarian Jews to labor camps in the Reich continued all summer. According to Götz Aly and Christian Gerlach, about one quarter of the 430,000 Hungarian Jews who were dispatched to Auschwitz in spring–summer 1944 were transferred to camps in Germany or Poland.[116]

By the summer of 1944 the Jews had become the main national group among the concentration camp inmates. There were 8,100 Jewish prisoners in Auschwitz I out of 14,300 inmates in mid-July of that year. Between mid-May and the end of July some 430,000 Jews from Hungary were transported to Birkenau, as well as 3,000 from France and 1,500 from Italy. Also sent were thousands from the Terezin ghetto, from the Westerbork transition camp, from worksites at Sosnowiec, and more than 2,000 from Corfu. By mid-August 60,000 Jews from the liquidated Łódź ghetto were among the arrivals and another 430 French Jews.[117] Not all the arrivals in these transports underwent selection and were chosen for labor. If the estimate of the number of Hungarian deportees is taken as representative, however, it appears that about one quarter of the Jews brought to Auschwitz in spring–summer 1944 were fortunate enough to be selected for labor in the camp and were sent to one of the subcamps or transferred to other concentration camps.

Between April and October 1944, 47,000 Jewish prisoners arrived at Stutthof: 22,268 of them had been transferred from Auschwitz, 8,982 from camps in Kovno and 15,851 from camps evacuated in the Riga area. At Groß-Rosen and its numerous subcamps, there were some 60,000 Jewish prisoners in the second half of 1944, who accounted for about one half of the total prisoner population. Of this total, 26,000 were women from Hungary and Poland.[118] There were 9,837 Jewish prisoners at Buchenwald in November 1944, about 16 percent of the total, and by the end of December their number had risen to 15,477, about one quarter of the total. There was a similar number of Russian prisoners; the French accounted for 16.5 percent of the prison population and the Poles 7.5 percent.[119] Maurer, who was in charge of assigning prisoners to labor sites, issued a special instruction regarding Jewish prisoners. It was permissible to move them freely between the Buchenwald subcamps in accordance with labor requirements but totally prohibited to transfer them to other concentration camps.[120] Thus, in late 1944, the Jews became the main national group even in the subcamp network of a veteran concentration camp in the heart of the Reich. Oswald Pohl testified after the war that, at their numerous meetings, Himmler never ordered him to adopt a harsh or special policy toward Jewish prisoners in the camps: "With me he spoke only of prisoners, since he knew precisely which prisoners I was dealing with."[121] This knowledge was undoubtedly shared by the entire system. When Jews or other prisoners were selected for labor, it was because they were capable of working, regardless of their nationality. However, in his speech about the 200,000 Hungarian Jews, Himmler made it abundantly clear that extermination and labor were not conflicting aims. Exploitation of the labor of Jews and other camp prisoners was undertaken for the sake of the war effort, but victory could not be complete without the extermination of the Jews, in particular the children and women who were of limited economic value but could prove highly dangerous in the future.

From the moment the prisoners reached the camps and labor sites in the last years of the war, their lives proceeded along a time axis between their physical fitness at one extreme and their liquidation at the other. They could move in only one direction, and reaching the end of the line was only a question of time. The concentration and labor camps in the last stage of the war had become installations for slow extermination; selections were not carried out within minutes of arrival, as had been the case on the Auschwitz ramp, but over days and weeks as a result of hard labor. Those who were incapable of enduring the effort and fell sick, collapsed, or were injured and disabled due to the working conditions were murdered on the spot or evacuated from the camp to other camps that absorbed these walking dead. Majdanek, at the end of 1943, was a major destination for prisoners who had undergone this selection and whose lives were now considered worthless. Dozens of transports brought tens of thousand of prisoners there from Dachau, Buchenwald, Flossenbürg, Neuengamme, Auschwitz, Mauthausen, Sachsenhausen, and Ravensbrück. At least 30 percent of the prisoners from many of these transports perished at Majdanek after several weeks.[122] In early 1944 Bergen-Belsen also began to serve the needs of this project.[123]

This reality can only be explained by the fact that in the last year of the war the camps became vast labor and extermination installations that housed prisoners of all races and political affiliations who had been classified as dangerous enemies of the Aryan race. These prisoners were merged together into a faceless collective entity, devoid of identity apart from the instrumental identity that could be exploited until it ceased to be of use to the war effort. It was these masses of prisoners who set out on the evacuations and death marches when the great retreat began in winter 1944–1945. They were to be the last victims of Nazi genocide.

CHAPTER TWO

The Circumstances of Evacuation

On June 17, 1944, Himmler issued a general directive, unique of its kind, concerning the security situation in the concentration camps. It was sent out by Richard Glücks 10 days after the Allied landing at Normandy, and it was addressed mainly to the Supreme SS and Police Commanders, the HSSPF (Höheren SS- und Polizeiführer) in the various districts of the Reich and the occupied territories. This group of senior SS officers enjoyed special status; they not only controlled the police and the SS in their areas, but also wielded supreme authority on sensitive ideological and political issues. For example, when transports of forced laborers *(Zwangsarbeiter)* from eastern Europe left for the Reich, it was they who decided on the status of the dispatched laborers, on the basis of racial criteria. Himmler often entrusted to this group of 40 SS officers, in whose loyalty he had implicit confidence, responsibility for executing the most sensitive and problematic tasks, such as dealing with the Jewish question.[1]

Odilo Globocnik, the SS and police commander of Lublin district, was the prime mover behind the measures for Germanization and the planned demographic revolution in the Generalgouvernement. He was also in charge of implementing the program for extermination of Polish Jewry.[2] Friedrich Katzmann, the HSSPF of Eastern Galicia, was assigned major responsibility for managing the plan for liquidating the Jews of the region in 1943. In recognition of his outstanding achievements in achieving these aims, he was promoted in April 1943 to the position of HSSPF of Danzig and Western Prussia; in this capacity he was responsible for evacuating Stutthof concentration camp.[3]

Jürgen Stroop, HSSPF of Lwów, who had acquired considerable experience in liquidating local Jews, was ordered by Himmler in April 1943 to organize the liquidation of the Warsaw ghetto. Stroop, as we know, completed the job rapidly and with brutal efficiency within a few weeks in April–May of that year.[4]

Instructions and Interpretations

Dozens of copies of Himmler's directive were circulated to the HSSPF, to senior WVHA officers, and to RSHA officers. The fact that it was so widely circulated throughout the SS, to economic agencies and to those responsible for the police and for political security, indicates the importance that Himmler attributed to running the concentration camps at a time when the war was entering a new phase. Under no circumstances did Himmler want to forfeit control of the hundreds of thousands of prisoners who, in summer 1944, played a vital role in the war production system and were an important source of income for the SS. The directive, *Sicherung der Konzentrationslager A-Fall* (Security of Concentration Camps in Case A) stated that

> camp commandants continue responsible to the WVHA for all general administrative matters except during alert periods *(A-Fall)*, when the HSSPF *(Höhere SS und Polizei Führer)* assumes complete control of Concentration Camps in his *Wehrkreis* and the camp commandants become members of his staff. The HSSPF is, henceforth, responsible for the military security *(militärische Sicherung)* of all Concentration Camps and Work Camps *(arbeitslager)* in his district with the exception of Special Purpose Camps *(sonderlager)* and Political Sections *(politische Abteilungen)*.[5]

This directive determined the framework of the SS's responsibility for the camps and the way they were to be administered. Its unspecific terminology and failure to deal with a wide range of logistic and organizational problems stemming from the management of hundreds of thousands of prisoners were among the factors that turned the evacuation of the camps into a voyage of murder and horror.[6]

The directive did not define precisely what "Case A" might be. After the war, a number of possible interpretations were explored. *A* could be interpreted as a state of attack *(Angriff)*, a revolt of prisoners or uprising in the camp *(Aufstand)*, a state of alert or a general instruction regarding a state of emergency, or some undefined and unanticipated situation *(Ausnahmezustand)*. The issue was debated at the Nuremberg tribunals because of the need to ascribe legal responsibility for implementating the measures that led to the savage murder of hundreds of thousands of prisoners.[7]

Senior officers in the concentration camp system remembered Himmler's instruction of June 1944 vividly. Rudolf Höß, commandant of Auschwitz until November 1943, who from early 1944 headed Unit D-I in Office D of the WVHA, referred to the question in his testimony of April 15, 1946, at the Nuremberg trial of Ernst Kaltenbrunner. When asked how he had learned that the camps were to be evacuated at the end of the war and who had given the order to evacuate them, Höß replied:

Originally there was an order from the Reichsführer, according to which camps, in the event of the approach of the enemy, or in case of air attacks, were to be surrendered to the enemy. Later on, due to the case of Buchenwald, which had been reported to the Führer, there was—no, at the beginning of 1945, when various camps were within the operational sphere of the enemy, this order was withdrawn. The Reichsführer ordered the Higher SS and Police Leaders, who in an emergency case were responsible for the security and safety of the camps, to decide themselves whether an evacuation or a surrender was appropriate.[8]

After the war, Gerhard Maurer, head of D-II, also referred to Himmler's directive in his deposition of July 1947:

I remember that in the middle of 1944 Himmler issued an order to the Higher SS and Police Leaders according to which, in the case of "A," the concentration camps and work camps located in the district of command, were automatically subordinated to them [the Higher SS and Police Leaders]. Upon receipt of this order the Higher SS and Police Leaders had to get in touch immediately with camp commanders to prepare for taking charge of the camps in the "A" case.[9]

Wilhelm Burger, who was head of D-IV from June 1943, also remembered Himmler's directive, but a little differently:

Toward the end of 1944 I noted down an order received from Himmler regarding the concentration camps, which stated that, in the event of what appeared to be "Case A" (approach of enemy forces), authority should be transferred to the HSSPFs. They would be required to concern themselves with the prisoners who, in this case, should be evacuated (by vehicle or on foot). They would be in charge in this eventuality of supply of food, clothing and accommodation for the marchers.[10]

There is no question as to who was responsible for this directive. Himmler was the only individual who could have sent it out. Oswald Pohl even speculated that the source might have been even more senior. "I am convinced that the instructions, particularly that which stipulated that all concentration camps and labor camps must not remain in place but should be evacuated in accordance with the military advance [of the enemy] came from Himmler, if not from Hitler."[11]

Himmler's underlying motives in issuing this directive in June 1944 are partly indecipherable. In that month there was immediate danger that the concentration camps would fall into the hands of the enemy, particularly those on the eastern front, in Lublin district, and in the Baltic states. It was Pohl who called Himmler's attention, about two months before the directive was issued, to the security situation in the camps. Pohl spoke of "Case A" as early as April 1944 in a report to Himmler on the situation at Auschwitz. In it he described the situation in the three main camps, which housed 67,000 prisoners at the time. He did not explain the precise reasons for the deterioration in the security situation, but wrote that

> 2,000 SS men are available to guard the inmates of Camps I and II, including the staff of camp headquarters, who are to be detailed in Case A. In addition, there are 650 guards available for subsidiary camps of Camp III.
>
> SS Obergruppenführer Schmauser keeps a company of police of about 130 men, in readiness by the middle of this month. This company shall, if necessary, be used for additional security of Camp II. It will therefore be billeted in the close vicinity of this camp.[12]

Pohl went on to list a series of measures that had been adopted: tightening of security around the camp, construction of an electrocuted fence, and reinforcement of a series of bunkers and positions in order to protect what he called the "inner ring" of the camp. All these measures were being handled by the SS, but if Case A should arise, the "outer ring" should be backed by Wehrmacht troops. As for the 1,000 Luftwaffe men stationed at Auschwitz, Pohl did not suggest taking them into account, unless the emergency situation developed concurrently with an air attack on the camp installations and if there was also danger of an uprising of inmates, who might try to escape.[13] The fears of a prisoners' uprising as the Red Army approached the camp were shared by SS personnel at Majdanek.[14] In any event, a month later Himmler approved Pohl's measures for strengthening the security network at Auschwitz.[15]

Although Pohl was concerned with specific circumstances in the Auschwitz camp system, his assessments were undoubtedly colored by the situation in Lublin district and the decision taken in Berlin between March 20 and 25, 1944, to evacuate prisoners from Majdanek. The WVHA conveyed that order to the camp commandant, Martin-Gottfried Weiß (who in fall 1943 had moved from Dachau to Majdanek), and was apparently formulated jointly by Pohl and Glücks.[16] Nevertheless, in his report to Himmler, Pohl did not propose reorganizing the security arrangements in the camps. Andrzej

Strzelecki surmises that what lay behind Pohl's proposals regarding Auschwitz was fear of the combination of an Allied aerial attack and an internal uprising, supported by military action by the Polish underground from outside. There is substantial evidence that the Polish underground was in fact making preparations for this kind of action on the assumption that an Allied attack on the economic formation at Auschwitz was only a matter of time.[17] Such an attack, directed at Auschwitz III and industrial installations in several of the subcamps, was not to take place until August 1944, but Pohl, who focused his efforts on the smooth functioning of the production system under his jurisdiction, was already alert to these dangers by spring 1944. In his report, he was particularly concerned with the threat of an air attack on the I. G. Farben Works at Auschwitz III.[18]

In May Himmler, as noted, approved the suggestions about Auschwitz. A month later, when he issued his directive, he realized that situations such as might occur in Majdanek and Auschwitz—namely, a combination of an Allied onslaught and the danger of an internal uprising—could also arise in the coming months in other camps, creating a wide range of local security problems. "Case A," as he envisaged it, encompassed a wide range of possible scenarios, and not solely a prisoners' uprising or an air attack.[19] As in many other cases, Himmler, like other Reich leaders, preferred to draw a wide picture and to leave considerable room for maneuver to the local authorities on whose loyalty and efficiency he could rely. He preferred to assign responsibility for dealing with the situation to a single central authority and charged the HSSPFs with the task instead of the WVHA, which had been the sole authority according to Himmler's 1942 directive. The WVHA remained in charge of the economic aspects of the camps, but responsibility for security was entrusted to senior SS officers. They concentrated on administration of internal security and terror methods and on special projects undertaken in Himmler's service.

Against this background, the confused nature of Höß's testimony regarding Himmler's intentions in summer–fall 1944 is understandable. Those responsible for the camps, both in Berlin and in the field, were genuinely perplexed at the time. Himmler's directive made no mention of the need to evacuate the camps but was devoted solely to the problem of military security in the area. There is no evidence that, prior to June 1944, Himmler ever issued an order stipulating that the camps were to be handed over in toto to the enemy.

Maurer and Burger understood that Himmler's directive regarding "Case A" implied evacuation of the camps or preparations for such a move, under the responsibility of the local HSSPF. But it may well be that senior officers in the camp system did not necessarily perceive the June 1944 directive as a categorical order to evacuate. They understood that it was essential to upgrade security, but not necessarily that they were to organize the hasty evacuation of tens of thousands of prisoners and certainly not that they were to murder them en masse. Moreover, it was unquestionably convenient for Pohl to blame Himmler and Hitler for the evacuations that were to occur several months later, since he himself was dealing, at most, with the security and defense of Auschwitz's production lines. However, one cannot ignore the fact that his April 1944 report on the security of the camps in the frontline area created a snowball effect, so that eventually, seven to eight months later, the system degenerated into a series of never-ending death marches.

Not all HSSPFs reacted to Himmler's directive in the same way. Some took it very seriously. Karl Hermann Frank, HSSPF of the Bohemian and Moravian Protectorate, went on a tour of a series of Flossenbürg's subcamps under his jurisdiction in August 1944. He subsequently sent a report to Pohl, describing the security measures adopted in conjunction with the camp command. The commandant of Groß-Rosen also prepared a report, apparently at the joint request of Frank and the HSSPF of Silesia, Heinrich Schmauser, on the number of prisoners and the security threats in several of the subcamps in Lower Silesia in the Protectorate.[20]

There were also other interpretations of Himmler's directive. One of the dozens of copies probably reached Walter Bierkamp, SIPO (Sicherheitspolizei—Security Police) and SD commander in Radom district in the Generalgouvernement. On July 21, 1944, he issued an order to the SIPO and SD commander in Tomaszów subdistrict, in which he wrote:

> I again stress the fact that the number of inmates of the SIPO and SD prisons must be kept as low as possible. In the present situation, particularly, those suspects handed over by the civil police need only be subjected to a short, formal interrogation, provided there are no serious grounds for suspicion. They are then to be sent by quickest route to a concentration camp, should no court martial proceeding be necessary or should there be no question of discharge. Please keep the number of discharges very low. Should the situation at the front necessitate it, early preparations are to be made for a total clearance of prisoners. Should the situation develop suddenly in such a way that it is impossible to evacuate the prisoners, the prison inmates are to be liquidated and their bodies disposed of as far as possible (burning, blowing up the building etc.). If necessary, Jews still employed in the armament industry or on other work are to be dealt with in the same way.
>
> The liberation of prisoners or Jews by the enemy, be it the WB[21] or the Red Army, must be avoided under all circumstances, nor may they fall into their hands alive *(leben in die Hände fallen)*.[22]

This order raises a number of questions. Bierkamp did not deal with the concentration camps and was not responsible for camp security. He could not have ordered the murder of inmates of labor camps that were also under the authority of private economic elements, particularly those connected to Speer's ministry. When he issued the directive, the labor camps in Radom district with Jewish inmates, including factory camps belonging to private concerns, were being evacuated, and the prisoners were being transferred to other camps in Germany or to Auschwitz.[23] But the timing of his orders, so close to Himmler's directive and when the wave of evacuations of camps and detention installations in his area had begun, indicates that he was familiar with Himmler's instruction and was open to an interpretation that was most likely acceptable to those in charge of the camps in the East. At a time where there was danger that prison installations housing dangerous enemies of the state would be liberated by enemy forces, and when there was no possibility of moving prisoners elsewhere, it was necessary to ensure that they were liquidated. In such a case, economic considerations or constraints of the armaments industry were not relevant. They were all to be liquidated, prisoners in general and Jews in particular.

Evacuation Patterns, Summer 1944: Majdanek

The advance of the Red Army in spring 1944 drove the Wehrmacht back more or less to the 1939 pre-invasion border between the Soviet Union and its neighbors to the west (Poland and the Baltic states). Moreover, massive manpower and equipment losses had been inflicted on the Germans, and a wide-scale Red Army summer offensive was anticipated.[24] In light of these circumstances, the question of the ability to maintain a series of camps close to the front line required immediate response. Majdanek was the first camp that needed to be evacuated.

The organized evacuation of the camp began on April 1, 1944. This move had been expected and so came as no surprise to the Polish underground and the camp inmates, who were apparently aware of the plans by the last week in March. Several days previously, the *Delegatura* (underground representatives in Poland of the government in exile in London) reported that evacuation was imminent, although the destinations of the transports were not entirely clear.[25]

The evacuation began with the transfer of 84 children aged 2 to 8 and several women to Dzierżążnia near Łódź. On April 2 a transport of 1,150 Polish and Russian prisoners was taken to Natzweiler-Struthof in Alsace. Five hundred of the prisoners in this transport were sent on to Bergen-Belsen. A transport of 800 prisoners left on April 6 for Groß-Rosen. Several other transports conveyed prisoners from Majdanek to Auschwitz; the first with 2,200 prisoners on April 8 and the second, with 1,881 prisoners, the following day. On April 13 another transport left Majdanek with 1,239 prisoners, men and women, who had been in the camp sick bay. A further transport of 1,327 women and children (38 of the total) also left for Auschwitz on April 16. Two days later the Jewish women and children were selected and sent to the gas chambers. Some 600 prisoners, 480 of them men, were sent on April 15 to Płaszów near Kraków. On April 19, 1,345 women prisoners were sent to Ravensbrück.[26]

The prisoners were transported aboard densely packed cattle cars and under appalling sanitary conditions, but still, most of them eventually reached the destination camps. Left behind in Majdanek were 2,000 disabled prisoners, most of them Russian POWs, and 200 inmates, 85 of them Poles and the remainder other nationalities, who were employed in the camp. Their task was to destroy administrative material and other evidence of what had been done there.[27]

On July 7, 1944, when the Red Army was already a stone's throw from Lublin, the last stage of the evacuation began. Some 1,250 disabled and wounded Russian prisoners were transferred to Mauthausen. On July 10, as part of the preparations for retreat, the Germans perpetrated mass murder of inmates in the Gestapo prison, housed in Lublin's ancient fortress. On July 20–21, a day before the Red Army entered the town, the last remaining 8,000 prisoners were evacuated. They were joined by another 229 prisoners who had worked in one of the functioning German factories in Lublin. This convoy of prisoners marched toward the small town of Kraśnik, and reached Ćmielów, where they were loaded onto a train and transported to Auschwitz.[28] This transport was the only one dispatched from Majdanek that gave some indication of what was to occur during the evacuations of the following winter. Only 608 of the 1,200 prisoners, 452 men and 156 women, who set out on the journey reached Auschwitz on July 28. The rest, unable to endure the grueling pace demanded of them, were killed by the guards during the march.[29]

The first stage of the evacuation of Auschwitz also belongs to the evacuation period of summer–fall 1944. In March–April of that year in a special operation, the Germans evacuated 7,000 Polish prisoners to various camps in the Reich. Strzelecki attributes the decision to the escalation of Polish underground activity in the camp and fear of security problems, as evident from the correspondence between Pohl and Himmler that month. By September 1944 about 13,000 Slav prisoners had been transferred from Auschwitz, most of them Poles and Russians, but also some Czechoslovakians and other nationalities.[30]

However, these evacuations were apparently internal transfers of prisoners within the labor system of the camps in accordance with changing needs, as was often the case in that period, rather than the beginning of an evacuation process. In April 1944 many of the evacuated Majdanek inmates were transferred to Auschwitz, as were thousands of Jews from Greece and western Europe and later from the liquidated Łódź ghetto and, of course, from Hungary. The number of inmates rose sharply and rapidly and approached 140,000 in mid-August; 30,000 of them were Hungarian Jews who were not absorbed into the camp and were merely in transit before being sent to other camps.[31]

Despite the indubitable impact of the Polish underground's activities in the region and Pohl's fears of a prisoner uprising, it appears that the Poles, Russians, and Czechs were moved to camps in Germany because the decision to transfer Jewish prisoners to camps in the Reich had not yet been taken. When the decision was finally made, in May–June 1944, and further to the evacuation of the Slav prisoners, the transfer of tens of thousands of Jewish male and female prisoners to labor camps in the Reich was set in motion. As the labor needs of these camps became increasingly urgent, Poles, Russians, Jews, and others were sent without special selections. This process continued uninterrupted throughout the summer and fall and led, within a few months, to a significant decline in the number of prisoners in Auschwitz. All in all, 65,000 prisoners were evacuated from the three main Auschwitz camps by January 1945.[32]

Evacuation Patterns, Summer 1944: The Jewish Camps

The advance of the Red Army through the Baltic states in July 1944 led to the evacuation of inmates of camps in the Reichskommissariat Ostland. According to Pohl's report to Himmler, there were 3 operative concentration camps and 30 labor camps in Ostland in April 1944, in Kovno, in Riga-Kaiserwald, and at Vaivara in Estonia.[33] This figure is incomplete, however, for it does not include all the special labor camps for Jews *(Zwangsarbeitslager für Juden)* established in Ostland. These camps were established after Himmler gave the order, in June 1943, to liquidate the functioning ghettos in Ostland. Between mid-September and mid-November 1943, some 20,000 Jews, mainly from the Kovno, Minsk, Riga, and Vilna ghettos, were assembled in labor camps. In 1943–1944 there were 35 such camps in Lithuania, 13 in Latvia, and about 8 in Estonia. Responsibility for the administration of these camps was entrusted to the commanders of the SIPO and the SD (Kommander der Sicherheitspolizei und des SD—KdS) in Ostland. Although these camps were set up for Jews, in several cases adjacent smaller camps were established for non-Jewish slave laborers. Still, the great majority of the slave laborers in the concentration camps in Ostland in 1944 were Jews from the Baltic states and elsewhere.[34]

In July 1944 it was decided to evacuate the camp that was still operating in the Kovno ghetto area. On July 7 the German officer in charge of the ghetto-camp, Wilhelm Göcke, informed the head of the Judenrat (the Jewish administrative council under Nazi occupation), Elhanan Elkes, that the evacuation of the remaining Jews from the ghetto would begin on the following day. He spoke of evacuation by boat to Tilsit.[35]

Göcke's men apparently attempted to persuade the remaining Jews that they were being sent to labor sites and that no harm would befall those who reported for evacuation in accordance with instructions.[36] The Jews were convinced that transfer to Germany meant certain death. They knew nothing, of course, of the change in the policy decided on by Himmler of exploiting Jews in essential industries. They hoped to be saved at the last moment if they stayed in place just a few more days until the Red Army arrived. When it became known that the ghetto was to be evacuated, considerable panic ensued, and many tried to find hiding places and avoid reporting for evacuation.[37] Between July 10 and 12 the Germans conducted a thorough and violent search for those in hiding:

> We try to get into the *malina* (bunker) very fast and to close the entrance. We managed to get into the *malina*, closed the entrance, then they inserted gas through the ventilation opening. Of course we ran fast to breathe air from outside. They took us out, stood us by the wall; we looked at one another and said: this is it, it's over. Suddenly they received an order to take us to the *komitet* . . . and they gave us our clothes . . . at two in the afternoon we began to move . . . toward the Kovno railway station.[38]

Some of these hiding places had been prepared in advance, but the Jews could not remain there because of the danger of suffocation once the Germans began setting them alight. Some of them emerged, others were pulled out by the Germans and dragged, sometimes half-dressed, beaten and humiliated along the way, to the assembly point.[39] Other Jews reported as ordered and waited for the evacuation to commence, seated on their bundles.[40] The murders were committed mainly when Jews tried to escape en route to the railway station.[41] German bullets killed 36 Jews during the final evacuation of the ghetto.[42]

Still, mass liquidations, such as those perpetrated in previous years during searches prior to deportations of Jews for extermination, did not occur in Kovno in July.[43] The need to keep the slave laborers alive was paramount. All in all, some 8,000 Jews were evacuated that month from Kovno ghetto and several labor camps in the region. On July 13 the evacuees reached the railway station at Tiegenhof, where the men were separated from the women. The men were transported by train that same day to Dachau and from there were transferred to subcamps at Kaufering in Bavaria, not far from Landsberg. The women were taken to Stutthof in several transports during the month of July.[44]

More than 5,000 forced laborers from the Riga ghetto passed through the Riga-Kaiserwald camp after its establishment in summer 1943. Most of them spent only a short time there and were moved on to a series of other labor camps in the region. When the date of the final evacuation arrived in summer 1944 there were still about 12,000 Jewish forced laborers in Latvia in a series of camps. They included survivors of the Riga Jewish community, but also Jews from the Reich and the Protectorate, as well as Jewish women from Hungary who arrived in spring 1944 and women transferred from the Vilna ghetto.[45] Most of these *Arbeitsjuden* (work Jews) were evacuated aboard several transports in August–September 1944. Most of them arrived at Stutthof, and others were taken to Neuengamme subcamps in the Hamburg region or other camps.

One of the labor camps to which Jewish prisoners were brought from Riga-Kaiserwald was Dundaga in northern Latvia. The Jewish prisoners were lodged in flimsy cloth tents, 18 to 20 of them per tent. They were employed in the backbreaking task of constructing a training camp for the Wehrmacht in the heart of a forested area. Their labor included paving roads, chopping down trees, and constructing buildings and installations. The mortality rate at Dundaga was particularly high; in winter 1944 between 10 and 20 prisoners perished daily. "The Holy One blessed be He takes us in *minyanim* [minyan = a quorum of 10 for prayer]" was a common saying among the Dundaga laborers.[46]

In May 1944, 5,000 Jewish women from Hungary arrived at the camp, having been transferred from a labor camp in Riga. They were brought on open cattle cars, and lodged in tents like the other inmates, under appalling conditions. They found it hard to adapt to the circumstances since most of them did not know Yiddish, Russian, or German and could not endure the working conditions. Their work included uprooting and dragging tree stumps brought from the forest by horse-drawn equipment; when the horses were not available, four women took their place.[47] Not surprisingly, the mortality rate among these women was high. According to one witness, not more than 3,000 women out of the group that arrived in May 1944 survived until the evacuation of the camp in August. There were unverified claims by prisoners that mass murder was perpetrated in the camp when it was evacuated in August 1944 and that all males and females under the age of 17 and over 30 were murdered, with only 500 prisoners being left alive.[48]

The Germans did not apparently conduct organized slaughter of thousands of prisoners during the evacuation of the camp. No mass graves were uncovered there by the special Soviet commissions of inquiry that visited the region several weeks after the evacuations.[49] It should be recalled that in the summer and fall months of 1944, the concentration camp commands generally followed the basic instructions Himmler and Pohl had issued regarding the transfer to the Reich of prisoners capable of working. In any event, when the date of evacuation of Dundaga arrived, the Jewish prisoners regarded the move with total skepticism. As was the case elsewhere, they were convinced that the evacuation spelled death for all of them. After all, since so many Jews had been murdered "who needs a few hundred Jews who've been left alive?"[50]

However, the process of slow, unplanned, and naturally occurring killing took place in Dundaga as well in the familiar form of "selection by stages," as in all concentration and labor camps. The fact that almost all the prisoners in the camp were Jews certainly gave those responsible for the camp no cause or motivation to improve living conditions. The resounding proof of this is the tragic fate of the Jewish women from Hungary, who could not tolerate the physical exertion and the abominable living conditions and faced daily selections. Many of them perished in the brief period they spent in the camp.[51]

Another group of Jewish prisoners who experienced the summer 1944 evacuation at first hand were those who worked in the Gęsiówka labor camp in Gęsia Street, erected on the ruins of the Warsaw ghetto in July 1943. Some 3,680 Jews from Auschwitz were sent there to work, most of them of Belgian, French, Dutch, and Greek nationality. They arrived in four transports, between August and the end of November 1943.[52] Their task was to dismantle all the valuable reusable materials in the ruined and abandoned ghetto and to prepare the area for a large park.[53]

By early 1944 thousands of laborers had died in this camp. Consequently another 4,000 Jews, quite a few of them Poles, were brought in from Auschwitz in November 1943. Before they set out by rail, they were allotted rations (bread, margarine, and sausage) for the journey. When this group arrived, there were apparently no more than 550 or so Jews left alive from the first group of laborers, who had been sent the previous summer.[54] The site was constructed along the lines of a camp, with all that entailed, although it was located in the middle of a town. There were eight or nine fenced barracks with several hundred prisoners in each, a kitchen, and service storerooms. In addition to the Jewish prisoners, there were several hundred Polish prisoners whose number rose to more than 2,800 in the final weeks before liquidation of the camp. Several dozen German prisoners also labored there.[55]

The prisoners transferred to Gęsiówka were employed, as noted, in the meticulous dismantling of the ruins of the ghetto. It was a Sisyphean task.

House by house, wall by wall, the ghetto was taken apart, and the piles of bricks removed were carefully cleaned of the old plaster and heaped up in orderly stacks to serve for future construction purposes. Prisoners often perished when walls collapsed on them, since many of the buildings had been almost totally destroyed after suppression of the uprising.[56] During the camp's brief existence, hundreds of tons of dismantled building materials, metals, and wood and hundreds of thousands of bricks were dispatched for reuse elsewhere.[57]

The living conditions in the camp were atrocious. The daily rations were meager: about 9 ounces (250 grams) of bread, less than an ounce (20 grams) of sausage, half a quart (half a liter) of soup, and several potatoes.[58] The main problem, however, was not the food, since the location of the camp and the fact that Poles also worked there created various opportunities for obtaining food by other means. The greatest problem was the absence of minimal hygienic conditions. The barracks were infested with lice, and epidemics and filth were rife, resulting in a high death rate. Prisoners who arrived there from Auschwitz in 1943 remembered it as worse even than the camp they had left, particularly because in Gęsiówka there were no accessible water faucets as there had been in other camps.[59] At first, prisoners who fell sick were sent back to Auschwitz.[60] The good relations with the Polish laborers were almost the sole ray of light. In return for valuables found among the ruins, the Poles bought food and clothing on the Aryan side of the city for the Jewish prisoners. The Jewish prisoners, for their part, collected dismantled wooden building materials for the Poles, since there was a severe shortage of firewood in Warsaw.[61] The opportunities for barter with the Poles and the fact that the ghetto residents deported to Treblinka had left various assets behind that could be sold apparently explain why, relative to other camps, the Jewish prisoners did not starve.[62]

An improvised crematorium operated on the site, among the ruined houses, and a special unit of prisoners burned the corpses, most of them victims of the raging epidemic of typhus. Prisoners were also murdered in the Pawiak jail adjacent to the camp. In order to improve the efficiency of prisoner liquidation, work was begun on a permanent crematorium; it was completed by June 1944 but was never used because the camp was evacuated.[63]

On July 27 preparations began for evacuating the camp. Prisoners who reported to the infirmary because they feared they were unfit for the evacuation trek were assembled and murdered. All in all more than 300 sick prisoners were liquidated before Gesiówka was evacuated.[64] The remaining prisoners marched for three days, practically without food or water. Before they set out, they were given half a loaf of bread each but very soon found themselves unable to eat because food only intensified their thirst.[65] From time to time they scavenged vegetables and fruit along the way in the small Polish towns they passed.[66] Prisoners caught trying to obtain food were summarily shot by the SS guards who accompanied them. The corpses were piled onto the trucks that followed the convoy. In the evenings, the corpses were unloaded and buried in mass graves.[67] Yet, the worst enemy in the hot July days was apparently acute thirst:

> It was summer, and the roads in Poland were dusty. We suffered greatly from thirst. In the evening barrels of water were brought but they were not of great help. We were allowed to go over to the Vistula to drink. Some people waded in deeper and were shot . . . when we passed sewage, I took a pot I had with me, collected sewage water and poured it through a hat. That was how I filtered the water and I drank it. . . . We started digging with spoons and reached water. We dipped cups in the hole and brought up cloudy water.[68]

The sight of guards shooting prisoners was stamped indelibly on the memories of the survivors, who also recalled how the guards drank from their water bottles while firing. Some of the prisoners clutched the tin plates they had received in the camp throughout the march, in the hope that they would succeed in collecting a few drops of the rain that fell from time to time.[69] Several Hungarian Jews tried to wipe the sweat off their faces with handkerchiefs and to wring the cloth into their mouths, although the high salt content only increased their thirst.[70]

After a three-day march, the prisoners reached Zychlin and were loaded onto open freight cars, 90 of them per car, in intolerably crowded conditions. The heat and the lack of water turned the evacuation into a nightmare. Before they were loaded onto the cars, each prisoner was given a can of meat that was immediately opened and devoured, but the salt content of the meat soon created tormenting thirst. There was no water, and some of the prisoners, in their desperation, tried to damp their lips with urine, again intensifying their thirst.[71] The lack of water sent people out of their minds.

> We received no water, and were forced to take out our gold teeth in order to obtain a little water. There was supposed to be absolute silence in the freight cars. Several people went mad because of thirst. If someone made a sound, the SS immediately fired into the car, so that every bullet threaded three people.[72]

After a four-day journey, they reached Dachau. About 120 Jewish prisoners and an additional group of Polish prisoners had been left behind to collect the remaining equipment and liquidate the camp. They were saved from extermination by the Polish uprising that broke out in early August 1944, in which some of them participated.[73]

Superfluous Jews in the Balkans

Particularly lethal was the evacuation in summer–fall 1944 of Jewish slave laborers from Yugoslavia, on the southern margin of the continent. A few thousand Hungarian Jews worked for the Hungarian Labor Service (Munkaszolgalat) in mines in Bor district, about 124 miles (200 kilometers) southeast of Belgrade. In view of the military situation and the withdrawal from the region, the Germans decided to evacuate the slave laborers on September 17, 1944. About 6,000 Jewish laborers from Hungary were divided into two groups: the "first step," who were to leave immediately, and the "second step," who were to be sent later. Some 3,000 "first-step" laborers set out on their journey on September 17, accompanied by about 100 Hungarian guards. Their destination was Hungary.[74]

These Jewish forced laborers sensed that the front was collapsing and that the Germans were retreating under pressure. In view of this retreat and the Yugoslav partisan activities, they were filled with dread, sensing that nobody had further use for them. However, they were under Hungarian protection and were being evacuated northward toward the Hungarian border, so that "there was hope that all the same we would be returning to the homeland," according to one of the survivors. The urge to leave as fast as possible drove many of the prisoners to seek inclusion in the "first-step" group. It was universally believed that those who were evacuated early had a better prospect of survival than those left behind for days or weeks in the camp.[75]

Before setting out, the Jewish forced laborers were given a loaf of bread and one can of food. After only two or three days, the convoy had turned into a slipshod mass of people, straggling along without order or organization. From time to time, a prisoner collapsed and was shot by the Hungarian guards. There were apparently not many such cases before they reached Belgrade on September 25. On the other hand, 146 Jews who fled the convoy and were caught by local Germans (of Schwebian origin) were murdered in cold blood near the village of Jabuka. Subsequently, another 250 were murdered by the local German militia, which was also composed of local residents. Those who survived the murders reached Cszevenka on October 6, 1944. Some 800 of them continued toward Sombor. The others remained at Cszevenka and were handed over to the SS, to men of Prinz-Eugen's 7th Division, who had been reinforced by SS recruits of Bosnian origin.[76]

A bloody massacre was launched at 9 p.m. on October 7. The Jews were led in groups of 20 to 30 to a pit 44 to 55 yards (40 to 50 meters) long and 9 to 11 yards (8 to 10 meters) wide and shot on the brink. The firing continued until about 4 a.m. One of the survivors described the scene:

Between 7 and 8 October 1944, they started to take groups of twenty and suddenly we started hearing shots. It was machineguns and apparently rifles. . . . I was also in a group of twenty. That's how it went, groups of twenty, I don't know how many of them. . . .

Where we were . . . we saw a kind of mound and behind it a pit. And on the mound SS men with rifles were standing and they ordered the groups to stand in front of them. And the groups were coming and they shot them and people fell and that was it, over. . . . I must have been in the middle of a fall, so the bullet didn't hit me. Afterwards, because I said it was a group of about 15, 20, so about ten or fifteen groups came after and fell on top of me, dead or dying . . . after the lull, when it was over, the SS men started coming over again to see if someone was still alive and they also threw a few grenades. Luckily for me, several of my friends were still lying on me and they protected me . . . and at dawn, I suddenly heard that things had quietened down.[77]

About 700 Jews perished in the course of this massacre.[78] The remainder of the group set out at 5 a.m. for Sombor. En route, they fell victim to random killings, perpetrated by passing German and Hungarian soldiers.[79] In contrast to the bitter fate of the first group that set out from Bor, the prisoners from the "second-step" group, who were evacuated only at the end of September 1944, were liberated in most cases by Yugoslav partisans.[80]

The Jews who worked in the Hungarian labor battalions were not concentration camp inmates. They were in the charge of the Hungarian army and, this being so, Pohl and Himmler's instructions concerning the need to preserve the prisoners did not relate to them. Seemingly, there was no connection between the fate most of them suffered and what was happening in those same months in concentration camps in Poland and Germany. Nonetheless, the killings perpetrated during their death march displayed similar elements to the evacuation of the large Polish concentration camps several months later.

These murders took place during the retreat of the German and Hungarian armies from the region and the constant skirmishes with Yugoslav partisan units. Predictably, the first stage of the killing was perpetrated by local civilians of German origin. They identified the Jewish escapees with the Serbian-Yugoslav enemy. The fact that they were Jews and that they were being aided by the local Serbian population was known and only heightened the urge to liquidate them. The entire region was in disarray, which made it easy for local civilians to decide to play a part in their own defense. The murder of Jews, naturally enough, was part of their effort.

Like the prisoners at Dundaga in Latvia, the Hungarian Jewish laborers at Bor did not delude themselves into believing that anyone wanted to keep them alive. It was obvious to them that, since they were Jews, the moment they began to be a burden to the guards of the convoy, the guards would take immediate steps to be rid of them. Nonetheless, these laborers continued to trudge along, starving and exhausted, although they could have tried to escape at least during the first stage of the evacuation. They lived in the hope that they would cross the Hungarian border before someone decided to kill them: "It was a march of people who fostered a kind of fantasy of reaching the Hungarian border to the north."[81]

Once the survivors of the first acts of slaughter were handed over to the SS, their fate was sealed. The highways were densely crowded with military equipment and retreating forces and had to be kept clear for that purpose. There was absolutely no valid reason to march some 1,500 Jewish laborers along and supervise them when it was not clear what use they were and how they were to be moved northward. The SS men did what their colleagues had already done in thousands of previous cases: they led the Jews to the pits and exterminated them there.

The West: Natzweiler-Struthof (September 1944–April 1945)

As the American and French forces advanced into eastern France in summer 1944, the Natzweiler-Struthof concentration camp in Alsace was gradually evacuated. This camp was set up in May 1941, and the first 270 prisoners were brought in two transports from Sachsenhausen. On the eve of the evacuation in summer 1944 there were 23,000 prisoners in the camp, 13,000 of them in dozens of small subcamps and labor camps. Most of these camps were located east of the Rhine on German soil and others to the west of the river, close to the border between the Reich and the occupied region of France and north to the border with Luxemburg.[82]

Natzweiler-Struthof was not one of the worst camps in the concentration camp system. Even close to the date of the first evacuation of the camp, in June 1944, the death rate was not drastically high there, particularly when compared to the situation at the time in other camps, such as Mittelbau-Dora. That month 274 prisoner deaths were recorded at Natzweiler-Struthof. Moreover, the national and ethnic groups that were the main target of Nazi murderous plans were not strongly represented in the camp: there were almost no Jews or Gypsies, and the number of Soviet POWs was not particularly high. Most of those sent there were French, Norwegian, Belgian, Dutch, or German political prisoners. When the camp was evacuated in September 1944, the French and Alsatian prisoners accounted for some 40 percent of the prisoners. In several of the subcamps, there was a higher proportion of prisoners from eastern Europe and the Balkans, between 12 and 30 percent.

They were mostly Poles, Russians, and Yugoslavs who had been interned there in 1943.[83]

Friedrich Hartjenstein, commandant of Natzweiler-Struthof, gave the evacuation order on September 1, 1944. In the order he noted that the instruction to evacuate had reached him by telephone from Office D (Concentration Camps), namely, from Glücks. Then he went on to name the officers responsible for organizing the evacuation and listed the destinations. He also ordered that the telephone and teleprinter infrastructure be left intact, to be dismantled in orderly fashion by the camp command after the prisoners left.[84]

It was, in fact, a well-organized evacuation. On September 4, 5,518 inmates were transferred from the main camp to Dachau and another 401 were sent on September 20. By the end of September all the labor camps west of the Rhine had been evacuated and the inmates transferred to other camps in Germany or dispersed among other Natzweiler-Struthof camps east of the Rhine. All in all, 8,460 prisoners were transferred.[85]

The evacuation of this camp bore witness to the fact that, in early fall 1944, the WVHA did not consider the closing down of the camp system to be especially urgent. Even after the inmates were dispatched east of the Rhine, dozens of labor camps continued to operate in the area, only a few of them populated to full capacity. Several of them were quite large: Leonberg near Strasbourg had more than 1,160 inmates at the end of September; in Neckarelz there were close to 3,000, in Dautmergen some 2,000, and in Vaihingen some 2,200. In all, there were 13,400 prisoners in the subcamps and labor camps after the main camp was evacuated. Moreover, even after evacuation of the main camp, prisoners from camps in the heart of Germany continued to arrive in the subcamps east of the Rhine. In the last 10 days of September approximately 800 prisoners from Dachau arrived in the two labor camps.[86] While the evacuees from Natzweiler-Struthof were wending their way to Dachau, other prisoners were moving in the opposite direction. The system continued to function and to shift prisoners in accordance with labor requirements and supply possibilities, and Natzweiler-Struthof continued to function in fall 1944 as a concentration camp and a slave labor system, with all that this implied.

The testimonies of Natzweiler-Struthof prisoners confirm the assessment that the murderous activities that accompanied the evacuations from eastern Europe did not occur during the evacuations in Alsace and along the Rhine, even in the later stage from mid-March 1945. One of the evacuated camps was Neckargerach near the Neckar River, east of the Rhine. It was not evacuated in the first wave because it was not in immediate danger of falling into enemy hands in summer–fall 1944, as were the camps west of the Rhine.

It was evacuated only on March 26, 1945, and the inmates were earmarked for Dachau. The sick prisoners, 200 out of the 800 evacuees, who were not fit enough to march, were left behind and were due to be sent by rail, but did not get farther than the Kochendorf subcamp, a little south of Neckargerach. About 20 of them apparently perished in the course of the evacuation.[87] The other prisoners began the walk to Dachau.[88]

> Fortunately, it did not deteriorate into a death march, although the situation became very tense. For a week we were given nothing to eat, except for once, but despite it all we all reached Dachau and later returned home safely. On our way to Dachau, only one man lost his life, a French comrade whose name, regrettably, I can't remember.[89]

Kochendorf camp was established in September 1944 in the depths of a salt mine near this small town. It was intended to be the site for manufacture of engines for jet aircraft. More than 1,800 prisoners were housed there; about 700 of them were Jews, mostly from Hungary, who had been sent from Auschwitz and were considered to be skilled craftsmen. The harsh working conditions in the depth of the mine claimed numerous victims in the few months of the camp's existence.[90] About 1,250 Kochendorf inmates (including sick prisoners from Neckargerach) set out on the evacuation march on March 20, 1945, and reached the village of Hütten a day later. They were feeble and starving, having received no regular rations for several days. On the joint initiative of several guards and several local families, food supplies were organized for them for the four days they spent in the town. Despite the objections of the guards, the local mayor succeeded in visiting the site outside town where the prisoners had halted and saw that 200 of them were in very poor condition. They were too weak even to drink water. On his instructions, milk, bread, apples, and other foodstuffs were supplied to them. He even succeeded in rounding up four trucks in order to transport the sick prisoners. The entire project was organized with the help of local residents and the commander of the local Volkssturm (People's Militia).[91]

Evacuation of the Natzweiler-Struthof camps east of the Rhine gained momentum in mid-March 1945 due to the advance of the American and French forces. Most of the prisoners in these camps were evacuated to Dachau and others to Neuengamme. In the first half of April, quite a few of the Natzweiler-Struthof evacuees succeeded in reaching Dachau before the final chaotic two weeks in the German concentration camp system.[92] But even then, in that atmosphere of pandemonium, the inmates were not massacred. For example, the Schörzingen subcamp, which lay north of the Danube, was evacuated relatively late, on April 18, 1945. On April 16 the prisoners were told that they should prepare their belongings for departure. Two days later the 650 inmates were called out of their barracks and arranged in groups of about 100 each. Some 40 guards accompanied the march.

About 4,000 prisoners evacuated from several southerly subcamps of Natzweiler-Strutof were roaming the area at that time. After walking for three days, the Schörzingen evacuees reached the shore of Lake Konstanz, the meeting point of the borders between Germany, Austria, and Switzerland. During the march they were given 7 pounds (3 kilograms) of potatoes daily. With the French army advancing rapidly in this area, the accompanying guards tried to divert the march to a more southerly route. Upon reaching the town of Ostrach the guards fled, leaving the prisoners to their own devices. Thirty-seven prisoners perished during this death march. A neighboring subcamp, Schömberg, was evacuated in similar fashion on April 18. The prisoners were prepared for departure and received half a loaf of bread for the journey; the small staff burned the few documents in the camp office, and the march set out on its way. The guards intended to bring the prisoners to Dachau. There were several shooting incidents along the way when prisoners who lagged behind were killed. On April 21 the guards fled because French troops had already moved into the area, and the prisoners were released.[93]

Nonetheless, brutal killings did take place on some of the death marches from Natzweiler-Struthof. In one case, the victims were prisoners from the Hessental subcamp in Schwäbisch-Hall. This was one of the most easterly camps of Natzweiler-Struthof, located east of the Necker River. It had been established relatively late, in October 1944, and initially had 600 inmates. The number rose to 800 in December 1944. SS-Hauptscharführer (Sergeant-Major) August Walling commanded the camp from the beginning until the evacuation. The inmates worked for the armaments industry on the production line of Messerschmidt Me-262 jet planes, Hitler's secret weapon, which was intended to shatter Allied domination of the skies over Germany. In all, 182 of the prisoners perished during the brief operation of the camp.[94]

As was true of other Natzweiler-Struthof subcamps, the evacuation of Hessental was not conducted chaotically, as had been the case in concentration camps in Poland several months previously. The preparations began at the beginning of April upon news of the advance of American forces in the region. On April 3 trucks arrived in the camp, carrying 200 evacuees from Kochendorf, who were in very poor physical condition. This group had been evacuated with the other prisoners on March 30. The circumstances that arose while they were at Hütten recurred frequently in spring 1945 in various geographically remote labor camps. The commandant of Kochendorf, Augen Bütter, who was in charge of the evacuation, decided that there was no point in dragging along a large number of sick prisoners, many of them Jews. He reasoned that they would not be able to withstand the rigors of the journey and, in any case, were not needed for labor purposes. The 50 weakest prisoners were singled out and liquidated at Hütten. Hessental agreed to accept the other 200.[95] When the date to evacuate Hessental came around on April 5, no locomotive was available and the prisoners began to walk southward to Dachau and its subcamp, Allach. Before they set out, 17 prisoners were murdered, apparently because of escape attempts, as were several others who were too weak to walk.[96]

One of the investigators on the commission of inquiry established immediately after the war by the French Ministére des Anciens Combattants (Ministry for Veteran Affairs) retraced the route of this march in February 1947. The commission focused on places where there was information on the murder of French prisoners during death marches, and made every effort to locate the sites of these murders in order to bury the victims in the homeland from which they had been deported. Mainly through conversations with mayors of small towns and villages and other witnesses, the investigator discovered several mass graves of prisoners from the Hessental death march. In Sulzdorf, which the prisoners had reached on the first day, the remains of 17 corpses were found, 8 of them identified as French. In Ellwangen, which the march reached on April 7, 36 corpses were exhumed. Other corpses were discovered in towns along the route, but the largest mass grave was uncovered in the village of Zöbingen, where 42 corpses had been buried. Almost all the victims were apparently among the 200 sick and feeble prisoners from Kochendorf who had set out on the march despite their infirmity.[97]

The massacre at Zöbingen was perpetrated in a way that would often be repeated during the spring 1945 death marches, in Germany and Austria in particular. Thirty-seven of the murdered prisoners were killed by guards' bullets, evidently because they could march no farther. After the killings, the victims were buried by a battalion of Volkssturm men. They were elderly civilians from the region, who were no longer eligible for ordinary military service and hence had been drafted into the popular militia established in October 1944 under close supervision of the Nazi Party. Its main task was territorial defense. In order to help in the burial chores, the Volkssturm men took five prisoners with them, who dug the graves of their comrades. They were then shot in the back of the head and buried with the others.[98] These groups of murderers, all local residents, were to play an important role in liquidating camp prisoners in the final weeks of the war.

Characteristics of the Prologue

The evacuations that took place in summer–fall 1944 at the southern, eastern, and western margins of the Nazi realm intimated what was to occur several months later. To the west, in the Natzweiler-Struthof camps, there were almost no incidents of mass slaughter of evacuated prisoners, at least during the first evacuation period in fall 1944. This was apparently because the distances covered were relatively short, transportation was more convenient than in the eastern areas, and also because of the timing of the evacuation. It was only in April 1945, in the stormy days of the end of the war, that circumstances changed and the inmates of several subcamps of Natzweiler-Struthof also fell victim to slaughter. Nor should we forget another central factor: the identity of the prisoners. Many of the inmates of Natzweiler-Struthof and its subcamps were western Europeans, and only a minority were Jews or came from eastern Europe.

In contrast, in the East as early as summer–fall 1944 there were clear indications of what was going to occur several months later. Quite a few of the camps evacuated in this period were populated by Jewish, Polish, or Russian prisoners. The murder of the Jewish laborers at Bor and the killing of camp laborers in the ruined Warsaw ghetto demonstrated that preservation of the lives of the slave laborers was far from being a supreme economic consideration, which dictated the attitude toward prisoners or the manner of evacuation. The SS soldiers, German or other, and the Wehrmacht troops were ready to take these needs into consideration only to the extent that they did not create unnecessary complications, did not involve them in complex dealings with the logistics of evacuation, and did not pose a real or imagined danger to their own personal safety. When those involved were Jewish prisoners, the economic consideration was usually a low priority. These were the main factors that determined the narrow borderline between life and death on the death marches that began in early 1945.

CHAPTER THREE

Waves of Violence and Acts of Annihilation

When the Red Army's great winter onslaught began in January 1945, the imbalance between the two armies was so great that the Wehrmacht had little or no prospect of checking the Russian race into the heart of the Reich and onward to Berlin. Marshal Ivan Konev on the First Ukrainian Front and Marshal Georgy Zhukov on the First Byelorussian Front had a total of 2 million men under their command. Facing them, along the 558-mile (900-kilometer) stretch from the Baltic countries in the north to the Carpathian Mountains in the south, were some 400,000 exhausted, battle-weary German soldiers who doubted their ability to halt the Soviet war machine. Their military equipment, in particular artillery and tanks, was inferior in scope and quality to that of the Red Army.[1]

The slackening of military discipline, which was now quite common, had begun even before the complete military collapse of the past few months. At the beginning of 1943 German officers were forced to employ increasingly draconic measures to maintain order and discipline in the front line. Hitler himself referred to this problem in a special order of the day. Soldiers were frequently caught trying to desert and were summarily executed. It was no rarity to find within the German ranks men who hoped for rapid death in battle rather than capture by the Soviets. Some took emotional leave of their distant families and tried to reconcile themselves to the fact that they would never see them again. Yet, their fear of falling captive and the knowledge that they constituted the last barrier against the influx of Soviet troops into the hinterland were translated into a stubborn and fierce resolve to fight, even though the odds were against them.[2]

The Soviet attack, which began on January 12, 1945, triggered panic-stricken flight of the civilian population from all the areas where the Red Army was expected. Albert Speer, who visited Upper Silesia at the end of January 1945, brought back to Berlin a series of photographs of the region. They afforded a glimpse of the human drama unfolding there: tens of thousands of German civilians were fleeing the Soviet guns. When shown the pictures, Hitler refused to discuss them. He went into an uncontrollable rage whenever he was informed of an additional collapse of defense lines in the East and insisted on total evacuation of the population and of all industrial and military equipment and total destruction of infrastructures in evacuated areas.[3] With a tenacity that can only be explained by psychopathological criteria, Hitler refused to approve tactical retreat and reorganization of the eastern front along logical defense lines that would take into account the total inferiority of the German army. The attempts of his generals, headed by Heinz Guderian, chief of the General Staff, to persuade him of the hopelessness of such tactics were to no avail.[4] Hitler and Goebbels, adrift in a world of historical fantasy, decided to appeal to the German public through the press and explain that this war was a modern version of the Punic Wars between Rome and Carthage. It was a struggle between European civilization and the barbarism that had invaded it from without, a war in which victory could be achieved only through the collaboration and supreme courage of leaders and nation, as in the case of Rome's triumph over Carthage.[5] The Nazi newspaper, the *Völkische Beobachter,* explained to its readers what the war was about. It surveyed the historic role of the Mongols in the human and political fabric of the Soviet Union and argued that the Soviet regime attributed great importance to the integration of the Mongol nation. Some 800,000 Mongol troops were serving in the Red Army, which was now about to invade Germany, the paper wrote.[6]

The German army, however, was disintegrating. Units were falling apart, while hungry soldiers were resorting to looting the property of the local population. There were reports of retreating soldiers who forcibly dragged women and children off the trains evacuating them from Eastern Prussia westward and took their place. Nazi Party activists were among the first to board these trains. There were quite a few cases of desertion, and field courts martial handed down death sentences, carried out on the spot, against soldiers who deserted or tried to escape.

"Along the road we saw German soldiers who had been hung. There were signs around their necks saying: 'I was a coward and I tried to run away,'"[7] wrote a 13-year-old boy, describing the sights he saw from a refugee train heading from Posen westward. For Polish prisoners who arrived in labor camps in Lower Silesia after the suppression of the Warsaw uprising in summer 1944, the sight of dozens of German soldiers hanging on trees along the roadside was resounding proof that the end of the Third Reich was at hand.[8]

The Horror from Out of the East

The social repercussions of the military breakdown were as far-reaching as the military implications. The highways, roads, and railway stations of western Poland, Eastern Prussia, and Silesia were crammed with hundreds of thousands of men, women, and children, all making their way westward. It was this sight, more than any other, that characterized the eastern front at the beginning of 1945. The imminent arrival of the Red Army evoked ungovernable dread, and the urge to flee was the main driving force. Horror stories spread like wildfire, in which the Soviet troops were depicted as the emissaries of Satan, sowing death as they advanced. Horst Wegner, then 16, remembered his encounter with them:

> We walked to Kolberg on the Baltic Sea, about 30 miles away. The Russian tanks caught up with us just before we reached Kolberg. The infantry sitting on top of the tanks started to shoot wildly all over the place. My father got shot right through his thigh. We were near a farmer's house, and sneaked into the barn to catch our breath and rest a little. I was dog-tired from pushing my mother on the bike. The Russians found us and pulled us out of the barn. They were Mongolians. They had huge scars and pockmarks on their faces. And they were draped in jewelry—they wore watches up to the elbows. They came in and pulled out everyone wearing anything military—a military coat, for example. They were taken behind the barn, shoved against a wall, and shot. They weren't even all Germans; some of them were foreigners. They even shot the private who had bandaged my father's leg.[9]

During this wave of evacuation and flight, social solidarity was totally subverted. A boy evacuee recalled how families were torn apart and lost their loved ones in the great flight, how the sturdy dragged the weak out of the trains, hurled their belongings onto the platforms, and took their place, and how peasants slaughtered their beasts and left the carcasses at the roadside so that the animals would not fall into Soviet hands. Old people who had lost their wits were a common sight on the crowded refugee trains.[10] One of the U.S. Army intelligence reports described the collapse along the eastern front:

> The current Russian offensive in the East which has brought in its wake a mass movement of an estimated 4,500,000 refugees has brought into sharp focus a problem which is likely to be one of the most critical confronting Military Government during the early stages of the Occupation in Germany. . . .

It is doubtful whether history has ever witnessed a mass movement of people to compare with the hasty and disorganized trek of millions now taking place in Eastern Germany.

As invariably happens in refugee movements, the people affected are primarily women, children, old people and invalids, although even the Germans admit that a large number of able-bodied men, who should be remaining in their factories or fighting with the Volksturm, have joined the trek.[11]

Villages and towns, in particular in Eastern Prussia and Silesia, from which German nationals fled in January–February 1945, became ghost settlements after the exodus. Dogs and cats, abandoned by their owners, prowled the streets of the deserted towns.[12] In many houses, cooking pots were left on the gas burners and plates on the table when the householders fled without finishing a meal. Open churns of fresh milk were left standing outside cowsheds or houses. The doors of shops gaped open, exposing the merchandise on the shelves.[13] "The roads are full of refugees, carts and pedestrians . . . now and then carts packed with people and suitcases go by, followed by envious looks from those on foot. Again and again there are jams. People are gripped by panic as the cry goes up: 'The Russians are close,' " wrote someone who fled.[14] Prisoners from the Stutthof subcamps, who were also evacuated at the time, never forgot what they saw:

> And as we walk along, I will never forget this, hundreds of Germans are fleeing like us. They look the same, the heroes. They are fleeing, on horse-drawn carts, on foot, the heroes are fleeing like us, and they look so pathetic, just like us.[15]

There were horrendous sights in the towns of Eastern Prussia after the Soviet troops entered: ruined, smoldering churches; human corpses and animal carcasses lying side by side in the streets and among the ruins; overturned, charred trucks and vehicles. The plague of violence and murder did not spare the old, the women, and the children. In quite a few small towns, almost all the girls and women were raped savagely, regardless of their age. Such atrocities were often perpetrated before the eyes of husbands and children, and all members of the family were subsequently murdered. Female corpses were often obscenely abused.[16]

The driving emotion among the population was primeval terror at the thought of the approaching Red Army. They were convinced that they could suffer no worse a fate than to fall into the hands of the conquerors from the East. Tales of the atrocities that awaited those who did not escape spread by word of mouth and appeared in the press. They described in detail the atrocities the Red Army troops were committing: mass murder, torture of POWs, unbridled looting, and above all, brutal rape of German women. Josef Goebbels wrote in his diary:

We have similar reports of atrocities from the eastern territories. They are truly horrifying. They cannot be repeated in detail. From Upper Silesia in particular information coming in is shattering. In certain towns and villages all women between the age of 10 and 70 were raped innumerable times. This seems to have been done on orders from above since the behaviour of the Soviet soldiers leads one to think that there is a definite system.[17]

Word of the events along the eastern front in January–February 1945 found its way not only to Goebbels's diary. The crumbling Nazi regime made every effort to transmit the details to the German population at first hand. At the beginning of February the *Völkische Beobachter* published the eyewitness account of a woman who described how two Soviet soldiers entered her house at midnight on January 15, 1945. They were completely drunk, went into the kitchen, and began to devour whatever they found in the larder. "We didn't know when they would leave. Then we heard the first shots in the village. My two sons, aged 18 and 20 and my husband were taken by the soldiers and shot."

She went on to describe how she was raped and how other women and girls in the village were also raped by the soldiers. Most of the young men were left alive in order to be deported to labor camps in the Soviet Union, the paper concluded.[18]

A German officer described what occurred in Burgwasser in Oppeln district. Most of the civilian population fled in terror even before the Bolsheviks arrived. Not more than 25 families remained behind. When the Red Army troops entered, they began to loot all the property and valuables they could seize. Cameras and watches were coveted in particular. A man of 70 was shot in the street. Several girls who had remained in the village were raped by the soldiers.

Detailed accounts were published about incidents of rape in the village of Raschütz in Eastern Prussia. They began when an 18-year-old girl who was walking down the street was seized by the soldiers and raped. Other sexual assaults took place inside the houses. The soldiers broke in and raped women in their homes, regardless of age. A woman of 50 was also raped. In many cases, these acts were committed before the eyes of small children. Girls of 14 and 15 also fell victim.[19]

This wave of violence toward the German civilian population in the eastern territories was sanctioned by the senior military command. The ambivalent message that Soviet troops received as to their treatment of German civilians was easily interpreted as license to act as if the victims did not deserve humane treatment. In spring–summer 1944 the Red Army's anti-German political propaganda became increasingly extreme, now calling for a tougher and more brutal final effort to root out fascism. It emphasized the need to subdue the Nazi beast on its own soil—in other words to pursue and destroy it en route to Berlin.[20]

Rape on a wide scale had already occurred during the Russian invasion of Rumania. In Budapest too and elsewhere in Hungary, women and girls were sexually assaulted. The Russians did not regard the Rumanians and Hungarians as part of the Slavic family. In Poland, Czechoslovakia, Bulgaria, or Serbia, in contrast, incidents of rape were sporadic and marginal compared to Hungary and in particular to Germany.[21]

The Soviet military command had not anticipated the intensity of the violence toward the German civilian population of Eastern Prussia and Silesia. It was no rarity to find Soviet-occupied villages where all the women aged 12 to 30 were raped, food, alcohol, and valuables were looted, and the village was then burned to the ground. The accounts of rape were so numerous that they can scarcely be considered random or local events.[22] Red Army reports described many cases of violated German women who subsequently committed suicide. Some died as a result of repeated rape.[23] Needless to say, this harrowing experience affected the lives of hundreds of thousands of women:

> What does it mean—rape? When I said the word for the first time aloud, Friday evening in the cellar, it sent a shiver down my spine. Now I can think it and write it with an untrembling hand, say it out loud to get used to hearing it said. It sounds like the absolute worst, the end of everything, but it's not.

An anonymous Berlin woman wrote these words in her diary in May 1945.[24] The acts of brutal violation were to haunt the victims for many years after the war.[25] Such was the revenge of the Red Army soldiers against the nation that had transformed their country into a wasteland and slaughtered millions of its citizens during the war years.

The mass rape of some 1.9 million German women by Soviet soldiers (between 840,000 and 980,000 in Berlin alone out of a female population of 1.4 million) in the last few months of the war and after the surrender[26] apparently had a stronger impact on many Germans than any other experience. Many found it difficult to view the end of the war as an occasion of liberation from a regime in which they had lost faith because they perceived the victors, in particular the Russians, as sexual occupiers.

In the British and U.S. armies a particular effort was made to impress on the troops the distinction between the German people and the Nazi regime and to instill the conviction that not all of the civilian population were to be regarded as the enemy. Such efforts failed in the case of the Red Army because they did not stem from the senior command. It became evident that many Russian soldiers did not perceive the struggle against Germany as a liberating and humanitarian mission to the German people. They viewed the occupation of Germany mainly from their own personal perspectives, having themselves experienced occupation by a force that had perpetrated terrible war crimes on their soil. American and British soldiers had never lived under oppressive occupation, but for the Red Army, the war years were a traumatic era that dictated their conduct toward the German civilian population.[27] This attitude was reinforced by the belief that they had come as an army of liberation to free their fellow countrymen, held in degrading captivity as laborers for the Germans. Many Russian troops also harbored suspicions as to the fidelity of the wives or girlfriends they had left far behind, and this too fueled the outburst of sexual violence toward German women. And finally, their encounter with the relatively comfortable and prosperous bourgeois lifestyle of German civilians in Eastern Prussia and Silesia, which contrasted so sharply with their own miserable and drab lives at home, also contributed to the frenzied outburst of violence, destruction, and looting.[28]

Brutality, a fathomless desire for revenge, and the looting, murder, and rape of the civilian population were the hallmarks of the soldiers *(homo sovieticus)* who came from the East and invaded Germany. In the weeks before the capitulation in early 1945, the ideological and propaganda concept of "Soviet subhumanity" *(Das sowjetische Untermenschentum)*[29] became a tangible reality for millions of Germans, infiltrating their homes and threatening their lives. Many Germans were beset by fear of bestial revenge, and their immediate reaction was mass panic-stricken flight. This fear was later to find expression in outbursts of violence against what was perceived as a demonic threat. In the course of this chaotic period of headlong flight, as millions of civilians, soldiers, civilian officials, and party activists and their families escaped westward, the great concentration camps in Poland were also evacuated.

From Evacuation to Death Marches: Auschwitz, January 1945

The final evacuation of Auschwitz was set in motion by an order issued on December 21, 1944, by Fritz Bracht, Gauleiter and Reich commissar for defense of Upper Silesia. The instructions were to evacuate from Upper Silesia all POWs, forced laborers, and concentration camp inmates and transfer them to Germany, to locations from which they could be dispersed for labor assignments. Bracht attributed even greater importance to the potential labor force than to production installations or machinery. He stipulated which elements in the police and in the Gau (party regional administration) offices would be responsible for different aspects of the evacuation. The district commander of the SS and the police was placed in charge of the evacuation of the camp inmates, in accordance with Himmler's orders of summer 1944.[30] In Silesia, Ernst Heinrich Schmauser, whose headquarters were in Wrocław, was in charge.

Almost a month after Bracht circulated his orders regarding evacuations from Silesia, no arrangements were yet underway for the final evacuation of the Auschwitz inmates. On January 12, 1945, the Red Army launched its wide-scale winter onslaught, with the operative objective of ending the war in Europe within 45 days. After less than two weeks, the Soviet forces were advancing west of Danzig in northern Poland and had liberated most of southwestern Silesia.[31] Schmauser was not clear as to how he was supposed to deal with the prisoners under these circumstances. He telephoned Pohl, apparently at some date after January 12 when it was already evident that the Red Army would reach the camp within a few days, and asked what he should do. The answer he received in Himmler's name in mid-January 1945 was that not a single healthy prisoner was to be left behind in the camps under his jurisdiction.[32] The precise date of this order is unknown, but it was certainly received several days, if not hours, before the actual evacuation began.[33]

The confusion that prevailed in the highest echelons of the SS command regarding the evacuation of the concentration camps was again demonstrated on January 19, 1945, the day after the prisoners left the camp. Pohl then dispatched directives to the camps in Ostland and Russland-Nord, announcing that responsibility for the camps in those areas was being transferred to Friedrich Jeckeln, the HSSPF Ostland. The WVHA staffs of the camps were ordered to return to Berlin at once.[34] There was almost nothing new in this order, for these arrangements had been decided on in principle six months previously. Pohl recalled after the war that, since Himmler had informed him in October 1944 that the Stutthof camp was to be evacuated when in danger of falling into Soviet hands, the new instruction was seen as an order to implement Himmler's directive.

There is no evidence that Himmler ever issued a sweeping designated order to evacuate all the concentration camps in Poland, as is confirmed by Schmauser's confusion. Moreover, Pohl claimed that what Himmler had conveyed to him the previous October was not a general instruction applicable to all the camps in Poland. By the time the actual evacuation arrived (January), it was necessary to refresh the instructions in order to take action. The familiar cumbersome bureaucracy had been rendered even more inefficient by the circumstances of winter 1945, so that the orders had not yet caught up with the requirements of the situation. The case of Schmauser demonstrates that those responsible for the camps had no clear idea as to how to act; should they evacuate all the prisoners or only some of them, or should they leave the camps as they were? Nor did Pohl know whether Himmler's instructions were to be applied to all the camps or whether all the prisoners were to be transferred to vital labor projects in the Reich. In any event, the order he issued related exclusively to Stutthof and not to the large concentration camps in Silesia, Auschwitz, and Groß-Rosen.[35] Examination of the winter 1945 orders regarding the three large-scale camps in Poland suggests that, in the end, the camp commandants alone were expected to deal with the complex and insoluble logistic problems. Despite the involvement of more senior WVHA officials or HSSPFs, it was the commandants who dealt with the problems directly. It was not uncommon, particularly in the later evacuation period, for the Gauleiters or SS and police commanders to take no interest in the fate of the camps after they had transmitted the orders to the camp commandants.[36]

Bracht's December 1944 order and its addenda regarding the overall evacuation of Silesia detailed the way in which the prisoners were to be transferred. It took into consideration the measures to be adopted during evacuation of various groups: civilians, military, civilian administration, POWs, and camp prisoners, as well as the railway schedules, the evacuation of vital equipment, and the preferred destinations for prisoners earmarked for industrial labor. The order also specified several central subcamps of Auschwitz as candidates for evacuation.[37] In practice, however, nothing was done until the actual day of evacuation arrived.

On January 18, 1945, the evacuation of some 56,000 Auschwitz prisoners was set in motion. About 2,200 inmates from several of the subcamps were transported by rail directly to camps in the Reich. Another 8,000 were left in the main camp and in Birkenau, and another 500 or so, mainly sick inmates, were left in several subcamps that were not evacuated. Many were dying and all were unfit for marching. The prisoners left behind were convinced that they were fated to be murdered within the next few hours by the SS men. For this reason, quite a few made the effort to join the convoys of evacuees despite their poor physical condition and consequently collapsed en route.[38]

To be left behind in the camp was frequently perceived as a certain death sentence. In such remote subcamps as Golleschau, where most of the prisoners were Jewish, this conviction was particularly valid. This work camp had been operative since summer 1942, and the inmates labored in a cement factory. Toward the end of 1944 there were 1,100 prisoners in the camp, more than 1,000 of them Jews. The order to evacuate was received on January 19. The prisoners were assembled on the parade ground, received a meager portion of food for the road, and began the march toward Wodzisław Śląski. For most of them, this journey was a traumatic experience. They had no idea what the future held in store, and they were convinced that the end result of the evacuation could only be extermination. The 37 sick prisoners left behind were also certain that the guards would slaughter them all as soon as the convoy had left the camp. But it was precisely this small group that was liberated several days later by the Russians.[39]

There were also prisoners who were strong enough to join the march, but who nonetheless decided to remain in the sick bay and to exploit the turmoil around them in order to hide and await the Russians. Among those who set out on the trek, some also undoubtedly realized that remaining behind held out better prospects of rescue than setting out into the unknown.[40] Those who remained in Auschwitz and were not evacuated were liberated by the Red Army on January 27, 1945.

What occurred in the sick bays during the evacuation of Auschwitz was also an indication of the chaos prevailing in the camp. One of the Jewish nurses working there was told by a guard that they were due to be evacuated and that they would be collected within a few hours. The sick inmates watched as huts went up in flames, and they heard the explosions around them as the Germans made a last effort to destroy the camp, its buildings and contents. The sight convinced them that the guards would be coming any minute to kill them all.[41] But the camp guards were busy with the evacuation and took little interest in the prisoners lying in the infirmary.

> We were in the hospital. Our things were in the bunker and we see on the street in front of the lager there go crowds of SS men, soldiers are marching, automobiles, tanks at high speed, and there walk Polish people and Reichs-Germans and Volks-Germans with wagons, and they transport their clothes and move on. We see that something was in the offing. That liberty is coming for us.[42]

Dozens of sick prisoners, some scarcely able to stand, emerged from the barracks that were now burning and roamed half-naked in the snow, the rags that had served them as bandages trailing off their bodies. At those moments, Auschwitz breathed its last. "Then it seems all over. . . . The Germans were no longer there. The towers were empty." Thus Primo Levi described the camp.[43] Those left behind, almost all of them no longer of use as a labor force, were spared the encounter with the last stage of the Nazi genocide— the death marches.

Yet, despite the evacuation, the extermination of the Jewish camp inmates was not yet over and done with. The last massacre of Jews in Birkenau took place between January 20 and 25. After most of the prisoners had been evacuated and only the sick and frail were left, a small group of SS and SD men from the Political Section (Gestapo) continued to destroy the remaining documents and other evidence that needed to be obliterated before the Russians arrived. They apparently completed the job during the afternoon of January 25, some 48 hours before the Red Army arrived, and made plans to leave. But before they left, they murdered some 300 sick Jews in Birkenau. The SD personnel separated the Jews from the other sick prisoners, who were not harmed. This was the last group of Jews murdered in Auschwitz.[44]

It will be recalled that none of the written or oral instructions issued by Himmler or Pohl from summer 1944 onward hinted in any fashion whatsoever that the evacuated prisoners were to be exterminated. Rather, they suggested the contrary; they generally emphasized their importance to the German war effort and the need to transport them in good shape to the various labor camps. And yet the period of the death marches, which began in January 1945 and lasted about five months, was marked by a bloodthirstiness that reached unprecedented heights of brutality and horror.

Wilhelm Reischenbeck was the commander of one of the convoys of prisoners evacuated from Auschwitz.[45] He related that, on January 17, 1945, Richard Baer, the last commandant of Auschwitz, told the guards assigned to accompany the columns of prisoners that they were to shoot any prisoner who tried to escape the column or who lagged behind. Baer also told them to carry out this order without hesitation and emphasized that they were responsible for ensuring that any prisoner incapable of continuing the march be removed from the convoy. Only those able to march should remain, he declared.[46]

Reischenbeck's testimony is problematic: because he himself was one of those responsible for this death march, it was convenient for him to shift responsibility to Baer. While Baer would probably have had no qualms about giving such an order, it is doubtful that it would have reached all the guards or that they would have attributed any significance to it. Baer did not devote particular attention to the evacuation and appears to have been totally uninterested in the entire project. Rudolf Höß claimed that this was the case and that a large part of the responsibility for the havoc and for the horrors that were perpetrated during the evacuation rested with Baer, who did not bother to prepare the camp for the events.[47] Additional proof of Baer's negligence and failure to prepare for the evacuation was provided by Hans Schurtz, head of the Political Section in Auschwitz. He claimed that at the end of 1944 Baer was shown Schmauser's evacuation plan, but displayed scant interest in it.[48] When the date of the evacuation arrived, Baer left posthaste with senior officials of his staff and moved to Groß-Rosen, where the new provisional command of Auschwitz was to be located and to which many of the evacuated prisoners were to be sent.[49]

Several of the people in charge of the Auschwitz subcamps, on the other hand, realized that it was essential to continue to preserve the prisoners. For example, on January 14 or 15 (three or four days before the evacuation) the Jewish kitchen workers in the Janinagrube subcamp adjacent to the Polish town of Libiąż made a particular effort to bake loaves for the prisoners in anticipation of the evacuation.[50] In some cases the prisoners were given general instructions on the day of evacuation and were briefed to a certain extent. A group of prisoners in the Sosnowiec II camp were assembled on the day of evacuation, January 17, and the "block elder" (Blockälteste) reassured them, "No, don't be afraid! We are not going to be shot. They are taking us with them. They have brought carts, but they haven't yet managed to find horses. It looks as if we will have to push them."[51] At Gliwice on January 20, 1945, several prisoners awaiting the trains due to transport them westward heard SS soldiers discussing the fate awaiting the prisoners. They said that the Germans needed these prisoners to serve as a security belt against the Russian onslaught that was driving them westward.[52]

Whereas inmates of the camps evacuated in summer–fall 1944 had received prior information, the hasty evacuation of Auschwitz caught some of the prisoners unready for what was to come. They were aware that the camp was about to be liquidated because the Germans were busy destroying documents and office equipment and loading vital equipment onto trucks. They could also hear the distant boom of the Red Army artillery to the east. But the actual exodus from the camp was unexpected and was carried out hastily and in an atmosphere of pandemonium. It was obvious that the guards had not been properly prepared for this move:

> One morning there was suddenly unusual noise, and the SS roused the dying women, who were sleeping, worn out from their labors, with unprecedented sadism. Within minutes we were standing ready in lines of five; each of us was given a loaf of bread, which the starving women ate immediately . . . we wrapped our feet in newspapers before shoving them into our heavy wooden clogs so that we would be warmer on the road, which was covered in a thick, slippery layer of snow. None of us knew what lay ahead.[53]

In other blocks, in contrast, the prisoners had prepared for the evacuation and had even been told several hours ahead to prepare for departure. In some cases, block leaders assembled the prisoners under their charge and told them that they were being evacuated from the camp because as soon as the Russians arrived they would be executed, whereas in Germany they were needed as a labor force.[54] The prisoners who received this briefing were afraid to leave the camp because they felt that what lurked beyond the camp gate was far more threatening than the familiar routine within. "We were sad at leaving. We were afraid to leave. We knew what we had in Auschwitz, but we were not sure what dangers awaited down the road. At the same time we were excited that the war was about to end."[55] Prisoners with contacts and initiative equipped themselves with food and warm clothes before the march began. Some packed their personal belongings in a sack or bundle that they could carry with them.[56]

The testimony of the survivors confirms the assumption that confusion and disorder reigned on the day before the evacuation and that organization was haphazard.[57] Although some prisoners knew what was happening and prepared for the journey, others knew almost nothing and did not have time to make any preparations whatsoever before leaving. Those who were in the know or were among the groups prepared for the first departures succeeded in laying their hands on a few items of clothing or sturdier shoes.[58] Some prisoners took advantage of the turmoil to conceal loaves of bread stolen from the camp storehouse in their bundles.[59] A few of the guards were ordered to execute any prisoners who collapsed or tried to escape, while others briefed the prisoners and conveyed a reassuring message. But all this was instantly forgotten once the prisoners set out on their trek. Along the snow-laden roads of Silesia a very different reality emerged.

From the moment the prisoners walked through the gate of the camp and began their march westward or southwestward, they added to the human load on roads that were already densely packed with long convoys of retreating soldiers and civilians. A senior Nazi jurist in Katowice, Silesia, witnessed this total disorder in late January 1945 and described it:

> Developments in the situation in Upper Silesia are reflected in today's general communiqué, to which I now refer. The excessively rapid turn of events has inevitably resulted in the evacuation of prisoners. The previously determined evacuation routes had to be partly abandoned because the roads were either too congested or within the range of enemy action. The traffic jams on the roads resulted from the fact that around 1,500,000 of the people living in the endangered areas were now on the move, some in pedestrian columns. For days on end, huge convoys of vehicles slowly moved down the few roads leading west or south west. In addition to that, there were the retreating columns of the Wehrmacht and police. Finally, the prisoners of KL Auschwitz were also sent out on these roads—apparently 50,000 men and women, along with thousands of British and Russian prisoners of war. I have been told that of 3,000 men in one particular POW column only 1,000 reached their destination. Bearing in mind the total disorder on the roads, made even worse by enemy attacks from the air, I do not find this hard to believe. Basically words

cannot describe the horrific scenes. The countless human corpses, dead horses and upturned vehicles were scattered along the roads. The state of security deteriorated considerably from 20 to 23 January—according to the security police *(Sipo)* commander—because 8,000–9,000 concentration camp prisoners could not be evacuated and had to be left behind totally unsupervised.[60]

Rudolf Höß, who toured Silesia during the January–February 1945 retreat, also described the chaos along roads crammed with convoys of panic-stricken civilians, dragging behind them through the snow baby carriages heavily loaded with the personal belongings they had managed to rescue, while alongside them walking skeletons plodded through the snow aimlessly, without clear destination or purpose.[61] In this disastrous situation, the Auschwitz prisoners became a security threat rather than an economic asset. They were the last to be taken into account in the long columns of groups in flight. The military, the police, civilians, vital equipment, POWs, all these were higher priorities. There was little room for this dangerous ragged mob among the masses fleeing to the old borders of the German Reich, and there was no impediment to merciless slaughter.

As the evacuation proceeded and the columns of prisoners began to move toward the place where they were scheduled to board trains, it developed into a scenario of unceasing slaughter. The columns stretched for miles. The guards at the tail of the column often lost contact with those at its head, and when they wanted to convey a message or to halt the column, they often fired into the air by agreed signal.[62] Once they left the camp, the prisoners were under the total responsibility of the guards, who, as noted, had received no clear instructions, although in general they realized that the killing of problematic prisoners or failed escapees would not cause problems for them. This state of havoc generated the conditions that transformed the evacuations into gruesome death marches. The aimless wandering that often characterized the evacuation gradually took on an absurd and threatening aspect. The prisoners grasped immediately that the longer the march, the slimmer their prospects for survival. They also soon realized that often their guards had not received instructions as to what to do with them. A survivor of one of the Auschwitz subcamps described the situation:

> After a day's marching the order was given to go back. We waited for seven hours at night back at the place we had left. Why? What was the reason? We learned that the Russians had attacked and cut off the passes and so, once again, we turned back. Then we turned again in a different direction. Three times we were given orders after a few kilometers to turn back and try another direction.[63]

Conditions along the way were appalling. In many cases, the prisoners had wolfed down the ration they had been allotted in the camp, consisting of a hunk of bread and a can of food, as soon as they received it. They were given no more food along the way. Their constant fear that the trek along the densely crowded roads would eventually end in their extermination was heightened by the difficulty of walking at a rapid pace in harsh weather, while hunger gnawed at them:

> No food had touched my lips all the day before. Others "snatched" whatever they could—grass, snails, potatoes left in the fields—but my throat was blocked, although my stomach was growling with hunger. I had nothing else, so I ate snow. My whole body shook with cold. . . .
>
> The march went on for days and nights and nobody knew where we were being taken. If they want to mow us down somewhere with machineguns, why don't they do it immediately? Or, perhaps there are special installations for that? Perhaps they are taking us again to some new installation for killing by gas? But it seemed that there was no need for any of that; at least two-thirds of the prisoners were already lying lifeless by the roadside. In a few days all of us would suffer the same fate.[64]

The ability to survive the death march often depended on whether the prisoner had succeeded in procuring comfortable shoes and a warm garment before leaving. Those who set out into the icy cold wearing wooden clogs soon found it hard to keep up with the column. In some cases, as the column advanced through the snow and ice, prisoners threw away the few belongings they had brought with them from the camp, including bundles of blankets and clothes that weighed them down and made it impossible for them to keep up the pace dictated by the guards.[65] The idea of escape was not inviting because most of the prisoners, in particular the Jews, were not familiar with the region and did not know how the local villagers would respond to requests for shelter.[66] Only a few hours after they left the camp, the guards began to shoot at prisoners who stumbled. So many of the prisoners who set out on the march were sick, wounded, and too feeble to stand that the guards regarded it as a minor problem to rid themselves of those who straggled or fell.[67] Some prisoners recalled vividly that the guards did not differentiate between men and women.

> Those who stopped, everyone who would fall on the road, was shot, no difference whether it was a man or a woman. You see, we left after the women . . . and we saw en route many dead bodies of women lying on the ground. We marched at night and we had to rest during the day, so that the people should not see us being led through, and evenings when it was dark we marched on again.[68]

The story of one of the columns of prisoners is typical of what occurred. They left Auschwitz-Birkenau on January 18, 1945, in a group of some 14,000 prisoners in all. The column consisted of 2,500–3,000 prisoners, almost all of them Jews from Hungary, France, and Poland.[69] There are few known details about the first lap of this death march from the camp to Mikołow, a distance of 20 miles (32 kilometers). After marching about 12 miles (20 kilometers) they reached Gliwice on January 20. The next day they were loaded onto a train and transported southward to the town of Rzędówka-Leszczyny, where additional small groups of prisoners from several subcamps were already waiting. Thirteen years later, in 1958, a mass grave was uncovered there, containing about 290 corpses. These were apparently the bodies of prisoners who had died aboard the train and others who died or were liquidated while in the town.[70] From there the prisoners set out on a 124-mile (200-kilometer)-long death march that passed through a series of small towns and villages on the roads stretching westward to Groß-Rosen. They entered the Protectorate (Nazi-annexed territories of Bohemia and Monrovia, 1939–1945), returned to Silesia, and advanced northward toward Dzierżoniów and from there to Groß-Rosen. At least a thousand of them died or were murdered in the first stage of this death march, the 34-mile (55-kilometer) stretch from Auschwitz to Gliwice, the 12-mile (20-kilometer) train journey to Rzędówka-Leszcyny, and another 19 miles (30 kilometers) to the town of Racibórz. In other words, about 30 percent of the prisoners perished or were murdered in less than a week. There is no precise information on the number of prisoners murdered later, although information on the locations where prisoners were murdered during this march was collected in late January–early February 1945 in the towns and villages through which they passed.[71] Years later, the death march from Auschwitz reminded the survivors of a well-known historical event:

> And then the march began, and in order to compare it somehow, anyone who has seen the film about the 1812 Russian-French war, and the scenes of the retreat of the French from Moscow, the snow-covered soldiers, the soldiers with crystals of ice on their lips, on their moustaches, soldiers without head coverings and with a layer of snow, and soldiers retreating with torn boots and toes protruding from the torn leather, soldiers who collapsed out of weakness, starvation—it was nothing compared to the hell of the retreat, of the death march.[72]

The roads of Upper Silesia were strewn with mass graves of prisoners murdered during the evacuation of Auschwitz. For example, the grave of seven shot prisoners was found in Marklowiec; in Orzepowice a mass grave of 13 Auschwitz prisoners murdered there on January 24 was uncovered;

the corpses of between 45 and 48 prisoners were found near Wodzisław Śląski; and a grave was uncovered at Rybnik, containing the corpses of about 290 Auschwitz prisoners who froze to death between January 18 and 20 while halted in the town. Most were Poles, and the rest were Belgian, Dutch, Czech, French, Russian, Yugoslav, and Jewish.[73] The corpses of 34 prisoners who had been shot were exhumed in the vicinity of Jastrzębie Zdrój.[74] In the village of Borowej not far from Gliwice, 30 corpses were brought to the cemetery for burial.[75]

After the war it was almost impossible to ascertain the identity of the thousands of victims of these massacres. In one exceptional case, 10 corpses of prisoners who had been shot were discovered in the town of Stary Biedruń. Polish investigators who examined them concluded that they were Jewish prisoners, apparently murdered on January 24, 1945. They were dressed in prison garments and had been in very poor physical condition. Among them was Edmond Asewicz from the Warsaw area, who was identified through a letter found in his pocket. Also identified was Josef Zigler from Łódź, through a letter from his children found in his pocket and bearing his ghetto address. In all cases there were bulletholes in the skulls, and the meticulous investigators even noted the calibers: 7.65, 8, and 9 mm.[76] Almost the only personal details recorded by the investigators were height and prisoner's number and occasionally also national origin. In one case, a committee of inquiry uncovered a mass grave containing 23 corpses in the town of Neisse. Several of them had the letter F (France) or H (Holland) sewn onto their garments. In Gräflich-Wiese the corpses of 32 prisoners were found, almost all of them with the letter P (Poland) sewn onto their clothes.[77]

These acts of slaughter were by no means conducted clandestinely. The Polish residents of towns and villages the prisoners passed saw the columns of human beings dressed in rags trudging through the snow and the armed German guards shooting those who fell by the roadside.[78] Quite a few residents of Rybnik saw the hundreds of dead victims. Sometimes the murders were committed in courtyards adjacent to the villagers' homes. The murderers did not even try to conceal their identity. One of the Polish peasants in whose courtyard several prisoners were executed even remembered the names of the soldiers: Rudolf Paszuta, Henrik Wojtas, and Gustav Gulik.[79] The liquidation of prisoners along the evacuation routes was reported by members of the German police and gendarmerie in the towns they passed. The policemen submitted reports whenever they found corpses by the roadside. There are extant reports from Silesia and from villages in the Protectorate along the route of the death marches from Auschwitz and Groß-Rosen.[80]

Quite frequently, peasants and town residents took pity on the prisoners passing through and tried to throw them food, evoking angry responses from the guards who were afraid that the prisoners might disperse, causing unnecessary delays. Sometimes, often on the initiative of the village women, prisoners who succeeded in escaping found shelter in local homes.[81] Among the Auschwitz evacuees who found such shelter were Jewish prisoners and Soviet POWs who were not fluent in Polish, a fact that made their concealment even more difficult.[82] Sometimes villagers identified the slaughtered victims as Jews and carried the corpses left lying by the roadside to mass graves in the local Jewish cemetery.[83]

The evacuation of the numerous Auschwitz subcamps was also beset with problems. The order to evacuate inmates was frequently received at the last moment, creating total disarray and precluding any organized preparation for departure. This was the case in Neu-Dachs in Jaworzno, one of the largest of these subcamps. On January 17 there were some 3,500 prisoners in Jaworzno, among them 400 to 500 who were too sick and feeble to walk. The Jews constituted the largest group of prisoners, since 1,500 of them had been brought there in late June 1944. There were about 200 to 250 guards and staff in the camp.[84]

On the previous night, one of the factories had been bombed, and some of the prisoners working there were killed or injured, but the crews were sent to work as usual on the following day. At 4:30 p.m., earlier than usual, the prisoners who had been laboring outside the camp were brought back to their huts and hurriedly ordered to prepare to leave.[85] "Suddenly we receive the order that everyone is to go into the barracks and take their blankets and everything they have, then go out and stand in groups of five by the gate, and that we were going to leave through the gate."[86]

It is by no means clear when the commander of Jaworzno, Bruno Pfütze,[87] received the evacuation order from the main camp at Jaworzno, what detailed instructions it contained on how to deal with the prisoners, or what the guards and SS personnel were to do. Another unanswered query is whether, when the prisoners were hastily readied for departure, any plan existed as to evacuation methods, transportation, and destinations.[88] But in light of the confusion and disarray that accompanied the evacuation of the main camp, it is not surprising that the orders handed down to the subcamps were even more confused and incomplete.

In the last few hours in Jaworzno, nobody knew exactly what to do. This was particularly evident in the treatment of the sick prisoners who were incapable of moving. About two or three days after the Auschwitz evacuees set out on their odyssey, Ernst Heinrich Schmauser, the HSSPF, apparently gave orders that sick prisoners were not to be left behind to fall into Russian hands.[89] This order came too late, both for the Auschwitz prisoners and for many other prisoners in the subcamps. At 9 p.m. on January 17, the sick prisoners were summoned out of their huts in Jaworzno for a special parade. They were told that they would be leaving the camp within the hour, on their way to Mysłowice, and from there would continue by rail. By 10 p.m. all the prisoners in the camp were out of their barracks and ready to leave. They left between 10:30 and 11 p.m. However, despite what they had been told several hours previously, the sick inmates were not sent with them. Fate was kinder to these 400 prisoners than to their fellow inmates, for whom another few months of suffering and death lay ahead. The prisoners left behind were liberated several days later by the Russian troops.[90]

After a rapid night march, the Jaworzno prisoners reached Mysłowice on the morning of January 18 and continued on their way. The first victims, whose number is unknown, were murdered by the guards on the night of the rushed departure. No train was awaiting them in the town, and they continued on foot with only one stop in a factory building in one of the small towns on the way. At 3 a.m. on January 19 they reached Beuthen, halted for an hour's rest, and continued their march westward, reaching Gliwice that day. Although Gliwice was the main junction from which the Auschwitz prisoners were being evacuated, no boxcars awaited the Jaworzno prisoners to transport them westward. They marched on and reached Pyskowice, where the guards settled them for the night in a large barn. There they even received soup that had been prepared for them.

On January 20 this death march continued on its way south because the forward units of the Red Army were already in the area. The guards grew increasingly nervous because of the dangerous proximity to the Russians, and a few of them took advantage of the dark to flee during the night of January 20–21. This was also the most murderous night, indelibly stamped on the minds of the survivors. The frozen and exhausted prisoners halted for rest in a forest, and it was obvious that many of them were too weak to continue. Several guards, the most active among them Hans Stefan Olejak, passed among the prisoners and liquidated them coldbloodedly one by one. According to one eyewitness, Olejak himself murdered dozens of prisoners.[91] Born in 1918, a Polish-born *Volksdeutscher* (ethnic German living outside the Reich) with only seven years of schooling, he had been a passionate German nationalist from his youth. In September 1939 he joined a unit of the pro-Nazi Selbstschutz (paramilitary self-defense organization) established by the *Volksdeutsche* in Poland. Several months after the occupation of Poland, he joined the Waffen-SS and was among the first guards sent to serve in Auschwitz after its establishment in summer 1940. In June 1943 he was appointed Rapportführer (work detail leader) at Jaworzno and was second in the command hierarchy in the camp. Among his tasks was central responsibility for the death march.[92]

On the morning of Sunday, January 21, the Jaworzno evacuees reached the large Blechhammer subcamp, just as the evacuation of its 4,000 prisoners to Groß-Rosen was beginning. Because of Soviet military action in the area and the need for rapid evacuation, it was decided that those Jaworzno prisoners who were incapable of marching, apparently about half the group, would be left behind at Blechhammer. They remained in the camp for several days unsupervised, and the stronger prisoners took advantage of this fact to escape and hide until the Red Army arrived. After about four days, a Wehrmacht unit arrived in Blechhammer and moved most of the remaining prisoners out, transferring them to Groß-Rosen.[93]

There was good reason why so many prisoners from Jaworzno were too feeble to march on. During the four-day trek from Jaworzno, the weather conditions had been harsh, with temperatures dropping to −10 to −15°C. The prisoners marched half-frozen, and those who survived the shootings, crammed rags and paper into their shoes in order to protect their feet. By the time they reached Blechhammer, many had frostbitten feet and could not walk. The guards were so terrified that they would not succeed in delivering the prisoners to Groß-Rosen before the Soviet tanks caught up with them that they forced them to march almost without rest or stops for food supplies. It was a cruel race against time, and the night before they reached Blechhammer was the cruelest of all. Prisoners were beaten savagely to spur them on, causing many to collapse with exhaustion or to be murdered by one of the escorts.[94]

There were about 4,000 inmates in Blechhammer at the time of the evacuation, including prisoners from the subcamps transferred there during the first days of the evacuation. More than 3,000 of them were Jews, including a group of 200 women. Among the prisoners who were brought to Blechhammer from other camps, some realized on arrival that they were part of an overall evacuation of the Auschwitz camps and that the area was about to be occupied by the Red Army.[95] When the evacuation to Groß-Rosen began on January 21 each prisoner was given half a loaf of bread, a dab of margarine, some ersatz honey, and a slice of sausage. After leaving the camp, they received no food until they reached Groß-Rosen. The guards were elderly men whose conduct toward the prisoners was drastically affected by their fear of the approaching enemy and the imminent end of the war. Some of them encouraged the prisoners, promised them that liberation was at hand, and even offered them food. Others did not hesitate to pull the trigger and shoot any prisoner who stumbled or lagged behind.[96] At least once they were forced by order of the convoy commanders to retrace their steps and find another route since the road they were taking was too close to the front line. In the towns and villages they passed, the prisoners noted that the German civilian population had taken flight. This being so, it was sometimes easy to forage for something to eat in the fields and abandoned storehouses.[97] On February 2, 1945, the surviving prisoners from Blechhammer reached Groß-Rosen. At least 800 had perished or been murdered during the march.[98]

After the prisoners set out on their march, several hundred prisoners evacuated from other subcamps arrived at the abandoned camp at Blechhammer and continued on their way.[99] About 100 sick prisoners were left behind, including some from Jaworzno. During the panic-stricken flight, the guards had not conducted a careful inspection of the prisoners lying in the huts or in the revier, too feeble to leave. Quite a few prisoners heard about the death march from prisoners from other camps who succeeded in sneaking into the sick bays in order to avoid the evacuation. One of the prisoners, a Jewish physician from Czechoslovakia, undertook to treat the sick, and a group of prisoners in reasonably good physical condition scavenged for food.[100] In their search, they ransacked the guards' mess. "The soup was still on the gas stove in the SS kitchen. That was what their flight was like," an eyewitness stated.[101]

At noon on the day of evacuation, an armed unit of the Organization Todt reached the camp to see what was left in the factory where the prisoners had labored. They ordered the prisoners to dig a pit in order to burn the corpses. There was a supply of petrol in the camp that served to fuel the crematoria where the corpses of dead prisoners were burned.[102] The return of the Germans alarmed the prisoners, particularly after the Todt personnel caught several of them red-handed with equipment or food and shot them. When the Todt unit eventually left, a group of 10 prisoners, most of them Jews from Slovakia, decided to make their escape from the camp. This decision saved their lives.[103]

The prisoners awaiting the Red Army in Blechhammer spent several quiet days. But then, on January 26, 1945, a group of 100 to 150 SS troops arrived and began to destroy the deserted camp offices.[104] Afterward they started to murder the weak prisoners who lay inert on straw-filled sacks in the sick bay. They ordered those prisoners still able to stand to carry the corpses together with the sacks to a pit dug several days previously. They too were shot immediately afterward and thrown, some injured but still alive, into the pit on top of the corpses. The murderers then poured petrol on the straw and set it on fire. The injured prisoners who tried to escape the flames were shot. The SS conducted a thorough search of the camp, and all those rounded up were shot on the spot. Apparently, fewer than 10 prisoners escaped this slaughter.[105] On January 28 several of them made their way to Gliwice where they were taken in by the Soviet forces who had already reached the town.[106]

The identity of this group of killers is not entirely clear. Some of the handful of survivors of the massacre claimed that the killers were not SS men. "It was Germans from the front line who came—not SS . . . Wehrmacht—they seemed to come from the front, were given orders to kill us so that not a trace would remain."[107] Others claimed that the group had been SS soldiers.[108] The confusion may have stemmed from the fact that, before the final massacre, there had also been soldiers in the camp who had come to evacuate most of the prisoners. The reason for the decision to kill is also open to question. There is no way of telling whether Schmauser's order not to leave sick prisoners behind was the pretext for liquidating the sick prisoners at Blechhammer. The timing appears right because his order was given two days after the evacuation of the main camp and before the slaughter at Blechhammer. However, it is not certain that the murderers at Blechhammer knew about the order; what is evident is that the decision was taken on the spot without prior planning by the officer in charge of the unit. The fact that they were not wearing camp guard uniforms also hampers identification. They may have been Wehrmacht soldiers or, alternatively, newly recruited camp guards in army uniforms and not veteran concentration camp guards.

This phenomenon of a "second wave" of murderers who came to liquidate the sick prisoners left behind was not confined to Blechhammer. A similar incident occurred in the Tschechowitz-Vacuum subcamp, which was established in late September–early October 1944 and had about 600 inmates, most of them Jews and the rest Poles, Czechs, and other nationals. The evacuation of this small camp began on January 18. On the evacuation day the 560 prisoners were told to pack their belongings and prepare to leave. The sick, who were not capable of setting out on a march, were told that they would be evacuated on a special train. This persuaded many of the prisoners, who felt that they could not endure a march under wintry conditions, to remain in the sick bays. In all, 138 prisoners were left in the camp when the others left on foot.[109]

The prisoners remained there for three days, managed to find some food, and spent their time resting and awaiting the arrival of the Red Army. In the afternoon of January 21 a unit of 10 members of Organization Todt reached the camp. They ordered the prisoners to dig a pit 2 yards (2 meters) deep and 3 yards (3 meters) wide, claiming that it was needed for burial of the prisoners who had died. At about 8 p.m. that evening, the final slaughter of the Tschechowitz prisoners began. About five men in SS uniforms moved through the sick bays and executed the prisoners with pistols and automatic weapons. Few survived the massacre. Local Polish civilians heard the echoes of the shots and were told that sick prisoners were being dealt with. When the murderers left, one of the local inhabitants estimated the number of victims at about 100.[110]

The Tschechowitz-Vacuum prisoners marched northward to Gliwice and from there, together with numerous other prisoners from Auschwitz, were taken to Buchenwald. In the course of this death march 50 to 60 more prisoners were murdered by the escorts,[111] less than the number murdered by the liquidation unit in the camp they had left behind. All in all, at least 150 of the 560 prisoners who had been there on the eve of departure, perished during the evacuation.

The cases of Blechhammer and Tschechowitz prove that the prisoners were under threat of death even before they set out on the march. This was particularly true of the subcamps. It is impossible to establish whether the liquidation units that murdered the prisoners left behind were acting on the basis of a sweeping order or whether the massacres were local events. What is evident, in any event, is that such massacres did not occur in all the camps. However, those cases that did occur prove that at the time guards, random soldiers, junior officers, or local officials wielded almost limitless power to order and perpetrate murder. The scope of their authority was demonstrated during the death marches.

The Tzrebinia subcamp, whose inmates were mostly Polish and Jewish prisoners, received orders to evacuate on January 17, 1945. The prisoners were scheduled to be transferred to Auschwitz so that they could be evacuated with the other inmates of the camp. After the war one of the guards testified that the prisoners tried to elude the evacuation, but in the end the guards succeeded, with the aid of the kapos, in rounding them up and liquidating those incapable of marching. The prisoners reached Auschwitz a day later after a number of killings along the route.[112] The Libiąż subcamp (Janinagrube) was also evacuated on January 18. The prisoners traveled for 18 days on foot and by rail to Gliwice and were transferred from there to Groß-Rosen. Several weeks before the evacuation of the camp, on December 6, 1944, about 250 Aryan prisoners had been evacuated to Birkenau and from there to Buchenwald and Mauthausen. This meant that the Jewish prisoners constituted the main group among approximately 850 inmates on the day of evacuation. During the evacuation, the transport commandant, Heinrich Niemeier, issued clear instructions to the guards to shoot to kill any prisoner who stumbled or fell during the march. Apparently he himself did not commit many murders, but the other guards did not hesitate to pull the trigger. Survivors estimated that one of the guards, Woland, murdered between 20 and 50 prisoners during the march. Woland and Niemeier displayed particular devotion to duty in killing feeble Jewish prisoners.[113]

During the evacuation from Golleschau to Wodzisław Śląski, one of the men in charge, 49-year-old Josef Kierspel, was particularly active in urging guards to shoot any Jewish prisoners who collapsed. This death march of hundreds of prisoners lasted three days and covered more than 50 miles (80 kilometers). The evacuees were frozen and starving, and those who stumbled were shot by their escorts. Kierspel would stroll over, accompanied by a medic and a doctor from the column, check the prisoner's condition, and then order his liquidation. Some of the guards hesitated to pull the trigger, but he urged them to kill the wretched souls who were holding up the column.[114]

The guards were tense and nervous because of the haste of the retreat, particularly in small and remote places. This heightened their murderous instincts to a degree that astounded even those veteran prisoners who were only too familiar with the dimensions of brutality in the camps.

> And that's how it was, and anyone who lingered and didn't go back in very fast, was shot. And there was a shot and then another shot, real shots; they shot like you shoot stray dogs. And till then we hadn't seen anything like that. We'd seen hangings and we'd seen all kinds of things because of some crimes people were supposed to have committed. But suddenly we saw that people were simply abandoned to their fate, defenseless. They didn't pay attention and fired right and left without consideration for anything. And we saw the blood on the white snow, and we walked on.[115]

Joachim Neander defined these orders as "local liquidation orders" *(lokale Vernichtungsbefehle)*.[116] In other words, they were instructions to kill prisoners issued by any random guard or individual who believed, to the best of his understanding of the situation, that this was the right thing to do in the circumstances. This decision was usually taken because it was not possible to evacuate the prisoners to another camp due to their physical condition or the lack of suitable arrangements. Guards made innumerable decisions of this kind after evacuation of the camp and during the marches until the prisoners reached their destination, whether it was the main camp from which they continued the trek or a railway station. It was these local decisions that transformed the evacuations into murder routes and death marches. Issuing instructions to kill did not require a prior order from the senior command. Any junior sergeant or guard marching alongside the prisoners had sufficient authority to give such an order and carry it out. The fact that in many camps, particularly the subcamps, there was a particularly high proportion of Jews among the prisoners during the evacuation undoubtedly helps explain the ease with which such local decisions were taken and must have rendered them self-evident to the perpetrators.

The evacuees from Auschwitz and the subcamps advanced along two main evacuation routes. The first stretched 34 miles (55 kilometers) from

Auschwitz and Birkenau to the northwest as far as Gliwice. The second, a 39-mile (63-kilometer)-long southwesterly route, led to Wodzisław-Śląski. Those who arrived at the destination were loaded onto open freight cars and transported to various concentration camps in Germany. About 400 of the women prisoners from Auschwitz arrived in Bergen-Belsen, and another 7,000 were taken to Ravensbrück. Fourteen hundred prisoners reached Dachau; 500 Auschwitz evacuees were brought to Neuengamme; and about 9,000 ended up in Mauthausen[117] and 2,000 in Flossenbürg. The largest number, 14,000, were absorbed by Buchenwald.[118] At least 4,000 of these were transferred soon after to Mittelbau-Dora. Another 15,000 Auschwitz prisoners survived the march to Groß-Rosen, from which they were evacuated soon after.[119]

Flight and Murder: The Groß-Rosen Camps, February 1945

In the second half of January 1945 Groß-Rosen became a transit and re-routing camp for evacuees from Auschwitz and its own subcamps. A special new area ("field") was prepared adjacent to the camp, and more than 10 barracks were constructed to house the thousands of prisoners flooding into the camp. It was named Erweiterung "Auschwitz Lager" (the Extended Auschwitz Camp), but it was far from providing the answer to all the urgent needs. In the space of a few days, tens of thousands of weak and infirm prisoners were brought into the camp where no measures had been taken for their absorption. The conditions were appalling. Several barracks that would usually have contained about 100 prisoners each now housed 400, and no fewer than 1,000–4,000 prisoners were crammed into other barracks, with a capacity of 200 each. One barrack, Block 9, housed 1,800 inmates.[120] All in all there were more than 97,000 prisoners in Groß-Rosen and its subcamps on the eve of the evacuation in February 1945, rendering it the largest camp in the Reich at the time.[121]

The incoming prisoners scuffled, sometimes violently, for a little space, sometimes only a few square inches, where they could lay their heads. Since there was not enough room for all the arrivals, many spent the day outside the barracks and were forced to stand for hours at a time, or to lie in the mud beside the barbed wire fences.[122] The food rations were meager and were not distributed regularly. There was no longer any written record of the arrivals. One of the prisoners described the situation:

> As soon as we entered, we were left to our own devices without guards, like a
> flock of sheep without a shepherd, but there were SS men standing around.
> In the camp there were no barracks, no bunks, nothing except for earth and
> mountains and around the area were scattered thousands of corpses, thousands

of skeletons. Suddenly the order was given . . . to pick up the corpses and arrange them in lines. . . . Two men picked up each corpse, a man at each end
and threw the corpses . . . it grew dark and we continued to throw them one
after the other automatically. Our strength ran out and we sank down where
we were standing in order to rest a little. We crowded together in order to
keep warm and fell asleep.[123]

Although the prisoners evacuated from Auschwitz and its subcamps spent
only a few weeks in Groß-Rosen, it was indelibly stamped on their memories as a hell on earth.[124]

The entire camp stank of burned flesh and the smoke rose and rose. We were
concentrated in huts without anything, only walls, no beds, nothing. We were
jammed in one on top of the other, there was no room to sit, everyone had to
stand.[125]

There were piles of corpses everywhere so that there was no room for
new arrivals in the densely crammed barracks, and it was hard to distinguish between the dead and the living.[126] A Jew from Hungary who arrived
in Groß-Rosen with the Auschwitz evacuees wrote to his brother in 1946
that "Dante's Hell was a paradise compared to that."[127]

It will be recalled that Karl Hermann Frank, the HSSPF of Bohemia who
had jurisdiction over the Sudetanland during the evacuations, had sent instructions to the Groß-Rosen commandant, Johannes Hassebroek, as early
as November 1944 regarding the possibility of an evacuation. These instructions were based on Himmler's June 1944 directive on the evacuation
of those camps that were in danger of falling into enemy hands. Frank listed
13 subcamps in the Sudetenland that were in such danger. These included
10 labor camps for women, 2 camps for men, and 1 for both sexes.[128] However, nothing was done until January 1945 when the headlong flight from
Silesia began. In contrast, in the two weeks between the evacuation of Auschwitz in mid-January and the beginning of the evacuation of Groß-Rosen in
early February 1945, a certain effort was made to make appropriate preparations and conduct the evacuation in orderly fashion. In light of the conditions
that prevailed during the evacuation, little could be done to avoid repeating
the horrifying incidents that accompanied the evacuation of Auschwitz.

On February 6 the office of Richard Glücks in Oranienburg dispatched
an order to the camp command, informing them that Schmauser, who was
in charge of evacuating Auschwitz, would be responsible for evacuating
Groß-Rosen as well and that the prisoners were to be transported to Buchenwald, Mittelbau-Dora, and Flossenbürg. To a certain extent this was a
repetition of Pohl's order, sent to camps in Ostland two and a half weeks

earlier. It reiterated what should have already been known to those in charge in the camps since summer 1944. The additional detail that Glücks mentions is the names of the camps to which prisoners should preferably be sent. He was probably more up to date on this matter than Pohl.[129]

At the end of January 1945 Schmauser issued the evacuation order with regard to 15 subcamps of Groß-Rosen that were under threat from the Red Army. Hassebroek conveyed the order to the subcamps without specifying clear guidelines and procedures on how to deal with the prisoners who were candidates for evacuation or those too sick or feeble to march.[130] Here again the orders were baffling for the guards and the personnel in charge of the subcamps.

Albert Lütkemeyer was the commander of the Riese camps, which were established in spring 1944 and operated independently even though they were part of the extended network of Groß-Rosen. The inmates of these camps in the Owl Mountains labored on a megalomaniac and clandestine project (never completed), which was to include the Führer's headquarters. In summer 1944 there were 13,000 Jews there who had been transferred from Auschwitz.[131] When the evacuation of these labor camps began on February 16, 1945, Lütkemeyer did not know exactly what to do with the sick prisoners under his command. He decided to leave them behind, and they were subsequently liberated by the Red Army. Several hundred of them were hospitalized after the liberation in grave physical condition, but most survived.[132]

One of the camps in the Riese network was Lärche, which developed as an external commando of Kaltwasser. Quite a few Jews from Auschwitz, including some who had been deported from the Łódź ghetto, reached Lärche in fall 1944. This camp, like others in the system, was evacuated on February 11, 1945. The prisoners walked for six days to the Czech town of Gradlitz Choustnikov/Hradiště, receiving en route only a little soup and a hunk of bread. From there they marched on to Trautenau/Trutnov, where thousands of prisoners who had been evacuated from a series of subcamps of Groß-Rosen were loaded onto freight cars and transported through Prague to Flossenbürg.[133] Each car held about 120 prisoners, and their only sustenance was one small sack of bread per car. Among the 3,000 prisoners who traveled this route, including the Lärche inmates, only about 1,000 reached Flossenbürg alive.[134]

About 900 prisoners arrived at Gradlitz on February 19.[135] Amanda Heinrich, who lived in the town, remembered the groups of prisoners, who were gaunt and could scarcely stand. On the night they spent there, at least nine of them perished. When they left the town with their guards, 78 corpses of prisoners who had been murdered or died remained behind. Two local inhabitants dug a mass grave, and the victims were buried there.[136] The mass graves of victims of the death march in the Trutnov region were exhumed after the war. Physicians who examined the corpses noted, as in other cases, the horrendous physical condition of the victims, some of whom had not been shot but had simply collapsed where they stood and been left to die at the roadside.[137]

The prisoners were stunned by the brutal conduct of their escorts. They noted that not all the guards who accompanied them along the death march, particularly before they boarded the freight cars, were familiar to them from the camp. Some joined the march along the way, and from time to time they disappeared and other SS men took their place. These guards were totally indifferent to the fate of the prisoners, and all they wanted was to bring the columns of evacuees as fast as possible to the railway lines. They were anxious to make their escape when they could; even the commandant of Lärche camp, who had prepared the evacuation, vanished into thin air after a few days.[138] Among the escorts in the Protectorate were quite a few Slovak guards.[139] They preferred to flee before the column reached the camps in Germany. The German authorities in the Protectorate were confronted with a logistics problem, which was by no means simple: how to evacuate 8,000 to 9,000 prisoners, many of them Jews, while the front line was breaking up and the roads and highways were clogged with convoys of refugees. Under these circumstances, their lack of interest in the fate of the prisoners is not surprising.[140]

Hassebroek testified after the war that the personnel in charge of the sub-camps did not receive orders to kill the weak prisoners and that the order was to bring them to the nearest police station.[141] If we examine events at several subcamps, it becomes difficult to accept Hassebroek's statement at face value, particularly since he was clearly trying to absolve himself of responsibility for the deaths that occurred during the evacuation. It is also at odds with Schmauser's unequivocal instruction that no prisoners were to be left alive in the camps after the exodus. But there is no way of ascertaining whether such an order was transmitted to the subcamps during the evacuation. Matthias Heßhaus, the commandant of Halbau subcamp, who was in charge of a column of evacuated prisoners that eventually reached Bergen-Belsen, testified in court after the war that Hassebroek's order clearly specified that exhausted prisoners were to be shot. This appears to be another case of an expanded interpretation of orders issued in the camp before the evacuation. In September 1944, apparently while prisoners were being transferred to other camps, Hassebroek sent out a directive, based on instructions received from Office D, to the effect that any prisoner who attempted to escape was to be shot. In mid-December 1944, a few weeks before the evacuation of

the Silesian concentration camps, Glücks ordered the Groß-Rosen commandant to shoot Soviet security prisoners for fear that they would create problems at the time of evacuation.[142] It was only a short distance from these orders to the conclusion arrived at in the subcamps during the February 1945
evacuation that any flagging prisoner who created problems or hampered
progress was to be shot.

The inmates of Halbau, a not particularly large camp where some 1,200
inmates were housed in six or seven barracks, set out on their trek on February 10, 1945. Most of the prisoners were Poles, but there were also
Czechs, Russians, and Frenchmen among them. Shortly before the evacuation, a group of about 100 Jewish prisoners arrived and joined them.[143]
During the hurried preparations for evacuation, the guards told the prisoners explicitly that the sick were to remain in their barracks and not prepare
for departure. Between 70 and 120 sick prisoners were left behind, namely,
some 10 percent of the inmates, and a considerable proportion of them
survived.[144]

In any event, Heßhaus's testimony does not clarify whether an order was
given to liquidate debilitated prisoners, nor can we draw conclusions with
regard to those prisoners left behind. Heßhaus, like Reischenbeck at Auschwitz, who claimed that Baer had ordered the killing of prisoners unable
to continue the march, was directly responsible for the killing of prisoners
in the transport under his command. According to the testimony of the prisoners, such killings occurred on at least 20 occasions, with seven to nine
prisoners at a time being murdered. All in all, some 700 prisoners reached
Bergen-Belsen out of more than 1,000 Halbau inmates who set out on the
death march.[145] Because about 30 percent of the prisoners under his authority had been murdered, it was only natural for Heßhaus to try to shift responsibility to Hassebroek.

The evacuation of the Gassen subcamp near the Polish town of Jasień
reinforces the assumption that the commandants of the more remote camps
received patchy directives, although the general tone was clear. This camp,
which was not very large, had been established in September 1944 and in
the few weeks before the evacuation, it housed 700–800 prisoners, most of
them Poles and Russians and the rest of them French, Czech, Croatian, Rumanian, Belgian, Italian, and German. The commandant was 32-year-old
SS-Hauptscharführer (Company Sergeant-Major) Walter Karl-Heinrich
Knop, a veteran camp man who had been serving in the concentration camp
network in various positions since the mid-1930s.[146]

Knop claimed at his trial that in early February 1945 he had received a
written directive from the main camp to the effect that the camp was to be
organized for evacuation to Leipzig-Thelka, one of Buchenwald's subcamps.

The order also specified, he asserted, that all prisoners who were sick or unfit for marching *(Kranke und Marschunfähige)* should be shot before the camp was evacuated. He explained that this order was in line with the familiar instruction that prisoners should not be left alive to fall into enemy hands; the order was also intended to prevent delays and problems during the retreat in light of the advance of the Red Army in the East.[147]

However, no prisoners were killed in Gassen before the evacuation. Fifty-three prisoners, who were examined by a physician accompanied by a prisoner and were declared unfit to march, were loaded onto trains together with two or three guards and transported to Buchenwald. On February 12 the remaining prisoners were ordered out to the parade ground and given instructions regarding the evacuation. They were told that a prisoner who did not obey instructions and tried to escape would be shot without mercy. After the parade they were given a small ration of food for the road, and Gassen was evacuated. The prisoners proceeded on foot until February 22 when they reached Leipzig-Thelka. There are no statistics on the number who perished en route, but there were certainly no wide-scale killings during this death march. The Leipzig-Thelka records for March 20, 1945, list 580 prisoners from Gassen. Together with 53 sick prisoners evacuated to Buchenwald, 633 of the 700–800 inmates of Gassen at the beginning of 1945 survived the evacuation and reached camps in Germany.[148]

The court expressed doubt as to the existence of a written order of the type Knop had mentioned, and stated that no such order was known to have been given in any other of the Groß-Rosen camps.[149] Knop most probably found it convenient to cite the order if only to show that he had ignored it and had chosen to transport the sick by train to Buchenwald. Yet, whether he was deliberately lying about written orders or his memory had betrayed him, it was indubitably true that some kind of directive to leave sick prisoners behind in enemy hands did in fact reach him. Schmauser had transmitted such an instruction several days after the evacuation of Auschwitz, but because of the confusion that prevailed at the time, it most probably did not reach all its destinations. Hence thousands of sick prisoners were not evacuated. Whether the instruction to Gassen came directly from Hassebroek or from some other source, it is clear that it was a known operative order during the February 1945 evacuations.

This does not necessarily mean that the order was always carried out to the letter, and we cannot draw conclusions regarding all the Groß-Rosen subcamps that were liquidated in February. If the camp was located at a distance from the crowded evacuation routes and had a small prisoner population maintained in relatively tolerable conditions, so that not too many prisoners were "unfit to march," the inmates had better prospects of reaching their destination alive. This, for example, was the case in the small remote camp of Aslau in central Bohemia. It was established in May 1944 and housed some 500 prisoners who labored in the adjacent factory. Almost all were Polish political prisoners, and several were German, Russian, French, and Spanish nationals. The camp commandant was SS-Oberscharführer (First Sergeant) Wilhelm Gustav. There were no cases of extreme abuse or starvation in the camp, perhaps because 20 civilians worked alongside the prisoners. On February 11, 1945, the Aslau inmates were evacuated and marched for more than a month until they reached Mittelbau-Dora on March 16 or 17. Of the 500 evacuees, 483 reached their destination. The evacuation was carried out partly on foot and partly by rail, but the instructions Gustav issued to the escorts specified that prisoners were to be shot only in the event of escape attempts. For each prisoner who succeeded in escaping, a remaining prisoner was to be executed.[150] This may have been why the march, although protracted, was not marked by frequent killings. Whatever the cause, the fact remains that massacres such as occurred during other marches did not occur in this case.

The haziness of the orders handed down during the evacuation of the Silesian camps in winter 1945, together with the conditions prevailing during the marches, spelled death for thousands of prisoners during the evacuations from Auschwitz and Groß-Rosen. Neither Hassebroek nor Baer at Auschwitz ever gave a thought to the fate of the prisoners after they passed through the camp gates and set out in convoy. A new chapter had begun outside their sphere of jurisdiction. To the extent that they interpreted correctly the instructions issued by Pohl and Glücks in January–February 1945, they deduced that no prisoner still capable of laboring was to be left behind. This particular order was implemented scrupulously, but decisions as to the fate of the prisoners en route were left to the commanders and guards who were escorting them. As to those who could not be evacuated, local commandants tended to avoid mass liquidation. The sick were often left in the camp or evacuated as a group if the means of transportation were available. This was the case in Auschwitz and in the Groß-Rosen subcamps.

The evacuation of the Groß-Rosen camps proceeded in several stages. In the first 10 days of January, some 11 subcamps east of the River Oder were evacuated. The inmates were transported to the main camp and housed in the "extended Auschwitz." In the second, main stage, the central camp was dismantled, and most of the prisoners were transported by train to various camps deep within the Reich. Also evacuated were labor camps in the vicinity of the main camp in Lower Silesia, and the inmates were taken on death marches to camps in Sudetenland and the Protectorate. The final stage, in mid-April 1945, encompassed various labor camps that were still operating on the western bank of the Oder. This stage lasted until the eve of Germany's final capitulation in early May 1945.

The journey by rail from the concentration sites in Auschwitz and Groß-Rosen to camps in the heart of Germany, which lasted for several days, was an additional chapter in the lethal history of this period of evacuations and death marches. The congestion and lack of food and water in the densely packed freight cars killed hundreds of prisoners and threatened the sanity of the survivors:

> The doors were shut. We had no food with us, and now we tried to sit down. When eighty people sat down the others had no place where to stand, and there were many people who were very tired. It was not possible otherwise; one stood "over" another. We trampled on other people's fingers, and these people, of course, resisted and were striking at others, and so a panic ensued. It was so terrible that people went crazy during the trip and soon we had the first death among us. And we didn't know where to put the dead—on the floor they were taking up space—because they had to lie stretched out. And there it occurred to us—we had a blanket with us, so we wrapped the dead man into the blanket, and there were two iron bars in the car and so we tied him on above us.
>
> [It was] like in a hammock. But soon we understood that that won't do because we had more and more dead due to the heat in the car, and the bodies began to smell. And that is how we were travelling. There were the German troop transports retreating from the front because the front was receding, and they had to retreat further. All the tracks were blocked and we had to stand for days to let the troop transports through first, and at night one could not see a thing. And one was beaten and trampled. In my case it was so that my trousers, my prisoner's trousers, were torn longwise and I couldn't wear my trousers any more. And I remained in my underpants. And so without any nourishment, without a drop of water, and there was snow outside, the SS gave us nothing. And we—there was a mass of insane and dead people in the car and after continuous travelling for five days we arrived in Regensburg. And it was already night and the SS opened the doors and said: If we throw out the dead bodies we shall get some food. And so I myself, together with a friend, removed twenty-five dead bodies from this car and laid them outside in the snow, you see? And then we were given a piece of bread and a little beaker of soup.
>
> I had been standing all the way during this trip and I saved my life only because I had fastened to the car a piece of rope and held on tight. It was indeed utterly impossible. For instance, a friend of mine who withstood all these years in Auschwitz, went insane during the trip and attempted to attack us with a knife and four of use, even five, had to hold him, otherwise he would

have killed somebody. It was decidedly a panic. The whole car was in a tumult, and we heard later when we arrived in Dachau that in the open cars it was the same. At least there they had air, but part of the people froze to death. And when we arrived in Dachau there were more dead bodies than survivors.[151]

Conditions in the open wagons in which many of the prisoners were transported were no better than in the closed freight cars. One of the prisoners who endured the death march from Auschwitz to Groß-Rosen described the scene in the wagon in which he was transported:

We entered the wagons naked, nearly naked, with the thin trousers, no . . . no overcoat, in the snow. Food we did not get. And so in these wagons we traveled for six days and six nights without food. If you want to, don't believe me!

I myself cannot. . . . I myself can't believe that I have endured it! In every wagon there were every morning from ten to fifteen dead. For instance, we asked one another, "How many dead have you? And how many dead have you?"

We slept on the dead. We lay on top of the dead. One took off the shoes from the dead if he had other, worn out shoes. We sat on top of the dead like on a [word not clear], simply sat on top of them. We slept on top of them and everything, so high. . . .

Simply have gone out from hunger, plainly from hunger. Have gone out from hunger by day and by night. There were Greeks. Because they were so . . . the Greeks were more terrible. They wanted to commit a dreadful deed. We didn't permit them. They wanted to cut off flesh from . . . from the dead and roast it . . . and eat it, simply eat it. They asked if anybody has matches.

They had a piece of [wooden] board. But we said: "I will die together with everybody and shall not eat human flesh."

We did not permit them to do it. It was eaten in several wagons. It was eaten.[152]

The prisoners evacuated from Groß-Rosen were brought to several camps in Germany. About 2,300 reached Dachau, 4,000 reached Bergen-Belsen, 4,800 reached Mauthausen, and some 6,000 reached Buchenwald. About 9,500 of the evacuees from Groß-Rosen and its subcamps were brought to Flossenbürg. The camp that took in the largest number, more than 11,000, was Mittelbau-Dora. Several dozen apparently also reached Sachsenhausen.[153]

"They Were Pulling the Women by Their Hair and Shooting"

One of the evacuated Groß-Rosen subcamps was the women's camp at Schlesiersee. Established in fall 1944, it had housed Polish Jewish women prisoners, mainly deportees from the Łódź ghetto who were sent to Auschwitz, and a group of Jewish women from Hungary who were also deported to Auschwitz in early summer 1944.[154] In total, the camp, which was located on two neighboring farms, held about 1,000 women.[155] They were set to work there digging trenches under severe conditions and without suitable winter clothing.

> It was bitterly cold in Schlesiersee and since our clothes were inadequate, several of the girls wrapped themselves in the only blanket supplied during work. There were about three or four checks on all the women after they returned from work and anyone found wrapped in her blanket was sentenced to 25 whiplashes. . . . The girls were beaten till they bled. Out of about 100 girls I worked with, thirty suffered this punishment at least once. We were also beaten if our clothes were wet or dirty. It wasn't possible to prevent it because our work was digging anti-tank trenches in the snow.[156]

The exact number of women who perished in the three months of the Schlesiersee camp's existence is not known, but it was apparently several dozen.[157] The evacuation of this small camp began on January 20, 1945, and its commandant, Karl Hermann Jäschke, was in charge. The prisoners walked about 59 miles (95 kilometers), aiming for the camp at Grünberg. After five days of marching through snow and ice, in the course of which about 20 women were murdered,[158] they reached the village of Alt Hauland [Stary Jaromierz]. The Commission for Investigation of Nazi Crimes (Okregowa Komisja Badania Zbrodni Hitlerowskich) at Zielona Góra investigated this death march in 1967 and summed up its findings in a detailed report.

> The group consisted of prisoners of Jewish descent, mostly of Polish citizenship. "They spoke Polish." Some women had insignia on their clothes saying "Ost" which meant that they were from the territory of the Soviet Union. All the women were exhausted. They were wearing prison clothes and pieces of blankets around them.
>
> The column stopped in Jaromierz [Alt Hauland] to rest and get food. The German soldiers demanded that the residents of the village give them potatoes, boiled and prepared just like for the pigs to feed the prisoners. One of the witnesses, Gertrud Wociechowski, reported the following: "The women were exhausted and wearing tatters. At one point the women threw themselves [down] to eat red beets which were lying in storage on my father's farm, but the guards started to brutally beat them."

The savage massacre of 38 prisoners took place a day later, on January 25, 1945, in a forest near the village:

The German guards separated 38 women who were mostly exhausted and unable to walk farther. These women were not fed any more. Next, around 3:00 pm they were loaded onto 3 wagons which belonged to the farmers and transported to Nowe Jaromierz [Neu Hauland] with 7 guards assisting the transport. After reaching the nearby forest, the guards told the driver to turn right and 300 meters further to stop. Next, they began executing these defenseless women. They were executed in cold blood and in [a] most inhumane manner.

This slaughter was first investigated in 1960 by a local commission of investigation:

> In the course of the investigation, 38 human skulls were found as well as bones, which provide resounding proof of the number of women slaughtered. The corpses uncovered were interred in a mass grave in the Kargowa [Unruhstadt] cemetery. On the spot where the murders took place a memorial stone was later erected in memory of the victims of Nazi crimes.[159]

The murderers made no attempt to conceal the atrocities from the local population or to cover up the traces. Florjan Drzymała was a farmer who had been living there since 1940. He was about 20 years old when the group of Jewish women prisoners arrived in his village. He was unsure of the identity of the German guards, but he noticed that they were not wearing SS or police uniforms. When the prisoners reached the village, some of the guards went off to relax with a glass of vodka and food in the home of one of the local German landowners.

Oswald Tiehle, who was the German overseer of the village, ordered several farmers to prepare three wagons. One was supplied by the farmer for whom Drzymała worked, and it was he who drove it. The second was driven by a Ukrainian laborer, and the third by a local German settler, Wilhelm Milke. The three drove the wagons to the local school where the Jewish prisoners had been assembled. Drzymała described what happened subsequently:

> In front of the school I saw women sitting. They looked miserable and exhausted. The women were wearing rags and they were almost barefoot and their heads were wrapped in blankets. I realized the women hadn't eaten at all. The sitting women were loaded into wagons after some time. I would like to point out that when the village administrator ordered the wagons, he said that the women would be brought to the hospital in these wagons. I was convinced about that also. Together with the women on board there were also guards who got on the wagons and told us to go in the direction of Nowy Jaromierz [Neu Hauland].

When we got to the first forest they ordered us to turn right into the forest. Then, after about 300 meters, they ordered us to stop and they started shooting the women. They were pulling the women by their hair and shooting.

After murdering these women the guards permitted the other two wagons to go. I was ordered to accompany the guards further. I saw one of them ripped off the insignias "Ost" from the victims' clothing and putting them in his pocket.

I would like to point out that during these executions, one of the women said in Polish to another woman, "Farewell, *(servus)* Hela." I also would like to add that the village administrator from Nowy Jaromierz [Neu Hauland], Gutsche by name, brought to us two other women who also were killed while I was there.

It was one of the guards who told me there were 38 victims. The same guard also said they had executed many today. It meant to me in the sense that in previous days, they must have executed others along the way as well.

After burying these women, all seven guards ordered me to go in the direction of Kargowa [Unruhstadt]. The guards were drunk and they continued to drink. They even offered me some alcohol.[160]

In later testimony Drzymała recalled that he had heard one of the murderers say: "Thirty eight. Today there were many" *(Achtunddreissig. Dziesiaj tak dużo)*. From this he inferred that in the previous days they had murdered other prisoners. He also added details about the event:

Two of them were pulling the girls by their hair down the wagons and shooting them with rifles in the back of their head. When they were through, they sent the two drivers back and kept me. We pulled them to the trenches and laid them in rows of 3 or 4. Some had blankets, the tin bowls fell, so we picked them up and threw [them] on the top. If one moaned or moved her hand, they approached with a rifle and shot. When they were shooting, I and the old German, we held horses by the heads, because they were afraid and were jumping. They were shooting in the back of the head. There was a border trench between private and state woods. They were laid in a row 30 to 40 m. long. Some were covered with blankets, and with snow. When they finished, they drank some vodka and I drove those butchers away.[161]

The surviving prisoners continued their death march westward toward Unruhstadt [Kargowa]. A farm woman, Monika Fröhlich, passed them with her cart:

The prisoners of the column were walking very slowly because they were exhausted. They were helping each other in the column. Their clothes were rags;

they didn't have any shoes on their feet. Their feet were wrapped in rags and this is how they were marching in the direction of Kargowa.[162]

After a night's halt at Unruhstadt [Kargowa], the prisoners continued their march toward Züllichau. The guards chose a shortcut that passed through Reckenwalde, from where it was possible to cross a lake that had frozen over during that harsh winter. Two prisoners succeeded in escaping at Wojnowo and found shelter in a barn belonging to Jadwiga Kaczmarek. She talked to them after discovering them hiding in her yard, and they told her that they were Jewish. They remained there until the Red Army arrived.[163]

The massacre at Jaromierz was typical of the incidents that occurred during some of the winter 1945 death marches after the evacuation of the camps in Poland, particularly the subcamps. In the Groß-Rosen system quite a few small camps were located at a considerable distance from railway junctions, so that transportation of prisoners by rail was ruled out. Thus, often a small unit of middle-aged camp guards had to march prisoners to a camp dozens of miles away, from which, they believed, they would be sent on in the next stage of their journey. It was an exhausting trek; their frail, feeble charges were obviously unfit for any work and, by their very existence, were obstructing their efforts to accelerate the pace of the march through snow and freezing temperatures. In view of the muffled cannon fire of the advancing Red Army and the urgent need to end the protracted nightmare, it was not enough to shoot those who fell by the roadside. What was required was wide-scale slaughter to eliminate those prisoners who could no longer move forward. This was often perpetrated at stops along the route.

From Züllichau these Jewish women prisoners continued their hellish journey to Grünburg, a labor camp for women established in 1942 and converted in early summer 1944 into a subcamp of Groß-Rosen. At least 150 of them perished along the way.[164] In November 1944 there had been 971 Jewish women in the camp from Poland, Germany, and Hungary[165] who worked in the textile factory, manufacturing cloth for the Germany army.[166] After the arrival of the prisoners from Schlesiersee, the number rose to 1,800. This camp was evacuated on January 29, 1945. The guards divided the prisoners into two groups, each earmarked for a different destination. One group, consisting of 1,000 to 1,100 women, began a death march to Helmbrechts, a small town not far from Hof.[167] A small number of these prisoners reached Zwodau.[168] The two camps were subcamps of Flossenbürg in Upper Franconia.[169]

The second group was taken to Bergen-Belsen.[170] The evacuation conditions were atrocious. The prisoners made their way on foot to Jüterborg and there were loaded onto boxcars that transported them to the camp. During the month-long evacuation, quite a few of them perished, but there were no incidents of mass slaughter. Among the escorts there were conflicting attitudes toward the prisoners in their charge. Some SS men did not hesitate to shoot prisoners who collapsed. But, in contrast, a woman in charge of one of the groups prevented the guards from shooting feeble prisoners and even escapees.[171] The result was that the older guards, members of the Wehrmacht, did not treat the prisoners with extreme brutality. Sometimes they even collected clothes from the villagers and handed them out to the half-frozen women.[172]

These women walked approximately 400 miles (640 kilometers) in one month until they reached a camp in northern Germany. They were given no food, and their survival depended on their success in foraging for something to eat. This included frozen vegetables stored in the barns where they spent the night, or stray chickens, whose flesh was eaten raw. They were unable to digest solid food, and many died in agony as a result. In many cases the guards did not even bother to shoot prisoners who fell and simply left them to die in the snow beside the road.[173] The number of women who died during the evacuation and the death march to Bergen-Belsen is unknown, but it was apparently one-third to one-half of the 700–800 who set out from Grünberg.[174]

About 1,100 Jewish women prisoners left Grünburg on January 29 for Helmsbrechts on a death march that lasted five weeks, until March 6, 1945. They covered between 19 and 31 miles (30 and 50 kilometers) daily, along snow-covered routes, some of them without suitable shoes, with feet wrapped in rags. A few of them had prepared bundles before leaving Grünburg, consisting of a blanket, a garment of some kind, and the personal belongings they had managed to conceal. They very soon discovered that on this grueling and endless trek, any bundle was a superfluous burden. They wore the blankets or wrapped their bodies in them if only so that their hands would remain free to scrape up a little snow from the roadside to quench their thirst. If they were lucky they succeeded in plucking a little fresh grass sprouting through the heavy snow.[175]

Women who stumbled or seemed to the guards to be contemplating escape were shot on the spot. On some days between 10 and 15 women prisoners perished.[176] Sometimes prisoners managed to escape but were handed over by the local population or caught by the guards. They were then executed in front of the other prisoners as a dire warning to them. Jäschke, the commandant of Schlesiersee, was involved in the shooting of about five prisoners, apparently brought back after escape attempts. The other women were forced to dig burial pits in the frozen earth for their dead comrades.[177] Not many tried to escape: "Fear of death is so great that if you are not particularly brave ... there is always hope that tomorrow you will be saved."[178]

One day the women reached the village of Bautzen where they halted for the night. An unusually generous food ration was handed out: a loaf of bread each. The guards then discovered that several loaves were missing. Since none of the prisoners admitted to the theft, the guards (according to one version it was Jäschke himself who conducted the selection)[179] singled out every tenth prisoner and transported the selected group to a nearby forest, where all 50 of them were murdered.[180] Several other prisoners were taken to the site and made to dig burial pits for the dead victims, receiving a loaf of bread each for their pains. "We ate that bread ... it was bread of blood but we ate it. ... There were no feelings, no emotions apart from the terrible hunger."[181]

On March 6, 1945, the surviving 621 women prisoners reached Helmbrechts.[182] It is difficult to estimate how many Jewish women from Schlesiersee and Grünberg reached the German camps in February–March 1945 because the number who perished during the evacuation to Bergen-Belsen is not known. But certainly no more than 1,200 out of the 2,000 survived the march. In other words, about half of the women died or were shot (a few managed to escape) over a period of three to four weeks. Very few of those who survived the march lived to see the day of liberation.

Written Instructions and Verbal Realities: Stutthof

In January 1945 the Stutthof camp network was also in danger of falling into the hands of the Red Army. Stutthof had developed somewhat differently from other camps established in Poland after 1940. Until the beginning of 1942 it was not part of the IKL administration, and its inmates were almost all Polish prisoners from the Gdańsk area and Western Prussia. Its establishment was part of the ethnic purge project that included the liquidation of the Polish intelligentsia and political and religious leadership in those areas.[183] From the beginning of 1942 it was a regular concentration camp, and, like other camps, it began to serve as a center for the supply of forced labor for the war effort. The number of prisoners in the camp and its subcamps increased significantly in 1944. In Stutthof, as in other camps at that time, the Jews were a prominent national group among the incoming prisoners. The first transport of 2,500 Jews arrived from Auschwitz on July 9, 1944. During summer and fall 1944 tens of thousands of Jews evacuated from camps in the Kovno region and from Riga and Auschwitz arrived at Stutthof. The last transport arrived on October 28, 1944, and included

1,500 Jews. All in all, 23,566 Jewish prisoners were brought from Auschwitz; 21,817 of them were women, and the great majority from Hungary. Another 25,043 Jews were transported from the Baltic states, and here too a large proportion were women: 16,123. Among the evacuees from the camps in the Baltic states were some 150 children and adolescents. Other Jews arrived in smaller numbers in transports from other camps.[184]

In October 1944, after the evacuations and the retreat from the Baltic states, preliminary talks were launched to prepare the ground for evacuating the camp. The talks were attended by Fritz Katzmann (since 1943 HSSPF in Danzig), camp commandant Paul Werner Hoppe, and several senior officials of the WVHA. This preliminary planning, conducted in fall 1944, took into account evacuation routes, food supply to prisoners, and the amount of manpower required to accompany the evacuees. The emphasis in these discussions was on the need to transport healthy prisoners to alternative labor sites in German camps. Hoppe was apparently telling the truth when he claimed after the war that, according to Katzmann, Oswald Pohl had emphasized that not a single camp was to be allowed to fall into enemy hands and that prisoners should be transported and dispersed in camps within the Reich.[185]

Shortly before discussions of evacuating Stutthof began, plans for the construction of a gas chamber were set in motion. This was in mid-July 1944, when transports of Jewish prisoners from the Baltic states were beginning to arrive. Hoppe declared then that prisoners who arrived in poor physical condition should be liquidated, whether by a bullet to the head or by injection of poison. In mid-1944 the use of Zyklon B gas for wider-scale liquidation of useless prisoners was examined at Stutthof. A gas chamber was constructed where 4,000 inmates were liquidated before the evacuation, including Jewish females, mainly older women and children who would clearly be unable to withstand the evacuation conditions.[186] The number of women murdered in this fashion is not clear, but it was apparently several hundred.[187]

On January 8, 1945, several days before the onset of the wide-scale Soviet onslaught in the Baltic area, Katzmann issued an appeal to the German population in the Danzig region, calling for recruitment to the cause of the fatherland, in the spirit of the Führer's appeal.[188] Four days after the onslaught began, on January 16, 1945, Katzmann issued a directive declaring an emergency situation for the purpose of general evacuation of the population of the Baltic region and North Pomerania, to include the evacuation of Stutthof.[189]

The evacuation of the remoter subcamps of Stutthof began on January 20 and the prisoners were transported by road to the main camp. By January 23–24 the Red Army was less than 31 miles (50 kilometers) from the main camp. The area around the camp, not far from Danzig port, was teeming with more than 60,000 civilians and soldiers, heading for the port in order to leave by sea for Germany.[190] This disorder was at its height precisely at the time the prisoners were to be evacuated.

On January 25, 1945, Paul Werner Hoppe, commandant of Stutthof, sent out a detailed directive on the evacuation of the camp. Its tone and precise detailing suggest that it was prepared a day or two before the official date it bears. The evacuation was due to begin that same day at 6 a.m. Hoppe apparently delayed the final instructions until the last moment because he was trying to clarify both to Katzmann and to Office D (Concentration Camps) in Oranienburg that, in light of the situation in the region, it would be difficult to arrange for orderly evacuation of the prisoners and their rapid transportation to other camps. He suggested to Katzmann that they examine various evacuation options.[191]

Hoppe ordered that sick prisoners incapable of marching be left behind. He assigned the task of organizing the evacuation to Schutzhaftlagerführer Theodore Mayer, the officer responsible for prisoners in the camp. Alongside Mayer, he appointed another officer and one of the camp physicians, Dr. Laub. The order went on to state that the evacuation would proceed in a westerly direction toward the town of Lauenburg; a route map was appended. Also detailed were the number of columns of prisoners to be sent, the number of accompanying guards, ways of equipping them, and so on. Included were instructions on how to deal with the corpses of prisoners who perished during the evacuation: they were to be conveyed to a chosen spot and buried together. All such incidents should be reported to Mayer.[192]

There were 46,331 prisoners in the main camp and 22,521 in the subcamp when Hoppe sent out his order.[193] Concomitantly he circulated another order, headed Operational Plan *(Ablaufplan)*, which included a detailed plan of the evacuation routes. It also specified the routes and the time of departure of each column of evacuated prisoners. The first left at 6 a.m. as planned, followed by Column 2, Column 3, and so on. Column 6 was scheduled to leave Stutthof at 10 a.m. The columns were heading for the town of Nickelswalde, west of Stutthof, and from there were to continue to northwestern Pomerania toward Lauenburg. Several of the columns were later directed to the Baltic coast, most of them to the town of Puck.[194]

The fact that plans had been drawn up ahead of time ostensibly ensured an orderly and organized evacuation. On January 25, 1945, at 4 a.m., the prisoners were called out to the parade ground and divided up by block into columns, which left one after the other. Among them were Poles, Russians, Lithuanians, Czechs, Hungarians, Norwegians, Italians, Germans, and Jews.

Each prisoner was allocated 18 ounces (500 grams) of bread and 4 ounces (120 grams) of margarine.[195]

The instructions were not clear enough, however, particularly with regard to the prisoners left behind. After the war Hoppe testified that, because of the Red Army advance, the sick prisoners who were incapable of walking created a problem. Several days later, Hoppe claimed that on January 26 or 27 Katzmann sent him a new order, contradicting the previous one, to the effect that all sick inmates, regardless of their condition, were to join the evacuation marches.[196] All the same, after the columns left, 11,000 prisoners remained in the camp, and not all of them were sick or too feeble to walk. They were prisoners who had been classified as economically essential workers, who labored in the workshops or the camp administration.[197]

A large number of Jews made up at least three of the columns of prisoners that set out from Stutthof.[198] None of the evacuees were wearing clothes that could protect them against the wintry conditions, and many were barefoot. Every day the guards killed dozens of prisoners who were too weak to march on. On the other hand, at least some of the guards did not object when civilians at the roadside offered food to the prisoners. The guards and prisoners even conversed at times, speculating together about what the future held in store. A Lithuanian prisoner found himself exchanging views with a Lithuanian guard who had volunteered for the SS and served at Stutthof as to who was in a better position: the prisoner who was about to be liberated or the guard who had to contemplate his future after the war. Neither of them was willing to change places with the other. In some cases, the guards even tried to persuade German civilians that these prisoners were not a gang of criminals whose only desire was to murder innocent citizens and that they could allow them to spend the night in a barn in the farmyard.[199]

Hoppe's January 25 directives make no mention of the evacuation of the subcamps. An entirely different scenario was played out in the dozens of small camps stretching from Eastern Prussia to the south of Danzig district and central Pomerania. Thousands of prisoners perished during these evacuations, among them a large number of Jewish women who had arrived in those camps in summer and fall 1944.

In August 1944 a labor camp was established near the little Polish village of Szerokopas in Pomerania; it housed 500 to 600 Jewish women, about 450 of them Hungarian and the others from Poland and Lithuania. As was the case in other subcamps of Stutthof, winter took a devastating toll on the prisoners, and many of them died of hunger, cold, and hard labor. This camp was evacuated around January 13, 1945, with 150 of the surviving women prisoners beginning the march northward toward Danzig. Thirty women remained behind because they were too weak to leave. Apparently, one guard stayed with them, his task being to liquidate them. According to one version, these wretched women were killed by injections of poison. Later, people from the neighboring village saw the dead prisoners heaped on a wagon that was transporting their corpses out of the camp for burial.[200]

This policy of liquidating women too feeble to be evacuated was repeated in a number of places. Killings also occurred in the Gutowo subcamp in Western Prussia, where 1,200–1,500 Jewish women from Hungary, Czechoslovakia, France, Germany, Holland, Poland, and the Baltic states were incarcerated. Only about 1,000 of them lived to see the day of evacuation, January 17, 1945. The others perished from the backbreaking labor: digging antitank trenches in the frozen soil. About 200 to 300, who were too infirm to set out on the trek to the town of Nowo Miasto, which began in the early morning, were murdered by injections of kerosene, strychnine, or Lysol.[201] Similar liquidations also took place at the Hopeehill camps where approximately 50 women were selected and shot shortly before the evacuation began early in January.[202] Thirty sick inmates of the Kzremieniewo subcamp not far from Gotowo suffered a similar fate. On January 19, 1945, they were executed by poison injections on the eve of the evacuation.[203]

The liquidation of prisoners too infirm to march was common in the more remote subcamps south of the main camp, in the heart of Pomerania. These camps were located at a considerable distance from the main evacuation routes to the north, in the Baltic Sea area, and were evacuated as the Red Army came closer. The scope of the murders perpetrated in these small camps, where many of the inmates were Jewish women, was greater than that in the subcamps of the two other major camps that were being evacuated at the time—Auschwitz and Groß-Rosen, where the sick were often left to their own devices. This liquidation activity can be explained in part by the very restricted opportunities for evacuation in those areas, the fact that the inmates were Jewish, and the lack of instructions from the camp command as to evacuation procedures. In any event, without doubt every effort was made to leave no living prisoners behind.

The second stage of the murders occurred along the snow-clogged roads in the course of the odyssey. Some 200 Jewish women from Lithuania had been brought to Stutthof in July 1944 and were transferred soon after to the Steinort subcamp. Their labor assignments were not clearly specified: digging trenches, helping with local agricultural labor, and engaging in various service tasks. The conditions were harsh, but it was possible to supplement meager rations by collecting vegetables from the fields. At the end of December 1944 the small camp was evacuated to Proust, southwest of Stutthof. This evacuation was in no way conducted according to Hoppe's instructions:

We started out on foot. It was the end of 1944, winter, snow and ice. We were wearing summer clothes, frayed rags, without stockings and with torn shoes. . . . Along the way I found a pair of wooden clogs left behind by another transport. There were also clothes lying around but we didn't touch them. We only took shoes. The road was strewn with corpses, blood, scattered clothes . . . at night they took us into barns. They gave us no food at all.[204]

One of the Jewish prisoners transferred from Kovno, a Stutthof subcamp, described her trek with her sister to Proust:

Our urge to live gave us the strength to jump up and down and to bang our hands against our shoulders in order to warm ourselves and so as to shake the lumps of snow off the wooden soles of our cloth shoes. On this route the Germans did not kill many women. When they saw someone faltering and lagging behind the others they killed her. The thought came to me that they would kill us as well. I gripped my sister's hand, and the moment the German looked in another direction, and our lines were being supervised by a German of about sixty years old, we slipped into a courtyard where they were milling grain for flour. Suddenly an old German appeared there with a wagon in order to mill his grain. He saw us and immediately went over to the German who was leading our convoy and informed on us. The German immediately came over to the courtyard, hit us on the shoulders with his rifle, and shouted: Run and catch up with the others. . . . At that moment we thought our end had come. We joined the last rows where we had been walking. The German who was guarding us didn't come looking for us and we continued on our way.[205]

In the havoc of the evacuation from Western Prussia and Pomerania, where most of the Stutthof subcamps were located, the columns of prisoners trudging westward for hundreds of miles were a hallucinatory sight. A large proportion of the prisoners were Jewish women. When one of them collapsed and died, her fellow prisoners would rapidly strip off the rags she was wearing so as to add a little warmth to their own bodies. The sight of the corpses scattered along the evacuation route was branded forever on their minds. The guards, generally middle-aged men, walked over to prostrate prisoners and coolly shot them in the head. At night the evacuees were lodged in a barn, if one was accessible, or in other buildings that could be used for the same purpose. Sometimes they were given rations of food, organized haphazardly. In the morning they often discovered that they were lying on the corpses of those who had died during the night. This nightmare lasted for several weeks until the Soviet tanks caught up with the death marchers of the subcamps, particularly in Pomerania.[206]

In quite a few of the Stutthof subcamps, the women survived thanks to the fact that the Russians caught up with the convoys. This was the case with the 500 Jewish women inmates of Sophienwalde. The 300 to 350 who survived were evacuated at the end of February 1945. After walking for several days, the transport began to break up because the Russians were already in the region. Women began to escape and to hide in the forests, and between March 10 and 12 they were liberated.[207] Whenever the convoy reached areas that were about to fall into Soviet hands, the guards seemed to become less alert; the prisoners noticed that "they were frightened for their own skin." Those women who were fluent in Polish or Lithuanian and thought they could pose as Catholics, hid with Polish families in Pomerania who agreed to open their homes to them even though they were well aware that the haven-seekers were Jews.[208]

The familiar phenomenon of mass killing often recurred during the death marches from Stutthof. One of these incidents occurred along the evacuation route of Columns 3 and 5, which left the main camp on January 25 and on February 2, 1945, respectively. The prisoners were forced to march in a southwesterly direction to Proust and from there to the town of Kahlbude. On their way they passed the town of Parangenau. After the war, graves that had been dug between January 28 and February 3, 1945, were exhumed in the local cemetery of Parangenau, including those of 41 prisoners murdered there. Most of the victims were Poles, two were identified as Lithuanians, two as Belgians, one was Rumanian, and one Ukrainian. Five others were not identified by nationality, but only by the prisoner's number on their garments. Three were never identified. Where identifying details existed, the victims were also located by name on the extant camp lists.[209]

Murderers, Collaborators, and Witnesses: The Palmnicken Affair

Some of the prisoners evacuated from Stutthof and its subcamps passed through towns and villages in Prussia populated by German nationals. The encounter between the evacuees and the German population, who were apprehensive and on edge in the face of imminent military defeat, had critical implications for the fate of the prisoners. The circumstances generated mass killings in which elements completely unconnected to the camp personnel played a part. As the war neared its end, the number of prisoners in the midst of the German civilian population increased, and massacres of various dimensions occurred in a number of places.

In the Königsberg area in Eastern Prussia there were several subcamps: Jesau, Seerappen, Schippenbeil, Gerdauen, and Helgenbeil. There was another small camp in Königsberg itself. According to the last report issued by the Stutthof command, in January 1945 there were 4,500–5,000 prisoners in these camps, many of them Jewish women and even a few adolescents.[210] This camp, notorious for the grim conditions that prevailed there, was the most easterly in the Stutthof system and was located at a distance from the main camp.

Of the thousands of Jewish women transferred to Stutthof in fall 1944, about 900 were sent to Jesau. After some time, 100 Jewish men from Vilna were also brought there. They were roused each morning at 3 a.m. and left the camp two hours later for work: paving the access road to a military airfield. They were marched 6 miles (10 kilometers) to their place of work and at 7 p.m. started their march back to the camp. On arrival, they were given their main ration of the day: 9 ounces (250 grams) of bread and a dab of margarine. The evacuation of Jesau began on January 21. The destination was Königsberg, and the aim was to concentrate all the prisoners from the region there and then to transport them westward by sea. Prisoners who collapsed along the way were shot by the guards. When they reached Königsberg they were housed in an abandoned factory near the railway station in the north of town. Keenly aware that the SS guards had no orderly plan for what to do with them, they were uneasy.[211]

In Seerappen as well, most of the inmates were Jewish women from Poland, Hungary, and Czechoslovakia, but there were also French and Belgian male prisoners who had no contact with the Jewish women. The men labored for Organization Todt. The number of prisoners who died as a result of strenuous labor, filth, and starvation was relatively small. The killing of women prisoners by the camp staff was rare. On receipt of the evacuation order, the women were summoned out of the barracks and lined up in groups of five. They began to march accompanied by the camp guards and the Todt personnel:

> The route was horrible. All the time we were drowning in the deep snow. We had no shoes. We were wearing wooden shoes and the snow stuck to them and made it difficult to walk. Several dozen girls who collapsed were eventually shot dead. After superhuman effort, exhausted and starving, we reached Königsberg.[212]

The prisoners spent six days in the abandoned factory. The guards passed among them daily and dragged out dying prisoners, who were obviously too weak to continue the trek. They were taken outside and murdered. The group received no food, and some of them simply died of hunger. On January 26 this transport began to make its way in a northwesterly direction to Palmnicken, 31 miles (50 kilometers) away[213] on the Baltic coast. The weather was brutal. There was bitter frost,[214] and the prisoners lacked suitable clothing to protect them against the freezing cold.[215]

> The assembly point was the camp at Köenigsberg. Young women from the surrounding area came there, and there were about 3,000 of us, and maybe even more. Several days later we were told that we would move on; those who couldn't walk would be transported by trucks.
>
> As we were leaving the camp, we heard shots—our comrades were being executed. We were marched in heavy snow. The cold was fierce, and a freezing wind blew—this was the weather we had to cope with. We weren't allowed to rest at all; every moment shots were fired. Also, we weren't allowed to walk, we had to run. En route a large number of people were shot to death. They kept spurring us on until we were herded into a huge locksmith workshop in the town of Palmnicken. With frost-bitten hands, hungry and deprived of sleep, we waited for the end. We were told that we would not get food, [a] bit later it turned out that the local population gathered bread and potatoes and sen[t] them to us so that we wouldn't starve to death.[216]

The escorts and guards were a varied group. There were about 30 SS men and another 120 other guards and escorts. Some were members of Organization Todt. There were also Ukrainians, Lithuanians, Latvians, and Estonians.[217]

The road to Palmnicken was scattered with mass graves of murdered prisoners. In early February 1945, after the Red Army had liberated the area, a mass grave was discovered approximately 9 miles (15 kilometers) northwest of Königsberg, containing about 100 corpses, mostly female.

> Due to freezing weather the bodies had not decomposed and remained well preserved. It could clearly be seen how exhausted these people had been. All the bodies had the striped camp rags on them, tightened with wire used as a belt. A six point star of dirty yellow color was on their backs. . . . A five-digit number was tattoed on their palms of the hand.[218]

Another report, composed by one of the Red Army military commissions, drew a similar picture:

> An inspection revealed 4 graves in the marshland area of the woods. Three graves consisted of pits 1 to 1.5 m. deep; the fourth grave was shaped like a ditch, about 3 m. long, about 2 m. wide, and 1.5 m. deep.
>
> Eighty-six bodies were pulled out from these graves, including 80 bodies of women and six of men; all of them 20 to 40 years of age.
>
> These bodies were dressed in tatters made of fabric and paper bags, infested with lice, their legs shod in worn-out shoes with wooden soles.

On the left sleeve of the clothing of each body was a number and a six-pointed star. . . . The six-pointed stars were also found on the victims' clothes, on the back.

All the bodies were belted with telephone wires to which bowls and cups of cans had been fastened. In the pockets of the clothing of the bodies, pieces of fish, potatoes and turnip were found. . . .

All the bodies bore signs of extreme fatigue, were infested with lice, and bore unmistakable marks of hunger and disease.

The cranium of each body exhibited marks of bullet wounds, with extensive areas of the skull splintered. The bodies exhibited numerous injuries in the extremities and the chest, which indicates their having been shot point-blank with automatic weapons.[219]

These were the prisoners who had marched from Königsberg to Palmnicken, which they reached on January 27. About 2,500–3,000 prisoners survived the 31-mile (50-kilometer) march,[220] which means that at least 1,500 perished or were murdered in a period of 24 hours. Local residents testified after the war that, on the night of January 26–27, there were piles of corpses along the road from Königsberg to Palmnicken or at the edge of the forests close to the road.[221] The murders continued as the convoy of prisoners passed through the streets of the town, and the corpses were left lying in the streets.[222] The prisoners had the impression that the guards had become more murderously violent in the last stage of the evacuation. The guards wanted to move ahead at a rapid pace, but because they had not received clear instructions as to what to do with the prisoners, murder seemed the best solution, particularly since the group consisted of Jews.[223]

On January 27 the convoy reached Palmnicken,[224] a small town in Eastern Prussia with a population of 3,000, and the evacuees were lodged in a local factory building.[225] The presence of so many prisoners, and the fact that it was not clear when they would be taken away, how, and to where, created an atmosphere of unease and anxiety. The Red Army was practically on their doorstep. In the past few days about 5,000 refugees had also arrived—German nationals in flight from the advancing Red Army—adding to the havoc and aggravating the supply problems in the small town.[226] Local residents asked the SS guards what they were going to do with those Jews and were told that they were merely passing through the town and would be moved on when possible. They urged the townspeople to stay indoors while the prisoners were there and not to make contact with them.[227]

Two different groups were engaged in a race against time in Palmnicken. The guards and escorts, on one hand, were eager to leave as soon as possible, particularly since only a few dozen of them were members of the SS, and of these, some apparently made their getaway after the Jews had been housed in the factory.[228] The guards and Todt personnel were also very reluctant to remain with the prisoners in a place that was about to fall into Russian hands. The urgent desire to send the prisoners on their way without consideration for their fate was shared by the mayor, Kurt Friedrichs, who was head of the local branch of the Nazi Party (Ortsgruppenleiter), and several other local party activists. The fact that their motives differed from those of the guards was of little import for the prisoners. The guards feared being taken prisoner by the Russians, while Friedrichs and his colleagues did not want large numbers of prisoners to be released into the streets of their small town when the Red Army arrived.[229]

There was one group of townspeople, however, led by Hans Feyerabend, who were vehemently opposed to any measure that might lead to the murder of prisoners. A retired artillery officer who had fought in World War I and a respected local resident, Feyerabend was the commander of the local Volkssturm unit. He was ordered to deploy his unit to transport the prisoners out of town but flatly refused.[230] He was also heard saying that he would not permit a massacre like that of the Katyn forest, where Polish officers were slaughtered by the Soviets. It was he and his men who brought food to the prisoners.[231]

During the few days when the prisoners, most of them women, were held in the factory, the two viewpoints waged a silent battle between them. Several of the women prisoners noted that all kinds of discussions were taking place and saw that the guards were uneasy. But as long as they were allowed to rest without disturbance and were not summoned out for another arduous slog through the snow, they were content.[232] Feyerabend did everything in his power to ward off situations that endangered the prisoners' lives. His supporters guarded the factory in shifts and made sure that the guards and local Nazi Party members were doing nothing irregular.[233] Friedrichs, on the other hand, began to prepare the evacuation of the prisoners from the town. He gave orders to obtain horse-drawn wagons and recruited 50 to 100 young men, all members of the Hitlerjugend (Hitler Youth), who were allotted rifles for this assignment.[234] Several of them conducted a hunt for prisoners who had sneaked out of the factory, and executed those they caught. Some of these youngsters were sent home by Todt members or on their parents' initiative once the nature of their activities became known.[235] Rumors were rife in the town that the Jews in the factory were going to be liquidated.[236]

Feyerabend and his Volkssturm unit were a hindrance that needed to be removed. Friedrichs summoned the local SD elements to his aid, and they transmitted an order that a unit of 100 Volkssturm men was to be dispatched to reinforce defensive positions in the area. Feyerabend realized that he was the victim of a ruse aimed at leaving the prisoners unprotected. On January 30, 1945, after the Volkssturm unit had left town, he shot and killed himself. That night the fate of the prisoners in Palmnicken was sealed.[237] The Volkssturm force left in the town was now under the command of Friedrichs, who coopted the Hitlerjugend recruits into the unit. Rumors spread like wildfire to the effect that large pits were being dug outside town and the prisoners were to be liquidated there. On Wednesday, January 31, wagons were driven up to the factory. In his interrogation after the war, Friedrichs claimed that it was the SS who insisted on evacuating the prisoners from the town and that he had been convinced that, if he supplied the wagons, they would transport the prisoners elsewhere. The problem was, he asserted, that after the suicide of Feyerabend, who was an authoritative and influential figure, nobody was left to frustrate the SS's murderous scheme.[238]

There are two versions as to the date on which the prisoners were murdered. The first is that the liquidation occurred between January 30 and February 1.[239] The second version dates it several days later, between February 4 and 5. Reinhart Henkis estimates that the preparations for evacuating the prisoners to the coast began only after Friedrichs received word of Feyerabend's death. This must have been on February 1 since Feyerabend committed suicide on the night of January 31 and his death was not discovered on the same day. Moreover, according to one of the Soviet reports, residents of Palmnicken recalled that the prisoners who arrived in the town on January 27 spent eight days there before the massacre—approximately up to February 4 or 5.[240]

The discrepancies appear to stem from two causes: not all the prisoners arrived at the factory on the same day, and the massacre was not completed in a single day. The liquidation of prisoners who were hiding in the area continued for several days after the massacre. The German investigators who prepared the file on the affair concluded that the massacre was perpetrated on the night of January 31–February 1, 1945.[241] However, it can be concluded that, after the wide-scale liquidation on the first night, the killings continued.

On the night of the major massacre, the guards began to move the prisoners out of the factory. They were told that they were being taken to the coast and that boats would evacuate them from there. However, several of the women noticed that sleds loaded with machine guns were being added to the convoy.[242] The route to the coast was short, and 3,000 prisoners were dispersed along the shore under the guards' supervision. When the last group was in place, heavy fire was directed at the prisoners from automatic weapons. One of the few survivors of the massacre described what occurred:

Late at night we came to the beach. We reached a cliff and in front of us was a steep drop with the Baltic Sea below. It was a terrible sight. On both sides of the line stood guards with machine guns and fired into the approaching crowd. Those who were hit lost their balance and fell down the slope.... I don't know what happened to me but suddenly I felt something cold on my back. When I opened my eyes I saw the slope and people covered in blood were falling down it all the time and I was in the rough sea on a little projection of frozen earth on a pile of bodies, some of them wounded and still alive.[243]

Another survivor told her story:

And that was how the killing took place: each time they selected ten groups of five and sent them forward. As it turned out, we were on the Baltic Sea shore. The executions were carried out like this: they took 50 women at a time and made them run on the thin ice on the beach. There was ghastly darkness. We had to lie down on the ice and they immediately started firing at us from machine guns . . . I don't know how long I lay there. Suddenly I heard a yell from one of the murderers: "Get up fast and run."[244]

Heinz Pipereit, a resident of Sorgenau on the Baltic shore several miles south of Palmnicken described in May 1945 what he had seen:

On February 5, at night, as I walked down the seashore toward Sorgenau, I heard a great deal of infantry cannonade. I figured that this was a mass execution by machine guns. The next day, February 6, I went to the shore and I learned that the SS men were due to march a large number of women prisoners from Palmnicken to Pillau. In the shrubbery near the seashore and on the beach itself I saw many bodies of men and women. All of them, without exception, were scantily dressed, and some were completely naked. These were the poor souls who on the night of February 5–6, 1945 had been moved from the factory in Palmnicken to the seashore and there shot to death. Their naked bodies showed deep bruises which could have resulted only from blows by shot-heels [sic] and clubs. It's possible that some of these poor souls died from beatings and internal injuries, since they bore no marks of bullet wounds. I also observed many bodies, mostly of women, that had been cast ashore by the sea. . . . For two more weeks bodies, mostly of women, were cast by the sea onto the shore in the area of Sorgenau. Bodies were cast ashore not only near Sorgenau, but along the entire coast from Palmnicken to Rothenen.[245]

The Palmnicken affair did not end with the ghastly slaughter on the beach. At the village of Kraxtepellen northwest of Palmnicken, rumors spread about what had been perpetrated not far from there, and it was said that some Jewish prisoners had managed to escape and were roaming the district in search of shelter. A remorseless hunt was launched, and most of them were apparently caught and cruelly murdered, as the Red Army commission reported:

> Inspection of the sites of the savage extermination and burial . . . uncovered 263 bodies, of them 50 bodies of men, and 204 bodies of women, all of them aged 16–25. These bodies were laid in rows, in three to four layers; here and there however bodies were thrown haphazardly into the ditch measuring 1.6×2×3 meters. . . . Clothing on the bodies were rags and tatters of the kind characteristic of the camps—striped, with the numbers sewn on the front, and six-pointed stars on the back and the sleeves. Most of the bodies had foot-gear made of wood *(sabotes)* on them, though some legs were wrapped in rags. All the bodies were infested with vermin and completely emaciated. For the most part all the bodies of men exhibited injuries to the skull caused by shooting; splintered bones of the skull indicating shooting at close range. Some bodies bore marks of more than one bullet wound which indicates that the killing was carried out by an automatic weapon shooting detonating bullets. The skulls and the bones of the extremities of the bodies of most of the women were splintered, which indicates savage killing by blows with blunt instruments. The undergarments of some of the young women's bodies were torn and pulled down their thighs, whereas some bodies of the women were found in the posture of cynical abuse, their legs pulled up behind their heads, without any undergarments.[246]

This report was not composed for political propaganda purposes. The Red Army investigators, who included physicians, pathologists, forensic medicine experts, and several senior officers, checked and recorded what they saw with cool professionalism.

Several local people displayed humanity in the midst of this bloodbath. One of them, Günter Hartmann, hid several women prisoners, who had succeeded in escaping the massacre, in his barn, and several other local residents opened their homes to escaping prisoners. These were a handful of the survivors of the Palmnicken slaughter.[247] All in all, the number of survivors was estimated at some 200, 50 to 100 who escaped the shooting on the beach and the remainder prisoners who made their escape before the transportation to the beach, and found shelter in forests or in local homes.[248]

The massacre of 4,500 prisoners, which took place between January 26 and February 5, 1945, between Königsberg and Palmnicken, was an extraordinary event even in the violent and bloody annals of the evacuation of concentration camps and death marches in Poland in winter 1945. More than it typifies murderous incidents during death marches, it recalls the acts of total annihilation that destroyed the Jewish communities of Lithuania,

Ukraine, or Byelorussia in 1941–1942. It evolved as a local event because during the preparations for the evacuation of Stutthof, the need for evacuation measures appropriate for the remote camps in Eastern Prussia was not taken into consideration. A group of guards found themselves trapped with thousands of exhausted, starving, and lice-ridden Jews between the Scylla of the approaching Soviet tanks and the Charybdis of the Baltic Sea, which could not be crossed without suitable vessels.

One cannot ignore the connection between the liquidation that began in fall 1944 at Stutthof, several months before the evacuation of the camp, and the slaughter at Palmnicken. Frail, exhausted Jewish women, who were totally incapable of hard labor, were an obvious target for liquidation even before discussions of evacuation began. The guards who murdered Jewish women at Palmnicken were completing the task they had begun before the convoy of prisoners left the camp. Those who were no longer of any economic worth continued to be the target of mass liquidation in the months to come.

The process that led to the total liquidation of thousands of Jewish prisoners occurred within German towns and villages and before the eyes of the local population. For several days, two points of view clashed in Palmnicken: the first was that of the guards, who were eager to be rid of the prisoners before the Red Army arrived and to flee, and it was shared by the local civic leaders. The local leaders, however, did not necessarily insist on killing the prisoners; they would have preferred for them to be removed by the guards because they believed that the release of thousands of Jewish prisoners into a town of 3,000 inhabitants under Soviet occupation would be catastrophic for the local residents. These forces eventually prevailed over the viewpoint of Feyerabend and his supporters, who wanted to preserve the honor of their town and to save the lives of the ill-fated souls who had landed on their doorstep hours before the end of the war.

Some 113,000 prisoners were evacuated from concentration camps in Poland to Germany in January–February 1945. Of the Auschwitz evacuees, some 15,000 perished during the evacuations. Of the Stutthof evacuees, about 9,500 died, the great majority of them Jews. There is no way of estimating how many of the Groß-Rosen prisoners perished during the evacuations.[249] The situation that developed in Palmnicken was to be repeated during the last stages of the evacuations, in spring 1945. These took place in areas with German populations and in combat areas on German and Austrian soil. The fate of hundreds of thousands of prisoners who survived the evacuations of winter 1945 and were dispersed through camps in the Reich would depend on the decisions taken by their guards or by party leaders and others in the places where chance had led them.

CHAPTER FOUR

Administrative Chaos and the Last Order

By February 1945 it had rapidly become clear that the hundreds of thousands of prisoners who had been transferred to concentration camps in Germany represented a problem that had not been duly noted by the system. During the chaotic breakdown in the East transports were dispatched westward, but once the prisoners arrived at camps in the Reich, it became obvious that there were no means of housing and feeding them and keeping them alive, nor was it even certain that their labor was required. Rudolf Höß testified after the war that he became aware of the problem after only a few weeks, when the evacuation of Sachsenhausen was being contemplated, and he then mentioned it to Heinrich Müller, chief of the Gestapo. No place could absorb the prisoners, he reported, since the camps were overflowing; there was no possibility of feeding them, and, apart from several places that were still manufacturing for the armaments industry, none of the camps needed them.[1]

At the end of January, Müller learned of the situation developing in the camps. He ordered Höß to transmit precise instructions to the camps to prepare, before the evacuation date, lists of "dangerous prisoners" *(gefährliche Häftlinge)*. These were prisoners who were thought to be liable to instigate provocation when the enemy forces arrived, to collaborate and to menace the local population. They should be liquidated as quickly as possible before leaving the camp, Müller stated. According to Höß, this instruction was to be transmitted to the commandants of Buchenwald, Ravensbrück, Sachsenhausen, and Stutthof.[2]

Several of the commandants knew of this directive. Müller had even discussed the matter personally with Anton Kaindl, the Sachsenhausen commandant, who confirmed after the war that he had received such an order in early 1945. His final list, prepared by the political department at Sachsenhausen and submitted to Müller, apparently included the names of 200 to 250 inmates who, for security reasons, were to be liquidated or evacuated.[3] In early February 1945 more than 200 Sachsenhausen inmates were murdered, among them officers, Soviet and British POWs.[4] The selected prisoners were taken outside the camp and murdered by several of the guards and by the special Sonderkommando Moll unit, transferred to Sachsenhausen from Ravensbrück.[5]

The Sonderkommando Moll was a small and select unit within the concentration camp murder apparatus operating in early 1945. It was established by Johannes Schwarzhuber, a veteran and highly experienced concentration camp officer. In May 1933 he joined the staff at Dachau, where his career flourished and he was rapidly promoted to higher ranks and positions. In 1941 he was appointed commandant of one of the Auschwitz subcamps, and in March 1942 he became commandant of Auschwitz II (Birkenau), where he served until April 1944. After leaving Auschwitz, he moved back to Dachau as commander of the subcamp network at Kaufering. On January 12, 1945, he moved to Ravensbrück, where he served until April 1945. On arrival there, he established the Kommando Moll, a unit of no more than eight men, commanded by Otto Moll, one of his loyal officers from the Auschwitz days. Moll was in charge of the crematorium at Birkenau from May to September 1944, the peak months of the wide-scale extermination of Hungarian Jews.[6] When the evacuation of the camps in the East was completed, Moll transferred to Office D (Concentration Camps) and began to tackle the task for which his unit had been created: the extermination of sick and feeble prisoners before the camps were evacuated.[7]

"The Sick Here Gradually Pine Away till They Die . . ."

Ravensbrück was in a difficult situation in winter 1945 because of the severe outbreak of typhus in the camp.[8] On January 15, 1945, there were 46,000 women prisoners and 7,840 male prisoners in the central camps and the series of subcamps. The state of hygiene was appalling, the sanitary conditions had deteriorated, and the crowding in the prison barracks was unendurable.[9] All this was before the arrival of the evacuees from the East.

The commandant of Ravensbrück, Fritz Suhren, testified after the war that at the end of January and the beginning of February, he was occupied with the evacuation and transfer to the main camps of inmates of Ravensbrück's subcamps east of the River Oder due to the advance of the Red Army. Instructions to this effect had been received from Glücks's office, and possibly also from the local HSSPF, August Heißmeyer.[10] The instructions did not include specific details on what was to be done with the evacuated prisoners, but Suhren emphasized that it was clearly stated that escape of prisoners and their liberation by the Soviets were to be forestalled by every possible means, including the use of armed force.[11]

The liquidation of "dangerous prisoners" began almost simultaneously at Sachsenhausen and Ravensbrück. Parzifal Triete, an SS physician who served in Ravensbrück camp, said after the war that executions were carried out beside the crematorium and estimated that 50 prisoners at a time were liquidated. Two members of the camp staff executed the victims by pistol shots to the back of the head, and the corpses were then carried to the crematorium.[12] Schwarzhuber, who was the main figure behind the winter 1945 liquidation operation, reckoned that 150 to 200 prisoners were murdered by the Kommando Moll in that period.[13] In its final months of existence, Ravensbrück was transformed into an extermination camp. Between 150 and 180 male prisoners were liquidated in January 1945 in an improvised gas chamber as the overture to a wave of murderous activity. In the course of three months, until close to the date of evacuation of the camp, 5,000 to 6,000 prisoners were gassed.[14] Experts, who had gained their experience in operating extermination installations at Auschwitz, contributed their expertise to the construction of the gas chamber and to the mass extermination project at Ravensbrück in January–February 1945.[15] Almost all the victims were women.[16] The gas chamber was not large, about 10 yards by 5 yards (9 meters by 4.5 meters), and its capacity was a mere 150 prisoners at a time. It was built about 5.5 yards (5 meters) from the crematorium.[17]

However, the proficiency of the extermination experts from Auschwitz did not apparently extend to the ability to draw subtle distinctions between sick and unfit prisoners and those who could still be of some use to the system. Not all the victims were sick and elderly men, and among them were quite a few young women still capable of working.[18] The selections conducted in the camp were a daily nightmare for the women prisoners. The older women and the sick who were hospitalized in the revier or who lay prostrate in the barracks, lived in constant terror of being dispatched to the gas chamber in the next selection. Every day that passed without selection for death was a miracle.[19]

Quite a few women prisoners from the subcamps were liquidated in the gas chamber at Ravensbrück. One such camp, Uckermark, operative from 1942, changed its function in December 1944, when thousands of women were evacuated from Auschwitz. It was, essentially, no more than a provisional transit camp for thousands of women prisoners from the East who were earmarked for extermination. Their physical condition was particularly pitiable since they had already undergone one evacuation from the

East. Many of them fell victim to the devastating terror campaign, which lasted a few weeks.[20] One of the supervisors of the women SS guards, Ruth Closius-Neudeck, who was transferred to Uckermark from Ravensbrück in January 1945, explained:

> When I took over the Uckermark camp, there were about 4,000 prisoners of all nationalities there. When I left Uckermark, apprx. six weeks later, there were only apprx. 1,000 prisoners left. About 3,000 women were selected for gassing during my activities in Uckermark.[21]

Dr. Adolf Winkelmann, one of the physicians who carried out the selections, described them as follows:

> I selected for removal the prisoners unfit to work. I always did this together with Dr. Trommer. I knew that drafts went to the youth camp at Uckermark, but I did not know for what purpose. The selection took place in one of the roadways of the camp, or very rarely in a barrack. The prisoners marched in single file past Dr. Trommer and me. We could, of course, conduct only a very superficial examination, and people who were obviously sick, unfit to work or unfit to march, were picked out. The prisoners had their legs bare, so that we could see whether they were fit to march. It is possible that prisoners were examined in a barrack stripped to the waist. The barracks were unheated, and the last prisoners would have to wait about an hour. During my time at Ravensbrück, Dr. Trommer and I selected about 1,500 to 2,000 prisoners for outward drafts.[22]

Schwarzhuber, who claimed to have attended only one *Aktion* (assembly and deportation of prisoners for extermination) of women prisoners who underwent selections in the final period at Ravensbrück, described what he had witnessed:

> I attended the gassing. 150 women at a time were forced into the gas-chamber. Hauptscharführer Moll ordered the women to undress as they were to be deloused. They were then taken into the gas-chamber and the door was closed. A male internee with gas-mask climbed on the roof and threw a gas container into the room through the window, which he again closed immediately. I heard groaning and whispering in the room. After two or three minutes it grew quiet. Whether the women were dead or just senseless, I cannot say. I was not present when the room was cleaned out. I have only been told by Moll that the bodies were taken straight to the crematorium.[23]

Thus it was that Auschwitz, whose gas chambers and crematoria had been out of action for several months, stretched out a tentacle in spring 1945 to a veteran concentration camp in the very heart of the old Reich.

The responsibility for the decision to convert Ravensbrück into an operative extermination camp in its last few months of existence remained indeterminate. Suhren claimed that when he returned to Ravensbrück in mid-March 1945 he was told that Heißmeyer had given the order to construct the gas chamber.[24] Schwarzhuber recalled after the war having been told by Suhren that the order came from Himmler and that it had emphasized that all sick women unfit for evacuation on foot were to be killed.[25] He was unable to supply details as to precisely when and how he received it. Both Schwarzhuber and Triete claimed that the decision to establish a provisional gas chamber in order to liquidate incapacitated women prisoners was made simply because the killings by shooting had not proceeded at a satisfactory pace.[26] Closius-Neudeck too believed that the gassings were introduced because a very large number of women prisoners needed to be exterminated in a short period. As she explained, when only two to three women were scheduled for extermination on a particular day, they were shot. But when a large group was involved, they were sent to the gas chamber.[27]

There was a salient connection between the exterminations at Ravensbrück and Sachsenhausen in that period. Concurrently with the selections at Ravensbrück and the dispatch of prisoners to the gas chamber, the Sachsenhausen command began to liquidate inmates "unfit to march." In February–March 1945 about 4,000 infirm prisoners were selected; some were shot and others gassed.[28] It is evident that the planned liquidation of prisoners classified by the camp command as sick, dangerous, or unfit for marching was carried out in spring 1945 in almost all the concentration camps. The killings were perpetrated by shooting, in gas chambers if such existed in the camp, or by injection of poison.[29]

In Dachau, a gas chamber was constructed in February 1945, and there too experts evacuated from Auschwitz played a significant part in the extermination project. Heinrich Schuster was an Austrian prisoner who had been interned in Auschwitz, where he assisted the camp's physicians. After the evacuation of Auschwitz in January 1945 he arrived at Dachau, and there too he volunteered to help in dealing with the numerous cases of typhus in the camp. He was not a full-fledged physician since he had not completed his medical studies, but his partial qualifications sufficed for his tasks at Dachau. He continued to send sick prisoners to the gas chambers, as he had at Auschwitz.[30] In the final months one of the prisoners, Edgar Kupfer-Koberwitz, noted the catastrophic situation in the camp: on February 20, 700 prisoners died in Block 30; in Block 21 more than 20 died daily. In mid-March 1945 he wrote that in February 4,000 inmates had died of typhus.[31] As was the case in other camps, Zyklon B gas was used in the gas chamber at Dachau.[32]

The situation at Flossenbürg was similar. The arrival of transports of prisoners from the camps in the East led to a steep rise in the mortality rate in the camp. Between mid-January and April 13, 1945, 3,370 prisoners perished, an average of 42 daily. The peak month was February, when most of the transports arrived; 59 prisoners on average died each day. At the same time there was a considerable increase in the selective liquidation of prisoners designated for "special treatment" *(Sonderbehandlung)*, namely, those who were considered potentially dangerous since it was feared that they might attempt to escape or foment resistance. Most of these were Russians.[33]

In Mauthausen, mass murders of prisoners had taken place even before early spring 1945. A regular gas chamber was constructed in fall 1941 in the cellar of one of the buildings, and there too Zyklon B was the accepted murder method. The chamber was small: 4.1 yards by 3.8 yards (3.8 meters by 3.5 meters). Only 80 prisoners at a time could be gassed. The victims were almost always camp inmates, excluding one case in 1942 when a group of Soviet POWs were gassed.[34]

At least nine cases of liquidation by gassing of large groups took place at Mauthausen in April 1945. Some of the victims, arrested for political reasons, were sent to the camp for execution there by the Vienna, Graz, or Linz Gestapos. They were taken directly to the gas chamber without any record being made of their names. On April 20, 1945, Dr. Waldemar Wolter, SS physician in the camp, gave instructions that at least 3,000 of the 7,782 sick inmates should be transferred to Camp III (a section of the camp constructed in spring 1944, where most of the inmates were infirm and earmarked for liquidation) because they were feeble, sick, and nonfunctioning. In the end, 1,500 prisoners were sent to Camp III, and about 650 of them were dispatched to the gas chamber between April 22 and 25. The mass extermination continued until the end of the month, and some 1,200 to 1,400 men and women were gassed.[35] This was in addition to the 3,000 or so other prisoners who perished in the camp in the final weeks of the war as a result of the camp's inhuman conditions.[36] In Neuengamme as well, the massacre of sick prisoners began in fall 1944 and continued in the first few months of 1945. Between January and March, 6,224 sick prisoners were executed by poison injections administered by the camp physicians. In the first two weeks of April, another 1,800 prisoners were liquidated.[37]

In the same period, prisoners were liquidated in other camps by different means. In Buchenwald, for example, a section of the camp known as the "Little Camp," which had been a tent camp until 1944, was expanded to contain 17 prisoners' barracks. Thousands of prisoners evacuated from camps in the East soon filled those barracks. Each was intended to hold between 500 and 600 inmates, but 1,000 (and, in some cases, even 1,800–1,900) were packed in. The Little Camp was closed off and isolated from the rest of the camp. Hunger, disease, and death reigned there, and countless corpses lay sprawled between the barracks. The Jews who arrived from Auschwitz and Groß-Rosen on February 10, 1945, were thrown like discarded objects into a site that resembled a vast pigsty.[38] At the beginning of January there had been 6,000 prisoners in the Little Camp; by early April the number had swelled to 17,000. Extermination through starvation and disease produced results similar to active initiatives such as gas and poison injections, adopted in other camps: about 5,200 prisoners died in the Little Camp at Buchenwald in less than 100 days. In all, more than 13,000 inmates perished in the camp and its subcamps in January–April 1945.[39]

However, the most blatant example of extermination through epidemic and disease, as practiced in 1945, was Bergen-Belsen. It had started out as a small camp for the internment of groups of "Jews for exchange" *(Austauschjuden)*— that is, those who were to be exchanged for groups of Germans living in Palestine or other countries under Allied protection. With time it expanded into the camp where Himmler intended to hold 30,000 Jews as a bargaining card in the negotiations. In the last weeks of the war it was transformed into one of the most atrocious murder sites for Jews and other concentration camp prisoners.[40]

In early 1944 Oswald Pohl and other officials in the WVHA came to the conclusion that Bergen-Belsen was being underexploited and should be used more efficiently. As a result the camp was assigned a new series of tasks in March 1944: it became an absorption camp for sick prisoners from concentration and labor camps administered by the WVHA. In the cynical coded language of the WVHA, the camp was denoted a "rehabilitation camp" *(Erholungslager)* whose task was to rehabilitate sick prisoners in order to restore their capacity for work. By spring 1944, groups of prisoners from Mittelbau-Dora who could no longer keep up the pace required by the intensive construction work began to arrive at Bergen-Belsen.[41] They were housed in empty barracks without reasonable sleeping arrangements, received very little food, and were given no medical treatment. Its high mortality rate became a constant feature of the "rehabilitation camp." In the course of 1944 Bergen-Belsen rapidly became a vital cog in the "extermination through labor" machine, which was then approaching maximal production. In summer 1944 the camp was expanded to include a women's camp, and in the fall large transports of women prisoners from Auschwitz arrived in order to become slave laborers.[42]

In view of the anticipated large-scale evacuations from the East and the planned expansion of the camp, Josef Kramer was appointed commandant of Bergen-Belsen. Kramer had acquired considerable experience in the system.

His career was launched in April 1936 at Dachau; he moved on in 1938 to Mauthausen, and in 1940 to Natzweiler-Struthof, where he was promoted to camp commandant in 1942. In May 1944 Glücks appointed him commandant of Auschwitz II (Birkenau), but he held this position for only a few months. By fall 1944 Auschwitz was being dismantled and Bergen-Belsen was growing. In late November 1944 Glücks ordered Kramer to take up the position of commandant of Bergen-Belsen.[43] There were 15,257 inmates when Kramer arrived in the camp, and the number expanded rapidly in the last few months of the war. Prisoners were sent there from all over Germany, from Mittelbau-Dora, Ravensbrück, Sachsenhausen, and other camps. Bergen-Belsen became the main center for extermination of prisoners who were of no further economic value. By March 31, 1945, the number of prisoners had reached 44,060. Kramer realized that matters were spiralling out of control after he received instructions to absorb another 2,500 sick women from Ravensbrück. He appealed to Glücks that month to take immediate action in light of the situation:

At the end of January it was decided that an occupation of the camp by over 35,000 detainees must be considered too great. In the meantime, this number has been exceeded by 7,000 and a further 6,200 are at this time on their way. The consequence of this is that all barracks are overcrowded by at least 30 per cent. The detainees cannot lie down to sleep, but must sleep in a sitting position on the floor. . . . In addition to this question, a spotted fever and typhus epidemic has now begun, which increases in extent every day. The daily mortality rate, which was still in the region of 60–70 at the beginning of February, has in the meantime attained a daily average of 250–300 and will still further increase in view of the conditions which at present prevail.

The incidence of diseases is very high here in proportion to the number of detainees. When you interviewed me on 1st December, 1944, at Oranienburg, you told me that Bergen-Belsen was to serve as a sick camp for all concentration camps in North Germany. The number of sick has greatly increased, particularly on account of the transports of detainees, which have arrived from the east in recent times—these transports have sometimes spent eight to fourteen days in open trucks. An improvement in their condition, and particularly a return of those detainees to work, is under present conditions quite out of the question. The sick here gradually pine away till they die of weakness of the heart and general debility. As already stated, the average daily mortality is between 250 and 300. One can best gain an idea of the conditions of transports when I state that on one occasion, out of a transport of 1,900 detainees, over 500 arrived dead. The fight against the spotted fever is made exactly difficult by the lack of means of disinfection. . . .

Gruppenführer, I can assure you that from this end everything will be done to overcome the present crisis. With this letter I merely wanted to point out to you the difficulties which exist here. For my part, it is a matter of course that these difficulties must be overcome. I am now asking you for assistance as far as it lies in your power. In addition to the above-mentioned points, I need here, before everything, accommodation, facilities, beds, blankets, eating utensils— all for about 20,000 internees.

I want to assure you once again that on my part everything will definitely be done to bridge over this difficult situation. I know that you have even greater difficulties to overcome and appreciate that you must send to this camp all internees from that area; on the other hand, I implore your help in overcoming this situation.[44]

The number of prisoners who perished at Bergen-Belsen in the last four and a half months of the war, namely, from early 1945 until the liberation, has been estimated as approximately 35,000. When British troops reached the camp on April 15 there were about 60,000 inmates there, most of them suffering from typhus. Many of them died after being liberated.[45]

Bergen-Belsen's evolution in the final months of the war from a transit camp of secondary importance to the site of mass extermination cannot be explained solely on the basis of the conditions in the camp system after the large-scale evacuations from the East. Eberhard Kolb regarded this development as an intrinsic component of the Nazi concentration camp system. It converted a concentration camp, which had been established as an installation for imprisonment, punishment, and later, for labor supply, into an installation for mass extermination. Although this extermination was not preplanned, its scope was no smaller than that of installations established specifically for liquidating target populations, first and foremost among them the Jews. Bergen-Belsen is the prime example of this development. Therefore, it cannot be grouped together with the conventional concentration camps: Dachau, Buchenwald, Mauthausen, and others. Nor can it be included in the same framework as the camps for planned extermination: Sobibór, Treblinka, Majdanek, or Auschwitz.[46]

Israel (Reszö) Kasztner, the Zionist leader of the rescue committee in Budapest in 1944, arrived at Bergen-Belsen several days before the liberation of the camp. He noted in his 1946 report what Josef Kramer said to him about the situation there:

In Bergen-Belsen there are now about 67,000 inmates, among them some 53,000 "Star Jews" *(Stern-Juden)*. Most of them arrived here between January and March this year from various camps in the East. They arrived in poor condition and brought with them typhus, and as if that were not enough—in the last few weeks it has not been possible to bring in foodstuffs, because the Allies have destroyed all the access roads. Today there are more than one thousand typhus sufferers. For two weeks they have been unable to distribute bread, but there is still a reserve of carrots, potatoes, a little fat and meat for about eight days. Because of the worsening of the food situation, about 500–600 inmates have been dying daily. This is the situation regarding the *Stern-Juden* ["Ordinary Jews"], and apart from them there are some 7,000 "favored Jews" *(bevorzugte Juden)* here . . . on the basis of a previous directive, I ordered the transfer of these latter Jews to Theresienstadt.

Kasztner added, again quoting Kramer, that in early February there had been 81,000 *Stern-Juden* in the camp and some 8,000 *bevorzugte Juden*. Although additional transports had arrived since then, in early April there were only 60,000 Jews in all.[47]

Bergen-Belsen at the beginning of 1945 embodied the last stage of the Nazi murder machine. Its procedures lacked coherence and system. It not only liquidated prisoners through disease and starvation; it reduced them to a state verging on madness.

With us we carry all our distress, our decay, all the rags and shreds, the bundles of vast volume and meager capacity . . . we hear the wailing of the sick who are too many for us to be able to treat them one by one, and the groans of the dying, hurled into this vortex of transition, curses, skirmishes and sobbing. I had to soothe the sick women, bring them the chamber pots and empty them in the nearby latrines. The inside of the barrack was filled with the stink. The terminally ill lay sprawled on their bunks, dying slowly, rotting while still alive. . . .

I wrestled, truly wrestled with a woman who had lost her mind . . . it was essential to subdue her in order to prevent her from terrorizing other women . . . that night she leapt out of her bunk three times and each time I had to stop her . . . she begs and sobs . . . it is terrible.[48]

The situation at Bergen-Belsen and other camps was the direct outcome of the need for slave laborers, and of the inability and impossibility of maintaining them, the lack of places to which to transfer them, and the overall system rationale that it was preferable to be rid of and even to murder sick, feeble, and worn-out prisoners who were of no further value. In no other camp were the Jews so prominent a presence as in Bergen-Belsen in early 1945, and this fact undoubtedly exacerbated this unique situation. These were indeed unparalleled circumstances, a combination of planned and spontaneous extermination that existed in all the camps in Germany but took on monstrous proportions at Bergen-Belsen. The extermination activity in the concentration camps in the weeks and days before the evacuations was an inseparable part of the death marches chapter that began in January 1945 in camps in Poland, continued in the camps in Germany, and was to end in April–May.

The Beginning of April 1945: Bureaucratic Chaos

As if the catastrophic conditions in the camps due to the influx of prisoners from the East were not enough, those responsible for the camps, from Himmler through Pohl to Glücks and the various camp commandants, were caught up in a tangled web of confused interests and of instructions, counter-instructions, and incoherent directives transmitted and received in haphazard fashion. Those who paid with their lives for this administrative chaos were, of course, the camp inmates.

By the beginning of April Pohl was very anxious to dissociate himself from involvement with the camps. His attention was focused on planning the evacuation of the WVHA offices from Berlin to the south and on the destruction of incriminating documents. He was totally indifferent to the fate of the concentration camp inmates.[49] Himmler, however, did not leave him to his own devices. In mid-March 1945 Pohl, Rudolf Höß, and Enno Lolling, head of D-III (Statistics and Hygiene) in Office D, set out on a tour of several concentration camps. The objective was to inspect camp arrangements, hygienic conditions, labor systems, and the like. It was Himmler who ordered them to conduct the tour. In addition to this routine inspection, Pohl was to clarify to the camp commandants that the Jewish prisoners under their jurisdiction should be kept safe and treated decently. Pohl visited Neuengamme, Buchenwald, Mauthausen, and Bergen-Belsen. Richard Glücks visited two other camps, Sachsenhausen and Ravensbrück, for the same purpose.[50]

The problem of the Jewish prisoners aggravated the administrative disorder at the time. After the war Höß asserted that Himmler had given explicit instructions that everything possible was to be done to ensure that Jewish prisoners survived and received proper treatment.[51] Pohl, too, emphasized this matter at his trial, and Felix Kersten, Himmler's personal masseur, recorded in his diary for March several conversations with Himmler regarding the release of several thousand Jews and their transfer to Sweden or Switzerland.[52] Kurt Becher, the SS officer who toured Bratislava and Germany in March together with Kasztner and met with Himmler, also reported that Himmler told him that Jews would no longer be exterminated *(nicht mehr vernichtet)* in camps in Germany, and that he personally would ensure that during the evacuation of the concentration camps, the earlier directives regarding respect for human life would be honored *(Respektie-rung des Menschenlebens).*[53]

In March 1945 Himmler was trapped in a maze of amateurish and self-contradictory diplomatic activity as he attempted to implement hopeless and futile policies. Secret talks were being held at the time between Scandinavian and Swiss diplomats, representatives of the Red Cross, and Jewish organizations (the World Jewish Congress or the Joint Distribution Committee—JDC) on one side, and the German military and intelligence on the other. The objective was to try to arrive at certain agreements with senior representatives of the Allied armies in order to formulate capitulation settlements that would prevent Germany's total collapse and check the Soviet advance into the heart of Europe. In the course of these intricate contacts, the question of the fate of the concentration camp prisoners in general and the Jewish prisoners in particular was raised again and again.[54] As we know, these intensive discussions did not result in a dramatic rescue operation. The reverse was true; to a large extent these discussions only reinforced the general apathy with regard to the fate of the camp prisoners, especially the Jews.

The individual directly responsible for the catastrophic situation in the concentration camp system and for the deadly consequences was Heinrich Himmler. He was apparently preoccupied with the affairs of the camps during the week of March 5–12, 1945. According to Kersten's notes, on March 5 Himmler focused his attention on this issue. He reiterated Hitler's instructions that if National Socialist Germany was condemned to rack and ruin, then its most bitter enemies, now incarcerated behind barbed-wire fences, should also pay the full price. They should not be permitted to rejoice at Germany's devastation. However, a week later, Himmler changed his mind. He agreed that Hitler's directive, namely, that the camps were to be destroyed together with their inmates when the liberating armies approached, should not be sent out to the camp commandants. The camps should be closed down in orderly fashion; further murder of Jews was to be categorically prohibited. The concentration camps would not be evacuated and would be left intact until the liberators arrived, and the prisoners were to be given food rations that would suffice until the liberation. According to Kersten, Himmler even agreed to sign an order in this spirit. This was also the impression of Walter Schellenberg, chief of SS Counter-Intelligence, who in the last weeks of the war was also engaged in seeking channels of dialogue with the West.[55] These directives were put to the test two weeks later, when it was necessary to decide on evacuating two camps that were in danger of falling into the hands of the U.S. Army: Mittelbau-Dora and Buchenwald.

Joachim Neander, in his wide-ranging study of the evacuation of Mittelbau-Dora, claims that the evacuation of camps was a multistage process that recurred during various evacuations, from winter 1945 on. The first stage involved preparations for evacuating the camp *(Räumungsvorbereitungen)*, during which prisoners were transferred from the subcamps to the main camp, equipment and food were prepared, routes were checked, and so on. The second stage was the departure *(Abmarsch)*. The prisoners were assembled on the parade ground, divided into groups, and then left the camp, generally on foot, to an evacuation point where they were loaded onto trains. The third stage was the "cleanup" *(Nachlese)*, as prisoners, mainly the sick, who had been left behind were liquidated, buildings were blown up, the camp archive was destroyed or transferred, and traces of the horrors that had taken place were obliterated. The last stage was the transport, namely, the final evacuation of the prisoners to their destination.[56] It will be recalled that this planning did not stand the test of the situation during the months of evacuation and panic-stricken retreat from Poland, where conditions dictated a different kind of evacuation. On the other hand, in Mittelbau-Dora, an attempt was made to conduct the move in an orderly fashion.

Preparations for evacuation of the Mittelbau-Dora camp complex began in early spring 1945. The direction of the U.S. Army's advance through central Germany was not entirely clear, but since the camp and its many branches were of vital importance to the armaments industry, it was feared that the enemy forces would arrive before the sophisticated weapons industry could be evacuated to another site. It is unlikely that Hans Kammler, the key figure in establishing this military production network, was aware at the end of March 1945 of Himmler's indecisiveness and failure to adopt a firm policy on the camps. Even if he knew the situation, it is unlikely that he took it into consideration in any way. In late January 1945 Kammler ordered the evacuation from the camp of the production line of EMW (Elektromechanische Werke GmbH), which manufactured electromechanical equipment. This evacuation encompassed a series of production lines in several subcamps and about 4,300 laborers, some civilians, and the majority of the prisoners classified as "skilled workers." At that time, thousands of prisoners from the large camps in Poland, Auschwitz, and Groß-Rosen were beginning to arrive at Mittelbau-Dora, and one of the aims of the evacuation was to facilitate the absorption of these newcomers.[57] In late March 1945 Hitler invested Kammler with new powers relating directly to production at Mittelbau-Dora. He was now also responsible for producing the new jet aircraft, Messerschmidt Me-262, Germany's last prospect of changing the course of the war and undermining the total supremacy of the British and American air forces: "clearing our skies again," as Josef Goebbels phrased it.[58] After being granted these powers, Kammler was in charge of the most important military production lines in the armaments system: manufacture of the V rockets and the new jet aircraft. He was loath to abandon the so-phisticated production project he had built up in the past year and leave it to the Americans. As far as he was concerned, every possible effort must be made to transfer the prisoners and the production lines to a place where they could still be exploited.[59]

In view of the conditions at the front and the United States' total domination of German airspace, it was difficult, almost impossible, to evacuate the vast armaments industry built up in the mountain areas in fall 1943. Approximately one quarter of a million human beings were involved in producing weapons systems in the great complex at Mittelwerk, which, at the end of 1944, produced 22,384 Fi 103 flying bombs and 3,170 A4 rockets.[60] However, Hitler's explicit order that, under no circumstances, was equipment or means of assisting the enemy in their war against Germany be permitted to fall into enemy hands,[61] together with Kammler's single-minded determination to continue producing at least part of the sophisticated weaponry at a site that the fighting had not yet reached, motivated the large-scale evacuation of Mittelbau-Dora.

However, the great majority of the 41,000 prisoners on the site were far from being the "experts" required for production purposes. They were "construction prisoners," who labored at digging and maintaining the enormous production tunnels. They were considered expendable by those responsible for evacuating the military production project from Mittelbau-Dora.

The evacuation of Mittelbau-Dora was supervised by Richard Baer, the last commandant of Auschwitz. Baer came to Mittelbau-Dora in February 1945, replacing Otto Förschner, who was appointed commandant of the Kaufering camps in Bavaria.[62] Baer and the additional SS officers from Auschwitz who had been posted to Mittelbau-Dora brought with them the experience they had gained during the evacuations from Auschwitz. They began by separating the healthy prisoners who were still capable of production work from those who were of no further economic value. In accordance with Himmler's agreement with the president of the Red Cross, the Swede Folke Bernadotte, Norwegian and Danish prisoners were removed from the camp and sent to Neuengamme to be treated by the Swedish Red Cross.[63] On March 8, 2,250 sick prisoners were rounded up at Mittelbau-Dora and the subcamps and sent on a special transport north to Bergen-Belsen, which they reached on April 13. On March 21 another transport set out from Mittelbau-Dora with 800 prisoners who had recently arrived from Groß-Rosen and they too were dispatched to Bergen-Belsen. As was the case in other concentration camps before evacuations, the transfer of prisoners from the subcamps to the main camp was begun concurrently, and the sick and feeble were assembled separately.[64]

In March 1945 a new unprecedented situation arose in the Mittelbau-Dora camps. Some 16,000 prisoners from camps in the East, 10,000 of them from Groß-Rosen, had been added to the population all at once. The death rate in the camp in its last month of existence was very high: 5,000 prisoners perished in the weeks before the evacuation, apart from those evacuated to Bergen-Belsen, who were in such poor condition that their prospects of survival were close to nil. The overcrowding at Mittelbau-Dora had reached terrifying proportions; the camp had a capacity of 14,000, but in early spring 1945 it housed nearly 21,000 human beings.[65] Similar horrendous conditions prevailed in the subcamps. Hundreds of prisoners from Groß-Rosen were brought to Ellrich, one of the largest of Mittelbau-Dora's subcamps. "It was a terrible camp. It was a camp where they worked in the quarries and there were many Russians and Ukrainians, and there was a terrible smell because . . . they dug a pit and put the corpses there and threw in wood . . . and set it alight . . . and the smell drove us crazy,"[66] recalled one of the prisoners in the camp. But the catastrophic situation in the camp in the weeks before the evacuations is most vividly illustrated by the events in Boelcke-Kaserne, a local version of the combined planned-spontaneous extermination installations that functioned in all the camps at the time.

Boelcke was a Luftwaffe camp, built close to Nordhausen. In 1943 it was converted into a slave labor camp, whose inmates worked in the Jonkers engine factory. In summer 1944, 6,000 slave laborers were employed there, and it had become part of the Mittelbau-Dora complex. Concentration camp prisoners had not been sent there until then, and the first of them arrived only in fall 1944, when Mittelbau-Dora was becoming an independent concentration camp.

From the beginning of January 1945, sick and incapacitated prisoners were sent to Boelcke once the supervisors of the labor units decided that they were no longer of any use as workers. On arrival of the transports from Auschwitz and Groß-Rosen, which included hundreds of sick and exhausted prisoners, quite a few of them Jews,[67] the camp administration converted Boelcke into the "central camp for the sick and dead of the Mittelbau complex" (zentrales Kranken und Sterbelager des Mittelbau-Komplexes). The dying prisoners were concentrated in Blocks 6 and 7 in the camp. Boelcke slowly evolved into a death camp for 3,000 prisoners packed tightly into its barracks. These structures could not absorb the thousands of incoming prisoners, and hundreds lay inert on the floors and between the bunks. The dying received almost no food and very little to drink. In the final few weeks, approximately 100 prisoners died daily. A French prisoner who was transferred to Boelcke from Ellrich in early March 1945 related that when they reached Boelcke:

The train stopped, the door opened, and on the order to go out I jumped onto the ballast. I then saw the ultimate in horror: rail cars already opened, full of corpses and the dying that the SS pushed out of the rail car with their feet. Others jumped out, but having no more strength to get on their feet, were shot by the SS. . . . I was assigned to Block 6, and we received neither food or drink that day. We slept sardine-like, on the cement with a bit of straw—quickly reduced to dust.[68]

Until the end of March, bodies were removed and taken to the crematorium, but in the final days before the evacuation, the camp staff did not bother to move them. The dead lay alongside the dying, and often it was hard to distinguish between them.[69]

In the main camp, conditions were no less abysmal before the evacuation. About 300 prisoners died daily, just as they had in Bergen-Belsen at the beginning of April. For example, on April 5, 1945, the day Mittelbau-Dora was evacuated, 1,100 prisoners perished. Others, who were too feeble to join the evacuation, were consigned to Boelcke to die slowly there. On March 31 there were 3,855 prisoners in this death installation, 2,637 of whom were sick. Three days later another 1,200 prisoners were brought in. It is estimated that at least half of the 11,000 prisoners who were sent to Boelcke did not survive the war. Not surprisingly, the place was known to prisoners as the "living crematorium" *(das lebende Krematorium)*.[70]

On April 3 and 4, 1945, the RAF carried out two bombing raids on Nordhausen. The first raid began at 4 p.m. on Tuesday, April 3: 255 Lancaster bombers dropped more than 2,200 pounds (1,000 kilograms) of bombs and 3,600 pounds (1,600 kilograms) of napalm on the town. Thousands of civilians fled and sought shelter in the surrounding forests. The center and eastern sections of the town were reduced to rubble, giant fires broke out in the streets, and the old city was burned to the ground. About 8,000 of the 65,000 inhabitants of the town were thought to have been killed. "I looked around and it was like an abattoir of bodies, blood everywhere, and the corpses could not be identified. Everywhere body parts were scattered, there were rivers of blood and destroyed buildings,"[71] recounted one of the Boelcke prisoners who succeeded in fleeing the camp when the bombing began and tried to find shelter in the town. The inmates of Boelcke were also targets of the heavy bombardment because of the camp's location at the edge of the town. On the day of the raid, the camp held 3,855 prisoners, most of them too weak to escape. About 450 of them were killed in the raid.[72] The British aerial attack was a decisive factor that precipitated the decision to evacuate Mittelbau-Dora and its subcamps.

At the beginning of April the prisoners sensed that evacuation was imminent. The British bombing raid on Nordhausen was clearly visible at Ellrich, only 7 miles (12 kilometers) away. Giant flames lit up the sky, and, at Ellrich, the inmates tried to conceal their delight because they could see that their guards were tense and agitated. At the main camp as well, there was an atmosphere of disquiet and nervous anticipation. On April 1 Easter Sunday, the prisoners, to their surprise, were given a day's vacation. They gathered in groups between the barracks, shared their fears, and tried to guess what the coming days and weeks might bring.[73] They sought some cause for optimism in the circulating rumors that the authorities in charge of industrial production might be able to dissuade the SS from harming them in the last days of the camp's existence. Proof that the camp was about to be evacuated arrived two days later, when some 2,000 prisoners were transferred from Mittelbau-Dora to the subcamp at Harzungen as the first step on the way to final evacuation.[74]

Richard Baer did not give the order to evacuate the 36 camps in the Mittelbau-Dora complex until the morning of Wednesday, April 4, 1945, although the first group of prisoners, 4,000 Russians, had left the camp on the previous day. From Wednesday and throughout Thursday, trains evacuated the prisoners from the main camp and the subcamps. On April 4 the subcamps were evacuated to larger camps or directly to railway stations where prisoners from several smaller camps were rounded up and loaded onto trains. On April 5 and 6 almost all the prisoners from the main camp and the subcamps were evacuated. The last transport to leave the main camp, consisting of 4,000 prisoners, left on Thursday, April 5, at about 9 p.m. The prisoners were loaded onto between 80 and 100 open freight cars and were accompanied by 50 or so armed SS guards. The train traveled in a northerly direction to Osterode am Harz, and on April 9 it reached Münchehof. Dozens of prisoners on this transport were murdered by the guards. It was impossible to continue northward because of the advance of the U.S. forces, and so the transport, consisting now of 3,500 prisoners, turned south, back to Osterode am Harz. Left behind were 416 sick prisoners who were incapable of marching; they were liberated on April 10 at Münchehof by the Americans.[75] Thus it was the evacuees who were in the direst state who survived to see the day of liberation. The brevity of the interval between departure from the camp and the evacuation march, and the haste with which the guards were forced to choose an alternative evacuation route, leaving the weak and sick behind, created an exceptional situation. It spelled survival for those prisoners who would ordinarily have been the first to be liquidated on the death marches.

The last group, consisting of 1,000 inmates, were evacuated from the subcamps at Günzerode and Ellrich-Bürgergarten on April 10. They had separate destinations, and as a rule the columns did not succeed in reaching them. Most of the transports were earmarked for Neuengamme, but almost none of the groups ended up there. The Via Dolorosa of some 23,700 inmates evacuated from Mittelbau-Dora ended at Bergen-Belsen, generally between April 8 and 11.[76] After two or more weeks of a journey accompanied by incessant attacks by Allied aircraft, others succeeded in reaching Oranienburg (generally in the second half of April), where they were detained at Sachsenhausen. One group of 300 from the small Groß-Werther camp reached Mauthausen on April 15. Only a minority of the Mittelbau-Dora inmates, some 7,400, followed a direct route from the camp to their destination.[77] Most of the transports roamed the highways, suffering endless delays, mishaps, and transportation shortages. Several such convoys disintegrated as the march continued and the destination became increasingly uncertain. Some of the prisoners were fortunate enough to escape and hide until the U.S. forces or the Red Army arrived. Several groups of prisoners from Mittelbau-Dora's subcamps fell victim to one of the bloodiest massacres of the end of the war in the town of Gardelegen.

When the American forces entered Mittelbau-Dora on April 11 they found about 100 sick prisoners, who had been left behind at Boelcke. Many of them lived on for only a few days after the liberation. According to a report published by the Americans on April 16, 1945, 2,000 corpses were counted at the site.[78] The scenes of atrocity that met the eyes of the American soldiers who liberated Boelcke were to haunt them for many years to come.[79]

At Buchenwald as well, there was an atmosphere of uncertainty in early April 1945 with regard to the fate of the main camp. From the beginning of February, when thousands of evacuees flooded in from Auschwitz and Groß-Rosen, the camp was crammed to overflowing. The freight cars from which the prisoners were unloaded were filled with corpses, and those prisoners who had survived the nightmare journey were exhausted, starving, and injured. Many of them spent a few weeks in Buchenwald and were then transferred to one of the subcamps; they remembered their time in the main camp as worse than the entire period they had spent in Auschwitz.[80] In late March and early April 1945, when the arrival of U.S. forces was imminent, the transfer of thousands of prisoners began from the subcamps to the main camp. At the beginning of April there were approximately 60 camps for men and 26 for women in the Buchenwald complex. They housed about 80,000 prisoners, 50,000 of them in the main camp,[81] although the usual capacity was only 21,000. The familiar sight seen in other camps, of prisoners lying on the ground outside barracks with no place to rest their exhausted and emaciated bodies, was repeated at Buchenwald.[82] In addition, the camp administrators were in a state of confusion and indecision in the first week of April.

As noted, Pohl visited Buchenwald on March 20, 1945. It seems that even before his visit, Hermann Pister, the camp commandant, knew about Himmler's directive that Jewish prisoners were to be protected, with a view to transferring them en bloc to Theresienstadt when the time came.[83] In a conversation with the senior camp command team, including Pister, Pohl repeated Himmler's instruction that the Jewish prisoners were to be given suitable medical treatment and that every effort was to be made to keep them alive. Those who could not be saved should be allowed to die quietly. When Pister expressed his surprise and asked the meaning of this change in policy, he was told that Himmler wanted to protect the Jews in order to exchange them for "German interests." Nothing was said at this meeting about evacuating the camp or surrendering it to the advancing U.S. forces.[84]

On April 2 Pister convened his senior staff and announced that if no counterorder was received, the camp would not be evacuated and would be handed over in its entirety to the Americans. Pister explained that at the end of March he had received clear instructions from Berlin that the camp was to remain intact and the prisoners were to be handed over to the Americans.[85] He ordered that the Jewish prisoners be separated from the others and prepared for departure from the camp, having understood on the basis of the directive conveyed by Pohl in Himmler's name that this step was required of him.[86]

The underlying motive of Himmler's orders to transfer all the Jews in concentration camps in Germany to Theresienstadt is evident. However, practically speaking, in view of the transportation conditions in April 1945, it was a fantastic scheme, doomed to end in failure. He was motivated by the desire to safeguard a large number of Jews, who were to serve as hostages and bargaining cards in the negotiations he was then conducting. In any event, by the end of 1944, small groups of Jews began to arrive at the camp in the Protectorate, and the numbers increased in the last month of the war. In all, between mid-April and May 11, 1945, 12,829 Jews arrived in Theresienstadt, almost all of whom survived the war.[87] To a large extent the transfer of Jews to Theresienstadt was known as a "work instruction" in the camps of central and southern Germany and Austria in mid-April 1945, and the spirit of the order was known to commanders in the field.[88]

The decisions taken by the Buchenwald command at the beginning of April, to leave the camp intact and transfer the prisoners unharmed to the enemy, were meaningless in the case of the subcamps. On April 2, 1945, preparations began for evacuating one of Buchenwald's large subcamps, Ohrdruf SIII. This camp was located about 31 miles (50 kilometers) southwest of Weimar and had been established in early November 1944 when the subcamp complex was expanding. It began its operation with 1,000 prisoners, a number that had increased by March 1945 to more than 13,700. Ohrdruf became a vast subcamp with subcamps of its own.[89] When it was decided to transfer the Ohrdruf inmates to Buchenwald, the camp commandant received orders from the SD in Weimar to liquidate all dangerous criminal and political elements who might cause problems, but not to harm the Jewish prisoners. Before the Ohrdruf inmates set out on their death march to Buchenwald, more than 1,500 prisoners were mercilessly liquidated. Approximately 12,000 prisoners left on April 4, and of these only 9,000 survived to enter the gates of Buchenwald three days later. The other 3,000 were shot along the way by the guards, by units of Hitlerjugend, and by civilians who took part in exterminating these dangerous enemies of the Reich.[90]

A young soldier who entered Ohrdruf after the massacre wrote in a letter to his parents:

Dear Mom and Dad,

After having written so much about the beauties of the German countryside, this letter may sound a bit unusual, for it is going to tell something ugly, something uglier than I have ever seen, or expect to see.

I'm going to devote this whole letter to this one subject. There is nothing else to write about, true, but I have more sufficient reasons for centering my words about one theme. First, I don't want any other thoughts to distract your attention from the story I shall unfold below. And secondly [sic], I want this letter placed in a very safe place, for it is my personal memorandum of something I personally want to remember, but would like to forget. I want to remember because in remembering in years to come I shall better be able to control any inclination toward softening the peace given a bastard people. I want to forget because it is human to wish to erase unpleasant sights from your mind. My feelings were likewise confused toward seeing this. I want to see it, yet the likelihood of seeing it sickened me. But I went. Enough of a preface.

You have read in the newspapers and magazines of German concentration camps, the camps where slave laborers were confined, tortured, killed. You've read of this camp or that camp where dead were found piled high. In print, it seems perhaps true, but the thought never really finds its way into that "inner sanctum" of realization which is a result of personal experience. I, like all of you, read of these places, and murmered [sic], "How awful!"

Today I saw one of these places, saw it in all its horror, all its filth, all its death. It was discovered soon after we moved into this area. Stories of its ghastliness filtered back to me, stories to make your blood boil and your pulse quicken. I had to see it.

You approach it along a dirty road. The camp consists of a group of dirty, one storey, ramshackle barracks. Lying just outside the gate to the camp is a body—an SS trooper who dressed like a refugee and tried to escape with some of them when the Yanks came, but was recognized by some and clubbed to death. Good riddance. You enter the camp. You go down a path. Suddenly you're in sort of a courtyard. You halt. Your senses deceive you. To your right is a heap of riddled bodies, the mortal remains of perhaps thirty prisoners who were machine gunned in desperation by the Germany Army when the Americans were approaching. All of them lying there, just as they fell, all emaciated, starved, barely skin and bones. Among them an American Air Force lieutenant. Thirty of them, bloodied, riddled, dead.

You move down some more paths. You see a crowd around a little shed. You push your way to the front of the crowd around the entrance—then suddenly wish you'd stayed in the rear. Inside is a heap of perhaps forty bodies, stripped of all clothing, piled just like the logs in our basement, one on top of the other, some feet first, some head first, all dead, massacred. All foreigners who weren't of the "best stock," the scum of the earth, the ones who weren't supermen. Someone had thrown lime on the heap.

Then you enter one of the barracks. Most of them were barns, with straw mattresses laid along the sides as tightly as possible, much more tightly than any pinch-penny farmer would dare pack cattle in his barn. Then you go on. You see the crematory—a nice bit of machinery with two layers, huge steel doors at each end, neat little tracks from each direction so the victims could be rolled directly in and rolled directly out. A very neat and durable piece of machinery, that.

Then we went up the road for some distance. As we approached this next "attraction," it looked as if someone had been digging huge holes. Nearby was a charred piece of field—perhaps twenty feet by ten in dimensions. It looks as if someone had a log fire there at one time. As you get very close, though, you realize they did have a log fire, with human beings as logs. Visible are the forms of men—heads, backbones, ribs, legs, all blackened and charred. Here, too, the Germans were systematic. They constructed parallel rails, somewhat like a railroad, and placed them cross wise on this, making sure the rails were elevated so a draft would come up underneath the bodies. You go over the pits and find them partially filled with acid. Protruding above the surface of the acid you see a leg and foot, partially disintegrated. Just another of the scum. How many completely destroyed bodies lie in the acid, who knows?

This is the end of the tour. Until now, I felt that unlike our comrades on the other side of the globe, we were fighting an enemy with some semblance of Roman civilization, an enemy with some standard of decency which might be remotely compared to ours. That feeling was destroyed completely this afternoon. Probably a relative minority of the German people knew about or had any connection with this monstrosity. But the people as a whole must bear the blame for allowing such fiends to rule their nation.

I wish most of the people in America could have been with me today. They (-) have returned with a different outlook on this war, with a different conception of the nature of the enemy we fight here. The crime is horrible enough in itself; in releating [sic] it, be sure to note these were European slave laborers, not prisoners of war, save for the American Lieutenant.

I thought perhaps I could write this letter and somehow or other summon up the vocabulary and journalistic ability to relay most of the fiendishness of this spectacle. Re-reading I feel I have failed. But perhaps I have given you a glimpse of the tragedy I beheld today.

There's nothing more to write today. I'm safe and well, Mom and Dad.

All my love,

Al Jr.[91]

What occurred at Ohrdruf was a planned and systematic massacre, such as was also perpetrated on prisoners in subcamps evacuated in Poland several months earlier. However, when the German subcamps were evacuated in spring 1945, the narrow loophole that had often existed for those sick prisoners who were not capable of setting out on evacuation marches from the Auschwitz or Groß-Rosen subcamps and so survived was closed. There were no sick prisoners at Ohrdruf when the American troops entered. There were only empty barracks, a sickening odor of charred human flesh, and piles of corpses of prisoners slaughtered before the evacuation of the camp.[92] The possibility of leaving prisoners behind had not been contemplated. Their liquidation had begun at the end of winter, several months before the evacuations. When the evacuation date arrived, those who were not candidates for evacuation were summarily liquidated. They were no longer left to die a slow and certain death, or liquidated in the gas chambers of such camps as still had them, but were killed swiftly and instantly by the guards.

There were also cases that, fortuitously, ended less tragically. This was what happened at the subcamp for women close to Lippstadt. It had been set up in November 1944, and about 750 women labored there, almost all of them Jewish women from Hungary and Poland. They began their march northward toward Bergen-Belsen on April 2, 1945. Very soon, they realized that the guards had concluded that it was impossible to deliver their charges to their planned destination. After marching them for a day and a night, they locked them in a building along the route. The women feared that their fate was sealed, but on the third day they were taken out. One of the prisoners described their rescue:

We heard already the rumbling American tanks, and we were led into the woods. I don't know how they happened not to hit us. So he says (he still yelled then), "You band of Jew-pigs." And he left us alone with all the SS men and he himself ran away. So I said then to one of the girls, "You know, I don't know whether we shall survive, but he will not come back any more."[93]

Several hours later, the Americans arrived and the remaining guards surrendered. It is hard to explain why prisoners at Ohrdruf were massacred while the women of Lippstadt survived. The difference cannot, of course, be attributed to gender-based decisions, because in dozens of other cases guards murdered women as brutally as they liquidated men. Apparently, local circumstances explain the outcome. There is no information on a directive to the camp supervisors to liquidate the women prisoners. The camp at Lippstadt was located at a distance from Buchenwald, and hence its evacuation began two days earlier than the evacuation of Ohrdruf, even before the hasty retreats in the Weimar and Buchenwald areas. And as often happened, the more pressure and confusion accompanied the move, the more casual the calculations of those responsible with regard to the fate of the prisoners.

While the inmates were being transferred from the subcamps to the main camp, special attention was devoted to the condition of the Jewish prisoners. It was they who needed to be preserved and transferred to Theresienstadt. About 350 of them walked for more than a week from Niederorschel camp to the main camp. Before leaving, the camp commandant warned them not to attempt to escape since anyone doing so would be shot without warning. Not many of the Jewish prisoners in the group of evacuees made the attempt, either because they were given adequate food rations during the evacuation or because they often passed the corpses of prisoners shot while trying to escape.[94] Moreover, since their clothes bore the mark identifying them as Jews, they feared the hostility of the German civilian population: "we . . . were hated and feared," was the impression of one of the prisoners. A rumor spread like wildfire that a Jewish prisoner who had escaped had been murdered by a German farmer.[95] In all, between 12,000 and 14,000 Jews were concentrated at Buchenwald in early April 1945. Other Jews were sent directly from subcamps to Theresienstadt, and some 1,500 arrived there in the last days of April.[96] The main reason so many were transported was the availability of means of transport to the local authorities.[97]

The military situation in the Buchenwald area at the beginning of April only heightened the nervousness of those in charge of local affairs. Josias Erbprinz zu Waldeck und Pyrmont, the HSSPF responsible for Buchenwald, abandoned his center of operations at Kassel, moved to Weimar, and on March 31 transferred his office to Buchenwald. He showed no particular interest in either the evacuation of the camp or the fate of the prisoners, and instead focused his efforts on preventing unnecessary losses and damage when the U.S. Army arrived. On the other hand, Fritz Sauckel, the Gauleiter of Thuringia, brought considerable pressure to bear on Waldeck-Pyrmont to order the evacuation of the camp. Sauckel wanted to avert a situation whereby thousands of liberated prisoners would scatter throughout the region and, so it was claimed, menace the population of nearby Weimar. Waldeck-Pyrmont, who agreed with Pister on this issue, refused to wield his authority and proclaim "Case A"—in other words, to give the order to evacuate the camp—until he received explicit instructions from Himmler to do so. Waldeck-Pyrmont recalled after the war that such an order did indeed reach him from Himmler sometime at the beginning of April.[98]

Pister gave instructions at the beginning of April to prepare the Jews for evacuation, but by April 5 he realized that the rest of the camp was to be surrendered to the U.S. Army. On April 5 or 6 Pister received a cable from the KdS in Weimar, stating that Himmler had sent them a directive to limit the number of prisoners in the camp before the Americans arrived. If it was impossible to evacuate them by train, they should be sent on foot.[99] Pister estimated that Sauckel was responsible for the altered instructions. He claimed that Sauckel had approached Himmler and complained that he was unable to feed so many prisoners and that their number in the camp should be reduced as much as possible. Since it was not clear whether freight cars would be available to transport the prisoners, Pister instructed the camp physicians to carry out medical examinations and to select only those prisoners fit enough to be evacuated on foot. These prisoners later set out from Buchenwald to the railway station at Weimar.[100]

Thus Pister, a veteran concentration camp administrator, a bureaucrat who tended to evade independent initiative, found himself faced with contradictory and ambiguous instructions. He continued to hesitate, seeking confirmation that the order from Weimar had in fact been issued by Himmler and was not some local SD initiative. At 10 p.m. on April 6 he cabled Oranienburg, reporting that he had received orders to evacuate the camp. He wrote that the evacuation would begin the following morning, he asked how many prisoners were to be evacuated, and he reported that there were 48,000 inmates in Buchenwald. The following morning, just after 11 a.m., Glücks replied: 20,000 were to be evacuated, 1,500 of them to Dachau and the rest to Flossenbürg.[101]

Pister issued the evacuation directive on the same day. It was somewhat reminiscent of the order Hoppe issued at Stutthof, but was at odds with Glücks's instructions. Phrased precisely and clearly, it ordered the transfer of 5,000 prisoners to Dachau, with the remainder to be sent to Flossenbürg.

Thus the 3,060 prisoners who were capable of walking began the death march from Buchenwald to Flossenbürg, in the charge of SS-Obersturmführer Schneier.[102] Another two transports were organized, one of them commanded by 37-year-old Hans-Erich Merbach. In all, 120 guards and 10 commanders were assigned to the transports, and instructions were handed down as to the quantity of food to be allocated to the inmates (for two days). The prisoners were scheduled to set out from the camp at 1 p.m. for Weimar and there immediately to board the open freight cars that awaited them there.[103] Waldeck-Pyrmont claimed after the war that on April 6 he told Himmler that he and Pister believed that the prisoners could not be evacuated on foot and that the necessary number of freight cars should be provided; if these were not available, the evacuation should be suspended. Himmler, he said, did not accept this view and replied that responsibility for providing the required numbers of cars rested with the local HSSPF.[104] In any event, when the prisoners were examined, their physical condition alone was taken into account; no attention was given to the need for equipment, food supplies, and suitable footwear. One of the SS physicians who conducted examinations in the camp explained after the war that "many were wearing wooden clogs, but they had only to walk as far as the Weimar railway station, that is 10 kilometers [6 miles]." As the inmates left on April 7 and 8, Waldeck-Pyrmont stood at the gate of the camp and inspected them.[105] These prisoners did in fact march only as far as Weimar in the first stage, but later their transport suffered through one of the most traumatic of the death marches before it reached Dachau only a day before the liberation of the camp.

The question of who gave the order to evacuate Buchenwald remained unanswered even after it was discussed by the Nuremberg tribunal. According to Walter Schellenberg, the order came from Ernst Kaltenbrunner, head of the RSHA. Schellenberg considered that Kaltenbrunner received it directly from Hitler, thereby bypassing Himmler, who favored a contrary policy at the time. It was Kaltenbrunner who instructed the SD in Weimar to order evacuation of the camp. However, Schellenberg was referring to the evacuation of the "privileged" prisoners alone. This was a small group of prisoners with special status, who had been imprisoned at Buchenwald under preferential conditions. Among them was Leon Blum, who had been premier of France in the mid-1930s. This was not to be an odyssey of tens of thousands of prisoners.[106]

This explanation is not entirely commensurate with the facts. Kaltenbrunner argued, and justifiably so, that the sole individual who could have given the order to evacuate the concentration camps was Himmler. Kaltenbrunner even doubted that Hitler himself had given the order. Kaltenbrunner himself had no authority to deal with this matter at the beginning of April 1945.[107]

Only on April 18, 1945, when Himmler appointed him supreme commander of security in southern Germany, was he empowered to issue instructions in the name of the Reichsführer.[108] The authority behind the order to evacuate the Jews from Buchenwald, as well as the decision to send out more than 20,000 prisoners on April 6, was Himmler. Glücks then transmitted these instructions to Buchenwald in Himmler's name.[109] The sequence of events created an intolerable situation; in the course of only a few days, three different and contradictory evacuation orders were sent out, and the fact that the last of them was dispatched at the very last moment did not, of course, facilitate efficient planning. There were two reasons for this mayhem: the total collapse of Office D at the time,[110] and Himmler's inability to decide exactly what he hoped to gain from the fact that hundreds of thousands of prisoners, many of them Jews, were at his mercy and under his control. In view of the situation on the battlefield, there was something surrealistic about the administrative disarray, and its outcome was to influence the fate of the inmates of the various subcamps.

Pister dispatched 28,000 prisoners from Buchenwald, 8,000 more than he had been ordered to evacuate. Most of them were sent out on death marches and were not transported by rail.[111] When the Jewish inmates of Buchenwald were ordered to prepare for departure on April 4, they were gripped with panic. The Jews, most of whom had lived through the death marches and evacuations from camps in the East several months previously, made every effort to hide and avoid reporting to the parade ground. They scattered among the barracks, trying to find refuge, particularly among the political prisoners.[112] They had no difficulty in interpreting the order as a prelude to their execution before the arrival of the Americans:

> I said to myself, Efraim, you are not walking any more, you have walked enough. We hid in the sewage canals. In the canals there were ways down and iron pillars you could hold. In order to go down and clean them, there are hooks that you hold like a ladder, you go down. A few times I went down, and covered myself up, standing on that ladder. I waited till the *Appel* [head count] ended, and when the *Appel* ended, I got out.[113]

In the end, the guards succeeded in rounding up about 3,000 Jewish prisoners. They left the camp on April 7 and walked to Weimar, a 6-mile (10-kilometer) route strewn with corpses of prisoners shot by their escorts.[114] In Weimar they were loaded onto freight cars on a train heading south,[115] which, like many others at the time, was bombed on its way to Flossenbürg by U.S. aircraft. When the Jews reached the camp, it was already in a state of total breakdown. Food was no longer being allocated, and when several containers of soup were brought in one evening, the starving prisoners fought for it and many did not succeed in getting their share.[116] Some of the Jews evacuated from Buchenwald to Weimar by rail continued their journey until those of them who survived reached Theresienstadt.[117]

The non-Jewish prisoners who were evacuated to Flossenbürg reached the camp between April 16 and 20.[118] They were held there for several days under grim conditions, without sleeping quarters, food, or water,[119] and when the time came for evacuation of the camp, they set out once again on a death march to the south. The survivors of this transport arrived at Dachau a day before the camp was liberated by the Americans. Some 8,000 Buchenwald prisoners were murdered on these death marches before the convoys reached Dachau, or were liberated en route by the Americans. In all, between 13,000 and 15,000 of more than 48,000 Buchenwald inmates perished during the evacuation of the subcamps and the partial evacuation of the main camp.[120] That is, more than one third of the prisoners from Buchenwald and its subcamps were murdered or died in a period of three weeks because of the conditions on the death marches. This was the camp that Himmler at the end of March 1945 had decided not to evacuate and to protect its Jewish prisoners.

What occurred at Weimar as a result of the chaotic evacuation of Buchenwald had vital implications for many of the prisoners who survived the last three weeks of the war. From late 1943 on, the Buchenwald inmates, like prisoners in other camps on German soil, were a regular presence in the town. Large groups of prisoners and other slave laborers passed through the town on their way to their worksites or in transition between subcamps and the main camp. The laborers could be seen all over the town, at the railway station or in the streets as they carried out various tasks, and the townspeople, naturally enough, asked themselves various questions about their identity. They also witnessed numerous acts of violence against prisoners who were punished by the guards for petty theft. The violent treatment that had been commonplace in the camp now spilled beyond the fences and was witnessed by the civilian population.

Toward the end of the war, it was widely rumored in Weimar that the communist underground had taken control of the SS troops in the camp and was about to take over the town. These were not new reports, since it had been rumored since mid-1944 that an organized communist underground was operating in the camp.[121] In March–April 1945 the activists, including quite a few communist kapos, were making every possible effort to delay and sabotage the evacuation plans.[122] Fear of the rapidly advancing Soviet forces on the eastern front and of what was considered a communist rabble imprisoned close to home, contributed to the perception that the prisoners were a dangerous threat.[123] The influx of prisoners in the previous year, especially Jews,

Poles, and Russians, had exacerbated tensions in the area. These prisoners were in very poor health, emaciated and dressed in rags, and resembled walking skeletons. For the local population, however, they were a menacing sight. The guards tried to keep their charges at a distance from the civilian population in the towns and villages where they passed or halted for the night.

For example, on March 27, 1945, the prisoners in the Witten-Annen subcamp were evacuated and walked 81 miles (130 kilometers) in three days to Lippstadt. The local residents, who already had a subcamp for women in their vicinity, were nervous about the presence of so many prisoners close at hand several days before the liberation. A group of armed local Volkssturm forced the prisoners out of town.[124] In other places, such situations ended much more tragically.

In Weimar as well, the townspeople began to be apprehensive about the rabble assembled near their homes. The most fearful were those who had been employed in various tasks by the SS and had come into contact with the prisoners. They were convinced that the prisoners would slaughter them when the day of liberation came. The leaders of the political underground in the camp were also afraid that Weimar and its inhabitants would fall victim to prisoner violence, since they were aware that many inmates harbored an urge for revenge. They regarded the prevention of such acts of vengeance as one of their main tasks after the liberation.[125]

The turmoil that prevailed around the evacuation of Buchenwald and the fact that the camp was evacuated only in part apparently infuriated Hitler. Pohl related that, before leaving Berlin in mid-April for Dachau,[126] he talked to Glücks, who told him that Hitler demanded to know who had given the order to evacuate Buchenwald. Word reached Berlin that prisoners liberated by the Americans on April 11 had walked out of the camp into Weimar in search of food, clothes, and medicines. Several incidents of clashes with the German population were inflated into hair-raising tales of violence by prisoners; these rumors spread like wildfire. This was only one part of a much larger puzzle. Kurt Becher, for example, told Israel Kasztner that Himmler had received information about incidents in which Russian prisoners released in the East had been equipped with weapons and joined the forces fighting Germany and were harassing the local population.[127]

When Hitler learned that Himmler was responsible for the confusion around the evacuation of Buchenwald, he declared furiously that if Himmler was not capable of executing orders to the letter (namely, emptying the camp and leaving no prisoners alive when the enemy entered), he should be relieved of responsibility for the project.[128] In any event, what occurred in Weimar after the liberation in no way fitted the descriptions of atrocities committed there. Liberated prisoners did in fact enter the town and there

were several cases of theft of food from shops or clothes hanging on wash-
ing lines, but no atrocities took place. After the liberation, political prisoners
in the camp made contact with antifascist civilians in Weimar, mainly in order
to organize aid for liberated prisoners and to supply food and clothing to the
camp.[129] Yet none of this was truly important to Himmler. The Führer's anger
and the web of rumors had made an impact. After the Buchenwald affair,
Himmler was much more purposeful in his actions.

On April 14, 1945, Himmler issued his last order regarding the concentration camp prisoners.[130] The tortuous path he had followed in the past
year with regard to the fate of the hundreds of thousands of slave laborers
in his prison installations had eventually led him to a conclusion that was in
line with his outlook and his previous policies:

> Surrender is out of the question. The camp must be evacuated immediately.
> Not a single prisoner must fall alive into enemy hands. The prisoners at Buchen-
> wald have taken action against the civilian population.
>   (-) Himmler.[131]

This order raised quite a few questions after the war because no clear and
unequivocal version existed. It was sent out to the commandants of Dachau
and Flossenbürg who had taken in the Buchenwald evacuees. It may well be
that on April 14 the order was sent only to Dachau and that a similar order
was received at Flossenbürg on April 18 by teleprinter. It is not clear whether
Himmler sent it directly or whether Pohl's staff brought it southward when
they fled Berlin.[132] In any event, evidence of the existence of the order was
found after the war in the diaries and memoirs of prisoners and the depositions of SS officers from Dachau.[133] But even if the circulation of the order
was limited and several versions were received, its basic principles were unquestionably plain to wide circles of position-holders in the collapsing SS
system and in the concentration camps. To a large extent it set the official
seal on instructions transmitted orally, alluded to indirectly or interpreted in
this manner owing to fears that incidents such as were said to have taken
place at Buchenwald would recur.

CHAPTER FIVE

Murder Is Rampant

Himmler's confused and indecisive orders created administrative chaos in the concentration camp complex in April 1945. As a consequence, the HSSPFs, the Gauleiters, and the concentration camp commandants, charged that month with organizing evacuations, were never certain which instruction to follow and from whom it came. The decisions they eventually took were the outcome of the situation in central Germany, which was almost entirely isolated as the Red Army approached from the east and U.S. forces came from the west. In nearly every case, the decision pointed in one direction: if not evacuation, then liquidation. In the final analysis, what determined the length of the interval between evacuation and liquidation, in particular in the subcamps, was the military situation and the ability to break through the ever-shrinking territory still under German control. This was the situation in the concentration camps in the north.

"Do What You Think Is Right"

Georg-Henning Bassewitz-Behr was the HSSPF of Hamburg, and Neuengamme was under his jurisdiction. When interrogated after the war, he said that he had known of a directive that came from Hitler himself, although it was transmitted by Himmler, which stated that "the Führer has made you personally responsible for ensuring that no prisoner falls alive into enemy hands" (*Der Führer macht Sie persönlich dafür verantwortlich dass kein KZ-Häftling lebend in die Hand des Feindes fällt*). Bassewitz-Behr could not state categorically when the directive reached him, but he was certain that it was on his desk at the end of March 1945.[1]

His last meeting with Himmler took place at the beginning of April 1945, but Neuengamme was not mentioned then, although the camp was in danger of falling into British hands. Himmler's sole allusion to the problem was the general directive which, as he emphasized several times, stemmed from the Führer. Bassewitz-Behr did not know whether Himmler had disseminated Hitler's directive to all the camp commandants.[2] As we know, Himmler did not do so. He may have transmitted the directive to Neuengamme and then modified his decision, as was the case with Buchenwald. It is also possible that Bassewitz-Behr interpreted it as he saw fit, or found it expedient after the war to shelter in the shadow of the senior decision maker in the Reich. The question remains unanswered. What is clear, however, is the conclusion he drew, namely, that in any event he was to continue evacuating the prisoners, and if this plan proved impractical, they were to be executed (*dass die Häftlinge immer weiter zu evakuieren seien; oder aber dass sie getötet werden sollten*). He claimed, however, that he had never intended to carry out the Führer's directive but planned to surrender the camp to the enemy if he did not succeed in evacuating it. Although this implied that he intended to flout an order, he succeeded in obtaining oblique permission to do so. In their last conversation, he asked Himmler what precisely he was to do with the camp, and Himmler replied: *"Tun Sie was Sie fur richtig halten"* (Do what you think is right). On the basis of this reply, Bassewitz-Behr prepared a plan to evacuate the prisoners to several sites in the Bremen area and elsewhere.[3]

In Neuengamme and its subcamps at the end of March 1945 there were more than 40,000 male and more than 11,000 female inmates. Like other camps at the time, it was crammed full: sanitary conditions were unspeakable, food and medicines almost unavailable. Between early January and the end of March 1945 more than 6,200 prisoners died there.[4] Even if Bassewitz-Behr wanted to evacuate this exhausted and starving population in orderly fashion, as he claimed, he lacked the means, the time, and the conditions. It is questionable, however, whether this was really of concern to him.

Max Pauly, commandant of Neuengamme, knew little about Bassewitz-Behr's conversations with Himmler. All the guidance he had was the well-known directive of summer–fall 1944, which stated that in the event of "Case A," the Hamburg HSSPF would be granted the supreme authority to decide the fate of the camp. When this came to pass in February 1945, Bassewitz-Behr ordered the evacuation of two of Neuengamme's subcamps, which were in danger of being occupied.[5] The evacuation of further subcamps began in late March and early April, mainly in the Hanover area. As in similar cases, the prisoners were mustered and given food for the journey, and the columns began the march to the evacuation destinations, which were Bergen-Belsen and the main camp.[6]

"At Any Rate. . . . They Are Pleading to Be Shot"

One of the camps evacuated at the time was a subcamp near Wilhelmshaven, an important port town and naval base in Upper Saxony. Established in September 1944, it housed some 1,100 prisoners. As the front line moved closer at the end of March 1945, it was decided to evacuate the camp to Neuengamme. On April 5 the first group of prisoners set out on foot for Hamburg, 124 miles (200 kilometers) distant. Only a few inmates were left behind, mainly those who had been in the sick bay during the evacuation. Also left were prisoners who had been caught trying to escape and had been brought back. A physician examined the inmates before the evacuation and decided who was to remain behind to be evacuated by rail and who was capable of walking. In all, 390 to 400 prisoners remained in the camp[7] and were scheduled to be sent by rail to Neuengamme. They were of French, Yugoslav, Polish, and Russian origin, and there was also a group of Hungarian Jews.[8]

On April 3 these prisoners were loaded onto four freight cars. There were about 100 in each of the first three cars, and 60 were crammed into half of the fourth car, the other half being reserved for the guards. The 12 to 16 guards were navy personnel,[9] between 30 and 55 years of age, who were no longer fit for active service. In charge of the transport was one of these guards, a junior officer named Rudolf Engelmann, who was joined by an SS-Oberschütze (Private 1st Class) from the Waffen-SS, 36-year-old Gustav Alfred Jepsen, a Danish national of German origin. He had been attached to the transport on orders from the commandant of Wilhelmshaven, since, as he explained after the war: "I had experience of this kind of work." Jepsen stated that the prisoners on this train were "so sick with tuberculosis, syphilis and open sores . . . that they were scarcely capable of walking." None of this deterred Jepsen from bringing his girlfriend, Ilsa Bähr, with him on this trip. She had come to visit a week before the evacuation and had been stranded in the camp because of various disruptions of passenger rail services. She rode the death train in order to get back to her home near Hamburg.[10]

On April 3 the inmates of Wilhelmshaven were evacuated to Bremen, which they reached the next day. The hygienic conditions on the train were horrendous, and food was in short supply. Hunger, filth, and lice tormented the evacuees, and at least 10 of them died on the first day. The guards, perturbed by news of Allied bombing raids on trains carrying prisoners, wanted to abandon the train as quickly as possible and deposit the prisoners at Neuengamme. On April 6 the train left Bremen, and a day later it reached Lüneburg. That morning and afternoon, the town was bombed by the U.S. Air Force. The railway station was heavily damaged and put out of action. Various installations, including local fuel reserves, were set on fire, and deafening explosions were heard throughout the town.[11]

The prisoners were locked in throughout the bombing raid. Most of the guards fled to nearby groves of trees in search of shelter, and only four of them remained to watch the prisoners. The cars turned into death traps for many prisoners. Although the sides were not particularly high, many prisoners were too feeble to climb over and escape, and they continued to crouch inside. Those who survived lay wounded on blood-soaked straw on the floor of the cars, wailing with pain and crying out for help. The guards began to drag the prisoners out of the cars to a nearby field, and in the course of this move, several prisoners were murdered.[12] Seventy-one of them perished during these bombing raids.[13]

The guards apparently faced a serious problem after the bombing: many of them had lost their rifles in the fires. During the night of April 7 Jepsen tried to obtain new weapons from the Gestapo and SD offices in the town. The guards complained that they could not guard the prisoners without weapons. Only after Jepsen promised a local officer that the weapons would be returned to the local police once new rifles arrived from Neuengamme did the officer agree to lend him rifles and 60 bullets from the police armory.[14] At the height of the mayhem, about 20 prisoners succeeded in escaping. They roamed among the houses in search of refuge. When a degree of calm had been restored, the corpses of the prisoners who had been killed in the raid were piled up beside the train. The survivors, many of them severely injured, were moved to a field near the home of a local farmer. The guards feared that prisoners would continue to escape and kept a strict watch on those who lay in the open field. The night was very cold and the prisoners lit scraps of paper they found there in order to warm themselves. During the raid, their clothes had been ripped and torn, and some of them had lost their shoes.[15]

Jepsen had no idea precisely what he was expected to do with the group of prisoners stranded near the railway station at Lüneburg. The locomotive was out of action, and no replacement was available. He sent a telegram to Neuengamme and asked for instructions. The reply ordered him to take the transport to Bergen-Belsen. He sent a second telegram, reporting that this was not possible. Many of the prisoners were dead, and others were not fit enough to be evacuated on foot. Close to midnight, Jepsen received an additional message that two vehicles would arrive the next morning to evacuate the prisoners.[16] On April 8 an officer and a physician from the camp arrived and told Jepsen that the two vehicles were on their way and would transport the prisoners to Bergen-Belsen. After some time, a truck arrived and took 68 of the prisoners. Two days later, a second truck arrived and took another 78. All of them eventually reached Bergen-Belsen.[17]

Meanwhile, those left behind, a number of them injured, lay sprawled on the ground near the railway station. Jepsen continued to search for a solution to his predicament and asked the SD and Gestapo what to do with the prisoners left in the town. He was told to liquidate them. On April 10, 1945, three days after the bombing raid, the commander of the local police, Otto Müller, and the mayor, Hauschild, took the initiative to bury the prisoners killed in the bombing or during the evacuation. Toward evening, they gathered the corpses and buried them in a mass grave dug in the Tiergarten forest about half a mile (1 kilometer) south of the railway station.[18] It was also the place to which the guards had fled for shelter several days earlier.[19] That day, Jepsen apparently made another attempt to meet with police or municipal officials in order to find a solution to the problem of the injured and sick prisoners at the railway station. He encountered flat refusals wherever he turned, and was told that what occurred at the railway station was not the concern of municipal bodies.[20]

On the same day a police officer came to tell him that since there was no suitable place in Lüneburg where the prisoners could be detained, they were to be shot.[21] The presence of the escaped prisoners who were roaming unsupervised apparently evoked considerable alarm in the town. On April 11 the local paper, *Lüneburger Zeitung*, printed a Gestapo warning to the population, stressing the danger posed by these people. A hunt for escaped prisoners began in the vicinity of the town and the nearby forest, with the participation of police and Gestapo personnel and local civilians.[22]

The police officer who came to talk to Jepsen removed several bullets from his pistol and handed them to him. When Jepsen asked him if this symbolic gesture meant that the prisoners were to be killed, the officer turned and left without replying.[23] Dozens of sick prisoners had remained in Lüneburg, and nobody knew what to do with them. On April 12 a physician with the rank of Unterscharführer (Sergeant) arrived and told Jepsen that they were all suffering from typhus and endangering the local population and hence should be shot. Under interrogation at his trial, Jepsen asserted that this order had even been written down and signed by the officer, whose name he could not recall.[24] However, it appears that Jepsen had no idea who had given the order to murder these prisoners, and it is unlikely that he cared. He decided to put an end to the interminable saga, on the assumption that someone in the town had decided that it was necessary to liquidate them. His excuse was that if he himself had given the order, it would not have been obeyed. On the evening of April 11 the group of killers passed among the sick, injured, and dying prisoners at the railway station and killed them one by one.[25] Jepsen did not have enough men at his disposal to carry out the task swiftly because some of the guards had been injured in the air attack and others had fled. They also lacked sufficient ammunition, and so it was provided by a local police officer.[26] In any event, he could not recall a single guard who refused to carry out the mission that began after Engelmann talked to the men.[27] Jepsen described his role as follows:

> I myself shot six, using only one round for each, except for one, whom I did not kill outright. I shot them through the heart so as to kill them with the least possible pain except for the one, whom I tried to shoot through the temple; this man did not die immediately so I shot him again through the heart. . . .
>
> A few days after the air raid, Ilse Bähr took a train back to Hamburg, but this took place before the internees were shot.[28]

The corpses of 244 prisoners who died in the aerial attack on the train or were murdered later by the guards and their helpers were later uncovered in mass graves on the spot. It will be recalled that about 400 prisoners had set out in the transport from Wilhelmshaven. Of the 244 corpses in Tiergarten forest in Lüneberg, 71 died in the bombing raid. Jepsen and his accomplices were responsible for the death of the other 173. Some of them died during the transport to Lüneburg and during the wait for evacuation transportation, which was delayed; most were massacred on April 12. Another 146 more fortunate individuals continued on their way to Bergen-Belsen. It is not known how many died along the way, but only 100 survived to the day of liberation.[29] Thus about 75 percent of the prisoners who set out on the death march perished within five weeks in a series of random or deliberate incidents: from the machine guns of the American bombers or the pistols of SS guards or weapons supplied by local authorities in the town where the transport was stranded.

The precise number of Jews among these victims is unknown. At the end of November 1944 about 200 Hungarian Jews who had been transferred from Auschwitz were sent to Neuengamme and from there to Wilhelmshaven. It is not known how many of them were among the 250 dead buried in the forest.[30] Of the Lüneburg victims, 167 were identified after the war. The great majority were French political prisoners; several others were Belgian, Italian, and Polish. Six were Jews from Hungary: Meir Friedman, Nikolas Klein, Ferno Mulner, Bela Müller, Martin Munk, and David Stadler.[31] Jepsen and his henchmen vanished from the town the day after the last murder. On April 13 they reached Neuengamme, and from there Jepsen made his way home to Denmark. He was apprehended and tried at Hamburg in August 1946 and hung on July 26, 1947.[32]

The slaughter at Lüneburg was the outcome of several factors that coalesced at a critical moment in time. It demonstrated vividly the major impact of the circumstances in Germany in April 1945 when transportation of prisoners reached an impasse. By mid-April there was, of course, no contact between Bassewitz-Behr in Hamburg and Max Pauly at Neuengamme and Alfred Jepsen and Engelmann at Lüneburg. It is possible that Bassewitz-Behr would have preferred orderly evacuation of the camps, although he knew that liquidation of prisoners was not a far-fetched option. Pauly tried, to the best of his ability, to ensure efficient evacuation of prisoners, particularly from the main camp. But in practice, in various corners of the disintegrating Reich where trains were stranded, there were men like Engelmann and Jepsen who had to decide what to do with several hundred prisoners who could not be shifted. In the chaos prevailing at the time, and in view of the fact that those responsible for transports came up against a blank wall whenever they tried to find ways of continuing the evacuation, murder appeared to be a logical solution. When Jepsen informed Engelmann that he had received orders from the SS physician to liquidate the prisoners, Engelmann replied: "Well, at any rate those people are half dead and they are pleading to be shot, so perhaps we'll shoot them."[33]

The British military tribunal that tried Jepsen determined that all the local municipal bodies, ranging from the mayor to the police chief and the railway officials, avoided any involvement in the affair and made no attempt to help the injured prisoners who lay out in the open. They most certainly did nothing to prevent the murders that were in the offing for several days.[34] The prosecuting counsel came to a definite conclusion:

> From various evidences by witnesses in connection with the case . . . the Court could gather that such very seriously meant threats of shooting were a matter of daily routine during the recent times, before the German collapse. One can express this as follows: National Socialism became all the more dangerous as it came nearer to its ruin.[35]

The Death Routes in Northern Germany, on Land and on Sea

At Neuengamme, Max Pauly continued to deal with the transfer of prisoners to other camps. He visited Hamburg in mid-April for a talk with Bassewitz-Behr. He was told that, in light of what had occurred at Buchenwald and the anticipated danger to the population of Hamburg, everything possible must be done to ensure that no prisoners fell into the hands of the Allies alive. At the very same time, between April 13 and 15, Pauly was informed that prisoners who had been the subjects of medical experimentation were to be killed before the evacuation. As a consequence, several dozen prisoners were liquidated at Neuengamme on April 21 and 23, including some who had been detained in the Gestapo prison installation in Hamburg and then sent to the camp for execution. Anton Thumann, one of the camp guards, admitted to having taken part in this massacre because he knew of the order that no prisoners must be left alive to fall into enemy hands.[36]

As the front moved closer, however, familiar problems arose. Bassewitz-Behr suggested to Pauly the following solution to the problem of evacuating the Neuengamme inmates: they should be moved toward Lübeck bay, and loaded onto boats, to be supplied by Karl Otto-Kurt Kaufmann, the Gauleiter of Hamburg.[37] The evacuation began on April 15 with the transfer of 2,500 sick inmates to Bergen-Belsen.[38] On April 19 and 20, 1,200 prisoners of Norwegian and Danish origin were handed over to the Swedish Red Cross. By April 29 another several thousand prisoners had been evacuated from the camp to several camps in northern Germany.[39] About 10,000 prisoners from the main camp were taken to the port of Neustadt in Holstein, where they boarded three vessels: 1,998 boarded the *Athen,* 4,600 crowded onto the *Cap Arcona,* and 2,800 were placed on the *Thielbek.* It is not entirely clear what was planned for these prisoners.[40] The move may have been part of a plan to transfer them to Sweden.[41] The boats, however, soon turned into death traps. They did not have enough fuel to set out to sea, there was a lack of water on deck, and no food had been taken on. The hygienic conditions were intolerable, and hundreds of prisoners died on the decks of the three ships within a few days.[42] Karl-Emil Grafenhorst was the commander of a small military unit affiliated with the submarine command of the German navy. His men suffered from various health problems and hence had been disqualified for active service; moreover, most were elderly and close to retirement from the navy. At the time, they were assigned mainly to guard duties and to rescue units near the port. On May 3 Grafenhorst received instructions from his commanding officer (CO) to post his men in the port area, since rumors had reached the town that prisoners were escaping the deportation ships and that some had murdered a woman and several children. He told his men that it was their duty to protect the German population against the prisoners, whom he described as subhuman beings who did not deserve to live. The unit was deployed throughout the port, seized prisoners who tried to hide, and killed them. The number of victims is not known for sure, but there were certainly several dozen. Since horror stories were being spread about the conduct of escaped prisoners, the guards were naturally anxious to move the vessels as fast as possible outside the range of danger to the innocent civilian population.[43] The solution, however, came from another direction entirely. On May 3 at about 3 p.m., British aircraft strafed Neustadt port in what was one of the most catastrophic events of the last days of the war. The three ships with their cargo of prisoners were hit, and giant fires broke out. The prisoners were trapped in the burning, sinking ships and were either burned alive or drowned. Some 7,000 of the prisoners drowned in the bay, and others were shot by the port rescue unit.[44]

The option of total extermination of the prisoners remaining in the camps was raised repeatedly in various forums in the last few months of the war, at work meetings and in talks between camp commandants in northern Germany and senior SS officers. Anton Kaindl, commandant of Sachsenhausen, testified at his postwar trial by a Soviet military tribunal in Berlin that this option was mentioned to him explicitly. On February 1, 1945, he spoke to the Gestapo chief, Müller, by telephone. Müller told him that he must find the means, either by gunshot, bombing from the air, or gassing, to liquidate the camp inmates.[45] Kaindl chose to interpret this directive leniently as referring to prisoners from specific target groups: the sick and the political inmates who were liable to prove dangerous during the evacuation of the camp. Indeed, on the day after his talk with Müller, the first 150 prisoners were executed. As noted, by the beginning of March about 5,000 prisoners had been liquidated in the camp.[46]

Müller's order to Kaindl raises several questions. Although Kaindl's testimony should be treated with the necessary caution, and consideration should be taken of his natural desire to shift the blame for the murder of thousands of prisoners to some senior figure, it may be assumed that Müller did in fact urge such a solution. The Soviet advance in Prussia and their imminent occupation of northern Germany were tangible threats. With Sachsenhausen only 12 miles (20 kilometers) from Berlin, the Gestapo chief was troubled by the prospect that it might fall into Soviet hands. His main concern was security issues, and so the fate of the prisoners was of no concern whatsoever to him; the liquidation of prisoners who could not be evacuated was a crucial need. Kaindl accepted Müller's instructions in principle. There would be no total liquidation for the time being; but killing of dangerous political elements or prisoners unfit for evacuation was to be implemented without delay.

There were more than 58,000 prisoners in the Sachsenhausen complex at the end of January 1945. Concurrently with the murders in the camp, large numbers of prisoners were being transferred southward and westward. In January–February some 20,000 prisoners were evacuated from

Sachsenhausen to Bergen-Belsen, Mittelbau-Dora, Mauthausen, Ohrdruf, and other camps. Several days before the final evacuation date of Sachsenhausen, 2,300 Norwegian and Danish prisoners were handed over to the Red Cross. They were sent to Neuengamme and joined the 1,200 or so prisoners from those countries who were later transferred to Sweden.[47]

Lieberose was a Sachsenhausen subcamp whose liquidation began in February 1945 as part of the transfer of subcamp inmates to the main camp. It was located close to the village of Jamlitz in eastern Brandenburg. The camp had been functioning since late 1943, and in summer 1944 numerous Jewish prisoners were brought in, mainly from Hungary. The conditions in the camp were abominable, and at the end of the summer some 500 prisoners who were no longer fit for labor were dispatched to Auschwitz for extermination. Approximately 1 percent of the 4,500 to 6,000 prisoners who passed through the camp in its final months perished there. Most were Jews from Hungary and Poland.[48]

On January 31, 1945, the commandant of Lieberose received orders to evacuate the camp. The order specified that some 1,000 prisoners who were no longer fit for labor were to receive "special treatment" (Sonderbehandlung). The others were to be transferred to Sachsenhausen.[49] The camp guards began to classify the prisoners into categories: the sick and elderly on one hand, and the prisoners in reasonable physical condition, who appeared capable of withstanding the conditions of the march, on the other. The first group was to be transferred to Bergen-Belsen.[50]

On February 2 the guards began to assemble the prisoners, and by 8 a.m. machine-gun fire was heard, which continued till the evening. Prisoners were moved by the guards from barracks to barracks, the Jews and the sick being concentrated in the same place. The guards then supervised the prisoners' digging of a 2-yard-by-2.5-yard pit, into which the bodies were to be thrown. Then prisoners were taken out of the barracks one by one by guards and identified, and once it was confirmed that they were Jews, they were shot. Other Jewish prisoners picked up the corpses and threw them into the pit. The liquidation of Jewish prisoners in the camp continued until February 4.[51]

The murderers were a diverse group. There were a few guards from the nearby factory where the prisoners labored, and a group of ethnic Germans from Yugoslavia who had been in Jamlitz since the end of 1943 and had been coopted to the camp administration as guards. All of them carried out their assignment unhesitatingly and even enthusiastically. One was heard calling out to a colleague: "Come with us. We are going to shoot the Jews. We'll get schnapps for the job."[52] Yet Jewish prisoners were not the only ones singled out for slaughter. There were political prisoners considered dangerous, and others who had informed against fellow inmates to the camp command.[53]

After the war, 1,236 corpses of murdered prisoners were discovered in a nearby village to which they had been taken for burial. Some 1,500 others were evacuated to Sachsenhausen.[54]

On April 18 Kaindl received the order for final evacuation of the camp. In contrast to the procedure in the camps that had been evacuated several months earlier in Poland or to the evacuation of Neuengamme, the local HSSPF was not involved in the evacuation order. August Heißmeyer had left his office in Berlin more than a month earlier because of the heavy bombings of the city and later claimed that he had no subsequent contact with anyone in the camp. He also claimed that he never gave an order to evacuate the camp, and certainly not to liquidate prisoners during the evacuation.[55] Kaindl said that it was Glücks who ordered him to evacuate the surviving prisoners from the main camp and subcamps and move them north to the coast, where they were to be taken out to sea and drowned (versenken).[56]

Although Kaindl's statements should be regarded with caution, the date of the order and its phrasing support the assumption that such an order did in fact reach him. Several days earlier, Himmler had issued the directive that no prisoners were to be permitted to fall into enemy hands alive. Glücks undoubtedly knew of this directive and its implications and, as a loyal bureaucrat, chose the suitable path of implementation. It is highly likely that the decision to send the Neuengamme prisoners to Lübeck and load them onto ships was also part of the directives that were bandied about among camp commandants in northern Germany in the second half of April 1945.[57]

The evacuation of the main camp at Sachsenhausen began on the night of April 20–21. The prisoners were summoned out of the blocks, arranged in groups of 500, and began to march in a northwesterly direction. The camp command faced a problem that was quite common during the spring 1945 evacuations: a shortage of escorting guards. Consequently, a group of German prisoners were chosen, most of them criminals but several "politicals." They were given uniforms and weapons and joined the SS guards. These members of the "prisoners' police" (Häftlingspolizei) treated their fellow inmates viciously and brutally in most cases.[58] Most of them were hardened criminals whose attitude toward the Jews, Poles, or Russians who were imprisoned alongside them had always been hostile and arrogant. These tough and violent men looked out for themselves above all and found it hard to maintain solidarity with other prisoners.[59] For many of them the approaching liberation held out no particular promise because they feared that the other prisoners would take revenge on them as soon as they were able. As far as they were concerned, the uniforms and new status were a preferred option, especially because it enabled them to try to disappear among the civilian population whenever the opportunity arose.

According to Kaindl's testimony, he had to transfer the Sachsenhausen prisoners to Wittstock and continue from there toward Lübeck, where they were to board ships on the way to "disappearing."[60] On April 22, a day after the evacuation began, Soviet and Polish units reached the camp and liberated it. There they found 3,000 sick prisoners, including 1,400 women, who had been left behind.[61] The reason the sick inmates were left, when strenuous efforts had been made in earlier months to liquidate large numbers of them, is unknown. It seems that this time the urge to leave before the Soviet troops arrived played to the advantage of those who were physically incapable of enduring the hardships of a march.

Fritz Suhren, the Ravensbrück commandant, received general orders to evacuate his subcamps in late January–early February 1945 to prevent prisoners from falling into Soviet hands, and the evacuation of the prisoners to the main camp began in March. The evacuation proceeded at a sluggish pace. About 3,000 women and 1,000 men in several camps were transferred to the main camp to await the evacuation.[62] More than 7,500 women prisoners were transferred in April 1945 to the Swedish Red Cross under the agreement between Himmler and Bernadotte. Most of them were from Scandinavian countries, but there were also women from Poland and other countries.[63] On April 21 Himmler met with Norbert Masur, the representative of the World Jewish Congress, and it was agreed to attach 1,000 Jewish women to a transport of women to be transferred from Ravensbrück to Sweden.[64]

The order for final evacuation of Ravensbrück apparently arrived at the end of March 1945, and Suhren claimed that it was sent through Glücks and Heißmayer.[65] The camp physicians were required to decide who was to be evacuated on the basis of vague and somewhat inconsistent criteria. One of them, the SS physician Dr. Adolf Winkelmann, testified at his trial that he received instructions to select for evacuation those inmates who were capable of continuing to work and fit enough to endure the conditions of an evacuation march. His testimony indicates that there was a clear correlation between the various components: labor, physical condition of the prisoners, and the situation along the front:

> As for working fitness, the case was that so and so many people were wanted to work: as for the fitness to march the case was that the Eastern Front came nearer and the camp was going to be evacuated.[66]

The conditions along the front and the advance of the Red Army meant not merely that there was only a very narrow corridor through which prisoners could be moved to northwest Germany, but also that to continue to utilize them as slave labor would be absurd. Consequently, in quite a few subcamps a number of women prisoners were left behind who could not be evacuated because of the Red Army advance. All the equipment, kitchen installations, barracks, and the limited means of subsistence had already been evacuated. These sick and feeble women were left to starve, exposed to the rigors of the weather. Quite a few died in the days just before the Soviet troops arrived. Among them were a number of Hungarian Jewish women who had been transferred to Ravensbrück from Auschwitz.[67] Such, for example, was the plight of the women inmates, most of them Jewish, who had been transferred, after arrival at Ravensbrück, to the Malchow subcamp. One of them described the second evacuation these women had experienced within several weeks:

> The walk from Ravensbrück to Malchow took a day and a night, a day and a night. And I was already so weak, and so were we all. One of them helped me on one side and the other on the other side and we slept as we walked. And that was how we moved on, and anyone who couldn't endure it fell and they shot her. They didn't give them a chance; they shot the girls on the spot. And once I needed the lavatory. I didn't know what to do. I stepped out of the line and there was no lavatory but there was a barn. So I went into the barn. I said to the girls: "I must go to the lavatory, it's impossible." I went to the barn and I went into the barn . . . and then we continued on our way till we reached Malchow.[68]

In Malchow, where there were about 900 women prisoners, conditions at the beginning of 1945 were unendurable.[69] Those prisoners who were lucky enough to continue working in the vicinity collected rotten vegetables from the fields near the camp, and this was all they ate.[70] "It was . . . a camp where there was hunger such as I can't remember, in Auschwitz there wasn't such hunger," one of the women prisoners recalled.[71]

When the time came to evacuate Ravensbrück, on April 26, there were 30,994 inmates in the camp complex. About 17,000 of them were in distant subcamps and could no longer be transferred to the main camp, where the others were imprisoned. Suhren estimated that about 3,000 of them were men. He claimed that the evacuation order was conveyed to him by Heißmeyer at the end of March and he understood that Glücks was behind it. As he said: "The suggestion I made to Heißmeyer to hand these people over in orderly fashion to the enemy or the International Red Cross was rejected. So I had to continue with the evacuation."[72]

The final evacuation came as a surprise to the prisoners. The front was within hearing range, and it was rumored in the camp that the prisoners would be left in place.[73] The relatively late date of the final evacuation raises several questions as to the intention to evacuate. The fact that a number of women prisoners were handed over to the Red Cross created the impression that the camp was not going to be emptied and that the inmates would stay put until liberated. Because of the delay, the evacuation turned into a panic-stricken flight, although the destination, as per Glücks's instructions, had been known for weeks. To Winkelmann, it was abundantly clear what fate awaited the evacuees:

> These people would have been in a very bad way; first of all they had very bad footwear, they had hardly proper clothing and no blankets. There would have been no shelter during the night and they would have to spend the night on the lawn or in the woods. There would have been no chance for them to look after the sick and there were bound to be many sick from cold. They would at any rate not get warm food and there was also some talk about a secret order that no prisoner be allowed to fall into Russian hands and that was the reason why everybody had to be evacuated to the west.[74]

The order that "no prisoner is to fall alive into enemy hands" was, therefore, also familiar to the authorities who dispatched prisoners from Ravensbrück. Winkelmann, who had served in several concentration camps and was among those who conducted selections at Ravensbrück, admitted at his trial that

> I heard of a secret order but I did not see it—namely that no prisoner was to fall into Russian hands and another version that the camp had to be handed over with only 2,500 prisoners. What part of this is true I do not know.[75]

On April 27, 1945, the women prisoners were taken out of the main camp and organized in groups of 300–500 in preparation for departure. At Ravensbrück as well, between 2,000 and 3,000 sick men and women who had been classified by the camp physicians during several weeks of selections as unfit for marching were left behind.[76] These selections were of course a farce because many more than 3,000 inmates were too feeble to withstand the grueling conditions of a death march. Winkelmann argued in his defense that 90 percent of the women were capable of marching 60 miles (100 kilometers) "if they had halts along the way and if they were not expected to march more than 17 to 20 kilometers [10 to 12 miles] a day."[77] It seems that he forgot what he had said on another occasion during his interrogation about the physical condition of the women prisoners and what they were wearing.

The camp guards, who were armed and used tracker dogs, inspected the barracks to check that no women prisoners were hiding there. Each woman received a package supplied by the Red Cross, but a considerable proportion of the contents had been looted by the guards and never reached the prisoners. The convoy included wagons, on which were heaped the equipment and belongings of the guards. Any suspicious approach to these wagons by prisoners spelled mortal danger.[78]

The prisoners evacuated from Ravensbrück were marched toward Schwerin, to which women prisoners from the subcamps had also been evacuated. One of the rumors that circulated among the camp guards was that a new camp was to be established near Lübeck for the prisoners from Ravensbrück and that the sick women would be sent to Bergen-Belsen.[79] It is unlikely that any of the guards believed this story. In one case, when women prisoners from the subcamp at Retzow-Rechlin were evacuated, they were led into a forest along the route and told that this was a rest place. Suddenly the guards began to fire at them indiscriminately. Those women still capable of running fled into the forest as the guards shot at them. What troubled the guards above all was the thought that they might be identified by the women prisoners after the war. Their panic at the prospect of being taken prisoner by the Red Army was a source of danger for the women. As the guards became increasingly frantic to escape the forces closing in on them, their fingers became lighter on the trigger. Often the guards halted at tailoring workshops or clothing stores in the towns they passed and demanded civilian clothes. After throwing away their uniforms, they fled to towns in the region.[80]

This was a relatively short death march, and it gradually fell apart as the columns of prisoners advanced toward Schwerin. The Red Army liberated the main camp and the sick inmates there on April 30. When the U.S. forces reached Schwerin on May 2 there were about 20,000 prisoners there from the camps evacuated in northern Germany—Sachsenhausen and Ravensbrück.[81]

On April 23, 1945, the first groups of prisoners from Sachsenhausen reached the vicinity of Wittstock. It was a high-speed death march; the prisoners marched in blocs of 500, and the guards rode bicycles alongside them. No food was supplied; the marchers tore out grass from the roadside and sometimes came across the carcass of a horse killed in an Allied air raid on the retreating German columns.[82] Several miles north of Wittstock, near the forest of Below, the guards led the prisoners, some 16,000 in all, into the forest to halt and await other columns so as to continue together on the way north. More and more prisoners arrived, including, after a few days, a number of women prisoners evacuated from the main camp at Ravensbrück.[83] In all, there were about 40,000 prisoners in the forest on April 29, consisting of the evacuees from Sachsenhausen and some of the evacuees from Ravensbrück.[84] Thousands of prisoners sprawled on the ground, among the trees, without food and water or suitable clothing. They tried to assuage their hunger by chewing leaves and grass and to ease their thirst by digging holes in the damp ground and collecting underground water.[85] Several prisoners who spent the last days of the war in Below forest jotted down on scraps of paper they found, or on remnants of the sacks in which they had wrapped their bodies or feet, reports of what they suffered there. They called the place *"das lager im Belower Wald"* (the camp in Below forest). After the war it became known as the death camp in Below forest. It was the most bizarre camp imaginable. Apart from thousands of starving and dying prisoners, there was no trace of the typical structure of camps. It existed for only a few days, but it claimed many lives.

A day after the prisoners were brought into the forest, several Red Cross trucks arrived with food parcels. One of the prisoners, Johannes Dötsch, wrote that these parcels contained canned meat, sausage, biscuits, butter, sugar, and even chocolate, coffee, tea, and cigarettes. However, for many of the prisoners the aid packages arrived too late. In the morning quite a few were found dead, having been unable to digest the food.[86] The escorts of the convoy had scant interest in the prisoners but made sure that they did not try to escape from the clearing in the forest. Those who did attempt to escape were shot instantly. The mass grave uncovered in the forest after the war contained 400 corpses of prisoners who died during the brief span of existence of the Below forest camp. In their testimonies, prisoners estimated that between 700 and 800 prisoners perished there.[87] The death march north to Schwerin was branded on the memories of the survivors as a total shambles:

> In the places we passed we saw bombardments and aircraft shooting and a retreating army. As we passed the villages we sought ways of snatching a potato. It was April. Here and there we saw explosions, dead, slaughtered cattle. Anyone who was able to, tore off a lump of meat and ran back into the line. People were shot. There were SS men who beat us all the time. We went on foot and alongside, every few meters, was an SS soldier and older men who guarded us—a lot of army men. There were people who stayed behind, because they couldn't go on—a lot of them. Some tried to escape and were shot. When we halted by a grove of trees or in a forest, each of us searched for something—a little greenery or something—one fine day the Red Cross found us. I think it was two days before the liberation.[88]

On April 28, on the joint initiative of the Red Cross and some of the prisoners in Below forest, 800 sick prisoners were taken to the nearby village of Grabow for medical treatment in a dispensary set up for them. By June 1945, 132 prisoners from this group had died.[89] There were acts of slaughter on this death march as well, sometimes only a few hours before the prisoners were liberated by the Red Army. One such massacre occurred at the village of Zapel-Ausbau, about 3 miles (5 kilometers) east of the town of Crivitz near Schwerin. At the edge of a nearby grove of trees, in a barn belonging to a local farmer, a group of 30 prisoners too weak to continue marching with the column were left behind. According to eyewitness accounts by local residents, they were sick, and after they were abandoned there, the farmers brought them food and water. The Red Army was expected to arrive within a few hours. At about 9 a.m. on May 3, 1945, an SS officer passed through the village, accompanied by several other SS personnel. They asked the prisoners which of them were Germans. Four spoke up; they were taken out of the group, given civilian clothes, and sent on their way. The remaining prisoners, mainly French nationals and Jews from Hungary, were left in the barn. Several minutes later, the farmers heard volleys of gunfire. When the shooting died down and it was clear that the murderers had gone, several farmers entered the site of the massacre. The 25 corpses of murdered prisoners were buried in a mass grave in a nearby grove.[90] Other groups of prisoners, who survived the death march from Sachsenhausen and Ravensbrück, were liberated by the men of the 49th Division of the Second Byelorussian Front between May 1 and 3 in the region between Ludwigslust and Schwerin.[91]

The massacre at Zapel-Ausbau was a local, random incident, enacted entirely as the last murderous whim of an anonymous officer who happened to pass through the village. The prisoners in the barn in no way threatened the local population and were about to be liberated at any minute by the Soviets. The fact that the German prisoners were spared indicates that the motive was ideological, possibly reinforced by the desire for revenge, in view of the imminent capitulation, and by reluctance to leave behind living witnesses to the events. The Zapel-Ausbau affair demonstrates the narrow and fragile border between survival and death due to random acts of murder perpetrated in the last minutes of the war.

One small group of evacuees from Sachsenhausen received different treatment during their death march in late April 1945. These were the Jehovah's Witnesses, 213 men ("Brethren") and 17 women ("Sisters") who were citizens of six different countries. They were assembled together with the last group of prisoners to leave the main camp and were actually dispatched separately. Although they were no sturdier than the others, none of them was harmed during the evacuation, and they were permitted to assist one another without being harassed by the guards. As they marched at the end of the column, they passed the corpses of those who had stumbled and been shot by the guards, but not one of them was shot. On one occasion they even received food packages allocated by the Red Cross as they halted by the road, apparently in Below forest. All of them were liberated by the Americans at Schwerin on May 3, 1945.[92]

"The SS Men Joked and Laughed during the Shooting"

From late 1944, and in particular from early 1945, at least 17 transports of prisoners from evacuated camps in the East reached Flossenbürg, which was located 74 miles (120 kilometers) northeast of Nuremberg. Approximately 12,000 prisoners were transferred there, a third of them from Groß-Rosen. Because of the proliferation of typhus in the camp and the fact that there was not enough room in the sick bay for all the sick prisoners, the camp commandant, Max Koegel, sent hundreds of the sick inmates to Bergen-Belsen at the end of January. The camp was in a state of dissolution because of the atrocious hygienic conditions and the shortage of manpower. In order to cope with the problem, Koegel selected several hundred German prisoners from the Reich *(Reichsdeutsche),* most of them criminals,[93] allotted them uniforms, and turned them into a kind of special police force. Their task was to supervise and report to the SS everything that happened in the prisoners' barracks.[94] They treated the other prisoners, in particular the Russians and Poles, with particular viciousness.[95] Because of its geographical location, close to the border of the Protectorate in southern Germany, Flossenbürg became the absorption center for transports from central Germany, when evacuations began there in the first half of April. For example, at least 6,000 prisoners evacuated from Buchenwald were taken there.[96] On April 14, on the eve of the evacuation of the camp, there were more than 45,800 prisoners in the Flossenbürg complex, 16,000 of them women.[97]

Koegel had apparently not realized until April 14 that he was going to be entrusted with the task of evacuating the inmates to the south. On that day, he began to evacuate some of the camp command, in particular the wives and children of the SS guards. Preparations for the transfer of prisoners to Dachau began on the following day.[98] This activity was in keeping with the routine orders followed in the camp system up to then. The Jews were to be sent to the south and kept safe there as hostages, and the camp was to be handed over to the Americans. This, more or less, was what Pister had understood in Buchenwald several days previously. However, within a few days the picture changed completely.

April 15 started out as just another day in the camp. For quite some time the prisoners, many of whom had labored in the Messerschmidt aircraft manufacturing works,[99] had been idle most of the time. No raw materials had arrived, there was no work for them, and the kapos (prisoner-functionaries) were indifferent to the situation in the workshops. But on that day the work crews were not sent out: they were confined to their barracks until 3 p.m., and then they were summoned to the parade ground. The Jewish prisoners were ordered to assemble in a separate group. As was often the case in other camps as well, the fact that the Jews were singled out immediately evoked fear that this was a selection that would end in extermination. The rumors that spread rapidly through the camp all pointed in this direction: the Jews would be liquidated and all others would be left alive. The fact that Jews who had just arrived from Buchenwald were attached to the group of Jewish prisoners seemed to corroborate the rumors.[100] At 5 a.m. on the following morning the Jews were again summoned out of their sleeping quarters.[101] Several SS men began to divide them into groups of 100 prisoners each, 1,700 in all. Each group was accompanied by eight guards who walked alongside them and at the head and foot of the column. The Jewish prisoners began the march from the camp gate toward the railway station 4 miles (6 kilometers) away. When they reached there, the train, consisting of both closed and open freight cars, was already waiting. and the prisoners were loaded aboard, 60 to 75 per car. The train, with its load of prisoners, guards, and equipment, set out for the south.[102] This evacuation of Jews from Flossenbürg was one consequence of the irresolute decision regarding Jewish prisoners issued by Himmler several weeks previously.

The evacuation of the remaining Flossenbürg inmates followed several routes. For example, the 2,000 prisoners who took Route A left the camp on April 17 and began the trek southward toward Dachau, which they reached on April 23. There were several categories of prisoners in this group: veteran Flossenbürg inmates, others who had arrived from Buchenwald between April 14 and 18, and a group transferred from Flossenbürg to Ohrdruf in March 1945, who had now returned.

All these "new" prisoners, who joined the "veteran" inmates, were renumbered a day before departure. Most of them had been transferred to Buchenwald several months before from Auschwitz and bore the numbers assigned them there. The number system used is not clear, and it is possible that their Auschwitz number was reported and registered together with the new number before they set out on the march.[103] In other words, within the span of a few months they had been registered and numbered two or three times in the camps they passed through. For these reason, it is almost impossible to trace the numbers and identities of the prisoners in the evacuation columns on the basis of the extant documentation, even when those lists were preserved.

At this time, efforts were being made to prevent the evacuation of camps in southern Germany. Kurt Becher, one of Eichmann's henchmen in Hungary, visited Himmler frequently during these weeks, while trying to devise his defense strategy for the postwar period. When Becher toured the collapsing Reich in April 1945, together with Israel Kasztner, he tried to curb the wave of evacuations of concentration camps and to ensure that Jewish prisoners would not be harmed. On April 15 he told Kasztner that he could not understand how, despite Himmler's assurance to him, some of the Buchenwald prisoners had nonetheless been evacuated several days previously. He attributed the move to the manipulations of Ernst Kaltenbrunner. He was of course misinformed, or perhaps preferred to believe that this was the case. Responsibility for the evacuation rested entirely with Himmler. In any event, Becher promised to make further efforts to ensure that Flossenbürg and Mauthausen were not evacuated.[104]

Becher traveled southward toward Mauthausen and passed through Flossenbürg on April 17, where he informed the senior command of Himmler's directive, which he wanted to believe was the official one—namely, that the prisoners were not to be evacuated. However, a day later a cable was received at Flossenbürg from Himmler to the effect that "no prisoner is to fall alive into enemy hands." On April 19 Koegel convened a meeting of all the camp staff. Immediately afterward, the hasty evacuation of some 25,000 to 30,000 inmates began, including those who had arrived from Buchenwald several days earlier. Their destination was the last camp in southern Germany to which prisoners could still be transferred—Dachau. In the haste and urgency of the evacuation, 1,527 sick prisoners from the sick bay were left behind. It was this group that the U.S. troops found when they entered Flossenbürg on April 23, 1945.[105]

The evacuation of the Jewish prisoners to the south was disrupted on the first day by U.S. aircraft, which strafed the train shortly after it set out. This was the first in a series of attacks in the course of the evacuation. The U.S. shells easily penetrated the wooden sides of the freight cars, and injured and killed quite a few of the prisoners. The guards leapt out of the cars and sped in search of shelter. The prisoners, weak and apathetic from starvation, ignored the aircraft circling above them and attacking the train. They rummaged through the belongings of the guards in search of food. When the aircraft withdrew, the SS men began to fire in the air and to collect the prisoners scattered around the train. Not all the prisoners returned. Several dozen perished, some in the raid, others at the hand of the guards who unhesitatingly liquidated those prisoners who had been injured. Only a few succeeded in escaping and hiding in the vicinity.[106]

Inside the freight cars, the mood was desperate. Some prisoners were losing their minds from hunger, and none could understand why they were not being killed on the spot instead of being transported like animals and starved to death. After only two days, quite a few had died in the packed cars. They had no water, and when, during one of the halts, Polish women who were laboring in the local villages tried to give the prisoners water to drink, they were driven away and threatened by the guards. At 5 p.m. on the third day, food was allocated. Each car received four loaves of bread, weighing about 4 pounds (2 kilograms) each, and each prisoner was given a dab of margarine.[107]

That same day, April 20, close to the small town of Schwarzenfeld, a massacre was perpetrated against this transport. About 750 of the Jewish prisoners who had left Flossenbürg on April 17 arrived there that day. Their train was stranded there after an aerial attack that put it out of action. About 30 prisoners died in the cars that day.[108] Many of them had been injured in the bombing raid and were unable to continue the journey. After the war, at least 140 corpses were discovered in a field close to Schwarzenfeld and were buried in a mass grave there, together with 44 others who had been murdered in the neighborhood. The circumstances of their death remained unknown after the war. An examination by the International Tracing Service in 1950 determined that 140 of them perished in a Luftwaffe raid.[109] It is indisputable, however, that the attack on the train was carried out by U.S. aircraft. Elsewhere it was established that these 140 prisoners died in the raid and were not necessarily massacred by the guards.[110] There is no way of verifying how many of them were killed by the aircraft and how many by the guards, but it seems that the murders perpetrated by the guards were not confined to a few injured prisoners.[111] One of the survivors described what happened:

> The SS men joked and laughed during the shooting . . . the prisoners were led in groups of 15–20, they had to lie on the ground and were shot in the nape . . . the commander of the transport saw what was going on and was not at all moved.[112]

When it was evident to the guards that the train was out of action and that the evacuation must continue on foot, they took care to eliminate prisoners who were liable to delay the column and cause difficulties. A local dentist in Schwarzenfeld, Max Hasender, was summoned to examine the sick and injured prisoners before the slaughter began:

> The SS medic told me that the injured prisoners who were unable to continue with the evacuation were to be shot. . . . I didn't actually see the shooting of the prisoners but I heard shots for two days after the air raid. I also saw a horse-drawn wagon loaded with corpses. . . . I saw about 20 to 30 corpses on the wagon. . . . On several of the corpses I saw bullet-holes in the head, in

the back, the shots fired while they were seated, and they were certainly not fired from aircraft guns, but from rifles or revolvers.[113]

The surviving prisoners were unloaded from the freight cars and divided into groups of about 100 each.[114] They were taken into the forest and set out on a long march. At first the dominant emotion was relief. The overcrowding and stifling atmosphere of the closed cars and the constant fear of the aircraft guns sniping at them were replaced by pleasure at being in the fresh air and the hope of finding suitable shelter in the event of another bombing raid. Their gnawing hunger was eased slightly by grass plucked along the way. The more fortunate among them found potatoes on the edges of the fields as they passed through villages. But the momentary relief was swiftly replaced by distress as they began to suffer agonizing bouts of diarrhea and prisoners fell to the ground writhing in pain.

It was raining heavily, and the death march continued toward Nuremberg. Progress along the mud-clogged forest paths was a nightmare. The weaker marchers could not tolerate the weather conditions and the hardships. Many suffered from fever, and others collapsed after being bogged down in the mud. They were shot without hesitation by the guards, who became increasingly dangerous as the march continued. The guards were now uneasy and tense because of the situation and also because all their equipment, including the food they had brought from Flossenbürg, had been destroyed in the train. They loaded the food and equipment they had managed to salvage onto wagons and handcarts, which the prisoners pushed.[115]

After another day's trek and after passing Nuremberg, the prisoners reached the small village of Stamsried. They were lodged in a barn for the night. The next day, April 22, one of the guards told them that they would be staying there for one more day and would receive food and coffee. During the afternoon they were given boiled potatoes. On April 23 the guards continued the march. The prisoners passed through Stamsried as the villagers gaped at them. After they had left the village, they suddenly heard the supervisor of the guards calling his men to gather at the head of the column. The procession began to disperse, and the marchers slowed their pace and then halted, clustered in small groups. The guards did not seem to care what they did and merely cautioned them not to leave the forest because, if they did so, they would be shot instantly. Soon afterward they vanished, leaving behind the wagons with their load of food and equipment, and even their uniforms, which they had exchanged for civilian clothes before leaving. About 600 Jewish prisoners in the column that had left Flossenbürg several days earlier lived to see the day of liberation.[116]

Not all the Jewish evacuees from Flossenbürg were fortunate enough to be liberated due to the flight of their guards and the arrival of the U.S. Army. Another group of Jewish prisoners, who had been transferred to Flossenbürg from Buchenwald a few days before the evacuation, continued their march and reached Theresienstadt at the beginning of May. This evacuation, which was one of the products of the fantastic scheme to use Jews as a bargaining card, deteriorated into a purposeless and murderous death march:

> We walked for several days as if we were in limbo, without food and exhausted, along the highways of the Sudetenland. Every day people fell by the road and we left them there. The echo of the shots was heard afterwards, they had been sentenced on the spot. Many of the friends who walked beside me kept saying to me: Mordechai, I've no more strength. And I, a shadow of a man, I encouraged them . . . they drank so much water that they had diarrhea and they asked for permission to relieve themselves by the roadside. If they sat down for too long, the Germans came over with their pistols and shot them in the head.[117]

This situation was the direct consequence of the disintegration of the evacuation columns in the last days of the war. Various groups that left the camps together, or were evacuated from one of the subcamps and were scheduled to head for the same destination, scattered during the evacuation in different directions. As a result, their fate was determined in different ways. After the war, one of the Jewish prisoners evacuated from Flossenbürg described the disarray along the roads of southern Germany at the time:

> And then there arrived . . . the comrades from Buchenwald . . . whom we had met on the road. And they had also gone through the same hardships. And we walked on. We walked again at night, and again we lay in the woods during the day. But this could not go on for long, because many people fell. Simply fell. And every meter there were corpses lying on both sides of the road. When one did not have the strength to go on, he would sit down. And a minute later he was lying already dead. To get us to Dachau . . . they could not bring us there, because the communications were disrupted. . . . And they could not bring us to that certain place where they wanted to exterminate us. But they took each group, took them into a forest and surrounded them, dug . . . ordered to dig their own ditches mass graves, and bury themselves. . . . And we were supposed to go to the place where we were going to be shot, but the road . . . we got lost on the road and walked in a different direction. And by this miracle we remained alive. . . . Our

group, the fifty people who kept together, who took the wrong road, succeeded in remaining alive.[118]

Another group of Jewish prisoners was evacuated from the subcamp near Regensburg, where there had been about 700 inmates. Most of them had arrived there in February 1945 after an 11-day trek from Auschwitz via Mauthausen, Oranienburg, and Flossenbürg. They journeyed in open freight cars without food, most of the time with nothing but snow to eat. From time to time compassionate civilians threw a loaf of bread into the cars, but only the strong and fortunate managed to seize some. The place they were brought to was not really a camp. It was a clearing in the forest where several trenches, reached by several steps, had been dug below ground. Above ground, a layer of straw served as a roof. This underground accommodation was damp and cold, and contained no bunks. The prisoners slept on the frozen ground, which was padded with a little damp straw. There was no real work for them, and Allied bombers flew overhead constantly, causing the guards to seek shelter under the trees. Prisoners died of cold and hunger daily. The corpses were burned in a primitive crematorium, which consisted of several metal rails on which the dead were laid; then a few logs were scattered over them and the pile was set on fire. This little camp was evacuated southward in mid-April.[119] Before departure the guards burned down the site, and several prisoners who were too weak to leave and lingered in the underground trenches died in the fire. After marching for five days, 170 prisoners reached Dachau.[120]

When Flossenbürg's more distant subcamps were evacuated, the guards did not hesitate, before setting out, to liquidate the sick prisoners incapable of marching. This was done, for example, at Flöha Chemnitz in Saxony, in the western section of the district of Freiberg. The inmates of this camp were evacuated on April 16, 1945. Before departure, the guards began isolating a group of sick prisoners from those who were due to leave. The selection was lax, so that some prisoners managed to infiltrate the group in the hope of evading the evacuation. When the SS men noticed what was happening, they dispersed the group and conducted an arbitrary selection of about 150 prisoners, who were loaded onto the trucks awaiting the evacuees. Some 135 other prisoners were sent back into one of the bunkers in the camp and were joined by another 53 sick prisoners from the two reviers. Altogether, 188 prisoners were excluded from the evacuation, and all of them were murdered by the guards. Almost all the evacuees were liberated on May 9, 1945, at Graupen Voitsdorf/ Krupka-Fojtovice in Czechoslovakia.[121]

The evacuations from Flossenbürg vividly illustrate the plight of concentration camp prisoners in the second half of April 1945. The familiar conditions of unplanned extermination, which played havoc with the inmates prior to the evacuations, prevailed in certain camps. At the more remote sites, where it was difficult to organize transportation or where the routes were blocked, the guards did not hesitate to murder those who were too debilitated to march. As long as it was possible to make a little progress and cover another few miles, bringing the survivors of the transport closer to a place that might be able to absorb them, the guards continued to spur them on, while liquidating those who lagged behind or fell. The moment it became evident that the roads were blocked, the guards were faced with two possible choices: to murder the prisoners under their charge and flee, or to escape and leave them behind in an isolated spot along the route. There were no hard-and-fast rules. The random element prevailed: it was the decision of a transport supervisor or local officials, or the reaction of the local population in the town where the prisoners were abandoned, that determined whether they would live or die.

In all, some 16,000 prisoners set out from Flossenbürg for Dachau, but only a few thousand of them reached the destination. Most of the groups of evacuees from the subcamps roamed Upper Bavaria in the last two weeks of April until they were liberated by the Americans. The last group was liberated on May 2. In all some 7,000 prisoners perished in the weeks of evacuation from Flossenbürg and its subcamps.[122]

"I Thought I Was Seeing a Group of Old People"

As noted earlier, in early March 1945, 621 Jewish women who had survived the death marches from Schlesiersee and Grünberg reached Helmbrechts. This camp, one of Flossenbürg's subcamps, had been established in late June–early July 1944. The first 190 women prisoners were brought there from Ravensbrück between July 19 and August 31, 1944, and more arrived in October, in November, and in January 1945. By February 1945 there were 594 women inmates,[123] most of them from Poland and Russia, as well as a small group of French women and some 25 German women. After the arrival of the Jewish women, there were 1,200 inmates. On April 13, 1,171 of them were evacuated, including the 580 surviving Jewish prisoners.[124]

In charge of the transport was Alois Franz Dörr, the Helmbrechts commandant. Dörr was born on January 11, 1911, in Hofingen, a little farming town with a population of 1,500, where his family had a small farm. After his father was killed in World War I he continued to live there with his mother, who remarried, and his siblings. He never learned a trade and did casual labor for farmers in the district. In October 1932 he became a member of the Nazi Party and the SA, and in January 1933 he joined the SS.

Two years later he volunteered for a year's military service in the infantry. From 1936, he was a member of the SS and from 1939, of the Waffen-SS. He then began his service in the concentration camp system, undergoing training at Oranienburg. In 1940 he took part in the fighting in France and later was assigned to Flossenbürg. In 1941 Dörr served for several months in a Waffen-SS division and later returned to Flossenbürg until mid-1943, where he was placed in charge of a Volksdeutsche unit recruited in Slovakia, Serbia, Croatia, and Russia, which was attached to the concentration camp guard units. In September 1943 he was transferred to the women's camp of Zwodau in the Sudetenland, and in January 1944 he was appointed commandant of Krondorf, a Flossenbürg subcamp. Five months later he was appointed commandant of the new women's camp at Helmbrechts. Dörr was a typical colorless junior camp administrator, and his career was far from brilliant. In early 1942 he was promoted to the rank of Unterscharführer (Sergeant) and stayed at this rank throughout the war.[125]

In charge of the women guards in the camp was 27-year-old Herta Haase-Breitmann. After only eight years of schooling she had been employed as a salesclerk. She volunteered for the Reich Labor Service for young women (Reichsarbeitdienst der weiblichen Jugend), established in the early years of Nazi rule, and spent six months there. In 1937 she married, was divorced four years later, and returned to her hometown of Chemnitz, again as a salesclerk. Her rise to the position of Dörr's right-hand woman during the bloody evacuation of Helmbrechts resulted from a combination of random circumstances. In 1942 she began to work in the large-scale German automobile concern Auto-Union, in Chemnitz, where she remained until August 1944, when one of the production lines was transferred to Ravensbrück. Haase-Breitmann was posted there and became a labor supervisor in the service of the SS. At the end of August 1944 she was sent with a transport of women prisoners from Ravensbrück to Helmbrechts. In the new camp she fulfilled several functions, and in early April 1945 she was appointed chief supervisor of a group of SS women guards. Her personal contacts with Dörr also contributed to her appointment to a senior position. For her, the camps were merely a place of employment. She never joined the Nazi Party and was not a member of any of its organizations.[126]

The administrative team at Helmbrechts was not large. At the end of January 1945 there were 12 male guards and about 20 female guards.[127] When the camp was evacuated in April 1945 the death march was accompanied by 23 to 27 male guards and a similar number of women guards.[128] They were a typical group. The men had almost all been recruited in the last wave of recruitment of camp guards, and of those identified after the war,

12 were aged 45–55, two were aged 35–45, and a similar number were in the 25–35 and 21–25 age brackets. The women guards were all between 21 and 37.[129]

It is not clear how many Jewish women were interned in the camp before the arrival of the death march survivors from Poland, but they were apparently a minority among the 600 inmates. Only in March 1945 did the Jewish women become the majority group. Their situation was infinitely worse than that of the other inmates. They arrived at Helmbrechts after weeks of strenuous marching, in many cases barefoot with feet wrapped in rags. Those who were shod were usually wearing the wooden clogs allocated in Polish concentration camps.[130] Their rations were meager: coffee and 10½ ounces (300 grams) of bread in the morning, 16 ounces (half a liter) of almost inedible soup at midday, and no supper.[131] The veteran non-Jewish women prisoners, in contrast, were treated better. Helmbrechts was not one of the worst of Flossenbürg's subcamps. The prisoners worked 12-hour shifts and received adequate rations. For breakfast they were given bread and coffee, at lunchtime soup, potatoes, and sometimes even meat, and in the evening bread, margarine, and added cheese or sausage. Those who worked in the adjacent factory even received extra rations.[132]

When the 620 Jewish women reached Helmbrechts, they were housed separately from the other prisoners under untenable conditions. Their barracks were overcrowded, more than 300 women per block; in the absence of bunks, they slept on the freezing floor on a thin layer of straw, without suitable clothing or blankets. They did not work and were treated with particular brutality by the women guards.[133] It is no wonder that in the few weeks that lapsed between their arrival and their departure on a second or third death march, 44 of them died.[134]

The decision to evacuate Helmbrechts was apparently taken before Koegel realized that an overall evacuation of Flossenbürg was necessary. As noted, Himmler's directive that "no prisoner is to fall into enemy hands alive" was not transmitted before April 14 at the earliest, and Koegel was unsure of how to organize and implement the evacuation. Dörr's decision to evacuate the camp was taken on the night of April 12 or in the early morning hours of April 13. He made up his mind during a hasty meeting with a group of male and female guards, at which they were informed that the evacuation would begin on April 13 in the morning. Max Reimann, a veteran concentration camp guard, who was placed in charge of one of the groups of women evacuees, was not at all sure whether the order had come from the main camp or had possibly been received several days previously but not reported before the hasty meeting. He recalled that Dörr had visited Flossenbürg several days before the evacuation of Helmbrechts and thought that the order might have been conveyed to him there. In any event, the guards were shown no written document.[135] Dörr tried to consult the Flossenbürg command as to what he was to do with the prisoners, but on April 12 he did not succeed in contacting the main camp. Communications with the decision makers in the north had been cut off, and the U.S. Army was only 31 miles (50 kilometers) away. Despite this breakdown of communications and the lack of clear directives, Dörr understood only too well that he was to do everything possible to prevent the prisoners from falling into American hands.[136] When the columns left the camp, the guards had neither maps nor other auxiliary aids to guide them.[137] All they took with them was a rough hand-drawn sketch of the route to the southwest and the destination— the women's camp at Zwodau. Some of the guards had gained the impression from Dörr's remarks that the ultimate destination was Dachau.[138] This appears to bear out the theory that Dörr must have received instructions or general guidelines regarding an imminent evacuation while at Flossenbürg several days earlier, since in mid-April Dachau was the destination of most of the subcamps in the region.

While the evacuation was being organized, it was decided that the women prisoners would be sent on foot in three columns, together with the guards. Each column was accompanied by several armed male guards and several women guards. These women were not armed but carried wooden truncheons and were supervised by Herta Haase-Breitmann. On departure, the prisoners were given a small ration of food, and the non-Jewish prisoners were given clothing and blankets as well as bread and margarine. It is not known what the Jewish women received.[139] Several prisoners walked at the rear of the column, pushing a handcart loaded with the guards' belongings.[140]

The evacuation of Helmbrechts was the result of a collective decision taken by the camp guards and their commandant, Dörr. The guards were undoubtedly aware that the camps were not going to be surrendered to the enemy. They knew that they had not received explicit instructions regarding the evacuation, they had not been told what the destination would be, and, moreover, they had no means of transportation at their disposal. The idea of liquidating prisoners during the evacuation was not broached during the hasty exchange of views in the hours before the columns left the camp. To the extent that the issue was discussed, it was only in reference to those who were liable to collapse during the march. It is not at all clear what exactly Dörr said to the guards. Some of them understood that they were to liquidate any exhausted women who could no longer walk, and others thought that it was categorically forbidden to kill these incapable of marching.[141] Whatever the case, a group of 40 Jewish women, who were in such poor condition that they could not join the evacuation, were not killed before the columns departed. Instead, they were transferred by truck to Schwarzenbach/Sale, the first stop on the route of the Helmbrechts evacuees.[142] As noted, it is unlikely that Dorr discussed the option of murdering feeble prisoners before leaving the camp. It was, rather, the way in which the evacuation decision was taken and the feeling of the guards that they were being left to their fate together with a group of more than 1,000 prisoners, half of them Jewish, exhausted, starving, and scarcely able to stand, that rendered this death march so murderous.

In the afternoon of April 13 the women prisoners set out on their death march. The highways were crowded with refugees, civilians roaming hither and thither in frantic search for refuge from the enemy armies advancing from the East and military forces retreating in disorganized fashion.[143] The customary method of coping with this situation was based on the trigger. The first prisoner was shot shortly after departure from the camp, at a distance of about 3 miles (5 kilometers). Another woman was killed at the edge of a forest. Several miles farther on, not far from the village of Mödlitz, two more were murdered:

> The two victims were taken among the trees by the roadside, because they were too feeble to keep up with the transport, and after a short distance they were shot to death. Both victims have head wounds. One of the women was shot through both cheeks, the second has a shattered skull. They lay side by side. On their clothes and on their drinking cups were numbers which could be identified. The witnesses who discovered the bodies do not recall the exact number.[144]

All the familiar characteristics of subcamp evacuations in the last weeks of the war could be identified here. The women guards acted brutally toward the prisoners and beat them mercilessly in order to spur them on.[145] According to Charlotte Stummer, one of the guards, they were acting in accordance with Dörr's order. She also admitted that she did not hesitate to act in this manner, and once beat a prisoner with particular savagery.[146] The killing at Mödlitz and other murders perpetrated on the first day of the march by the guards were aimed at liquidating prisoners who were slowing the pace of the march. The killings were perpetrated, even though Dörr and the guards had received no authority, and certainly no explicit instructions, to murder weak prisoners. Dörr, who witnessed the incidents from the first day on did nothing to prevent them or to stop their recurrence.[147]

The guards' intention was not necessarily to kill the weakest or sickest women or those whose survival prospects were nil, since prisoners in that condition had not joined the march and had been dispatched by truck. Because it was evident to the guards that their transport was on its way to nowhere and that it was no longer feasible to put these exhausted prisoners to work, their sole consideration was to remove obstacles to rapid progress. Ten prisoners were murdered that day.[148] The tribunal at Hof noted that it was impossible to positively identify the women murdered on the first day and it was not clear that all of them were Jewish.[149] Dörr claimed that the report he received at the end of the day was that the 10 prisoners had been shot while trying to escape.[150] It is obvious, however, that they were liquidated because they were holding up the column. There is no information about the killing of prisoners who tried to escape,[151] and it is very likely that all the victims were Jewish, for the Jewish women were in worse physical condition than the others.

When the prisoners reached their first stop for the night in the town of Schwarzenbach, they were led into a fenced orchard and slept in the open air. The sick and frail women, all Jewish, who had arrived by truck, were moved, on the intercession of the acting mayor, to a barracks near the local church. They received no food that night.[152] Six women died in the barracks during the night of April 13–14.[153]

The bizarre situation whereby prisoners too sick to walk were evacuated by tractor, while others, many of whom were no stronger than those incapable of marching, were forced to march, continued on the second day. The sick prisoners were loaded onto a wagon that was hitched to a tractor, together with 15 of the "healthy" prisoners who had spent the night in the open. Not only did they escape liquidation, but some of them apparently decided that it was preferable to continue the journey aboard the wagon rather than to collapse shortly after setting out and be shot by the guards. They made this choice despite their constant fear that the wagon passengers would become the target of extermination the moment the guards decided to be rid of them.[154] About 60 women rode in this "sick wagon."[155]

Dörr did not accompany the column of women. Astride his motorcycle, with Herta Haase-Breitmann riding pillion, he usually joined them in the evenings when they reached their next stop for the night.[156] This meant that, during the day, the power to decide the fate of the prisoners was invested, de facto, in the guards. On the night he caught up with them at Schwarzenbach, or on the morning of the second day, April 14, 1945, Dörr told the guards that they were not to shoot women too weak to march. The decision to attach the wagon to the column may have been made on Dörr's instructions.[157]

However, the rules of this murderous drama were manifest to Dörr and to the guards from an early stage: any woman who collapsed and was unable to move on was condemned to death. "It was inconsequential to him if several members of his guard unit murdered prisons for no reason," the tribunal stated.[158] Both Dörr and the guards were well aware of the desperate state of the Jewish prisoners, from whose ranks the victims came. There was almost no way of distinguishing between the prisoners lying in the wagon and those trudging alongside it. All of them were living skeletons dressed in rags and appeared to have scant prospect of surviving the freezing nights of early spring. Even if Dörr did in fact give explicit orders that sick women were not to be liquidated (and the tribunal doubted that this was so), it was obvious to the guards that this was not an iron-clad rule.[159] Dörr did not investigate each killing en route, and in the course of this disordered retreat, the guards had long since ceased to obey their superiors' orders. Thus, whether Dörr did indeed prohibit murder or whether he invented the story in his own defense, what determined the fate of the prisoners was the crucial moment when an exhausted prisoner fell by the roadside and a guard who happened to be walking alongside her reacted instantly. After the first day, however, fingers were not so light on the trigger, whether because of Dörr's order or because of the possibility of flinging another living corpse onto the growing pile on the wagon. Five women prisoners were murdered during the second day.[160]

Toward the end of the second day the prisoners reached the town of Neuhausen. On that day a new element was introduced into the saga of this death march:

In the afternoon, an SS Untersturmführer (2nd Lieutenant) arrived at Neuhausen. He came on a motorcycle as the emissary of the SS-Reichsführung (SS command). He talked to Dörr and briefed him that, according to orders from the Reichsführung, he was to seek out groups of concentration camp evacuees led by SS personnel, who were in transit because of the advancing US forces. He asked Dörr if any shooting had taken place during the march up to that point. [Dörr] confirmed this, and moreover, informed the emissary of the number of prisoners shot ... the emissary informed [Dörr] that, according to the SS-Reichsführung directive of immediate validity, no more shootings were to be carried out since negotiations were underway with the Americans and these were not to be disrupted. In addition, the emissary told him that the truncheons carried by many of the women guards were to be discarded. Finally he ordered him to destroy all the camp documents in the event that there was danger that the column of prisoners might fall into the hands of the advancing US forces. In such a case, the older guards should take the prisoners into the forest and simply release them.[161]

The column commanders understood that this officer was a senior messenger who was bringing with him no less than an order coming directly from Himmler.[162] We now know, however, that in mid-April Himmler did not issue an order that prisoners were under no circumstances to be shot. Hence the origin of the directive brought by the anonymous SS officer remains a mystery. Nor is it entirely clear what precisely Dörr said to the guards at Neuhausen. He apparently informed them that, according to the order brought by the emissary, no more prisoners were to be shot, but he also made it clear that there were ways of circumventing this order. In essence, the instructions issued upon departure from the camp had not changed greatly. Each guard was empowered to decide, on the basis of circumstances, how to act toward prisoners incapable of marching. Dörr did not state categorically that under no circumstances were prisoners to be shot. Nor did he order the guards to free all the prisoners if the evacuation could not continue because of advancing U.S. forces.[163]

At Neuhausen, Dörr discovered that the Americans were only 9 miles (15 kilometers) away. He ordered the destruction of all the camp documents that had been brought along and the immediate evacuation of the prisoners from the site. In the commotion that ensued, about 50 women succeeded in escaping. Several of the escapees recaptured by German soldiers were not killed but were taken to the local jail where they were detained until the Americans arrived. Several of the women guards who decided that the time had come to disappear took advantage of the situation and fled.[164] The impression, however, is that the order not to shoot at every opportunity had some impact on the conduct of the guards. On April 15, 1945, for example, no murders were recorded. Three women were left behind in a Czech village. Two of them died, apparently from exhaustion, and a third, who was in critical condition, was nursed by the people of Neuenbrand and survived. A larger number of prisoners who could not continue the march were left with a local farmer named Anton Wagner in a village along the route. He housed them in a local factory building.[165] In the following days, no further liquidations of sick prisoners occurred. However, on April 16 a young Polish woman tried to escape from the column and a guard chased her and shot her several times until she fell.[166] This incident confirms the assumption that only prisoners who made escape attempts were killed.

A dramatic turning point in this death march occurred on April 17–18, when the prisoners reached Zwodau. The women transported on the tractor-drawn wagon had reached there on the second day of the evacuation from Schwarzenbach. Also in the camp was a small group of Jewish women evacuated from Grünberg, who had never gotten to Helmbrechts but were sent directly to Zwodau, as well as other Jewish women from Ravensbrück and Freiburg. This latter group consisted of 140 Jewish women from Hungary who arrived in Ravensbrück in December 1944, were transferred on January 15 to a labor camp at Freiburg, moved to Flossenbürg in February, and from there on February 26 to Zwodau.[167] The women who had not undergone the death march to Helmbrechts and on to Zwodau were in much better shape than those who arrived on April 18. The living conditions at Zwodau were relatively tolerable, and up to April food rations were distributed. In the final weeks, the conditions in the camp deteriorated, the prisoners suffered from lice and filth, and the incidence of disease increased.[168]

In all, there were some 625 women prisoners, most of them sick and totally spent.[169] An Oberscharführer (Technical Sergeant) at Zwodau told Dörr that he was to lead the Jewish women as well as some 20 German women toward Dachau. For the other 580 or so prisoners, the death march ended at Zwodau. They stayed in the camp and were liberated.[170] Once again, two junior noncommissioned officers, camp guards stranded in a distant camp with hundreds of prisoners, had to make a decision that would seal the fate of many of the women. Dörr and the Oberscharführer he consulted at Zwodau had no contact with the command at Flossenbürg, for the telephone lines and radio communications were no longer functioning. It very soon became evident that it was impossible to reach Dachau. Instead of taking the Jewish women and the small group of Germans there, it was decided to try and make for the Austrian Alps, the place where the Reich's last stand was supposedly to be organized.[171] This was not the only group of prisoners from the camps in southern Germany whose escorts tried to take them to Austria in the last days of April 1945. Although it is plain that Dörr received no specific instructions on this matter, the fact that he decided to aim for that location shows that he knew of this plan, as did other officers in charge of death marches at the time who were heading for the mountainous areas of Austria.

On April 19, after a day of indecision and confusion, Dörr sent his last transport, consisting entirely of Jewish women, southward toward Austria. With no detailed maps, he chose the direction on the basis of incomplete information and a vague sketch of the route that was given to him on the spot. The Jewish women were divided into four groups, each in the charge of an armed male guard and a woman guard. The fourth group consisted of the sick women and was in the charge of Werner Jaritz.[172] Most of the prisoners proceeded on foot, and those who were unable to walk were loaded onto horse-drawn wagons or vehicles. The evacuation route, which passed through the Sudetenland, was not to Dörr's liking; he was reluctant to come into contact with the hostile Czech population, who were liable to hamper his progress. Consequently, he tried to avoid entering villages along the way and, if this was not possible, to limit the march to the main street. After the transport left Zwodau, he met up with it only in the mornings and evenings. During the day he rode his motorcycle and dealt with the organizational problems of the transport, such as finding resting places for the night or food for the prisoners.[173]

No mass murders occurred in the first week. The main adversaries of the marchers, the source of their suffering, were starvation and cold and the fact that they were at the end of their rope. On April 19–20 they spent the night in an open field, and morning light revealed the corpses of 12 of the prisoners. Dörr did not allow the marchers to spend the night in closed buildings, protected from the cold and damp, even when these buildings were available and were offered to him in the villages where the transport halted.[174] Although he does not appear to have separated Jewish women from German women, all the victims were Jewish, since their physical condition was immeasurably worse than that of the Germans. When Czech civilians attempted to hand food to the women as they passed by, the male and female guards responded with violence and even threatened to shoot prisoners if they accepted the food. Nonetheless, people succeeded from time to time in throwing loaves of bread into the wagon where the sick women lay prostrate.[175] On other occasions, during night halts, the villagers supplied soup and potatoes to the prisoners.[176]

Another 10 women perished on the night of April 22–23 and a similar number the next night.[177] On the twelfth day, April 24, the transport began to display the familiar signs of disintegration. In Horouschen/Horoušany district or Ronsperg/Poběžovice district, the convoy was strafed from the air. Several of the prisoners were killed, and others injured. One of them, Netka Demska, was taken to a nearby hospital, apparently by several German soldiers. The aircraft also scored hits on the horses hitched to the wagons, killing several.[178] The starving women clustered around the carcasses, tore off lumps of flesh and chewed them:

> Lola had a big piece of horse liver in her pocket. Some girls had enough courage to take knives and opened up the horses which had been killed in the strafing and took out the liver. I don't know, they just knew that the liver has value. Lola had a piece. I don't know how she had gotten it. Maybe she herself had cut a piece. Anyway, she gave me a piece and I sucked it and chewed on it for as long as it lasted.[179]

Prisoners who were strong enough took advantage of the commotion caused by the attack and escaped.[180] These incidents increased the unease of the guards and exacerbated their rough treatment of those women who were holding up the column. The column passed through a village one day, and the marchers spied a pile of beetroot leaves, which farmers had thrown away. The starving prisoners fell on the pile, infuriating some of the guards. One of them, Walter Kowliv, who was mentioned several times in postwar testimony as a guard who never hesitated to shoot prisoners, did so this time as well. Several of the women guards joined him and beat the prisoners with their truncheons in order to spur them on.[181]

On the night of April 24–25 another nine women died during a stop at Wilkenau/Vlkanov. The next day they entered the Protectorate and passed close to the village of Neugramatin/Nový Kramolin. The women, sensing that the guards were no longer paying attention to what was happening in the column, fled toward the closest village houses. The guards fired in the air in order to scare them and managed to round up most of them, but they did not fire into the group or directly at the escaping women.[182] The guards were often forced to cope with hostile Czech civilians who tried to pass food to the prisoners. As a result, Dörr accelerated the pace to reach Maxberg, a town with a majority of German residents, as fast as possible. That night, the march stopped at Maxberg/Maxov. On the initiative of the mayor and local residents, hot soup was prepared and brought to the women. The famished prisoners crowded around and fought over the food until it was impossible to dole it out in an orderly manner. Dörr ordered the guards to remove the cauldrons of soup, and most of the women were left without food for another day. Three of them died that night.[183]

The column of hundreds of scarecrow-like figures who could scarcely drag themselves along continued its journey through the forest trails of Bohemia. On April 28, 130 to 150 women were already in such poor condition that they were no longer able to walk. With the help of a local mayor Dörr obtained seven horse-drawn wagons to transport those who were too feeble to continue.[184] At the end of April and the beginning of May the region experienced a cold spell accompanied by heavy rain and even snow at times. As prisoners continued to collapse, the guards were spared the trouble of liquidating them by bullet. In the wagons several women died each day. The death march staggered on through mountainous areas, and in the last two days of April advanced only about 6 miles (9 kilometers) a day.[185]

The final days of the death march were once again particularly lethal, recalling the first days. On April 30 five prisoners died during the day. That evening the column reached the town of Unterreichenstein/Rejštejn, and during the night five more women died. The next night was one of the worst: 19 women perished while the transport was halted at Außergefild/Kvilda. In the morning, while the dead were being buried, the guards ordered that an unknown number of women, who were apparently dying, be flung into the mass grave.[186] Dörr continued to deny food to the dying Jewish women even when the local residents wanted to bring it. The food generally arrived once a day and included soup and potatoes.[187] The breakdown of transportation and the prisoners' fear that the day was swiftly approaching when Dörr would face the ultimate decision as to what to do with them spurred escape attempts by those still capable of moving. Several prisoners, including three German women, escaped on the morning of May 1. Dörr himself chased them and succeeded in catching all three. He threatened them with his pistol and said that it would be better if he shot them on the spot, but instead he beat them and returned them to the column.[188]

Another 13 women died on the night of May 2–3, when the transport was in Filz.[189] The next morning the survivors received soup prepared by the local population. As the guards loaded the emaciated, sick women onto the wagons, savagely beating them, a local farmer, who could not tolerate the sight, threatened a woman guard with his axe. When she aimed her pistol at him he retreated. After the column set out again on its way, several prisoners tried to escape and were murdered. On the afternoon of May 3 the death march reached the town of Wallern/Volary. The convoy now consisted of 175 women on foot and a line of wagons carrying another 150 sick women, which arrived later that night.[190]

On the twenty-second day of the death march of the Helmbrechts inmates, Friday, May 4, 1945, Dörr apparently realized that the game was over and decided to release the prisoners. He particularly wanted to avoid being captured, together with the group of prisoners, by the American forces. He decided to bring the prisoners to the Czech town of Prachatitz/Prachatice on the border between the Protectorate and Germany, release them there, and then return with the guards to German soil and attempt to hide.[191]

In order to cover the distance as rapidly as possible, some 40 to 50 sick prisoners were loaded onto a trailer hitched to a tractor or some other vehicle. Some of the male and female guards also rode on the trailer. The remaining sick prisoners, for whom there was no room, were left behind for the time being and were scheduled to be transferred to Prachatitz/Prachatice by some other vehicle or on a second round by the first vehicle. Those still capable of marching, about 170 in all, began the final trek.[192]

Several miles on, the vehicle carrying the prisoners was strafed by U.S. aircraft. Several of the women guards were killed and others severely injured, including Herta Haase-Breitmann. The prisoners were not hurt, and several of them took advantage of the situation to escape. Most, however, were too weak to move. After the attack 18 prisoners who were no longer able to walk were taken to a barn belonging to a local farmer and locked in. Three guards remained to watch the barn. The other women continued their journey on foot until they reached Prachatitz/Prachatice. They were detained there for one day and on the following day, May 5, the Jewish women among them were led to the border of the Protectorate, about a mile (2 kilometers) east of Prachatitz/ Prachatice. The guards told them to continue walking eastward and went away. The women found their way into Czech villages and were taken care of by local farmers. Several German women, who were also in this group, remained at Prachatitz/Prachatice and were also released.[193]

Meanwhile, the guards left with the sick women at Volary were anxiously awaiting the return of the transportation. When other vehicle owners in the town heard that the first vehicle had been attacked from the air, they refused to rent their vehicles at the disposal of the guards. The guards decided to give up the futile attempt to take their charges to Prachatitz/Prachatice, left them in the furniture factory building, and beat a hasty retreat.

On May 5 the three men who were guarding the 18 women in the barn realized that nobody was going to rescue them from their predicament. The three—Walter Kowliv, Michael Weingärtner, and Sebastian Kraschanky—took the 17 prisoners out of the barn (one managed to hide) and led them to a forest in the mountains near the village of Zuderschlag/ Cudrovice. They began to shoot them one by one and left the bodies lying in the forest. Three of the women, who were a little sturdier than the others and were able to walk, were ordered by the three guards to escape on the run.[194] When the Americans arrived they found, in addition to the 14 corpses in the forest, another 12 lying beside a wall several hundred feet from the barn. These women had apparently been murdered by the three guards on May 4 and 5.[195]

On May 6 the Americans entered Volary. There they found about 120 Jewish women of Polish and Hungarian origin in pitiful condition. They weighed between 66 and 88 pounds (30–40 kilograms) each, 111 of them were suffering from typhus and dysentery, and most were covered in suppurating sores. Many were almost toothless. Some were still swathed in the filthy torn rags they had been wearing throughout the months of evacuation.[196] A medical officer, Aron S. Kahn, who examined the survivors in the furniture factory at Volary, described his impressions to a U.S. Army interrogator:

My first glance at these people was a terrible shock. I could never have believed that a human being could be so degraded, so starved, so scrawny and still live. My impression at that moment was essentially hasty. What I saw in the end in that small room resembled a heap of rats heaped on top of one another, too weak to even lift a hand. In addition they were wearing filthy, worn clothes which did not fit them, shabby and torn. They were smeared in excrement which covered most of the floor. The explanation is that these women were suffering from severe diarrhea and had bouts every two or three minutes. They were too weak to step outside and relieve themselves there. One of the things that astounded me when I entered that barracks was the fact that I thought I was seeing a group of old people lying there and I estimated their ages as between fifty and sixty. I was amazed and stunned when I asked one of the girls how old she was and she replied: seventeen. To me she looked no less than fifty.[197]

Such was the appearance of the survivors of the death march that Dörr led to Helmbrechts. Twenty of these hapless women died in the furniture storehouse at Volary between May 3 and 6, the day the Americans arrived. Two more perished on the day of liberation. The rest were taken to a military hospital, but there another four died. On April 19, 625 Jewish women prisoners had left Zwodau on a death march that lasted two weeks. The bloody toll of that march amounted to at least 278. During the nights, 129 of them died of the bitter cold and of starvation. Another 49 were murdered by the guards because they were unable to walk farther or tried to escape. In many other cases, the circumstances of death are unknown.[198]

Helmbrechts: A Representative Case or a Unique Saga?

"The Germans showed their determination to transform the Jews into ambulatory skeletons and then corpses. . . . This march was simply a 'death march,' in effect a German march of extermination," wrote Daniel Goldhagen, summing up the Helmbrechts affair.[199] It is questionable, however, whether this categorical conclusion is a correct interpretation of what occurred at Helmbrechts in the few weeks during which the Jewish prisoners were detained in the camp and during the death march.

The Jewish women reached Helmbrechts after a long and grueling death march from Poland and hence were already in much worse physical condition than the other inmates. According to accepted camp procedure at the time, they were no longer fit for work; in other words, their allotted span of life in the selective extermination machine of the concentration camps in 1945 had ended. This was the main reason why Dörr did nothing to alleviate their condition, although there was sufficient available food and clothing in the camp. This also explains why no attempt was made to put them to work in the factory where the other inmates labored.[200] In other words, they were essentially condemned to death, as were tens of thousands of other prisoners at the time in Boelcke camp at Mittelbau-Dora, at Bergen-Belsen, at Ravensbrück, and dozens of other camps. They were left to die not because they were Jewish but because they were debilitated and hence not worth exploiting.

When Dörr was interrogated on the circumstances of the evacuation of Helmbrechts, he insisted that he had given no instructions to murder the prisoners and that, after he learned of the incidents of murder on the first and second days of the evacuation, he gave the order that prisoners were to be shot only during escape attempts. He was aware, he claimed, that the guards who accompanied the column of prisoners were committing murder not necessarily in cases of attempted escape but because their prisoners were too weak to march on. This was also in accordance with the directive brought by the messenger who met the death march en route.[201] Despite the difficulty in accepting his evidence as reliable, it appears that something in that spirit was in fact conveyed to the guards.[202] Herta Haase-Breitmann, who supervised the women guards, testified that

> in practice each guard decided for himself who to shoot, but together with that, the commanders of each group were authorized to instruct the guards under them to abstain from shooting women prisoners—but this did not happen. Dörr never gave the order that nobody was to be shot although he had the authority to do so. (*Dörr gab niemals den Befehl, niemanden zu erschießen, obwohl er die Macht dazu gehabt hatte*).[203]

One of the three men in charge of the groups of prisoners, Max Reimann, said that he had not known the purpose of the order given by Dörr and was not told exactly what he was to do as commander of one of the evacuated groups. He also said that he had no idea whether Dörr said anything about what was to be done with prisoners unable to continue marching. At most, he understood that they were to be evacuated on wagons.[204]

Generally speaking, Dörr acted no differently to most of the personnel in charge of the evacuation columns: he did not order murder, but neither did he forbid it. To be precise, he ordered that it be committed in clear cases of attempted escape, as did other commanders. The delegation of authority to the personnel in the field to decide on liquidation was not unusual and occurred in hundreds of death marches in those months. However, Dörr was aware of the particularly dire condition of the Jewish women, many of whom (and not only those transported by wagon) were walking skeletons. Reimann claimed that he warned Dörr on several occasions that the prisoners were not being fed and that they would collapse and die if they continued to be deprived of food and water. None of this, according to Reimann, was of any interest to Dörr, who was entirely focused on completing his mission, namely, bringing the prisoners to Dachau as fast as possible, as instructed.[205] Dörr also knew that along the way he could anticipate a number of cases whereby prisoners would keel over and be unable to continue the march, and hence would be murdered in cold blood by the guards. He left those guards considerable room for maneuver, since they were expected to prevent escape attempts by shooting at the escapees and also to avoid, at all costs, leaving prisoners behind.[206] In all this, Dörr did not differ from other supervisors of evacuation columns and death marches. The tribunal's conclusions concerning the conditions and motives underlying the murderous action, which Goldhagen omitted from his book, are relatively accurate:

> The objective of this evacuation was not clear to them [the prisoners] or to the guards, except for the defendant [Dörr]. The defendant regarded the prisoners not only as enemies of the state, saboteurs, destroyers of the German people, anti-social and criminal elements, but treated them as creatures who should scarcely be considered human. Accordingly, it was all the same to him if he was dealing with Jewish or non-Jewish women, Poles, Czechs, Russians, Hungarians, French, Dutch or any other nationality. He displayed a spark of humanity only toward the 25 German prisoners, several of whom, in Helmbrechts and later during the march, received special treatment and certain concessions . . . the life of the prisoner was worthless to him, and he himself perpetrated several murders or ordered them.[207]

It is beyond doubt that the Jewish prisoners suffered infinitely more than the others. Most of them received miniscule food rations compared to the others, and, whenever the column reached its night's halt, it was almost always the Jewish women who slept in open fields during the freezing nights, while the German women, whenever possible, spent the night in a barn or closed storeroom. The German group marched separately and at a distance from the Jewish women, who could scarcely drag themselves along. It was rare for German women to be beaten by the guards.[208] But the main difference between the groups was the horrendous physical condition of the Jewish women in comparison to the others. Their infirmity did not develop at Helmbrechts, where they spent only a few weeks, but was the result of the conditions they had faced in the previous year and the death marches they had undergone. As a consequence, toward the end of the death march, close to half of them could no longer move along and were loaded onto wagons. Those who lay there totally inert received almost no food and, in the mind of the guards, were doomed to slow death according to the "living crematorium" method practiced in the camps.[209] Dörr's inflexible orders to deny the prisoners a reasonable amount of food even when local residents wanted to supply it, his equanimity in the face of abuse and beating of prisoners, and his refusal to permit medical treatment for the sick prisoners even when it was available indicate that, as far as he was concerned, all prisoners, and particularly Jews, were "lacking in a human aspect" *(nichts Menschliches hatten)*.[210] The fact that almost all the dying women were Jewish merely made it easier for him to treat them as such and for the guards to decide to pull the trigger. However, it would not be incorrect to state that they would have done the same with a group of prisoners of different nationality in equally poor physical condition, and such was often the case.

The Helmbrechts affair can be seen as a mirror reflecting all the problems that accompanied the death marches during the last days of the war. The evacuation of the camp began at a time when the Jewish prisoners were being sent south from the main camp at Flossenbürg. Several of the decisions that Dörr took during the evacuation bear out the hypothesis that he was aware of the order that Jewish prisoners were to be transferred to the south. When the rigors of the journey and the problems entailed in moving the women prisoners began to delay the evacuation, he decided, on April 17, to continue the journey with the Jewish women and a small group of German women and to release all the others. In any event, he had no intention of murdering these prisoners: had this been his intention, he could have done so during the march without any particular difficulties. The guards, so it would appear, would not have hesitated to abet him on this matter.

When the guards killed prisoners mercilessly on the first day of the evacuation, Dörr took steps to stop the carnage, since he was familiar with the order to bring the women prisoners to Dachau. As a result, in the days that followed there were few incidents of murder. When they did occur, the victims were usually prisoners who had tried to escape, often non-Jewish women who were stronger than the Jewish women. Only in the last hours of the march, when three random guards found themselves stranded with a group of prisoners who were unable to walk any farther, and had received no instructions as to what to do with them, did they choose the option that many other guards also chose in those final months: to rid themselves of the unfortunate wretches before they themselves fled the U.S. troops, who were now only a stone's throw away. Yet then too, their aim was not to liquidate Jews: three Jewish girls who were capable of escaping were given their lives as a gift before the final slaughter began.

Throughout the march, the guards treated the prisoners with great brutality. There was nothing new in this, for they had acted similarly in the camp. The situation that evolved during the march merely encouraged such violence. The pressure to keep moving, the ever-closer echo of enemy guns, the Czech civilians who were reluctant to cooperate with those who were clearly losing the war, and the fact that with each passing day more and more prisoners died—all these meant that the lives of the women prisoners, which had been of some minute value when they could be exploited as a labor reserve, were now worth nothing. In this respect, nationality and origin were of little significance. Under similar circumstances at the time, non-Jewish prisoners were also liquidated and in the same manner. One can only surmise that the fact that the guards were aware that they were dealing with a group composed entirely of Jewish women heightened the already existing murderous motivation.

CHAPTER SIX

Dead Men Marching

Toward the end of April 1945, Bavaria and Austria were the last regions in the ever-shrinking territory of the Reich where groups of prisoners could still be moved from place to place. Two large concentration camps, Dachau and Mauthausen, and their hundreds of subcamps were still operating in the final two weeks of the fighting. A considerable drama was played out around the question of the evacuation of the two complexes; at its core was the tentative attempt—responsibility for which was never finally clarified—to eliminate all the prisoners remaining in the camps in one lethal blow before the Reich's ship of state finally sank into the depths.

Dachau: Liberation, Selective Evacuation, or Total Murder?

Ernst Kaltenbrunner was the senior SS officer and the supreme authority in southern Germany from April 19, 1945, and the order to liquidate the camps in the region could certainly have stemmed from him.[1] Berthus Gerdes, head of the Gau Administration (Gaustabsamtsleiter) of Upper Bavaria, testified at his postwar interrogation that, in mid-April, Kaltenbrunner handed down orders to Gauleiter Paul Giesler to prepare an operation for liquidating prisoners at Dachau and several large subcamps in Mühldorf and Landsberg districts, many of whose inmates were Jewish. The measures proposed in order to liquidate the tens of thousands of prisoners were mass poisoning or bombing from the air. Gerdes said that he was summoned urgently in the middle of the night for a discussion with Giesler, and Giesler told him that Kaltenbrunner had given clear orders that, so he claimed, came directly from the Führer. The operation was given the code name of *Wolke AI* (Cloud AI) and *Wolkenbrand* (Cloud of Fire). The first referred to liquidation by aerial bombing of subcamps and the second to poisoning at Dachau. The district health bureau was to supply the canisters of poison. Gerdes said that it was plain to him that the plan was essentially insane and could not be implemented. However, he was obliged to discuss it with two senior party functionaries *(Kreisleiter)* in Mühldorf and Landsberg in order to examine its feasibility. He tried, he said, to gain time on various pretexts, such as bad weather conditions and shortage of fuel and bombs, in order to avoid implementing the scheme. After several days, Kaltenbrunner ordered him to evacuate the large camps in eastern Bavaria, transfer the Jewish prisoners to the main camp at Dachau, and liquidate them there.[2]

Another theory attributed responsibility for this liquidation attempt to Gauleiter Giesler himself. SS officer Friedrich Karl von Eberstein, who was commander of the district police, testified at Nuremberg that, at the beginning of March 1945, he talked to Giesler in Munich. In 1945 the Gauleiters also functioned as *Reichsverteidigungskommissare* (RVK—Commissars for Defense of the Reich) and were the senior military authorities in their districts. Giesler asked von Eberstein to talk to the Dachau commandant and persuade him that, as soon as the American forces were close at hand, all 25,000 inmates of the camp should be shot. Von Eberstein refused to carry out the order and said that it was not within his powers to give orders to the Dachau commandant. Giesler insisted, saying that, in his capacity as RVK of Upper Bavaria, he would ensure that the camp was bombed. Von Eberstein replied that he did not think that it would be possible to find Luftwaffe pilots who would agree to cooperate. Giesler replied that if the scheme failed, he would seek a way of poisoning the prisoners. Von Eberstein testified after the war that, after this conversation, he sent a cable to Glücks saying that the camp should surrender and be handed over to the Americans. He showed this cable to Giesler who, so he claimed, was furious at him for having circumvented his authority, and hence his original plans encountered considerable obstacles.[3]

Rudolf Höß, who in the last two months of the war was partly involved in the chaos of the camp evacuations, said that he knew nothing of the scheme for liquidating prisoners or bombing camps in southern Germany. Apart from that, it was his view that such an operation could never have been implemented.[4] However, such plans were unquestionably under consideration in mid-April 1945. The commandant of Dachau, Martin-Gottfried Weiß, who was not in the main camp at the time[5] (Eduard Weiter was replacing him as acting commandant), stated at his postwar trial that he did in fact receive information on such a directive, which came from the office of Gauleiter Giesler. He said that it referred to the bombing of the camp. Weiß hastened to contact von Eberstein, who told him that under no circumstances would the camp be bombed.[6]

Naturally enough, Kaltenbrunner made every effort to absolve himself of responsibility. Hitler knew only too well who was responsible for the concentration camp, he declared, and it was not he. Directives to camp commandants could be issued by Himmler, Pohl, and Glücks in that order. He (Kaltenbrunner) had been given full authority over security matters in the district from April 19, 1945, onward, but this authority was confined to Austria. Consequently, he could have given orders with regard to Mauthausen but not Dachau. On April 19 he left Berlin for Prague, and from there he traveled to Linz. He was not in Bavaria during the mayhem of the Dachau evacuations. Hence, Kaltenbrunner argued, Giesler's testimony that it was he, Kaltenbrunner, who gave him the order in the Führer's name was incorrect. He had also known nothing of the existence of subcamps in eastern Bavaria where Jewish prisoners were being held, and, in general, he had no authority to give orders to the Luftwaffe.[7]

For quite a few individuals it was convenient after the war to pin the responsibility on Kaltenbrunner. One of them was Gottlob Berger, who in 1943 was chief of the SS Staff *(Chef des SS-Hauptamtes)*[8] and the senior SS officer in Munich. He submitted a deposition to the Nuremberg tribunal in which he wrote that

> the commandant of Dachau or his deputy telephoned about 12 o'clock and stated to me that he had received this order, that is, the order for the evacuation from Kaltenbrunner after he had been summoned by the Gauleiter of Munich, the Reich Commissar.[9]

Kaltenbrunner contested Berger's statement on the grounds that the individual empowered by Himmler was Berger himself, as supreme SS commander of Bavaria and the western regions.[10] This was in accordance with Himmler's well-known directive that in the event of a threat that the camps would fall, authority over them was to be transferred to the HSSPF.

Kaltenbrunner was authorized to make this kind of decision, including the decision to liquidate all prisoners. However, at Nuremberg, it was not determined that he was the authority behind the murderous initiative. In any event, on the basis of developments elsewhere, it would appear that Gauleiter Giesler's role was by no means marginal. The order von Eberstein received from Berlin in mid-March to surrender the camp without harming prisoners was undoubtedly in line with Himmler's conduct during those weeks. What von Eberstein could not have known was that the spirit of Himmler's instructions changed drastically after the Buchenwald affair, and by mid-April the directive that "no prisoner was to fall alive into enemy hands" was circulating within the system. On April 18 the commandant of Buchenwald, Hermann Pister, arrived at Dachau from Oranienburg and told the camp commandant, Weiter, to evacuate the camp to the Tyrol region in Austria.[11] Giesler, as the supreme political authority in the region, had access to this type of information, which is also in line with Weiß's testimony. It is not impossible that he was already pondering such ideas in mid-March, but he could only have issued the instructions in mid-April, citing the spirit of Himmler's directive.

It appears that Giesler interpreted Himmler's directive, as conveyed by Pister, to mean that it would be preferable to liquidate the prisoners. The time and place were suitable for such an initiative. The scope for retreat was diminishing, and the fighting in various places in southern Germany was beginning to take on the character of a fanatic struggle by small and disorganized groups of fighters. In mid-April the area was marked by almost uncontrollable anarchy. Acts of violence and killing for food had become common occurrences. Deserters and armed civilians roamed the villages.[12] Party extremists were also a source of terror.[13] In this situation the idea of liquidating tens of thousands of dangerous enemies who were about to be set loose did not appear to be a groundless scheme.

Nobody wanted to take responsibility for the camp now that the end of the war was at hand. It may feasibly be assumed that two paths of action were being broached at the time, involving Kaltenbrunner and local authorities such as the Gauleiters, Berger, or camp commandants in the south. The first option, which had been in the cards for several months, was to conduct negotiations for release of prisoners or to surrender them, unharmed, to the enemy forces. The second option was to deliver a final lethal blow in order to exterminate them all. Concomitantly with the exchange of views on liquidating the Dachau inmates, negotiations were being conducted for the release of groups of prisoners or their transfer to the Red Cross. Between April 12 and 19 Kaltenbrunner was in contact with the Red Cross president Carl Jacub Burckhardt regarding transfer of the 6,000 French prisoners to that organization. Rumors were circulated on April 19 about the negotiations.[14] On April 27, two days before the liberation, Victor Maurer, representative of the Red Cross, arrived at Dachau. A committee of underground activists had been established in the camp, and it succeeded in including Belgian and Dutch nationals in the group—in other words, all the western European prisoners. At the same time, Maurer conducted discussions with what remained of the camp administration regarding its surrender to the American forces.[15]

In the final week a race against time took place in Dachau between several forces. The camp underground, backed by external bodies such as the

Red Cross, attempted to exempt as many groups of prisoners as possible from the danger of evacuation and to leave the camp intact until the Americans arrived. This activity was conducted in defiance of the familiar instruction that no prisoner was to be left alive to fall into enemy hands, which such people as Giesler and the camp commandants could not or did not wish to ignore. From the moment that the western European prisoners were excluded from the circle of evacuees, the Russians, Poles, Jews, and Germans were earmarked for dispatch. These were also the prisoners evacuated from the subcamps to the main camp.[16]

Both prisoners and guards knew that the sands of time were running out. For the prisoners, the knowledge strengthened their resolve to delay the evacuation; for the guards, it served to reinforce their sense of powerlessness and their lack of motivation. One of Dachau's large subcamps, Allach, had 8,900 inmates on April 25, including prisoners who had arrived from Buchenwald and Natzweiler-Struthof about 10 days earlier.[17] On April 23 the leaders of the prisoners learned that they were scheduled to be evacuated southward to the Tyrol. They employed every delaying tactic they could to prevent departure. A form of passive resistance evolved, as the prisoners took advantage of the guards' confusion in order to cause delays: they did not emerge from their barracks when summoned for examination, they exchanged places among themselves so that the numbers would not tally, and so on. The rebellion was led by French, German, and Russian communist prisoners.[18]

This situation was only possible because the guards themselves were far from enthusiastic at the prospect of evacuation. They did not appear to know who was to be evacuated. On April 25 the French, Belgian, Dutch, Luxembourgian, Italian, Polish, and Yugoslav prisoners were removed from the list of potential evacuees. In practice, only the Soviet and German nationals remained. This group, 900 inmates in all, was evacuated from the camp and began a death march to the south. On April 28 the last remaining guards vanished. The Allach inmates were free.[19]

The largest concentration of Jewish prisoners in the Dachau complex in April 1945 was in the subcamps at Kaufering near Landsberg and at Mühldorf. There were about 7,500 Jewish prisoners in those camps out of a total of 16,300.[20] The camps had been established in mid-1944, in a period when the German armament industry was seeking secure production sites. Thousands of prisoners were brought there and employed by Organization Todt in constructing subterranean production installations, mainly for the Messerschmidt concern. After the camps in the Baltic region were evacuated that summer, thousands of Jewish prisoners were sent to Kaufering, and later, in November, Jewish slave laborers arrived in large numbers at Auschwitz as well. This, to a large extent, transformed those camps into forced labor camps for Jewish prisoners. The living conditions were grim, and the prisoners who had arrived from Auschwitz employed all the stratagems familiar to them from their years in that camp in order to forage for food, and obtain better labor assignments and places in the barracks. However, even these experienced prisoners soon turned violent and wild in the face of the conditions, and this, in turn, increased the mortality rate:[21]

> We wore only those striped uniforms, almost naked. All the food we received was only after we returned from work, a bucket, that is to say, a plate with a little soup, and from that we had to live. We lost weight, all of us lost weight, there were illnesses, abscesses, sores ... and the bodies outside the barracks where we lay were taken away and buried in pits prepared for that purpose.[22]

As in other camps, the death rate increased as the war neared its end, and the piles of corpses taken daily to the burial pit grew constantly. The Jewish prisoners who had been transferred from Groß-Rosen in the second week of February 1945 were stunned at the conditions they found. Skeletal figures teeming with lice, dressed in rags, and suffering from a variety of diseases shuffled aimlessly around the camp because almost no work was being done.[23] In several camps in the Mühldorf complex, 631 prisoners died between the end of August 1944 and the end of April 1945. In two other Mühldorf camps, the "forest camps" (Waldlager), where conditions were particularly harsh, over 640 prisoners perished in that period. When the Americans entered these camps, they found a mass grave with 2,249 bodies of prisoners who had died or been murdered in the days before the evacuation. The victims were not even included in the statistics recorded in the camp files. A total of 8,300 prisoners perished in the Mühldorf camps, 47 percent of the number brought there, in the year or so that the camps operated.[24]

The number of victims in the Kaufering complex is estimated at 4,300, but this figure is incomplete. It does not include the prisoners who died on the transports to the camp or those sent to their deaths at Dachau in the last few months because they were too feeble to work. In any event, the death rate in the Kaufering camps in the final period resembled that at Mühldorf and approached 50 percent of the total number of inmates.[25]

The evacuation of the Kaufering camps began on April 23. It was preceded by several moves to concentrate inmates of the smaller commandos in one camp. On April 29 two U.S. Army sergeants entered Kaufering 4, where sick and unfit prisoners from other camps were assembled, and wrote a brief report on what they saw:

> Our first sight of the camp was appaling [sic]. Inside the enclosure we could see three rows of bodies, approximately 200, mostly nude. We entered the

camp to look it over. The bodies were in all shapes and conditions. Some were half burned, others badly scorched. Their fists were clenched in the agonies of their death. Their eyes were bulging and dilated as though even in death they were seeing and enduring the horrors of their lives in prison. None were more than skin and bones. The camp had been partially destroyed by fire, these were the victims.

From there we went to another camp, known as Kaufering for our first interrogations. We interrogated one person who could speak English, but without much luck. He was lying in a filthy, stinking room on a pile of rotting straw. He was starved to the point of death. His body was deformed by paralysis and malnutrition. In addition to all this he was suffering from typhus. He was of no mental help to us because he was to [sic] weak that his mind could not function. . . .

About 3000 prisoners were at #4 when the Americans came close. The able bodied and sick who could walk marched away. When they were moved from camp to camp it was always a forced march without food or water. . . . After the walking cases marched away, the guards loaded two special trains. One got away all right, the other was bombed by the Americans. About 300 were unable to be put on trains so they were drenched with gasoline and burned alive.[26]

These scenes were repeated, as we know, in many subcamps that the liberating forces reached only hours after their inmates had been evacuated. In the Kaufering complex there were many Jews among the prisoners due to be evacuated southward in April 1945. The case of Kaufering is essentially an illustration of the vulnerability of Jewish prisoners as compared to other nationalities in light of the decision for specific liquidation of subcamps taken during the last days of the war. A number of Jews had been concentrated at Kaufering no. 4 not because it had been decided to liquidate them there, but because they were the weakest group among the prisoners in that camp complex. For example, those who arrived at Kaufering in summer 1944 had already spent some three years in the Kovno ghetto or other ghettos in Lithuania. They had survived the local *Aktions,* engaged in forced labor in the ghetto, been evacuated from there, and spent a short time at Stutthof; then they had undergone an arduous evacuation to Dachau and from there to Kaufering. Others, who had been detained for four years in the Łódź ghetto, were evacuated to Auschwitz in August 1944, transferred in January 1945 to Dachau, and from there to Kaufering.

The conditions in all these camps were abysmal. Several were situated in the heart of forests without proper living quarters. The prisoners dug narrow underground trenches that were roofed with wooden planks and branches for camouflage.[27] In March or April 1945, when few of them were still capable of standing upright or walking, they were transferred to Kaufering no. 4, which was another example of a "living crematorium." When the guards were ordered to evacuate the camps and decided to rid themselves of those too infirm to move, they found hundreds of Jews in this condition, lying on piles of stinking straw, scarcely alive. They had no qualms about deciding to murder them on the eve of the evacuation.

The evacuation of the Kaufering camps was hasty and disorderly, even by the standards of concentration camps. Many prisoners succeeded in making their escape, whether during the preliminary round-up, during the evacuation on foot, or when American aircraft strafed the train taking them to Dachau.[28] Fear of the American planes was often stronger than dread of the anticipated reaction of the guards to escape attempts.[29]

The evacuation to Dachau was also marked by acts of murder by the guards. "Anyone who was healthy, had no diarrhea, kept going . . . and anyone who just moved aside and said: I want a lavatory, I need to relieve myself—was killed on the spot."[30] The precise number of prisoners who died during this evacuation is not clear. It is estimated variously at between several hundred and 1,000 out of the 5,200 evacuated prisoners.[31]

The evacuation of the Mühldorf inmates began at the same time as the Kaufering evacuations, and the inmates of the smaller camps were transferred to the central camp. A train left from Mühldorf on its way westward with more than 3,000 prisoners aboard. In the late morning hours of April 27 it reached the outskirts of the town of Poing, some 11 miles (18 kilometers) east of Munich, where it was attacked by U.S. aircraft. The train stopped at the local station, and in the afternoon the prisoners began to descend from the cars:

> A railway official came out as we were standing in our carriages and told us that we were free. So we all left the carriages; most of the people began to run into the village in search of food and other things. I and two friends, one of them called Levin, stayed standing beside the carriages and after about 20 minutes, when everyone was rushing about in all directions, we heard shots . . . when they started shooting, I went back into the carriage and looked around to see what was happening . . . our guards came back and started shooting people.[32]

The dispersal of the prisoners throughout the town resulted in the familiar scenario. Hundreds of them roamed in search of food, not hesitating to snatch whatever they found, so that sometimes nothing was left for those who followed, as one of the prisoners reported: "I left the carriage with a few friends and we went into Poing. I tried to find something to eat in the houses but a few of the people from the transport were there and they had taken most of the food."[33] The atmosphere of lawlessness that prevailed in the town as a result of the prisoners' release soon persuaded the guards to reassemble them in the train while firing indiscriminately at roving prisoners.

Prisoners later estimated the number of prisoners shot in the town and the surrounding fields at 150 to 200. Most were injured, and at least 50 killed.[34] The guards did not put a stop to the killings even when the prisoners returned to the railway siding where the train had halted. Several of them continued to go from carriage to carriage and shoot prisoners, apparently those who had already been injured. More than 10 were murdered alongside the train.[35] Almost all the prisoners who witnessed the massacre at Poing stressed the major role played by the older guards, who were Luftwaffe men.

The transport continued on its way early in the morning of April 28 and reached Wolfratshausen; the next day it was again attacked by U.S. aircraft.[36] That evening it arrived at Tutzing, southwest of Munich. A local physician, who visited the train with a Swiss diplomat, estimated that at least 2,000 were prisoners aboard. He described what he saw:

> All the prisoners were suffering from severe malnutrition; they were nothing but skin and bone; their bodies were unbelievably filthy and swarming with lice. In addition, in the various carriages there were corpses alongside living prisoners . . . 45 people were suffering from severe gunshot wounds, and I am not sure how many had less severe injuries.[37]

The murderous evacuation of the Mühldorf inmates ended on April 30 when they were liberated by U.S. troops.[38]

At Dachau, the preparations for evacuation were proceeding at a sluggish pace. On April 23 the prisoners were no longer sent out to their workplaces. It seemed that a race against time was taking place. Since it was well known that the Americans were only several days' march from the camp, the political underground made every effort to disrupt the evacuation plans. A first group of 2,000 prisoners was prepared for departure, but there was no available locomotive for the evacuation train. On April 24 a group of prisoners "with privileged status" left the camp by truck for the Alps.[39]

The prisoners noted that the guards were packing their personal belongings and destroying papers and documents in the offices. At about 1 p.m. some 2,000 Jewish prisoners were ordered to report to the parade ground for evacuation, but their departure was delayed. They waited, ready to leave, and on the next day were loaded onto a train. By April 26 they had not yet left the camp. Various rumors circulated in Dachau as to what was to be done with these prisoners. One version was that the Jews were to be moved southward and liquidated on a mountain peak.[40] However, as time passed, quite a few of the Jews succeeded in slipping away and hiding in the barracks.[41]

On April 26 the evacuation began with the departure of 6,887 prisoners: 1,213 *Reichsdeutsche* (Germans of the Reich), 4,150 Russians, 1,183 Jewish men, and 314 Jewish women. They had been selected in accordance with the agreement between all the parties involved in contact with the SS heads at the time. The evacuees were divided into three blocs of marchers: the first consisted of 3,600 prisoners, mainly Russians, the second of 2,944 men, and the third of the 314 Jewish women and several men. Before leaving, they were given 10½ ounces (300 grams) of bread, 10½ ounces (300 grams) of sausage, 1 ounce (30 grams) of margarine, and a packet of cheese each. At about 9:30 p.m. the first group left the camp and began the march to the south.[42] This transport dispersed after a few days. In the end, most of the prisoners evacuated from Dachau, 5,000 in all, were liberated by the Americans on April 30 at Beuerberg, and another 360 close to Dürnbach. The last group of 2,000 prisoners who set out from Dachau proceeded southward on April 27. They did not get far, as the train carrying them was stranded at Wolfratshausen, apparently on April 29, and they continued from there on foot. The townspeople remembered the columns of starving prisoners who passed through their town, accompanied by guards in SS uniforms. They handed out bread and potatoes to the marchers while the guards looked on indifferently.[43] After they left the town more than 30 corpses of prisoners who had perished during the evacuation or in the town were collected.[44] Two days later the surviving Dachau evacuees were liberated by the Americans.[45]

Fritz Degelow was in charge of one of these groups, with about 100 guards under him. Their first stop was Munich. The local police placed five trucks at his disposal in order to transport those prisoners who were unable to march. The trucks left for the south on April 27 or 28, but Degelow lost contact with them when they were stranded en route without fuel and could not continue their journey. When the column reached Wolfratshausen after a slow march of 31 miles (50 kilometers), he ordered that the evacuation be halted because of the weather conditions. It was raining heavily, the roads were clogged with mud, and the prisoners were exhausted and unable to walk on. They received a little food from a Dachau subcamp in the vicinity. He wanted to leave the prisoners to their own devices until the Americans arrived, but he received orders from Munich to leave only Russians and Poles behind and to continue southward with the Jews and the Germans. On April 30 Degelow moved on with 3,000 Jews and Germans and reached Bad Tölz, where the guards deserted the death march and disappeared. He stated that 50 prisoners had reportedly died along the way.[46]

The convoys of prisoners evacuated from Dachau and its subcamps clogged the roads in Bavaria in the last week of April. In addition to the large transports that set out from the main camp, a number of groups from distant labor camps were also moving southward. As the days passed, the space for maneuver was reduced. The guards were only too happy to be rid of as many prisoners as possible and to melt into the civilian population before the Americans arrived. Thus, for example, in one case a small group of prisoners encountered another group along the road. Their guards handed them over to the escorts of the second group, who agreed to accept them in return for all the equipment, and in particular the food, in their possession. Once they were rid of their charges, these guards could take flight.[47]

The main concern of all the guards was to find the propitious moment to disappear. In almost all the groups evacuated from Dachau between April 27 and 30 the guards made their escape, leaving large numbers of prisoners alone. The prisoners, sensing the mood of their guards, became increasingly daring in their attempts to escape from the trains or the columns.[48] In contrast to previous evacuation periods, it was now evident to the prisoners that the orders the guards had received had become meaningless. From the moment they set out, it was clear to all the participants in the death march that it was no longer possible to transfer prisoners since no camp was available to absorb them. Under these circumstances, the guards usually preferred to make their getaway rather than to perpetrate mass murder of prisoners. Indeed, quite a number of them abandoned their prisoners during the evacuations.

Paradoxically, what disturbed the prisoners most on the evacuation trains were the U.S. aircraft that circled around them constantly and strafed any random means of transportation. They were sometimes more dangerous than the apathetic guards, who were preoccupied with plans to escape. In one such raid, on a train evacuating prisoners from Mühldorf on April 24, hundreds of evacuees were killed. "It was a worse slaughter than the Germans committed," said one of the survivors sorrowfully.[49] Fear of the bombings was so intense that even the thought that they would be forced to seek shelter among a hostile German population did not deter many of the evacuees from making escape attempts whenever possible.[50] Their escorts, naturally enough, did not hesitate to press the trigger and liquidate prisoners caught during or after the attempt.[51] However, relative to the evacuation of other camps, the number of victims of the death marches from Dachau was low, estimated at about 1,000 to 1,500.[52]

While the transports were leaving Dachau, thousands of prisoners evacuated from camps in the south in mid-April were being brought in. Many came from Hersbruck, a large subcamp of Flossenbürg. It held 5,863 inmates at the end of February 1945, 2,155 of them Hungarian Jews. The death rate in the last few months was appallingly high. In December 1944, 467 prisoners perished there, and in January 1945 another 250. In February 465 prisoners died, most of them newcomers from Groß-Rosen. In March the number rose to 741.[53] Some 3,800 prisoners were evacuated on April 13 and began a lengthy death march toward Dachau. Another 1,600 or so sick prisoners were transported by train and reached Dachau after a day or two.[54] About 70 of the prisoners died on the train before it reached the camp. At least 350 who were evacuated on foot were shot by their guards.[55] The death march of the Hersbruck prisoners lasted two weeks, and throughout this period they received no food, apart from what they managed to forage in the fields and forest. The guards fired instantly at anyone who lingered, attempted to escape, or was unable to continue walking.[56]

Some 2,000 prisoners eventually reached Dachau on April 24.[57] About 250 of them apparently died there the day after their arrival. Their corpses were immediately dispatched to the crematorium.[58] "We arrived like ghosts," said one of the prisoners. The arrival of thousands of sick and feeble prisoners in the camp only increased the internal havoc:

> And then, at Dachau, nobody wanted to supervise us because Dachau itself was in a process of evacuation. Thousands of prisoners were coming and going, in and out of the camp. And then, after they received us, they didn't give us any clothes. We were naked, just wrapped in blankets. And that's how I lived . . . and there was an advantage because I didn't have to report, I didn't have to report to headcounts or to go to work because I had nothing to wear. And so I waited . . . until the final liberation.[59]

A number of absurd situations arose in Dachau in the final days of the war. Simultaneously with negotiations with Red Cross representatives concerning the orderly handover of the camp, schemes were being devised for mass poisoning of the prisoners or their liquidation by aerial bombing. While the evacuation of prisoners of certain nationalities was being planned and implemented, other prisoners enjoyed relative security until the Americans arrived. While some of the guards were fleeing, the multinational underground in the camp was taking action to delay any attempt to evacuate the prisoners. At the same time that columns of prisoners were leaving on the last death marches, transports of dying prisoners were coming in from camps in the north. It is not surprising that, amidst this chaos, nobody paid attention to the death train that arrived in Dachau one day before the camp was liberated.

On April 28 the transport evacuated from Buchenwald on April 7 reached Dachau. It will be recalled that it consisted of 5,000 to 6,000 prisoners of various nationalities who had been sent southward at the beginning of the evacuation of the camp. The first leg of the evacuation was from Buchenwald to nearby Weimar, 6 miles (10 kilometers) away.[60] This brief death march claimed 300 to 350 victims. Merbach, commander of the transports, admitted that he himself had shot to death about 10 prisoners who tried to escape. In Weimar, the prisoners were loaded onto open freight cars, 90 to 100 per car. In all there were between 39 and 43 cars, some carrying equipment and food, such as sacks of potatoes, bread, margarine, and canned meat. In the first stage of the evacuation the CO lost control of events. The roads were crammed with refugees, the railway tracks were defective, and trains could not proceed smoothly. The evacuation train was bombed several times by the Americans. The transport took two weeks to cover a distance that in normal times would have taken one day, and the longer it took, the more prisoners perished.[61]

One of the French prisoners on the transport managed to jot down daily impressions of events along the route. The prisoners received a food ration on the average once every two days. It included 7 to 9 ounces (200–250 grams) of bread, a little cheese, and on some days a few potatoes or 16 ounces (half a liter) of soup. Other prisoners in the transport recalled that the food rations were even smaller.[62] On several occasions, when the train halted because of constant disruptions, the guards boarded the cars and murdered those prisoners who appeared unable to endure the conditions.[63] Merbach, who himself liquidated at least 20 prisoners, rode the train as far as Munich and on April 28 entered his destination, Dachau, with the transport.[64]

The train had left Weimar with about 5,000 living prisoners. During its three-week journey thousands died, whether of starvation or from the guards' bullets. When the doors of the cars were opened on April 29 as it stood not far from the camp, there were more than 2,300 corpses aboard, which were not even unloaded in the last stages of the evacuation. It is hard to estimate the precise number of victims of this death train, since there is no way of knowing how many corpses were thrown off the train en route.[65] There were hundreds of dying prisoners in the cars, lying prostrate on top of one another, so that it was not possible to distinguish the living from the dead. This was how the Americans found them on the day they liberated Dachau:

> As we approached the camp . . . the first thing we came to was a railroad track leading off the camp with a lot of open box cars on it. As we crossed the track and looked back into the cars, the most horrible sight I have ever seen (up to that time) met my eyes. The cars were loaded with dead bodies. Most of them were naked and all of them skin and bones. Honest, their legs and

arms were only a couple of inches around and they had no buttocks at all. Many of the bodies had bullet holes in the back of their heads.[66]

The flight southward was lethal for the camp inmates. The story of the Buchenwald–Weimar–Dachau death train illustrates this fact. At the end of the first week of April it was still assumed in the camp system that it would be possible to preserve some of the prisoners and that in the south they would continue to be of some use, whether as a labor force or as hostages. The camp guards, however, found themselves burdened for more than two weeks with a transport of dying prisoners, some of whom attempted to escape at every opportunity. There was no food available for them, and the longer the journey, the clearer it was that they could be of no further use, either as slaves or as human material for barter. Consequently, the guards passed through the cars, converting them into traveling extermination installations; those prisoners who did not die of starvation and exhaustion were shot in the head.[67] This was one of the most lethal transports even by the nightmarish criteria of the Nazi extermination apparatus in its last weeks of existence: at least 50 percent of the prisoners who set out on the evacuation died. This transport conveyed corpses to a concentration camp that was intended to absorb prisoners for purposes of labor or negotiations. The guards were undoubtedly determined to reach Dachau as fast as possible, to hand over their cargo to whoever was willing to accept it, and then flee. But when the train eventually reached its last stop, there was nobody there to receive the transport of death, and this was how the U.S. soldiers found it on April 29, 1945.

Mauthausen: The Final Refuge

On March 8, 1946, Kurt Becher submitted the following deposition to the tribunal at Nuremberg:

I, Kurt Becher, formerly a colonel in the SS, born 12 September 1909, at Hamburg, declare the following under oath:

Between the middle of September and October 1944 I caused the Reichsführer-SS Himmler to issue the following order, which I received in two originals, one each for SS Generals [Obergrupenführer] Kaltenbrunner and Pohl, and a carbon copy for myself:

"Effective immediately I forbid any liquidation of Jews and order that, on the contrary, hospital care [pflege] should be given to weak and sick persons. I hold you [and here Kaltenbrunner and Pohl were meant] personally responsible even if this order should be strictly adhered to by lower echelons."

I personally took Pohl's copy to him at his office in Berlin and left the copy for Kaltenbrunner at his office in Berlin. In my opinion, Kaltenbrunner and

Pohl bear the full responsibility after this date for any further killing of Jewish prisoners.

When visiting the Concentration Camp Mauthausen on 27 April 1945 at 9:00 am. I was told under the seal of strictest secrecy by the commandant in the camp, SS Colonel [Franz] Ziereis, that "Kaltenbrunner gave me the order that at least a thousand persons have still to die at Mauthausen each day."[68]

Once again there arises the question of Kaltenbrunner's involvement in the plan to murder large numbers of prisoners before the capitulation. No copy of the directive that Himmler allegedly conveyed to Becher on halting the extermination of Jews was ever found, and it is doubtful that it existed, although Himmler, as we know, engaged in considerable manipulations on the issue of the Jews in the camps in March–April 1945. Pohl, as noted above, was not particularly concerned about the fate of the Jewish prisoners in the last few weeks of the war. Kaltenbrunner, on the other hand, was the senior commander in Austria from mid-April 1945, and the question of his involvement in this type of directive was raised after the war from various directions.

Kurt Emil Schmutzler was the commandant of Wiener Neudorf, the sub-camp of Mauthausen. He claimed that two SS physicians from Mauthausen came to see him urgently on April 30, after they had been summoned that day to Ziereis's office. The commandant told him that he intended to liquidate the 60,000 inmates of Mauthausen and the large subcamps at Gusen before the Americans arrived. The plan was to stage an aerial attack on the camp, to exploit the incident in order to assemble the prisoners in the subterranean tunnels where they labored, and then detonate the tunnels. The two physicians had been asked to be responsible for the action.

The two physicians asked Schmutzler to intervene with Ziereis. Schmutzler testified that he talked to the Mauthausen commandant and told him that such an operation would prove catastrophic for the local residents, since the enemy forces would react with severe reprisals. He insisted that Ziereis open the camp and leave the prisoners to their own devices until the Americans arrived. Ziereis refused on the grounds that this would strengthen Germany's enemies and endanger the local population. However, a day later, Schmutzler related, Ziereis told him that he had changed his decision and given orders to halt the preparations for liquidating the prisoners.[69] Schmutzler did not recall any directives from Kaltenbrunner on this matter.

A further reference to the issue of liquidation of prisoners can be found in Ziereis's last letter, as recorded by Hans Maršálek, a former prisoner at Mauthausen. Ziereis fled on the night of May 2–3, 1945. Three weeks later he was found by a group of liberated prisoners, who summoned American soldiers. Ziereis opened fire at the soldiers, was severely wounded, and was taken to a U.S. military hospital, where he dictated to Maršálek a kind of confession and a last letter to his wife before dying on May 24. On the final murders, he wrote:

> According to an order by Himmler, I was to liquidate all prisoners on behalf of SS Obergruppenführer Dr. Kaltenbrunner; the prisoners were to be taken into the tunnels of the factory . . . and only one entrance was to be left open. This entrance was to be blown up by the use of explosives and the death of the prisoners was to be effected in this manner. I refused to carry out this order. This matter was the extermination of the prisoners of the so-called mother camp Mauthausen, and the camps Gusen I and II.[70]

All these testimonies by SS officers after the war were aimed, first and foremost, at absolving themselves of at least some of the guilt they had accumulated during the war years, and shifting it to their superiors. Himmler, Kaltenbrunner, and Pohl were sufficiently senior authorities for responsibility to be attributed to them. Kurt Becher had begun to construct his alibi in summer 1944 in Budapest, in the hope that it would hold fast after the war. Schmutzler played an important part in implementing the directive Ziereis transmitted to the Mauthausen subcamps in the Vienna area at the end of March 1945 regarding the liquidation of prisoners too sick to march, or those liable to create political problems if they fell alive into enemy hands. He was also responsible for a series of massacres of prisoners in a camp he commanded, which was evacuated at the beginning of April 1945.[71] There is firm evidence that in April 1945 Ziereis did, in fact, contemplate liquidating some 40,000 prisoners at Gusen by detonating dozens of tons of dynamite in tunnels.[72] However, these plans, to the extent that they existed, were no more than the fruit of murderous "brainstorming" by various authorities in southern Germany and Austria in March–April 1945. The general collapse of the system prevented the schemes from reaching the operative stage.

This being so, it is impossible to establish with certainty who was responsible for the initiative to murder tens of thousands of prisoners at Mauthausen in the camp's final days. However, as was the case in other camps as well, what determined fates at Mauthausen at the time was not some precisely worded order transmitted by a senior officer. There were two variables: the *zeitgeist*, which encouraged extermination of almost all those who were incapable of walking, or those who were considered politically problematic; and the fact that Mauthausen was essentially the final stop, from which it was no longer possible to move on elsewhere. The last camp still operating within the camp system was not capable of absorbing the prisoners who inundated it, a fact that encouraged murderous schemes.

On February 15, 1945, a transport of 2,500 arrived at Mauthausen, consisting of prisoners who had been evacuated from Sachsenhausen during the first wave of evacuations in January–February when it was feared at Orianenburg that the Russians would reach the Berlin area within a few weeks. During these months, Ziereis did not want to take in further inmates because the camp was packed full. He continued to insist on this matter in the following months, in particular in April, with the arrival of the survivors of the death marches from the camps evacuated to Mauthausen. Ziereis was overheard speaking angrily to the guards and those responsible for the groups of prisoners, and complaining that they had brought him a superfluous rabble, instead of getting rid of them along the road.[73] In this case Glücks rejected his request to take the transport elsewhere, but he did receive the go-ahead for liquidating some of the newcomers, apparently the sick and infirm.[74]

When the prisoners arrived at the camp and were unloaded from the train they were told that the sick, the injured, and those incapable of moving were to step forward in order to be taken to the sick bay. About 400 such prisoners stepped forward, some on their own initiative and others shoved by the guards who had noticed their conditions. Afterward

> the camp commander gave orders that these men should be stripped entirely naked in weather 18 degrees below zero. Several of them rapidly got congestion of lungs, but that did not seem fast enough for the SS. Three times during the night these men were sent down to the shower-baths; three times they were drenched for half an hour in freezing water and then made to come up without being dried. In the morning when the gangs went to work the corpses were strewn over the ground. I must add that the last of them were finished off with blows from an axe.[75]

The camp's deteriorating function caused by the large influx of prisoners, which raised the level of violence toward the more vulnerable prisoners, did not begin and end with this transport.[76] About three weeks earlier, on January 23, more than 5,700 prisoners had arrived from Auschwitz, and by the end of February the number of Auschwitz evacuees in the camp had reached 9,000. Because of the overcrowding, not all of them succeeded in entering the camp. One of the transports included prisoners who had walked from Auschwitz to Gliwice, where they were loaded onto boxcars without food and water and transported through Czechoslovakia and Austria. When they reached Mauthausen, they were left in the cars for a whole day until it became clear that there was no room for them in the camp. They were then redirected to Flossenbürg. In light of this odyssey, the high death rate on this transport, which a survivor estimated at about 50 percent, is not surprising. While the prisoners were in almost constant transit from place to place in search of a camp that would take them in, they threw the many corpses out of the open boxcars without burying them.[77] In February thousands more prisoners arrived from Groß-Rosen and Sachsenhausen as well as small groups of prisoners dispatched from the Gestapo in Slovakia and Austria. The number of prisoners in the Mauthausen complex (including the Gusen camps) rose steeply from 73,000 or so (about 14,000 in the main camp) at the end of December 1944 to approximately 85,000 (27,000 in the main camp) at the end of the first week of March 1945.[78]

At the end of March and the beginning of April rumors circulated in the Mauthausen camps about a plan to liquidate the prisoners before the capitulation. The prisoners in the Gusen camps were particularly apprehensive because of the trenches and tunnels that had been excavated in the mountainside where they worked, which seemed suitable for the implementation of the plan. Once transports arrived from the East, the number of prisoners at Gusen was greater than that in the main camp. In the second half of 1944 thousands of prisoners were transferred to Gusen, including some 4,000 Poles sent after the suppression of the Polish uprising in fall 1944.[79] Additional prisoners arrived from the camps in the East in the winter 1945 wave of evacuations. As a result there were more than 24,000 inmates in the three Gusen camps at the end of March.[80] Another camp whose prisoner population increased considerably in April 1945 was Ebensee: more than 18,500 prisoners were incarcerated there on April 23. From the beginning of March to early May, several days before the liberation, thousands of prisoners were transferred to Ebensee from the subcamps according to the familiar method of evacuating subcamps and concentrating the prisoners in a small number of main camps. In April about 4,500 prisoners perished in Ebensee because of the unspeakable conditions there. There too rumors spread that the prisoners were to be liquidated in a tunnel on the eve of the Americans' arrival, particularly after all the German prisoners were released on April 30.[81] One of the prisoners described the situation:

> Four people slept in each bunk; every night one or two of the four would die. Then I used to hold the hand of the dead man so that they would give him too some bread—I caught the hand like this and with my other hand I gripped the hand of the dead man, so that they would continue to give him a piece of bread.[82]

Transfer of prisoners from the subcamps to the main camp, to Gusen and Ebensee, occurred mainly in the first weeks of April. One of the evacuated camps was Wiener-Neudorf. It was located not far from Vienna in Lower Austria and housed 2,500 prisoners, who labored mainly for the military aviation industry.[83] It began to operate in August 1943 and the population usually consisted mainly of Yugoslav, Polish, Soviet, German, and Austrian prisoners. In 1944 small transports of Hungarians and Italians arrived. There were also a few French, Czech, and Belgian inmates. The few Jewish prisoners arrived only at the beginning of 1945, shortly before the evacuation.[84] Here too new guards, who were not an integral part of the camp team, arrived in 1944. These were Luftwaffe personnel, reassigned as guards; all of them were in their forties and fifties, born between 1890 and 1905.[85]

Preparations for evacuation of the camp began on March 26, 1945, when the sick prisoners deemed incapable of enduring death march conditions were separated from the others. They were examined by the camp physicians and sent to the revier. On March 28 the prisoners set out for work for the last time, and the camp awaited the final evacuation order.[86] Rumors spread rapidly among them. Among other things they were afraid that, in contradiction of what they had been told, prisoners incapable of marching would not be evacuated in boxcars but would be murdered.[87] On April 1 the commandant, Walter Schmutzler, summoned his colleagues for a meeting to discuss the evacuation. He told the guards that they were not to delay during the evacuation and that prisoners unable to keep up with the pace were to be shot. In charge of implementing this order were several SS veterans who were serving there. After the war, Schmutzler admitted giving the order:

> Several days before the evacuation of the camp, I convened a meeting on the evacuation at which . . . I informed the participants of the existence of secret evacuation orders which, among other things, included a secret directive that prisoners unable to stand or walk were to be shot.[88]

Schmutzler naturally chose to admit that he briefed his men about the existence of such a directive, but he did not confess to giving the order to implement it. In any event, he was with the group only part of the time during the evacuation.

The evacuation proceeded along familiar and routine lines. The prisoners were divided into three blocs, the first two consisting of 1,000 prisoners each and the third of 500–600. The two blocs of marchers were in the charge of two SS men, Luftwaffe recruits, one of whom was 52-year-old Otto Schrader; the third bloc was accompanied by veteran camp guards, several of whom had dogs with them. This was also the unit responsible for the murder of those who lagged or fell. The sick and exhausted had been assigned to this third group.[89]

The evacuation of Wiener-Neudorf began on April 2 at 6 a.m.,[90] and the evacuees reached the main camp 13 days later. Of the 2,518 prisoners in the camp, 2,490 set out on the march. The remaining 38, who were too weak to march, were murdered by the guards before the departure.[91] The evacuation conditions did not differ essentially from those of hundreds of other death marches in Germany and Austria at the time. The marchers received no hot food, and insufficient food supplies were taken along. They received a large loaf of bread, a can of peas, and a packet of margarine per prisoner.[92] Schmutzler preferred to load office equipment and the personal belongings of the guards onto the trucks that set out from the camp; hence there was no room for food. All the bread was devoured in the first two or three days. The columns covered about 19 miles (30 kilometers) daily under severe weather conditions and in heavy rain. Most of the nights were spent outdoors, a single blanket per prisoner serving as the only protection against the cold. The sound of shots began to be heard on the first day at the end of the column. Prisoners who collapsed were shot by the guards, who approached the unfortunates and aimed at close range. In the first four days 97 prisoners were murdered and 34 were able to escape.[93] Each day prisoners who could not keep up with the pace of the column were shot,[94] and all in all at least 146 prisoners lost their lives on this death march from Wiener-Neudorf to Mauthausen.[95] It seems likely that at least some of the prisoners had been earmarked in advance for liquidation. The fact that they were sent on the march when their physical condition was so poor appears to have been a way of delaying the liquidation decision to a later date, instead of executing it in the camp.

One of the guards whose role in the murder of prisoners during this march was investigated in 1991–1993 was Dominik Gleba. He was born in October 1921 in Ruda in Poland to a Polish Volksdeutsche family that had moved to Eastern Prussia in 1923. The family owned a farm, and Gleba, who in childhood was sickly and was forced to leave school as a result, began to help his parents in their dairy farm after his recovery. He was totally uninterested in politics, and his family too was indifferent to the political ferment in Germany in the first half of the 1930s. Like other young people in search of a dynamic social framework, Gleba joined the Hitlerjugend and engaged in sports in his spare time. He was short (5 feet 5 inches) (1.65 meters) and puny, and was often teased and harassed because of his appearance and height. His low self-esteem and lack of self-confidence triggered a nervous collapse, and he spent some time in a psychiatric hospital where he received psychotherapy. In 1942 he joined the Wehrmacht and shortly afterward was transferred to the Waffen-SS. He served for some time in Holland and, while there, became a fervent believer in Nazi ideology, finding in his unit the social connections he had been deprived of in adolescence. He was transferred to Mauthausen, and on July 10, 1942, he executed two Russian POWs in the camp. In this fashion, an apolitical individual, with low self-esteem and a history of failure and negative experiences, became a killer. At the end of 1943, he was transferred to Wiener-Neudorf, where he served until the camp was evacuated and the death march set out in April 1945.[96]

At the end of the first day's march, the commander of one of the groups, Weiß, ordered Gleba to shoot a prisoner who could not stand and was obviously unable to walk farther. Gleba knew of Schmutzler's instructions to liquidate prisoners in such cases. But in the course of the first day, when there were only isolated cases of prisoners who collapsed and were murdered, he refrained from doing so. Even when he was ordered to liquidate the prisoners that evening, he hesitated. He turned to one of his colleagues and consulted him, and the colleague told him that the instructions were quite clear and he should obey. Gleba was persuaded; the prisoner had been carried by his comrades all day, and it was clear that they could not continue to do so.

Gleba did not like the order he received, but he was accustomed to obeying orders and observing the rule that any order from a superior, in this case Schmutzler and Weiß, must be carried out. He was also afraid that refusal to obey could mean punishment and might even cost him his life. Schmutzler had clarified the point that, in a state of war, there was no difference between a Wehrmacht soldier and an SS soldier. Yet, it is now evident that this was not precisely the situation among the guards. During the evacuation, quite a few of them found various ways of evading orders to shoot prisoners, as ordered by Schmutzler. Such refusals were subtly presented, and since there was always someone else ready to pull the trigger, did not lead to punishment. For Gleba, reliance on official sanction from a higher authority made it easier for him to decide not to evade orders. He went over to the victim and shot him in the head. This gesture broke down all the barriers, and, from then on, Gleba took part in the murders.[97]

"These Dogs and Swine All Deserve to Be Dead!"

The death march of the Wiener-Neudorf prisoners claimed quite a few victims, but did not deteriorate into a massacre as happened with other death marches that flooded into Mauthausen at that same time. Such massacres occurred during the evacuations of Jewish prisoners transferred to the camp from a series of camps on the Austrian-Hungarian border. This stage lasted several weeks and was one of the most lethal.

On October 18, 1944, the Hungarian minister of the interior announced that he was ready for the deportation of 50,000 Jews, men and women, for forced labor within the Reich. Several days later the Hungarian dictator, Ferenc Szálasi, gave the go-ahead for the beginning of these deportations. The move was in line with his desire to render Budapest free of Jews when the city was in danger of occupation by the Soviet forces. These Jews would satisfy the urgent call for forced laborers needed to construct the fortified area known as the southeastern wall *(Südostwall)*, which would check the Russians and prevent the fall of Vienna. Over a period of four weeks, from early November to early December 1944, the Hungarian fascist regime handed over to the Germans more than 72,000 Jews, "lent" to them for labor purposes. The transfer of Jews continued afterward, but no precise records of the deportees were kept.[98] The Jewish slave laborers were sent to Hegyeshalom, a Hungarian border post on the route to Vienna. These groups were not all male; many of the deportees were women aged 16 to 40 who had been forced to report for duty as recruits for labor for "defense of the homeland."[99]

Dieter Wisliceny, an SS officer and one of Adolf Eichmann's men, said after the war that in November–December 1944, approximately 30,000 Jews were sent from Budapest to the Austrian border. They marched 124 miles (200 kilometers) in poor physical condition, he said, and were given almost no food. The order to dispatch them was given by Eichmann, and the Jews were to be transferred to the Gauleiter of Lower Danube (Niederdonau) for labor purposes. Wisliceny claimed that he himself was not happy to deal with these Jews because they were weak and, in many cases, diseased, but Eichmann insisted and even threatened to inform Himmler if he refused. Of the tens of thousands of Jews transferred to the border area in order to build fortifications, 12,000 were taken to Vienna and its environs. A small proportion of these were transferred directly to several concentration camps, mainly Sachsenhausen and Flossenbürg. Most of these deportees were women, and they were joined by several units of the Hungarian labor service.[100]

The Jews who were deported from Budapest set out from the beginning of November in groups of 2,000 to 4,000 daily and marched toward Hegyeshalom. The marchers, 70 percent of them women, were escorted by Hungarian policemen and gendarmes. Since the guards wanted to hand over the groups as quickly as possible, they urged the marchers on, and those who had difficulty keeping up were shot by their Hungarian escorts. Between 6,000 and 7,000 Jews were murdered along the way by the guards, and another 2,000 perished because of cold and starvation.[101] To avoid lagging behind the Jews discarded their food rations and the clothes they had taken with them, thereby exacerbating their condition. The march lasted seven to eight days.[102] When they reached Hegyeshalom they were in such a pitiable state that the Germans who took them over from the Hungarians concluded that they were no longer equipped to become an effective work force.[103]

The Jews were dispersed through a number of labor camps in the Gau of Niederdonau and in Styria/Steiermark. They were assigned strenuous tasks, which included digging trenches and canals and building fortifications. They were not the only laborers recruited for these tasks. Alongside them were Austrian and German civilian laborers, POWs, and foreign slave laborers from various countries.[104] The Jewish prisoners, however, had the worst living conditions. In February–March 1945 a severe typhus epidemic broke out in Styria Gau. Those prisoners who fell sick were liquidated systematically by SS men on the spot, together with groups of Volkssturm and young members of the Hitlerjugend. Of some 35,000 Jews who labored in camps in Niederdonau, more than 3,000 perished within three months from the bullets of the guards or as a result of the dire conditions.[105]

At the end of March 1945 Himmler held work meetings with the four Austrian Gauleiters in Vienna regarding the military situation in the East, and in accordance with the familiar procedure, he granted them full defensive authority in the evolving crisis. Various problems were raised, including the question of evacuating Allied POWs and civilian populations.[106] Baldur von Schirach, the Gauleiter of Vienna, who attended one of these meetings, claimed after the war that Himmler had requested that the commandant of Mauthausen, Ziereis, be present at the meeting where he conveyed explicit information regarding the Jews laboring in the border camps of the southeastern wall:

> I want the Jews now employed in industry to be taken by boat or by bus if possible, under the most favorable food conditions and with medical care, et cetera, to Linz or Mauthausen. Please take care of these Jews and treat them well; they are my most valuable assets.[107]

The Gauleiter of Styria, Siegfried Uiberrcither, in whose Gau thousands of Hungarian Jews were laboring in the Austrian-Hungarian border camps, also remembered Himmler's instructions. According to Uiberreither, these instructions were conveyed to him orally in March 1945 and at the same time were transmitted to the Gestapo. Himmler ordered that the transfer of Jews be carried out "in the accepted way" and demanded that Ziereis treat them properly.[108] Thus the familiar scenario recurred. Himmler gave instructions that these Jews be preserved for well-known reasons, while Ziereis preferred to remember the order, which did or did not come from Kaltenbrunner, to murder 1,000 prisoners daily. What was plain was the fact that the tens of thousands of Jews laboring in eastern Austria had to be transferred to Mauthausen. What happened to them en route differed completely from what had been planned at the Vienna meeting a week previously.

The evacuation of the labor camps along the southeast wall began in the second half of March 1945, and the familiar evacuation instructions were followed here as well. The instructions stipulated that the workers were to be rounded up and concentrated in one or two central camps and were to set out from there. Since the camps where the Jews were laboring did not belong to the concentration camp system,[109] the guards and escorts had to be provided by local bodies. To this end, administrative and organizational powers were assigned to party elements: district chiefs *(Kreisleiter)* or even heads of local branches *(Ortsgruppenführer)*. Himmler himself sent a directive in this spirit to the Gauleiters in the two Gaus where the camps were located. It was formulated in the spirit that von Schirach and Uiberreither recalled from the Vienna meeting: namely, the evacuation was to be orderly and the lives of the prisoners were to be strictly safeguarded.[110]

At the same time, local elements retained the authority to interpret the difficulties and disruptions caused by the military situation and to decide how to act. These party functionaries had the power to recruit local Volkssturm units, Hitlerjugend units, SS personnel, or local party activists. Operating together with them were other, more established units: Waffen-SS or Gestapo.[111] In this fashion, new elements from the civilian (party), military, and local police sphere joined the circle of murderers during the evacuations and death marches, which were usually manned by camp guards.

At the time, the Gauleiters were the supreme authorities in their districts. This group of several dozen party functionaries, most of them "veterans" *(alte Kampfer)* had served Hitler and the party from the initial period in the 1920s. Mainly members of the relatively well-established professional class, they had not necessarily suffered professional failures, unemployment, or personal instability before joining the party. A Gauleiter was usually a man who, even if his origins were lower middle class or even working class, enjoyed professional success and a high standard of living.[112] The Gauleiters had not joined the party in its early stages as a means of extricating themselves from professional or personal stalemates or social marginality, but were motivated by belief in an idea and a leader. They formed the most solid infrastructure of the party and the most loyal and closest associates of Hitler—apparently the only group in whose company he felt safe and open.[113]

When war broke out in September 1939, the issue of public morale took on particular significance for Hitler. His paranoia and obsessive fear that the home front would collapse once again because of defeatism and traitors, as he was convinced had happened in 1918, led him to transfer more and more powers relating to the security of the home front to these senior party functionaries, whom he trusted implicitly. On September 1, 1939, 13 Gauleiters in areas close to the front received appointments as defense commissars of the Reich. They still had too few real powers, but this situation changed in November 1942 when all 42 party Gauleiters were granted such powers. The reversal of fortunes resulting from the debacle in North Africa and later at Stalingrad led to the transfer of additional powers to the Gauleiters. They were now charged with responsibility for managing life on the home front. They wielded authority on issues of manpower, civil defense, education, slave labor, relations with the army and security bodies, economic affairs, and the like. They were also an active and major factor in the ideological radicalization of the regime in the last years of the war. Several Gauleiters were particularly active in dispatching Jews and Gypsies from their Gaus to the camps and to extermination: Goebbels in Berlin, Karl Otto-Kurt Kaufmann in Hamburg, and Baldur von Schirach in Vienna. After the assassination attempt on Hitler on July 20, 1944, and the appointment of Goebbels as Reich authority for total warfare (Reichsbevollmächtiger für den totalen Kriegseinsatz), the Gauleiters became even more powerful. On the basis of Hitler's decree of August 16, 1944, they were granted authority to receive information and to give orders to all government and state apparatuses or to economic and commercial bodies at the local level. In this capacity, they were essentially rulers of their areas. In the final months of the war, they exploited their status and powers in order to recruit civilians into the Volkssturm units they established. As the military crisis became increasingly acute in the second half of 1944, and large parts of the Reich were cut off from contact with the central region, the Gauleiters became the sole policymakers in the areas under their jurisdiction.[114] Their main recruited manpower resources were the Volkssturm units.

The establishment of these units in summer–fall 1944 was the direct consequence of the manpower shortage within the Wehrmacht after the military defeats in the East and the Red Army's entry into Eastern Prussia in August. For the first time since the outbreak of war, enemy forces had reached German soil. In addition, the rapid Allied advance into France and the incessant bombing of German cities caused a severe breakdown of morale on the home front. A component of this breakdown was the profound fear that if the military collapse continued, it would lead to an uprising of foreign slave laborers throughout the Reich. After the failure of the July 20 conspiracy, the party leadership arrived at the conclusion that supervision over the military and, insofar as possible, over German society as well, should be tightened. The assassination attempt and the fact that numerous Wehrmacht elements had been involved undermined the confidence of Hitler and the party leaders in the General Staff, which for some time had been waning. Hence, the effort launched in summer 1944 to recruit most of the available manpower in Germany for defense of the homeland was also motivated by a desire to establish units that would not be answerable to the military command. Hitler concurred with this plan and in September 1944 approved the establishment of a popular party militia.[115]

Underlying the Nazi leadership's outlook at the end of 1944 was the conviction that the war could still be turned around. The keys to the change were to be reinforcement of the will and motivation to fight, adherence to the objectives of the war, and bolstering of belief in the racial and biological supremacy of the Germans. The Volkssturm, under the ideological guidance of party elements, Gauleiters or Kreisleiters, were perceived as the main instrument for general mobilization of the nation. Their fervent determination to continue resisting would, so Josef Goebbels and Martin Bormann believed, reinforce the unyielding stand of the soldiers in the front line, who would be confident that they were backed by a resolute and united home front, ready to fight for its liberty.[116]

The militia was officially established on October 18, 1944, the anniversary of the battle of Leipzig in 1812. Although service was obligatory for all men aged 16 to 60, the party leaders, especially Martin Bormann, the originator of the force, perceived it not as the result of official coercion but as the expression of the widespread popular resistance of the German people. David Yelton asserts that the Volkssturm was the living proof of the absence of dichotomy between the German people and the party leaders, an absence in which the leaders believed. The party, in the final analysis, was the bearer of the will of the Volk, and the Volkssturm was the expression of this fact.[117] The ideological aspect of recruitment into the Volkssturm greatly preoccupied the Nazi leaders, and Bormann issued clear instructions on this matter on January 5, 1945. As the war approached its close, party elements increased their efforts to instill in the recruits a zealous fighting spirit, both ideologically and politically. The party-political aspect was so central to these units, and belief in their importance for military purposes was so strong, that in certain places, local party chiefs did all they could in spring 1945 to ensure that new recruits did not find their way into the ranks of the Wehrmacht but were recruited into Volkssturm units.[118]

The local angle, the struggle for the safety of the community and the family, was a major component of the underlying concept of the Volkssturm, and the party functionaries both controlled and guided it: from the Gauleiter who wielded the authority to command and organize the militia in his Gau to the Kreisleiter, the district leader, and down to the head of the local branch. The recruits into this militia were middle-aged farmers or laborers, World War I veterans bearing the trauma of defeat and no longer eligible for active service; their 16–17-year-old sons had joined the Hitlerjugend. This was the force assigned the task of reversing the trend to defeat and, by force of their fanatic belief in the regime and fear of foreign occupiers, warding off the military debacle.

The Volkssturm was the incarnation of the concept of the Nazi "national community" (Volksgemeinschaft), the popular community that was to erase all differences in social status, origin, or age and unite all people on the basis of race. It was the service framework for members of the local community, who had been raised together and lived side by side, and now bore arms together in order to defend the community. It was intended to be the popular expression of the will of the people to fight and never yield. The Volkssturm, so the party leaders believed, would solve an additional disturbing problem: the fact that, in view of the bombings and the military defeats, the sense of collective national responsibility was wearing thin, as was the desire to fight for a national goal.[119] But in the final years of the war, the Volkssturm recruits found themselves taking part in security activities that neither its members nor the founders of this militia had anticipated.

The distance between von Schirach's Vienna and the small towns of Burgenland and the Styria Gau on the Austrian-Hungarian border, where Jewish prisoners from Hungary were to be sent in April, was undoubtedly short in geographical terms, but immense in practical terms. The decisions taken several weeks previously in Vienna and the instructions to conduct the transfer in orderly fashion lost all meaning when the time came to organize a series of chaotic evacuations, rife with obstacles. In the familiar circumstances that ensued, the conditions for future perpetration of mass murder were born.

In general, the procedures through which the Jewish camps on the Austrian-Hungarian border were evacuated resembled those in the large concentration camps in Poland and Germany. Eduard Frantz Meissl, Kreisleiter of Fürstenfeld district, issued an evacuation order for several camps in his district on March 22, 1945, which was similar to the evacuation directive regarding the Polish camps that had been sent out several months previously, particularly the order issued by Hoppe at Stutthof. According to this directive, when the date of evacuation arrived in "a case of alert" *(im Falle eines Alarmes)*, the Jews in several camps in the district were to be brought together and led on a march westward along two designated routes, of 14 miles (22 kilometers) and 20 miles (33 kilometers), to a transit camp near the town of Bierbaum Zettling. In addition to detailing routes, the directive specified that the escorts of the prisoners be Volkssturm personnel and that two local party heads *(Ortsgruppenführer)* be responsible for organizing the evacuation and supplying the required escorts. Meissl's directive makes no mention of infirm prisoners incapable of walking, or those too weak to endure the hardships of the trek.[120]

The considerable similarity between Meissl's order and the orders circulating in the Polish concentration camp network from fall 1944 indicates that the evacuation pattern for the camps was well known to elements in the labor camps, including those affiliated with organizational frameworks without operative connections between them. No contacts existed between the local party apparatus in charge of the evacuations and death marches of Jewish prisoners from the Austrian-Hungarian border, and the supervisors of the concentration camps and the HSSPF in Poland. However, they issued similar operative instructions in the spirit of Himmler's familiar strategic conceptions, and this despite the fact that Himmler was anxious to ensure that the evacuation of Jewish prisoners in Austria be conducted in well-regulated fashion. In Austria as in Poland, there was little in common between the orderly instructions and the gory implementation.

One of the camps included in Meissl's directive was Strem, where 500 to 600 Jewish prisoners were detained. In charge of the evacuation was the local party head, Paul Schmidt, a 39-year-old businessman.[121] He claimed that he received very strict instructions from the Styria Gauleiter, Siegfried Uiberreither, with regard to escape attempts by Jews, which were to be prevented at all costs. For every Jew who escaped, Schmidt said, he was ordered to kill ten others.[122] Meissl gave him this order orally.[123] Another guard, Kurt Nussbaumer, who accompanied a group of Jews evacuated from Rechnitz to Strem, testified that, while Schmidt was in charge of the evacuation from Strem, it was Meissl who gave the order to murder any prisoner, Jew, Ukrainian, or other foreigner, who was too weak to continue marching. He did not specify how the order was given.[124] In contrast, Anton Unger, also a party head at Strem, testified that, on the eve of the evacuation of Strem, Meissl and Schmidt toured the camp together and that he saw Schmidt shooting two prisoners.[125]

Schmidt admitted that, during the evacuation from Strem, he killed four Jewish prisoners, two of them as they tried to escape.[126] Other accomplices in the murder of Jewish prisoners at Strem were members of the Hitlerjugend, one of whom was Josef Dex, aged 17. Like other boys of his age, he joined a Hitlerjugend company in October 1944 within the Volkssturm framework, and his 180-strong unit was deployed in aid to Wehrmacht units. The commander of the Strem Hitlerjugend, 23-year-old Karl Schlicher, gave the order to liquidate several Jewish prisoners during the evacuation of the camp. According to Dex, they were told that these Jews were suffering from typhus. The sick Jews were evacuated from the camp on horse-drawn wagons, but along the way several were taken off the wagons and murdered in a nearby forest.[127] At least 25 prisoners too frail to set out on the march were murdered in a forest grove close to Strem before the march left the camp. In all at least 100 Jews perished on the march from Strem to the place to which Schmidt was ordered to bring them.[128]

Uiberreither, it will be recalled, had attended the Gauleiters' discussion with Himmler in Vienna at the end of March 1945, on the eve of the evacuations from the border camps. He claimed that he had not been in contact of any kind with Kreisleiters in his Gau when the evacuations began in April 1945. All he did after returning from the meeting with Himmler was to brief several Kreisleiters about Himmler's instruction that, in the event of the Red Army approaching, the Jews were to be evacuated and were to be sent to Mauthausen in the usual way. He understood Himmler's instruction to mean that he was to take into account transportation difficulties and the state of the routes, but was to ensure that the prisoners did not suffer en route.[129]

Whatever the interpretation of "difficulties,"[130] and with all necessary caution, it is doubtful that Uiberreither gave explicit orders to murder Jewish prisoners before or during the evacuation. In the case of Strem, it is possible that Meissl issued such an order. In any case, an explicit order, whether written or oral, would not have sufficed to authorize the murder of prisoners on the death march. Examination of the incidents of liquidation during the evacuation of the Jewish prisoners to Mauthausen indicates that, for those responsible on the local level, it was enough to interpret the spirit of the order as they saw fit and to remember the identity of the evacuees.

Some time before the evacuation began, those sick prisoners who were manifestly incapable of enduring the march were liquidated in the camps. The case of Klöch, a camp close to the border with Yugoslavia, illustrates clearly how these murderous situations evolved in the border camps in Austria. On the eve of the evacuation, the local party leader, Anton Oswald, gave the order to murder at least 26 sick Jews. He described the circumstances that brought him to organize a mass murder operation:

I was IC of a working party of Jews who were building fortifications at Klöch. The strength of the party was 250 Jews. I remember that in February 1945 there was an outbreak of typhus,—under the following circumstances. In January a party of 54 Jews arrived. . . . That evening it was reported to me that they were unfit for work in the fortifications, so I put them on to snow clearing instead, and decided to bring the matter up at a conference to be held a few days later, suggesting that they should be removed. When I made this suggestion to . . . Anton Rutte,[131] at the conference, he said that the South Eastern fortifications had to be completed and that the Jews must work on them. This meeting was on the 5th February or thereabouts. . . . The Doctor was sent for, who examined the sick. The Doctor's name was Haring, who diagnosed typhus. The Doctor said he would report this at once to the Kreisleiter so that medical supplies could be sent to prevent the disease from spreading.

I wrote immediately to Rutte and asked for transport for the sick to go to hospital, as the conditions in the camp were unsuitable for isolating the sick. A week passed and nothing happened, so I wrote a second and more detailed letter to Rutte saying that the cases had increased and that he should take immediate action to send the sick to hospital otherwise I could not guarantee that the fever would not spread to the whole camp. After the second letter, I was sent on a course to Paubegg, and ten or eleven days later, I returned on 1 or 2 March to report to Kreisleiter Lill, who told me there would be a conference the following day and so I need not return at once to Klöch.

At this meeting, I met Huetter, one of my men from Klöch, and asked him what was the news from Klöch. He told me that a Commission had visited Klöch and had decided that the Jews who had typhus were to be shot. I asked him how that could be, and he replied that the SS would come and shoot them. I protested and said I wished to have nothing to do with that and if medical supplies cannot be obtained, I do not want to know or see anything. I also told him that it was not in my power to change the decision, but wanted to have no part in it. When I came back to Klöch, I went to my office and my men wanted to tell me about this. I told them I know all, and did not wish to hear anymore. . . .

My political superior was Lill. . . . I intended to visit Lill in Mureck to ask him to try to prevent the shooting and take other measures. I could not fulfill this intention as Lill came to Klöch the same evening. He told me he knew it was terrible, but there were no hospital or medical stores available, there was no alternative. I told him it was not my duty and was told I must do it to save the other workers. I asked him who he thought must carry out the execution, he replied, you and your staff. I asked him to give this order himself to my staff, as I did not want to do it myself.

He answered that he had not got time for that and I said that I didn't want it on my conscience, I could only [do] what I was doing, and that he was responsible. Lill detailed the men to take part and I replied that they probably would not want to, but as it was an order, I had to carry it out. I got the names from Lill but I hesitated for 10 days to execute the Jews. . . .

As I could see no other possibility, I detailed those men whose names I got from Lill—until then I had not warned them, and told them that on the Gauleiter's orders the sick Jews must be shot. The [sic] protested but I told them that Lill had detailed them by name and as they were Volkssturm men, they had to obey orders. They said they were not murderers, and it was terrible for them. I explained the whole situation to them and at length, they agreed, though they were still unwilling.

I intended to take only the worst cases as I thought the others might recover. I sent a man to their billets and he asked the Jewish Doctor whose name may have been Fedor, to select the worst cases. He selected 26 as the worst cases and fetched them outside where they were put in the lorry. Those 26 were taken away and were shot. I was present when they were shot. I took part in the shooting myself, with a machine pistol. The other men who took part in the shooting were—Alois Ullrich, Huetter Anton (now dead), Koren Franz, Sablatnig Anton, Sattler (first name not known), and one other whose name I am not sure of. The Jews were shot in a forest called the Gruisler Wald, S.E. from Klöch.[132]

A particularly brutal massacre took place in Rechnitz in Burgerland. On the night of March 25, 1945, at least 180 Hungarian Jews were liquidated in a massacre led by the local Gestapo commandant, Franz Podezin.[133] Another incident occurred in the small town of Jennersdorf, where a small labor camp for Jews from Hungary had been established at the end of 1944.[134] The order to evacuate the Jews was sent by Anton Rutte, party Kreisleiter,[135] and received by Dr. Luckmann, who was the head of the party branch in Jennersdorf. Apparently, Luckmann was not pleased at the order; he argued that there were not enough recruits in the town capable of carrying it out and managing a group of prisoners. This group consisted of some 30 exhausted prisoners who were being held in the local school, where a sick room had been prepared for them. Rumors were rife in the town that these prisoners were scheduled to be liquidated, but when Luckmann was informed of this, he retorted: "Let's not talk about that matter" *(über diese Sache ist nicht zu sprechen).*[136]

Wilhelm Mohr, a soldier in the Waffen-SS Das Reich Division, found himself involved in the murder of this group of Jewish prisoners. At the end of October or the beginning of November 1944[137] a special SS construction battalion arrived in Jennersdorf. It consisted of 900 to 1,000 Bosnian Moslem recruits, whose task was to work on the large-scale project for construction of the southeastern wall.[138] Several months later, in February 1945, two companies of about 300 Waffen-SS men arrived in the town; one of them apparently also included Bosnian Moslem recruits and Croatian Volksdeutsche.[139] Mohr, who then held the rank of Oberscharführer (Technical Sergeant), recalled after the war that in March 1945, when he and his unit were posted in the town, he received orders to take a group of about 30 sick Jews from the school and to liquidate them. They were not told the origin of this order. His reaction, he said, was to polish off a bottle of schnapps, and several of his colleagues did the same. This group of murderers was relatively heterogeneous and included Croatian Volksdeutsche, in addition to German SS soldiers.[140] They were armed with pistols and automatic weapons. The Jews, most of whom were too infirm to join the evacuation to Graz, were led outside the town and shot there. Franz Paul, one of Mohr's fellow soldiers, remembered the incident, and he too had no idea who had the authority at the time to issue the liquidation order. They received it through their Oberscharführer, a man named Maier.[141] Naturally enough, the fact that the origin of the order was unknown did not prevent several members of the unit from carrying it out faithfully. In all, no more than 33 SS men took part in this slaughter of sick Jewish prisoners. Mohr, Paul, and a third man, Karl Amlinger, were tried for the murder of the Jewish prisoners at Jennersdorf, a task in which they were assisted by two or three Volksdeutsche.[142] The murders apparently took place on one of the days between March 21 and 28, 1945, since the Waffen-SS unit left the town during that week.[143]

Also characteristic was the massacre in Balf camp, south of the Hungarian border town of Sopron. About 1,500 Hungarian Jews worked on the site, which was evacuated on March 28, 1945. Prisoners who were too sick to endure the evacuation remained behind. On March 31, 1945, 176 of them were murdered by an SS unit, whose identity was never fully clarified after the war. The Jewish victims were led to antitank trenches that had been dug some time before by the prisoners themselves[144] and ordered to stand alongside them. Two SS men armed with automatic weapons apparently began to shoot these feeble human beings, who fell into the trenches. The massacre lasted half an hour, and then one of the killers turned to his colleague and asked: "Have they all been finished off?" (Sind sie alle kaputt?) Then the murderers left. Several prisoners survived the slaughter, because the killers were careless in checking that all of them were dead. Once they were sure that the Germans had gone, they crawled out of the mass grave.[145] On April 1, 1945, at about 9 a.m., Red Army forces entered Balf.[146]

One of the bloodiest massacres during the evacuation of the Jewish prisoners from the border occurred close to the town of Eisenerz. A large convoy of between 6,000 and 8,000 prisoners, who had left Graz on April 4, passed through the town on April 7. They were led in three columns by Volkssturm, Gestapo, and Ukrainian Waffen-SS men. Since there were only a few guards, it was necessary to coopt local Volkssturm units along the route as reinforcement.[147] Throughout the journey, the guards murdered prisoners who collapsed and could not move on. On one occasion, a group of 20 Jews tried to escape but were caught by the Waffen-SS guards and murdered in a nearby ravine in this mountainous area.[148] The long column proceeded through the Präbichl Pass in the Alps close to Eisenerz, making for the town of Hieflau.[149] The decision to murder the Jews on the march to Mauthausen was apparently taken by the Kreisleiter of Leoben district, Otto Christandl, who had held the post since 1938. He was the supreme political authority in the district at the time and, in accordance with the political and military structure of the Reich at the end of 1944, was empowered to deploy the Volkssturm units.[150] The order was implemented by a group of recruits from one of the Volkssturm units in Eisenerz.

Since November 1944 Adolf Schumann had served as senior commander of the Volkssturm units in the town. By occupation he was a policeman, whose main task was directing traffic and keeping the peace in the sleepy little Alpine town. He related that on Saturday, April 6, 1945, he learned that a transport of 3,000 to 4,000 Jews, which was on its way from Hungary to Mauthausen, was due to arrive in his town. The police and Volkssturm units at Eisenerz received orders to be ready to accept this transport, which was to cross the Präbichl Pass, and accompany it to Hieflau. The Eisenerz police chief, Ernst Bilke, told Schumann that he had assigned two policemen to this task, and asked for the assistance of one of the Volkssturm units. Schumann passed the orders on, as received, to the Volkssturm unit chosen as escorts, quite a few of whose members were SA men. He emphasized that the marchers were Jews and were to be shot only in the event of escape attempts. He asserted after the war that if he had known in advance what was about to happen, he would have placed greater emphasis on the orders.[151]

The massacre at Präbichl was by no means a spontaneous occurrence, but neither was it carefully planned. On April 1 the problem of the march of Jews from the Austrian-Hungarian border camps to Mauthausen had been raised in a talk between Christandl and Schumann. Christandl had apparently also discussed the murder of Jews en route to Mauthausen with the Gauleiter of Styria, Uiberreither. One of the conjectures examined after the war was that the decision to liquidate as many Jews as possible en route resulted from the fact that Mauthausen was full to overflowing in April and there was no room for another large group of prisoners.[152] This fact was also known in one way or another to the commander of the Volkssturm company that was designated to accompany the prisoners, as well as to several of the group leaders in the company.[153]

On the evening of April 6 the group leaders held a meeting. The Volkssturm company was commanded by Ludwig Krenn, a veteran Nazi and member of the SA since 1933. He was too old for active service during the war and was 46 at the time he directed the Präbichl massacre.[154] The company, which was a fairly typical Volkssturm unit, consisted of 69 men, the youngest born in 1914 and the oldest in 1891. Most of them were between 38 and 45 years of age.[155]

On the eve of their mission, the Volkssturm men gathered in the unit canteen for a get-together meal and received a half-liter of wine each, in view of the coming operation. Krenn addressed his men, and the canteen manager heard him say:

The Alarm Company has been instructed to take over a transport of Jews on the Präbichl tomorrow. These dogs and swine deserve all to be dead. If among you there is a coward, he must report himself right away, for tomorrow will be too late. If tomorrow anyone goes cowardly on me, I will finish him off personally.[156]

As in other such incidents toward the end of the war, the question of who gave the order has never been entirely clarified. Schumann claimed that he never issued such a order, but whether Krenn received the instructions from Christandl directly (which was not customary in the chain of command within the Volkssturm but could certainly have happened in this case),[157] from Schumann, or from Anton Eberl,[158] who was Schumann's second in command, it is clear that Krenn displayed particular initiative and enthusiasm. He was known among his men for his brutal conduct and his ideological fanaticism.[159]

The men were ordered to report for duty in Sunday, April 7, 1945, at 5 a.m., at the unit's assembly spot, and at 6:30 they reached the Präbichl Pass.[160] On the morning of April 7 Krenn addressed them again and told them bluntly that their mission was to kill the Jews.[161] As he put it, if the Jews did not attempt to escape, they should be helped to do so. He also insisted on knowing if any of them felt they were unable to shoot and promised that after the operation, they would all received schnapps and cigarettes.[162]

That morning Schumann received word that there had been previous cases of killings of Jews. He claimed that he hastened to instruct one of the unit commanders that, under no circumstances, were weapons to be used except in cases of escape attempts or refusal to obey orders. That afternoon, one of his subordinates telephoned him and told him that something had gone wrong at the Präbichl Pass and that the men of Krenn's company had liquidated Jews. The massacre began between 4:00 and 4:30 in the afternoon[163] and apparently lasted only 15 minutes.[164] One of the men in Krenn's company described what happened:

> The order given to us by Krenn meant that we had to fire on any Jew who was no longer able to move on. There were, as I have been told, 7,000 Jews in troop order, following one after the other. They started at the Hotel Reichenstein and moved to the Präbichl Pass, very slowly, according to their state of health. Krenn and his assistants were always after them, pushing them on with the butts of their rifles and with sticks. The distance between the different troops became larger and larger and when people fainted or fell to the ground, Krenn and his assistants began to fire on them. In heaps they fell, 5 or 10 at a time, often they were badly wounded. Krenn's assistants rushed with their pistols in their hands to those who were lying on the ground in their death struggles, and shot them. I saw with my own eyes how this ill-famed Neumann came with his pistol in his hand to one man, who was lying on the

ground covered with blood; this man, when he saw Neumann, pulled together all his strength and asked Neumann to let him live, but Neumann took his pistol and fired into the mouth of this man. The man fell backwards and was dead.

During the march I tried to count the number who were killed, but this was impossible, because if any of our people had seen me doing this they would have killed me. Another reason I could not count them we [sic] because they shot amongst the people with their Tommy guns and a great many were lying on the top of each other. At my estimation there were about 120 to 150 persons killed. All this happened between the Hotel Reichenstein and the Präbichl Pass.[165]

Schumann visited the site of the murders and met with Krenn and Eberl. They reported that the transport had reached Eisenerz and that everything had gone smoothly. Schumann persisted and asked how they could say that when people had been murdered. The reply was that this had been done because the Jews had tried to escape. Schumann described what he saw:

Every few paces there were dead bodies, and all the bodies were on the route of the transport, so that the report that they were trying to escape was wrong. We turned round half way up and Bulke then gave orders to stop all civilian traffic on the road. When asked, Krenn then stated, "Yes, they showed insubordination and refused to march on." When I said that refusing to march was not insubordination he shrugged his shoulders. I then ordered Krenn to go with the police. Bulke wanted to make the first enquiry and then arrest Krenn.[166]

This massacre, it appears, was not perceived as irregular by the perpetrators, as Schumann went on to state:

I then spoke with some of the guardsmen but found that they did not understand the wrong that they had one [sic]; to the contrary, they were satisfied and said it was a pity to drive on so many persons. That opinion was held especially by Wilding, Neumann and Mitterboch.[167]

The death blow inflicted so suddenly on the Jews making their way through the mountain pass was unexpected. They had not been ready for such treatment and apparently did not understand what was happening. Those who continued the march picked their way between the corpses of their comrades as they fell, sometimes at their very feet.[168] One of the surviving women described the scene:

We had to climb up a hill. I was among the first in the column and since the line had scattered, we had to wait at the top of the hill for those who were lagging behind. I could see that the previous guards who were Volkssturm men had been replaced by guards from the SS. . . . When people reached the top, the guards began to drive us downhill and at the same time to fire at us. Those who were firing stood behind trees or bushes and fired from their hiding places but after a short time they came out but continued to shoot. I saw them aiming and firing . . . then an SS man arrived on a motorcycle and ordered them to stop shooting.[169]

At least 250 Jews were murdered in a brief span in this bloody slaughter.[170] It was halted only after the transport commander, an SS man, intervened. He even submitted a complaint to the Gestapo in Graz.[171]

Whenever the columns of Jews left camps in Styria district and began their death march northward to Mauthausen, the consensual murder machine went into full operation. On April 11 or 12, 1945, a column of 1,000 Jewish evacuees from Judenburg reached Trieben. By the time they reached the town, more than 10 of them had been liquidated by several of the guards, SA men. In charge of the transport were several SA men and one of the Volkssturm commanders, Franz Puchner. They had 19 guards at their disposal, SA men who served in the Volkssturm and several other Volkssturm personnel, civilians who were not SA men. Puchner, who was born in 1903, was the commander of a Volkssturm unit in the village of Fohnsdorf, several miles northeast of Judenburg. He described what occurred:

> In March or April, I don't know exactly, I got an order, together with 19 other men of the Volkssturm, to come to the courtyard of the school in Fohnsdorf. These men were present. . . . These men were all living in the Gemeinde of Fohnsdorf. In Pöls I had to take the command of the transport. . . . I was told that near the bridge at Judenburg a Jew should have been shot . . . the next day it was reported to me, that SA Egger had shot a Jew who tried to escape. . . . I told all my men not to shoot.[172]

Josef Eger was a 44-year-old Volkssturm member. He described his role in the murder of Jewish prisoners as follows:

> In the end of March or the beginning of April I was called to the courtyard of a schoolhouse in Fohnsdorf. From there we went by lorry to Judenburg and to the Stubaple. We didn't know what we had to do. When the transport arrived, we learned that we had to escort Jews. We stayed for the night at Wöllmerdorf. The next day we went through Judenburg and toward Pöls. On the way there I had to shoot a Jew near the village of Strettweg because he had opened his arteries. . . . I tried to shoot him in the neck. I think I missed him. . . . I shot another Jew . . . because he tried to escape. We had orders to shoot in case a Jew tried to escape or would not obey, because they were suspected of spotted fever.[173]

This was a reality that was repeated endlessly. Two or three Volkssturm men were ordered to accompany a group of Jewish prisoners for a short time as they plodded slowly through their village and on to the next one on their way to Mauthausen. Over that short distance, some of the Volkssturm guards turned into murderers. At the beginning of April, Stefan Knaus, a 42-year-old Volkssturm man, and several of his comrades received orders to accompany a group of Jews coming from the direction of Graz. When the prisoners passed the village of Frohnleiten, one of them went over to Knaus and pleaded for a chunk of bread in return for his boots. The commander of the column, Franz Iskar, who was riding his bicycle alongside the column, warned Knaus not to dare to agree. Farther on, several prisoners tried to tear lumps of flesh off carcasses of horses lying at the roadside. Then too Iskar threatened to shoot anyone who did this. Some time later, prisoners began to collapse, unable to continue walking. One of the guards, Rupert Schmer, shot them. About 19 prisoners were shot by the guards along the 9-mile (14-kilometer) stretch of road.[174] A more wide-scale massacre occurred near the village of Frensdorf. Twelve Jewish prisoners were taken, on orders from Kreisleiter Johann Brandber, to the cellar of a building in the village and shot there.[175] In the town of Gratwein as well, several Jews unable to continue the march were murdered. They were led to a bomb crater and shot by one of the guards. This murder was committed before the eyes of local residents, who heard the Jews pleading for their lives before being shot.[176]

This death march spent about a week in Upper Danube district along the route northward to Mauthausen. The guards and escorts were almost always members of the Volkssturm and local gendarmerie from the towns and villages the columns passed. About 5,000 to 6,000 Jewish prisoners who marched northward along two or three axes reached Mauthausen in the third and fourth week of April.[177]

During the unbridled murder activities in Styria Gau, the victims were not only Jews. During the evacuation of camps in this area, the liquidation of prisoners incapable of walking as far as Mauthausen or of proving useful there apparently spread like wildfire. One such incident occurred in the Mauthausen subcamp in Hintenberg, about 2 miles (3 kilometers) from Lauben. This camp had been established in mid-August 1944 with some 600 inmates, mostly Russian, Polish, Austrian, German, and Yugoslav. By the eve of evacuation, the number had risen to approximately 800. The guard team was composed of about 15 SD men, Austrians and Germans, and another 80 Ukrainian guards. About 40 sick prisoners were murdered by the Ukrainians shortly before evacuation of the camp on April 4, 1945.[178]

The evacuation of some 18,000 Jewish prisoners from camps in western Hungary, in the Lower Danube Gau, and the Sopron and Köszeg districts began at the end of March 1945. One of these camps was Engerau, now Petržalka, in the Bratislava area in Slovakia. About 3,000 Hungarian Jews as well as Jews from Czechoslovakia who had been sent to Hungary in 1943 as laborers reached this camp in March 1944.[179]

Alfred Waidmann was one of the senior functionaries in the area. He was a 42-year-old Vienna-born electrician and a veteran Nazi, who had joined the party in 1930. He belonged to the group of "veteran fighters" in the Austrian party and as such enjoyed considerable prestige in the former Austrian capital. In October 1943 he was appointed Kreisleiter of District no. 8 in the Gau of Vienna, a position he held until the end of the war. In addition to his post in the party ranks, he was also responsible for construction on the section of the southeastern wall fortifications where Jewish prisoners from Engerau labored. Waidmann was involved in preparations for evacuating the camp. After the war, he related that his instructions regarding the evacuations were very clear. He handed down the Gauleiter's directive that the Jews were to be equipped with food and that the sick prisoners were to be treated. The Jewish prisoners were even supposed to be separated from the others, since they were to be dispatched by rail to a destination that was not known to him. And, in fact, before departure, each prisoner was given one and a half kilograms (about 3 pounds) of bread and a ration of butter and cheese.[180]

In this camp, which was dismantled on March 29, 1945, the guards conducted a massacre of prisoners whom they considered too frail to undertake the march. The number of victims remains unknown. According to one evaluation, about 480 Jews were murdered there in 1945, but how many of them perished before the march set out is not known.[181] What is evident is that those who perished before the evacuation were killed with great savagery with pistols and daggers. Some of the killers were apparently intoxicated at the time. After the prisoners left the camp, another massacre took place. The Czech investigators who examined the mass grave exhumed there after the war found 48 corpses of prisoners who had been liquidated by policemen or other accompanying party members.[182] Waidmann claimed that he did not know who was responsible for the killings at Engerau before the evacuation began. He heard about them later and was told, so he said, that between 60 and 65 prisoners were liquidated.[183]

Who ordered the killing of 60 Jewish prisoners (or 100 according to other sources) at Engerau immediately before the evacuation? Various speculations were raised after the war, but there was no clear answer, despite the fact that those suspected of perpetrating the massacre were tried over a lengthy period (from 1945 to 1954).[184] Among other theories, it was suggested that the order was given by engineer Dr. Erwin Hope, who was directly responsible for Engerau and several nearby camps or by one of his assistants. It was also suggested that the order came from the local mayor, who was reluctant to allow dozens of sick prisoners to remain in the camp because they would be liberated by the Red Army and would bear witness to what had happened in the town.[185] Be that as it may, it is quite clear that the decision was taken at the local level, in the field, immediately before the evacuation began. It did not differ from similar decisions taken at that time elsewhere in respect to the evacuation of Jewish prisoners from camps on the Austrian border. The Austrian courts succeeded in establishing that some 600 Hungarian Jews perished in the camp, including the victims of the massacre on the eve of departure.[186]

About 10,000 of the Jewish prisoners in the Sopron area and in the border camps of the Lower Danube Gau were evacuated to the northwest in the direction of Mauthausen. Other were led southward and evacuated together with the prisoners in the Styria Gau.[187] Prisoners in the Sopron area understood only too well that they were being evacuated because the Russians were approaching. They could hear the muffled roar of the cannons in the East, and the guards could not conceal their desire to move westward as fast as possible. Those who collapsed and could not keep up with the rapid pace were shot. On one occasion, they were led into a quarry near the town of St. Margarethen in Burgenland, north of Sopron, where some of them were slaughtered. Some of the SS men fired into a group of prisoners who were resting there,[188] and others rolled heavy boulders down on them from the hilltop. About 20 prisoners were killed in this way. "Anarchy prevailed," as one of the survivors said. "They acted as they saw fit where the Jews were concerned."[189]

This death march continued on its northwesterly journey and reached the small town of Stotzing. When the prisoners passed through, about 200 people took part in a massacre. The victims were chosen at random, and the perpetrators too were a random and varied group. "These murders were committed by SS soldiers as well as civilians," said one of the survivors. In one of the villages, Austrian farmers lined up on both sides of the road with long sticks and beat the prisoners brutally in order to spur them on as fast as possible.[190] The evacuees from the Sopron area eventually reached the town of Gramatneusiedi, where they were loaded onto a train that transported them to Mauthausen.

The death march to Mauthausen through the Styria Gau lasted about two weeks. The prisoners who were evacuated through the Lower Danube Gau were more fortunate, since their journey lasted only a few days, mostly by rail. The number of victims of these evacuations was estimated after the war as 22,000 to 23,000.[191] If we take into account that about one-third of the 35,000 Jews who labored in the border camps in Lower Danube perished before the evacuations, namely, between December 1944 and March 1945, then at least 45,000 of the 76,000 Jews handed over by the Hungarian Arrow Cross to the Germans at the end of 1944 perished in the border camps and on death marches in spring 1945. This figure does not include prisoners who died in camps in Styria because no records exist on this, nor those who died in the few weeks that the survivors spent in Mauthausen and Gunskirchen before the liberation. Even by the familiar yardsticks of the genocidal apparatus in the last weeks of the war, this was a particularly lethal operation.

That civilians were involved in the murder of prisoners during the death marches in Austria is indisputable. The authority and responsibility assigned to party leaders, Gauleiters and Kreisleiters, to supervise this evacuation activity introduced into the circle of murderers various groups that had not been involved when the Polish camps were evacuated. The Volkssturm, the civil defense militia without uniforms, received directives, which were sometimes open ended and left to their discretion, to murder prisoners. And they carried these orders out without soul-searching. Sometimes the crimes were committed by Austrian civilians even in the absence of explicit orders or on the basis of vaguely worded instructions, as was the case at the Präbichl Pass. Krenn, for example, singled out a group of several men from his unit for the liquidation operation, which he organized with great efficiency, since he was confident that they would not hesitate to take part.[192] Although he gave permission for those men who did not want to join the transport to stay behind, there are no known cases of evasion of duty, even if only a small number actually participated in the shooting. This phenomenon of voluntary participation in the killing of Jews even when it was permissible to refrain without penalty is familiar from similar cases in Poland.[193]

The Kreisleiter's motives for this large-scale massacre inevitably differed from those of the Volkssturm men. The Kreisleiter perhaps felt that it would be advisable to rid himself of as many Jews as possible before the survivors reached Mauthausen where, in any event, there was no room for them. The local residents were impelled mainly by the desire to drive out a rabble that, unfortunately, had been stranded on their doorstep in the final days of defeat. The moment problems arose or someone gained the impression that the Jews were lagging behind or even trying to escape, they were shot mercilessly. The fact that they were Jews made the task easier. In southeast Austria, humiliation and beatings administered by farmers were common occurrences. Those units usually identified with the traditional murder apparatus, namely, SS personnel, operated alongside these civilians, but they were not the sole players on the bloodstained stage of evacuation of Jewish prisoners from the border camps to Mauthausen in March–April 1945.

The readiness of civilians to participate in the slaughter of Jewish prisoners passing through their settlements deserves fuller attention. Those who confessed, such as Josef Eger, naturally cited the orders they received, but also added the reasoning behind the acts: the Jews were diseased and it was feared that if they escaped, they could infect the local population.[194] In another case, one of the Volkssturm men in the Styria area claimed that it was obvious to him that the order to shoot prisoners who tried to hide, or were incapable of marching on, came from the authorities in the Gau, even though it was not always precisely clear what the source was. Although the killing of prisoners was not always ordered explicitly and sometimes even a half-hearted instruction to avoid killing was given, the targets were prisoners, moreover Jews, who were regarded as enemies. Hence the orders were not questioned or scrutinized closely. There were, of course, also cases in which commanders of Volkssturm units instructed their men to kill Jews unhesitatingly, but often the men who carried out the murders had no need of an unequivocal instruction: they acted even in the absence of such orders.[195]

"A Dead Man Had Risen from His Grave and Walked"

The situation at Mauthausen, as noted, was catastrophic even before the Jews from the border camps began to arrive. Between January 1 and May 3, 1945, 8,734 Jewish men and women prisoners were brought in, many of them arriving from Auschwitz in January–February. They were in immeasurably worse physical condition than the other inmates. At the end of March 1,401 of the 8,081 prisoners in the sick bays in the camp were Jews.[196] These figures, however, relate only to those registered in the camp books and are far from reflecting the actual numbers of incomers.[197] The Jews who arrived from the border camps were never registered. In order to absorb the thousands of Hungarian Jews who had survived the death marches and were flooding in, 14 giant tents were erected. In mid-April Jews from the main camp, or those evacuated from large subcamps like Gusen, were also housed there. Most of them were prisoners who had come from Auschwitz several months earlier.[198]

Despite the ghastly living conditions in the camp, the situation there was still considered reasonable compared with conditions in the tent camp.

Thousands of prisoners were housed in barracks that often held more than 800 prisoners each instead of the planned 400 or 500. The food rations could not guarantee survival, but the prisoners continued to receive soup made from chard and 3.5 ounces (100 grams) of bread daily.[199] More than 4,000 people were crowded into the tents, whose actual capacity was about 2,500. Since there was not enough room for all, many simply lay outside on the muddy ground in the rain and cold of early spring. The Mauthausen tent camp was the beginning of the final chapter in the saga of evacuation and death marches of the close to 20,000 Jewish prisoners in Mauthausen at the end of April. They were all survivors of the camps and the marches, some having survived Auschwitz and its evacuation and others the Hungarian-Austrian border camps and death marches from there. However, what occurred in the tent camp was imprinted on the memories of the survivors as worse than anything they had experienced before:

> People were dying of hunger. We searched for single grains of wheat in the straw scattered on the floor of the tents. Many people totally lost their humanity, they moved about with a terrifying expression, like the living dead. They had lost all their will and their urge to live . . . there was a large pit and people defecated into it. Once one of us fell into the pit and remained standing there, half his body buried in the filth, leaning on a spade. I don't know if it was out of unwillingness or exhaustion that he did not even try to climb out.[200]

The stay in the tent camp was an experience totally detached from time, place, and reality for many of the prisoners. Since there was no longer any obligation to work, they passed the time lying aimlessly in the tents or outside them, starving, enfeebled, crawling with lice and filthy, and among piles of corpses that grew higher each day.[201] Many were totally apathetic and had lost any existential purpose: "We no longer had a sense of time. Not night, not day, you couldn't see anything any more. No sense of time and no sense of anything," as one of the survivors described the mood.[202] Starvation, despair, and the incessant struggle for a patch of space in the overcrowded tents reduced relationships to hitherto unknown depths. A bitter dispute developed between prisoners from Hungary and those from Poland or Lithuania, which deteriorated into enmity accompanied by violence. Since the Hungarians had arrived before the Jews from the main camp, it was they who seized the internal management roles. In the constant battle over every crumb of food, these positions were of considerable significance. Loss of control because of the gnawing hunger led to cases of cannibalism, in particular after bombing of the camp claimed the lives of several prisoners, and their torn corpses lay scattered near the tents or by the fences.[203]

The concentration of the Jewish prisoners in a separate camp in April 1945 was probably the direct consequence of Himmler's directive, given at a meeting in Vienna several weeks previously, and his order that this valuable resource was to be preserved at all costs. This was apparently also the reason for the evacuation of the tent camp to Gunskirchen that began in mid-April. Gunskirchen was one of the last subcamps established in the Mauthausen complex. It came into being in December 1944 in a forest near the town and consisted of several barracks for prisoners with 500 inmates and about 150 guards.[204] When it was decided to convert it into an absorption center for Jewish prisoners from Mauthausen, the non-Jewish prisoners were returned to the main camp. In the second half of April about 15,000 Jewish prisoners were transferred there from the Mauthausen tent camp. Logistically speaking, this was a strange decision. The transfer of 15,000 prisoners from the main camp to Gunskirchen, 34 miles (55 kilometers) distant, disrupted the movement of the retreating armed forces since their route crossed two important bridges over the Danube. Those in charge at Mauthausen wanted to be rid of the tent dwellers, who constituted a health hazard and a danger to all the camp inmates; hence they exerted pressure on August Eigruber, Gauleiter of Upper Austria, to order the evacuation of the Jews to Gunskirchen. It appears that Himmler's instruction that these Jews were to be preserved, even if it became evident that there was nobody to whom they could be sent and no authority able to conduct negotiations over their fate, was sufficient to launch an evacuation. Although the Jews were not sent to Gunskirchen for purposes of liquidation, as in other places, the evacuation itself claimed many victims in the course of countless incidents of murder along the route.[205]

The departure was also marked by rampant killings in the tent camp. A group of German guards proceeded from tent to tent and murdered all prisoners who appeared incapable of standing upright.[206] Along the route, some 1,500 prisoners who collapsed or lagged behind were liquidated. They were buried by inhabitants of the villages they passed.[207] In a number of cases guards fired at random into the columns of marchers in order to urge them on because of their uneasiness in the prevailing chaotic circumstances.[208] During the three days of this march, almost no food was allocated, and on those occasions when scant amounts were given out, only a few marchers received them. "We grabbed greenery, leaves, worms we found along the way," said one survivor. In other cases, prisoners succeeded in digging up potatoes in the fields and eating them raw. Sometimes villagers set out buckets of water or dry loaves of bread by the roadside. The fortunate few who snatched them were able to ease their hunger and assuage their thirst to some degree.[209]

The death march from Mauthausen to Gunskirchen, one of the last such marches, was also one of the most phantasmagoric. It was obvious to the guards that this entire journey was leading from nowhere to nowhere and that there was no underlying purpose. Prisoners noticed that the elderly guards accompanying them were almost totally indifferent to what was going on around them and to their charges. When they halted for the night the guards took out their own rations, which were also of poor quality, scraped off the mold that had accumulated on their bread due to the dampness, and threw the moldy crusts to the prisoners lying nearby. "They didn't care . . . they looked at us as if they were looking at a starving cat that sits beside a man who is eating and he throws it something and the cat darts at it and eats it." The few who continued to carry out their murderous task scrupulously were the veteran camp guards, who rode their bicycles alongside the column and behind it and killed all the marchers who were too feeble to continue.[210]

Gunskirchen was the continuation of the Mauthausen tent camp, but conditions there were even grimmer. The few barracks were not capable of housing thousands of prisoners. About 2,500 prisoners were crammed into each hut. The prisoners sprawled on the damp and muddy ground, which was not even padded with straw. The congestion was intolerable.

> We couldn't lie; there was no room to lie down. They sat us down, our knees had to be bent or spread, the next one in line in the same position . . . as if we were being packaged for the night. One was sitting between the knees of the other, and then it was night and these people, exhausted, sick, could not control their bodily functions and their orifices.[211]

Many found no space in the barracks and were forced to lie outside. Some even preferred to be outdoors, since the stink and the incessant quarrels inside maddened them. Those who were not sufficiently close to one of the openings at either end of the barracks were unable to go out in order to relieve themselves. The stink inside was indescribable:

> Everyone did it on the spot, on the spot. On top of one another. I went to sleep, in the morning there was a corpse beside me. One on top of the other, a corpse here, a corpse there. We were like that all the time. Full of lice. There were lice like ants, I brushed them off, and again I was covered in lice. Lice like ants, full, full, full.[212]

It was almost impossible to leave the filthy crowded barracks and go out into the open air. The prisoner was required to push his way through hundreds of prisoners lying or sitting crowded together, to tread on the dying who were too weak to move, and to take beatings from those who objected to being trampled on.[213] Hundreds of feeble prisoners lay outside, crawling on all fours like dogs from place to place.[214] "We simply trod on one another. Every day hundreds died there. Died of nothing. There was no need to kill people. We didn't do anything there. We waited to die."[215] Food was distributed meagerly, usually one loaf of bread for 10 to 20 prisoners and sometimes even a little soup and turnip.[216] At Gunskirchen as well, there were cases of cannibalism:

> People there died like flies. First of all, lack of food, lack of conditions and the death rate was catastrophic. There was no food and people ate human flesh. It turned out that they cut flesh off human beings and ate it. . . . They didn't give food, there was crowding and we saw that we were going to die of starvation—they simply starved us slowly. People reached a state of prostration and there was no flesh on their bodies. The people, when they were released, they were skeletons—just bones.[217]

On May 4 the last of the German guards in the camp left; they were almost all older recruits who had been assigned to the concentration camps in the last year of the war.[218] Those prisoners who were still capable of walking began to emerge from the barracks and to advance toward the approaching American forces. The first U.S. soldiers who encountered them heard from them about the camp in the nearby forest. When they approached the site they encountered the corpses of those prisoners who had tried to walk toward them but had been too weak to continue.[219] An American officer from the 71st Infantry Division, one of whose units liberated Gunskirchen in the afternoon of May 4, 1945, recorded what he saw several hours after his arrival:

> I visited the camp today. The living and dead evidence of horror and brutality beyond one's imagination was there, lying and grawling [sic] and shuffling, in stinking ankle-deep mud and human. excrement. . . . It was not possible to count the dead, but 200 emaciated corpses would be a very conservative estimate. For the most part they had died during the past two days, but there were many other rotting bodies inside the barracks beside living human beings who were too weak to move.
>
> It is practically impossible to describe in decent or printable words the state of degradation in which the German guards had permitted the camp to fall. Located in a dense patch of pine trees, well hidden from the main highway as well as from the air, the site was well suited for the slimay [sic], vermin-infected living conditions that existed there. To call the camp a pig sty would

be doing injustice to a self respected pig. The sight was appaling [*sic*] and the odor that reached you a hundred yards from the camp site was nauseating.

Traveling into the camp along a narrow wagon road was an experience in dodging the multitude of dazed men, women and children fleeing from the horrors of this living hell. The natural impulse of these people after the Americans arrived was one of hysteria—a desire to escape—to leave that place forever behind them. The road was clogged with hundreds, but many did not get far. Dozens died before they had gone but a few hundred yards from "hell hotel" prison. . . .

We entered the first buklding [*sic*] . . . which was originally built for 300 but now housed approximately 3000. Row upon row of living skeletons, jammed so closely together that it was impossible for some to turn over, even if they could have generated enough strength to do so. Those too weak to move defecated where they lay. The place was crawling with lice. A pair of feet, black in death, protruded from underneath a tattered blanket, just six inches from a haggard old Jew who was resting on his elbow and feebly attempting to move to us.

A little girl, doubled with gnawing pains of starvation, cried pitifully for help. A dead man was rotting beside her. . . . Few of those remaining in the building could stand on their feet. The earth was black and a chilled wind gave out the smell of death and filth. Small fires of straw added to the revolting odors that filled the air.[220]

On the day of liberation the Americans counted 5,419 survivors.[221] These were usually prisoners who had been unable to leave the camp on the previous day, when the guards took off. After the war, mass graves of prisoners who perished during the few days this death installation existed were found; they contained 1,220 corpses. The precise number of victims of the death installations for Jewish prisoners at Mauthausen in those last days of the war is unknown.[222]

The appearance of the prisoners who had ended their death march at the last stop, Gunskirchen, was almost indescribable. "Many of the living people looked dead. Bones covered in skin with almost no sign of flesh, sunken cheeks and deeply sunken eyes and a glassy expression, the expression of the living dead. The human visage had become monstrous, he stumbled as he walked and when he succeeded in taking a few steps, it seemed that a dead man had risen from his grave and walked," recalled one of the survivors.[223] "The skin of the survivors was loose and wrinkled, their cheeks hollow, the skin wrinkled around their expressionless, staring eyes. Their teeth were broken and rotting, protruding from their open mouths," recalled an American Jewish army physician who visited the camp.[224] Thus, as the war reached its last day, the visual distinction between the living and the dead was obliterated: that fine distinction that had existed several months previously, before the prisoners set out on the death marches, and had fostered the illusion that these people could still function as slave laborers or as hostages to the last-minute attempt of the master criminals to save themselves. The march to Mauthausen and from there to Gunskirchen demonstrated the absence of this distinction in practice.

The bodies of prisoners who died during the evacuation of Auschwitz-Birkenau lie in the snow along the main road of the camp immediately after its liberation. © USHMM, courtesy of Mark Chrzanowski.

A group of prisoners evacuated from one of the camps in the vicinity of Dachau. © Yad Vashem / Photo: Soviet soldier.

The burial of 56 prisoners massacred during the death march from Buchenwald to Grafenwald. U.S. Army Signal Corps / Photo: PFC Chapman.

The charred remains of bodies burned by the SS right before the evacuation of Ohrdruf. © USHMM, courtesy of Patricia A. Yingst.

A young German
walks by the victims
of the death march
from Flossenbürg to
Namering: 800 Russians,
French, and Czechs.
NARA.

German civilians forced to bury the victims of the Namering death march. NARA.

Above: Corpses of the prisoners
in the barn at Gardelegen.
© Yad Vashem / Photo: U.S. Army.

Right: One of the bodies burned
at Gardelegen. © Yad Vashem / Julius
Mintzer.

The burned bodies of Gardelegen prisoners before burial. © Yad Vashem / Photo: U.S. Army.

The site of the Gardelegen massacre in 1945. © Yad Vashem / Photo: Soviet soldier.

On orders of the American Army, the inhabitants of Gardelegen head out to bury the massacre victims. © USHMM, courtesy of NARA, College Park / Photo: Josef E. Von Stroheim.

The cemetery where the Gardelegen victims are buried. © Daniel Blatman, 2002.

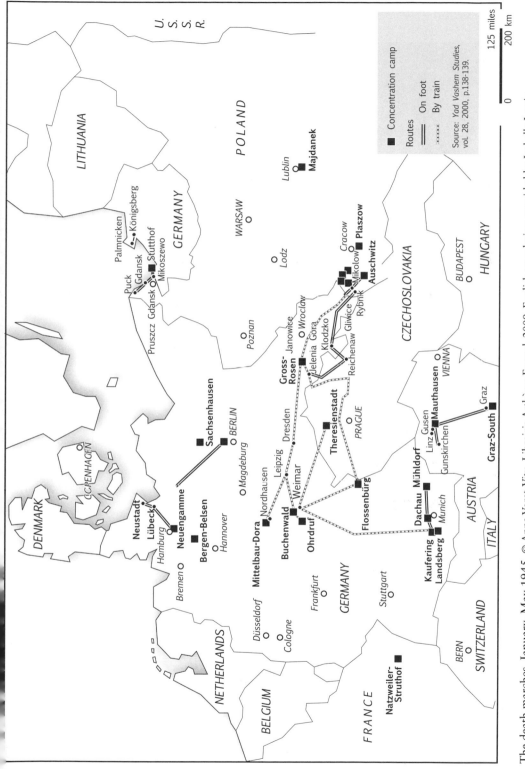

The death marches, January–May 1945. © Anne Varet-Vitu, Librairie Arthème Fayard, 2009. English translation provided by Isabelle Lewis.

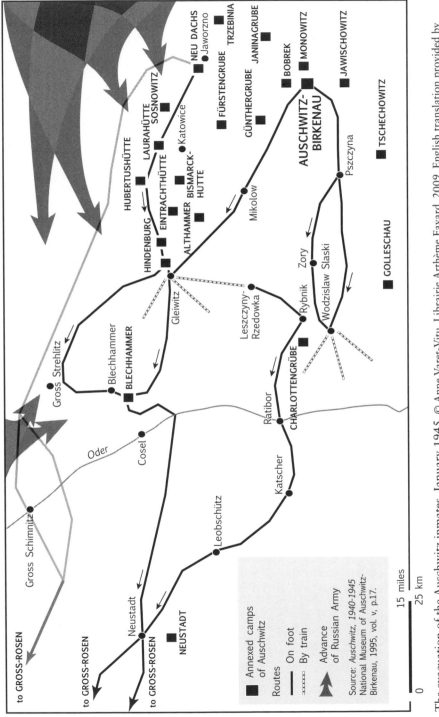

The evacuation of the Auschwitz inmates, January 1945. © Anne Varet-Vitu, Librairie Arthème Fayard, 2009. English translation provided by Isabelle Lewis.

The following labels appear on the map:

to GROSS-ROSEN

NEU DACHS
Jaworzno
TRZEBINIA
FÜRSTENGRUBE
GÜNTHERGRUBE
JANINAGRUBE
BOBREK
MONOWITZ
JAWISCHOWITZ
HUBERTUSHÜTTE
LAURAHÜTTE
SOSNOWITZ
Katowice
EINTRACHTHÜTTE
ALTHAMMER
BISMARCK-HUTTE
AUSCHWITZ-BIRKENAU
TSCHECHOWITZ
HINDENBURG
Mikolow
Pszczyna
Zory
Wodzislaw Slaski
GOLLESCHAU
Gleiwitz
Leszczyny-Rzedowka
Rybnik
Gross Strehlitz
Blechhammer
BLECHHAMMER
Ratibor
CHARLOTTENGRÜBE
Oder
Cosel
Katscher
Leobschütz
Gross Schimnitz
Neustadt
NEUSTADT
to GROSS-ROSEN
to GROSS-ROSEN
to GROSS-ROSEN

Annexed camps of Auschwitz
Routes
On foot
By train
Advance of Russian Army

Source: Auschwitz, 1940–1945
National Museum of Auschwitz-Birkenau, 1995, vol. v, p.17.

0   15 miles
    25 km

The death march of prisoners from Helmsbrechts. © Anne Varet-Vitu, Librairie Arthème Fayard, 2009. English translation provided by Isabelle Lewis.

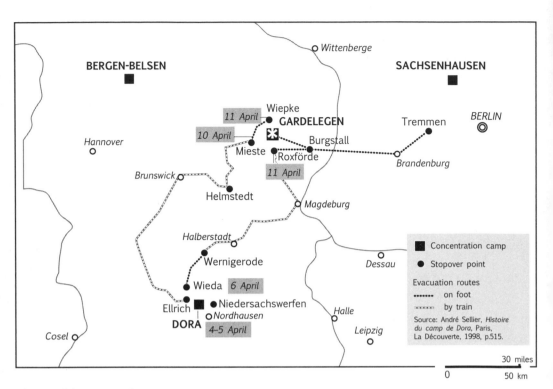

The Gardelegen tragedy. © Anne Varet-Vitu, Librairie Arthème Fayard, 2009. English translation provided by Isabelle Lewis.

PART TWO

Criminal Communities

CHAPTER SEVEN

A Society in Collapse

The mood of German society in September 1939 in no way resembled the state of mind that had prevailed in the Second Reich in August 1914. The warlike fervor that had engulfed Germany and the rest of Europe in summer 1914 was nonexistent in the fall of 1939. Before the German invasion of Poland most Germans idolized Hitler for his success in transforming Germany, rapidly and bloodlessly, into a state that wielded political power and had achieved unprecedented territorial expansion. He had liberated the Saarland, armed the Reich, annexed Austria and Sudetenland, and established the Protectorate of Bohemia and Moravia. The shame of Versailles *(Schmach von Versailles)*, as most Germans perceived it, had been expunged.

September 1939 was a different story. The invasion of Poland was about to lead to hostilities with the Western powers, and most Germans feared a recurrence of the scenario they had lived through once before, in 1914.[1] The American journalist William Shirer, who was in Berlin at the time, wrote in his diary on August 31, 1939: "Everybody against the war. People talking openly. How can a country go into a major war with a population so dead against? People also kicking about being kept in the dark. A German said to me last night: 'We know nothing. Why don't they tell us what's up?' "[2]

The atmosphere was gloomy; people were resigned to the inevitable, yet dreaded the future. The Jewish intellectual, Victor Klemperer, depicted the mood in Dresden on the outbreak of war:

> At the butcher's an old dear puts her hand on my shoulder and says in a voice full of tears: *He* has said that he will put on a soldier's coat again and be a

soldier himself, then Goering. . . . —An old gentleman, very friendly, brings the blackout order: Terrible, it's war again.[3]

The military victories in Poland did not alter this mood, since they did not improve the prospects for a political and military settlement with Great Britain and France, which could put a rapid end to the new European conflict. Even the favorable results of the campaign against Denmark and Norway did not evoke a fervent reaction. It was only after the capitulation of France and the Wehrmacht's triumphant entry into Paris in June 1940 that public opinion underwent a dramatic change. A wave of enthusiasm swept the country, and adoration of Hitler and what was seen as his unparalleled strategic and political genius reached new heights.[4] "The reputation of the Führer has risen immeasurably even among the half-hearted and grumblers, because of the tremendous successes. Clergymen who seldom bothered to address one with the 'German greeting' now greet one orally and in writing with 'Heil Hitler,' " it was reported in June 1940 from Darmstadt.[5]

"It [the conquest of Paris] was always a wish dream of millions here. And it helps wipe out the bitter memories of 1918 which have lain so long—twenty-two-years—in the German soul," wrote Shirer.[6] The glorious victory that would end the war seemed closer than ever. "[We] were the first pilots to walk down the Champs Elysées after France capitulated. We made plans to be the first ones to walk down Bond Street in London as well," thus a Luftwaffe pilot described his emotions.[7]

Almost without exception, the German population was excited at the thought of the possibilities opened up by the new German empire: the unprecedented economic potential offered by the new territories, the prospect of tempting careers in public administration and private commerce and industry, and the conviction of Germany's military and political might and unshakeable inner strength. The "New Order" of Heinrich Himmler and the SS envisaged an empire grounded on racial principles and demographic engineering. It was in its initial stages of implementation through schemes for large-scale settlement of German farmers in the areas annexed from Poland.[8]

While terror against Jews and Poles was raging in Poland, while the murder of innocent civilians was an everyday occurrence in occupied Polish cities, while hundreds of thousands of Jews were being uprooted from their homes, rounded up for forced labor, deported and imprisoned in ghettos,[9] life in Germany proceeded more or less as usual. Although blackouts, temporary shortages, and rationing cards for food and basic products were unpleasant indications that it was wartime, all these were seen as short-lived inconveniences, to be borne only until the imminent victory. The regime made every effort to maintain the semblance of prosperity; thus, for example, in summer 1940 the population of Berlin enjoyed an abundant supply of fresh vegetables, eggs, and bacon dispatched from occupied Holland and Denmark to German markets.[10] War, terror, and the atrocities in the East were far removed from the everyday life and awareness of German civilians. The morale of victors *(Siegermoral)*, as Norbert Frei called it, characterized the public mood in Germany in summer 1940.[11]

There were several reasons for this collective reaction, one of which was a reluctance to know what was really happening and an inability to gauge the true political situation. The most important reason was the fact that, for many Germans, the war had blurred the distinction between revisionist foreign policy and the Nazi *Lebensraum* plan for additional "living space" with all its genocidal implications. The military victories captured the imagination of German civilians and affected their ability to take note of what accompanied those victories. The entire society was exhilarated by the amazing successes on the battlefield. When problems began to surface in 1941, this exhilaration was replaced by anticipation and hope that the gains would soon be resumed. The day-to-day difficulties and the exhausting struggle for means of subsistence, which worsened as the war continued, particularly after the invasion of the Soviet Union—all these impaired the German people's willingness to confront the political realities. Another important factor was the propaganda and organizational effort that the regime invested in creating a national community *(Volksgemeinschaft)* which, in the early days of the war, was a vital component of internal policy and of the administration of the civilian population.

In order to create an alternative to the rigid class-ridden structure of German society, Nazism preached the theory that the sole differences between the equal individuals of the nation *(Volk)*, who were united in a racial partnership, were those stemming from achievement-related abilities rather than class affiliation, origin, or family ties. After the outbreak of war, and especially after the invasion of the Soviet Union, Nazi propaganda expounded the ideology of the *Volksgemeinschaft*: the shared destiny of battlefield and home front, the community with a single destiny *(Schicksalsgemeinschaft)*, united in the struggle for its future and its survival.[12] The Third Reich succeeded in making its presence and influence felt in wide spheres of civilian life, including the individual domain, which was naturally and intuitively resistant to any intervention from above. This success was particularly striking in the education system and in the socialization process of the young generation. It succeeded to a large extent in shaping and maneuvering the youth subculture, the creative and entrepreneurial spirit of the young generation,[13] the workplace, the rural lifestyle, and extensive areas of household management. In order to understand the inner dynamics of society in the

Third Reich, we need to examine the experience of young Germans in youth organizations, the everyday exertions and coping methods of housewives, and the processes of professional mobility in the workplace.[14]

The hopelessness of this war was not internalized for some time and not only because the regime had succeeded in making an impact on various areas of everyday life. Once the fears of 1939 had dissolved, the war was perceived for some time as a continuum of triumphs, and no objections were voiced on the home front. The man and woman in the street, if they were at all interested in knowing what was happening outside the borders of their own country, could learn about the hardships and the devastation war had brought in its wake only from the stories brought home by soldiers on leave. The war arrived on their doorsteps only in 1942, when the massive bombardment of German cities began, and at first the population did not doubt that the regime was capable of tackling the challenge. The authorities hastily repaired bomb damage and, to the best of their ability, restored normal life. But beneath the surface, there was growing fear that Germany was powerless in the face of the British and U.S. air attacks. Word of the Stalingrad catastrophe in late January 1943 came as a shock. The steps that led to the proclamation of "total war" only put the seal on what most of the German public had already realized for themselves.

Total War and Terror: 1943–1945

Twice—in 1943, and some 18 months later, in 1944—the Nazi authorities announced the institution of an emergency regime of "total war" *(totale Krieg)*. The first announcement was made on February 18, 1943, at the Berlin Sportspalast by the minister of propaganda and Gauleiter of Berlin, Josef Goebbels, shortly before the military debacle at Stalingrad and the surrender of the 6th Army, commanded by General Friedrich Paulus, to the Red Army.

"Wollt ihr den totalen Krieg?" (Do you want total war?) was one of Goebbels's most important speeches. On a platform decorated with swastika-emblazoned flags stood a giant banner that read, *Totaler Krieg—Kürzester Krieg* (Total war—briefest war). According to contemporary press reports, Goebbels addressed an audience of 15,000. After starting out by praising the heroism of the troops in the front line, he declared that he wanted to present a realistic and true picture of the situation, since the German people wanted to know the truth. For two hours he attacked Germany's enemies, in particular those who claimed that the confidence of the German people in their Führer was waning, that their spirit had been broken by the defeat in the East, and that the nation no longer believed that

Hitler was leading them to the ultimate victory. A special section of the speech was devoted to an attack on international revolutionary Jewry, which was sowing terror and anarchy, hunger and distress. The threat was intensifying, Goebbels declared; it had already brought the Anglo-Saxon world and Russia to its feet, and it was now planning to subdue the entire European continent.[15]

Before listing the anticipated changes in the lives of German citizens, Goebbels stressed the effectiveness and advantage of these steps. Employing his tried and tested rhetorical techniques, he reiterated the slogan that had been chosen to lead this campaign: "total war is the briefest." Then he moved on to discuss the popular support he sensed on all sides, particularly the pressures being exerted by the working class on the government to adopt tougher internal measures. He denounced people who were wasting their time in places of entertainment that could only provide material satisfactions, and who were concerned only with the needs of their stomachs, who shopped in luxury stores and purchased luxury goods. He did not spare the bureaucracy in various state institutions which, he claimed, were doing nothing and squandering time on absurd and useless tasks. His wrath was also directed at haute couture stores and beauty parlors and other places where the prosperous and influential whiled away their time. All these places of frivolous entertainment would disappear, Goebbels cried. Only cultural institutions that served the needs of the wider public, such as theaters, cinemas, and concert halls, would endure.

Goebbels went on to detail the steps to be taken: tightening of belts in the economy, changes in the labor system, the referral of new workers to the armament industry in order to free more manpower for service in the front line, and the introduction of compulsory labor for women. At the climax of his speech, he put 10 questions to his mass audience, to which they responded with roars of support. His questions related to the readiness of the nation to continue making sacrifices for the sake of the war effort, their desire for total war, their total confidence in the Führer, their readiness to reinforce the eastern front with manpower and military equipment, their consent to the introduction of compulsory labor for women, and their uncompromising commitment to doing everything possible for the army, for victory. In order to inflame his audience even further, Goebbels declared that the British and American press were reporting that the German people were not willing to undertake the effort and the sacrifice that the war demanded; he urged the masses to prove to Germany's enemies that the opposite was true. The impassioned crowd, almost all of them known supporters of the Nazi Party who had been carefully selected as the suitable audience for the event, responded with hysterical declarations of support.[16]

The theory of total war was not invented in 1943; its roots lay in the modern theories of warfare developed after World War I. As a result of the expansion of military capacity on the ground and in the air, and the increase in the potential power of fighter planes, it was posited that the battlefield where armies clashed was no longer the sole arena of hostilities between warring countries; all of the enemy's territory was a battlefield.[17] In the second half of the 1930s the destructive power of aerial bombardments, as demonstrated during the Spanish Civil War, strengthened this strategic theory.[18] In 1935 Erich Ludendorff, renowned World War I military leader and Hitler's associate in the failed putsch of November 1923, published his book *Der totale Krieg*. In it he wrote that total war called for total mobilization and a *totale Staat,* a situation whereby the army and the people *(Volk)* constituted a single integrated unit, supplying basic requirements and military needs. In order to achieve this objective, what was required was *totale Politik* as well as a wide-ranging propaganda machine that would convey this message to the people. In total war, he wrote, the most important factor, one that would decide the fate of the war, was the morale of the people and their sense of unity. Only strong morale and national cohesion could endow the people with the ability to support the battling armed forces and to work for the army.[19] Faith in victory was the key to overcoming all the difficulties stemming from war and from the action taken by the enemy. This unity of morale and morality, according to his national *(volkisch)* theories, could be achieved only by a people that maintained strict biological hygiene and racial purity.[20]

The definition of a state of total war is naturally open to different interpretations. Several factors need to be taken into account before decisions are taken to impose far-reaching changes on the lifestyle of a nation in order to adapt it to the demands of the circumstances. First among these factors is the situation on the battle fronts, but also important are the ability of the economy to face the challenges of waging war and the ability to mobilize the population for this purpose. In the first years of the war these conditions clearly did not exist. The Wehrmacht's blitzkrieg in 1939–1941, which brought resounding victories, fostered the illusion that the home front and the civilian population were not vulnerable and hence were not required to make any special effort.

The era of rapid victories with few casualties came to an end in the middle of the first year of the war in the Soviet Union. Despite the Wehrmacht's impressive military gains and the occupation of vast Soviet territories, a huge number of German soldiers paid with their lives for these triumphs once the fighting turned fiercer and bloodier. By March 1942, 1,107,830 of them had been killed, some 35 percent of the total German military force that invaded the Soviet Union on June 22, 1941. The percentage of loss of equipment, in particular tank and heavy equipment, was also high. It was manifest that in order to cope with this military burden and to win the war in 1942, extraordinary efforts would be required.[21]

Goebbels soon awoke from the euphoria of the victorious campaign in the East in summer 1941[22] and by the second half of 1942 apparently contemplated declaring a state of economic emergency and total mobilization of society for the war effort. At the end of December 1942 he discussed this plan with Martin Bormann, head of the Party Chancellor's Office (Chef der Parteikanzlei) and one of the individuals most closely associated with Hitler. In early January 1943 Goebbels spoke openly about this matter with senior officials of his ministry.[23] He claimed that "the German population will not blame us if they are forced to wear rags for several months; but they will never forgive us if they are forced to be beggars all their lives."[24] However, the plan was not put into practice before the crisis generated by the Wehrmacht's military debacle at Stalingrad.

Steps that would dramatically change the lifestyle of the German population could not be taken without coordination between several elements and several highly influential individuals who controlled the German economy, industry, and manpower resources. Both Albert Speer, who was in charge of armaments, and the heads of the Wehrmacht were interested mainly in stepping up the recruitment of manpower for military production purposes. Robert Ley, head of the German Labor Front (Deutsche Arbeitfront), and Fritz Saukel, who was in charge of recruiting manpower, wielded centralized powers on these matters. In light of the internal relations in the Führer's headquarters in early 1943, it was impossible to introduce any far-reaching changes on the home front without the cooperation of Martin Bormann. From 1941 onward, Bormann held sway, to all practical purposes, over the power centers of the party through his position in the Chancellor's Office, and in April 1943 he was also appointed secretary to the Führer (Sekretar des Führers). He was Hitler's closest confidant in the later years of the war, and Goebbels, who was familiar with the internal balance of power within the Nazi leadership, arrived at an agreement with him at a meeting in late December 1942, with Hitler's knowledge and sanction. They concurred on the need to reduce the standard of living of the German population, in particular the more prosperous elements, in order to mobilize manpower and equipment for the war effort.[25]

Goebbels, who was a close observer of the mood of German society, understood only too well that, in the first stage, the path to maximal mobilization of population resources lay through propaganda. If the war was to be defined as a life-and-death struggle *(Krieg auf Tod und Leben)*, the public must be primed to receive it by means of effective information. In January 1943 he began to prepare public opinion for the formal proclamation of a state of total war. Thus, for example, in an article he published on January 24, 1943, in *Das Reich,* under the heading *Die Optik des Kriegs* [The optics of the war] he expounded his view that, in the prevailing situation, changes were necessary in the structure of society. The goal he set was both total recruitment for the sake of victory and the psychological transformation of individuals, but he also wanted to achieve total remolding of society and to create a "fighting community" *(kämpfende Gemeinschaft)*. In the article, he wrote of the need for radical changes in the individual lifestyle, namely, frugality, renunciation of luxury and self-indulgence, and mobilization for the sake of the war economy.[26]

On January 30, 1943, Goebbels read out a brief statement from Hitler at the traditional meeting at the Berlin Sportpalast on the anniversary of the Nazis' ascendance to power. It was a very important traditional event that Hitler had exploited several times in the past in order to issue statements of major significance on foreign policy and policies toward Jews. On this particular date, when the capitulation of the 6th Army at Stalingrad was imminent, Hitler refused to appear in public and agreed only to allow Goebbels to read out his speech. Among other things, it stated that "the heroic struggle of our soldiers on the banks of the Volga must serve as a warning to each and every one of us to act to the maximum in the struggle for the liberty of Germany and the future of our people, and, in effect, for the preservation of our continent in general." Goebbels added his own interpretation of the Führer's statement: "From the expanses and the depths of our nation there arises the cry in our ears calling for the most comprehensive efforts of total war."[27]

Hitler reiterated these principles of total war to a large degree at a meeting on February 7, 1943, with Gauleiters and Reichsleiters. He listed the main points of the measures that Goebbels had asked him recently to approve, but that he had refused adamantly to do until the defeat at Stalingrad. The crisis that Germany was suffering was mainly psychological and must be overcome by similar means, he declared. The Gauleiters were exhorted to mobilize in order to start a regime of cutbacks, abolition of the excessive rights of privileged sectors, and introduction of austerity and sacrifice.[28]

Whether or not Hitler saw Goebbels's February 18 speech in advance, it is unquestionable that the main points it raised were acceptable to him. The guidelines had already been agreed on.[29] At its core was an aggressive propaganda campaign, accompanied by measures aimed at transforming Germany into a mobilized society, fighting with ideological fervor to overcome an enemy that threatened its survival in the East.

Goebbels, however, was hoping for more than delegated authority in the sphere of propaganda and recruitment of the masses for total war. In light of the impressive propaganda impact of his speech, he wanted Hitler to give him a range of executive powers that would grant him influence over various internal sectors, mainly in the sphere of the economy and mobilization of manpower for the war effort. To a large extent, he was aspiring to the status of a quasi-chancellor for the home front, a position that would have undermined some of the authority wielded by others, such as Minister of the Interior Wilhelm Frick, Minister of Armaments Albert Speer, Reichsmarschall Herman Göring, head of the German Labor Front Robert Ley, and General Plenipotentiary for Labor Deployment Fritz Sauckel. However, it was not only the hostility, suspicion, and Byzantian power struggles characteristic of the Reich leadership that hampered implementation of centralization and of rational administration of manpower and economic resources.[30] Hitler himself, who agreed as to the important role of propaganda and psychological impact in mobilizing of national resources for "total war," and the need to reform the manpower system, refused to assign these powers to the propaganda minister, mainly because of his reluctance to surrender an iota of his own close control over every aspect of national life.

By 1942 the war was having a severe impact on the urban working class, and the bombardment of German towns and cities placed an additional burden on their ability to face everyday hardships. The shortage of basic commodities was now common, and economic distress was evident in the poorer urban quarters long before it was felt in villages and small towns. British intelligence reports indicated that unrest was beginning to spread through various sectors of German society, notably among farmers and women who were being forced to report for work in industry. Hitler feared that increasing the burden would affect the popularity of the regime and aggravate social and class tensions.[31] But his main concern was that measures as drastic as those Goebbels wanted to introduce would generate discontent that could endanger the stability of the regime. Hitler was firmly against imposing drastic cutoffs, reducing of living standards, mobilizing women by coercive means for industrial production, and all other emergency measures. The threatening shadow of a return to 1918 conditions haunted him. His nightmare was the thought that if dissatisfaction and internal tension grew, they would once again foster conditions conducive to revolutionary activity. His greatest trauma, the conviction that enemies within had stabbed the nation in the back, was one of the cornerstones of his political theory.[32]

Hitler saw no reason to introduce sweeping and radical measures on the home front, even if the situation called for a draconic state of emergency, as implied by the declaration of total war. Even after Stalingrad he persisted in his absolute belief in the final victory, his confidence in his military and political skills that were supported by Divine Providence, and his optimistic view that his will and personality could transform the debacle into a future military triumph. In any case, all matters pertaining to the political and economic organization of society at home were of scant concern to him in 1943, and he preferred to leave the constant squabbles between his ministers and advisers permanently unresolved.

Hence, the main impact of Goebbels's speech was confined to the propaganda sphere, and it was perceived as an official proclamation that the war had moved on to another stage, which called for new measures.[33] SD reports reveal that by summer 1942 quite a number of Germans had begun to realize that the war against the Soviet Union was going in a disturbing direction. From 1939 these reports, which examined the public attitude toward the war, were composed scrupulously on the initiative of Otto Ohlendorf, head of Hauptabteilung (Department) III in the RSHA and later commander of Einsatzgruppe D. They were a vital instrument in examining the mood of the population regarding the war and the regime, although Hitler and Goebbels tended to criticize them on the grounds that they were drawing a dark picture *(Schwarzmalerei)*.[34] By early 1943 most German civilians were aware that the war had reached a critical watershed and that victory was far out of reach, if at all attainable. They preferred to hear the blunt truth about the situation and to know how to prepare for what was to come. In this respect, Goebbels's speech was, for many Germans, a sign that greater hardships lay ahead.[35]

Goebbels's announcement of the closing down of bars and luxury hotels, a ban on gambling on horse races, compulsory recruitment for essential labor, restriction on the employment of domestic servants, and cancellation of workers' vacations did not leave a strong impression on wide sectors of the public. In any case, in winter 1943 their daily diet was restricted to potatoes, red cabbage, a meager quantity of meat from time to time, and bread. Victor Klemperer referred to the proclamations only in passing. He was, on the other hand, greatly troubled by another threat implicit in Goebbels's speech:

> But when I think of Goebbel's speech of February 18 in the Berlin Sportpalast, then I take Richter's opinion and warning completely seriously, Richter gave me the *Dresdener Anzeiger* of the nineteenth with the text of the speech . . . the speech contains a threat to proceed against the Jews, who are guilty of everything with the "most draconian and radical measures" if the foreign powers do not stop threatening the Hitler government because of the Jews.[36]

Klemperer understood only too well the Reich leaders' administration methods and priorities. The ban on gambling on horses encountered a num-

ber of obstacles because of the pressure brought to bear by party functionaries, who enjoyed considerable profits from this activity. Even Hitler was
forced to devote attention to this particular weighty issue at the height of the
military crisis.[37] However, the first stage of the new state of emergency that
Goebbels initiated was the deportation of the last of the Jews in Germany,
including 7,000 who were still working in Berlin in February 1943. This was
a step on the path to realizing the goal of creating a militant, homogeneous,
and racially pure community whose members would stand shoulder to
shoulder, ready to withstand those enemies who wished to destroy it.[38]

The dimensions of the military catastrophe were rapidly becoming evident in 1943. The entry of the United States into the war and the inexhaust-
ible resources it brought with it to the Allied war effort; the change of fortunes in the North African campaign and the loss of the foothold in Tunisia;
the Allied landing in Italy and the deposal of Mussolini, together with the
situation in the East—all these were clear indicators of the direction the war
was taking. Aerial bombardments of Germany were increasing. In late July
1943 the RAF executed a series of raids on Hamburg, the worst Germany
had experienced so far. Giant fires destroyed whole areas of the city, and there
were 40,000 dead. Everyday life in the Reich had become a hell.[39] Toward the
end of 1943, there was a growing threat of an Allied landing on the western
front, and Hitler and senior Wehrmacht officers were convinced that it would
occur in spring or summer 1944.

Despite all these signs, as late as June 1944, about a month before the assassination attempt on his life, Hitler told Goebbels that he was still not
convinced that all the harsh measures demanded by the total war situation
should be adopted, and emphasized his conviction that obstacles could be
overcome by accepted methods. He preferred to continue to wait but promised that, should conditions change, he would not hesitate to sanction
strong-arm methods.[40] The abortive assassination attempt of July 20, 1944,
changed the picture dramatically. On July 22, at a meeting of several ministry heads and other senior officials, Chef der Reichskanzler (Head, Reich
Chancellary) Hans Heinrich Lammers proposed that Goebbels be granted
wide powers to carry out total reorganization of internal life in Germany.
The ways of achieving this aim had been detailed in a memo Goebbels submitted to Hitler two days before the assassination attempt.[41] On July 23 the
leading figures of the regime met at Hitler's headquarters in Eastern Prussia,
and there the Führer approved the new powers to be held by his minister of
propaganda.[42]

Goebbels's role in the rapid foiling of the plot to kill Hitler and stage a
coup in the Reich[43] persuaded Hitler to appoint his faithful minister of
propaganda "Reich Authority for the Total War Effort" on July 25. On the

following day, in a radio address to the nation, Goebbels proclaimed, for the second time, full national mobilization for total war.[44] This time German civilians clearly felt the changes. Life in Germany, which was being conducted in the shadow of aerial attacks and constant severe shortages, took a new turn.

In summer 1944 the familiar ideological basis for total mobilization of the nation for the coming self-destructive struggle remained unchanged. The National Socialist vision was set against world Jewry, which was said to be behind an implausible alliance between Anglo-American capitalism and Soviet Bolshevism.[45] By the end of August 1944 Goebbels had taken a series of steps, some in collaboration with Fritz Sauckel. All factories working for civilian needs were required to slash manpower and to close down nonessential production lines. The same order was given to financial institutions, such as banks and insurance companies. The workers rendered jobless were to be redirected to the armaments industry. Students at universities and high school pupils were also assigned to the armaments industry. The objective was to recruit several hundred thousand workers for the war economy. The maximum age for women workers was raised to 45, and all women from 17 to 45 were required to join the war effort. The regime hoped that in this way it would succeed in recruiting more than 900,000 women. All forced laborers who were being employed in service tasks, including servants, nursemaids, and cleaners, were to be redeployed in industry. Their places would be taken by older German men and women, who were not able to work in industry for health reasons or due to unsuitability.

Far-reaching changes also occurred in cultural life. Artists of all kinds, musicians, painters, and stage artists, were required to report for work in the armaments factories. As a consequence, art schools, municipal orchestras, and theaters were closed. A special edict stipulated that the character of public life was to be adapted to the needs of total war. The result was a ban on lavish receptions, festivals, gallery openings, and large-scale ceremonies. Some 30,000 people who had worked in various cultural institutions were directed to the war effort. The number of public service employees was drastically curtailed. Such vital services as the post and telephone were reduced in scope and now became cumbersome. The posts of public archivists and municipal officials were cut, thereby affecting the public's access to basic services. The number of newspapers was reduced, and their staffs were reassigned to war work. In August 1944 all vacations in the public sector were canceled, and the working week was extended to 60 hours.[46]

However, in summer 1944 Goebbels hoped to institute a revolution of much greater scope. He wanted to create a socioeconomic reality based on unique wartime socialism *(Kriegssozialismus)* wherein all class and social borders would be obliterated and the bonds that united society would be strengthened, thanks to a common ideological goal. He believed that the heavy burden being borne by German society, and the common suffering caused by the casualties battlefront and the deaths and damage at home due to carpet bombing by the Allies, would help to promote this new social solidarity. In an article published in June 1944 in *Der Reich,* Goebbels described the new society emerging under the trauma of bombardments, a society liberating itself from the burdens of civilization *(Ballast der Zivilisation)* and creating a new purged, purified, and truer social order. Because of the aerial bombing, Goebbels declared, a new society was being created, devoid of social tensions and imbued with a unique sense of shared destiny.[47] The theory Ludendorff had expounded in the 1930s regarding the existential need for social cohesion based on racial purity in a state of total war is clearly discernible in the theories of the propaganda minister. In any event, public shock in the wake of the abortive assassination attempt against the head of state at a time when the country was fighting for its survival facilitated the introduction of a draconic emergency regime.[48] From past experience, which had taught him that any worsening of the military situation led to radicalization of anti-Jewish policies, Klemperer considered that in July 1944 "there was a simultaneous possibility, if not probability, that we would be butchered in the course of evacuations."[49]

By its final year of existence when it was fighting for its life, the Third Reich had lost all resemblance to the Weimar Republic, with its rich and exciting cultural life, its art, theater, and music, which had flourished until the late 1930s. Between fall 1944 and the end of the war aerial bombardments destroyed 12 percent of the country's economic infrastructure and approximately one quarter of the homes. Nearly 1.11 million soldiers were killed on the two fronts between August 1944 and the end of January 1945, the worst month of the year casualty-wise: 451,742 German troops were killed that month.[50] More than 10 million refugees from Eastern Prussia, Silesia, and the Balkans inundated the ruined German cities and the rural areas, creating an insoluble humanitarian problem because of the shortage of housing and food supplies.[51] Germany became a drab Spartan country, moldering and destitute, the predominant landscape of its towns and cities now consisting of heaps of debris. It was a state whose blood was being let on the altar of a hopeless attempt to survive under fanatic leaders who were detached from reality.

The waning of faith in the war and the growing evidence that many Germans now blamed their leaders for the catastrophes that had beset the country were very tangible dangers for the rulers.[52] The heavy aerial bombings and the shortage of suitable air-raid shelters contributed to the mood of mistrust and the sense of alienation. SD reports indicated that in the towns and cities, as well as in the countryside, the population feared that soon there would be no buildings fit for human habitation.[53] This mistrust grew in the winter months and the early spring of 1945. The hostility toward the Nazi Party, its political functionaries, and their propaganda messages could no longer be ignored.[54] And yet that same society continued the bloodletting for many months until the final capitulation.

Hans Mommsen dwelt on the factors that, in his estimation, influenced the transformation of Germany in the final years of the war into a society fighting a hopeless and deadly war with inexplicable tenacity. As he perceived it, as long as Hitler was alive, it was impossible to put in motion a move to accept the conditions the Allies stipulated to end the war. Goebbels's central position in the leadership after July 1944, the establishment of the Volkssturm several months later, and the conversion of the Gauleiters into commissars for Protection of the Reich—all these symbolized the direction in which the Nazi leadership was propelling German society. The party reverted to the days of the "period of struggle" *(Kampfzeit)* of the early 1920s. It was assumed that the weaknesses of German society and the military disasters resulted from the fact that bureaucrats or skeptical and unreliable officers had taken over the leadership of the state and the army. In order to restore the nation's fighting capacity and faith in victory, the party needed to take over all powers. It alone was capable of making a radical change and mobilizing the will and faith of the masses. It was precisely the collapse of the state apparatus due to the military defeats, the advance of enemy forces, and the growing chaos that enabled extreme elements within the party, the SS, and the Gestapo to take control of systems that were in a state of dissolution and through them to organize mass mobilization. All this was entirely in line with Hitler's profound conviction that the entire war situation could be reversed through resoluteness, faith in ultimate victory, and unconditional readiness to die for the sake of the ideology represented by the party.[55]

Internal terror accompanied by savage anarchy now prevailed in everyday life in those territories as yet unoccupied by the Allies, particularly in the West. This terror intensified in early spring 1945. On February 15 Hitler ordered all state apparatuses, and in particular the SS, the police, and the Nazi Party, to take firm action against any attempt to sabotage Germany's fighting power. The intention was to liquidate anyone suspected of shirking a task and spreading demoralization or defeatism, whether civilians or soldiers. Those heads of Volkssturm units in small towns who refused to continue resisting, thereby condemning their home areas to total destruction by American gunfire, were tried and hung summarily by party activists.[56] In

Franken thousands of Germans were executed in spring 1945 in this fashion. In various places, in particular on the western front, military or police personnel fired into the homes of civilians who flew white flags in anticipation of the American occupation.[57] In rural areas the Gestapo hunted down and arrested those suspected of committing crimes against the racial laws by sheltering forced laborers *(Zwangsarbeiter)*. This threat heightened the atmosphere of disintegration and despair among many German civilians.[58] The more fanatic supporters of the regime; frustrated soldiers who had deserted or been cut off from their units; gangs of slave laborers and criminal elements—all these engaged in robbery and looting.[59] Caught between the desire to escape and thus survive the relentless heavy bombardment of their homes and fear of falling victim to the long arm of the party, Germans were trapped in a morass of violence, disorder, and fatalism. For all these reasons individuals retreated into their own private world, trying to do whatever possible to protect their immediate families or communities. Many lost interest in the state and in wider society, seeing themselves as unwilling victims. Economic activity was almost entirely at a standstill, and people worked only to ensure minimal survival. Totally disconnected from the system at large,[60] they clung to life *(überleben)* in order to survive the nightmare months until the war came to an end.[61] But this dogged adherence to life often led them to adopt brutal and murderous defensive measures toward those elements perceived as threats to the integrity and safety of the family and the community.

The Murder of Foreign Slave Laborers

At the end of September 1944 there were close to 4 million forced laborers in Germany. The interminable bombardment of urban industrial concentrations created a new reality for the workers. The spreading chaos led to slowdowns and sometimes to total cutoff of food supplies to the camps where they were housed. In summer 1944 the phenomenon of foreigners escaping their workplaces and roaming unsupervised in constant search of food was increasingly widespread. They moved in gangs, often violent in character, and found shelter mainly in the debris of ruined and deserted buildings. They were a major factor in the burgeoning urban black markets and created the infrastructure for the development of a new underworld, composed of local Germans and slave laborers, mainly from the East.

In the atmosphere of uncertainty and collapse in the final months of the war, foreigners, whether male or female, were seen as an additional threat. These aliens were not necessarily associated with the underworld and with illegal or violent action. Even a group of 25 Russian women who had been employed in a concern near Leipzig and were evacuated from there to South Bavaria found themselves coping with the alienation and hostility of Germans. These women, some under 20, had been abandoned in a village near Rosenheim by a Swedish engineer who was employed by the Germans. They tried to enter the town in search of a haven until the American forces arrived:

> The people of the village would not let us in. We went to the mayor. Also to the *Lagerführer* because there was a *Lager* in that village, but neither the *Lagerführer* nor the mayor would take us in. We sat on the street with the little belongings that we still had. We were all wet. It poured, but still our pleading was of no avail, and since I was the senior among them I had to go plead everywhere while the whole party sat on the street and wept. . . .
>
> And still they didn't want to have anything to do with us. We remained there still the whole day on the street in the rain. Time and again we went to the mayor and pleaded. Finally we asked him to give us at least shelter in the school building. So he told us he expects a great deal of military men and the school already has been billeted. All houses are already billeted. There is no room for us, for twenty-two people.[62]

The growing number of foreign laborers wandering without supervision was of great concern to the Gestapo. It was feared in particular that escaping slave laborers, clustered in gangs that sometimes resorted to violence, were liable to sabotage fighting efforts on the German home front. Although there may have been a few among the escaping or abandoned slave laborers with political backgrounds, their main objective was to obtain food and survive until the end of the war. At the end of 1944 Cologne became the focal point of this phenomenon. As the front approached from the West and more and more slave laborers were evacuated there, gang activity increased. Also concentrated in the city at the time were quite a few Gestapo and SS personnel who had been transferred there from Paris or Brussels after the liberation of those cities by the Allies. Outbursts of violence began to occur between the gangs, mostly from the East, and the SS. In early 1945 gang members were arrested and executed. This marked the beginning of a campaign against foreign forced laborers, which in March–April 1945 spread to other places in Germany.[63]

In the final months of the war, the forced laborers, in particular those who had been detained in "labor education camps" (Arbeitserziehungslager— AEL), were one of the main groups marked out by security elements as potential dangers. There were about 200 such camps in Germany, and, unlike the concentration camps, which were under the WVHA's responsibility, they were administered and supervised by the Gestapo. Most of the inmates were slave laborers caught committing various crimes, in particular shirking work, theft, or maintaining forbidden ties with the German population. Allied POWs were also sent to these camps, as were German citizens, although the number of the latter decreased toward the end of the war.[64]

In the last months of the war, the inmates of these camps fell victim to a series of brutal killings that recalled the occurrences in the concentration camps, though on a totally different scale. In fall 1944 the Gestapo in the towns where these detention centers were located faced the problem of what to do with the prisoners. It was feared that escaping prisoners would perpetrate violent crimes against the civilian population. In September 1944 discussions were held on this matter in Düsseldorf. Himmler issued a clear directive to the effect that the camps for foreign laborers were not to be left standing and must be evacuated before the enemy arrived. Rudolf Batz, the last commander of the Dortmund SD, said after the war that there were explicit instructions to evacuate all forced laborers from camps "for the security of the fighting units and to protect the civilian population."[65] In those camps where preparations were made for evacuation, careful selection took place, and lists of prisoners earmarked for liquidation were drawn up. The criteria for selecting the victims were not entirely straightforward and in any event did not apply only to workers from the East, since almost all nationalities were selected. Most were Russian and French, but others were Belgian, Dutch, Italian, Polish, Portuguese, Hungarian, and even Swiss.[66]

Between October 25, 1944, and early March 1945 the killing of prisoners was carried out in AEL camps in the Cologne area. The last killing occurred on March 1, 1945, as the Allied forces reached the outskirts of the city. All in all, some 300 forced laborers were murdered in Cologne,[67] and systematic slaughter of forced laborers also took place in Dortmund. At least 14 Russian forced laborers were murdered in one of the AEL camps on February 4. On March 7 another group of about 30 Russian workers were taken to a nearby forest and liquidated. A few days later a further 15–20 laborers were killed, on March 30, 42 more, and on April 7 an additional 60. The wave of murders in Dortmund continued right up to April 9, the day the American forces entered the city. Foreign forced laborers were liquidated by the Gestapo or the Kripo in other cities as well. On April 5 the Hanover Gestapo perpetrated a wide-scale massacre of 154 American and British POWs in one of the AEL camps. The POWs, most of them in civilian clothes, were taken from the camp in two transports to the Seehorst cemetery outside town. A large pit was dug in the cemetery and they were lowered into it in groups of 15 and shot by the Gestapo troops, who were standing round it.[68] The total number of victims of the selective massacre of forced laborers in AEL camps under Gestapo administration was estimated at 1,000.[69]

This wave of murders was the consequence of the political and security situation, mainly in the western areas of Germany, which had been a combat zone since early 1945. By March of that year there were large concentrations of forced laborers in those areas and the food shortages, the highways clogged with retreating Wehrmacht units, and the general pandemonium impelled many of them to escape and hide in towns as well as in the forests and the countryside. There they constructed flimsy camps, foraged for food in local farms, and awaited the liberating armies. Such was the situation near Arnsberg in the Westfalen-Sud Gau, where thousands of forced laborers wandered the area, some on their way east, others simply hiding and waiting. The local security authorities were uneasy, for they were convinced that the escapees would take part in resistance activities against the German civilian population as soon as they felt sufficiently confident after the enemy forces arrived.[70]

A 600-man unit of operators of the German secret weapon, the ZV2 rocket, was stationed at the time in the Arnsberg area in a forest near Warstein. Between 800 and 1,000 forced laborers from the East were also in the vicinity at the time. The unit commander was the SS General Dr. Hans Kammler, an engineer. Seeing the laborers as he drove through the district in his car, he declared that everything possible should be done to rid the area of this dangerous horde, who were wandering without supervision in the midst of a civilian population. He was heard saying that these people would be compelled at a certain stage to take violent action against the German population because they needed to adopt the guise of antifascist fighters if they wanted to be accepted back into their home societies and regimes. Apart from this, he said, there were serious food shortages, and as long as the rabble lingered or passed through, they would be consuming vital food supplies that were intended first and foremost for the German population.[71]

It seems that Kammler's claims about the danger posed by the forced laborers at Warstein, many of them women and children, fell on responsive ears. On March 20, 1945, an *Exekutionskommando* force (murder squad) was formed hastily, consisting of men from the rocket unit. The force entered a nearby military installation that had been converted into a temporary center for foreign laborers, and brought out 14 men, 56 women, and one 6-year-old in his mother's arms. These laborers were loaded onto trucks, driven out of town, and murdered. The next day the action was repeated. The force chose 80 laborers, this time apparently only young men who were identified with certainty as laborers from the East. They were taken out in groups of 15 to 20 by the soldiers, murdered, and, like the first group, buried in a mass grave. By the time this wave of slaughter gained momentum, Kammler was no longer in the vicinity. This did not prevent repetition of the crime several days later when 35 men, 21 women, and 1 child were murdered. In total, at least 208 forced laborers from the East were massacred in these few days.[72]

These killings and the murder of prisoners during the evacuation of concentration camps share several similarities. The ideological aspect seems to have been similar. The foreign laborers who roamed unsupervised through bombed cities or rural areas often resembled camp inmates. They were dressed in rags, starving and filthy, lacked papers attesting to their legal status since most of them had fled their workplaces, and were sometimes even armed. Although they had no political aspirations or particular urge to take their revenge on German civilians, they often took the law into their own hands and acted violently, particularly when searching for food. The predominance among them of laborers from the East, in particular Russians, heightened the suspicions of the local population. These people represented everything that Nazi ideology had warned against: the demonic threat posed by a violent and inferior race, the Slavs, the Asians, and the Bolsheviks who had come out of the East to infiltrate Germany's towns and cities.

However, there was an obvious difference between these laborers and the camp prisoners. The camp inmates who were evacuated were in immeasurably worse physical condition; they were so feeble and emaciated that their wretched appearance evoked compassion. By the time they reached residential areas, most of them had spent weeks on death marches since the previous summer or winter. They could scarcely stand and were certainly unarmed, and there were almost always guards with them who did not hesitate to liquidate them mercilessly and without rhyme or reason. And yet German civilians considered them a threatening element, sometimes even more so than the foreign workers.

The Massacre at Celle: "To Cleanse Our Forest of Communists"

Celle, a town with a population of 65,000, located some 22 miles (35 kilometers) northeast of Hanover, was no different from other towns in northern Germany in the last months of the war. It was bombed by American aircraft for the first time on February 22, 1945. By early April it was evident to the townspeople that Celle was about to fall into British or U.S. hands and that there was no danger of Soviet occupation. The few small army units stationed there were not equipped to defend the town against the occupiers. On April 8 there was no unusual turmoil, no panic-stricken flight of civilians, and no significant fear of air raids, inasmuch as the town contained no large industrial concerns or important army bases.[73]

On April 7 the inmates of Salzgitter-Bad and Salzgitter-Drutte, two sub-camps of Neuengamme located near Salzgitter, not far from Braunschweig, were evacuated. At the end of March there had been 2,862 men and 472 women in the two camps, from almost all the occupied countries. Most were Russians, Poles, and Ukrainians, but there were other nationalities too: Belgian, Dutch, Czech, Yugoslav, Hungarian, Italian, Lithuanian, and others. Some of the Polish prisoners and almost all the Hungarians were Jews. On April 5 preparations began for the evacuation of Drutte, and on the night of April 7–8 the camp was vacated.[74] The camp guards were particularly jittery, and some of them fired over the heads of the prisoners as they boarded the train in order to urge them to move faster. At the same time, some of the "block elders" prepared the prisoners for departure and told them to take whatever they could, especially clothes.[75]

These evacuees were joined by inmates of two additional camps: Salzgitter-Watenstedt and Salzgitter-Leinde. On March 25 there had been 1,854 men and 729 women in these two camps, many of them Jewish women from Hungary. They were evacuated on April 6 and 7 to Braunschweig and attached to the transport scheduled to move north to Neuengamme, which set out on April 7 after 10 p.m. There were 84 boxcars on the train, with 60 to 80 prisoners crammed into each of them. They were given a little food for the journey, as was the routine for most evacuations at the time: about 10.5 ounces (300 grams) of bread and about 2 ounces (50 grams) of margarine.[76] On April 8, after traveling 48 miles (78 kilometers), the train halted at Celle.[77] It is not known how many of the inmates of the Saltzgitter-Leinde camp were aboard the evacuation transport at the time. For example, the sick inmates from Sattzgitter-Watenstedt were transported to Neuengamme separately. Nor are there records of how many prisoners perished during the evacuation. In any event, according to the report of a British commission of inquiry on the events in the town, the transport that stopped at Celle on April 8, 1945, consisted of some 3,000 male and 800 female prisoners. Also aboard were 200 male guards and 32 women guards from the women's camps.[78]

On April 8 Celle suffered a second aerial bombardment, heavier than the earlier attack, which had been directed against the factories in the Salzgitter camps. From the early evening hours, 132 U.S. B-26 bombers attacked in several waves. The raids wreaked devastation; fires broke out in a number of places, and enormous clouds of smoke rose above the town. People fled for their lives and tried to find shelter in forests outside the town. The streets were filled with casualties, with children straying in search of their wounded parents, and with old people whose injuries had not been treated. That evening, in the absence of any local authority who could take control of the situation, Celle was in a state of total disarray.[79] The raid had taken the inhabitants completely by surprise, and they could not understand why their town, devoid of industrial concerns or important military installations, had been chosen as the target for such a heavy bombing raid. At least 122 citizens perished in the attack, but the number of dead was apparently even higher because many were buried under the debris of their homes and others died in giant fires. Thousands were left homeless.[80] Apparently, one of the targets was Celle's railway station, where two or three trains were then standing. One was a prison train from the Neuengamme subcamps and the other a military train carrying army units and equipment, military vehicles, explosives, and fuel. When the bombs began to fall on the trains a giant fire broke out, and there were a number of explosions. The aircraft that bombed the railway station flew at low altitude, and their hits were accurate and deadly. For the prisoners in the train, the attack was a death trap. Many of them were injured by direct hits, while others were caught in the burning cars and died in the flames or from detonation of the explosives on the adjacent army train.[81] It is not entirely clear whether the casualties resulted from the direct hits on the train or from the explosions and fires. In any event, those who were saved claimed that they had been targeted directly by the aircraft and they could not understand why they were the object of the Allied attack. The pilots could not have been unaware that this was a prisoners' train. They were flying so low that they could see the striped uniforms worn by camp inmates.[82]

The interior of the cars was an inferno. Wounded prisoners sprawled helplessly, and body parts, pools of blood, and corpses were strewn all around. The cries of the wounded rose up high. When the prisoners realized that they were the target, those who were unscathed began to break out of the train and flee as far as possible from the station in search of shelter. Their terror of the planes was greater than their fear of the guards. In any case, the guards had already escaped and found shelter in a grove of trees half a mile (1 kilometer) west of the station.[83]

When the raid ended, the guards began to round up the thousands of prisoners who had fled into the forest and bring them back to the station. Night fell and the search was not easy, particularly because many of the escapees ignored the guards' call to return. At this point a process began that ended in disaster for many of the prisoners.

Gangs of prisoners wandered through the town, particularly that district closest to the forest, in search of food and water. The people of Celle, panic-stricken because of the general disorder in their town, watched in terror as starving people in striped uniforms roamed among their houses and tried to scrounge food. Windows had been shattered and walls blown down by the bombardment so that the houses now gaped open, and the prisoners peered in and demanded food. The householders were so alarmed at the thought of what the prisoners might do to them that many spent the night in cellars and subterranean storerooms for fear of falling victim to violence.[84]

On the night of April 8–9, 1945, an officer named Eberhard Streland entered the forest with 80 men from his unit in search of escaped prisoners. The soldiers were allocated 60 bullets each for their weapons. Before setting out on their mission, they were briefed by an officer who told them the following: a large group of prisoners had escaped from the train during the bombing. They had succeeded in seizing weapons unloaded from the army train, and some had even found and donned uniforms belonging to the station firefighting crew. These prisoners were endangering the civilian populations, and a unit of the Waffen-SS was already operating in the forest against them. The mission of the new group was to capture the prisoners and return them to the station.[85]

Needless to say, none of this was true. The prisoners were unarmed, and it is unlikely that they would have lingered after fleeing the train in order to replace their prison garb with firefighters' uniforms. Several of the prisoners, however, were not wearing the familiar striped garments and in several cases had received civilian clothes from compassionate local residents who realized that their identifiable clothes put them at risk.[86] Those groups of prisoners who had managed to evade their pursuers and were hiding in the forest were afraid to emerge before the British forces arrived for fear that their clothes would betray them and they would be murdered.[87] Almost none of the prisoners were German, and most were from eastern Europe. Even if they were fluent in German, they could not have concealed their origin because of their wretched appearance and obvious state of malnutrition. However, no motivation speech or fabricated story was required to convince the local residents that they were dealing with an armed and a violent gang. Superstitious dread was rife at the thought of thousands of roaming prisoners.

Dozens of armed men entered the forest at Celle on the night of April 8–9 and conducted a relentless manhunt. They were an unholy mixture of uniformed personnel and civilians: camp guards, SA personnel, soldiers from the army train, local policemen, members of the Volkssturm, and party functionaries. The stalkers were joined by soldiers from a nearby base. Apart from these units of various security forces, however, groups of civilians also organized spontaneously in order to hunt down the prisoners. Among them were boys aged 14–16 who did not hesitate to fire at prisoners caught in the forest.[88] In the prevailing atmosphere after the heavy bombardment it was not difficult to obtain weapons and organize a posse.[89] The British report described the event:

After the raid was over and before the prisoners could proceed to this gathering point a number of SS soldiers, assisted by civilians, commenced a roundup of the helpless prisoners. An unknown number of prisoners were caught and shot. Others were beaten to death while others who had gathered in groups were fired on at random. The wounded were killed by a shot in the back of the neck. Many prisoners tried to escape but were too weak to do so, and were eventually caught and shot without mercy. Shooting went on through most of the night, and continued until midday Monday 9th of April, no quarter being given to the prisoners who were being hunted like animals. Many prisoners were begging for mercy and pleaded to be allowed to live but were laughed at by those taking part in this persecution, and who shot the prisoners dead on the spot, leaving the bodies lying where they had fallen. Many civilians tried to assist the prisoners by rendering first aid and supplying refreshment but were themselves threatened and abused by those taking part in this persecution of the prisoners.[90]

This atrocity was perpetrated without any special effort to conceal the actions from the local residents. Throughout the night, there was incessant shooting in the forest. On the morning of April 9 quite a few local people saw the prisoners who had been apprehended in the forest being led by their captors to the railway station, but the firing in the forest continued sporadically. Wilhelm Sommer, who was 13 when the massacre took place in Celle, remembered that corpses of people shot by men in uniform lay on the outskirts of the forest. He talked to his mother about the identity of those people and, 45 years later, still remembered being told that "somehow it's possible that we are talking of Jews."[91] It was widely rumored in Celle on April 9 that about 1,000 Jews had been shot by the SS and the other guards that night.[92]

The local citizens were convinced that it was essential to hunt down the dangerous criminals and return them as quickly as possible to the SS, who were experts in dealing with them. One German prisoner was in a group of about 150 prisoners who were caught in the forest by several armed Volkssturm men. He appealed to them and asked why they were being handed over to the SS, since the war would be over any day. "We need to cleanse our forest of communists who are hiding there," the Volkssturm man replied. As punishment for having dared to ask such a question, the prisoner was shot and killed.[93]

On April 9 the results of the massacre could be seen on almost every path in the forest. Corpses of prisoners lay everywhere. A number of civilians and Volkssturm personnel began to collect the bodies and convey them to newly dug mass graves. Local people, clutching spades, began to dig pits and to throw in the corpses. Young members of the Hitlerjugend were recruited in order to help collect and bury the dead; all this time the killings continued. Wounded prisoners who had not been liquidated during the night were shot before being thrown into the mass graves. Despite the frantic effort to bury all the victims, when the British forces entered the town on April 12 about 100 corpses and dozens of injured prisoners were still lying in various places near the station or in the street. The injured prisoners were taken to a military hospital. "Belsen in microcosm," was how the British investigators described what they found at the heart of a medium-sized German town as they liberated it. They estimated the number of victims of the Celle massacre at 800.[94] Another 200 to 300 had died during the air attack on the train.[95]

Approximately 1,100 prisoners were assembled in the forest by the manhunters and taken to a concentration spot at the railway station, and from there they made their way on foot to Bergen-Belsen. An unknown number of prisoners succeeded in evading the bullets of the stalkers and hid in the forest or in the cellars of humane local residents, who sheltered them[96] until the British troops arrived, two days after the hunt and the massacre. In all, about 1,500 of the 3,700 prisoners on the transport that stopped at Celle on April 8, 1945, lived to see the day of liberation.[97]

In general, the camp prisoners who roamed the bombed towns and cities of Germany in mid-April 1945 were perceived as a threatening and dangerous group. When most of the evacuees from the Neuengamme subcamps passed through Lower Saxony, the population was warned of their presence. In Hanover, for example, the Kreisleiter issued a special proclamation on March 30 to the effect that, in the course of the evacuation of military forces from the region, hostile elements would also be evacuated and would be passing through the town. It was strictly prohibited, and highly hazardous, he warned, to give shelter to prisoners or to hostile elements if they escaped and begged for help. No contact was to be made with any individuals who appeared to be refugees, were wandering without supervision, and were of unknown origin.[98] On April 11, the day of the massacre of a group of prisoners who were stranded in Lüneburg, the local paper published a notice headed: "Beware escaped concentration camp prisoners!" It warned the populace of the dangers of any contact whatsoever with these dangerous enemies and described the prisoners as a violent, wild, and uncontrolled rabble.[99]

During this period of total dissolution, as the army retreated, thousands of forced laborers roamed unguarded, and unrelenting Allied bombardments created devastation and panic, the escaped concentration camp inmates were widely believed to pose a serious threat. The security forces identified with the collapsing regime needed no persuading that these dangerous enemies must be liquidated. The Celle affair attests to the fact that, after 12 years of constant indoctrination, many ordinary citizens had internalized this point of view. On April 8 the situation in the town deteriorated in a matter of hours into a state of total chaos that fostered rumors and subsequent panic. These, in their turn, created the dynamics that led to the murderous events. In the final days of the Third Reich quite a number of local residents were convinced that, in the state of total chaos and in the absence of a central authority capable of restoring order, the thousands of released prisoners were a hostile, violent rabble and a dangerous threat.

CHAPTER EIGHT

Marched toward Gardelegen

On Sunday, April 14, 1945, the 2nd Battalion of the 405th Regiment of the 102nd Infantry Division of the U.S. 9th Army, which was fighting its way through central Germany, advanced toward Gardelegen from the northwest. Not far from this historic town was a Luftwaffe base. On its way to capture the base the battalion passed through the town of Estedt, without which it would not be possible to secure their entry to Gardelegen. In Estedt the American forces encountered resistance from a German paratrooper unit, equipped with rifles, automatic weapons, and antiaircraft guns. The 405th Regiment force was accompanied by the 701st Tank Battalion.

That day the Germans had succeeded in capturing an American officer, Lieutenant Emerson Hunt, the liaison officer between the 405th Regiment and the 701st Tank Battalion. He insisted on being interrogated by an officer of rank equal to or higher than his own. Hunt was taken to the command headquarters (HQ) of the Luftwaffe base near Gardelegen. He told his interrogator that U.S. tanks were only half an hour away from Gardelegen and that if the town continued to resist and did not surrender, the tanks would launch a heavy shelling, whatever the cost in human life and in damage.[1] The German officer decided on the spot to surrender, so as to save the town and its inhabitants from destruction and prevent further casualties. He sent Hunt back to the American lines, accompanied by one of his officers with a surrender offer. By the evening of April 14, 1945, the town had surrendered to the U.S. forces.[2]

Gardelegen is a small town in the Altmark region of Upper Saxony, about 25 miles (40 kilometers) north of Magdeburg. It was apparently settled at the beginning of the second millennium, but the town began to develop only from the early twelfth century. From 1358 on it was one of the Hanseatic towns of northwest Germany, but had to withdraw from the league in 1488 after its inhabitants participated in riots that broke out in protest against taxation on Garley-Bier, the special beer brewed there. In the early sixteenth century Gardelegen had 1,500 to 2,500 inhabitants, but, owing to economic sanctions, it suffered a long period of recession and economic stagnation.

The town preserved its agricultural character for centuries, and petty trade and industry did not develop on a large scale, nor was it a center of trade fairs. The local market was mainly a source of products of the region and the town. From 1539 onward, as the Reformation spread, Gardelegen became a Protestant town. Not until 1900 was a new Catholic church constructed. Despite the introduction of trade and a small amount of industry into the urban economy in the mid-eighteenth century, the town remained a small farming community until the end of the nineteenth century, remote from the centers of economic and political activity.

In 1880 Gardelegen began to integrate into the economic and industrial frameworks of the Second Reich. An electricity power station and a gas production concern were established, bringing change into the lives of the local farmers. A working class began to emerge, composed of inhabitants who worked in the newly established factories. The workers in the electricity and gas enterprises labored under rigorous conditions 48 to 56 hours per week. Although it was a district town (Kreishauptstadt), almost no state officials settled there.

Of particular importance in the annals of the town and its economic development were its reciprocal relations with the army. In 1725 Prussia moved a permanent military unit to the Gardelegen area, and it remained there until the French occupation in 1807. In 1867, a permanent Prussian base was established near Gardelegen. The fact that the base was close at hand had an impact on the economy and social life of the town. There were 6,000 inhabitants at the time, and after the base came into existence, quite a few military families came to live in the town. Gardelegen's history up to the end of World War II is interwoven with the military presence. The last years of the Wilhelmian empire were a period of prosperity and development. The economy flourished, and the society, typical of small provincial towns, was stable, politically conservative, and marked by complacency and confidence.

With the outbreak of war in 1914 the town was swept by a mood of patriotism, so that the military defeat of 1918 came as a heavy blow. After the war, there was an influx of new residents, who emigrated from Posen district after its annexation to Poland. The democratic reforms and principles of liberty and equality promoted by the newly established republic were not welcomed in Gardelegen. The local Social-Democratic Party (Sozialdemokratische

Partei Deutschlands—SPD) was relatively conservative in its views, and plans for social-democratic changes did not succeed.

The people of this small town in Upper Saxony were mostly concerned with their everyday lives and the welfare of their families. The town attracted people in search of employment or of a Christian community. The stability was impaired toward the end of the 1920s by economic upheavals, at a time when the influence of the SPD was at its height in Gardelegen. The political tensions simmering between right and left in Weimar Germany were felt there as well. Both the Communist Party (Kommunistische Partei Deutschlands—KPD) and the SPD were highly active, in particular among the trade unions, but in 1930 the Nazi Party caught up with the left-wing parties. The growing number of local Nazi supporters came from various political circles, including the Social-Democratic ranks. In many cases, the motives for support were not necessarily ideological, and in any event the reasons for the Nazis' increasing popularity in the town were the same as those in other parts of Germany.

In general, in the early days of Nazi rule, life in Gardelegen did not differ from life elsewhere in the Altmark. In 1936, the situation changed after several Wehrmacht installations were established in the area. The first of these was a military cavalry school *(Remonteschule)* that had a strong impact on the local economy. Quite a few families became involved in the activity of the base, supplying provisions and services or working there, and it also utilized various urban services. Families with small children settled in Gardelegen because of the new employment opportunities.

In 1939 an airfield was constructed near the town, which served mainly as a technical base for the repair of engines and aircraft *(Reparaturflugplatz)* for the Luftwaffe, and it too contributed to the local economy. A paratrooper's base *(Fallschirmjägerregiment 1)* was also established, and a new district hospital was set up to meet growing needs. The presence of three army bases promoted environmental development, and road networks and access roads were expanded. On the eve of World War II Gardelegen had slightly more than 10,000 residents. From the mid-1930s, the town had a young and dynamic population whose contacts with the military were a source of income and of local pride. The Nazi regime was undoubtedly beneficial to the town.[3]

There is documentary evidence that a Jewish community existed in Gardelegen from 1344. The Jews owned pawnshops or engaged in trade, typical occupations of the Jews of Germany at the time. In 1510 they were expelled from the town after a blood libel, having been accused of murdering a Christian child. In 1565 a few Jews returned to settle there, but they were expelled again eight years later.

In the first half of the nineteenth century Jews began to return to Gardelegen in response to the political changes introduced by the French occupation. In 1840 there were 40 Jews in the town, and several Jewish families made valuable contributions to economic and cultural life. Salomon Friedmann owned a large trading company; Siegmund Hess was a musician who set up the town orchestra.

After World War I, the Jewish community shrank considerably as the younger generation left for larger towns. When the Nazis rose to power, there were only 60 Jews left in the town and its environs. During the November 1938 pogrom *(Kristallnacht)* Jewish property was damaged and destroyed, including a synagogue built at the beginning of the nineteenth century. The district party newspaper *Der Mitteldeutsche* published a long article after the pogrom, declaring that there was nothing for the Jews to do in Altmark. By the beginning of the 1940s there were few Jews in the town, all of them married to Germans.[4]

When men of the U.S. 102nd Infantry Division occupied Gardelegen on the evening of Saturday, April 14, 1945, they were unaware that they were about to come face to face with one of the most ghastly war crimes perpetrated on German soil in the last days of the Third Reich. The Division had been established in 1921 in Missouri and Kansas as a U.S. Army reserve unit, but up to September 1942 it existed essentially only on paper. That month, about 15,000 troops were recruited into the Division from those two farming states and were sent to a training base in Texas. They were not assigned to active service until 1944 and instead spent most of their time in training bases in the southern United States. On September 12, 1944, the Division, with all its equipment and manpower, boarded ship in New York and set out for Europe, disembarking at Cherbourg in order to join the U.S. forces in France in anticipation of the invasion of Germany.

On April 3, 1945, the Division crossed the Rhine, its main mission being the liquidation of the remaining German pockets of resistance. Four days later, the troops reached a spot some 50 miles (80 kilometers) from the town of Bielefeld, and took thousands of POWs. On April 12 the forces advanced in an easterly direction toward the Elbe. At this stage of the fighting, there was almost no German resistance in the region, and the 102nd, 35th, and 84th Divisions advanced so rapidly that the sole danger they faced was from random German units that passed them in their retreat toward the Elbe. At the end of that day the regiments of the 102nd reached the vicinity of the town of Gifhorn, several dozen miles west of Gardelegen. The next day they continued their advance. The 406th Regiment moved to the north of Gardelegen toward Osterburg on the banks of the Elbe. The 1st Battalion of the 405th Regiment made for the town of Stendal, northeast of

Gardelegen. The 2nd Battalion of the Regiment moved toward Gardelegen from the northwest.[5]

On April 14 the 2nd Battalion was involved in a fierce battle in the forests northwest of the town of Wiepke. After quitting the Schwiesau region at 7:30 a.m. the force encountered heavy automatic weapon fire near Wiepke from inside the forest and the town itself. The advance was checked because the terrain conditions around the village were to the advantage of the German force. The battalion summoned an artillery unit and, with the aid of a tank company, succeeded in overcoming the resistance and capturing Wiepke at 10:50 a.m. The troops left the village and moved southward, where they again encountered resistance from light weapons and antiaircraft guns, the latter fired by a paratrooper unit in the north section of the town of Estedt. In order to overcome this relatively tenacious resistance, an additional tank unit was brought in to reinforce the battalion in its effort to occupy the town.

Meanwhile, the 3rd Battalion of the 405th Regiment had received orders to overtake the 2nd Battalion and advance in a northerly direction. The force captured the town of Bismarck at 1 p.m. and awaited further orders. When the 2nd Battalion met up with strong resistance, the offensive plans were modified. The 1st Battalion skirted the 2nd and undertook the original mission of occupying Stendal, the main town of Altmark. It was occupied at 11 p.m. after mild enemy resistance. The 3rd Battalion, which also encountered no real resistance, advanced toward the town of Borstel. After rallying its forces at Estedt at 4 p.m., the 2nd Battalion continued the attack from the south. However, it encountered heavy resistance near the town and in particular in the surrounding forests, and once again the artillery was called in. Then a German paratrooper on a motorcycle with sidecar, bearing a white flag, appeared from the direction of Gardelegen. Seated in the sidecar was Colonel Kurt von Einem, commander of the paratrooper base near Gardelegen. He had heard from Lieutenant Emerson Hunt of the danger the town would face if the Germans did not surrender unconditionally. Von Einem, who was looking for the American CO in order to surrender, reported that there were 400 to 500 German soldiers in Gardelegen. The CO of the 405th Regiment, Colonel Lorin Williams, received the German officer and they agreed on total capitulation of all German forces, at 7 p.m. in Gardelegen. In a ceremony held at the German Luftwaffe base, the 500 German troops surrendered to the Americans. Another 300 arrived shortly afterward in order to hand over their weapons.[6] Several minutes after 7 p.m. the HQ of the 102nd Infantry Division received the following telegram:

Gardelegen (Y48442) is surrendering to our 405th Inf at 19:00 with 800 PWs and many American PWs. Request that all your units be informed not to fire in Gardelegen . . . as this was part of surrender agreement. Request that you assume control of town as soon as practicable.[7]

Twenty-five U.S. officers and men who had been captured before the German surrender were released. After the capitulation of Gardelegen, the HQ of the 405th Regiment was moved to Stendal and began to operate from the town at 11:50 p.m. on April 14. The entire Altmark region was now occupied by the U.S. 9th Army.

This marked the end of another battle between U.S. forces and the remnants of the German army in the last stages of the war. As was the procedure on other occasions when units of the 102nd Division entered towns or districts where fighting had just ended, they received orders to remain in the area. A unit of the 2nd Battalion of the 405th Regiment was left there in order to ensure that all German forces had capitulated, since reports had been received of gunfire directed at U.S. troops as they advanced eastward. Meanwhile, the 405th was ordered to take over supervision and administration of the town.[8]

On Sunday, April 15, a group of 15 men from the 2nd Battalion of the 405th Regiment set out on a routine patrol near the town. At an early stage of the patrol, they apparently encountered a young Pole, dressed in a ragged concentration camp uniform and scarcely able to stand. One of the soldiers jotted down in pencil on a scrap of paper a summary of the story the young man, Edward Antoniak, told them. This is what he wrote:

Edward Antoniak—18 years old
   Wielin Poland
   (1) Worked in Poland three years
   (2) Came to Riethausen, Germany, worked in factory for one year (laborer)
   (3) Brought to Gardelegen two days before the crime
   (4) 200 Jews, 300 Frenchmen, 400 Russians, 600 Poles—ranging from 18–50 years of age
   (5) Were killed because not in favor of Nazis. German soldiers in control. 10 escaped during night of Friday April 14

   Were marched to Gardelegen. Those who couldn't march were shot. Herded into building and thought they were going to spend the night. Floor was covered with straw which soaked with gasoline. At 18.00 fire was set to straw. Those who tried to get out of building were shot and other escapists were dispersed with concussion and fragmentary grenades.

   Meals consisted of 6 raw potatoes for 3 weeks. Ditches were dug before victims were brought to Gardelegen.[9]

It is not clear whether this brief and slightly confused summary of Antoniak's story was written before the soldiers reached the site of the massacre or whether they found him, one of the few survivors, after witnessing the consequences of the deed itself. Nonetheless, when they continued their patrol, they climbed a small hill not far from the town. From there, they spied, some distance away, a burnt brick structure, which was still smoking. When they approached the building, a nightmarish sight met their eyes. Hundreds of charred corpses, dressed in the remnants of prison camp uniforms, were lying in several trenches that had been dug hastily alongside the building. The doors of the building, which was revealed to be a large barn, were also charred, and from beneath the doors were protruding the heads or hands of murdered prisoners. When the soldiers opened the doors, they discovered hundreds of horribly distorted charred corpses inside, all glued together.[10] It was the most harrowing experience those men underwent throughout the war. One of them wrote to his mother several days later:

Dear Mother,

Yesterday I saw something I'll never forget. It was one of those war crimes that the Germans are noted for. This time the Americans came up too fast and they weren't able to cover up their crime. It took place in a large barn in the town of Gardelegen.

It started out that the Germans were bringing some two thousand Russian prisoners of war from East Prussia on a march to Hannover. While marching to their destination, about one thousand Russians weren't able to continue the march on account of the light meals they were getting. By that I mean two potatoes for each meal. As they dropped out, they were killed where they fell. The balance were to be taken to Hannover, but the Americans were already east of Hannover, and put about five hundred of these prisoners of war in a large barn in which the floor had a light layer of straw and potatoes soaked with gasoline.

They closed the doors and put the place on fire and BURNED THEM ALIVE. The balance of them were told to dig trenches around the barn and when they got through digging, they were lined up along the trenches and shot and buried. Some were buried alive.

The Americans moved up so fast that they weren't able to get rid of the evidence. Only two men escaped and that is how the story was told.

I was up to see the mass [sic] and words can't explain how bad it was. I took a few pictures of the place and bodies. Now I wonder how many American boys met the same death.

It would be a good idea if you told some of the people about it so that they will know just rotten these Germans are. Even a dead German isn't good because he stinks.

I guess this story must already be in the newspapers back home. It's the real dope and much worse than I can explain in a letter. I don't think the Japs are half as bad.

I hope you didn't get sick reading this. I just thought I'd let you know what's going on.

Love . . . [11]

The details and facts reported by the young soldier are not necessarily exact, but every line in his letter reflects his deep emotional shock and his burning rage at the murderers and the entire German people. In the first hours and days after discovery of the barn and the adjacent pits with hundreds of charred corpses of prisoners, it was not possible to clarify the details and answer the grim questions underlying the bloody massacre: who had they been, these individuals slaughtered so cruelly several hours before the Americans arrived? What were the circumstances that led to this deed and, of course, who were the murderers and what were their motives?

The Cave and River Prisoners

As noted, in mid-1944 the Mittelbau-Dora complex began to expand, and within a few months a series of new camps had come into being, most of them with no more than several hundred to a thousand inmates. Because of the expansion of the factory network and its wider dispersal, prisoners were now housed at a considerable distance from their places of work. Consequently, the camp command decided to set up camps closer to the worksites so that inmates would not waste time walking to and from work.[12] In the spring the authorities began the transfer southward, outside the range of Allied bombers, of the large-scale Junkerwerke aviation concern, which had operated in Dessau, Bernburg, and near Leipzig and Magdenburg. The site chosen was north of the main camp, Dora, not far from the town of Niedersachswerfen.[13]

Concomitantly, work began on the infrastructure for a subterranean production complex east of Nordhausen for other factories of the concern, the Junkers AG Schönebeck enterprises. They were constructed inside the large Heimkehle cave complex in the southern Harz Mountains. The existence of this natural 1-mile (2-kilometer)-long network of underground caves and grottos has been known since the mid-thirteenth century. Because of the gypsum content of the mountain soil, subterranean rivers flow through the caves, creating lakes and natural cisterns, and the air is extremely damp. The Junkers aircraft production concerns were transferred to these caves, which were excavated, extended, and prepared for this particular use. In addition, industrial areas were prepared near the town of Rottleberode and a camp was constructed for the prisoners who worked there. The first section built was Rottleberode A5, which began operating on March 13, 1944. At first it was a subcamp of Buchenwald and was affiliated with Mittelbau-Dora from October 28 of that year.[14]

The camp at Rottleberode was located on the site of an old factory that produced chemicals, apparently from the local gypsum, and it consisted of two buildings. One served as a storehouse, mainly for tools and other camp equipment, and also contained the services and the kitchen. The prisoners lived in the other building, part of which served as a revier (sick bay). The prisoners' quarters were divided into four separate blocks, with 200 to 300 inmates each. The bunks were mostly on two levels, and each prisoner received a straw mattress and two blankets. They had neither pillows nor lockers.[15] There were separate quarters in the building for the kapo and the "block elder" (Blockältester). The first consignment of inmates to reach Rottleberode consisted of 200 prisoners from Buchenwald. In the first months of the camp's operation, it housed 380 inmates.[16] By June 1944 the number was 700, on November 1 it rose to 819,[17] and in December it reached 930. By the end of 1944 there were 1,000 inmates, and by early 1945 some 1,100.[18] The prisoners at Rottleberode were of Russian, Polish, Czech, French, Belgian, and Dutch nationality, and there were several Luxembourgian nationals and 5 or 6 Germans.[19]

The first commandant of Rottleberode, who arrived with the Buchenwald prisoners, was Heinrich Grabowski. He was born in Danzig, but his family apparently originated in western Poland. Grabowski was remembered by the survivors of the camp as a decent commander, who prohibited arbitrary punishment, particularly while the prisoners were at work.[20] When he was replaced after six months it was rumored among the prisoners that he had been dismissed because he was too lenient.[21] Shortly after he left a new SS officer, Bendig, replaced him, and in November 1944 command was taken over by Erhard-Richard Brauny, who had been serving at Mittelbau-Dora in junior command positions since September 1943.[22] His deputy was Hermann Lamp. The guard team consisted almost entirely of Luftwaffe veterans who had been reassigned to guard duties in the concentration camps in 1944.[23] The oldest among them was Franz Putz, who was 58 in 1944, and the youngest was 40-year-old Walter Triebner. Apart from the guards, several staff members of the SS concentration camp network held various command positions.[24]

The small group of German prisoners fulfilled almost all the internal functions. The Lagerältester (camp elder) was Hubert Hagen, a 49-year-old political prisoner.[25] But the dominant figures among the prisoner functionaries in the camp were two other prisoners. The first was Walter Ulbricht, the *Häftlingsschreiber* (inmates' clerk), a German who had been classified as an antisocial element. He had been arrested in 1941 for vagrancy and evasion of work and was interned at Buchenwald. The other was Karl Paul Semmler, a political prisoner and communist who was arrested and released several times in 1933 and finally sent to Buchenwald in 1938. At the end of March 1944 Semmler was among the first prisoners dispatched from Buchenwald to the new camp at Mittelbau-Dora.[26] He was appointed kapo and in December 1944 was transferred to Rottleberode. His good relations with the camp command, which were based also on his lengthy imprisonment at Buchenwald and Mittelbau-Dora, led to his promotion to chief kapo *(Oberkapo)* of the camp with responsibility for eight or nine other kapos, most of them also Germans,[27] each of them in charge of about 100 prisoners.[28]

The prominence of German prisoners among the concentration camp "aristocracy" was a common phenomenon in many camps. Not only criminals or antisocial elements but also quite a number of communist political prisoners held positions in the camps. The communist prisoners, who were of German, Polish, French, and other extractions, often helped organize underground resistance.[29] This stratum, as Wolfgang Sofsky writes, received everything denied to ordinary prisoners: enough food, warm clothing, and sturdy footwear. They had normal haircuts and were clean-shaven. They were not obliged to work, and when they were sick, they received effective treatment in the camp dispensary. They could also entertain themselves, and they spent their leisure time in sports contests or in other cultural activities. They were the only inmates who lived what could be described as reasonable lives. They were also agents of the terror apparatus that controlled the lives of the prisoners.[30]

In the first few months, there were two labor units in Rottleberode, which worked in two separate commandos. Their work was particularly strenuous, and the damp in the tunnels deep under the mountains had a ruinous impact on their health. The working day lasted 12–13 hours and was divided into two shifts.[31] The morning shift began at 3:30 a.m. when the prisoners were roused. They stood at attention beside their bunks and were given a breakfast of coffee and a ration of bread. Approximately seven minutes later they reported for morning lineup, which lasted half an hour; then they set out for work.[32] Initially, they walked from the camp to the worksite, but after some time special cattle trucks were introduced to transport them there. They were allowed a day's rest every second Sunday.[33] In the first two months of the camp's operation, until about May, the prisoners received their food from the main camp at Dora. From May on, the procedure was changed, and they were given rations earmarked for prisoners engaged in strenuous construction tasks. They included a daily portion of

21 ounces (600 grams) of bread, 2 ounces (50 grams) of margarine, and 3 ounces (80 grams) of canned meat or sausage. They were also allocated a quart of soup daily and coffee in the morning.[34]

Jews arrived at Mittelbau-Dora relatively late. The first transport of about 1,000 Jewish prisoners reached the Mittlebau-Dora network at the end of May 1944. These prisoners were sent to Ellrich-Juliushütte and Harzungen following Himmler's decision to transfer Jews from the camps in the East to camps that were working for the munitions industry. At the end of September 1944 another transport of skilled Jewish artisans from Natzeiler-Struthof in Alsace reached Mittelbau-Dora.[35] At Ellrich, the largest of the subcamps of the Mittelbau-Dora network, there were 803 Jews in mid-February 1945 among the 7,686 inmates. At Harzungen in mid-December there were 173 Jews.[36]

No more Jews arrived at Mittelbau-Dora up to January 1945. From the second half of the month, several transports arrived that had been evacuated from Auschwitz and Groß-Rosen, as well as Jews from labor camps evacuated in the Częstochowa area.[37] In all, 16,000 prisoners evacuated from concentration camps in Upper and Lower Silesia were brought in, and it is estimated that about one quarter of them were Jews. In several camps, Jews accounted for 10 percent of the total prisoner population. This was the case in Harzungen and Boelcke. After the first Jews arrived in Mittelbau-Dora in May 1944, they were assigned the most difficult tasks in the construction units, with poor prospects for long-term survival. The Jews suffered abuse at the hands of the SS men, the kapos, and those in charge of the work units. In order to keep the labor units homogeneous and prevent friction among the laborers, the camp commandants and supervisors tried to avoid accepting Jewish prisoners, particularly in the smaller camps. They believed that, since the Jews were despised by the other prisoners, their presence could only generate tension and disrupt work procedures. Hence, from late 1944, when the number of Jews in the Mittelbau-Dora network was still relatively small, they were dispatched only to larger camps such as Ellrich and Harzungen, and almost none were to be found in the smaller subcamps.

Only one other ethnic group, the Gypsies, were treated in similar fashion. In early 1945 there were approximately as many Gypsies as Jews in the camps: about 600 in Dora, 365 at Ellrich, and 479 at Harzungen. However, unlike the Jews, they did not receive special attention from the camp personnel. At Harzungen there was even a Gypsy inmate who served as kapo, and others filled various administrative functions. There is no evidence of Jewish prisoners ever holding positions in the camp network.[38] In August 1944 a subcommando of the Rottleberode camp, Stempeda B-4, was opened about 2 to 3 miles (4 to 5 kilometers) from Rottleberode. The inmates were employed on the backbreaking task of excavating a tunnel not far from a river-bed. They cleared rocks from the riverbed, which were detonated in the tunnel in the heart of the mountain. Their task was to raise the stones out of the frozen water and load them onto wagons, which were dragged away. In the first few months, 50 prisoners labored at these tasks, after walking from Rottleberode to Stempeda and back every day. In the first stage, prisoners from Mittelbau-Dora were apparently taken to Stempeda.[39]

The Stempeda commando underwent a dramatic change at the end of January 1945. On January 17, 2,740 Jewish slave laborers were evacuated from the Hugo Schneider Aktiengesellschaft-Metalwarenfabrik AG (HASAG) armaments enterprise at Częstochowa and moved to Buchenwald. After less than two weeks, 1,000 of them were sent to Mittelbau-Dora.[40] On January 29 approximately 500 were sent from Dora to Rottleberode, about 445 of them Jews from Buchenwald.[41] These Jewish prisoners constituted the main group sent to the lethal labor commando at Stempeda.

At the beginning of February there were 525 prisoners at the site, 450 of them Jews. The rest were mainly Russian, Polish, and French,[42] which were the dominant nationalities among the inmates of Rottleberode and Mittelbau-Dora. Stempeda was the only commando in the entire Mittelbau-Dora complex where Jews were the largest national group.

In that period, three barracks were constructed beside the river at Stem-peda, only 110 yards (100 meters) from the worksite. In the prisoners' dor-mitory, there was a kitchen, where they received their meals, as well as a room for the kapo. Yet, it seems that not all the laborers lived in those bar-racks on a permanent basis, since Stempeda did not become a regular sub-camp.[43] Some of the laborers continued to walk to work every day from Rottleberode. The working day began between 5 and 6 a.m.; there was a break at noon, when the guards went into the barracks to eat. The prisoners were not fed, waited about 45 minutes until the guards finished eating, and then returned to work. At about 6 p.m. a lineup was held, and the prisoners then walked back to Rottleberode, where they received their evening meal.[44] Labor at Stempeda was divided into 12-hour shifts, the groups exchanging shifts every week.

The taxing conditions inside the tunnels, the damp, the cold weather, and the strenuous labor were not the only sources of suffering for the prisoners. An atmosphere of savagery and abuse prevailed at Stempeda; no such treat-ment was detailed in the postwar testimonies of other prisoners at Rottle-berode in particular and Mittelbau-Dora in general. Those Stempeda pris-oners who faltered and were incapable of continuing to drag rocks out of the water were immersed forcibly in the river until they drowned.[45] The guards and supervisors beat the prisoners with sticks and rubber hoses whenever they stopped to rest. In many cases prisoners were required to carry equipment from Rottleberode to Stempeda at the end of the working day. Those who collapsed under the load were shot by the guards.[46]

Several survivors of Stempeda singled out for mention one of the kapos, an inmate of Gypsy origin named Hermann Ebender, who was particularly brutal. Ebender, born in 1909, had been imprisoned at Auschwitz-Birkenau since May 1943 and arrived at Mittelbau-Dora after the Gypsy family camp there was liquidated in August 1944. In 1984 he was indicted in Germany for 17 cases of abuse of prisoners and involvement in murders in the period when he was a kapo at Stempeda.[47] One particular incident was recalled vividly by several survivors. Ebender executed a Jewish prisoner who collapsed into the river and was unable to continue working by inserting a rubber tube into his throat until he choked to death.[48]

Several other prisoners who were employed in the camp treated the Jews differently from the other prisoners. A prisoner named Yaakov Plat remembered a man of Polish origin who was in charge of one of the labor units at Stempeda and abused Jewish prisoners, and Yosef Feigenbaum, another prisoner, remembered a young German kapo who helped Ebender to throw feeble prisoners into the river.[49] The Jews were even afraid to go to the revier because one of the medical orderlies, a black prisoner named Johnny Nicholas, was hostile to Jews.

The Johnny Nicholas affair was one of the strangest in the annals of Rottleberode. Nicholas was born in Haiti and served in the French navy. In 1940, when France capitulated, he was in Paris, registered as a medical student. During the German occupation he joined the underground and obtained false papers attesting to his U.S. nationality and his profession of gynecologist. He was fluent in several languages, and in the Resistance his task was to help rescue British pilots who had crashed in France and try to smuggle them back to Britain. In November 1943 he was caught by the Gestapo, and two months later he was sent to Buchenwald. In May 1944 he was sent to Mittelbau-Dora and in November he reached Rottleberode. He was a political prisoner, but despite the color of his skin, he was not singled out for abuse. The camp guards were apparently convinced that he was an American and their attitude to American prisoners was usually circumspect. Nicholas also succeeded in persuading the camp doctor that he could serve as a medic. He began to work in the sick bay, and prisoners recalled his dedicated efforts, which often saved sick prisoners from lethal injections.[50] On the other hand, Jewish prisoners feared him because it was rumored that he did not hesitate to liquidate sick Jews.[51]

As a result of the influx of a large group of Jewish prisoners into Rottleberode in January 1945, and the assignment of most of them to Stempeda, the mortality rate in the camp rose. Several survivors were convinced that it was the camp commandant, Brauny, who ordered severe treatment of Jewish prisoners and that the decision to send them all to Stempeda on arrival was his. Jewish prisoners were rarely exempted from work when sick and sometimes suffered physical punishment. On several occasions Brauny himself was seen beating Jewish prisoners, particularly when he was drunk. He was abetted by his deputy, Hermann Lamp, who was directly responsible for the commando at Stempeda.[52]

Walter Ulbricht, who was the registrar of the prisoners, stated after the war that in the year he worked at Rottleberode, from March 1944 to the evacuation in April 1945, there were 10 deaths of prisoners: three sick prisoners died and another seven were executed because of escape attempts or other grave disciplinary misdemeanors. The figures he cited were far from being accurate, and he may have been referring to the last period. He also said that between February and the beginning of April 1945, 30 corpses of Jewish prisoners were brought from Stempeda and that they displayed signs of abuse.[53] Jewish survivors cited higher figures.[54] The corpses were loaded onto wheelbarrows and at the end of the working day were taken to Rottleberode. Several of them were buried in the camp, but most of the victims were taken to the crematorium at Mittelbau-Dora.[55]

On the other hand, the figure given by Ulbricht for Jewish prisoners who died at Stempeda is more or less in line with the data in the last report on the mortality rate in Rottleberode and Stempeda between February 6 and March 28, 1945. The report notes that 52 prisoners died in the two camps. During this period, on the eve of the liquidation of the camp, living conditions deteriorated drastically. The fact that some 16,000 evacuees from Auschwitz and Groß-Rosen, all of them in very poor physical condition, were relocated to Mittelbau-Dora also led to a rise in the death rate in the network camps.[56] According to this report 26 of the prisoners who died in Rottleberode were Polish Jews from the transport sent from Buchenwald—in other words, Stempeda prisoners. Thus, after the Jewish prisoners reached Rottleberode in January 1945 and were sent to work at Stempeda, they accounted for about 50 percent of deaths in the camp.

Another 43 prisoners, who died in the last week and a half that the camps were in existence, between March 26 and April 4, 1945, were not classified by nationality.[57] If we rely on statistics from the previous period,[58] at least 21 or 22 of them were Polish Jews from the Częstochowa–Buchenwald–Dora transport, bringing the total number of Jewish prisoners who perished in about two months at Stempeda to 47 or 48 at least out of the 445 who arrived there. In other words, in the two months during which Jews labored at Rottleberode and Stempeda, at least 10 percent of the total number died, approximately one prisoner every two days. This explains why the few survivors regarded it as a death camp in every sense of the word.[59]

Brauny's decision to transfer the Jewish prisoners who arrived at Rottleberode to commando Stempeda is not surprising. The desire to isolate the Jews from other prisoners, to the extent that this was a practical option, was shared by various commanders and administrators at Mittelbau-Dora. Stempeda was a particularly tough camp, which claimed the lives of many of the prisoners who labored there, and there was a need for able-bodied workers. The Jews who arrived from Częstochowa were in better physical condition than those brought from the evacuated concentration camps in Poland; this fact, too, probably influenced the decision to send them all to Stempeda. However, the arrival of so large a group of Jews unleashed violence and brutality. The strenuous labor that claimed so many victims was compounded by the camp functionaries' hostile attitude toward the Jews. They were more brutal toward them than to any other nationality in the camp. This policy was not dictated by the senior camp command, but was rather the outcome of local conditions and decisions taken by local commanders which, during the last months of the war, had an increasingly strong impact on the fate and survival prospects of concentration camp prisoners.

Evacuation: Rottleberode

At the end of March 1945 the 1,100 prisoners[60] in Rottleberode and about 400 in its subcommando at Stempeda sensed that something dramatic was about to occur. It was widely rumored that the camp was about to be evacuated and that the Americans were only a few days' march from the camp. During the night of April 3 work was suspended on the production lines and at worksites, and all prisoners were returned to the camp. On the following day as well, they were not sent out to work. In the late morning hours the prisoners began to return their tools and other equipment to the camp storehouses. They were permitted to keep their prisoners' garments, blankets, and personal dishes. After returning the equipment each received a can of meat weighing 30 ounces and a loaf of bread.[61]

In early April the guards at Rottleberode were also in a state of tense anticipation, but few preparations were under way to ensure efficient evacuation. At 2 p.m. on April 4 the SS men began to show signs of panic. The ex-Luftwaffe guards were told that they were to remain at their guard posts and make sure that the prisoners did not become disruptive. In the SS barracks bonfires were lit and equipment that had not been earmarked for evacuation was burned together with some documents. There was almost no interaction between the guards and the SS men. After some time, the Luftwaffe guards received orders to pack their belongings and prepare for evacuation. They began to collect their possessions and food supplies, which were packed in special cardboard boxes. Nobody told them what their destination would be or how the evacuation was to be carried out.[62]

The evacuation order that Baer issued on April 4, 1945, was brought to the Rottleberode commandant, Erhard Brauny, by messenger from the main camp. The order stipulated that all work in the camp was to cease immediately and that prisoners and accompanying guards were to report on the next day, April 5, to the railway station at Niedersachswerfen.[63] An external commando of Mittelbau-Dora, code name "Emmi," had been operating there since summer 1944 at the site of an old mine. The main work there was the dismantling of parts of V2 rockets that had been rejected for use because of faulty manufacturing or mishaps.[64] The directive made no mention of the evacuation route or its destination.[65] Brauny had apparently prepared in advance a list that contained certain details about the prisoners, which he was due to submit to Hans Häser, the Gestapo officer at Niedersachswerfen who was coordinating the evacuation of prisoners from the area.[66] The evacuation arrangements were completed within a few hours, and some 1,400 prisoners from Rottleberode and Stempeda were summoned out for a last lineup at about 8 or 8:30 p.m. They were divided into four large blocs of 350–400 prisoners each, subdivided into groups of 100.[67] One bloc of 400 prisoners was in Brauny's charge, and a second bloc of 1,000 prisoners was led by Hermann Lamp, his deputy. The two groups set out on April 4 in the evening, the larger group at about 9 p.m. and the second about two or three hours later.[68]

The distance from Rottleberode to Niedersachswerfen was about 11 miles (18 kilometers). Brauny's group walked all night, since the heavy bombardments of the area in previous days had damaged road and rail infrastructures. The roads were already crammed with civilians and with laborers from the industrial complex at Mittelbau-Dora, who were also leaving the area. The column of prisoners advanced to the northwest through Stempeda, Buchholz in der Nordheide, and Harzungen. It was not an easy trek. The route passed through mountainous terrain, and the paths were clogged with mud due to the rains. The weary prisoners were also carrying the personal belongings of the camp guards. The equipment collected before the evacuation was loaded onto wagons, which were dragged along by one group of prisoners and pushed from behind by another group. Because of the thick mud and the many bomb craters, the guards were forced to leave some of the wagons behind at the roadside.[69]

The first victims, unable to endure the rapid pace, collapsed at this stage of the evacuation. Several prisoners succeeded in escaping under cover of darkness. Walter Ulbricht made his escape near Buchholz[70] at about 4:30 a.m. on April 5. An aircraft apparently flew over the convoy, creating panic among the prisoners and guards who feared that it was about to strafe them. It is not clear whether the aircraft did in fact attack the column, but Ulbricht and another prisoner succeeded in escaping and hiding near Rottleberode until the Americans arrived several days later. When Ulbricht retraced his steps to Rottleberode after escaping, he discovered several corpses of prisoners who had been shot and left by the roadside.[71]

Brauny and his group reached the railway station at Niedersachswerfen in the early morning hours of April 5. Brauny realized that he needed to proceed northward, although he may not have known the destination: were they to move in the Hamburg direction, to Neuengamme where transports from Mittelbau-Dora had been sent, or Bergen-Belsen, where transports were being sent since it was now clear that Neuengamme was inaccessible? In any event, Brauny was forced to linger with his charges at the Niedersachswerfen railway station because he was scheduled to await the arrival of Lamp's group. Hans Häser, who received from Brauny a list of prisoners who had left Rottleberode, told him something to the same effect. When Brauny saw that Lamp had not yet arrived, he set out on his bicycle back toward the camp to find out what had happened to the other group. He did not find Lamp, who had decided to take another route, and so he returned to Niedersachswerfen on the evening of April 5.[72]

During the wait at the railway station soup was handed out to the prisoners, though possibly not all of them received a portion.[73] They were also given a can of meat or sausages each and one loaf of bread for every two prisoners; during the day they were allowed to brew coffee. Other prisoners arrived the same day. At noon a train consisting of 15 open boxcars arrived; 10 of them were already loaded with prisoners from Mittelbau-Dora and Boelcke. There were between 500 and 600 of them, and many were in very frail condition. The prisoners waiting at the station were loaded onto the cars, about 50 to 60 in each. Four cars were reserved for the guards and two for the equipment and food, including the blankets and clothes of the prisoners. There were about 50 guards and their supervisor, Friedrich Teply, assigned two to each car. At midday on Friday, April 6, the evacuation train left the Niedersachswerfen station.[74] The number of prisoners in Brauny's charge had risen to about 1,000, although he had no statistical data on this transport since he had given the papers he took from Rottleberode to Häser.[75]

In the first stage the evacuation train halted at Ellrich-Bürgergarten, where the prisoners from SS IV Construction Brigade were housed. A group of 350 prisoners (150 sick and 200 Jews) from among the 1,000 inmates of the camp was attached to Brauny's transport. Among them were some who had been evacuated that same day from Woffleben camp. This small subcamp of Ellrich, established in 1945, had 840 inmates at the end of March, who performed taxing excavation work and lived in two barracks under inhuman conditions.[76] Apparently, only the sick or severely debilitated Woffleben inmates were sent to Brauny's transport, as was also the case with the prisoners of IV Construction Brigade at Ellrich-Bürgergarten. The group of prisoners who boarded the train at Ellrich also received a little food before leaving, including half a loaf of bread and about 18 ounces (500 grams) of margarine per prisoner.[77]

At this stage there were about 1,400 prisoners on the transport. It is evident that Brauny's transport contained a particularly high proportion of sick, exhausted, and feeble prisoners. It seemed most unlikely that they would be capable of enduring the hardships of the journey and continuing to labor for the war economy somewhere in Germany. There was also a higher proportion of Jews among them than in other groups evacuated from Mittelbau-Dora because of their dominant presence at Rottleberode and Stempeda and because of the additional Jewish prisoners who had joined up with the transport at Ellrich-Bürgergarten.

On Saturday morning, April 7, Brauny's transport continued on its way to the Osterode railway station, where six freight cars were waiting, with about 300 prisoners from the Ilfeld subcamp. The prisoners in this small camp were evacuated on April 4 or 5 and led on foot to Osterode, in the charge of the commandant of Ilfeld, Werner Wachholz. They covered this distance, about 37 miles (60 kilometers), in less than 48 hours and reached Osterode in a state of exhaustion.[78] There is, however, another version of the evacuation from Ilfeld. According to one eyewitness, the prisoners were prepared for evacuation on April 4 at 11 p.m. They left Ilfeld on April 5 at 9 a.m.; the deputy commandant, Hermann Rose, was in charge of the column. The prisoners walked about 4 miles (6 kilometers) until they reached the railway station at Niedersachswerfen at about 10:30, and there they joined Brauny's transport. In any event, Rose was in charge of the transport when it set out, and it was he who reached the Gardelegen area with the prisoners.[79] When it left Osterode, Brauny's transport consisted of nearly 1,800 prisoners aboard a train with about 20 freight cars. In the first three days of the evacuation they had covered a distance of about 62 miles (100 kilometers), proceeding in a northwesterly direction in an attempt to approach its scheduled destination, Neuengamme.

That day, April 7, not far from Osterode, as the train was setting out northward for Seesen, it came under its first heavy air attack. Two U.S. bombers strafed the train, the engine was put out of action, and several of the freight cars, carrying guards and a group of sick prisoners, were damaged. Three SS men were killed and five were injured. The planes were apparently aiming at the engine, which was damaged beyond repair. A relatively large number of guards were injured because they were traveling in the first car.[80] The planes were flying at a low altitude, about 33 to 44 yards (30 to 40 meters), and the pilots could not have failed to see that the open cars were carrying prisoners and not military or industrial equipment.[81] When the train halted during the attack, the prisoners were hastily disembarked and began to scatter into the nearby fields. A local medical orderly together with the prisoner medic, Johnny Nicholas, began to treat the wounded guards and prisoners.[82]

When the raid ended the guards tried to round up the prisoners. Although there are no precise figures on the number of prisoners who managed to escape, it was probably several dozen. A group of young men from Osterode and nearby towns, including boys from the Hitlerjugend and several Volkssturm soldiers, came to the aid of the guards.[83] Brauny claimed after the war that it was not he who summoned them, although he was encountering problems with the guards, some of whom had fled during the raid while others were reluctant to linger when the Americans were so close at hand.[84] In any event, during the air raid and the manhunt several prisoners were killed, and their comrades buried them in a mass grave in a field beside the track. It is not known how many of them were killed by the U.S. planes and how many by the bullets of the camp guards or local inhabitants. Two Russian prisoners were murdered by one of the guards when they tried to break into the car where the food was stored.[85]

Shortly afterward a new engine was brought from Osterode, and the transport was able to continue on its way, though not for long. Some 6 miles (10 kilometers) north of Osterode, near the town of Badenhausen, the air-raid sirens again sounded. The train came to a halt, and the scene was repeated: prisoners leapt out of the cars and hastened to find shelter by the roadside, among the bushes, and in the fields. This time a large number of prisoners did not return to the train and hid in the surrounding fields; the guards again began to round them up. The Volkssturm personnel and other local civilians played a more active part on this occasion. Civilians quite often took part in hunts for prisoners who fled evacuation trains. Local residents recalled after the war that not only did civilians take part, but some even shot and murdered prisoners.[86]

After the air raid, the train was diverted to a new route, in accordance with Brauny's decision to change the destination. It headed for Braunschweig and the town of Gifhorn, northeast of the town where it had halted. On April 8 Brauny received word that the routes to the northwest in the direction of Hanover were not passable because of the situation on the front and that he was to continue in a northeasterly direction in order to bring the prisoners as close as possible to Oranienburg, to Sachsenhausen. As the train made for Braunschweig, prisoners on the transport heard the guards saying that their destination was Stendal in the Altmark, to the northeast, and that they would have to cross the Elbe in order to reach Oranienburg.[87]

Brauny's decision to divert the train raises certain questions, even in the event that he received instructions to do so, and it is by no means clear who could have transmitted them. It was an unconventional decision in view of the other evacuation routes from the Mittelbau-Dora camps. Almost all the transports that left the camp for Neuengamme eventually reached Bergen-Belsen. Some of the Mittelbau-Dora evacuees reached Ravensbrück; the prisoners from Groß-Werther reached Mauthausen, and other groups were stranded in various places during the evacuation to the north. Only a few groups of prisoners headed for Oranienburg. Some 150 of the 2,000 inmates of Harzungen, who were evacuated on April 4, headed there and were liberated by the Soviets on May 9. Also taken there were about 100 inmates of the small camp at Rußla.[88] In the final analysis, however, these were relatively small groups that headed for the camp on foot when they were unable to continue by rail for various reasons. The largest transport of prisoners that was scheduled in advance for Oranienburg was that commanded by Brauny's deputy, Hermann Lamp, consisting of 1,000 prisoners from Rottleberode. It is possible that the two men discussed this option on the eve of departure on April 4, when they did not know whether it would be possible to reach one of the large concentration camps in the north. Be that as it may, both men chose at an early stage, to some extent because of circumstances, to lead their transports northeastward and not northwestward. Brauny's decision to take the prisoners to Oranienburg sealed the fate of almost all of the marchers, who were to die a cruel death within a few days.

Brauny's evacuation march continued toward Gifhorn. One of the possibilities raised is that the train reached Gifhorn and from there turned eastward, taking the main Hanover–Berlin line as far as Oebisfelde. However, it seems more feasible that Brauny preferred to take the side routes in order to avoid air attacks. Prisoner testimony suggests that the train traveled mostly at night through forested areas along side tracks. It seems, therefore, that it did in fact turn to the east in the Braunschweig area, continued to Helmstedt, and from there went northward on a minor track. In the late night hours of April 7–8 the transport reached the town of Mariental, from there continued through Weferlingen, and then reached the station at Oebisfelde.[89] By whichever route, it halted at Oebisfelde on the night of April 8–9. The next morning, April 9, the transport traveled another 8 miles (13 kilometers) in an easterly direction and reached the town of Mieste in Altmark, 9 miles (15 kilometers) west and slightly south of Gardelegen. This was its final destination by motorized transport. The train entered Mieste station at about 8 a.m.[90]

On April 9 Brauny's evacuation train covered a very short distance. That day, the U.S. aircraft were attacking railway tracks and other transportation routes, and the train was apparently held up on several occasions because of information that the route eastward was impassable. About 6 miles (10 kilometers) east of Mieste, near the town of Solpke, the rails had been completely destroyed by bombing that day, and it was impossible to continue toward Gardelegen and from there to Stendal. The engine had been damaged again during one of the raids and would be out of action for some time. Mieste was the place where Brauny hoped to find another engine or, alternatively, to repair the existing one. It will be recalled that in the Gardelegen and Mieste areas there were several army bases and Luftwaffe technical units which, so the transport commanders hoped, would be able to supply the technical know-how and means of repairing the damage.[91]

Between their departure from the camp on April 4 and their arrival at Mieste five days later the prisoners received no supplementary rations in addition to the food they had received before leaving and during their wait on the first day. Most of them had devoured their ration, usually a loaf of bread, a can of food each, a dab of margarine, by the end of the first day. There was no regular distribution of drinking water, and the prisoners held out their shirts or jackets into the rain or dipped them in puddles on the floor of the freight car.[92] While the train was standing at Osterode station several prisoners succeeded in improvising soup from potatoes they found or that the guards gave them.[93] The overcrowding in the open cars, the harsh weather conditions, the constant rain, and the lack of all sanitary measures turned the floor of the cars into a morass of mud and filth on which the exhausted prisoners sprawled. When the train halted at Mieste, there were 1,740 prisoners in the freight cars. When a lineup was held at the station about 1,340 of them reported for the count. Another 400 or so, who were too feeble to climb down, were carried by their comrades. Eight corpses were also unloaded and were buried by the prisoners in a mass grave in a nearby field.[94]

The 1,000 other prisoners who left Rottleberode on April 4, under Hermann Lamp, followed a different route. Shortly after their departure Lamp decided not to steer a course for Niedersachswerfen and headed for Stolberg instead, 4 miles (7 kilometers) northeast of Rottleberode. From there the transport continued its death march to the north, through Quedlinburg, and along side roads toward Haldensleben, until it eventually reached Genthin. Several guards gained the impression that Lamp, throughout the march, was seeking a way of loading the prisoners onto a train and transporting them to Bergen-Belsen and that only near Haldensleben did he conclude that it was more realistic to aim for Sachsenhausen. One night the transport halted in a large barn near the town of Drackenstedt, 9 miles (15 kilometers) south of Genthin. During the night several armed men, members of irregular units established at the end of the war by Nazi Party functionaries in order to wage guerrilla warfare, entered the barn. Apparently aided by the camp guards, they murdered 58 prisoners who were unable to continue the death march. Most of the prisoners in this transport boarded a train at Genthin and reached Sachsenhausen on April 16, where they joined the prisoners evacuated from Sachsenhausen several days later. The more fortunate among them, who survived the second death march, were liberated by the Americans or the Russians in early May.[95]

Evacuation: Construction Brigade III

The evacuation of the camps of the *SS-Baubrigaden* (Construction Brigades), which belonged to the Mittelbau-Dora complex, began on April 6. These special construction units were established in early 1942, in parallel to completion of the reforms in the SS economic system introduced by Oswald Pohl and Hans Kemmler.[96] The increasingly urgent construction needs of the empire being built up in the East became the main factor underlying their establishment, and Kammler undertook direct responsibility for their administration. They were to fulfill an important function in furthering building projects in Poland, Germany, and other countries, and in exploiting concentration camp inmates in these projects. The Construction Brigades were an important instrument for the SS in early 1942 as it became involved in large-scale economic projects and expanded its contacts with private industry. In February 1942 three brigades were established, each consisting of several building units *(Baukompanie)* of concentration camp prisoners, with 200 laborers per group—a total of 2,400 to 4,800 in each brigade.[97] Inmates of Sollstedt, Hohlstedt, Osterhagen, Nüxei, Mackenrode, Ellrich-Bürgergarten, Wieda, and Gunzerode camps in the Mittelbau-Dora complex labored in the brigades. In October 1944 they numbered 5,100, and by the time the evacuation of these camps began in April 1945 only 3,100 were left.[98]

The general evacuation directive for the construction brigade camps was received at the end of March 1945. Kammler, who was directly responsible for them, sent out a directive on March 28 to the commanders of Construction Brigades III and IV, whose prisoners were dispersed through several of the Mittelbau-Dora camps, to the effect that they were to exercise discretion with regard to evacuation. The commanders in the field, he wrote, were to decide whether to evacuate the camps or, when necessary, leave them intact—in other words, surrender them to the enemy.[99] Kammler was therefore authorizing them to decide whether or not to evacuate and when. At the time he did not apparently display any particular interest in the fate of the construction laborers in Mittelbau-Dora. He was focused mainly on the final mission his Führer had entrusted to him: direct responsibility for the efforts to produce jet aircraft. In this situation, the decisions with regard to evacuation of the construction brigade camps were taken in practice by the three local commandants: Kurt Merkle, Fritz Behrnes, and Erich Scholz. As in other cases, the power they were given to decide on the final date of evacuation was a source of perplexity to them. The order to evacuate Construction Brigade III, consisting of prisoners from Wieda, Mackenrode, Nüxei, and Osterhagen, arrived before April 5, but it is not known who received it or who sent it. On April 6 the evacuation of Brigade III to Sachsenhausen began. The inmates of the Brigade I camps (Sollstedt and Hohlstedt) were evacuated on April 5 and 6 and eventually arrived at Mauthausen. The Brigade IV camps (Ellrich-Bürgergarten, excluding some 350 sick prisoners who were sent on Brauny's transport, and Günzerode) were evacuated only on April 10. Because of the delay in evacuation all escape routes were blocked, and the prisoners were liberated five days later by the Americans.[100]

Of particular interest is the decision of the commandant of Ellrich-Bürgergarten, Erich Scholtz, to send the sick prisoners and the 200 Jews with Brauny's transport. It will be recalled that these prisoners boarded the train carrying the Rottleberode evacuees on April 6, while the remaining camp inmates, some 700 in all, were not evacuated until April 10. Scholtz claimed after the war that a day before the evacuations from Mittelbau-Dora began, namely, on April 3 or 4, he visited the main camp but, in the atmosphere of pandemonium, nobody could supply him with details of evacuation dates or advise him as to the means at his disposal and the direction he was to take. Scholtz testified that he moved the sick and the Jews to Brauny's transport so that, when the time came for him to evacuate Ellrich, he would be able to do so more easily and without being hampered by the need to deal with sick and exhausted prisoners.[101] It seems likely that the Jewish prisoners at Ellrich, who had been sent from Auschwitz and Groß-Rosen in January–February 1945, were in particularly poor physical condition and hence were included in the group of sick prisoners. Scholtz and his deputy, Otto-Georg Brinkmann, left Ellrich a day or two before the departure of the remaining prisoners on April 10 and did not accompany them.[102]

The first stage of the evacuation of Construction Brigade III was the transfer of prisoners from Mackenrode, Nüxei, and Osterhagen to Wieda.[103] All labor at Osterhagen was suspended on April 4. For two days the prisoners were confined to the camp and were idle, and their impression was that the guards had no idea what was going to happen. The prisoners realized that a massive retreat from the area was under way because they saw convoys of soldiers and equipment passing through the camp and heading for the north and west. In great trepidation they began to pack their belongings in anticipation of the moment when they too would be evacuated. On April 6 they were evacuated on foot and walked 9 miles (15 kilometers) to Wieda. There were more than 1,000 inmates there, and the space allotted was too small to take all of them. On the night of April 5–6 another air raid took place, and panic broke out among the prisoners, in the course of which several were injured and crushed.[104]

Some 900 prisoners from three camps of Construction Brigade III were moved to Wieda on the morning of April 6 and reached the camp that afternoon. The next day all of the prisoners at Wieda were evacuated. Together with the prisoners from Wieda itself, the convoy consisted of about 1,130 prisoners, but the group was divided into two. About 800 of them, who were more robust, began a march of more than 12 miles (20 kilometers) along winding and difficult paths through the Harz Mountains. In the first stage they walked to Braunlage and passed through at a rapid pace. There was apparently an air raid while they were there. After leaving the town they continued north to Wernigerode, where they were lodged in several deserted barracks of a small Buchenwald subcamp, Richard, which had operated from March 1943 to November 1944.[105]

They were waiting for a group of about 340 sick prisoners who had been too weak to walk the distance.[106] Lucien Colonel, who had been imprisoned at Nüxei and was transferred to Wieda before the final evacuation, related that at the time of the evacuation from Wieda he weighed only 79 pounds (36 kilograms). In March 1945 he had been sent to the revier and was almost too weak to move. When they reached Wieda on the evening of April 6 they were taken into an old building in the camp. The next day they were loaded onto three freight cars, more than 100 per car, and transported to Wernigerode. According to another testimony the sick prisoners were transported to Wernigerode in trucks and not by train.[107]

The transport of 1,130 prisoners from Construction Brigade III set out for the north on April 9, its destination Braunschweig. At this stage, and perhaps even before the train set out from Wernigerode, the commander, Kurt Merkle, deputy chief of Construction Brigade III, left the transport. From that moment on SS-Sergeant Kemmnitz was in charge.[108] The closed boxcars in which the Construction Brigade III prisoners were evacuated, in contrast to the open freight cars of the Rottleberode prisoners, were large enough for the passengers to be able to sit during the journey. There were guards in each car. After 24 hours the prisoners began to suffer from severe hunger, having consumed their meager ration of a loaf of bread and a dab of margarine on the first day. At one of the train's stops soup was doled out to them. Several of them were fortunate enough to find a few potatoes, which they cooked in the cars.[109]

On the night of April 9–10 the train halted at the small town of Jerxheim, and on April 10 it turned sharply eastward toward Magdeburg on its way to Sachsenhausen. During the night of April 9 four prisoners died in the cars, and they were probably not the first to perish during the journey. Several of the sick prisoners who had been taken on at Wieda had died on the way to Wernigerode. When the train reached the western suburbs of Magdeburg in the late evening of April 10, there were only 1,124 prisoners alive.[110]

The train entered Magdeburg a few days after the town had suffered a heavy air attack. On the night of April 3–4 the RAF bombed the town, destroying the few structures still standing after a previous raid in mid-January. Some 15,000 inhabitants died in this attack; vast fires raged and thousands abandoned their homes and fled to the surrounding villages.[111] The Magdeburg railway station was totally destroyed, as were the tracks leading to the Elbe and several of the bridges over the river. The rapid U.S. advance, and the fact that American forces had already crossed the Elbe east of Magdeburg had finally blocked off this route. The entire Magdeburg area was in a state of chaos because of the German retreat, and the rail network was heavily overloaded. The transport was forced to wait its turn.[112]

The only option was to advance northward along side tracks. Kemmnitz apparently wanted to continue to Stendal and from there to attempt to move eastward, to cross the Elbe, and try to reach Sachsenhausen. On April 11 the train passed through Groß Ammensleben, Haldensleben, and Roxförde; it finally halted at 5:30 p.m. at the Letzlingen railway station, about 31 miles (50 kilometers) north of Magdeburg and 7 miles (12 kilometers) southeast of Gardelegen.[113]

Evacuation: Hanover-Stöcken

An external commando of Neuengamme had been functioning in Stöcken, the western suburb of Hanover, since July 1943. The inmates worked in an old established concern (Akkumulatorenfabrik—AFA), which had been manufacturing batteries for submarines since World War I. Prisoners from all over Europe labored in five labor camps in the Hanover area in the second half of 1943. In summer 1944 these camps became subcamps of Neuengamme. In late 1944 the camp took in Jewish prisoners who had been evacuated from the Łódź ghetto after its liquidation and then sent to Auschwitz, to Neuengamme, and from there to the camps in the Hanover area. A total of more than 4,000 concentration camp prisoners worked in private concerns there.[114]

The battery production factory at Stöcken was the first of the Hanover camps to put camp prisoners to work on its production line. In October 1943 500 such workers were housed in a camp not far from their workplace. As far as the SS were concerned Stöcken was an ideal camp, a model of success in exploiting concentration camp prisoners in private concerns. The distance to work was short, and the prisoners were guarded by about 15 SS men, almost all of them older naval personnel assigned to this duty in summer 1944. The kapos, who were German prisoners, were in charge of internal administration and work schedules.[115] The professional management was entrusted to engineers and the civilian administrators of the factory. Production was expanded in early 1944 to meet the increasingly urgent needs of the military, and the number of prisoners in the camp exceeded 1,000. There were 10 to 15 barracks, and the prisoners were of diverse nationalities: German, Polish, French, Russian, Belgian, Danish, a small group from the Baltic countries, and Italians, Czechs, and Greeks. As noted, there was also a small group of Jews. The German prisoners were mainly political detainees or homosexuals. The French and Danes were mainly Resistance fighters, and the Russians were POWs. It seems that there were also no deaths in the camp until late March–early April 1945.[116]

Preparations were beginning at the time for the evacuation of the labor camps in the Hanover area. As was the case elsewhere, here too the orders were not clear in the first instance, and the commander of this group of camps, Kurt Klebeck, did not know precisely what he was to do with his prisoners in view of the approach of enemy forces. On April 1 he received a telephone call from Max Pauly at Neuengamme, who talked to him about the Hanover camps, and conveyed explicit orders to the local commanders. Klebeck claimed that it was evident to him that the source of this directive was Himmler himself. Klebeck handed it down to the camps under his responsibility, among others to Paul Mass, who was in charge of Stöcken. According to the order, all prisoners from Stöcken were to be transferred to Bergen-Belsen.[117] Mass remembered the precise wording of the order: "No prisoner is to be allowed to fall into enemy hands."[118] Wilhelm Genth, one of the guards who accompanied the group of prisoners evacuated on foot to Bergen-Belsen, testified that before they set out they were told explicitly that the order to evacuate the camp came from the RSHA and that the guards and prisoners were to be transferred to Bergen-Belsen.[119] The phrasing is identical to Himmler's statement to the HSSPF of Hamburg, Bassewitz-Behr, in late March–early April 1945, and it is reasonable to assume that Pauly transmitted this operative instruction as such to the camps in the Hanover area. The prisoners at Stöcken naturally hoped that they would succeed in staying put in their barracks until the Americans arrived.[120]

On the eve of the evacuation, at the end of March, prisoners evacuated from Neuengamme's subcamps near Braunschweig arrived in Stöcken. They were on their way to the main camp, in accordance with the procedure for evacuation of the subcamps that had been put into motion at the time. The transport consisted of 400 to 450 sick prisoners, who were to be sent on to Bergen-Belsen, also in accordance with the decision of the Neuengamme command. They reached Stöcken aboard buses supplied by the Swedish Red Cross and were accommodated in several separate barracks. The mortality rate was high, and some did not live to see the day of liberation. Several survivors reported after the war that some of the prisoners perished at Stöcken in the last few days before the camp was liquidated.[121]

At the beginning of April there were 1,500 prisoners in Stöcken.[122] Klebeck, who arrived on April 3, ordered Mass, the guards, and Wilhelm Genth three days later to prepare the prisoners for evacuation.[123] About 1,000 prisoners who were fit enough to walk began their trek northward on April 7 and reached Bergen-Belsen the next day in the afternoon. Quite a few of them collapsed along the way and were shot by the guards.[124] The 500 sick prisoners left at Stöcken were in no condition to be evacuated on foot. They were left in the barracks, although the guards who remained behind had no idea what to do with them.[125] Klebeck, who was still in the area, reminded the guards of the directive that no prisoners were to be allowed to fall into enemy hands. However, he insisted that it was essential to arrange for a means of transportation for those unable to walk. After the war he claimed that, in accordance with the instructions he received, he gave orders to leave the sick prisoners in their barracks and meanwhile to organize a train or wagons to convey them to Bergen-Belsen. Under no circumstances did he order the murder of sick prisoners, Klebeck declared.[126] Indeed, these prisoners were not killed while they were awaiting evacuation; it was the 24-hour interval before the evacuation that sealed the fate of most of them. Klebeck stayed behind when the convoy left for Bergen-Belsen. According to him he spent the day trying to obtain some form of transportation for the sick. Only after he located freight cars, and responsibility for the evacuation was taken over by the Hanover police, did he leave Stöcken for Bergen-Belsen.[127]

The prisoners left behind in the barracks were in critical condition. They were almost too weak to move; many were naked or wrapped in a single thin blanket.[128] Late in the evening on Sunday, April 8, the guards informed the prisoners that they were to be evacuated from the camp. The departure was organized hurriedly. They were loaded onto four freight cars, about 100 per car, and several loaves of bread were thrown into each car, but no water was supplied. Several of the prisoners, who were obviously too weak to tolerate these conditions, were shot before the train set out.[129] The prisoners realized that their destination lay to the north, at Bergen-Belsen, but they were transported only as far as the Herrenhausen station, northwest of the center of Hanover. The train stood in the station until 11 p.m. because no one was able to organize the continuation of its journey.[130] From the moment the transport reached Hanover, it lacked a commander and evidently had almost no guards, and it was not clear who was in charge. The guards who had set out with the transport seized the opportunity and abandoned their charges at the station.[131] Those of the prisoners who were still able to move apparently fled. Since the train could not continue northward, it turned east to Gifhorn and traveled from there to Fallersleben and Wolfsburg. It then continued along the track eastward and slightly to the north toward Gardelegen until it reached its last stop, Mieste, on April 9 between 4 and 6 p.m.[132]

When the doors of the car were opened, a harrowing sight was revealed. About 400 sick and emaciated prisoners were sprawled motionless on the floor of the cars. Most were wearing prisoners' striped uniforms and were shod in wooden clogs. Quite a few of them were naked, particularly the weaker prisoners who had been dispatched hastily. In the confusion at Stöcken, nobody had bothered to cover them as they were dragged out of their barracks and thrown onto the cars. Because of the cold weather, some of them had frozen to death en route.[133] Many lay inert, smeared in excrement and filth, and it was difficult to distinguish between the living and the dead. A nauseating stink rose from the cars, and it was almost impossible to enter them. Even prisoners who had arrived on Brauny's transport from Rottleberode were horrified at the sight of these wretched human beings.[134] About 60 corpses were removed from the cars. Another 20 to 25 prisoners from the Stöcken transport died in the following two days while the prisoners were waiting at Mieste station. The dead were buried in a mass grave dug by prisoners beside the track.[135]

Two evacuation trains were stranded at the Mieste railway station on the evening of Monday, April 9, with a passenger load of more than 2,000 prisoners. A third train, which apparently arrived on the same day, was carrying military equipment and a group of military escorts, and was headed for Frankfurt. It too was unable to continue its journey. The small town of less than 2,000 inhabitants was transformed overnight into an assembly spot for thousands of prisoners evacuated from concentration camps and their agitated guards, who were terrified of being stranded with their prisoners as the Americans came closer. The railway station staff at Mieste made it clear to Brauny that he could not continue eastward before the tracks were repaired and that there was no way to locate a new engine to replace the damaged one because any available engines would be placed at the disposal of the army.[136] The prisoners overheard the guards discussing the situation as they waited at the station. It was impossible to find a way of continuing the transport in view of the military circumstances, they said, except for a transport to Heaven *(Himmelsfahrtstransport)*. In any case, the "swine and red dogs" *(Schweine und rote hunde)* did not deserve to live once they were of no further economic use.[137]

Waiting

The first night of the wait at Mieste, between April 9 and 10, was a night of suffering for the prisoners. When Brauny's transport reached the town and the freight car doors were opened, containers of water were brought in by several residents who lived close to the station. In all about 11 quarts (10 liters) of water were distributed, mainly to the prisoners in the worst condition. As night fell the prisoners were loaded back onto the cars without receiving food. They could hear the guards, gathered in a nearby tavern, singing and playing music. As morning dawned several prisoners took the containers from the previous night and went off in search of water. One of the guards who accompanied this group, which included the kapo Karl Semmler, refused to allow them to enter the town in search of food. He said that Brauny had prohibited any contact of the prisoners with the local civilian population.[138]

Tuesday, April 10, was a day of turmoil and considerable confusion for the guards. Although Brauny had been told that no engines were available, and the state of the railway tracks east of the Elbe was uncertain, he persisted in his search for ways of continuing the evacuation. He contemplated requisitioning horse-drawn carts from the local farmers for the sick prisoners, and continuing the journey on foot with the rest.[139] The prisoners noticed that Brauny was moving to and fro between the station and the town, talking to various people and to the guards, who also appeared at a loss.[140] Meanwhile, prisoners were dying, either of starvation at the station or while trying to slip away in search of food to ease their gnawing hunger. Several of them tried to break into a flour storeroom not far from the station; seven or eight of them were caught by the Luftwaffe guards and shot. Dying prisoners were also shot during the wait. Franz Unverdorben, one of the Ellrich guards on the transport, shot two or three dying prisoners. In all, 25 were shot by the guards while awaiting the decision to continue the evacuation.[141] At least one prisoner was murdered in the street while roaming in search of food.[142] On May 11, 1945, 86 unidentified corpses of prisoners who died or were murdered while their transport was halted at Mieste, were exhumed from a mass grave in the town.[143]

The situation was a source of anxiety to the town's notables, first and foremost the mayor, Adolf Krüger. He had been a Nazi Party member since 1931 and was active in a local party in this small provincial farming town in central Germany. When the prisoners arrived on April 9 he immediately appealed to the district council *(Landrat),* seated at Gardelegen, for enough food to feed the 2,000 or so prisoners stranded there. He apparently received orders from the Landrat to supply the food himself, but he refused and shifted responsibility back to the council.[144] Dr. Daue, the Landrat commissar responsible for these matters, ordered the dispatch of foodstuffs to Mieste, including potatoes, cabbage, meat, and coffee.[145] Albert Borges, commander of the Gardelegen gendarmerie, ordered two store owners, a butcher and a greengrocer, to prepare crates of food and arranged for them to be sent to Mieste in two trucks.[146] A day later, on April 10, a small quantity of food reached the prisoners. According to Krüger it consisted mainly of potatoes, a little meat, and coffee. The food was distributed to the prisoners on Tuesday afternoon. It was the first time they had received any food since arriving in Mieste and, indeed, since they had left the camps five days earlier. Several sacks of potatoes were divided among the prisoners in each freight car, so that each of them received about four or five potatoes. The more robust prisoners lit small fires and baked the potatoes. Some were too feeble to move, and a watery potato soup was prepared for them.[147] None of the survivors recalled receiving meat or coffee. On the other hand, they heard local residents near the station saying that it was a shame to feed these criminals and that it would be better to liquidate them all.[148]

Krüger did not consider it his duty to look after these prisoners, particularly since the regular supply of basic goods for the town's residents and the refugees staying there was also encountering considerable problems.[149] He wanted to feed them, not because he feared that they would starve to death, but because he was afraid that hunger might drive them to leave the station in search of food or to escape and try to find shelter in the neighborhood until the Americans arrived. He was concerned that the explosive situation might deteriorate into total anarchy and that the presence of 2,000 starving and unsupervised prisoners could lead to catastrophe. His fears were reinforced by the complaints of several local residents that roaming prisoners had broken into their houses or the storerooms in their yards and stolen food.[150] His main task, as he saw it, was to rid the town as fast as possible of these prisoners, and he did not find it necessary to try to alleviate their distress until the Americans arrived. Krüger began to exert pressure on Brauny to find a rapid solution to the problem and to leave town with his thousands of prisoners.[151] One of the Mieste tradesmen even heard Krüger say that the sick prisoners, who were incapable of walking and could not be removed in any other fashion, should simply be liquidated.[152]

It was becoming increasingly difficult to guard the prisoners. Quite a few guards from the original camp team, particularly those from the SS, left on April 10 and 11. It was they who most greatly feared falling into American hands, and they were the first to disappear. Brauny now suffered from a shortage of guards, which naturally made it easier for prisoners still capable of doing so to escape and hide.[153] He too seems to have realized that he could not continue to detain the prisoners at the railway station and must continue the journey by all possible means. On April 10 horse-drawn wagons arrived at the station and preparations for departure began. Neither the remaining guards nor the prisoners knew what the destination was and what fate awaited the transport.

Brauny could not explain to his postwar interrogators why he decided to continue the evacuation after he discovered at Mieste that his preferred destination, Bergen-Belsen or Sachsenhausen, was unattainable. Nor could he explain precisely which authority decided that the prisoners should be transferred to Gardelegen and concentrated there in one place where they could be supervised efficiently. However, he agreed that this had been the best way to act under the circumstances. Apart from that, he claimed, the prisoners were, in any case, incapable of walking because they were wearing wooden clogs and, in general

> there was no use to continue because too many of the prisoners were weak and could not continue and I had to give them a long rest. . . . We left in the afternoon from Mieste and [after a] short stop we arrived toward morning at Gardelegen.[154]

It may be assumed that Brauny considered this to be his last assignment with the transport under his command. He understood that he could not bring the prisoners to a camp that would take them in, not necessarily because of the state of their health but because the railway lines were not functioning and no engine was available. At this stage responsibility for the transport was being transferred from the guards and the officers who had brought them from Mittelbau-Dora to the local authorities in the Gardelegen area. From the moment the prisoners became a tangible presence in their area the problem was theirs, and they were required to provide satisfactory solutions, at least until the Americans arrived. The process began when it became necessary to feed the prisoners stranded at the railway station in Mieste and continued when the search commenced for a site capable of housing such a large number of prisoners and isolating them from the local population.

It is not known who decided to transfer the prisoners to Gardelegen. Karl Leppe, the acting mayor of Gardelegen, received warning of the arrival of the prisoners and began to seek a place able to absorb all of them. He was helped in this task by the senior police office in Gardelegen, Rudolf Ringstmeyer.[155] One possibility that was broached was to find a solution in the style of the "Jewish houses" *(Judenhäuser)* where the Jews who were left in the town in August 1941 had been concentrated. At the time, as was the practice elsewhere in Germany,[156] the last seven Jewish families were rehoused in a guarded building where they were permitted to live under the supervision of the local police. Twenty-one of the Jews who lived there were sent to extermination camps, and in October 1942 only nine Jews remained in Gardelegen, all of them married to non-Jews.[157] It soon became clear that the method employed to deal with several dozen Jews before deporting them would not work with 2,000 prisoners. The possibility was then raised of exploiting the stables in the army riding base in the town, which trained horses for military purposes.[158]

The Death March

On Wednesday, April 11, U.S. tanks were already less than 12 miles (20 kilometers) from Mieste. That morning, at about 8 a.m., the town railway station was attacked, and a bomb fell on the track where the prisoner train was standing. This U.S. bombardment created renewed panic among both the prisoners and the guards. The prisoners fled in search of shelter in the fields and among the trees beside the station. The guards, who sensed that they were losing control, began to fire wildly and indiscriminately at their charges. They began to round them up and bring them back to the station, and again murdered some who tried to escape. The guards shot 17 of them, but a few succeeded in getting away and hiding.[159] When the panic died down and most of the prisoners had been returned to the train, two slave laborers—a Pole and a Russian—arrived and reported that the Americans were about 8 miles (13 kilometers) from Mieste and were due to enter the town within a day at the latest. It was evident that if the guards wanted to assemble the prisoners in a suitable place before the American occupation, it should be done immediately.

It seems, however, that, in the general disarray that prevailed, the guards were not convinced that there was enough time at their disposal to take action. Brauny assembled the remaining guards and the kapos and told them the news. One option discussed was to leave the prisoners where they were and hand them over to local authorities, such as the Volkssturm or local army units. The decision to transfer the prisoners to local authorities at Gardelegen was the upshot of this discussion.[160] Brauny told his men that prisoners able to walk and in relatively good condition were to be taken off the train and assembled for the beginning of the evacuation. The sick were to be left in the freight cars. There were also persistent rumors that 300 sick and feeble prisoners were to be liquidated.[161] While these preparations were afoot a large group of Rottleberode guards decided that the game was over; about 20 of them took to their heels immediately after the aerial attack.[162] It is difficult to estimate how many guards abandoned the transport between April 5 and 11; there had been two or three guards in each car, about 60 in all. Desertions had already occurred during the journey to Mieste, particularly after the bombing raid on the train. The transport from Hanover-Stöcken arrived in Mieste almost without guards. By the time the evacuation march from Mieste to Gardelegen set out, only about 40 to 50 of the original guards were left.[163] If more than 1,800 prisoners were to be moved from Mieste to Gardelegen on foot, more guards would be needed. They were recruited on April 10 and 11 almost spontaneously, and undoubtedly in haphazard fashion from almost all the military or party frameworks still functioning in the area.

In the two days the transport spent at Mieste, various volunteers came to the station to reinforce the small group of guards, and thereby prevent what the local inhabitants feared above all, namely, escape of prisoners who might then hide in the town. On April 10 a unit of 12 to 16 local Volkssturm men, commanded by Erich Rust, reported to the station; civilians, sometimes armed with hunting rifles, also apparently joined the guards on their own initiative and without having been recruited.[164] They volunteered because they were terrified that the prisoners constituted a threat to their families and property. The most significant group of guards, however, were Wehrmacht and Luftwaffe soldiers from the local bases.

The largest base in the Gardelegen area was the central paratroopers placement base (Hauptuntersuchungsstelle der Fallschirmjägerarmee), which reassigned Luftwaffe personnel who had been classified as redundant. They underwent medical testing, and those found to be suitable were sent to the paratrooper unit affiliated with the Luftwaffe. Those unsuited for this type of service were transferred to various training tasks. During 1944 the camp processed more than 10,000 such men, and in March 1945 there were still 2,000 to 3,000 personnel there. It was also the base with the largest arsenal of weapons in the district: automatic weapons, grenades, antitank bazookas (Panzerfaust), and flamethrowers.

Also based in the area was the 101st Technical Unit (Flughafenbetriebe KP 101) of the Husum airfield, which in early April 1945 had been transferred to Gardelegen. It consisted of some 350 soldiers with no combat background or training, who were armed with outdated weapons, rifles, and antitank launchers. Until early April there were still several Messerschmidt 1092s in the airfield close to Gardelegen, but during that month they were moved eastward to the airfield at Stendal; only troops remained there. There was also a detachment of soldiers who had formerly served in the Tank Corps, who were equipped with light weapons, mainly mortars and rifles, as well as a unit of military police, whose main tasks in April 1945 were to seek out and capture deserters who were trying to reach home before the Americans could take them prisoner, or to direct the traffic as the military forces retreated eastward.[165] The two senior commanders of the two large bases were Oberstleutnant (Lieutenant-Colonel) Kurt von Einem, commandant of the Luftwaffe paratroopers base, and Oberst (Colonel) Walter Miltz, commander of the Luftwaffe base, who was in charge of all technical units within this framework.[166] Quite a few soldiers from these bases were to play a central part in deciding the fate of the prisoners assembled at Gardelegen.

On April 11, when the prisoners set out, the number of guards was the same as before, but the composition of the group had changed completely since they left Mieste. Among the 60 or 70 guards at the Mieste railway station,[167] the SS men and veteran guards who had left Mittelbau-Dora with them were now in the minority. It was now a random group of guards *(zufällig eingefundene Wachmannschaften)*[168] consisting of men from various units, Volkssturm members, Hitlerjugend boys, anxious civilians, and the remnants of the veteran guards group. They had one thing in common: concern for the welfare of the local population. From now on, local elements were to determine the fate of the evacuees from Mittelbau-Dora and Hanover-Stöcken.

That same day, around noon, after the panic caused by the air raid had subsided, the transfer of the prisoners to Gardelegen began. By 2 p.m. there were about 20 horse-drawn wagons at the station. The prisoners who were no longer able to walk were lowered from the cars by their comrades and loaded onto the wagons. They lay motionless on the straw on the wagons.[169] Those prisoners who could walk were divided into two groups, although the classification is not clear. The first group seems to have consisted of prisoners from Construction Brigade IV from Ellrich (Jews and sick prisoners) and most of the prisoners from Rottleberode and Stempeda. The second group consisted of most of the Ilfeld prisoners and some from Rottleberode.[170] The fact that prisoners from various camps were dispersed among the groups indicates that it was not necessarily the guards who divided them up. The prisoners probably did this themselves, and the natural choice was to remain with familiar people and not to march among strangers. Before leaving, the prisoners received several potatoes as provisions for the journey.[171]

The distance from Mieste to Gardelegen is about 9 miles (15 kilometers), but the two groups marched through forest trails and side roads in order to avoid exposure to the U.S. aircraft flying over the district. The chosen route, therefore, was long and passed through little villages to the west and north of the town, the aim being to reach Gardelegen from the north.

The first group began to march eastward toward Gardelegen. After a few miles, near the village of Wernitz, the paratroopers guarding the column singled out the weak prisoners who were finding it hard to walk and shot them with automatic weapons. Halfway to Gardelegen, near the small village of Solpke, the prisoners were directed off the main road onto forest paths. After walking for several hours, they stopped for a brief rest as darkness fell. They continued their march toward Breitenfeld and then farther north toward the village of Zichtau, where the prisoners were permitted to rest for an hour, and then moved on southward toward Gardelegen. They passed Wiepke,[172] and the villagers watched them as they passed. They looked like ghosts as they staggered along in their wooden clogs, and they gave off a strong stench. As they passed through one of the villages, a Russian slave laborer managed to hint to Karl Semmler, the communist kapo from Rottleberode, that he would do well to find a way to escape, since a cruel fate awaited them.[173] The prisoners continued their march through the villages in the direction of Estedt, reached Berge, and walked south toward Gardelegen. They arrived there between 4 and 5 a.m. on April 12[174] and entered the town from the direction of the railway station. They marched along Bahnhofstraße, stumbling and swaying and clutching the personal dishes that they had carried all the way from Mittelbau-Dora.[175] Although this was the fastest evacuation column and hence had the least victims, several prisoners were murdered during the evacuation by the guards.[176] Brauny was one of the escorts of this group and arrived at Gardelegen with the prisoners.[177]

The second group also set out for the north toward Breitenfeld, but shortly after they left Mieste, U.S. planes appeared overhead and they fled into the forest.[178] In order to round up the scattered prisoners, a group of armed civilians joined the guards and pursued the escapees into the forest.[179] The column of prisoners continued on its way and reached Estedt and then, for unknown reasons, instead of turning south and entering Gardelegen, continued northward toward Wiepke. At about 10:30 p.m. a German officer on a motorcycle passed them and told the guards that they were marching straight toward the American tanks. The guards panicked and ordered the prisoners to turn back, thrashing them and shooting those who were slow in carrying out the order.[180] The column retraced its steps and advanced into the forested area between Breitenfeld and Estedt. From that moment there was unrest in the column. The guards, soldiers from the nearby paratroopers base and local Volkssturm men, were terrified that by dawn they might be captured by the advance units of the U.S. force that was approaching Gardelegen. The prisoners realized that liberation was only a few hours away. Hundreds of them fled into the forest under cover of darkness, and about 120 suddenly found themselves unguarded.[181] The guards had either simply taken to their heels or had allowed the prisoners to escape amidst the confusion.[182] The prisoners could not grasp where their guards had gone and why they were now free. They split up into small groups of five to seven men each and began to seek shelter and, above all, food.[183] Some were unfortunate enough to be caught during the savage manhunt conducted in the forest. Others succeeded in gaining another few days of grace.

On April 11 Wilhelm Berlin, mayor of Estedt, was already aware that prisoners were crossing his village on their way to Gardelegen. He saw the first group pass through on its way south, and so did local farmers.[184] Berlin, who was 66, had served as mayor since 1927. He had been a member of the Nazi Party since 1940, but was not involved in political activity. The fact that escaped prisoners were roaming the forests around the village and that the American army was due to arrive at any moment was a source of great anxiety for him and for the 400 or so inhabitants. They felt that their public safety and security were being threatened.

At about 3 a.m. on April 12 Helmut Hockhaup, a paratrooper officer from the Gardelegen area, came to Estedt and called out the members of the local Volkssturm unit. They were ordered to join in the hunt for prisoners hiding near the village. Several of them refused because they realized the practical implications of the order, while others joined in unhesitatingly.[185] A nocturnal manhunt was launched in the forests around Estedt and in the village itself. Forty-year-old Henryk Kostrzewa, a former Polish soldier, was one of a small group of Polish slave laborers who were working for local farmers. He had been laboring in Germany since 1939, when he was taken prisoner in the September 1939 campaign. At 5 a.m. he heard shots from the forest near the village. After a short time, some people he had never seen before came to the house of his employer and demanded that Kostrzewa be sent with a shovel to the little restaurant in the center of the village. When he arrived there he found another eight forced laborers, all of them equipped with shovels. A man in an SS uniform and another group of soldiers were waiting for them. The nine laborers were taken to the forest, and there the soldiers told them to begin digging a pit. At the same time a wagon arrived with 15 corpses of prisoners and another 20 to 25 who were still alive. The soldiers ordered Kostrzewa and his comrades to unload the corpses. The surviving prisoners refused to climb down, but the soldiers shoved the Poles aside and dragged them off the wagon. The Poles then threw the corpses into the pit they had dug. Kostrzewa described the horror he witnessed:

> The prisoners who were alive were lined up on the edge of the ditch, and were ordered to kneel down facing the ditch. The soldiers then came along and shot the prisoners in the back of the head. Those who didn't fall into the grave after being shot were pushed in by the soldiers with their feet. Then the second wagon came with about 30 prisoners and five dead prisoners. They were taken off the wagon and we had to give them our shovels and they had to throw a thin covering of dirt over the bodies in the ditch. Even then, legs, arms and heads still showed. These prisoners were then lined up along the ditch and had to kneel down. They also were shot in the back of the head. I saw a Polish brothers [sic] who told the soldiers they didn't do anything and why do you want to shoot us. The soldier said "keep quiet" and shot them both. . . . All the soldiers were enjoying themselves and smoking cigarettes.[186]

After some time another wagon arrived with 15 prisoners. They too did not want to climb down and pleaded with the soldiers to spare them. They were dragged off the wagon and murdered in the same fashion as the previous group. When the nine slave laborers finished burying the victims they returned to the village. On the way they met a local farmer driving a wagon carrying another six or seven prisoners. He had found them hiding in his barn and immediately informed the soldiers, two of whom came and took them. The nine Poles were taken back to the forest and witnessed the murder of these prisoners, who were shot in the back of the head. Then they covered the corpses with soil and returned to the village. On the way they saw yet another wagon with six prisoners, but this time they succeeded in keeping their distance from the soldiers. The Poles feared that if they were again forced to bury victims, their luck would no longer hold and they, in their turn, would be killed in order to cover the traces of the crime. On their way back to their employers' farms, Kostrzewa and his friend witnessed another murder, this time of two prisoners caught in a village street and shot on the spot by the soldiers.[187] Not only foreign laborers but local farmers as well were summoned to bury the dead. In several cases, corpses of the murdered prisoners were heaped onto wagons and transported to the burial trenches in the local forest.[188]

Word of the massacre at Estedt reached the Americans on April 19, when they interrogated captured German soldiers. The following details appeared in the report of the interrogation:

> POWs consistently denied any connection with either of the foregoing, but admitted having seen the bodies of two political prisoners (identified by striped

clothing) in the woods by Estedt . . . 6 km, of Gardelegen. This info was transmitted through channels to Div CIC, who visited the area with PW Nachtigall on 19 April 45, and there found the bodies and graves of a large number of prisoners who had been killed by shooting or having their skulls cracked. CIC questioned the Burgermeister of Estedt as well as a number of other local people and French and Polish liberated prisoners, and found that knowledge of the affair was quite widespread. Among other facts ascertained was that a 3rd Co of an unidentified Para unit from Gardelegen had furnished escort guards for the prisoners killed at Estedt, and the man directing the affair was named Helmut Hockhauf.[189]

The interrogator, Lieutenant Kenneth Russ, conducted a thorough inspection of the mass graves of prisoners murdered at Estedt on May 9, 1945. He discovered two pits to the west of the village, identified through the fresh mounds of soil above them. They were located only about 295 yards (270 meters) from farmhouses. When they began exhuming the graves, the interrogators found it difficult to estimate the number of corpses. It was decided to transfer the victims to the local cemetery for proper burial. The mayor, Wilhelm Berlin, was ordered to supply the necessary manpower for the task. The graves were exhumed on May 11, with 60 corpses found in the first pit and 30 in the second. A third burial pit was discovered, containing four corpses. Others were discovered in pits dug by the farmers, which were scattered over various sites around the village. In all, 110 corpses of victims of the Estedt massacre were laid to rest in the village cemetery.[190]

Word of the massacre raging at Estedt reached Gardelegen. On Thursday afternoon, April 12, Berlin received a telephone call from Gardelegen, apparently from one of the heads of the Deutsche Arbeitsfront (German Labor Front—DAF) who told him that he must put an immediate stop to the manhunt in his village. Berlin was ordered to collect the stray prisoners and to transfer them en masse to Gardelegen to the riding barracks. By Thursday afternoon, 80 to 100 prisoners had been assembled at the firefighters' station at Estedt. These survivors of the Ilfeld transport, which had been almost entirely liquidated during the massacre, were transferred to Gardelegen and at about 5 p.m. were brought to an assembly point in the stables with the rest of the Brauny transport.[191]

That same afternoon another 100 or so escaped prisoners were caught in the forest, most of them apparently from the group abandoned by their guards on the previous night. Nine paratroopers led them to the spot where, early that morning, the large-scale massacre had been perpetrated. Preparations began for the liquidation of this group. They were ordered to strip, and six of them began to dig pits. Ludwig Lewin, who was among them, testified that he lay naked on the ground and waited to die. At the last moment he suddenly heard shouts from a man who had just arrived, who told the soldiers not to murder the prisoners.[192] It was Hans-Joachim Korts, son of the head of the local Nazi Party branch in the village. He conveyed to the soldiers the order Berlin had received, to the effect that all the prisoners were to be transferred to the riding barracks at Gardelegen.[193] They were sent to Gardelegen almost without guards, accompanied mainly by several prisoners, who served as kapos.[194]

The third group of prisoners, the last to leave Mieste on April 11, probably during the evening, consisted of 300 sick prisoners who were evacuated aboard wagons.[195] Most of the prisoners in the group were from Hanover-Stöcken and had been in desperate condition by the time they reached Mieste two days earlier. This column now had almost no guards, since there was little danger that the prisoners would be strong enough to escape. Hence only two or three SS guards and several kapos and Hitlerjugend boys accompanied them; the wagons were driven by members of the Volkssturm.[196] The convoy of 15 to 20 wagons took a different route to the other two groups because it was not easy to advance along the narrow forest trails. They took the direct route to the village of Solpke, where the prisoners were lodged for the night in a barn belonging to a local farmer named Fritz Schulze.[197] The next morning the group continued on its way to Gardelegen alongside the Solpke-Gardelegen railway line, reached Weteriz, south of Gardelegen, turned in a northeasterly direction, and entered Gardelegen in the late evening hours of April 12. They too were lodged in the cavalry school.[198]

Graves of prisoners shot along the way by the guards are scattered along this route. "The SS and the Hitlerjugend laughed as they turned us, we phantoms, into targets," related one of the survivors.[199] The prisoners on the wagons saw their comrades lying lifeless, often naked, by the roadside as they passed.[200] It seems that the guards did not hesitate to shoot any prisoners who appeared to be dying or were so debilitated that they would obviously be unable to make the journey.[201] A group of 12 to 15 sturdier prisoners were chosen to accompany the sick, their task being to bury by the roadside those who died during the evacuation. Several of them estimated that they buried between 15 and 20 victims.[202]

The death march of the three groups from Mieste to Gardelegen claimed more than 200 lives in the day and a half, from the afternoon of April 11 to the morning of April 13. Within a radius of 3 to 6 miles (5 to 10 kilometers) north and south of the town were the scattered graves of 110 prisoners murdered at Estedt, 33 at Wernitz, 23 at Solpke, 10 at Zichtau, and 8 at Berge, as well as the victims of the death march of the sick prisoners.[203]

Hunting Zebras

A transport of about 1,130 prisoners from the Construction Brigade III camps had stopped at Letzlingen, some 7 miles (12 kilometers) southeast of Gardelegen. As noted, they reached this small town in the afternoon hours of April 11. When their train finally came to a stop there was utter confusion in the station. The last car, containing the belongings and equipment of the guards, was uncoupled from the train and pushed onto a siding. The equipment was unloaded and each guard collected his personal belongings. Kemmnitz, the junior camp guard who had been given command of the evacuation train without prior preparation, did not know how to proceed in view of the blockage of roads and the destruction of railway tracks. He told the guards that they must decide what to do: whether to kill the prisoners or let them go. It appears that during this conversation two U.S. aircraft flew overhead and strafed the train. The hesitations of the guards, together with the rumor that the train was stranded and there was no solution to its plight, increased the prisoners' fear that a massacre was imminent. On orders from Kemmnitz the train doors were opened and hundreds of prisoners fled toward the groves of trees west of the station. In the ensuing turmoil some of the guards did not know what to do and began firing at the escaping prisoners. At least 25 corpses were found there after the war.[204] The fleeing prisoners were pursued, mainly by Luftwaffe troops. From this moment on the Letzlingen transport was split into several groups that took different evacuation routes.

As night fell on April 11 some of the SS guards left in Letzlingen began to discard their uniforms and put on civilian clothes. Quite a few of them vanished during the night, leaving hundreds of prisoners without sufficient supervision.[205] Other guards began to patrol the station, armed with pistols and rifles; the prisoners were not sure who they were.[206] Letzlingen was a small town, with less than 1,500 inhabitants. The situation was reminiscent of what had happened at Mieste when transports were stranded there, but the problem was now even more acute because almost all the guards had gone. The local residents were anxious to rid themselves of the prisoners.

Hundreds of prisoners remained at the station under Kemmnitz's supervision, but he did not succeed in restoring order. Several of the remaining guards rounded up a group of several dozen prisoners and began to march them eastward to Colbitz, about 9 miles (15 kilometers) away. These prisoners were all liberated later by the Americans. About 200 prisoners, most of whom had been caught in the forest after escaping, also set out eastward under the supervision of several guards from Nüxei and a few kapos, their destination Sachsenhausen. They reached the Elbe on April 12 and crossed it in small boats. Most of them, however, did not live to see the day of liberation. Many were murdered along the way by their guards and only about 50 finally reached Tremmen, 12 miles (20 kilometers) from the western suburbs of Berlin. The survivors of this death march were liberated by the Red Army on April 29 or 30.[207]

Another 600 or so prisoners set out eastward with Kemmnitz along side roads in the hope of crossing the Elbe before the Americans arrived. The sick and frail were loaded onto 16 wagons, and the convoy advanced along the narrow roads and forest paths. They reached Dolle, a village of 600 inhabitants, about 7 miles (12 kilometers) southeast of Letzlingen. From there they were scheduled to continue on foot, but not all of them were strong enough to do so. The familiar scenario was repeated: the locals were afraid that they would be forced to take responsibility for dozens of prisoners until the U.S. forces arrived. A massacre was perpetrated in the village before the transport continued on its way. In 1949 a mass grave with 66 corpses of slaughtered prisoners was exhumed at Dolle. According to the postwar investigation, quite a number of local residents and district Volkssturm men took part in the murders.[208] The 500 or so surviving prisoners of this transport marched another 6 miles (10 kilometers) eastward to the village of Burgstall, where an extraordinary rescue operation took place amidst the prevailing ritual of murder.

Two other groups of prisoners, who had been caught in the forest on the night of the wide-scale escape, marched toward Gardelegen. The first, consisting of between 40 and 60 prisoners, reached the town on the morning of April 12 and was taken to the riding barracks.[209] The 125 prisoners in the second group, who began the march to Gardelegen on the night of April 12, did not walk directly to the town but were taken to Jävenitz, 6 miles (10 kilometers) east of Gardelegen. They reached the village in the evening and were lodged in a barn, where they were given several potatoes each. The next morning several guards, who appeared to the prisoners to be soldiers, came and took them into the forest close to the small village of Hottendorf. At 8 a.m. they were told to run into the forest and await the Americans there, and then to come out and surrender. When they began to run the guards opened fire at them, but shortly afterward the guards left them there and went.[210]

A hunt for escaped prisoners was launched in the forest between Jävenitz and Hottendorf, mainly by the local Volkssturm and the Hitlerjugend. This time as well, their objective was to defend their homes. Jävenitz was a small village with 1,000 residents, and Hottendorf was even smaller, with a population of no more than 300. The dedicated young men who set out to defend their homes did not hesitate to tell the truth to the people of Jävenitz when asked the purpose of the operation: "We are going hunting, to shoot zebras" *(Wir gehen auf Jagd, um die Zebras abzuschießen)*.[211] At least four prisoners were shot by the Hitlerjugend boys close to Hottendorf, and no attempt was made to conceal the murders, which were witnessed by local residents. After the war a local man described how the prisoners were caught and pleaded for their lives, and how the boys shot them without turning a hair.[212]

Johannes Bieneck, aged 16, was a member of the Hitlerjugend in Jävenitz. He heard from a Feldwebel (sergeant) who passed through the village that escaped prisoners were roaming the nearby forest, and he was asked to go to the village mayor and to tell him to send the Volkssturm to collect them. The mayor told him that it was not Volkssturm's responsibility to deal with such problems. When he returned to the Feldwebel and gave him this answer, the latter ordered him to summon his comrades and to follow him. They were given weapons and a small amount of ammunition and set out to hunt down prisoners. They caught four and brought them to the village. Fifteen-year-old Fritz Kallweit also joined the zebra-hunters, but was apparently too young to be given a weapon. He did not manage to do much since he got lost in the forest and returned home without finding a single prisoner. Seventeen-year-old Ulrich Freitag was also asked by the soldiers to help in the search for escaped prisoners. He received a rifle and ammunition and was ordered to stand at the edge of a grove of trees and catch prisoners. He heard shots in the forest but did not know who was shooting.[213]

Whatever the identity of those who shot the prisoners as they tried to hide in the forest outside Jävenitz—soldiers, Volkssturm members, or Hitlerjugend boys—their hunt produced impressive results. An American officer, Captain Luther Gowder, examined the graves in the Jävenitz area after the war. In his report he concluded that 35 corpses of Polish and Russian prisoners were buried in the area and 17 pits were dug, 13 in the Jävenitz cemetery and 4 in the Hotendorf cemetery.[214] Another 22 corpses were exhumed close to Roxförde, about 6 miles (10 kilometers) southwest of Gardelegen.[215] These prisoners were probably murdered before the transport of the Construction Brigade III prisoners reached Letzlingen on April 11.[216]

By the evening of April 13 the hunt was over. More than 100 prisoners had been caught and rounded up in a street in Jävenitz. The need for guards was urgent, and the community leaders in Jävenitz and Hotendorf appealed to Gardelegen for more Volkssturm personnel to take these prisoners to the riding barracks in the town.[217] No reinforcements were available, and at approximately 7:30 p.m. the prisoners began to march toward Gardelegen, guarded by a handful of Luftwaffe soldiers. When they reached Gardelegen about an hour later there was nothing that could be done with them. The riding barracks were empty, and not far from there the liquidation of the prisoners in the barn outside town was in its final stages. The head of the Nazi Party branch in Jävenitz, Schweinicke, told one of the local farmers, Erich Mattis, to hitch his tractor to two wagons and to drive to Gardelegen, in order to return the prisoners to Jävenitz. At midnight Schweinicke and Mattis reached Gardelegen. Schweinicke tried to persuade the guards to leave the prisoners somewhere in Gardelegen until the arrival of the American troops, probably the next day. However, the guards refused to continue guarding the living and breathing evidence of the horrific crimes that had been perpetrated in the area and decided to free themselves of responsibility for the fate of the prisoners. There being no alternative, the prisoners were loaded onto the wagons and returned to Jävenitz. They reached the village between 4 and 5 a.m. on Saturday, April 14, where they were herded into a barn and fed by the farmers. They were told that they could go wherever they chose.[218] American tanks were advancing along all the routes in the area. No further manhunts could be conducted.

CHAPTER NINE

The Burning Barn

By the late evening of Thursday, April 12, 1945, between 1,050 and 1,100 prisoners, who had succeeded in surviving murderous assaults in various towns and villages on their route, had been rounded up throughout the Altmark and were massed in the cavalry school at Gardelegen.[1] This spacious building, which had served as a base for the army units stationed in Gardelegen since before World War I, was located at the edge of town in Bismarckstraße. In 1936 it had been converted into a cavalry school for military purposes. There were stables for the horses and wide areas where horses and riders were trained. The prisoners were assembled in the stables and the open areas.[2]

The town administrators, mainly the acting mayor, Karl Lepa, and the senior police officer, Rudolf Ringstmeyer, made the decision to round up prisoners from all over the region who could not be moved on because of the military situation and the blockage of routes to the north or east. They came to this conclusion even before they knew how many prisoners were stranded in their district. On April 11 reports were received that several prisoners had escaped the evacuation columns at Mieste or on the way there. In their frantic search for food, they had entered the town and were seen in the streets. But these were isolated cases, and Lepa believed he could contain the problem by locking the prisoners in several buildings until the Americans arrived.[3] This solution soon proved to be impractical, not only because there were so many prisoners but also because the local inhabitants objected to having them nearby, since rumors were rife that they were diseased, violent, and dangerous.[4] The cavalry school barracks appeared to be a feasible alternative.

Decisions

The barracks were vacant because they had been emptied of their four-legged occupants in good time. The commander of the installation, Lieutenant Colonel Friedrich Hilmer von Sherr-Thoss, had removed most of the horses on April 10. He had been commander of this base since August 1944, after having served for some time on the eastern front. After the war, he did not explain why he decided to evacuate the animals on that particular day, but it was probably because the Americans were close at hand. In any event, almost all the horses, close to 300,[5] were transferred to Seethen, 12 miles (20 kilometers) northeast of Gardelegen on the way to Bismark. Sherr-Thoss's departure left his deputy, Josef-Rudolf Kuhn, as the senior officer in charge of the site, assisted by a soldier named Martin Domno.[6]

Kuhn was 37, a Nazi Party member who had been a professional soldier since 1927. He had never held a significant appointment, and, since he was a farmer by occupation, most of his postings had involved dealings with animals rather than with rank-and-file soldiers. As far as he was concerned, the army was a place of employment; he lived in Gardelegen with his wife and three children. In October 1943 he was promoted to the rank of Rittmeister (Cavalry Master Sergeant), specializing in the training of horses. At the beginning of August 1944 he was posted to Gardelegen, where he was in charge of the animals and maintenance of the stables until November 1944. Then he was transferred to the Cologne area for several months, and on April 9, when his unit retreated eastward, he returned to Gardelegen. There were 50 soldiers at the base. When Sherr-Thoss left on April 10, taking a large group of soldiers with him, Kuhn remained behind with 30 men, mainly in order to complete the transfer of the remaining horses to local farmers. He too was anxious to leave as quickly as possible to avoid being captured by the Americans.[7] However, his plans went awry, and three days after returning to the cavalry school, on April 12, he faced a complex situation.

Kuhn was interrogated four times after the war, and gave four different and somewhat inconsistent versions of the events that had forced him to deal with more than 1,000 concentration camp prisoners at the site under his responsibility. The first version was given to U.S. Army interrogators in April 1945. On that occasion he said that on the evening of Wednesday, April 11, he received a telephone call from some army officer in Stendal, who told him to prepare the stables for the absorption of prisoners.[8] In August 1946 he was interrogated in Dresden by Red Army investigators. This time he told them that he had been left in the barracks by order of Sherr-Thoss so as to complete the arrangements for transfer of the horses to the local population before the Americans arrived. He said he had had nothing to do with the arrangements for the prisoners.[9] In later testimony, in 1961, he said that he received the telephone call on April 11 at 3 or 4 a.m. and that it came from someone in the military command in the Gardelegen area.[10] According to yet another version, given during his interrogation by the East German police in May 1950, he claimed that he was told that the prisoners would be staying only a few hours until arrangements could be made to evacuate them northward.[11]

That Kuhn knew in advance, before the prisoners arrived, that they were coming is beyond doubt. He apparently received word on April 11–12 late in the evening, perhaps even after midnight. Moreover, he was certainly notified by some person of authority in the army. The cavalry school was a military installation, and no other authority could have given orders to accommodate the prisoners there. However, it is unlikely that any high-ranking officer from Stendal was involved, since at the time the entire region was in a state of upheaval and the defense lines had collapsed. The only military authorities who could have conveyed such an order were local commanders in the town and its environs.

Colonel Fritz-Karl Walter Miltz was the senior military officer in the district and had been serving there for some time. In September 1940 he took over command of the Luftwaffe forces and the air force garrison close to the town, and from early April 1945 he served as military commander of the town and was in charge of the forces defending it *(Kampfkommandant der Stadt Gardelegen).*[12] On April 11 a local police officer, probably Ringstmeyer, informed him that a group of more than 1,000 prisoners had set out from Mieste, where their train had been stranded, on the way to Gardelegen. In this conversation, Kuhn was told that the district party head, Kreisleiter Gerhard Thiele, wanted to house the prisoners in the cavalry school in the town until their journey could continue. Miltz agreed to lodge them there.[13]

The frenetic efforts of the authorities in Gardelegen attest to the fact that, when the prisoners left Mieste on the afternoon of April 11, it was not clear where they were to be detained and for how long. The civilian authorities at Gardelegen, including Lepa and Ringstmeyer, wanted a site where they could be detained en masse, in order to forestall violent action on the part of unsupervised roaming prisoners. Under the pressure of events they were unaware, or perhaps failed to take into consideration, that there were hundreds of these prisoners. The moment it became known in Mieste and throughout the district that a solution existed in Gardelegen, the evacuation columns began moving in that direction. It was clear to the commanders of the transport, which had split up into a number of groups, scattered throughout the district, that the prisoners were to be concentrated in Gardelegen until the Americans arrived, and then handed over to them. Some prisoners had succeeded in escaping from the death marches, but even they, weary of roaming the forests and terrified of the manhunters, decided to make for the town, surrender, and spend the last few hours before the liberation in the cavalry school.[14] The civilian population of the villages to the north of Gardelegen who saw the prisoners pass by on April 11 and 12 also knew that escaped prisoners were to be sent there. Those who succeeded in surviving massacres en route were also sent to Gardelegen. As noted, in one case it was not even necessary to escort the prisoners from Mieste to Gardelegen. Fear of another massacre was greater than the desire to remain free.[15]

Brauny was naturally happy to bring his prisoners at long last to a place where he would be freed of responsibility for their future, and the same was true of the other escorts, who had brought the prisoners from Letzlingen or Jävenitz. It soon transpired, however, that Lepa and Ringstmeyer were unable to cope with this horde, and they were forced to appeal to a more powerful personage who would decide what to do with the evacuees. That individual was Kreisleiter Gerhard Thiele, who was in charge of the security of the district's civilian population.

On the morning of April 12 the future appeared quite promising for those prisoners who had already reached the stables. At 8 a.m. a guard came and ordered them to line up outside. They had marched all night at a rapid pace with Brauny and had arrived only a few hours earlier. They were exhausted from their efforts, and it took them some time to exit the stables. Once all those capable of standing had lined up, they were taken to a barracks that served as a kitchen and were given bread and a bowl of soup. They were so famished, not having received food since Mieste two days before, that many wolfed down the food within seconds. There were no SS guards in the vicinity, and apart from soldiers serving in the base, there was no special supervision.[16] Some of the prisoners heard the guards saying that it was a pity to give them food, since they didn't have much time left.[17]

That morning Kuhn did everything he could to rid himself of the prisoners. At about 8.30 a.m. he telephoned the mayor, Lepa, and asked him to arrange for the transfer of the prisoners since, he said, a military base was not an appropriate place for detention of concentration camp prisoners. Lepa assured him that the prisoners would not be there for long, but he could not give Kuhn what he wanted—trucks to take them away. He advised Kuhn to ask the army for assistance. Miltz too, however, told Kuhn that he could not supply trucks.[18]

All that day Thiele was occupied with attempts to find ways of ridding himself of the prisoners who, so he believed, were endangering the welfare and safety of the local civilians. His first step that morning was to telephone Miltz, the senior military commander in the area, and tell him that he had a problem with guarding the prisoners. There were not enough guards, he said, and he must have more manpower to ensure that they did not escape and prowl freely through the town. He demanded responsibility for the guard and escort units (Begleitkommandos) dealing with the prisoners. In other words, he wanted soldiers from his base to be assigned to guard duty. Thiele explained that the situation was spinning out of control because many of the original guards had left and the rabble (Gesindel) were a threat to the town. Miltz refused to accept responsibility for the prisoners. He seems to have realized, even if Thiele did not spell out the facts, that taking responsibility for the prisoners would entail sending his men to liquidate them. He told Thiele that there was no obligation to obey such an order since, so he said: "I am a soldier, not a murderer" (Ich bin Soldat und kein Mörder).[19]

Thiele understood that, despite his standing as the supreme authority on matters of regional defense, he would not succeed in recruiting Miltz's Luftwaffe men for the task of liquidating the prisoners. At about 9 p.m. that day, he again telephoned the cavalry school and talked to Kuhn. He told Kuhn to inform the commander of the transport as follows: an increasing number of prisoners were escaping, breaking into houses, stealing, looting, raping women, and turning the local population's life into a living hell. These prisoners should be executed. Kuhn insisted that this order be transmitted to Brauny but did not succeed in locating him that night.[20]

By Thursday morning Brauny realized that the fate of the prisoners he had brought to the stables in Gardelegen had been sealed. At about 11 a.m. he talked to Thiele and asked him to ensure that the prisoners were fed. Thiele replied that he could not help him on this matter. At the Mittelbau-Dora trial after the war, Brauny reconstructed their conversation:

> Brauny: I didn't get the exact wording but the Kreisleiter said it would be better to shoot all the prisoners.
> Question: What else did he say?
> Brauny: Because they were breaking into the places around here.
> Question: How did he suggest the shooting be done?
> Brauny: He wanted to send me ammunition.[21]

After his conversation with Thiele, Brauny hastened to share the facts with Friedrich Teply, who had been in charge of the guards at Rottleberode and had been by his side throughout the march to Gardelegen. Teply said immediately that they could not do such a thing.[22] But Brauny understood that neither he nor Teply, a weary, middle-aged concentration camp guard, had the power to prevent Thiele from carrying out the plan. When Brauny realized that the decision had been taken and the moment of truth was approaching, he obtained a bicycle and on Friday, April 13, at about 8 a.m. he left town.[23]

> I left with my bicycle. That cavalry captain who was in charge of the detail in the caserne asked me, "Where do you want to go?" I said, "I want to go away with my comrade. I am coming back again." Then I went to Neudorf [sic] and there was a parachute unit from Gardelegen there. We were told to either return our weapons or fight with them. I did not return my weapon and I stayed with the unit.[24]

Brauny rode to Kloster-Neuendorf, about 2 miles (3 kilometers) east of Gardelegen, where he found a uniform and transformed himself from an SS concentration camp soldier into a rank-and-file soldier. Two days later he was taken prisoner by the Americans.[25] His postwar explanation of why he left so suddenly is far from convincing. He was well aware that, as commander of the transport and the senior SS escort, he was liable to be found responsible for, or at least an accomplice in, the murder of the prisoners, and all this only hours before the arrival of the U.S. forces. He chose to beat a hasty retreat in good time and to leave Teply to face the music.

Friedrich Teply was almost 59 in April 1945. He had served in the Austrian army in World War I and joined the Nazi Party in 1938. He was not called to service until June 1944, and then, like many other veterans, was sent as a guard to Mauthausen. He was then transferred to Mittelbau-Dora, and, at the beginning of October 1944, he was posted to Rottleberode. He was in charge of guard duties in the camp, records of guards, duty assignment, and so on.[26] After the war, he explained his predicament at Gardelegen to his interrogators:

> I am an old man and I did not know how to deal with the prisoners. . . . He [Brauny] had been with the SS for 12 years. . . . I think he was a professional soldier and 12 years is a long time and I think if a soldier is 12 years with the SS he knows all the routines of service.[27]

Brauny's flight and the fact that the prisoners were now Teply's responsibility removed yet another obstacle to the implementation of Thiele's plan. It is feasible to assume that Brauny was not necessarily motivated by moral considerations when he decided to dissociate himself from the planned massacre. He was apparently anxious to prepare the ground for his future efforts to prove that he was not guilty of mass murder. Brauny was not a local man, and nothing he had heard since reaching Mieste about the threat to the safety and security of the local population made a strong impression on him, particularly in view of the tangible danger of being captured by the Americans and being charged with murder. However, reluctant to stage a confrontation with Thiele, he found flight to be the most convenient solution.

Together with his efforts to recruit support in the army or among the SS guards, Thiele approached the force that was available and entirely under his authority, namely, the local militia, the Volkssturm. There was a Volkssturm battalion in Gardelegen, composed of four companies. Its commander was Hans Debrodt, a man of 60, who had been a party member since 1933. He was a clerk by occupation and had not been called up for military duty because of his age. Debrodt was one of the most active and dedicated party members in the town, unquestionably loyal to Thiele and to the party. His postwar interrogation revealed that Thiele resolved to liquidate the prisoners even before the first groups reached the stables in the early morning hours of April 12.

On Tuesday, April 10, a meeting was held in the offices of the party's district administration *(Kreisleitung),* presided over by Thiele and attended by the Volkssturm company commanders; Paul Marx, head of the local DAF; the local party branch chairman;[28] and other party functionaries. The subject on the agenda was what measures to adopt in order to defend the townspeople at a time when the German forces were retreating and the Americans were due to arrive, and what to do with the mass of prisoners who were unable to continue their journey. No concrete decisions were taken, so it appears, since little could be done to change the situation. On Wednesday, April 11, the local party functionaries met again. Thiele announced that the prisoners were in Mieste and were due to arrive in Gardelegen within the next 24 hours. "We will be forced to deal with such a quantity of prisoners and so it will be necessary to liquidate them here," Thiele told the gathering.[29] Marx announced that the prisoners would be concentrated in the stables of the local cavalry barracks.

It was obvious that mass extermination of more than 1,000 prisoners could not be perpetrated in the center of town. On Thursday morning, April 12, the consultations continued in the Kreisleitung offices. Thiele sent a 16-year-old boy on a bicycle to locate a barn or large storehouse outside town. The site found suitable was a barn on the Gut Isenschnibbe farm, about a mile (2 kilometers) northeast of the town. It had once been owned by an aristocratic family named Lippe-Detmold, but had been requisitioned from the family and by 1945 was abandoned and empty, held in trust by the local authority.[30] The barn was situated on an isolated hillock, and there were no houses around it. Thiele learned of the location of the barn from Kuhn, who recommended moving the prisoners there from the barracks.[31] It seemed to be the ideal place for implementing the Kreisleiter's scheme.

At noon on Thursday Debrodt was at the Kreisleitung, busy burning documents, as ordered by Thiele. Several party functionaries were there with him, including one of the Volkssturm company COs, Walter Pannwitz,

Paul Marx, and Bernsdorf, an SA member and head of the Gardelegen Gestapo. They exchanged views on Thiele's decision:

> The general idea was that it was not good, but it was necessary. Pannwitz said: "When the Kreisleiter does that job he does it only in the interests of the population." Some said it was impossible, others said the Kreisleiter must know that it is necessary.[32]

On Thursday afternoon Thiele drove in his car to the riding barracks, but it is not clear if he held any discussions there. He was probably on his way back from the armory outside town because there was a considerable amount of weaponry of various kinds in the car.[33] At 4 p.m. he arrived back at the Kreisleitung and brought the weapons with him: a machine gun, about 150 grenades, and 150 cartridge belts. He left the weapons in the building and ordered Debrodt to recruit some of the Volkssturm men. He was referring to a group of about 10 men from each company, who had undergone intensive training, had received uniforms and helmets from the local army stores, and were armed with rifles and bullets.[34] They were nicknamed "the ruffians" *(Rabauken)*.[35] They were ordered to set out the next morning and seek out escaped prisoners, who were roaming the neighborhood. Any aliens caught roaming, who were beyond a doubt concentration camp prisoners, were to be shot on the spot. At about 9 p.m. Thiele telephoned Debrodt at the Kreisleitung offices, and told him that all necessary preparations had been made. The prisoners were to be transferred from the riding barracks to the barn outside town and would be exterminated there.[36]

The problem continued to preoccupy the small group around Thiele until late in the night between Thursday and Friday. At midnight, Thiele again telephoned his colleagues and advised them of his progress. He said that he had examined the possibility of liquidating the prisoners by machine gun, rifle fire, and antitank launchers. The best way, though, would be simply to set fire to the barn and not allow them to escape. It was essential to bring along flamethrowers in advance, since the barn that had been selected was constructed of bricks and not wood, said the Kreisleiter. After he had briefed them on his activity in the past few hours, his colleagues discussed what they had heard: "Several of them said it would be good for the population, nobody had serious objections."[37]

At 3 a.m. Debrodt went to brief Ringstmeyer. He told Ringstmeyer that the Volkssturm were going to take part in the hunt for escaped prisoners in the area. Ringstmeyer recalled that in their conversation at night they agreed that the Volkssturm, the police, and other municipal bodies must take action to ensure that the prisoners did not remain in Gardelegen.[38] He advised Debrodt not to cooperate in the hunt for escapees. They would return to the barracks on their own initiative, he said.[39]

Thiele's decision to murder the prisoners was definitely taken before their arrival, apparently on April 11. He had no difficulty in presenting his plan to the local party men, who accepted it with restraint and understanding. On April 12 he made all the necessary logistic preparations to ensure that the plan would be carried out the next day. That evening he began to urge the authorities who were responsible for the prisoners in the stables to put the plan into action. At about 9 p.m. he telephoned Kuhn and told him that it was necessary to shoot the prisoners because some of them had escaped, broken into houses, seized weapons, and raped women. Kuhn was evasive and referred him to the transport commander, arguing that the prisoners were not his responsibility. Kuhn realized that the intervention of a senior, powerful political functionary in this matter would not bode well for anyone abetting Thiele.[40] He did not succeed in contacting Brauny that evening and told Teply what Thiele had said.[41] The Kreisleiter telephoned Miltz at about 10 p.m. in an additional attempt to involve the army in his plans. He demanded the army's help; the prisoners were terrorizing the population, he said, and it was the army's duty to defend civilians. He also demanded that the army supply him with large quantities of gasoline and weapons. Once again, Miltz adamantly refused to cooperate and said that the separation of army and party must be maintained. Furious, Thiele declared that he was recruiting the Volkssturm and that the liquidation order would be carried out.[42]

Logistics

Thiele's instructions to Kuhn on Thursday, namely, that the prisoners were to be killed, were greeted with reluctance and prevarication at the cavalry school. On Thursday night, Thiele realized that if he did not take the initiative, Gardelegen would fall into American hands and hundreds of prisoners, thirsting for revenge, so he believed, would prowl the streets. At about 3 a.m. on Friday morning, he again telephoned from home to Debrodt and screamed at him: "Yes, they must be shot! I have so much to do and I can't have this worry; they must be shot. Yes, Heil Hitler, Debrodt."[43]

In addition to Thiele's efforts to mobilize soldiers and guards for the barracks, groups of Volkssturm were also brought in. Hermann Holtz, CO of Company 1 of the Gardelegen Volkssturm battalion, was ordered by Debrodt to summon his men on Friday at 3 p.m. to the Kreisleitung offices for further instructions. Debrodt told him that they would be assigned to guard duties near the railway station and in the vicinity of the adjacent food storehouses in order to capture escaping prisoners. These instructions were passed on inefficiently, and only a few men reported for duty. Debrodt, infuriated at the small turnout, harangued the civilians because of their irresponsible attitude toward the town's security problems. He made absolutely no mention of the guard duties that were the pretext for the meeting:

> In Kakerbeck all men fled in the woods because they did not want to be taken prisoners by the Americans, who approached in the meantime. When there were no German men in the village the unguarded prisoners took their chance to go around the village robbing and pillaging. Nearly all women and children were raped by the prisoners. When the Americans did not enter, the men of Kakerbeck came back in their village and arrested a big part of the prisoners. So, you see how dangerous and earnest the situation is now. I expected of every member of the Volksstrum [sic] that he follow up every order immediately. Those who disobey the order will be shot.[44]

Kakerbeck is a village with less than 1,000 inhabitants, some 11 miles (18 kilometers) north of Gardelegen. Rumors of alleged atrocities committed there by prisoners had reached Gardelegen and fueled the collective terror. There is no proof that such acts occurred in the village, and the source of the rumors is unknown. None of the columns of prisoners on the trains stranded at Mieste or Letzlingen ever passed through Kakerbeck, which lay to the north of their route. There may have been incidents of looting or other violence perpetrated by foreign slave laborers working there, who found themselves free before the Americans arrived, but there is no clear proof of this either. However, Thiele, Debrodt, and other civilians at Gardelegen, had no need of more substantial evidence. They were convinced that the rumors were reliable in view of the criminal nature of the "rabble."

The efforts to arm the group of Volkssturm men who reported to the Kreisleitung early on Friday afternoon indicate that what was being planned was not the publicly announced hunt for escaping prisoners in the surrounding forests. Debrodt told the group of Rabauken that they were to equip themselves with Panzerfäuste (recoilless antitank weapons) and rifles. The problem was that the armory was outside town, and there were apparently no more launchers in stock. Debrodt did not know who had taken them and thought it might have been one of the company commanders on his own initiative.[45] In any event, the Gardelegen Volkssturm had no need of antitank weapons in order to round up exhausted prisoners in the forest. Such weapons, which were of limited effectiveness against tanks, proved highly efficient when used to murder 1,100 prisoners crammed into a brick barn. Several of the Volkssturm men claimed after the war that they were told that they were going to be moved northward, in order to establish a defense line against the Americans, and that this was why the Panzerfäuste were needed.[46] However, the commanders of the Volkssturm battalion made no reference to such a plan because it was obvious that all military resistance had long since collapsed.[47] Thiele never contemplated using this group of elderly and fearful men in a hopeless battle against American tanks.

In any case, the mobilization of the Volkssturm proceeded at a sluggish pace. Gustav Palis, an army paymaster at a base near Gardelegen, was also the secretary of Holtz's company. Like the other civilians, he knew that a large group of prisoners had been brought to Gardelegen. On Friday, April 13, he and several other members of the company received instructions to report to the Kreisleitung offices and await orders.[48] Palis passed the message on to several of his comrades, including Fritz Rose, when they arrived. After hearing Debrodt's motivation speech, they were sent to await instructions at the Lindenthal tavern about a mile (2 kilometers) southeast of the exit from Gardelegen in the direction of Kloster-Neuendorf. They reported there at 4:30 p.m. While they were waiting, Thiele arrived and told them, according to Rose: "You are to come back to the Kreisleitung, and the prisoners at the cavalry school are to be taken to the barn where you will shoot them."[49]

Fifteen or sixteen of the Rabauken, the more skilled and better-armed Volkssturm men, also reported for duty to the Kreisleitung on Friday. They too were sent to the tavern. Several men from other Volkssturm companies also came, as did two additional commanders, Wilhelm Becker, CO of Company 3, and Walter Pannwitz, CO of Company 2.[50] They too were sent to wait at the tavern.[51]

Wilhelm Biermann, aged 47, was a resident of Kloster-Neuendorf and a member of the Volkssturm. He also reported to the Kreisleitung and heard Debrodt describing the conduct of the escaped prisoners and declaring that it was essential to kill them wherever they were encountered. Biermann went to the Lindenthal, which was near his home. With him were three of his colleagues: Wilhelm Hausmann, Arno Brake, and Willi Niebel.

On the way, at the edge of town, we stopped two people who had escaped from a concentration camp. They were dressed in camp prisoners' uniforms and were engaged in robbery at the edge of town. . . . They themselves were from Czechoslovakia and we did not ask them how they had escaped from the camp. Willi Niebel was drunk and wanted to murder these Slovaks on the spot but Hausmann wouldn't allow it and prevented him all the way to the tavern. I and Arno Brake escorted the Slovaks. When we arrived at the Lindenthal with the Slovaks, I reported to company commander Pannwitz who was commanding us . . . he immediately executed the Slovaks. Niebel and Hausmann delayed and so, on Pannwitz's orders, I and Brake led the Slovaks several meters away from the tavern and executed them. Brake murdered one and I the other.[52]

Arno Brake, then aged 45, also described the complex operation conducted by the Volkssturm:

> When we arrived [at the Kreisleitung], Battalion CO Debrodt made a speech and said more or less that in our areas there were a lot of escapees from among the concentration camp prisoners and they were robbing us and raping our women and it was our job now to catch them and execute them. Then he told us that we must go to the Lindenthal tavern in the forest and if, on the way, we met any of the escaped prisoners, we must immediately execute them. When we received the order, we four, I and Wilhelm Biermann, Wilhelm Backe, Willi Niebel went to the Lindenthal. As soon as we left town and were on our way, we met a man dressed in civilian clothes. Biermann asked him for papers. The man replied to Biermann in an unknown language which I didn't understand but I think it was Russian or Polish. So Biermann told him to wait and went off to a little barn we had passed and I went with him. We went because, before we left town, local people told us there was a man lying in the barn, so we took him with us as well. Biermann talked to the second man also in a language I didn't understand, and the detainee replied and I can state that they understood one another. We took the two detainees with us and brought them to the Lindenthal and when we reached it, Pannwitz, the commander of our district, ordered us, me and Biermann, to execute the detainees and we did it near the Lindenthal.[53]

Hausmann, or perhaps Becker,[54] was the fourth member of this group, and it is very possible that there were five of them.[55] It is not known if the two victims were Slovaks, Poles, or Russians. What is evident, however, is that for Biermann, Hausmann, Niebel,[56] and Brake, the capture of the two roaming prisoners vividly illustrated the danger cited by the commander only a few hours ago. They were convinced that prisoners liable to commit robbery and rape were wandering freely several hundred meters from their homes and their families in their village. As they perceived it, shooting the prisoners in cold blood was an act of self-defense.

The Volkssturm men who were sitting in the tavern on Friday afternoon and discussing the security situation in their neighborhood were agitated. None of them were willing to take responsibility and tell the others what to do, since Debrodt did not appear until the evening. They heard the shots outside the tavern and knew that roving prisoners were being liquidated.[57] At 6 p.m. Debrodt came and told them that there was no possibility of arming them all, and so the weapons would be distributed only to the 15 Rabauken. The others could wait at home meanwhile.[58] The men stayed in the tavern, drinking and making merry till 10 p.m., when Holtz and Debrodt arrived again and sent them all home, noting that they should be ready to be called out at any moment for an important assignment.[59]

Friday was the last date when Thiele could carry out his plan to eradicate the threat to the townspeople's safety. The Americans were due at any moment, and more than 1,000 vengeful prisoners would then be set free, backed by the occupying army. But when he examined the manpower at his disposal, the situation did not appear promising. Miltz had refused to provide men, and Kuhn had also evaded collaboration. Thiele knew that the small group of armed Volkssturm men at his disposal would obey his orders to the letter; about 30 SS guards from the camps who were with the prisoners in the cavalry school could also be recruited without difficulty.[60] Thiele apparently estimated that he needed more guards to escort such a large group to the murder site and to prevent mass flight when the killings began. A partial solution was improvised from an unexpected direction. On Thursday afternoon, one of the SS guards came to Kuhn and asked him for army uniforms for about 20 men. Kuhn sent him to the storeroom. His assistant, Martin Domno, who was in charge of the stores, handed over the requested uniforms to the SS man, an Austrian master sergeant named Deple.[61] In the late afternoon, Kuhn saw several of the prisoners emerging from the stables and donning uniforms. The SS guard also requested weapons for the new recruits. Kuhn did not recall seeing distribution of weapons to the prisoners.[62] A Polish prisoner, Kazimierz Drygalski, described the moment when he was transformed from a concentration camp prisoner into a uniformed guard:

> On 12 April someone from the SS came to the camp [cavalry school], singled out all the German prisoners and took them to another barracks. That day, Obersturmführer Deple came and called out the Poles from Posen and Silesia, including me. There were seven in all. This Obersturmführer said that we were being freed from the camp and were going to serve in the Germany army. Later in the evening, I was given a uniform, a jacket and trousers. On 13 April, Deple told me that the whole camp was to be executed by shooting. At 6, I was given a rifle and ordered to kill. I declared that I didn't know how to shoot a rifle.[63]

The metamorphosis of prisoners into guards apparently took place in two stages. In the first instance, 10 German prisoners were selected, most of whom had already served as functionaries in the camps. Adolf August Pinnenkämper, who had been at Ilfeld and was now at Gardelegen, was selected together with nine others who had been in his group. Deple, who chose them, told them that their task was to supervise the prisoners. The next day, April 13, they discovered that the prisoners were to be liquidated.[64] In the second stage, the guards began to single out Volksdeutsche from Czechoslovakia and Poles from Silesia. Andrzej Fankenberg, a Pole from Wroclaw, who was 19 when he was selected and given a uniform and a weapon, explained why he agreed to take part: "I had spent three years in concentration camps and I thought that there was only one step to take until the liberation, and, in any case, they were going to shoot us all."[65]

In all, 25 such prisoners were selected,[66] most of them Germans from the Reich, several Volksdeutsche, and Poles who declared themselves to be Volksdeutsche.[67] At the height of the crisis, there was no time to check their ancestry. Six of them were Polish nationals and one was Czech.[68] About 12 prisoners were taken from the barracks at 3 a.m. on Friday morning and escorted by several guards into town. Among them was Karl Semmler, the German communist kapo from Rottleberode. They took a large wagon with them, which they hauled manually. In town they stopped at the Kreisleitung building, where two large barrels of gasoline were brought out from a nearby hut and loaded onto the wagon. The prisoners returned to the cavalry school at 4 a.m. with the barrels.[69]

The recruiting and arming of German prisoners and Volksdeutsche for guard assignment was not uncommon at the time, although in Gardelegen, it took on far-reaching dimensions. Camp guards often exploited prisoners, usually Germans, when they encountered manpower problems during evacuations. During the evacuation to Gardelegen, the kapos served the function of escorts and guards and were sometimes given weapons.[70] Nevertheless, what occurred in the cavalry school on Thursday raises a number of questions with regard to the identity of the authority who initiated the move: Friedrich Teply claimed that it was not he. He described the events that day:

> There was a man who wore a brand new flier's uniform and one morning he came to see me accompanied by several other Germans and after that one man who had gotten clothing from somebody was supposed to have been an air force officer and because they were German they wanted to get clothing supplies too. [sic] It was early in the morning. I told them that I have no right to do that. I told this to the ones who wanted to get clothing supplies.[71]

Teply soon changed his mind. He admitted that he could not withstand the pressure of the German prisoners, who were eager to receive uniforms and thus be differentiated from the rest of the prisoners. He found some old uniforms that were not in use and handed them out. He said that he decided to act fairly toward this small group and not to discriminate among its members; apart from that, he thought that they intended to exploit the uniforms in order to escape, and this would help them save themselves. In addition, these prisoners were promised cigarettes and liquor.[72]

It appears that the initiative to transform some 25 prisoners into guards was taken on Thursday by various people in the cavalry school itself, and not by Thiele. None of the people who worked with Thiele in the 48 hours before the massacre recalled him mentioning such a move, particularly since it was totally at odds with his outlook and his perception of the prisoners. To give German weapons and uniforms to Poles, communists, or German criminals would have seemed to an ardent Nazi like him a desecration. The matter was apparently decided between Kuhn and Teply, who were under constant pressure from Thiele on Thursday to send their men to liquidate the prisoners. Kuhn admitted that he had a group of soldiers at his disposal in the barracks but did not consider himself under obligation to utilize them in order to carry out Thiele's plan, or, alternatively, to try and foil it.[73] The selection of prisoners was organized by the guards who had accompanied them from the camps. Only they were acquainted, more or less, with the prisoners and could therefore select the candidates.[74] By expanding the group of guards and escorts, Teply, and in particular Kuhn, could achieve with maximum efficiency what they wanted most of all: to be rid of the prisoners as fast as possible so that the imminent massacre would not occur while they were in charge, and so that they would not be forced to carry it out.

There is no clear indication as to who supplied the weapons and uniforms distributed to the prisoners who were selected to serve as guards. It could not have been difficult to find 20 old military jackets, but allocation of weapons was a different story. The rifles given out to the prisoner-guards could have come from the cavalry school arsenal or the nearby Luftwaffe base, where weapons and uniforms were available. The commander of the cavalry school barracks, von Sherr-Thoss, claimed after the war that there had been no weapons in the base he commanded and had abandoned several days before the massacre; they could only have come from the Luftwaffe camp, he said.[75] Kuhn too claimed that when the prisoners received uniforms from the camp stores on Thursday, he did not see them receiving weapons as well.[76] If the uniforms were in fact distributed on Thursday afternoon as Teply also claimed, then the weapons could have been handed out only on Friday afternoon, with the beginning of the transfer of prisoners to the barn.[77] On Friday the distribution of rifles could only have taken place at the cavalry school, but it is certainly possible that they were brought from the nearby Luftwaffe base by the soldiers who arrived from there on Friday afternoon to reinforce the guards. In any event, not all the prisoner-guards received weapons. For example, Fritz Waisar, a Czech, declared that he did not know how to use a rifle and was left alone. Several of the Poles and Germans did the same.[78] Others were given carbine rifles and about 30 bullets each. In some cases, the weapons and ammunition were of different manufacture and hence of no real use.[79]

By the morning of April 13 the logistic preparations had been completed. The quota of guards and escorts had been increased, sufficient fuel had been brought to the riding barracks, and it was now possible to begin transferring the prisoners to the distant barn. It was then that Brauny decided that the time had come to take to his heels and disappear. At about 11 a.m. Debrodt telephoned Kuhn at the cavalry school and asked him what was happening about the Kreisleiter's order to shoot all the prisoners. Debrodt appears to have been angry at Kuhn because of the delay and spoke to him abusively. Kuhn repeated what he had told Thiele the previous day: he was not responsible for the prisoners, and on this matter, Thiele should appeal directly to the SS men who were in charge of them. An additional telephone conversation from the Kreisleitung to the cavalry school took place between 2 and 3 p.m., one of several that afternoon. This time it was Thiele himself on the line. Kuhn agreed to summon the most senior SS man he could find at that hour, now that Brauny had vanished. It was Friedrich Teply. Teply talked to Thiele and afterward said to Kuhn: "It has to be done. It's a matter of self-defense. When necessary, the Kreisleiter can do anything he thinks necessary."[80]

The question the two men faced was what exactly was to be done. Teply and Kuhn realized on the afternoon of April 13 that they could no longer dodge Thiele's instructions, and their goal was now to do everything they could to ensure that their role would be minimal. It did not, of course, occur to them to take the 30 soldiers under Kuhn's command or the guards under Teply and try to prevent Thiele and his accomplices from transferring the prisoners to the farm outside town, although they knew what the implications were.

However, Teply adamantly refused to give the order to murder the prisoners, even when he talked to the Kreisleiter on Friday, several hours before the transfer of the prisoners to the barn.[81] He reconstructed his conversation with Thiele:

> The Friday before the Saturday we left the Kreisleiter called over by phone and gave us the order to finish off the prisoners.
>
> *Question:* To whom did he give the order?
> *Teply:* Brauny wasn't there and I went to the phone and I refused. I said, "We are guards."
> *Question:* Did you tell Brauny about the order?
> *Teply:* I didn't see him anymore.
> *Question:* Did you tell anybody?
> *Teply:* I told the guard down in the yard that the Kreisleiter requested this from me but I refused it.
> *Question:* Did the Kreisleiter tell you how to kill these people off?
> *Teply:* No, he only said, "We should finish them off." And I only said, "We are guards, we have to do this?"

Question: What happened with the prisoners?

Teply: After two hours he called again. He requested that we should lead the prisoners into a barn and we should set the barn on fire. I refused to do so. At night he called again between 5:00 and 6:00 at night. He heard from all sides that in the town a lot of robberies and burglaries were going on by the prisoners. The prisoners had to march from the caserne right away and he gave us another building. It was something like a barn. This barn was located about 15 minutes away above the caserne in the middle of an open field.[82]

Teply explained in detail to his interrogators why he agreed and why he objected during his conversations with Thiele and Debrodt. In the first conversation, with Debrodt, he refused to cooperate with the scheme and chose to take refuge behind the definition of the role of "guard" in order to avoid taking part. By the second conversation, with Thiele himself, the tone had altered. Thiele persuaded him at length and told him that he had received a series of telephone calls and appeals from mayors of villages and towns in the region who had complained that escaped prisoners were terrorizing the local population. Teply, still trying to evade the order, said that the prisoners in his charge were not doing anything and were concentrated in one place under supervision. The Kreisleiter then said that the quality of the supervision was questionable and it was by no means certain that the guards would stay put for long. Thiele insisted forcefully that the prisoners be moved to the barn.[83] At this stage, Teply no longer voiced objections to the redefinition of his duties and the nature of the assignment; the guards would merely escort the prisoners to a place selected for them because their presence in the town was causing suffering and damage to the population. What precisely was to happen to them in that barn he did not ask since this was not his job as guard. Most probably, he had no need to ask penetrating questions, because his talks with Thiele clearly indicated what the answer would be.

Kuhn also preferred to dodge the problem of the prisoners. As far as he was concerned, the transfer of the prisoners to the barn outside town was an ideal solution. He too was able to take cover behind the understanding between Teply and Thiele: the prisoners would be taken to a new location, a site more suitable than the cavalry school in the heart of the town, where they would be unable to cause damage and alarm the peaceful citizens. This guaranteed that no mass murders would take place in the base he commanded. He chose not to give instructions of any kind to the soldiers under his command and left them alone to decide, on an individual basis, what they wanted to do in the face of the approaching storm.[84]

That afternoon an additional group of guards arrived at the cavalry school to reinforce the unit taking the prisoners to the barn. They were young soldiers from the nearby Luftwaffe base. Among the guards was a group of Volkssturm members, apparently from the armed group sent from Kloster-Neuendorf, and a group of DAF men in green uniforms. Together with some 30 camp guards and 20 prisoners who agreed to bear arms, the guard unit now consisted of some 80 men. Several of the SS soldiers had guard dogs.[85] Just before 5 p.m. another telephone call was received from the Kreisleitung. This time it was Walter Pannwitz, one of the Volkssturm company COs, who asked Kuhn if he had sufficient men to carry out the murder assignment and if the prisoners had already left the stables. Kuhn said that they were being taken out at that very moment and were lining up for transfer to the barn. He added that it would be better if the crime was not committed as planned.[86]

The death march of the Mittlebau-Dora and Hanover-Stöcken camp prisoners set out on its last journey.

The Barn

Between 4 and 5 p.m. the 1,100 prisoners in the stables of the cavalry school at Gardelegen were ordered to line up in groups of 100 on the large parade ground in the center of the base. There were eight such groups, consisting of 100 to 120 prisoners each. Simultaneously, three horse- and tractor-drawn carts were brought in, and the 180 prisoners who were too feeble to march the mile walk to the barn were loaded onto them.[87] In addition, a small truck set out from the barracks to the barn, carrying barrels of gasoline and crates of ammunition, including about 1,500 bullets. This ammunition had been brought from the Luftwaffe base, probably together with the small group of soldiers sent from there.[88] During the preparations for the transfer of the prisoners to the barn, Thiele himself arrived in order to supervise but did not stay long, since he saw that the prisoners were starting to leave.[89]

From early Friday morning the prisoners sensed that something was about to happen. The information that trickled down to them was that they were about to be transferred elsewhere, and there were even rumors that they were to be taken to Hamburg.[90] There were also counter-rumors to the effect that there was something ominous about the planned move to the barn. The Polish prisoner, Romuald Bąk, heard several guards joking and saying that there was going to be a pogrom like the pogroms in the Polish ghettos.[91] Karl Semmler related that there was unease over the fact that barrels of gasoline had been brought along and that the prisoners who brought them from the Kreisleitung heard the guards saying that the barrels were to be taken to the barn.[92] In any event, the column of prisoners covered the short distance to the barn in an hour and a half. The last groups of the column arrived there between 6 and 7 p.m. Teply went with the barracks guards. He positioned his men in a close chain around the prisoners, between 6 and 12 for every 100 prisoners.[93] This time the guards were careful to ensure that nobody escaped, and, in fact, almost none succeeded in making their getaway. There were no killings along the way to the barn.[94] The groups that set out first stopped to wait for the others to catch up with them, to prevent a long wait before they were all assembled at the barn. It was no less important to ensure that the gasoline and ammunition would already be there when the prisoners arrived. After about half an hour, at 6 p.m., when the tractor carrying the equipment passed them, the groups resumed their march to the barn.[95] When they reached it, Teply beat a hasty retreat and returned to the cavalry school.[96] The short route to the barn passed through cultivated fields, and a prisoner found several potatoes scattered on the track and put them in his pocket. One of the guards burst out laughing and said: "You won't be needing potatoes any more" (Kartoffeln brauchst Du nicht mehr.)[97]

The red-brick barn to which the prisoners were led was 27 yards (25 meters) long, about 9 yards (8 meters) wide, and 4.4 yards (4 meters) high. There were two identical wooden double-winged doors facing one another on the longer sides. These doors were about 3.3 yards (3 meters) high, enough to enable the passage of a medium-sized truck or a tractor. There were two narrower entrances on the shorter sides. The floor was concrete with a concrete base about 20 inches (50 centimeters) high at each corner, which held the wooden beams that supported the entire structure. There were also beams embedded in the floor, branching up into wide-angled triangles in order to provide further support for the columns holding up the roof.[98] Outside the southwestern wall of the barn was a small wooden storehouse, where the fuel and ammunition crates that arrived with the prisoners were stored.[99]

The guards told the prisoners to sit down outside the southwestern entrance to the barn, for the other three apertures were closed.[100] The guards were dispersed around the group and the building to await the arrival of the last groups and the unloading of the sick prisoners from the carts. The equipment was unloaded from the tractor-drawn cart.[101] By about 6:30 p.m. all the prisoners were assembled there. Just then a group of about 20 soldiers from the local paratroopers camp also arrived, two of them riding motorcycles. They were very young, 18 to 20 at most, and brought with them a considerable quantity of weapons for the task they were about to carry out. They had automatic rifles, a crate of hand grenades, several Panzerfäuste, and one or two flamethrowers.[102] This was the main task force that Thiele had wanted to assemble, but he had failed until that day because of the objections of local senior military officers. The arrival of the 20 young paratroopers with their weapons permitted the final stage of the liquidations to begin. Shortly after these soldiers went into action, Teply and other older guards from the detachment of veteran camp guards left the area.[103] During their brief wait outside the barn, the prisoners saw the guards taking in the barrels of fuel. They could not have known then that this gasoline was being poured onto the straw and the potato sacks scattered over the floor of the barn.[104] The floor was covered with a 24-inch (60-centimeter) layer of straw, which in some places was 59 inches (a meter and a half) high.[105] While the preparations were under way, an American plane flew overhead and fired a few bursts at the site. Both prisoners and guards panicked, and the prisoners began to flee into the barn to hide. In the ensuing confusion, the guards fired at the prisoners in order to hurry them into the barn. This marked the beginning of the massacre, between 6:30 and 7 p.m. on April 13, 1945.[106]

At this stage Teply was still on the spot. The guards soon saw that the 1,000 or so prisoners jammed into the building were making attempts to get out. He described the event:

> *Question:* What was done to keep the prisoners from opening the door? What did you do?
> *Teply:* When I left the door was half-way open.
> *Question:* What was it that stopped the prisoners from escaping through the open door?
> *Teply:* The guard chain was standing there and I guess the door was closed later on.[107]

The prisoners could smell the gasoline as it soaked into the straw covering, and tried to get out of the building.[108] The soldiers and guards reacted with bursts of automatic fire at the entrance. It was quite dark inside the barn. Only faint predawn light filtered in through the cracks in the walls and the open door. For 20 to 30 minutes the trapped prisoners heard the guards walking around outside but were afraid to continue their efforts to break out for fear of being shot.[109] After another 20 minutes or so, at about 7 a.m., one of the guards came in through the door the prisoners had used and threw a lighted cigarette or match at the straw. A giant flame erupted from the gasoline-soaked straw within seconds, and the prisoners began to beat at it with the potato sacks or the blankets they had brought from the cavalry school. They soon succeeded in extinguishing the flames.[110] All this time, the guards continued to fire at the entrance to deter the prisoners from trying to make a getaway. After a short time, another guard came in and threw a firebrand or burning rag at the straw, which rekindled the flames with great force.[111] This time as well, the trapped prisoners succeeded in damping down the flames before they could spread.[112]

The prisoners now understood that if they did not break out of the barn as fast as possible they were doomed to be burned alive. Several Russian prisoners tried to break down the northeastern double door, opposite the door through which they had entered. They succeeded in bursting it open by pressure from within.[113] There were shouts of encouragement as prisoners urged their comrades to break out and try to overcome the guards, since they were doomed if they remained inside. Then all hell broke loose. The guards reacted to the escape attempts with heavy automatic gunfire. They had apparently decided to force the prisoners to try to escape, so as to liquidate them at the entrance.[114] At least 50 grenades were thrown into the barn, killing dozens of prisoners and intensifying the desperate efforts to break through the doors. Very soon a pile of corpses was heaped high at the two entrances, preventing any possibility of further escape.[115] In addition, the hand grenades helped to ignite the straw faster. The fire spread and caught the straw and the wooden beams. The 180 or so feeble and starving prisoners who had been brought along on carts, and were now lying on the straw, were the first to be burned alive.[116] Many of the prisoners lost consciousness and dropped to the burning floor because of the fire, the smoke, and the heat. The smoke rose high and could be seen throughout the district and in Gardelegen itself. Teply saw it when he arrived back at the cavalry school after leaving the site of the massacre several minutes before it began:

> I saw the smoke when I was down there, but I don't know who did it. Only one of these young people could have done it. This was nothing but smoke and I saw it but I was far away. In the morning I went to the medic and asked for some tablets.[117]

The inferno in the burning barn, the frantic scurrying from corner to corner, and the cruel death of their comrades were described by the few survivors in their postwar testimony. Edward Antoniak said:

> I went in the south west door and to the east end. There was an odor of gasoline on the straw which was piled about two feet deep. I believe the fire was started by grenades. The flames were about twelve feet high. I ran to the north east corner to escape the flames. I was wounded in the head by a grenade thrown by an SS man. I next ran out the north east door. One guard fired at me and missed. I fell down and the guard believing me dead did not fire again.
> The firing lasted all night until daylight. Bodies were piled about five feet high in front of the door.[118]

Romuald Bąk remembered that

> fire was burning all around. People started weeping, screaming, sobbing, calling for help, cursing. And all the time shots were being fired from rifles and machine guns on either side through the entrances. . . . People were sprawled in the fire. They begged to die.[119]

There were screams for help in different languages: Russian, Polish, French, Hungarian, and Dutch. From inside the burning barn, there rose the sound of the Marseilles being sung by French prisoners, most of them members of the French Resistance who had been interned at Mittelbau-Dora; the Internationale sung by Soviet POWs; and the Polish national anthem.[120]

The flames and the shootings that began after 6:30 p.m. continued until close to 10 p.m. At one stage the soldiers used flamethrowers they had brought with them, and at about 8 p.m. several bombs were fired into the barn from the Panzerfäuste.[121] At about 10 p.m. the young paratroopers saw that their mission had been completed and left. However, armed men from the groups of guards continued to move around outside the barn, checking if any surviving prisoners might be trying to escape under cover of darkness. Shots were heard until about 2 or 3 in the morning. Several of the murderers, apparently local civilians, continued to patrol the site in search of living prisoners. When they found them, they shot them mercilessly.[122] It was only toward morning, at 3 or 4 a.m., that silence reigned again for several hours.[123]

Escape from the inferno was a matter of chance and of resourcefulness, and few managed it. First, it was necessary to survive the murderous onslaught on the helpless prisoners inside the barn, and then to wait until it was completely dark outside. Evgeny Katev succeeded:

> I was thrown by the explosion to the north side of the barn and there was about 8–10 men on top of me. They were killed by the explosion. I couldn't move and was there the whole night.[124]

Romuald Bąk succeeded similarly in saving himself. "I lay on the floor protected by many corpses of those who had tried to save themselves, dead people, wounded people."[125] Vassili Mitofanovic Mamoshuk was saved by playing dead and lying motionless beside several of his slaughtered comrades until night fell.[126] Several prisoners in better physical condition succeeded in climbing the support beams inside the barn and clung to the wooden triangles that held up the ceiling. In this fashion, they evaded the bullets of the killers and the flames that consumed the straw below them.[127]

When darkness fell, several prisoners succeeded in slipping out of the barn. One of them was Szobel Aurel, a Jewish glove manufacturer from Budapest:

About 21:00 hours April 13th I was with two other prisoners and we crawled out through a hole we had dug under the door in the southeast corner of the barn. A Polish man was fired and a police dog came along and barked at him. Then a German soldier came over and shot the Polish man. The soldier and dog then went toward the back of the barn in the north side. I crawled toward the southeast . . . one other man followed me.[128]

The young Pole, Mieczysław Kołodziejski, a 23-year-old from a small village in the Opoczno district,[129] managed to stay with his father throughout the evacuation from Mittelbau-Dora and up to the incarceration in the barn. They tried to stay together and to escape through one of the doors:

We tried to get out the N.E. door and my father was shot at the door. I was able to get out and heard the guards say they were running short of ammunition. I saw a German soldier with a pistol shooting the man near the barn and I went back into the barn. . . . I then crawled out the N.E. door and saw a machine gun on the ground firing toward the barn. The fire has been starting again inside the barn and smoke was very heavy. I escaped to the S.E. to some woods. I stayed there in the woods for two days.[130]

A 22-year-old Polish student from Lvov, Włodzimierz Wosńy, managed to slip out of the barn in the dark in similar fashion:

I dug a hole near the S.W. door to get fresh air. In the meantime machine guns were being fired through the doors killing many people. Some tried to get out the door and were killed by machine guns or rifle fire. I stayed by the door until 23:00 hours when I escaped through the S.W. door and crawled along the south side of the barn toward the south east, . . . I was wounded on left side above the hip and twice on the back. Outside I was hit by a bullet on the outside of the upper left arm . . . between elbow and shoulder.[131]

Between 25 and 27 fortunate prisoners made their getaway in almost miraculous fashion. Karl Semmler stated that 22 prisoners succeeded in emerging alive from the barn: 16 Poles, 2 Hungarian Jews, and a Czech.[132] However, the actual number of survivors was slightly higher. Several prisoners escaped the bitter fate during the commotion when the U.S. plane flew overhead. At least two French prisoners were able to escape and were not included in Semmler's statistics.[133]

When the massacre was over, the barn looked like a scene from Dante's Inferno. Near the southeastern door lay at least 30 bullet-ridden corpses. Nearby were another 10 or so corpses of prisoners who had succeeded in getting out but were shot a few feet from the door. In the southeastern corner of the barn lay another 80 bodies, and by the northeastern door a similar number. The most gruesome sight, at the northwestern entrance, were about 150 corpses, many shattered by hand grenades. Dozens more were scattered at various distances from the entrances. These were prisoners who had succeeded in breaking out but had been shot before going far. Clouds of smoke were still rising inside the barn, although the flames died down after midnight. An acrid odor of burnt flesh hung in the air.[134]

When the murderers left, and before the task of obliterating the traces of the crime began, several prisoner-guards remained behind, their task being to prevent prisoners from escaping. Nobody was interested in them now, and they had no idea what they were expected to do. Several of them went off to sleep in a small hut near the barn, and two or three continued to patrol among the corpses and even went into the barn in order to shoot dying prisoners who still displayed signs of life. Several other prisoner-guards, who had not taken an active part in the massacre and did not fear for their fate, went back to the cavalry school. They returned the weapons they had not used and awaited the Americans.[135]

Before midnight Thiele launched the final stage of the Gardelegen massacre. The aim was to cover up what had happened, insofar as possible, before the arrival of the Americans, who were expected the following day. At 11 p.m. he telephoned Hans Debrodt, the loyal Volkssturm commander, and told him that the prisoners had been liquidated in the barn and that it was impossible to leave the site as it was. He insisted that Debrodt immediately go to the barn and check if enough fuel remained to burn the building and the remaining corpses. Debrodt objected and told Thiele that he could not start rounding up the Volkssturm and transporting fuel in the middle of the night. Thiele was livid and said he would deal with the matter himself with the help of several soldiers.[136]

Thiele knew precisely what had happened in the barn, and by midnight he realized that it was unthinkable to leave the site in its present condition. He had not been there during the massacre and apparently did not go there at midnight to see for himself what had happened, but he was well aware of the details. He probably received the information from the murderers themselves, from one of the Volkssturm men, or from the soldiers who reported to him. At about 2 or 3 a.m. on April 14 he telephoned the acting mayor of Gardelegen, Karl Lepa, roused him, and demanded that he immediately dispatch the local firefighter brigade and its technical unit to the barn to bury the corpses. He told Lepa what had happened, and the mayor realized that it would be best to keep his distance from this affair. He told the Kreisleiter to do his own dirty work and cut off the conversation. He then reported to Ringstmeyer what Thiele had said.[137]

Thiele did not give up. He stressed that he needed a large number of men to bury the dead and try to obliterate all traces. On that night (between

April 13 and 14); he telephoned heads of local party branches *(Ortsgrup-penleiter)* in the neighboring villages and demanded that they report to the barn with their Volkssturm units.[138] The cover-up operation now became a wider regional project.

At 4 a.m. on Saturday, April 14, 61-year-old Paul Scherinkau, commander of the local firefighting unit, was awakened by a telephone call. He was told to report immediately to the police station in the town and to bring his men, equipped with spades. When he arrived, 15 firefighters were already there. They set out immediately for the barn and reached it shortly after 5 a.m. Fifty local residents were already gathered there, farmers from Kloster-Neuendorf and Berge, who had been ordered by Thiele to come. The Kreisleiter was also present, and it was he who instructed this group of civilians where to begin digging the graves. Thiele also said that if they could not make progress, the best way to cover up all traces would be to pour large quantities of gasoline into the barn and try to destroy the corpses that way. However, Scherinkau was not willing to be involved.[139]

At about the same time August Bomm, the 49-year-old owner of the local laundry, who was in charge of the municipal technical unit, was told to bring his staff to the police station. This unit was responsible for maintenance of the municipal water system and electrical network, as well as for various technical repairs. They brought various tools, spades, and other equipment that could be used to dig burial trenches in order to obliterate signs of the crime. Ten men reported for duty and set out for the barn, which they reached before 6 a.m.[140]

At 6 a.m. Debrodt came to the home of Hermann Holtz, the CO of Volkssturm Company 1, woke him, and told him to mobilize his men within the hour; they should bring food and water with them for the next few hours, he said. Debrodt told Holtz that hundreds of prisoners had been murdered in the barn and that the corpses needed to be buried. Holtz ordered several of his men to round up the others.[141] One of these was 59-year-old Gustav Palis, a local clerk. Palis asked what had taken place, but Holtz told him only that they were to report for duty with spades in order to dig a large pit for dead prisoners. He refused to give details about the identity of the murderers.[142] At about 7:30 a.m. some 25 Volkssturm men made their way to the barn. Holtz had not been told by Debrodt what precisely they were to do there, since Debrodt had said that he would receive detailed instructions on the spot. Holtz and his men reached the barn at about 8 a.m. There were several soldiers there, commanded by an elderly sergeant. He told Holtz that he and his men were leaving, and left behind weapons and a small amount of ammunition. Holtz did not understand the purpose of this equipment. To the north of the barn, the firefighter unit and the technical unit personnel were already busy digging burial trenches.

Thiele arrived again, dressed in the uniform of a Wehrmacht soldier, as Holtz's men were preparing to join the grave-diggers. Holtz asked the Kreisleiter for instructions as to what his men were to do. Thiele said that the murdered prisoners had been dangerous criminals, and so, if any of them were left alive, they were to be shot without hesitation; the corpses were all to be buried. Holtz informed his men that the Kreisleiter's order was to bury the corpses and they were to do so without hesitation.

At 9 a.m., just as the firefighters and the men of the technical unit were preparing to leave, 60 Volkssturm men from Company 2 arrived with their CO, Wilhelm Becker, and men of Walter Pannwitz's Company 3, although Pannwitz himself did not accompany them. Gustav Palis, who was in this group, described what happened after he arrived:

> When we reached the barn I saw that four Volkssturm men were on guard . . . there was a group of firefighters with their vehicle, about 20–25 of them, and 20 men from the technical unit who had buried the burnt bodies. Beside the barn they had dug a trench 30 meters long, two meters wide and 3 meters deep, and they were throwing the bodies in and covering them with soil. The firefighters group and the technical unit had been working since 6 am, and Holtz's Volkssturm group started digging pits and burying the corpses . . . among the burnt bodies was one who was still alive, and one of the firefighters, Runge, who lives in the town, called one of the Volkssturm, who was armed, to murder him. The man, Franz König, fired one shot from his rifle at the burnt man but didn't kill him, only wounded him in the shoulder. So I took König's rifle and shot one of the burnt men and he was killed. It was a German.[143]

Holtz and Becker discussed what had occurred and agreed that the Kreisleiter's order to the Volkssturm to carry out this dirty job was inappropriate. However, they had little choice at this stage. Thiele was already on his way east in an effort to make his getaway before the Americans arrived. The Volkssturm men, all local residents, were left with the flagrant evidence of an appalling crime of mind-numbing savagery, and with hundreds of corpses lying on their doorstep. The only thing that could be done was to try to inter them all that morning. They continued to dig the burial trenches and to bury the bodies, which were lying scattered inside and outside the barn. It was not easy to persuade the elderly Volkssturm men to drag the charred and bullet-ridden corpses out of the barn and stack them in the trench. Becker, in any event, managed to slip away from the area after a short time and left Holtz in charge of the Volkssturm.[144]

Although 12 hours had elapsed since the massacre began there were still dying and injured prisoners at the site, who pleaded for an end to their suffering. When Holtz went into the barn, which was still thick with smoke, he encountered one of them. He knew that the Kreisleiter had ordered that the prisoner, who was pleading for his life, was to be shot. Holtz called one of his men and ordered him to kill the wounded prisoner. The man refused. Holtz could see that his men were losing patience and were no longer capable of digging the graves since they could hear the groans and calls for help of the wounded. He picked up his rifle and shot the prisoner. Immediately afterward another prisoner was discovered lying injured at the northeastern end of the barn. Palis shot the poor wretch in the head.

Becker, who also came to tour the site, told Holtz that other prisoners, with varying degrees of injury, were lying in the area farther away from the entrance to the barn. Holtz told him that the Kreisleiter had ordered that all of them be liquidated, and ordered him to take his car and drive to the Kreisleitung to ensure that someone would take responsibility for carrying out this assignment. He refused to order his own men to do it, partly because he was afraid that they would refuse.

It is impossible to estimate the number of prisoners murdered in the last round of the Gardelegen massacre, in which the Volkssturm played the active part. Holtz declared at his interrogation several weeks after the massacre that there were quite a few victims, and that some were not severely injured and could easily have been given first-aid treatment, and left to await the arrival of the Americans. Palis and several other Volkssturm men undertook to deal with the prisoners on the left side of the barn. Some prisoners still tried to escape when they realized that they were to be liquidated. They were shot instantly by the Volkssturm, and their corpses were thrown into the trench.

At about 11 a.m. Wilhelm Becker, who had gone to the Kreisleitung to find a solution to the problem of liquidating the surviving prisoners, returned to the barn. With him were two or three men in Luftwaffe uniforms, one of them a junior officer. They began to deal with the wounded prisoners, who were still lying in the smoking barn. When the soldiers entered they immediately encountered two prisoners, who staggered out, followed by another two. Three of the four were shot immediately. The soldiers then went over to the burial trench on the southern side of the barn, and there they shot one or two prisoners lying inside the trench who were still showing signs of life. After about 45 minutes they left.[145] From the place where he was lying, among the charred corpses of his comrades, the French prisoner Georges Crétin watched the scene:

From inside I hear the sound of spades and hammers. I can see civilians digging a pit and beginning to pull out the corpses of my friends with the aid of hooks and pitchforks and drag them to the pit. From time to time there are shots, apparently in order to liquidate those who are still alive. At noon I hear from afar cannon-fire. I see the civilians listening. I think they are going off to eat but after that I don't see them again.[146]

The murders and the burial continued until nearly noon. Then Palis left and returned to town in order to look for Thiele and tell him that his men were tired and could not continue the exhausting work. After all, he said, they were elderly men, not young enthusiastic soldiers, and the strenuous physical labor, together with the emotional pressure, had worn them out. "My men were shattered after several hours in the barn,"[147] he claimed after the war.

At noon, Holtz understood that he would not succeed in completing the task, particularly since his men were gradually slipping away. The Americans would be arriving in a few hours, and the last thing he wanted was to be caught at the scene of the crime with his men. He ordered them to collect the weapons left at the site and take them to the cavalry school. At 3 p.m. Debrodt came to his house and asked if the job had been completed. Holtz told him that they had not managed to bury all the corpses and that at least 200 were still scattered in the barn and around it.[148] Debrodt made a further effort to complete the chore. At 3 p.m. another 30 Volkssturm men were sent to the barn, and worked there until 5:30. Debrodt went with this group and, once they had started work, he mounted his bicycle and rode home. When he reached his house, he heard that the town was due to surrender to the Americans at 7 p.m. He immediately sent one of the Volkssturm men to tell the men in the barn to hurry home.[149] "Night fell and there were several injured Russians and Poles inside the barn . . . dragging themselves out from among the corpses. It was clear that nobody was supervising us any more and everyone who could move, left the macabre place," George Crétin said. Total silence now reigned. Inside the barn lay several wounded and burned prisoners, whom chance had left alive after 24 hours in hell.[150]

The next day, April 15, when the Americans had occupied the town but had not yet discovered the atrocity that had been perpetrated nearby, Holtz met Pannwitz in the street. Pannwitz asked him why he had not escaped like some of the other people implicated in the massacre. Holtz was astonished: "I had no reason to escape. What I did, was done in the framework of my obligation as a soldier to obey orders, and I have no connection with the massacre."[151]

CHAPTER TEN

After the Flames

Burgstall is a small village of 500 inhabitants about 22 miles (35 kilometers) southeast of Gardelegen and about 6 miles (10 kilometers) east of Dolle. The prisoners in Kemmnitz's charge, who had been stranded at Letzlingen, passed through Dolle on the way east. Dozens of them were murdered in Dolle by the Volkssturm and local civilians, in a very similar scenario to others that were being played out throughout the district at the time.[1] The remaining prisoners on this transport, about 500 in all, continued their march eastward and entered Burgstall on April 12, 1945. They included about 200 Russians, 150 Poles, and 60 to 70 Germans, as well as Yugoslav, Italian, Norwegian, French, Belgian, and Dutch nationals. Also among them were an unknown number of Hungarian Jews.[2] They were accompanied by about 50 guards, most of them middle-aged Luftwaffe recruits and the rest camp-SS personnel.[3]

The prisoners entered the village in three columns, most of them scarcely able to stagger along. Following them was a cart loaded with dying prisoners and corpses. Many of the marchers had injuries and were suffering from severe frostbite, since most had no blankets or suitable clothing. The local villagers brought them water and bread.[4] The reaction of the guards to contacts between the prisoners and the local inhabitants was apparently inconsistent. Some did not intervene and did not prevent the villagers from talking to the prisoners, while others ordered the villagers to keep their distance.[5]

The situation in Burgstall was almost identical to that in Gardelegen and other nearby villages and towns. The Americans were due at any moment, and it was obvious that the march of this group of exhausted prisoners eastward and across the Elbe could not continue under the prevailing transportation conditions. The local administration had been informed of the scheduled arrival of a large group of prisoners. Hermann Pett, a 54-year-old local lawyer and notary, discussed the matter with Reinhold Möhring, the local Ortsgruppenleiter. Möhring told Pett that he had received instructions from the officer in charge of the prisoners to take steps to execute them as quickly as possible.[6] When the prisoners arrived, one of the guards went to the home of the mayor, Bürgermeister Andreas Lehse, and informed him of the existence of the order. He demanded that Lehse find a suitable site for the killings. Lehse refused to have anything to do with the plan and sent the transport heads to Möhring, the highest authority on the spot.[7] Meanwhile, the prisoners had been settled for the night in an open field near the village.[8]

A debate ensued in Möhring's office, and voices were apparently raised as the participants differed as to who was authorized to decide the fate of the prisoners. It seems that the commanders of the transport had brought a document containing the order to liquidate the prisoners. The source of this document has never been clarified. Ursula Stachetski, a typist in Möhring's office, recalled that she heard the SS men say that the order came from the highest echelons of the SS.[9] It is most unlikely that SS soldiers who happened by chance on a small village would have been in possession of a written order from the senior SS command. It is more feasible to assume that, in order to rid themselves of the prisoners, they improvised a document to be displayed to the local authorities in the event that problems arose. Whatever the explanation, they did produce a document of some kind, since Pett read it and declared that it did not meet the required legal criteria. First, he said, it was not signed properly, and further, in order to execute an order to kill the prisoners, the law demanded a separate order for each prisoner; a collective order was not valid. Any such order should be signed by the camp commandant and should include precise details of the reasons that the sentence had been passed. The SS man who conducted the argument with Pett insisted that this was not a case of punishment; they were dealing with a group of prisoners who constituted a security threat and hence, must be eliminated.[10]

Pett's legal arguments, cited in order to gain time until the Americans arrived and to prevent the guards from recruiting local assistance in order to create the conditions for a massacre, were fully backed by Möhring. He contended, with Pett's legal backing, that under the existing emergency regulations, he was the supreme security authority in the village and the camp guards had no standing there. He declared that he intended to issue a directive prohibiting any attempt to harm the prisoners and that he had the authority to do so.[11]

When the debate continued into the late afternoon, the SS men realized that there was nothing to be done. They decided to beat a hasty retreat so that they would cross the Elbe before the few remaining escape routes were closed off. The 500 prisoners left behind in the village were handed over on April 13 to the American forces when they took the village.[12] During the night they spent exposed to the cold in an open field, eight of the prisoners perished. Several of them were apparently shot by the guards.[13] This, however, was the only large group of prisoners from the Mittelbau-Dora transports that had set out 10 days earlier for the Altmark who survived, thanks to the initiative of local authorities.

In the case of Gardelegen, the murder machine was set in motion by the local political security authorities, whereas in Burgstall, their counterparts, aided by local civilians, foiled the SS attempt to liquidate prisoners. Various reasons can be cited to explain the difference: the fact that the American forces had already reached the outskirts of Burgstall at the time the attempt was made to organize a massacre, or the refusal of the local population to cooperate and organize such activity. But the dominant factor, in the final analysis, was the personality of the two civilians who nipped the initiative in the bud. Pett was opposed to the Nazi regime, and his political views were no secret.[14] Möhring was a local party functionary in a small village in a remote area, but this did not inevitably transform him into a mass murderer. The collaboration between the two of them, backed by the local population, generated this unique rescue operation.

Burial and Commemoration

Colonel Edward Beale was the first American investigator to conduct a thorough examination of the massacre site at Gardelegen. In his report, he estimated that there were 300 bodies lying in and around the barn. Although he examined the site on April 17, three days after the killings, he reported that the straw and the corpses were still smoking. On the eastern side of the structure he saw two large trenches, about 6.5 yards by 2 yards (6 meters by 1.8 meters) each. These trenches had been partly covered by soil, but body parts were still visible despite the hasty efforts to conceal them. To the north of the building was another trench of similar dimensions, which was also partially covered with soil. The beginnings of a fourth trench could be seen farther north, parallel to the third, but the burial posse that had labored there in the early morning hours of April 14 had not completed their chore.

Numerous bloodstains were found, as well as torn and scattered garments. Beale also reported considerable quantities of cartridge belts, unused boxes of ammunition, and several Wehrmacht helmets. Rifles and Panzer-fäuste weapons were also found abandoned at the site.[15]

In the days after the barn massacre, the story was revealed to dozens of Allied war correspondents and photographers. The first report appeared on April 17 in the *New York Times*. It consisted of the testimony of one of the survivers, Gaza Bondi from Hungary. He told the American soldiers who found him that 700 prisoners had been immured in the barn and burned alive by a group of 16-year-old boys in SS uniforms.[16] In the days that followed, a wider and more accurate description was published.[17] Other U.S. newspapers published the story at length, accompanied by the testimony of the survivors, described the events that led up to it, and the reaction of the U.S. troops who discovered the horror.[18] They were outdone by *Life* magazine, which published a series of gruesome close-up photographs of charred and twisted corpses. The central photograph in the article depicted stunned American soldiers staring at a heap of corpses of prisoners murdered in the barn. According to the caption:

> The Holocaust of Gardelegen took place on Friday, April 13. German SS guards tried to burn between 500 and 1,000 prisoners to prevent their being liberated by the advancing Americans. There are approximately 150 corpses on the warehouse floor. In the background are three soldiers of the US Ninth Army, who took Gardelegen on April 17 and found the building still burning.[19]

While the details are not entirely accurate, this illustrated report, including a series of horrific pictures from Bergen-Belsen and Buchenwald, nonetheless contributed significantly to the U.S. perception of the character of the Nazi enemy and the essence of the war the United States had been fighting in Europe.[20]

On April 18 the mayor of Gardelegen and a group of local dignitaries were taken to view the atrocity that had taken place on their doorstep. The commander of the 102nd Infantry Division, Major-General Frank Keating, ordered that all the physically capable men be summoned in order to give the victims a proper burial. About 300 men were ordered to report to the municipality building and to bring tools with them. The local civilians were terrified that the soldiers were going to take revenge for what had happened.[21] They were led to the barn, escorted by the soldiers, and when they reached the spot, were brought face to face with the horror. One of the American officers said to them: "This was done by Germans!" *(Das haben Deutsche gemacht!)*.[22] Then the local citizens were ordered to bring out the corpses of prisoners who had been trapped in the flames and to exhume those who had been interred hastily in the trenches. There were a number of uncontrolled outbursts of fury from the soldiers, who hit diggers whom they suspected of shirking the task. Also present were several prisoners who had survived the massacre and who urged the soldiers to kill various local residents whom they thought they recognized as participants in the massacre.[23]

At first the Americans contemplated burying the victims in the mass grave whose excavation had begun close to the barn. However, after about two days the Division command ordered that they be buried individually. A military cemetery was prepared, in accordance with the burial regulations of the U.S. Army, about 500 feet (150 meters) from the barn. On the day it was completed, April 22, the entire population of Gardelegen was ordered to report to the town square, where each was handed a wooden cross, about 3 feet (1 meter) high. They were taken to the new cemetery where they planted the crosses next to the graves. The burial operation continued until April 24. The 1,016 bodies of the victims of the Gardelegen massacre were interred in the military cemetery; 586 of them had been exhumed from the burial trenches, and 430 were removed from the barn itself.[24] In fact, 1,018 graves were dug, as also reported in the final report of the U.S. investigators. The bodies of two prisoners found close to the Lindenthal tavern accounted for the extra graves.[25]

Identifying the corpses was no simple task. Most of them were misshapen, charred, and hence unrecognizable. Only four were identified by name. Another 301 were identified by the prison numbers on their garments. Others, in most cases prisoners who were shot outside the barn by soldiers and guards before they could enter, were identified later by nationality. Among them were 60 Poles, 52 Soviet citizens, 27 Frenchmen, 17 Hungarians, 8 Belgians, 5 Germans, 5 Italians, 4 Czechs, 4 Yugoslavs, 2 Dutchmen, 1 Mexican, and 1 Spaniard. In all, 711 prisoners were never identified and remained nameless.[26] Several of the graves in the Gardelegen military cemetery are marked with wooden Stars of David. This is due to the intervention of a small group of Jewish prisoners who had been evacuated to Mittelbau-Dora from Częstochowa and had labored at Stempeda. They succeeded in escaping from the death march from Mieste to Gardelegen and hid near Estedt. After the Americans arrived, as word of the massacre spread throughout the region, they came to see the site. It was they who singled out the Jewish corpses from the others when the cemetery was prepared at Gardelegen. All they could do was to try to identify which of the dead prisoners bore the mark of circumcision. These victims were then buried with a Star of David at their head. None were identified by name.[27]

On April 25, 1945, the cemetery was inaugurated, and a full military burial ceremony was held. Colonel George Lynch, chief of staff of the 102nd Division, delivered the main address at the ceremony. He said that it was being held in honor of hundreds of prisoners from the Allied forces who had been murdered there. Turning to the German civilians who were present, he declared that for years he had been accustomed to thinking that the atrocities of the Nazi regime were Allied propaganda. The question of the historical responsibility for these deeds was clear, as far as he was concerned:

> Some will say that the Nazis were responsible for this crime. Others will point to the Gestapo. The responsibility rests with neither—it is the responsibility of the German people. . . . The immediate perpetrators of this crime will be punished. But that is neither enough to restore respect for the German people, nor sufficient to compensate for the lives of our murdered comrades.

Lynch concluded by saying that it was the historic responsibility of the town to tend the cemetery so that it would remain a symbol of liberty and love of mankind, and would help the Germans to return to the human fold.[28] The plaque affixed to the gate of the cemetery read, in German and in English:

> Here lie the Allied Prisoners of War who were murdered by their captors. They were buried by citizens of Gardelegen who are charged with responsibility that the graves are forever kept as green as the memory of these unfortunates will be kept in the hearts of freedom-loving men.[29]

The text of the plaque was, of course, remote from the facts that were known to the 102nd Division. Few of the murdered prisoners were POWs (the number is by no means clear),[30] and the cemetery was certainly not established on the initiative of the people of Gardelegen. It was practically forced on them by the Americans. However, since it was a military cemetery, those interred there could not but be classified as murdered POWs. The phrasing of the plaque indicates the desire to pass on to the local populace responsibility for commemoration rather than for complicity in murder.

In the weeks after the murders in the Gardelegen area became known, corpses of victims were collected, on the initiative of the American force, from several other provisional burial sites. Near Jävenitz, more than 30 corpses were exhumed from no fewer than 17 provisional burial pits in the wake of the manhunt for escaped prisoners. All these victims were given a proper burial in cemeteries in these towns after a full military ceremony.[31]

Immediately after the murders were discovered the Americans launched a thorough interrogation of those prisoners who had survived and of dozens of inhabitants of Gardelegen and the district, including quite a few Volkssturm men who had been involved in one way or another. Those questioned included several prisoners who were appointed guards during the transfer of the prisoners from the cavalry school to the barn. In all, the Americans recorded 99 testimonies on the affair and arrested 26 individuals on suspicion of involvement in the massacre.[32] The detainees were held in the 9th Army's detention camp in Ziegenhain, and several of them, mainly Volkssturm group heads, committed suicide. One of these was Hans Debrodt, close associate of Gerhard Thiele. His wife, Elsa, was arrested on April 23. A day later, she hung herself in her cell.[33]

The investigation of crimes in the Gardelegen area was not exhausted in the first year after the war. On July 1, 1946, the district was handed over to the Soviet occupation authorities, and on July 25 the Americans transferred the file on the Gardelegen massacre to Red Army investigators. About two weeks later, Robert Sales, an advocate from the office of the U.S. Army Prosecutor of War Crimes, recommended that the file be closed. A list of individuals suspected of perpetration or of complicity in the crime was also handed over to the Soviets.[34]

Sin Lieth at the Door (Genesis 4:7): Shaping Memory

From the first few months after the war the population of Gardelegen uniformly believed that one man alone was to blame for the ghastly massacre that had occurred there, namely, Gerhard Thiele. It was he who organized it, and his accomplices were all confirmed Nazis, in particular the SS soldiers who had brought the camp prisoners to the town. The townspeople felt that they were the victims of Nazi manipulations that had left them with perpetual evidence of the crime perpetrated near their homes.[35] Until mid-1948, at least, the massacre in the barn seemed to have been erased from public consciousness: "The massacre in the barn was tabu as far as the population were concerned, as if it were a wall" *(das Massaker in der Feldscheune [war] ein Tabuthema in der Bevölkerung. Es war wie eine Mauer")*, explained one of the Gardelegen residents.[36] The site was neglected and abandoned, and because of the scarcities in the Soviet-occupied zone and later, in the DDR, the remains of the barn were dismantled and the bricks reused for building purposes.[37] In 1945–1950, and in particular before the DDR was established in October 1949, the area underwent an accelerated denazification process. Hundreds of thousands who had been members of the Nazi Party lost their jobs. Tens of thousands were placed on trial, and hundreds were given long prison terms or death sentences. A series of special internment camps were set up, several of them in former concentration camps (Buchenwald, Sachsenhausen, and others). Tens of thousands of Germans were held there, as were other nationals in the Soviet-occupied areas who were suspected of Nazi activity and support. After 1990 the mass graves of prisoners who died there after the war were discovered. There are various estimates of the number of individuals imprisoned and murdered in these special camps, which were totally detached from any contact with the civilian population and were reminiscent of the Soviet gulags. They range from 122,000 prisoners and 43,000 deaths according to Soviet statistics to 240,000 prisoners and 95,000 deaths according to American and West German sources.[38]

It was in the course of this intense period of internal purges, which led to the creation of a new state structure with Stalinist features, that patterns of memory of the Nazi regime began to emerge. In mid-1945, organizations of "victims of fascism" (Opfern des Faschismus—OdF) began to be established in Soviet areas, mainly by liberated camp inmates with political, socialist, and communist backgrounds. By the end of that year, such organizations existed in almost all districts in the Soviet-occupied zone.

Naturally enough, the communists held the central role in these organizations. They brought with them a heritage of resistance to Nazism that was fundamentally communist in character; they emphasized, among other things, that communists were the first, and to a large extent, the main victims of the Nazi regime. After the return of the German communist activists who had been in Moscow during the war, including the future head of the new German communist state, Walter Ulbricht, contact was established between the returning political functionaries and the antifascist ex-camp inmates. The consequence was the forging of the concept of collaboration between all the components of the antifascist struggle, with its clear message of communist resistance and victimization.[39]

The political identity of the DDR and the shaping of its national character entailed processing the National Socialist experience. This identity was based entirely on confrontation with the Nazi dictatorship and its social, economic, and political structure. As a state whose essence was antifascist (antifaschistischer Staat), the DDR grounded itself on the political myth that evolved around German resistance to Nazism. Its legitimization derived from the basic assumption that an antifascist movement had existed in Germany throughout the period of Nazi rule. For years the DDR portrayed the German Federal Republic as a state incapable of tackling the heritage of Nazism and devoid of anti-Nazi identity, and as having retained structural, ideological, and economic elements of the Nazi regime.

As part and parcel of its effort to nurture the antifascist heritage, the DDR represented itself as the sole alternative in Germany to National Socialism. This was the central project in all spheres of life, the ideological core and the objective of education. At its heart was the emphasis on communist resistance as the main agent of the struggle against National Socialism. This communist resistance had two parallel components: that which existed illegally in Germany itself and that which was organized in exile, in the Soviet Union. This heritage was fostered zealously because of its existential significance. It was a living legacy in all political frameworks and in the everyday life of all sectors of East German society. The patterns of living, social norms, and social activity in general were constructed and shaped in its name.[40]

The political-ideological pattern of memory also shaped attitudes toward the victims of the Nazi regime. In ruling Communist Party circles in the Socialist Unity Party of Germany (Sozialistische Einheitspartei Deutschlands—SED), numerous debates were devoted to identifying the victims. After the DDR was established, criteria were adopted that distinguished between two groups of victims. The first was the group without clearly defined identity. Jews were almost nonexistent, or at most were mentioned in passing, as were such groups as Gypsies, Jehovah's Witnesses, or homosexuals.[41] All these were classified as ordinary citizens of various nationalities, an innocent population that had been persecuted by fascism. The second category consisted of fighters, namely, members of the resistance movement, who were classified as communists. In practice, in the commemoration ceremonies held in the DDR in the early 1950s, most of the victims were described as ordinary people whom the Nazis decided to murder; no clear motives were cited (racism, anti-Semitism, social deviations, etc.) apart from vague references to the murderous nature of fascism. These ceremonies and rituals, which began to be held annually, were not dedicated to the memory of the victims. They always emphasized the heroic character of the resistance, the commitment of the fighters, and the educational message of their actions. The fighters were set up as the model for future generations in the long march to freedom and peace.[42]

These messages were soon given form in the memorial sites that began to appear in the early 1950s. The sites of former concentration camps were the prime object of commemoration. Whereas in the Federal Republic, it was mainly survivors who launched the first commemorative projects, in the DDR it was the state that first began to deal with the camp sites within its territory after the dismantling of the special Soviet camps, first and foremost Buchenwald. It was the DDR that designed and established national memorial sites in the camps *(Nationale Mahn und Gedenkstätten)*. Planning of the Buchenwald site began in 1951 and encompassed not only the camp, but also sites in the nearby town of Weimar and places where prisoners were murdered and mass graves of camp prisoners had been exhumed. The "boulevard of the nations" *(Straße der Nationen)* at the center of the memorial site emphasizes the multinational character of the victims of Nazism as well as the uniform path of resistance. The statues reflect the rationale that is at the heart of the DDR's message from the 1950s of commemoration and perpetuation. They portray prisoners supporting one another in postures of revolt, tenacity, and determined resistance. Underlying all this was a clear message: the desire to demonstrate the existence of another, antifascist Germany. The Buchenwald site was designed as resounding proof of the victory over fascism; the forces of resistance, within the camp and outside it, are meant to symbolize a single essence of liberty and the common struggle. All were antifascist fighters with a single unifying ideal, and their message links the past to the present.[43]

In establishing the memorial site for the victims of the Gardelegen massacre, it was necessary to contend with three issues that rendered the task particularly complex. First was the fact that the Americans had already laid the foundations for commemoration of the victims and established the model by setting up a cemetery, by identifying the victims as Allied fighters, and by imposing the task of preserving their memory on the local townspeople. The second issue was the looming shadow of the past and the well-known fact that this massacre was not the exclusive work of savage fascism but was also perpetrated by ordinary individuals who were now citizens of the new, socialist and antifascist Germany. Third, it was necessary to merge this site, which, as elsewhere in Germany, was established as a national memorial site, into the official message of all the sites commemorating victims of the Nazi regime.

The hesitant and multistage development of the memorial site at Gardelegen attests to the problems entailed. The process began in 1946 when a group of Jewish survivors set up a natural unhewn rock beside the military cemetery, marked with a plaque commemorating the Jews who died there.[44] When the state undertook the task of commemoration, the rock was already in place and could not be removed. The official design of the barn site, adjacent to the cemetery, began in 1950, and it was inaugurated in 1953 as a "memorial site for the victims of fascism" *(Mahnmal für die Opfer des Faschismus)*.[45] The remnants of the original barn were dismantled, and a wall of brown brick was constructed, with a wide opening at its center, recalling the original barn wall. A row of trees was planted beside the wall. The plaque affixed to the wall contained a very different text (in German) from that set up only dozens of feet away by the Americans in 1945.

You are standing before the remnants of the wall of the barn where, on 13 April 1945, one of the cruelest crimes of fascism was perpetrated. The night before the liberation, several hours before the Allied forces entered, 1,016 antifascist resistance fighters of various nationalities *(internationale Widerstandskämpfer gegen den Faschismus)* were burnt alive. If at any time you should feel defeatism or indifference in the struggle against fascism and imperialism, draw strength from the unforgettable memory of our dead.[46]

In 1965 a series of memorial stones on which were carved the names of the countries of the murdered prisoners were placed along the road leading to the barn site and the memorial wall. The countries included Belgium, France, Poland, the Soviet Union, Italy, Yugoslavia, Mexico, Holland, Czechoslovakia, and Hungary. The original plaque affixed by the Americans in 1945 was removed, in view of U.S. military activity in Vietnam, and, its message was lost. The plaque was not replaced until after the DDR had disappeared from the world map.[47] In 1971 a new element was added to the site. A monument by the Magdeburg sculptor Joachim Sendler was erected in front of the reconstructed barn wall. The sculpture, which resembles the statues of antifascist warriors at other commemorative sites in East Germany, portrays Albert Kuntz, a well-known communist activist, one of the heroes of the antifascist struggle and a prominent figure in the East German pantheon. Kuntz died in Mittelbau-Dora on January 23, 1945.[48]

In 1963 the commemoration of the victims of the Gardelegen death march was extended to other murder sites in the district. A 22-mile (36-kilometer)-long "path of national memory" *(Nationaler Gedenkweg)* was inaugurated, which passed through Mieste, Estedt, Jävenitz, Letzlingen, and other small towns. Memorial stones were placed at intervals at sites where mass graves had been discovered. This road follows the regional highway and borders forest sites where at least one corpse of a murdered prisoner was discovered.[49]

In the mid-1960s, therefore, the message of the memorial site in the Gardelegen area was complete, conforming entirely to the official party line. The message at the American site had been erased, and the new plaque redefined the identity and legacy of the victims. The link between U.S. imperialism and its West German ally was also emphasized. The role of ordinary citizens in the acts of murder, that gruesome specter, was now buried deep, and nobody contemplated exhuming it.

Because of the proliferation of memorial sites to the victims of fascism in the Gardelegen area, it became the focal point of East German commemorative activity in the late 1970s. In 1975, a procession—the "Dora-Gardelegen memorial march" *(Dora-Gardelegen Gedenkmarsch)*—was held for the first time and was an annual event until the late 1980s. This early political-didactic event has features in common with the present-day annual March of the Living of Jewish youth to Auschwitz on Israeli Holocaust Memorial Day. The opening ceremony was held on the parade ground at Mittelbau-Dora with the participation of hundreds of young boys and girls, members of the party youth organization, Freie Deutsche Jugend (Free Young Germans), and the Junge Pionier (Young Pioneers) youth organization. They then marched north to Magdeburg, where they were greeted by representatives of the East German army. The memorial procession continued on its way to

Mieste and from there, on foot, along the *Nationaler Gedenkweg* to Gardele-gen. On the last day of the trek, an official ceremony was held at the massa-cre site with the participation of Red Army soldiers, veteran antifascist fight-ers, and several survivors of the massacre who came from the Soviet Union, Poland, and France for the occasion.[50] The speeches placed special emphasis on "fascist violence" and its consequences, and from the 1960s on, docu-ments and testimonies on the events at the barn were prepared and distrib-uted to the youngsters.[51] The political message continued to emphasize the link between the fascism of the 1940s and the oppressive imperialistic capi-talism of the 1970s. The young generation was taught, for example, that whereas Allied planes had created havoc and ruin in the last weeks of the war among German civilians, Soviet planes had merely dropped pamphlets aimed at the population, Germans and others, exhorting them to join in the communist struggle against Hitlerism.[52] Thus the victims of the massacre in the barn became part of this popular struggle, and their depiction as antifas-cist liberty fighters received its authentic expression.

As part of the ceremony, the ritual of 1,016 rose columns *(Rosenstöcke)* was performed. The young people, most of them local, placed a column of flowers at the foot of each grave.[53] This memorial ceremony helped to re-lieve the local population of the weight of historical responsibility. The burdensome chore of tending the cemetery, which had been imposed in 1945, was revoked. The socialist state reassigned it, as an educational task, to the party youth organizations.

The commemorative efforts and the transmission of the heritage of anti-fascist resistance required living heroes in addition to the graves of victims. In the 1960s there were two suitable candidates. The first was Ludwig Lewin, a Jew from Pomerania. He was imprisoned in Auschwitz, and when the camp was evacuated he was sent to Mittelbau-Dora and then to Rottleberode, and he was on the transport that arrived in Gardelegen. When the prisoners were summoned to the parade ground of the cavalry school before being taken to the barn, he succeeded in slipping away, and was one of the prisoners sent to bring barrels of fuel to the barn. He remained in Gardelegen after the war, joined the Communist Party, and worked in the local textile factory.[54]

Lewin, however, did not fit the role of heritage transmitter. He was of Pol-ish origin, found it difficult to settle down after the war, and remained in Gardelegen for personal reasons. He was far from being a leader and was certainly not a veteran party man. Better suited to this role was another prisoner: Karl-Paul Semmler. Born in 1904, he had been a member of the German Communist Party from 1923 and was active in its organizations, including the special defense units established during the street battles with the Nazis in the early 1930s. In 1934 he was arrested and sent to a concentration camp, and in 1938 he reached Buchenwald. There he was active in communist resistance circles and in 1943 was one of the first prisoners sent to the newly established Mittelbau-Dora camp. In December 1944 he was transferred to Rottleberode, and there, like other German prisoners, he became a kapo. Semmler was a "veteran number" *(alte Nummer)*, the term used for long-term prisoners (who were exclusively German), and his good relations with the camp command were based on his status. At Rottleberode he was chief camp kapo *(Oberkapo)* in charge of all the other kapos.[55]

Semmler was one of the survivors of the massacre. After the war, he settled in Lugau, joined the police force, and later moved to Weimar. After retiring for health reasons, the consequence of his long years in the camps, he was recognized as a "victim of fascism" (OdF). From then on, he dedicated himself to commemoration of the victims of the Gardelegen massacre, and he became the main spokesman of activity around the memorial site that was established in the early 1960s. Semmler died in 1969 at the age of 64.[56]

Semmler was selected in the late 1950s as a suitable bearer of the heritage. He was invited to be the main speaker at the first memorial ceremony for the massacre victims, organized by the Gardelegen municipality in 1959.[57] However, buried within his biography as a communist freedom fighter was his history as a camp kapo, as well as the troubling and unresolved question of his actions on the day of the massacre. For example, there was the story told by Kazimierz Morus, a Polish prisoner from Warsaw, who was one of the prisoners given uniforms and assigned to guard duty. Morus remained behind in the cavalry school, claiming that he did not know how to shoot a rifle and was sent with several other prisoners to bring the barrels of fuel to the barn. He related that it was Semmler who distributed the uniforms to the prisoners assigned to guard duty at the barn.[58] Semmler himself told his American interrogators in 1945 (this was the first of several versions he gave over the years) that he was one of the German prisoners who were given uniforms and sent as guards. It is possible that, as he was known to have been a kapo, he was given the task of distributing the uniforms at the cavalry school. According to his first testimony, he was one of the prisoners who took the fuel to the barn.[59]

In his later testimony on the transport from Rottleberode and the Gardelegen massacre, Semmler referred to himself in the third person as "Paul." There too he refers to his special status as a veteran prisoner in charge of a group of prisoners. It is he who often addresses the SS guards and tries to clarify details about the prisoners, asks permission to bring water from the nearby village, and endeavors to persuade them that the physical condition of the prisoners and the conditions they face are lethal. He also relates that he received several cigarettes from one of the guards for distribution to his comrades. One of the guards even briefed "Paul" on the conversations of the transport commanders in the fateful interval they spent in Mieste.[60] Obviously, an ordinary prisoner would not have been able to converse with the guards without risking a bullet to the head.

All these details were erased from the official propaganda message of the memorial site at Gardelegen in the early 1960s. This propaganda stressed the central function of the communist Semmler in communist resistance activity in the camps, his lengthy service in the Communist Party, his contribution to the struggle against Nazism, and his good relations with the Soviet prisoners. Yet, the truth was by no means so simple. The ambivalent nature of his actions was well known to the East German secret police (Staatssicherheitsdienst—Stasi). Concomitantly with his selection as the spearhead of the official state memorial message at Gardelegen, he became a police informer. This was not, as we now know, an unusual status in the oppressive atmosphere that prevailed in the DDR. However, after his death, various troubling questions began to surface. In the mid-1970s, the 1945 U.S. records investigation file on the Gardelegen massacre was released; it contained testimonies of prisoners who attributed to Semmler a role in the atrocity. Evidence that accumulated from various sources cast light on the problematic role of communist prisoners who served as kapos. Semmler was gradually phased out of the memorial activity at Gardelegen in the 1970s and was replaced by survivors who had escaped from the barn at the very last moment, including some who had never been communists.

Diana Gring states that the Semmler affair clearly illustrates the neofascist nature of the DDR's attitude toward memory of the Nazi period. Semmler was, in the final analysis, a zealous communist and a brave opponent of Nazism for many years. He paid for his political convictions with liberty and health. As long as his biography suited the needs of the regime, he was honored. When it was no longer possible to conceal the fact that he had apparently collaborated with the system that oppressed him, he became anathema to the system of which he felt himself part and was transformed into its victim. He once said that the function of the camp kapo was to act under crossfire *(zwischen zwei Feuern)* between the camp guards and the prisoners. In his life after the liberation, he appears to have been caught between two fires, the past and the present.[61]

Sin Lieth at the Door: Revision

The decade that began in 1990 undid old theories. All at once, truths whose validity had not been questioned for more than four decades were subjected to examination. The cemetery and memorial site outside the little town in

Upper Saxony, which had nestled in the safe bosom of official memory under the previous regime, were suddenly placed under scrutiny. To this end, unfamiliar tools were exploited: newly opened archives, documents, and disinterested research that did not hesitate to ask troublesome questions and to provide blunt conclusions.

In 1995, the local Gardelegen newspaper published a long series of articles on the Gardelegen affair, written by the director of the municipal archive and museum, Dr. Herbert Becker. The first article was devoted to the arrival of the prisoners in the town and their concentration in the cavalry school. The townspeople did not know who they were, what they were doing there, and where they were being taken, he wrote. All they could see was that they were wearing concentration camp uniforms. The guards who accompanied the prisoners told curious bystanders that these were dangerous criminals who were being taken to the barn and would be detained there. It was only after the massacre that the local population learned of the tragedy that had taken place so close to home.[62]

When the prisoners reached the town, some escaped and wandered the streets without supervision. The local minister, Wilhelm Franz, encountered four of them, who had foreign accents. They told him that they were prisoners from one of the Neuengamme subcamps. He understood that they were Dutch, took them into his home, and sheltered them. Not all the prisoners who met local residents were as fortunate. Two prisoners were taken in by Paul Schönian and given food and drink, but shortly afterward were caught in the street and shot by two soldiers in paratrooper uniforms.[63] A separate chapter in these articles was devoted to the unique rescue operation in Burgstall.[64] Naturally enough, Thiele's central, almost exclusive responsibility for the crime, was emphasized throughout.[65] All the articles stressed the contrast between the attitude of the townspeople toward the prisoners, and that of the army and SS who persecuted them and liquidated them mercilessly.

Becker adhered to the basic facts of the affair as detailed in the report of the U.S. interrogators and in other sources uncovered in the early 1990s in German archives. The issue of the local populace's involvement in the crime is not discussed. To the extent that there is any reference to a local resident, it is in one of two contexts: assistance and attempts to hide escaped prisoners (as did in fact happen in several cases) and the exploitation and manipulation of local residents by Thiele and his men, for example, for burial of the corpses. Thus, several years after the fall of the Berlin Wall, the 1945 U.S. narrative was again incorporated into the local collective memory.

In 1998 the German scholar Joachim Neander published a booklet in Magdeburg on the Gardelegen affair. Neander devoted considerable research to the concentration camps and, in particular, Mittelbau-Dora. Summing up, he wrote that the murderers who participated in the Gardelegen massacre consisted of the following: party functionaries, members of the SA, SS, and Waffen-SS, Luftwaffe troops, soldiers from the cavalry school, paratroopers, policemen, members of the Hitlerjugend and Volkssturm, the Reich Labor Service, camp prisoners (kapos), men of the auxiliary technical units, and firefighters. "It was a representative profile of the German male civilian population of the district," he asserted. *(Das war ein repräsentativer Querschnitt durch diedeutsche männliche Bevölkerung im Kreisgebiet.)*[66]

That year, Herbert Becker began to raise questions regarding the circumstances of the massacre, its perpetrators and victims. First, he looked into the issue of the number of victims. The mythical number, reiterated in U.S. reports and adopted in the DDR by the shapers of commemoration patterns, was 1,016. However, Becker argued, close examination had revealed that the Americans did not specify that the 1,016 victims had been murdered in the barn, but were referring to 1,016 corpses collected in the barn area for burial in the cemetery. Only later were they all classifed as having been murdered in the barn.

Were all the dead who were buried in the military cemetery in fact victims of the massacre? Becker wondered. For example, one of the prisoners, Josef Pamuta, testified that when the prisoners were transferred from the stables of the cavalry school to the barn, a number of corpses of prisoners who had perished there were left behind. Walter Neubauer from Estedt related that he took about 100 prisoners, some dying and others already dead, to the barn. It was plain from this testimony that not all the 1,016 corpses uncovered in the barn had been murdered during the massacre, and that quite a few of the prisoners were already dead when brought there. The 1,016 figure was incorrect and should no longer be cited as the number of victims of the massacre.[67]

In another article, Becker questioned the structure of the cemetery and the accuracy and veracity of the details intended to perpetuate the memory of the prisoners. If one counted the burial areas of the cemetery, he claimed, the total was 1,023 graves. Did this mean that 1,023 prisoners were buried there? It will be recalled that the U.S. report referred to 1,018 graves (1,016 Gardelegen victims and two corpses found at Lindenthal). The source of one other grave is known. The former prisoner Wilhelm Fentzling, who died in 1952, asked before his death to be interred alongside his murdered comrades, and his request was honored. The identity of the other four corpses is wrapped in mystery.

Another problem relates to the identifying numbers of the prisoners as recorded on the wooden crosses. Two numbers, 48194 and 2890, were discovered to belong to two prisoners who survived the massacre (Karl Semmler and Edward Antoniak, respectively): Semmler died in 1969 and Antoniak was still alive in Poland in 2000. It is evident that the Americans were unable to record the numbers with complete accuracy. This raises the question of the actual number of victims and their identity.[68]

Discussion about the Gardelegen cemetery in recent years arose from a combination of factors. The U.S. unit that supervised the construction of the military cemetery left quite a few issues unsolved with regard to the identity of the corpses. In their final report, after completion of identification and burial, they wrote:

> This is to certify that 1016 bodies are buried in Gardelegen Military Cemetery. . . . The burying took place between 21 to 25th April 1945 with full military and religious services rendered at 14:30 hours on 25 April 1945. . . .
>
> From the barn were taken 442 charred and twisted bodies and from the trenches were removed 574 bodies bearing evidence of starvation, shooting and beating. In spite of the difficulties encountered, it was possible to "identify" 305 of the total bodies. This "identity" consists of POW numbers obtained from a metal tag around the neck, or the number stenciled on flap of shirt pocket, or the number tattooed on left forearm.
>
> The other 711 bodies must *forever* remain unknown because of the physical impossibility to determine any identification due to the completely burned or totally mutilated condition of the bodies.[69]

Several months after the war, the French government began to seek out the burial sites of French political prisoners who had been deported to concentration camps in Germany and perished in the camps or on death marches; the aim was to bring them to burial in their home country. The French military commission that examined the Gardelegen cemetery on the basis of information received from the U.S. Army estimated that among the 1,016 dead buried there, between 150 and 200 were French. Seven prisoners were identified by name; in all, 29 French victims were identified in the first stage.[70] In September 1948, 34 corpses of French and Belgian prisoners were transferred from the Gardelegen cemetery to the military cemetery in the French zone of Berlin. When this cemetery was eliminated in 1951–1952 the corpses were reinterred in France.[71]

In the first few postwar years this preoccupation with the victims and their graves helped fuel rumors of a revisionist nature as to the identity of the buried victims. Some claimed that local German civilians who had been shot by U.S. soldiers in enraged reaction to the crime were buried there. Others conjectured that the extra graves were those of individuals whom Soviet authorities immediately after the war suspected of Nazi sympathies. After the collapse of the DDR, this theory naturally gained popularity.[72]

After 1990, the familiar and unambiguous message as to the identity of the victims, namely, antifascist fighters, was also put to the test. It was no longer possible to believe Karl Semmler's story, once his role as kapo and collaborator with the notorious Stasi became known. Rumors and speculations as to who had been interred in the cemetery surfaced frequently, especially after Becker contributed to the revisionist campaign by asking questions. When the district authorities debated the allocation of funds in order to alter the memorial site—for example, by removing the communist statue and renovating the weather-beaten wooden crosses—Becker argued that it was inappropriate to launch any kind of commemorative activity there since some of the dead were not worthy of commemoration. "Not only antifascists and Jews lie there, but also quite a number of petty criminals."[73]

Nowhere can one find substantiation for any theory capable of refuting the unequivocal conclusion of the U.S. investigators in 1945: 1,016 prisoners, who were murdered savagely in the barn outside the town, are buried in the Gardelegen cemetery. Even if several of them were already dead when brought to the barn, they perished in the cavalry school or on the way to the barn. The report written after completion of the interment notes specifically that marks of severe violence, shooting, and abuse were found on the corpses in the trenches alongside the barn.

The original plaque removed from the gateway of the cemetery in the mid-1960s was restored in 1989, but with time it fell into decay, so that it was necessary to prepare a replica, which was affixed in 1990. In 1995 some of the original explanatory plaques were removed, and others, displaying different messages, replaced them. The buildings of the cavalry school were also destroyed.[74] Yet the Gardelegen affair has not yet faded into history.[75] The disquieting issue of the role played by the ordinary civilian population in acts of murder during the breakdown of the Third Reich remains on the agenda, as does the question of what conclusions can be drawn and how they can be expressed at the memorial site.

The Mills of Justice

The U.S. investigation of the events at Gardelegen culminated in a list of 27 individuals suspected, on the basis of documentation, of having taken part in the massacre. This was but one of a series of investigation files that were later handed over to the Soviet occupation authorities in the period when there was still cooperation between the military judicial authorities of the American and Soviet zones.[76] In summer 1946, when the files were transferred, almost none of the suspects were in detention in U.S. Army interrogation installations. The list included Helmut Stumf, aged 19, Hitlerjugend member; Max-Albert Stumf, aged 36, a teacher, party member, and SS man; and Hans Heisser, aged 56, a farmer who had been a party member since 1938 and was drafted as a Rottleberode guard in 1944. Also on the list were Alfred Schmidt, a 43-year-old tool manufacturer; Rudolf-Wilhelm Kampe, a cattle merchant, aged 47; and Otto-Anton Beckelmann, aged 53, manager of the Gardelegen flour mill—all three of them members of the Volkssturm.[77]

Other listed suspects were Erich Gotthard and Richard Bischoff, butchers and meat marketers in Gardelegen and Rudolf Ringstmeyer, the local police chief.[78] Then there were Volkssturm unit commanders and men: Arno Brake,[79] Herman Kohle (or Mohle),[80] Wilhelm Biermann, Hermann Holtz, and Gustav Palis. Also listed were Franz Unverdorben, one of the older camp guards at Ellrich,[81] and two prisoners who became guards: 26-year-old Adolf-August Pinnenkämper, one of the German prisoners who were given uniforms and against whom there was testimony that he murdered several wounded prisoners in the barn,[82] and the Polish prisoner Kazimierz Drygalski, aged 22, who was also identified by survivors as a participant in the murders.[83] All these men, however, were small fry who happened to be in the barn area or who murdered prisoners somewhere in the district. They did what they thought should be done or what they were ordered to do. Three additional suspects of different weight, who at one time or another were present at the defining moment of decision making, and whose decisions led to the massacre, were Erhard Brauny, Friedrich Teply, and Rudolf Kuhn, commander of the cavalry school barracks.

Teply appeared as a witness at the Dora-Nordhausen trial (the trial of Arthur-Kurt Andrae and others), which was held before an American military tribunal at Dachau between August and late December 1947. None of the men on the above-mentioned U.S. list of suspects were defendants at this trial.[84] Teply gave evidence in the case of Erhard Brauny, who was also never charged with regard to his role in the Gardelegen events. Brauny was sentenced to life imprisonment because of his service in the camps, and in particular his role as commander of Rottleberode, but was not found responsible for what was done to the prisoners he led to their deaths. He died of leukemia in jail in Landsberg on June 16, 1950.[85] Kuhn was interrogated at length by the Soviets on his role in the atrocity but was not tried for lack of evidence.[86] Several suspects were tried by Soviet military tribunals (Sowjetisches Militärtribunal—SMT), established in the Soviet-occupied zones in order to try German civilians suspected of Nazi crimes and war crimes, but also of "antirevolutionary activity." They included members of the SS, SA, or other police bodies. In August 1947 the Soviet occupation authorities promulgated Order No. 201, which transferred judicial powers from the Soviet military tribunals to German civilian courts. This order provided the main legal basis for the subsequent DDR system that placed Nazi war criminals on trial.[87]

In 1947 two suspects thought to have participated in the massacre, Erich Gotthard and Richard Bischoff, were sentenced to long prison terms. They were released at the end of January 1956, and both men moved to the Federal Republic. Ringstmeyer, who was convicted for his role in transmitting Thiele's orders, was also released and moved to Bielefeld in the German Federal Republic in the early 1960s, where he resumed his career as police officer.[88]

In 1950 other suspects—Brake, Biermann, Holtz, Palis, Pinnenkämper, Drygalski, and Unverdorben—were handed over to the East German authorities by the Soviet authorities. Brake was executed on April 3, 1951, Biermann on November 8, 1951, and Palis on April 6, 1952. However, not all the suspects were brought to trial. Hermann Holtz disappeared in 1955 and his fate is unknown, as did the Pole Drygalski. Unverdorben died on May 17, 1960.[89] Thus, in the late 1950s, the curtain came down on the prosecution of the small group of individuals interrogated and found guilty of taking part in the massacre of prisoners in Gardelegen district. As for Gerhard Thiele, he appeared to have vanished from the face of the earth.

In 1959 an investigation began in West Germany into the role of the Gauleiter Rudolf Karl Jordan in the Gardelegen affair, and Thiele's name was cited as the individual with major responsibility for the events. A preliminary inquiry revealed that, for a brief period after the war, Thiele was in U.S. captivity, was interrogated, but was released without being charged.[90] Only toward the end of the 1990s was the manner in which he evaded punishment fully revealed. Thiele left Gardelegen in his car, wearing an army uniform, apparently between 8 and 9 a.m. on the morning of April 14, 1945, after ascertaining that the Volkssturm and other units were continuing to bury bodies.[91] His wife, Rosemaria Thiele (Kaufmann), declared after the war that the last time she saw him was in Stendal before his arrest by the Americans. She claimed to have no knowledge of his actions that month because she was not living in Gardelegen in the final months of the war. In any case, she said, after the end of April she never saw him again.[92] Rosemaria Thiele continued to live in East Germany after the war and worked as a medical assistant. In June 1962 her marriage to Thiele was dissolved by a court, which accepted her declaration that she had no idea what happened to him after the war and had lost contact with him. The only information in her possession, she said, came from a distant relative who told her that he died after the war.[93]

As noted, Thiele was arrested by the Americans on April 17, 1945, and although he was wanted for his role in the Gardelegen massacre, his captors apparently failed to make the connection between their detainee and the Kreisleiter from Gardelegen district. He was registered at the POW camp as Gerhardt Thiele, Wehrmacht officer. His personal details, as recorded in his file, were altered. His birth date was given as January 13, 1914 (he was actually born in 1909), and his place of birth was given as Werdau in Saxony. Thiele declared that he was a professional soldier and said he had been a member of the Nazi Party only from 1933 to 1936. As to his military service, he said that he had served in France in 1940 and in Russia from 1941 to 1944.[94] During the six months he spent in an American POW camp, where he was even used as an interpreter because of his fluency in English, no one connected Thiele to Gardelegen. The search for Thiele, the murderer, focused on information that he had succeeded in fleeing southward and was hiding in the Harz Mountains or had found his way to Berlin. In any event, on January 30, 1946, Thiele was released from the camp.[95]

The cover-up operation began after he was released from U.S. captivity. Shortly after his release, he spent some time in Thale with his wife and children, one of them a 1-year-old, born toward the end of the war. His wife, naturally enough, did not report these facts to the interrogators. Thiele, afraid that the Russians were stalking him, spent nights away from home on several occasions. Once he was almost caught and then decided that it would be best to relocate to the U.S.-occupied zone. He then changed his name to Lindemann, but apart from that, altered nothing in his basic biography: he preserved his original birth date and even his place of birth, Stettin.

Between 1947 and 1950 Thiele changed his address several times as well as his occupation. He lived in Herten, Karlsruhe, and Cologne and finally in 1951 settled in Düsseldorf. During this nomadic period he worked at random tasks, once appearing as an actor and a singer in a theater troupe in southwest Germany, at other times employed in trade. After settling in Düsseldorf, he became a commercial broker and flourished. He prospered and even found a new female companion, though they never married. The couple lived a comfortable, bourgeois life in a large house. After his identity was revealed, people in his postwar social circle in Düsseldorf said that he was a popular man, charming and well liked, particularly by women. He was fond of sports, enjoyed drinking, and had many friends. None of those who knew him in his reincarnation ever dreamed that he was a mass murderer.[96]

When the Ministry of Justice investigators in Munich began to search for material about Thiele in 1961 and approached the DDR authorities, a number of obstacles arose. In that period there was almost no legal cooperation between the Federal Republic and the DDR and almost no information passed between them. Witnesses living in the DDR who could have cast light on the affair were not permitted to travel to the West to testify. Cold War calculations hampered the investigation.[97]

The East German authorities exploited the Thiele affair in the 1960s in their propaganda against the Federal Republic, claiming that West Germany was evading the task of bringing Thiele to justice, although they knew he was living there under false identity. This claim was part of the DDR's official line, which asserted that the Federal Republic was not doing enough to uncover the identity of thousands of Nazi criminals living within its borders. In practice, however, the DDR failed to hand over the information in its possession to West German investigators.

It was known in East Germany that Rosemaria Thiele played a central role in preparing the infrastructure that enabled her husband to escape to the West. After the war she engaged in illegal trading in gold and sent her husband considerable sums of money after his escape. This money enabled him to fabricate a solid identity as Gerhard Lindemann, respectable businessman, backed by the necessary documents, fake family ties, accommodation, and sources of income. His common-law wife, Margaret-Gertrude Glandien, knew nothing about the Gardelegen affair. He told her about his career in the Wehrmacht and his capture by the Americans after the war, but, naturally said nothing to suggest that he had been a Kreisleiter. Nor did she know that from the 1960s on, he transferred monthly sums to his wife and children, who were still living in Thale. Only in 1997, when Thiele was no longer alive and the criminal police of Magdeburg filled in the missing details regarding his evasion of punishment, did she learn about the massacre for which her life partner had been responsible almost 40 years earlier.[98]

In the 1960s and 1980s, the State Attorney's Office in Munich and later in Göttingen conducted an extensive inquiry into the Thiele affair. A search was instituted for witnesses, some of whom had died, while others were living in the DDR. By 1981, the investigating police and judicial authorities had accumulated detailed information and a relatively precise picture of Thiele's movements in the first few postwar years, his identity subterfuges, his changes of address, and so on. All this raises a particularly disturbing question: why, despite the difficulties caused by his change of name, was Thiele never uncovered, and why was no effective search ever conducted to track down his place of residence?[99]

Thiele's new life in West Germany was a known fact to elements in the ruling party in the DDR. In 1957 Rosemaria Thiele submitted a request to join the party, and two years later she was accepted.[100] However, in the early 1960s, the Chief Attorney's Office of the DDR merely informed the West German investigators of the Gardelegen massacre that Rosemaria Thiele had not seen her husband since the day he was arrested by the Americans. Information on her major role in his disappearance, and the fact that she knew where he was living, never crossed the Berlin Wall.

After the fall of the DDR, all these facts inevitably sparked numerous rumors as to Thiele's real function after the war. Investigators from the Wiesenthal Institute also began to investigate the affair.[101] Wiesenthal himself, in a 1992 newspaper interview, cited the possibility that Thiele had worked for the Stasi in return for nondisclosure, which could explain the smoke-screen that shrouded him in East Germany.[102] Investigators from the Institute met with Rosemaria Thiele, who was then 71, for a conversation. As a result of their research, two articles appeared in German newspapers, giving details of Thiele's disappearance in 1946 and noting that the East German authorities had concealed information from their West German counterparts. The conclusion was that the key to understanding the affair was the fact that Thiele was a spy, working for the Stasi, which, naturally, had no interest in exposing his true identity.

East German archives opened up during this period, and a flood of information poured out. Numerous theories and speculations on the working methods of the Stasi filled the press. But none of this information provided proof of any connection between the Nazi criminal in hiding and the East German secret police. The Stasi never contacted Rosemaria Thiele, and there was no evidence that it was behind her continued contact with her husband.[103]

After the unification of Germany in 1991, all the documentation on the Thiele affair was concentrated in the offices of the State Criminal Police (Landeskriminalamt—LKA) in Magdeburg and in the Stendal Attorney's Office. In 1992, partly as a result of the activities of the Wiesenthal Institute, the investigators received information on Thiele's new name and place of residence in Düsseldorf. It was not too late to issue an arrest order and try to bring him to justice for the atrocity for which he had been responsible 47 years previously. In this case, however, the mills of justice ground exceedingly slowly. Nobody disturbed the tranquil life of the respectable retired gentleman from Düsseldorf in his sunset years. Thiele died at the ripe old age of 83 on June 30, 1994.

The Thiele affair is a uniquely striking illustration of the impotence of the legal authorities in Germany in bringing a murderer like Thiele to justice. Bernard Daenekes served for many years as the senior investigator in the Central Bureau for Investigation of Nazi Crimes in Ludwigsburg and the Criminal Department of the Upper Saxony police in Hanover. He dealt with the Thiele affair from 1962 on and examined hundreds of testimonies and personal files of individuals suspected of complicity in the Gardelegen massacre. After retiring in 1986 he continued to follow the affair until it was fully exposed in 1997. According to Daenekes, this case was unique in that so many of the interrogated witnesses failed to emphasize Thiele's role in the affair and pointed an accusing finger almost exclusively at the SS guards.[104] This was in total contradiction of the conclusions of the U.S. interrogators in 1945. The conspiracy of silence that played down Thiele's role should not surprise us. After all, although Thiele was the instigator and organizer, the perpetrators were local townspeople.

In 1997 the fact that Thiele was living in Düsseldorf was no great secret. In the 1960s some Gardelegen residents, at least, knew of this, and a few even visited him there.[105] But even at that early stage of the investigation, when the West German authorities approached the DDR legal authorities in their search for material on the affair, the official stance of the Magdeburg Attorney's Office was that, as far as they knew, Thiele had died in 1947. The office even instructed the party branch in Gardelegen to adopt this as the official response.[106]

The obfuscation of the affair, which hampered investigators in their search for the murderer, raises various questions. The Thiele case and the massacre of concentration camp prisoners at Gardelegen was a Pandora's box, and it was convenient for many to leave it closed and sealed until after the death of the murderer. To open it up at a criminal trial would have summoned up the specter of local collaboration in this horrendous affair and would have drawn into the vortex many who preferred to keep their distance. As in many other cases where prisoners were murdered during death marches and evacuation of concentration camps, most of the killers of prisoners from the subcamps of Mittelbau-Dora and Neuengamme in Gardelegen district were never brought to justice. Not one of the dozens of soldiers who played a major part in the killings was ever caught and tried. Of the dozens of others from diverse groups of murderers, few were tried, and of those, some were soon released. And the man who bore major responsibility for the massacre lived out his life peacefully without being brought to reckoning for his actions.

CHAPTER ELEVEN

The Murderers

Research on Nazi genocide has dwelt to a considerable extent on the identity of the individuals behind the acts of murder. It has long since been concluded that the murder of European Jews and of other ethnic and political groups was a collective act, and that responsibility cannot be attributed solely to one particular narrow sector of murderers. The killers included senior functionaries and decision makers, fanatic Nazis, Einsatzgruppen (special operation units) soldiers who pressed the triggers beside burial pits in the Ukraine and in Lithuania, and gas chamber operators in the concentration camps. The genocide was the collaborative work of diverse groups of murderers from various sectors of the state, the regime, and the society: the SS, the military, the police, the party, the civilian administration, economic bodies, occupation authorities in the East, the concentration camp administration, and so on. Raul Hilberg defined it as "apportioning of the criminal labor" (arbeitsteiligen Täterschaft).[1]

Gerhard Paul distinguished between two categories of murderers at the two poles of the lethal activity. The first consisted of those who can be classified as planners at the local level, who were responsible for the everyday administration of the operation and were present during the event itself. They included the HSSPF, the commandants of the concentration camps and extermination installations and their henchmen, the commanders of the Einsatzgruppen and the personnel of the murder units in the East, as well as the officials of the occupation administration or the economic network who took part in the management of the deportations, the seizing of Jewish assets, or the organization of the slave labor system. At the other extremity was the large group of individuals whom it is difficult to define with accuracy.

They could be faceless officials of the occupation apparatus who did not deal directly with Jewish affairs or, conversely, the wives of concentration camp commandants who lived on the site and, by their very presence and the fact that they were raising families there, provided the social legitimacy for the apparatus of oppression and murder. Then there were the officials of the SD, who never left their offices in Berlin, or Pohl's economists and proponents of modern technology and bureaucracy. Without the contribution of all these individuals, genocide on such a monstrous scale could never have been perpetrated.[2]

The question of the central role of ideology *(Weltanschauung)* in the motivation of the murderers lay at the core of historiographic polemics for many years. The academic debate, which reached its height in the mid-1990s in studies by Christopher Browning and Daniel Jonah Goldhagen, focused on the murderers who did not belong to the senior echelon of decision makers and lacked direct access to those levels. Thomas Sandkühler argued that those who organized and perpetrated the Nazi genocide in tens of thousands of places did not know and could not have known whether decisions or directives to murder Jews did or did not exist. They could only have figured that an order had been issued "in the spirit of the Weltanschauung" *(Befehl in Weltanschaungsachen)* that was connected in one way or another to the senior echelons of the Reich, if not to the Führer himself. This was enough to enable them to internalize the required sanction for the killings.[3] The distinction between motivation inspired by a deliberate lethal ideology, and the legitimization of ideological murder acquired and assimilated under specific circumstances, is nebulous and may, in fact, be nonexistent.

Uniformed Murderers: The Camp Personnel

In those places where it was Germans who perpetrated the murders (in contrast to gangs and civilians, such as Ukrainians, Lithuanians, and Poles in the eastern territories), the killers were usually uniformed men. They included camp guards and men of the Waffen-SS, Wehrmacht, the gendarmerie, the order police, auxiliary units of Volksdeutsche, and others. Most of the murderers during the evacuations and death marches were concentration camp personnel and hence belonged to the uniformed category. Service in defined military or semimilitary frameworks promoted a certain sense of shared destiny and collective responsibility, which helped considerably to expand the circles of accomplices in murder. The unique *Kameradschaft* (brotherhood and shared destiny) that evolved among members of the same unit was not confined to combat frameworks. It also existed in those uniformed units that did not take part in specifically military operations but, owing to local circumstances, became involved in terror operations against civilian populations or in the murder of Jews.[4]

Two distinct groups that were serving in the concentration camps in early 1945 fulfilled separate functions during the evacuation of the camps. The first consisted of the senior camp-SS administration (*Konzentrationslager* SS), and included the camp commandants, their deputies, or senior functionaries, namely, department heads *(Abteilungsleiter)*, and so on. Karin Orth regards them as the core group of murderers and describes their political, professional, and even social common denominators. The group, which consisted of about 320 individuals, displayed all the political and ideological characteristics of senior functionaries of the regime. They had usually served in the concentration camp system from its early days and were promoted from post to post during the 1930s and after the outbreak of war. They constituted a relatively stable element within the system, although some members left in order to serve in SS fighting units. Most were too young to have seen combat in World War I but were certainly old enough to have absorbed the myths created in the 1920s around that war and the exploitation of those myths by the extreme right during the Weimar Republic. Quite a few of them came from families with military backgrounds. They were, in the main, of middle-class origin and had completed elementary or middle school studies, though most had not graduated from high school. When they did continue their studies, it was usually in vocational or commercial schools. They belonged manifestly to that social class that had suffered more than any other from the economic crisis that befell the republic. Their families had been impoverished, and experienced unemployment and loss of economic and social standing. A considerable number had themselves known unemployment and privation in the early 1930s.

They were associated with and even active in nationalist and radical *völkisch* (populist) organizations. This activity led them at an early stage to the Nazi Party, the SA, and the SS. All the concentration camp commandants had been party members before September 1931, some even from the mid-1920s. In the 1930s, the concentration camp system opened up new career opportunities. The concentration camp network, like the SS as a whole, was a prestigious organization as far as the regime was concerned, and service within it was of military and security significance. These men, who were in their early or mid-thirties, entered the camp system and by the time war broke out, had become the human infrastructure on which the system rested. It was they who kept it functioning until the end.[5]

As noted above, in summer 1942 Pohl introduced far-reaching changes into the concentration camp command, his aim being to reform its administration by giving priority to economic considerations and efficient management of manpower. To this end, new commandants were appointed. Most of the older generation of commandants had been born in 1900–1905, which means that they were at least in their late twenties when the Nazis came to power. Most had been active even earlier in nationalist and *völkisch* organizations or in the party, and were considered to be veteran fighters *(alte Kämpfer)* of the movement and its ideals.[6] The younger men who entered the system as a result of Pohl's reforms were a new generation, most born after 1910, and hence in their early thirties when appointed in 1942. This was true of Paul-Werner Hoppe, Johannes Hassebroek, Max Pauly, or Fritz Suhren, who were promoted following the reforms in the administration of the camps.[7]

For the first time since this unique system was established, key positions were being held by men who had grown within it, but had not necessarily spent their former careers in the concentration camps. Nor were they identified with the traditional training methods of the "Dachau model" devised by Theodor Eicke. Some had begun their service in other SS frameworks, in particular the Waffen-SS. Others had seen combat or at least had some contact with the war in the East and the mass slaughter of civilians that accompanied its initial stage, before taking up command positions in the camps. The inmates of the camps they headed from 1942 on differed from the detainees of the mid-1930s. Political prisoners in preventive custody *(politische Schutzhäftlinge)*, then the dominant category, were replaced in the late 1930s, and especially after the outbreak of war, by categories such as habitual criminals *(kriminelle)* or antisocial *(asoziale)* elements. Once territorial expansion began, there was an increase in the number of Polish prisoners and then of Russians, Soviet POWs, and finally Jews, who from 1944 on were the dominant and central group. The National Socialists viewed these prisoners as a hostile collective, enemies of the race and of the nation with which the young generation of camp-SS was totally identified.[8]

This group of senior officers played a secondary role in the mass murders perpetrated during the evacuations. At most, they were responsible for organizing the evacuation, and, on this matter, they hesitated at length and did not seize the initiative. On the eve of the large-scale evacuations of the camps in the East in January 1945, 37,674 men and 3,508 women were serving in the camp system. Between 80 and 90 percent of them were guards *(Wachmannschaften)*—namely, all those who did not work in one of the "professional" departments, which engaged in record keeping, administration, and organization of the prisoners' lives and the camp routine, labor, secretarial tasks, medical care, or in the political section *(politische Abteilung)*, which was under the Gestapo's jurisdiction.[9] They were guards, members of the camp guard units *(Wachtruppe)*, and camp-SS of a different kind. Most were posted to the camps in the period of expansion from 1943 on, when hundreds of subcamps were being established and the labor network was expanding. They had no connection to the "Dachau model," and many had not come from the ranks of the SS. When they arrived in the camps in the final years of the war, the system was already fixed in a pattern of terror and murder and had created modes of slow and selective killing, exploiting labor as the instrument for implementation. They were a different breed from the veteran camp-SS, but they were the dominant factor in the killings during the last months of the war. On May 9, 1944, Hitler issued a directive empowering Himmler to recruit soldiers close to or over 40 (born in 1906 or earlier) for guard duty in the concentration camps. In mid-1944, in response to this directive, some 10,000 Wehrmacht men who had returned from the Crimean peninsula and men of the air defense or technical noncombatant units of the Luftwaffe and even the navy were posted to the subcamps of the concentration camps.[10]

Willi Mirbach was one of the thousands drafted into this service. He was born in July 1904 into a family of textile laborers and was never a member of any political party. Even after 1933, he did not join the Nazi Party. He was drafted on May 27, 1940, and assigned to a Luftwaffe intelligence unit. In August 1944 he was transferred to Mittelbau-Dora. Initially, he was sent to the Harzungen subcamp and then to Rottleberode. He later claimed that this was the first time he had ever seen a concentration camp.[11]

Friedrich Teply, who remained, reluctantly, in charge of hundreds of prisoners at Gardelegen after Brauny left, was recruited at the end of June 1944. Born in July 1886, he was much older than Mirbach. He had served in the Austrian army in World War I and was a Czech national until that country was divided by the 1938 Munich agreement. Teply joined the Nazi Party in June 1938 for no significant ideological or political reasons; his neighbors had done the same, and apart from that, his son wanted to join the Luftwaffe and become a fighter pilot. Like other Sudeten Germans, Teply grasped which way the wind was blowing, and membership of the party on the eve of annexation to the Reich seemed a wise move. Because of his age, he was not drafted until summer 1944. In August of that year he was assigned to guard duty at Mauthausen, but the camp command rejected him because of his age. He spent several months in a transit camp in Linz and in October was sent to Rottleberode. There he was placed in charge of the prisoners' records and was given responsibility for a group of guards. Unlike Mirbach, he was not posted there after transfer from a Wehrmacht or Luftwaffe unit. From his first day in the armed forces, he served in the camp-SS and bore the rank of SS-Hauptscharführer (sergeant-major).[12]

Another elderly guard posted to the camps was Otto Schrader, born in 1893, who served at Wiener-Neudorf from August 1944 and guarded the prisoners on the march from Mauthausen in early April 1945.[13] A similar case was Franz Unverdorben, born in Königsberg in 1902, married with eight children, a farmer with only eight years of schooling. After leaving school, he worked on the family farm. In 1926 he went to work as a sanitary laborer because of the dire economic situation, and several years later he returned to the family farm. He too was never a party member and had not previously belonged to any previous political or military organizations. Unverdorben was not drafted until April 1944 because of his age and his limited qualifications. When he was finally summoned, he was sent as a simple laborer to the Luftwaffe construction unit. In October he was transferred to the camp-SS and sent to Ellrich.[14]

Paul Letmath, one of the murderers of the women at Helmbrechts, also belongs in this category. Born in November 1894 in Müssen, he was the younger son of a landowner. He completed eight years of elementary schooling and then attended a vocational school. He had no regular occupation and was a casual laborer until World War I. Letmath served in the army until 1918 and was demobilized with the rank of corporal. After the war, he returned to various laboring tasks and married in 1928. He had no connection with the Nazi Party and its organizations. In April 1944 he was conscripted to serve in the Grenz und Landesschutz (border and homeland defense) guard unit. In accordance with the arrangements made in May 1944 for older recruits, his unit was posted to Majdanek in July 1944, and a month later he was assigned for a short time to Auschwitz. From there Letmath was sent to Flossenbürg, and at the end of September or beginning of October 1944, he was posted to Helmbrechts. During the evacuation, he was one of three commanders of columns of women prisoners. He was indicted for murder and for giving orders to murder women prisoners in early May 1945, the last days of the death march from Helmbrechts.[15]

Max Reimann, his counterpart in another group of women evacuees from Helmbrechts, came from a similar background. Born in July 1896, he served as a soldier in World War I, and several days before the outbreak of World War II he joined a Grenz und Landesschutz unit. In 1940 he was posted to Breslau and later volunteered for service in the Waffen-SS. Because of his age, he was no longer qualified for combat service and hence was sent as a guard to Buchenwald and then to Dachau. From now on, the concentration camps were his service framework. In July 1942 he was posted to Groß-Rosen and was then transferred to other camps until the wave of camp evacuations began in the East in January 1945. He arrived at Flossenbürg with a transport of prisoners from Groß-Rosen. From Flossenbürg he was sent as a guard to Helmbrechts.[16]

Other elderly guards who came from elsewhere to serve in the camps were assigned as escorts of convoys during the period of the death marches.

Even in the diverse gallery of camp guards in 1945, the career of Wilhelm Genth is of particular interest. This guard from Hanover-Stöcken, who accompanied the prisoners from the camp to Bergen-Belsen on April 7–8, 1945, was charged with the murder of several prisoners during the evacuation. Born in Mannheim in 1894, he was 49 during the evacuation, had served during World War I as a medical orderly, and in civilian life was a musician. In 1934 he joined the SA in his hometown as a musician and played at official ceremonies and events. He continued his musical career in various party frameworks and by July 1938 was already a member of the SS. His unique occupation brought him in September 1939 to Dachau, where he continued to serve as a musician. By then he was in an SS reserve unit.[17]

In November 1940 Genth's musical career in the camps came to an end and he was assigned to regular service. In his postwar testimony Genth did not explain why this change occurred, and it is possible that he was not asked. Whatever the reason, he served for several years in labor camps in France and Luxembourg and toward the end of 1943 was transferred to Oranienburg, where he took part in an advanced course for medical orderlies. Up to this stage, he had no contact with concentration camp inmates, since the camps where he served in the West had not been part of the concentration camp network. Genth's career again changed direction after he graduated from the six-week course. He heard about a camp in the Lublin area and thought that it would be challenging and interesting to serve there; after graduation, he was sent to Majdanek.[18]

Genth served in Majdanek only until January 15, 1944. He was then transferred to Vaivara in Estonia, one of the most brutal of the labor camps to which the survivors of Lithuanian and Latvian Jewry were sent in fall 1943. Genth, a mature and relatively experienced man, was appointed head of the camp administration *(Lagerleiter)* in addition to being chief medical orderly. For about a year and a half, until the end of the war, he was part of the oppressive system that exploited arduous slave labor and carried out death sentences against Jewish prisoners in the concentration and labor camps. He served in camps in the Baltic countries until September 1944 and was then transferred to Neuengamme, where he continued to serve as a medical orderly, and from there to Hanover-Stöcken, where he fulfilled the same function.[19]

Genth gave an exact description of the situation in which he became a murderer. Among the prisoners he led to Bergen-Belsen were a number who could not keep up with the pace. Together with a Czech prisoner who was a physician (Dr. Wenzel), he constantly checked the condition of the marching prisoners. On the first or second day of the evacuation, one of the marchers collapsed. The Czech doctor told Genth that, unfortunately, nothing could be done for the prisoner, and it would be best to put him out of his misery. Genth went over to the prisoner and shot him. He did the same to another prisoner, after the doctor was heard saying: "There isn't much to be done here" *(Da ist nicht mehr viel zu machen).*[20] He murdered a third prisoner at his own discretion without asking the doctor for his "diagnosis."[21] He did so, he explained, because the order given before departure by camp commandant Paul Mass was clear to him: namely, that no prisoners were to be left behind alive.[22] And thus, a middle-aged musician from Mannheim, who was not even a party member when he began making music in the SA unit in 1934, became an accomplice in the murder of camp prisoners toward the end of the war.

These novice guards, who were transformed within a few days into skilled killers, were operating in a reality that required them to summon up instantaneously an internal mechanism that would help them to become part of that reality. It was a relatively complex process of "professional" socialization. Willi Mirbach described what happened when he arrived at Ellrich with a group of new guards on the way to their final posting. They attended a lecture by an SS officer about the camp, their tasks, and their contacts with the prisoners. They were told that they would be dealing with filth, human ordure, and that the prisoners should be treated accordingly: they were political enemies, saboteurs, and dangerous criminals. Any conversation or contact or negotiations with them were strictly forbidden. The guards were divided into groups of 20, under the command of a noncommissioned officer (NCO) and were sent to Harzungen. They were lodged in two long barracks outside the camp fence. Their food was prepared in the camp kitchen, together with that of the prisoners, and they were served in the guards' mess by prisoners. Theirs was a difficult security task, drab and without glamour, and they felt that it was repulsive, violent, and risky. There were 600 prisoners in the camp, supervised by 60 guards, and Mirbach was one of those assigned to escort and guard them. They were roused every morning at 4:20 a.m. and had to be ready by 5 a.m., with their prisoners, for the head count. Thirty guards were positioned on both sides of the prisoners as they stood on parade. The commando CO, a former NCO in the Luftwaffe, counted the prisoners and was responsible for their orderly transfer to the workplace. When the head count and registration were completed, the prisoners set out in columns, the guards marching on either side. It was a three-hour trek to Niedersachswerfen, where the prisoners worked. After bringing the prisoners to their destination, the guards spent the day cleaning their personal weapons and uniforms and doing other routine chores. At the end of the day, they accompanied the prisoners back to camp on another exhausting march. The work day ended at about 11 p.m., and the next morning at 4:20 it began again.[23]

Their relations with the camp-SS personnel were based on mutual suspicion. The experienced SS soldiers tended to be contemptuous of this gang of elderly men sent to guard enemies of the state and called them *Schlipssoldaten* (necktie soldiers)—in other words, they considered them a group of lazy incompetents who could not be trusted to display toughness and determination when required. The Luftwaffe men, for their part, believed that the SS men were blatantly indifferent to their duties and lethargic in their attitude. At the same time, they feared them and were convinced that, in times of crisis, the SS would blame the newcomers for any problems encountered with the prisoners.[24]

The thousands of guards who were given the task of evacuating hundreds of thousands of prisoners from camp to camp in the final months of the war left behind very little documentation of their conduct. Christopher Browning estimates that it is very difficult to investigate and to expose the motives and motivations of the ordinary men who perpetrated horrific crimes during the war. They did not belong to the higher echelons of a clearly defined organization identified with perpetration of war crimes, they were moved from place to place within the system, and they were not part of an orderly bureaucracy. Even when they joined an organization that committed war crimes, it was in the capacity of reserve units, which took part in later stages and were junior elements in the system.[25]

That said, the murder of the Jewish women prisoners near Stary Jaromierz, for example, illustrates the central role these guards played in the massacres that occurred in those months. The Polish farmer Florjan Drzymała, who witnessed murders, recalled vividly that the uniforms of the guards were identical to those of the Wehrmacht troops and that he saw no SS men in the vicinity: "I stress that the guards who committed the murder were relatively elderly and they were wearing green army uniforms."[26] Thirty years after his first testimony to the Polish commission of inquiry, Drzymała recalled clearly that they were elderly *(stare dziady),* although he was not entirely sure whether they were soldiers or older Volkssturm men.[27] Jan Wojcienchowski, a Polish slave laborer in the area where the women prisoners worked, reported that "he saw Nazis in black SS uniforms, and yellow Wehrmacht uniforms, leading a transport of women prisoners through Ujścia." A similar report was given by another Polish slave laborer who was interrogated on the affair. The Polish commission wrote in its conclusions that "the perpetrators of the murder were Wehrmacht soldiers" *(zbrodni tej dokonali żołnierz Wehrmachtu).*[28] The conditions that prevailed during the evacuation marches generated countless situations whereby these elderly guards became murderers. At the end of March 1945, as the Americans drew closer to Sonneberg, the Buchenwald subcamp, preparations began for evacuation of the inmates. The camp was evacuated in two stages. The first group of prisoners set out on April 1 or 2 and the second on April 9 and 10. The destination of this evacuation by foot was the Sudetenland. The first group apparently consisted of the sick and feeble prisoners, and the second of the remainder, 470 in number. There were quite a few older prisoners, mainly Jews from Poland who had arrived during the winter after being evacuated from camps in the East. Also in the group were Hungarian prisoners (Jews), French, and Belgian.[29]

Be. was one of the guards who set out with the death march of the Sonneberg prisoners. He was a 48-year-old laborer, a veteran of World War I who was conscripted in 1916. In 1940 he was drafted into the Wehrmacht and spent four years in a rear unit in Hanover. In September 1944 he was transferred to the SS and sent to Buchenwald. With him in the group was his colleague Otmar Böh, who was two years his junior and had served in the same unit in Hanover. Neither had any political background; they had never been Nazi Party members or active in any organization affiliated with the party. As the column advanced, the exhausted prisoners began to collapse and were no longer capable of standing upright. Be. asked his colleague what to do with one of them, and Otmar Böh replied, "Shoot him! Or do you want to carry him on your back?" *(Schiessen Sie ihn tot! Oder wollen Sie ihn auf den Rücken nehmen?)*. Be. shot at least six prisoners who could not move on.[30] How did they perceive their task, these elderly guards who found themselves serving unwillingly in one of the regime's most flagrant apparatuses of oppression and murder? Did the fact that they were in charge of thousands of prisoners, who were clearly identified with the enemies of the regime, color their attitude during the death marches? Were they capable of differentiating between the prisoners they guarded; did they treat prisoners differently on the basis of nationality, ethnicity, or gender?

The older men who served in units that were attached to the murder apparatus or helped it in various ways were usually marked by low motivation, and were indifferent and apathetic with regard to ideological issues.[31] The guards posted to the concentration camps mostly served for relatively short periods and did not particularly like this assignment. However, many of them had been exposed—even before being confronted with the decision to liquidate their victims during the death marches—to the violence and killing that characterized Nazism's ideological struggle against its enemies. They were attached to the apparatus at a totally different time to the Ordnungspolizei (Order Police—Orpo) or the older soldiers who had been posted to the East in 1941–1943 and were involved there in the fight against partisans or in the murder of Jews. The Orpo operated among civilian populations, and their activities were particularly savage and violent, claiming numerous victims. Violence, terror, and killing of Jews or Soviet partisans were important components in the operational activity of their units, even if they had not been trained specifically for such missions. The system encouraged them and created rewards and acknowledgment of their actions. They were not necessarily motivated by the guiding spirit of the party ideology. Most of them naturally regarded their victims as a marginal and an inferior group, and it was immaterial to them whether they survived or were savagely exterminated. What was important to them was the fact that their actions, the cruel manhunts, the killing of Jews and of other enemies, had been legitimized by the system they served and that the approval was granted lavishly.[32]

To a large extent this process also existed among a number of the older guards and death march escorts. The system they served gave them all the legitimization and ideological backing they needed to perpetrate murder. Such was the case with Wilhelm Genth, the musician turned murderer, who was trained in various camps before arriving at the decisive moment when he himself had to pull the trigger. The case of Ernst Föl. was also characteristic of this group of killers. Born in 1910 in Lauscha in Thuringia, he joined the party in 1930 and a year later became active in the SA. In 1939, when he was 29, he was recruited into the Wehrmacht and served in France and later on the eastern front. Because of his age, he was transferred from active service to the Protectorate and then to Yugoslavia, specifically for action against partisans. The struggle in Yugoslavia was ferocious, and violence and terror were employed against the enemy; groups of civilians were often liquidated as a form of collective punishment. In September 1944 Föl., like other older soldiers, was assigned to guard duty at Buchenwald. He was one of the most active murderers of prisoners during the death march from Sonneberg in April 1945.[33] When his operational background is examined, this fact ceases to be surprising.

Most of the older concentration camp guards tried to erect a distinct barrier between themselves and the system they were serving. They usually served in small and remote subcamps, and they often tried to exploit their civilian occupations in order to be assigned duties, such as supervision of construction work or responsibility for electrical maintenance, which did not entail close contact with the prisoners. The camp commandants, who at the time were struggling with a number of maintenance problems because of the shortage of skilled manpower, were happy to exploit these experienced men for local needs. Those who were assigned specifically to guard duties, escorting the prisoners to their workplaces or supervising them there, generally tried not to be too deeply embroiled in the system they served. Many of them tried to spend as little time as possible in the prisoners' camp and as much as possible in their own quarters.[34]

Even when the prisoners set out on their evacuation marches, the older guards tried to avoid overinvolvement in dealing with them and left the important decisions to those in charge of the evacuation, namely, the veteran camp-SS.[35] The instructions they received before setting out (to the extent that such instructions existed) did not include more than a general directive to shoot any prisoner who tried to escape.[36] However, when, as often occurred, the columns they were guarding were wandering aimlessly and various prisoners were lagging and holding up the column, the permission to murder escaping prisoners was expanded into far-reaching license to kill indiscriminately whoever they chose. Heinrich Häger, aged 54, who was sent to Mauthausen in December 1944, admitted that he murdered prisoners at Gunskirchen because they were no longer able to walk or because they refused to obey orders. Survivors of the camp saw him shooting prisoners at random. Willi Bruening, aged 46, murdered several prisoners during the evacuation of one of the Mauthausen subcamps to the main camps. They were all outdone by 62-year-old Werner Grahn, who was sent to Mauthausen in February 1944 as an interpreter. Shortly before the liberation, he murdered between five and eight Polish inmates who were working for him as interpreters. He apparently also murdered at least 30 Jews in the tent camp before the departure on the death march to Gunskirchen.[37] The conversion of a large number of older men, with diverse social backgrounds, into a group, many of whose members mercilessly liquidated the prisoners in their charge, can be understood only if one takes into account their incubation period during their months of service in the camps.

Between the senior command level (camp commandants and department heads) and the guards who were drafted at a later stage, there was an additional category that played a central part in the murder of prisoners during the death marches; these were the NCOs or, rarely, the junior officers of the camp-SS, who commanded the evacuation columns. They were a vitally important element in the implementation of the killings. They were the second command circle of the camp system, the junior staff, and differed from the senior cadre that administered and commanded the camps. When men from this group attained command positions in the system in the last year of the war, it was almost always in a subcamp for which they were responsible during the evacuation.

These were the SS men who commanded the columns of prisoners during the death marches—for example, Alois Franz Dörr, commandant of Helmbrechts, who was in charge of the death march from the camp, or Hans-Erich Merbach, born in 1910, who was in charge of the evacuation from Buchenwald to Dachau, and outranked Dörr. Merbach's career began in the concentration camps in 1940 at Buchenwald, and he served in Auschwitz from 1942 until the camp was evacuated. He was then transferred to Buchenwald, where he was placed in charge of the evacuation in April 1945. Another case was that of Oscar-George Helbig, born in 1913, who joined the SS in November 1933 and the Waffen-SS in September 1939. From 1940 to October 1943 he served at Flossenbürg and later fought on the eastern front for a year. In December 1944 he was posted to Mittelbau-Dora.[38] Another of these SS men was 36-year-old Alfred Jepsen, who was responsible for the massacre at Lüneburg. Jepsen served in the Wehrmacht until 1941 and then moved to the Waffen-SS. For a time he fought on the eastern front before being transferred to concentration camp service. He served at Neuengamme and was, among other things, Kommandoführer (work shift commander) of the Danish prisoners. In November 1944 he was appointed deputy commandant of the subcamp at Wilhelmshaven and, as such, in April 1945 was assigned as one of the officers in charge of the evacuation that ended in the bloody massacre of hundreds of prisoners.[39] This is manifestly also the story of Erhard Brauny, commandant of Rottleberode, who was in charge of the transport to Gardelegen. Born in 1912, he was a bachelor with eight years of elementary schooling. He attended a commercial college for three years but never graduated, and hence, had no diploma. Brauny joined the SS in 1932 and the Waffen-SS in November 1939. His career in the concentration camps began in 1937 at Buchenwald, and he passed through several camps before reaching newly established Mittelbau-Dora in September 1943. In November 1944 he commanded the subcamp at Rottleberode.[40]

For the middle and lower levels of command of the camp-SS personnel, terror and violence toward the inmates of the subcamps were the rule even before the death marches began. The regime that Brauny instituted at Rottleberode, and in particular his decision to man the death-dealing commando at Stempeda mainly with Jewish prisoners, reflected his outlook. Prisoners in the camp noted that when he beat prisoners, particularly when he was drunk, they were almost always Jews.[41]

Merbach, for example, who was in charge of the death train where hundreds of prisoners perished on the way to Dachau, was found guilty of at least 10 murders he committed with his own hands.[42] Alfred Jepsen, it will be recalled, also admitted murdering several prisoners.[43] But it was not necessarily the convoy commanders who had previously commanded subcamps who pulled the trigger. Elois Dörr was charged with giving the order to kill women prisoners who tried to escape or collapsed, or with having transmitted such an order through his close assistant, Herta Haase-Breitmann, but there was no incontrovertible evidence that he himself ever pulled the trigger.[44] Erhard Brauny, who led a transport of more than 1,000 prisoners to their deaths at Gardelegen, succeeded in slipping away at the last moment, so as not to be implicated in the event when it occurred. He too was never found guilty of the direct killing of prisoners.

Yet, a light hand on the trigger was often the clear characteristic of these SS men. Thirty-one-year-old Richard Kühler, an SS sergeant who served at Ohrdruf, was one of the SS men who were on the spot when the camp was dismantled and the able-bodied prisoners were transferred to Buchenwald, although it is not clear if he took part in the murder of the sick inmates before the death march set out. Later he was one of the escorts of the evacuation to Flossenbürg. The train, as noted, was strafed by U.S. planes and the evacuation was disrupted. Kühler murdered between 8 and 12 wounded prisoners after the attack.[45] SS Corporal Paul Kaiser, aged 37, murdered an unknown number of Jewish prisoners on the way from Mauthausen to Gunskirchen. Josef Wurst, aged 25, who was a guard at Flossenbürg and set out with the prisoners to Dachau, admitted having murdered three or four of them en route.[46] The two groups—the older soldiers who had been attached to the camps and the various camp-SS personnel—did not necessarily decide to participate in killings during the death marches for the same reasons. In the case of the attached guards, the decision was generally the product of circumstances and not of basic ideological motivation. These men, in most cases, were far from being fervent and loyal Nazis. Their charges were "human material" devoid of all importance, lacking faces or nationality, ethnic or sexual identity, and it was all one to their guards whether they lived or died. But it was only the presence and formal responsibility of the camp-SS officers and NCOs that enabled the massacres to take place.

For the older guards, the permission to murder prisoners the moment a problem arose licensed the killings, which became a "sanctioned massacre."[47] The authority figure, namely, the commander of the evacuation who represented the source of the legitimization, was present throughout. Nobody forced the guards to take part in the killing, and in fact quite a few of them refrained.[48] The decision to take part stemmed, above all, from the fact that in many cases these enfeebled prisoners had become a liability and were delaying the rest. The guards attributed the crimes to the totalitarian system to which they belonged and to its heads, and did not necessarily consider themselves responsible for the consequences of the atrocities they committed.[49] The presence of the SS, the source of authority, provided the ideological justification for their actions, since the victims were concentration camp prisoners: criminals, Slavs, communists, Soviet POWs, and large numbers of Jews. For the camp-SS personnel, the question of legitimization was of totally different significance. They came from a system that had been engaged for some time in exterminating the unproductive elements immured in the camps. Hence it is unlikely that they felt the need for legitimization.

Another group of SS men, who were not part of the camp-SS, namely, the Waffen-SS soldiers, took part in the murder of Jewish prisoners in camps on the Austrian-Hungarian border. This bunch of murderers did not usually take part in the evacuation of concentration camp prisoners, but many of them had acquired years of experience of murder operations against civilians in the East or the Balkans.

Karl Amlinger was one of the defendants charged with the murder of prisoners at Jennersdorf. Born in 1908, the only child of a middle-class family, he received a regular education, completed high school studies, and went on to study law, although he never completed his clerkship. Amlinger joined the party in April 1933 and was a member of the SA. From April 1940 he was a member of the Waffen-SS, was briefly assigned to Dachau, then served in Finland and France, and from early 1944 fought in Yugoslavia. His accomplice in the murders at Jennersdorf, Wilhelm Mohr, had a similar career. Mohr was 24 when the Jewish inmates were murdered at Jennersdorf. After eight years of elementary schooling, he went out to work. Drafted in December 1939, he preferred to serve in the Waffen-SS rather than the Luftwaffe. He too saw combat in a number of places, including Prague, Norway and the eastern front, and northern Russia in summer 1942. He then fought in Yugoslavia. Franz Paul, the third defendant at the Jennersdorf trial, was 25 in 1945. Born in Czechoslovakia in the Sudetenland, he was a poor student who barely scraped through elementary school. In October 1938 he volunteered for the Reichsarbeitsdienst (Reich Labor Service—RAD), and in May 1940 joined the Waffen-SS. Paul participated in the occupation of Norway in 1940, but most of his combat service took place from February 1942 on the eastern front in the fight against the partisans.[50]

It was by chance that these three murderers—Amlinger, Mohr, and Paul—found themselves in a situation where they had to liquidate a group of exhausted Jewish prisoners during death marches. In their previous service, they had not been in contact with concentration camp prisoners, and there is no information that they were involved in the murder of Jews. However, they served in a system that for years had trained them for relentless combat that would include, when necessary, the liquidation of specific groups earmarked for extermination. All three of them served for some time on the eastern front and in the antipartisan campaign in northern Russia or Yugoslavia. As they themselves testified, they had no idea who issued the directive to murder these Jews; the information reached them through one of the sergeants in their unit, who received it from the head of the local party branch, who had received it from the Kreisleiter. The moment the local decision-taking system created the required legitimization for murder, all that was needed was to find the individuals who would pull the trigger. In this case, these three soldiers from a Waffen-SS unit stationed in the district were the executioners.

Uniformed Murderers: The Military and the Police

Lieutenant-Colonel von Einem, age 54, CO of the paratroopers placement base at Gardelegen, was in charge of the only troops in the area with combat experience and the only reasonably sized arsenal. When he received orders on April 11 to evacuate his camp, he was at a loss as to how to do it. Von Einem gave the order to offer armed resistance until the last moment. Most of the soldiers still on the base realized that they would have to retreat at their own discretion since there was no organized plan for withdrawal. Some began to leave in disorganized fashion, heading eastward, and quite a number of them were taken captive by the Americans.[51] About 400–500 of them remained in the base and continued to fight until the final capitulation on the evening of April 14.[52]

Von Einem was interrogated by the Americans on April 15. He had a colonial background, having managed sugarcane plantations in Cuba before World War I. After fighting in that war, he was called up again in 1938, served as a staff officer until 1943, and was then posted to the eastern front. In September 1944 he was appointed commander of the base at Gardelegen. He gave the order to fight to the end, although it was obvious that his unit would not be able to prevent occupation of the town by the U.S. forces. Von Einem explained his decision as follows:

> I am a soldier—I fight as long as possible. The basic idea of National Socialism, as expressed by Hitler, is sound—improved physical standards of the people, closer community of interests within the nation etc. But I do not accept the parasites who attached themselves to the party, nor the atrocities and other crimes committed by them. . . . Nevertheless, regardless of my political views, which are National-Monarchist, I believe that the soldier is an organ of the State, and the State is the instrument of the people. Therefore, my duty to the people is transmitted though the agency of the State—whatever State is may be.[53]

The motivation of German fighting men on the western front at the time when the Reich was breaking apart has not been investigated as intensively as the motivation on the eastern front. It is quite clear that up to the very last months of the war, Wehrmacht soldiers were one of the sectors that most fervently supported the regime. This support was unrelated to their geographical origins or education or political views. Many of them backed the regime, concurred with its political aims, and, as long as they were directly involved, were willing to fight, to give their lives, and even to take brutal action in order to do their duty as they understood it. They believed, among other things, that Germany's enemies had no right to live.[54]

The assassination attempt against Hitler in July 1944 reinforced the faith of frontline soldiers in their Führer and their adoration of him. Although the military situation did not appear promising, many continued to eagerly respond to the messages of Nazi political indoctrination officers in the armed forces (Nationalsozialistische Führungoffiziere—NSFO). Those messages were a symbol of stability and optimism, preserving the familiar old-established values of their world. These soldiers, particularly on the eastern front, often perceived themselves as crusaders, risking their lives in defense of European civilization against Bolshevik barbarism. There were quite a number of manifestations of breakdown, weariness, and apathy, particularly during the panic-stricken flight from Silesia and Eastern Prussia, but as the war came closer to home, to Germany, the faith of the fighting soldiers intensified. They continued to fight with uncompromising fanaticism, both because they were convinced that they were defending their homes and families, and because they saw in their mind's eye the values of the *Volksgemeinschaft*. These values hold the key to understanding the outlook of these soldiers. They were the expression of social integration, integration with the state, with the Reich, and with the Führer whom so many of them revered. The internalization of these values by an entire generation of young people was the central manifestation of the regime's success in transmitting to the generation of fighting men the fundamental infrastructure of the values of National Socialism.[55]

These soldiers were inspired by a sense of *Kameradschaft,* particularly from fall 1944 on, as the Soviet forces pressed deeper into areas with German populations. The sense of mission, the belief that they were the sole barrier between the front and their homes, families, and communities, that they alone could avert the apocalyptic catastrophe, was very real.[56] It was a political soldiership, as Ute Frevert denotes it, and it was the crown of the individual's service on behalf of the state. The fact that the enemy were usually defined as *Untermenschen* (subhumans) only reinforced their conviction that they were engaged in a national mission.[57]

As we know, most of the concentration camps in Germany were liberated by the American, British, and French forces. To what extent were the values described above also internalized by soldiers on the western front, and did they serve there too to enhance motivation? Josef Goebbels devoted untiring efforts through his propaganda channels to proving that American power was illusory, nothing but *"amerikanischer Bluff."* He depicted the United States as a decadent plutocracy, morally inferior, an intermingling of races *(Rassengemisch)*, incapable of continuing strong in the long run. He constantly attacked American hypocrisy, and claimed that Anglo-American occupation would be no less dangerous than Bolshevik occupation. It was "the Jew Morgenthau" who was behind the American scheme to impose starvation and deprivation on the German people, he declared.[58] Occupation by the Anglo-Saxon powers held out the threat of mass unemployment and wretchedness for millions of Germans. Unbridled American capitalism would bring back inflation and the chaos that had prevailed in Germany before the rise of the Nazi regime. Chaos, hunger, unemployment, and scarcity—those were the essence of America's message to the German people.[59]

The propaganda minister maintained his blind belief that the German soldiers were continuing to fight with diehard resolve against the Anglo-Saxon enemy even in the weeks before the surrender.[60] However, it seems that his messages did not necessarily influence the motivation of German troops on the western front. After the Allied landing in Normandy, German forces began to retreat eastward into the Reich. The fighting became increasingly slack, now lacking one of the central elements that had inspired the ideological fanaticism of the war in the East: they were no longer engaged in an ideological battle, defined as a "race struggle" *(Rassenkampf)*. Moreover, both soldiers and officers on the western front were repelled by the battle orders transmitted to them, in particular by party functionaries who instituted terror tactics in areas close to the front and interfered in fighting units.[61] Von Einem said this explicitly to his American interrogators:

> I told the NSFO [Nazi Education Officer] that I was running the unit and that he should keep his nose out of it. As a result I was ordered to Berlin to answer charges on 19 counts. Including accusation of orienting my officers in daily talk on the military situation instead of a political question, of kissing the hand of ladies, and of keeping one permanent aide instead of rotating the job.[62]

The involvement of military units and their commanders in all stages of the massacre at Gardelegen is undeniable, but the motives of rank-and-file soldiers and of officers differed. Josef-Rudolf Kuhn and Martin Domno, who were in charge of the cavalry school at Gardelegen, were by no means frontline fighters. Both were middle-aged, lived locally, and regarded the base as a place of employment rather than the site of military service. Most of the soldiers at the installation were evacuated before the prisoners arrived, and those who remained were supposed to dismantle the base before the Americans arrived.[63]

On the basis of the various versions Kuhn gave in his postwar interrogations, it is difficult to establish any specific motivation for his actions with regard to the prisoners. In the various conversations he conducted while he was, in effect, responsible for the prisoners, who were lodged in an installation where he was the supreme military authority, he did his best to rid himself of them before the Gardelegen Kreisleiter, Gerhard Thiele, could put his scheme into action. Kuhn tried to draw a clear distinction between his dealings with the prisoners and his position as the officer in charge of the cavalry school, but admitted that he had been aware of the rumors about escaped prisoners and the atrocities they were allegedly committing against innocent civilians.[64]

As noted, Kuhn lived in Gardelegen with his family. He was not a young combat soldier imbued with a sense of mission and with ardent belief in the Führer. Still, he was a member of the Nazi Party and had been a regular soldier since 1927. All he wanted in the hours before the Americans arrived was to become a civilian once again and to keep his family safe. He was particularly apprehensive about being taken captive. In 1950 he confessed that the force at his disposal on the base could easily have prevented the removal of the prisoners from the stables and their transfer to the barn. In other words, Kuhn knew that the transfer of the prisoners outside his sphere of responsibility meant that they were going to be killed mercilessly. His tortuous attempts to claim, after the war, that all he had wanted was for the prisoners to be moved outside town and held there until the Americans arrived are far from convincing, since he understood only too well, from his conversations with Thiele, that Thiele had no intention of allowing the prisoners to fall into enemy hands alive.[65]

The senior officer in the district, Colonel Miltz, had also been a local resident for five years, since taking over command of the Luftwaffe forces and base near Gardelegen in 1940. Although he agreed to lodge the prisoners at the cavalry school,[66] he adamantly rejected any attempt to involve him in solving the problem they created. He refused to provide trucks for transfer of the prisoners to the barn, and he was not swayed even when Thiele tried to persuade him that they posed a serious security problem for local residents and that he should give the order to shoot those of them who were roaming unsupervised.[67] Notwithstanding, on the day of the massacre, a group of soldiers from his base were dispatched in order to reinforce the guards on the way from the stables to the barn.

It is not clear who issued the directive to these troops to go to the cavalry school and join the guards and escorts who were taking the prisoners to the barn. Nor is it clear whether this directive was in fact even given. These young soldiers were members of the ground force crews, as distinguished from the technical staff of the airfield, and their tasks were confined mainly to guard duty and security work. Their personal weapons were a random collection of rifles of diverse makes no longer in use at the front. In the days before the American occupation of Gardelegen, some of them were sent to man four defensive positions around the town. The rest remained at their base and played no part in the symbolic defense efforts.[68]

Some of these young men had been posted to the area only a few weeks before the occupation. Most were in their mid-twenties, unfit for active combat, and had been assigned to nonprofessional auxiliary units of the Luftwaffe. In April 1945 they were idle and unsure what was expected of them. One of them, Heinz Claus, aged 21, testified that they knew of the arrival of the prisoners, and it was evident to them, as to the rest of the population, that these were dangerous elements. They were Jews and camp inmates *(Juden und KZ-Häftlinge)*, as he defined them, some of them armed, and were to be treated as a security problem.[69] Max Barella, a technician at the Luftwaffe technical base at Gardelegen, related that he saw one of the groups of prisoners in their striped uniforms and that they looked pitiful as they staggered along. He added immediately, however, that there were rumors that they were harassing the local population.[70] The transfer of this group of young men from their guard duties at the edge of town to the stables in order to escort the prisoners to the barn, was not a particularly complex maneuver, particularly since they believed that they were dealing with Jews and dangerous prisoners. Thiele or his representative were able to carry out the transfer without difficulty.

Men from the paratroopers placement base also took part in executing of the death sentences against prisoners. The CO, Lieutenant-Colonel von Einem, made not the slightest reference in his interrogation to the fact that it was he who sent 20 soldiers from his base to the barn on the evening of April 13, 1945. It was these men, as we know, who brought the appropriate weapons and began to carry out the massacre.[71] Some of the soldiers in the Gardelegen area had apparently taken part in liquidating prisoners the day before the massacre.

Willi Baum, aged 21, who had served in a combat unit, was posted to Gardelegen in 1944 after being wounded in battle in Italy. He was fortunate enough to be sent to a base that happened to be close to his hometown of Stendal, northeast of Gardelegen. On April 10 he was one of the soldiers from the base sent on a security assignment or patrol to a spot about 2 to 2.5 miles (3 to 4 kilometers) south of Gardelegen. When the patrol reached their destination, they encountered a group of camp prisoners, some of whom were not wearing striped camp uniforms. They had apparently escaped from a column that had arrived in the district. Several of them were shot by the soldiers. One of the testimonies on this incident suggested that Baum himself took part in the killings.[72] It will be recalled that the manhunt for prisoners hiding in the forests near Estedt was led by an officer from a nearby paratroopers base. Soldiers from that base took part in the liquidation of the dozens of prisoners they caught.[73]

At the time when men from the units stationed in the Gardelegen area were playing a decisive role in the massacre of prisoners from the Mittelbau-Dora death march, the Wehrmacht was disintegrating on the western front. Troops dressed in ragged uniforms were retreating eastward or southward in disorderly fashion, trudging apathetically through small towns and villages. Many had been cut off from their units, were starving, and pleaded with civilians for food or water, in some cases resorting to violence. They made a sorry impression and, in many cases, reinforced the civilians' fears that they were totally vulnerable and that there was now no power capable of defending them or supplying protection in this interregnum period between the collapse of the former regime and the arrival of the conquering forces.[74]

Small groups of soldiers of this description without their COs were scattered through the Gardelegen district on that fateful day. In the past they had belonged to crack units of the army or the Luftwaffe, but now they had lost all sense of purpose.[75] Caught between confused orders to retreat and von Einem's determination to fight to the end, these men were now stationed in various sites around Gardelegen, and the sole enemy they encountered before surrendering to the Americans were the nomadic camp prisoners. They were convinced that these prisoners were dangerous adversaries who were terrorizing the local citizenry; they even reported this information to their officers in the local bases.[76] Some of them had been posted to Gardelegen after serving for long periods in Poland or fighting on the eastern front. Ulrich Röttger was one of them. Like Willi Baum, Röttger had been wounded in the front line and assigned to a noncombat unit.[77] These men had brought with them from the battlefields, particularly in the East, a tradition of unrelenting battle against the enemies of the nation, and it was obvious to them that the Jews and the dangerous prisoners belonged in this category. Some of these men were of local origin and were undoubtedly anxious to defend their homes. Hence, even without formal orders or directives, dozens of them took part in the hunt for prisoners in the forests,[78] in escorting the prisoners to the site of the massacre, and in the killings in the barn.

Wehrmacht units perpetrated two massacres of prisoners who had been evacuated from Langenstein-Zwieberge, the Buchenwald subcamp. This camp was established in summer 1944, and in April 1945, on the eve of its evacuation, it held more than 4,000 inmates. When it was evacuated on April 9 the prisoners made their way on foot toward the northeast as the American forces advanced from the west and the Red Army advanced from the south toward the Elbe. The transport was caught in an area where retreating German units were conducting a desperate and hopeless rear action.[79]

The motivation of the Wehrmacht soldiers who murdered the camp prisoners is ostensibly more difficult to define than that of other groups of murderers. It is patent that, in cases where soldiers took part collectively in these murders, it was always when the prisoners arrived in a district where the soldiers were about to surrender, and the massacres took place in the last days or hours of the war. This was true of the Gardelegen massacre as well as the massacre of the Langenstein-Zwieberge prisoners. The killings of camp prisoners were, above all, a reflection of the frustration and fury of the German soldiers, as manifested in violent assaults on those identified as enemies of the nation, on whom these emotions could be vented. The realization that it would be best to liquidate the dangerous rabble before the U.S. forces arrived, in order to protect the hinterland, was undoubtedly also a factor. The Wehrmacht men did not differ essentially from any other murderers who liquidated prisoners during the death marches in April 1945.[80]

At Celle, a group of local reserve policemen played a major role in organizing and perpetrating the murder of prisoners who fled into the forest.[81] Two police officers, Otto Schwandt and Albert Sievert, were ordered by the Celle police chief to take a detachment of policemen and try to restore public order after the heavy bombing. They began their task after midnight on April 8–9, 1945, and as far as they were concerned, this meant, first and foremost, suppressing the unrest caused by the presence of unsupervised prisoners in the town.

About 60 prisoners caught roaming were taken into the forest by the policemen and several SS men from the camp personnel who had been aboard the train with them. Schwandt gave the order to shoot the prisoners. Some tried to escape but the policemen fired at them, and several were wounded and fell to the ground, bleeding heavily. When one of the perpetrators, a laborer and former soldier named Otto Amelung, hesitated to shoot wounded prisoners, the policemen spurred him on with cries of "Don't be a coward, you're an old soldier, come on, shoot them!" Amelung overcame his hesitation and shot four helpless wounded men in the back of the head.[82]

Party Functionaries and Mayors

In the wake of the changes in internal security arrangements after the events of July 1944, the Gauleiters became the major authorities in the outlying German districts. As the dissolution of the central regime gathered momentum in spring 1945 it became increasingly difficult to administer the expanses of the Reich, and the Gauleiters now held full responsibility for security in areas under Allied attack. Thus dealing with the evacuation of the camp prisoners passing through their Gau became part of their job.

Gardalegen district was part of the Magdeburg-Anhalt Gau, whose Gauleiter was Rudolf Karl Jordan. Jordan was relatively typical of the Gauleiters. Of middle-class origin, he was the fourth and youngest child in the family. His father, a merchant, made sure that his children received a good education, and Jordan completed elementary studies, three years of preparatory courses, and a teachers college. At the end of the 1920s he worked as a substitute teacher, but his activities in the Nazi Party lost him his job.

Like other middle-class Gauleiters, Jordan did not join the Nazi Party because of his failures in civilian life or because of the frustrations of unemployment.[83] He joined in the mid-1920s, was an active member, and after being dismissed from his teaching position, he became a full-time party functionary. He served from 1929 as reporter and editor of the party organ, *Der Fuldaer Beobachter*. In 1931 he was appointed Gauleiter, a year later he was elected to the Prussian Landtag (state assembly), and in 1933 was elected to the Reichstag. From 1937 he was Gauleiter of Magdeburg-Anhalt, residing in Dessau.

Jordan was arrested by the British on July 30, 1945, and handed over to the Americans for interrogation regarding his role in the Gardelegen massacre. He claimed that at the time of the massacre he had not been in the area because he had relocated to the small village of Schierke in central Germany in early March, having transferred his family there from Dessau in 1943 because of Allied bombings. While living in Schierke, he said, he only visited Dessau once in his capacity as Gauleiter and Reichskommissar for district security.

"Gardelegen was of no interest whatsoever to me in March–April 1945," he told his interrogators. He and his staff were busy dealing with defensive measures against the incessant air attacks, and the transports of concentration camp prisoners were not the responsibility of the Gauleiter. Jordan said a directive stipulated that, if prisoners could not be dispatched eastward or westward because of the situation at the front, the party's popular auxiliary organization (Nationalsozialistische Volkswohlfahrt [National Socialist People's Welfare—NSV]) was responsible for supplying food and accommodation for them. It was not the concern of the army or the security bodies to deal with them. He himself, he insisted, never had any dealings with the prisoners. In any event, Thiele did not inform him in April 1945 that camp prisoners had arrived in the district, and Thiele was fully responsible for the district he administered.[84]

In July 1946 Jordan was handed over to the Russians. He was tried and sentenced to 25 years imprisonment but was pardoned in 1955 and returned to the German Federal Republic. His German interrogators concluded that it was impossible to determine if he had been responsible for the order to murder the prisoners at Gardelegen or if Thiele bore the sole responsibility.[85] Whatever the case, Jordan was never brought to trial with regard to the massacre in the barn.[86]

It is unlikely that Jordan was involved in the decision making that led to the massacre. The killing of prisoners during the death marches was initiated from below, by the thousands of people involved in guarding and managing the transports at the local level. This is also true in the case of Gardelegen. The local party functionaries, rather than the Gau heads, played the central part in the events.

The local level of party leaders, the local branch heads *(Ortsgruppenleiter)*, were the main human infrastructure of the party from the 1920s. These hundreds of thousands of local activists and branch leaders in the outlying regions played a major role in the mid-1930s in the party's efforts to reach into every household in Germany. The local groups *(Ortsgruppe)* played a propaganda and political role, bringing National Socialism's message to German society and were also charged with the task of supervising and controlling it from within.[87] After the outbreak of war, these leaders were allocated tasks of vital ideological significance. The party leadership entrusted them with guardianship of the spirit and soul of the "home front" and responsibility for ensuring that the great betrayal that had led to the myth of the stab in the back *(Dolchstoßlegende)* in 1918 would not be repeated. Beyond the organizational and administrative roles they fulfilled, these anonymous activists were the main mediators between German society and the party and Reich leadership.[88] They played a central part in the last months of the war in organizing and manning the Volkssturm units.

Unlike this infrastructure of branches in peripheral areas, built up in the 1920s, the district administration (Kreisleitung) was a relatively new system. It came into being within the party structure only in the first half of the 1930s, mainly in the wake of the vast increase in the number of party members after the rise to power. It was necessary to create an administrative function with political status and authority, somewhere between the Gauleiter and the local party groups that had also expanded vastly. The Kreisleiter and his office were intended to provide the answer to this need.

The people who served this function carried out a number of important tasks. They were responsible for the operative budgets in their district, for propaganda, for the media and the party press, as well as for matters pertaining to employment, the economy, and supervision of racial policy. The Kreisleiters were, to a large extent, the central factor in the success of the policy of unification *(Gleichschaltung)* of party and state over the years.[89]

When war broke out, they understood that their function, as the party leadership expected, was to be the coordinating link between the various party organizations in their districts and the internal security apparatuses. After July 1944, because of their good relations with the Gestapo and with party groups in their districts, they played a key role in implementing the policy of internal terror that evolved in the Reich.[90]

Most of these party activists were relatively young. In 1933, for example, there were 111 Kreisleiters in the party. About 17 percent (19) were aged 21–30, 68.5 percent (76)—31–40, 1.8 percent (2)—41–50, and only one was over 60.[91] Most had been born between 1903 and 1910 and hence had not fought in World War I and were not part of the generation of young frontline soldiers *(jüngere Frontgeneration)* as were the Ortsgruppenleiters at the local level. Their connection to the *Volkische* national movement was established during the Weimar Republic, an era of confusion and political and economic tension. Many of them were members of nationalist organizations and youth and student movements through which they found their way to the Nazi Party. They were mostly young, imbued with ideological motivation and firm political convictions, and many of them were well educated. Quite a few had studied medicine or auxiliary medical professions or had been teachers. They were unswervingly loyal to Nazi ideology and, in their party activities before 1933, did not hesitate to take violent action against the party's opponents; they were characterized by their drive for advancement and promotion of their careers within the party framework.[92]

Gerhard Thiele was a typical representative of the Kreisleiters. He was born on April 29, 1909, in Stettin; his father was a low-level state official, and his mother died when he was 9. He attended a public gymnasium in his hometown between 1916 and 1925 and later spent four semesters at the universities of Tübingen and Greifswald. Thiele did not complete his studies owing to financial straits. On January 1, 1931, he joined the Nazi Party and at the same time began to teach English, French, and physical education at a private school in Pomerania. On November 30 of that year, he was dismissed because of his party activities. In June 1932 he was appointed group leader in the Nazi youth organization Deutsche Jungvolk. In 1933 he joined the National Socialist teachers union, advanced through a number of educational-party appointments, and in 1937 was appointed head of the Hitlerjugend district school. Two years later he married Rosemaria Kaufmann, who bore him three children. That year he was drafted into the Artillery Corps. In 1940 he took an active part in the campaign in France and later served on the eastern front, in Byelorussia. For some time, he was released from service and returned to the Hitlerjugend but was called up again and continued to serve in the Wehrmacht until 1942. In April 1943 he was released on the grounds that the party needed him. In May 1944 he graduated from the institute for the training of senior party functionaries *(Reichsparteischule)* and was appointed Kreisleiter of Gardelegen district.[93]

On Friday afternoon, April 13, 1945, several hours before the massacre began, Gerhard Thiele was occupied with the final effort to implement his plan to rid the town of the prisoners. When Kuhn made one of his feeble attempts to extricate himself from the Kreisleiter's grip, Thiele insisted unrelentingly: "It has to be done. It's a case of self-defense. When necessary, the Kreisleiter can do whatever he thinks fit." After the massacre, when he told the Volkssturm men to go out and bury the corpses, he told one of them who claimed that this crime would cause irreparable damage to the town: "They're dead now, did you like it when they were alive, raping women and children?"[94]

Thiele's wide-ranging authority and the security situation were ostensibly the two variables that influenced his decision to liquidate the prisoners. It is interesting to note that the question of who was the supreme authority in matters pertaining to the prisoners did not trouble the men who were directly in charge of them, namely, the guards and camp-SS personnel. Brauny was interrogated on this and asked why he agreed to take orders from Thiele regarding the fate of the camp prisoners when it was well known that the HSSPF and not the Kreisleiter was empowered to decide what to do with the camps and their inmates. Brauny said that this had been the case before the evacuation of the camps, but once the prisoners were en route, it was by no means clear who was responsible for them and from whom orders should be received. Apart from that, he claimed that "the Kreisleiter had the authority to issue all kinds of directives and it was he who gave the orders. He was the supreme authority on all combat matters."[95]

Thiele would probably not have become a mass murderer but for the unique situation in Gardelegen in April 1945. His personal file contains no records or hints of criminal-racial activity, and he was never a member of the SS.[96] His political path more closely resembles the career of a party functionary and bureaucrat, an administrator, so that it is particularly difficult to classify him as belonging to one of the familiar groups of Nazi murderers.

Thiele's case, however, is only one example of the direct responsibility of local Nazi functionaries for the murder of concentration camp prisoners in the closing weeks of the war in Germany and Austria. The liquidation of thousands of Jewish evacuees from the camps on the Austrian-Hungarian border to Mauthausen could not have been implemented without the guidance and assistance of those functionaries. It was Edward Franz Meissl, Kreisleiter of Fürstenfeld district, who issued the evacuation order for the camps under his jurisdiction.[97] Otto Christandl was the source of authority for the murderers who perpetrated the massacre of Jewish prisoners at the Präbichl Pass.[98] Alfred Waidmann, one of the Kreisleiters of Vienna, was involved in the massacre of Jewish prisoners at Engerau.[99] The Ortsgruppenleiters made free and limitless use of the orders transmitted by the Gauleiters or Kreisleiters, each according to his tendencies and understanding of the general security situation in his domain. Thus, for example, Paul Schmidt understood that the need to prevent the escape of Jewish prisoners at all costs, according to the directive from Gauleiter Siegfried Uiberreither, as conveyed by Kreisleiter Meissl, meant that he had a free hand to shoot any of them as the situation demanded at any given moment.[100] Anton Oswald, another local party functionary, directed the massacre of dozens of Jewish prisoners in Klöch camp.[101] The head of the party branch in Celle, Mengershausen, took part in the hunt for and murder of escaped prisoners in his town.[102]

In almost every small town or village the prisoners passed in spring 1945, the town leaders were involved in one way or another in dealing with the problem they posed. This was true of Krüger in Mieste, Lepa in Gardelegen, or other mayors and heads in the district. In places where the party functionary was not particularly active, the mayor of the town or village took the initiative for "defensive" action against roaming prisoners. This was the case in Ermsleben in Upper Saxony. On April 14 or 15, the mayor of this small town convened an emergency meeting in the municipality to discuss a "search operation" *(Suchaktion)* against prisoners in camp uniform who had been seen in the streets. Local inhabitants were sent to hunt for prisoners, and two of them, Walter Kno., and Fritz Mei., both aged 50, caught three of them. On April 16 another meeting was held in the municipality, and the mayor reported that he had received an order from the Gestapo command or the police at Halle to execute prisoners caught wandering unsupervised. The fate of the three apprehended prisoners was sealed; they were killed by Kno. and Mei. and apparently several other local citizens.[103]

It is not surprising that these men almost always acted according to the same pattern. There was a breakdown of communications at the time regarding transmission of orders. When directives were transmitted with regard to prisoners wandering in the midst of the civilian population, each recipient understood them as he saw fit, and adapted them to his outlook or to local circumstances. The decision they took was almost always the same. In this fashion, a large group of political officials, many of them drab functionaries, found themselves responsible for part of the final murder operation conducted by the Nazis.

Nonetheless, these murderers can certainly be included in the category defined by Gerhard Paul as "criminals with a world outlook" *(Weltanschauungstäter)*.[104] A crucial element among the perpetrators of Nazi genocide, they were believers in National Socialism and regarded their victims as dangerous enemies threatening the integrity of the German people and nation. Many of them had party careers spanning more than a decade, and, from the early stages of those careers, they were inspired by the National Socialist spirit. In spring 1945 men such as Thiele, Meissl, Schmidt, or Anton wielded extensive powers in civilian and security matters in the new hierarchy of responsibility created in the final months of the Reich. Once the framework fell apart, the Kreisleiters or Ortsgruppenleiters remained the sole authorities in charge of the security of the population. Those prisoners who were roaming freely were a threat to the safety of their townspeople and so it was only natural for them to take decisions that were colored by their weltanschauung and their understanding of their responsibility. The consequence was elimination of the prisoners in order to eradicate the threat they posed. These functionaries, however, could not have succeeded so fully in implementing their decisions without the extensive cooperation and aid of other factors.

Mobilized Citizens

Party functionaries were, as noted, a central factor in the recruitment and organization of Volkssturm units in fall 1944. In practice, in various areas, the basic organizational unit of the Volkssturm largely resembled its counterpart in the party.[105] The administrative system of the Volkssturm was contained within the party and was not part of the Wehrmacht, despite its paramilitary tasks. The unit heads underwent screening and examination on the basis of political criteria. The party expected these men to serve as an example of ideal political loyalty and dedication. The Volkssturm was a militia with the characteristics of a National Socialist popular army and as such was of major importance toward the end in the strategy of warfare and the survival efforts of the regime. From the military viewpoint, its objective was to train men to operate as an auxiliary support system for the Wehrmacht, to try to isolate enemy units that infiltrated German territory, to help slow down the enemy advance, and to neutralize treacherous internal elements or foreign workers who were endangering the security of the hinterland and weakening its resolve. The success of these missions depended, above all, on the party's ability to recruit these groups of civilians for the national struggle and to inculcate in them a zealous fighting spirit. Hence the local political functionaries, including the Kreisleiters, were of vital importance in the mobilization.[106]

The recruits served in a number of capacities. From October 1944 many of them were employed in digging defensive trenches and antitank obstacles on the eastern front. The Gauleiter of Eastern Prussia, Erich Koch, conducted a widespread recruitment campaign into the Volkssturm and made extensive use of them, including as combat units equipped with Panzerfäuste.[107] On the western front, however, the Volkssturm was not a fighting unit with particularly strong motivation. In most places, these units surrendered to the Americans without a fight, and in many places white flags were hung on windows when the Americans approached. In spring 1945 German civilians on the western front had very little desire to fight and were ready even to risk facing rampaging party terror rather than continue fighting for a lost cause and endangering their property and their homes. The fact that the western Allies usually refrained from taking captive older men who surrendered unarmed and without resisting, and simply allowed them to return home, made it easier to adopt this line.[108]

To regard the Volkssturm as a mobilized unit is problematic, even if we take into account that these men did not volunteer for service but were forced to join the militia. In early 1945 these recruits, in contrast to the young Hitlerjugend, were far from eager to bear arms and fight. They were older men, armed with faulty weapons, and had received no effective military training that could have instilled in them confidence in their abilities. Their greatest fear was that, because they were a popular militia without uniforms, they would be treated like partisans and would be executed as soon as they were taken captive. Withdrawal into the local community and family circle characterized a number of sectors of German society in the final months of the war, and these men as well were mainly concerned for their families and homes. They did not even try to understand the political moves of the dying regime or the complex security issues. The collapse of the system and the absence of a source of authority that could inspire confidence led them to place trust solely in those who were in charge of security at the local level. "When the Kreisleiter does his job, he does it only in the interest of the population,"[109] said Walter Pannwitz at a meeting of Volkssturm group leaders in Gardelegen the day before the massacre. This was also true of the Volkssturm recruits who came under the authority of Kurt Friedrichs at Palmnicken at the end of January 1945. These men took part in the evacuation of Jewish prisoners from the town and helped create the conditions that enabled the SS to perpetrate mass slaughter on the seashore.

The prisoners were present in the everyday lives of the local population from the very beginning. In certain camps, such as Mauthausen, groups of prisoners could be seen going to and from their workplaces, and the townspeople often witnessed the abusive conduct of the guards toward them.[110] In almost all the camps this phenomenon became a routine sight from the second half of 1942, as the subcamp network and the number of external worksites increased. In Dachau, for example, two external commandos of camp prisoners were brought into the town in November 1942 and June 1943, and more than 750 prisoners labored there in two armaments factories. Hundreds of Buchenwald prisoners passed through Weimar on their way to worksites, and the local population witnessed the conduct of the guards. Prisoners could now be seen outside camps, in contrast to the 1930s when they were usually confined behind fences, and their presence evoked constant unease in the local residents. As the war approached its end, this unease turned into constant fear of the inevitable moment when this dangerous, violent, and vengeful rabble would be freed and unleashed on the German population.[111]

The local-popular mobilization of the Volkssturm units in order to liquidate prisoners was a phenomenon that recurred in countless places. Paul Bötter, born in 1902, had been a member of the party and the SA since 1934. With the exception of a very short period, he took no part in military service of any kind during the war. In 1944 he joined the Volkssturm unit established in his hometown, Frankenhain in Thuringia. He and his comrades were given clear instructions by the party heads in the town that if they encountered prisoners of war or escaped prisoners, they should execute them. When the evacuation of the local subcamps began in the second week of April, a group of five prisoners from one of Buchenwald's subcamps, which was situated not far from Frankenhain, passed through the town. The number of SS men accompanying this small group is not known, but they asked for the assistance of the local SA and Volkssturm in order to liquidate the prisoners. Bötter was one of the volunteers for this task. Nobody ordered him and nobody forced him to take part.[112]

A similar case was that of Kurt Pfützner, born in 1909. Born into a working-class family (his father was a builder), he attended elementary school and had several years of vocational schooling. He served in the army from November 1939 to June 1942 in a technical rear unit, and he joined the party at this time. He was demobilized because of health problems in August 1942 and was not recalled up to September 1944. That month he was sent, as an SA recruit, to the Generalgouvernement and after some time was posted to Kehrum, a small town with a population of several hundred in North Rhine-Westphalia. He returned to his hometown, Gera, in April 1945 and joined the Volkssturm. From there he was transferred with his unit to Thuringia, between two small towns, Caasschwitz and Hartmannsdorf. On April 13 a group of evacuated prisoners was marched along the road between the two towns. Several of the Volkssturm men, including Pfützner, escorted the group on their way. Several meters beyond a field of corn they had passed, the escorts murdered several prisoners who were too weak to continue the trek.[113]

Volkssturm men played a significant role in escorting and murdering prisoners from the subcamps of Buchenwald. Groups of militia men hunted and liquidated escaped prisoners, often on the initiative of local authorities. In one case, in Parkstetten, the Volkssturm unit leader persuaded his men to set out on a "hunt" for the usual reasons: in light of the threat posed by the escaped prisoners, he said, the Volkssturm could not stand idly by and must intervene.[114]

In the Gardelegen area, popular recruitment for this task proceeded at a particularly rapid pace, against the background of the upheavals and traumatic changes the little town was experiencing in the final two months of the war. On March 15, 1945, the town was attacked by U.S. B-24 bombers. Gardelegen itself was not the main target because there were no strategically important sites there. The brunt of the attack was directed at the nearby Luftwaffe base and the railway lines in the area, as part of an overall attack that day throughout the Altmark.[115] The main damage was inflicted on the local church, which was set on fire and most of which collapsed. Fires broke out at several other sites, and local residents fled to the fields outside town. Gardelegen was not prepared for this kind of aerial attack. Children could not find their mothers in the general confusion, and long after the attack ended, people were afraid to return home. About 50 civilians died in the raid; it was a traumatic experience.[116]

The general atmosphere in the town had been very tense for months before the attack and was exacerbated by the raid. More than 3,000 German refugees passed through the town in the first few months of 1945; they were refugees from the eastern front in search of shelter in towns that were clearly about to fall into the hands of the English-speaking forces. They brought with them stories of atrocities in places that had been occupied by the Red Army.[117] In mid-April this small town, which was awaiting enemy occupation and had been invaded by more than 1,200 freely roaming Russian slave laborers and several dozen Poles,[118] and by refugees in search of accommodation, received transports of prisoners from Mittelbau-Dora and Hanover-Stöcken.

One cannot overestimate the powerful impact on the local mood of the rumors concerning the identity and conduct of the escaping prisoners and the danger they posed. The townspeople were convinced that they were facing an existential threat. Annalisa Hennig, a Gardelegen-born woman, who was 22 when the prisoners reached the area, saw them as they were led to the cavalry school. She recalled a group of people in "criminals' clothes" (*Sträflingskleidung*).[119] Otto Künnemann, a postal clerk who lived in a nearby village, related that the local farmers were terrified of the prisoners and of what they might do.[120] Particularly interesting is the case of Wilhelm

Biermann, aged 49, a farmer who lived in Kloster-Neuendorf with his wife and 23-year-old daughter. He was a veteran of World War I, who had been in Russian captivity until 1922 and returned filled with fierce resentment against his captors and fear of what they were capable of. He joined the party in 1937 but was not called up for service during the war and only joined the Volkssturm in April 1945, namely, a few days before the Americans arrived. What convinced him to take part in defensive operations was the rumor that the prisoners had robbed outlying houses in the village.[121]

The destructive impact of these rumors in this case is not, of course, unique. Rumors usually spread rapidly when there is no available source of reliable information, in particular in wartime. The situation in Gardelegen in April 1945 was characteristic of circumstances in chaotic times, when reports of atrocities play on the most primordial fears of a population bewildered at the lack of reliable information. Such rumors can prove to be a force capable of inspiring popular mobilization, a sense of shared destiny, and a belief that collective effort will help achieve the supreme common objective.[122] In the case of Gardelegen, the aim was to prevent killing, rape, looting, and violence against members of the community.

One reason the rumors spread so rapidly was that the authorities incited the population by means of press reports and verbal persuasion, as in the case of Thiele. Beyond this, however, the rumors were wrapped in a smoke-screen of vague information on the true identity of the outlandish and repulsive individuals who had arrived on their doorstep. Inhabitants of Gardelegen who visited the cavalry school in the 24 hours that the prisoners spent there, either in order to bring food supplies or for other reasons, reported that they were behaving like animals, snatching at the food. They noted the violent conduct of the stronger prisoners toward the weaker, the filth that surrounded them, their lack of concern for hygiene and for elementary human relations.[123] Unsurprisingly, rumors of the way the prisoners behaved as soon as they were free fell on fertile ground and were backed by "facts" from reliable sources, which were taken as gospel truth.[124] These same prisoners were due to be liberated very shortly when the Americans entered the town.

Social behavior fueled by rumors can move in various circles and among other things can lead to outbursts of violence. This occurs when the social organism is in a vulnerable state. War, epidemics, riots, and collapse of order are naturally destructive, and rumors can then have a dangerous catalyzing effect.[125] At the time this was the state of German society in general, and in Gardelegen and other towns in Upper Saxony in April 1945 in particular.

The Volkssturm in Gardelegen were functioning in this atmosphere in April 1945. These mobilized citizens believed that their mission was to defend their

families rather than to perform national security tasks. One of the Volkssturm unit COs exploited the rumors about the prisoners' acts of atrocity in a
nearby village as the main theme of his motivation talk to his men, in which
he explained why Thiele's orders must be carried out.[126] Other commanders
and men of the Volkssturm accepted these rumors as incontrovertible
truth.[127] This conviction was apparently shared by large sectors of the local
public; Karl Lepa, mayor of Gardelegen, confessed that he had heard quite a
few townspeople saying that the prisoners should be liquidated and that the
area was in great danger.[128] This was the social infrastructure that supported
the massacre.

In such a potentially violent atmosphere, the distinctions, already breached,
between citizens wearing the Volkssturm armband and those who were not
serving in this militia were completed obliterated. Richard-Rudolf Bischoff,
aged 33, a butcher, was not a member of the Volkssturm. He had been living
in Gardelegen since 1939. During the afternoon of April 13 he rode his bicycle home as usual from his work in the local abattoir and on the way went
into the butcher shop owned by his colleague, Erich-Rudolf Gotthard.[129]
Gotthard was 35, and he too had never served in the army, but as a local
resident and business owner he had volunteered for Volkssturm service
when the local units were established in 1944.

Their conversation that day was not necessarily devoted to their common
occupation. They talked about the subject that was a source of anxiety to
the whole town: the presence of hundreds of prisoners and the threat they
posed to the community. Deciding to study the problem at close hand, they
mounted their bicycles and rode to the cavalry school, arriving before the
evacuation to the barn began, and returned with shocking descriptions of
what they saw there. They were particularly outraged by the conduct of the
prisoners, their violent and bestial behavior, and the way they fought over
food when it was provided.[130]

It seems that Bischoff and Gotthard, along with an unknown number of
Volkssturm members and other civilians, were present in the barn during
the massacre. The possibility that they took part was raised after the war,
but it was never proved beyond a doubt. It is evident, however, that the two
were there after the massacre when an effort was made to bury the corpses
as rapidly as possible before the Americans arrived. One of them, and perhaps both, was seen murdering at least one prisoner as he lay dying.[131]

A similar picture emerged with regard to the slaughter of 22 or 23 prisoners in the village of Röxforde, 6 miles (10 kilometers) south of Gardelegen. As
noted previously, some prisoners from the transport stranded in Letzlingen
were murdered there. The killers were acting in defense of their homes, and
several members of the same family often took part. Among the Volkssturm

men who murdered the prisoners at Röxforde were two farmers, 31-year-old Gustav Lüb. and Emil Gro., and they were assisted by Gro.'s 47-year-old wife, Erna. When the group of prisoners passed through the village, escorted by several camp-SS men, some prisoners escaped. A savage manhunt was launched, with the hysteria surrounding it having been fueled by rumors about their crimes. The local people needed no persuading that the prisoners were highly dangerous. They stalked them and killed them mercilessly.[132]

As noted, the line between mobilized citizens operating within a command hierarchy and arms-bearing citizens operating at their own discretion was almost nonexistent at the time. In Celle, where prisoners were murdered by a diverse group of killers, including policemen, soldiers, SS guards, and Volkssturm members, the participants included civilians whose organizational affiliation was not clear; they may or may not have been acting within the Volkssturm framework. Among them were the tradesman Heinrich Luhmann, the electrician Oscar Carlowitz, and a stove-builder named Heinrich Giesemann.[133]

There was no shortage of examples of popular mobilization. At the end of March 1945 a group of prisoners were evacuated from Niedersachswerfen, a Mittelbau-Dora subcamp, and on their way passed through the small town of Breitenstein. The familiar rumors were bandied about among the inhabitants, namely, that people had been attacked by escaped "zebras." Richard Lat., a 35-year-old forester and his 30-year-old wife, Marianne, lived in Breitenstein. Lat., who had not been involved in political activity before 1933, joined the party in 1937 and became a member of the SA. He served in the armed forces between 1941 and 1943. In 1945, he was not a member of the Volkssturm. On March 26 Ella Roc., a 14-year-old girl who worked in the Lat. household, reported that she had seen several "zebras" searching for food on the farm. On April 6 two prisoners were caught in the yard, and Ella Roc. witnessed their cold-blooded murder by Richard Lat.[134]

In the last weeks of the war, escaped prisoners were a tangible demonic threat. At Mauthausen, in winter 1945, dozens of complaints of citizens regarding robbery and violent acts by escaped prisoners were recorded. These reports were hair-raising: they described incidents of rape, severe violence, abuse, and murder. Their reliability is in question because alongside them are reports that the starving escapees were merely searching for bread or shelter and caused no harm to local residents. In the final months of the fighting, there were a number of massacres of camp prisoners in the vicinity of Mauthausen and its subcamps. Among the participants were some of the SS guards and quite a large number of Volkssturm men and Hitlerjugend boys. In Mauthausen, both older and younger men rallied in order to take part in security operations that were critical, so they believed, for their personal safety. This wave of violence had a silencing effect on other civilians, who were uneasy at the infiltration of Nazi murderous methods into civilian society, but they could do little because of the widespread public approval for the manhunts. They also feared that if they hid escaped prisoners and were reported by nosy neighbors, they would not be able to escape punishment at the hands of the SS.[135]

These relentless manhunts were repeated in the same manner in countless towns and villages. In April 1945 a transport of prisoners crossed the little village of Görsdorf in East Upper Saxony on its way from Pockau to Komotau/Chomatov in Bohemia. Three prisoners escaped from the transport and hid in the village. On April 13, 47-year-old Max Fei., a veteran local Nazi activist, who was in charge of the local gendarmerie, approached a group of villagers and asked them to launch a search for the escapees. Among them were Edmond Ric., aged 48, Paul Br., aged 43, and Karl Fra., aged 39. The first two, who were not party members, came from simple working-class families and had only a few years of elementary schooling. The third had been a party member since 1933. On April 15 they set off to hunt down prisoners and a day later caught three, who were murdered by two members of the gendarmerie in the courtyard of Ric.'s house. The three men buried the corpses.[136]

Anton Oswald and the six Volkssturm men under his command, who murdered 26 sick Jews at Klöch, also lacked experience of this kind of operation. Anton, who had been a party member since 1933, was 31 when he received orders to kill a group of prisoners, all of them Jews, who had been laboring on the southeastern fortification, but were of no further use. His inner conflict and attempts to evade the mission appear to have been entirely authentic. At first he merely protested against the idea that SS men might come to murder sick prisoners in the camp he headed, and said that he did not want to know about it. When he realized that it was he who would have to do the job with his men, he tried to shift the responsibility for selecting the participants to his superior, the Kreisleiter. When the Kreisleiter chose men at random, Anton was obliged to confront them and tell them that they must do as they were told since they were members of the Volkssturm and were obliged to obey. The final stage in the evolution of this low-ranking party functionary in a remote Austrian province into a mass murderer was inevitable: "I took part in the shooting myself with an automatic pistol."[137] After all, how could he demand such a thing of his men without himself taking part?

In April 1945 all these mobilized civilians came face to face, almost always for the first time, with concentration camp prisoners. In many cases, what they saw reinforced their prior convictions. It seems that this group of older murderers, who took part in the local massacres at the time, and whose number will never be known, belong in the category that Paul denoted "murderers from utilitarian motives" *(ulititaristisch motivierte Täter)*.[138] They had been living for more than 10 years in a political and social atmosphere in which anti-Semitism, xenophobia, and fear of the faceless Slav/Jewish/communist/criminal rabble confined in the concentration camps were dominant in propaganda and public discourse and outlook. They did not belong in the category that gave the orders *(Befehlsgeber)*, and they probably would not have initiated and organized the liquidation of prisoners without the guiding and coordinating hand of some party or police authority. Yet, the rabble that was now invading their hometowns in threatening numbers posed a security danger as far as they were concerned. In any case, the survival of the prisoners was of no consequence at a time when the entire system was breaking down and physical existence was being weighed in the balance. The advantage to be derived from liquidating them was immediate and was perceived as an existential issue: these civilians felt that they were protecting their homes, families, and property.

The Hitlerjugend was another group that operated in the gray area between the civilian population and the mobilized military units. If the Volkssturm were a militia under the control and direction of the radical elements that headed the party at the time, the Hitlerjugend was, in many ways, the protégé of the SS, and in particular of the Waffen-SS. In view of the changes that took place after the declaration of total war in early 1943, it was decided to establish a special Waffen-SS division composed of 17- to 18-year-old members of the Hitlerjugend, but it was not uncommon to find 16-year-olds among them. In summer 1943 the recruits into the 12th SS-Panzer Division Hitlerjugend, 10,000 youngsters in all, began their training. All of them were volunteers. By June 1944 they were fighting on the western front against the Allied invaders.[139]

In the second half of 1944 the recruitment of Hitlerjugend members into the Waffen-SS was greatly expanded. Gottlob Berger, the chief recruitment officer of the SS, received permission to recruit 20 percent of the 17- to 18-year-olds into the SS fighting units but, as in the past, there were a number of 16-year-olds among them. At least 150,000 boys and young men of those ages served in the Waffen-SS in the last six months of the war.[140]

The sharp transition from a militaristic scout-like youth organization with uncompromising ideological orientation to an elitistic military framework was a vitalizing experience for these young men. However, not all of them were drafted into combat units within the SS framework. Those who were not recruited were attached in fall 1944 to Volkssturm units in their hometowns. In winter 1945 these boys, particularly on the eastern front, were fighting shoulder to shoulder with older men from the Volkssturm, often without backing from any real military force. They were given hand grenades and Panzerfäuste and ordered to block the advance of the Soviet tanks.[141] Klaus Granzow, born in 1927 in Stolp in Pomerania, joined the Hitlerjugend in May 1943. He had no idea what was expected of him in the thick of the fighting, but what was stamped on his memory most clearly was the panic that seized the fleeing women, the rumors of rape, and the destruction and burning of villages by the Red Army. This was, to a large extent, the battle order that shaped his fighting motivation and that of his comrades.[142]

As a rule, these young fighters were infused with fighting spirit and ideological fervor. Their faith in the regime and its aims recalled that of their slightly older comrades in the disintegrating Wehrmacht. At the beginning of 1945, Hitlerjugend members in southern Bavaria began training in guerrilla (Werwolf) tactics in anticipation of the final stage in the struggle against the Western invaders. After the occupation of Franconia in April 1945, several sabotage and assassination attempts were made against U.S. troops. In the Nuremberg area, young boys and girls from the Hitlerjugend and its female counterpart, the German Girls Alliance (Bund deutscher Mädel—BDM), were caught with various weapons in their possession. In their interrogation, they declared that their only desire was to continue fighting the U.S. tanks and the enemy that had invaded their country. Boys of 12 and 13 proclaimed, bluntly and unequivocally, their hatred for the Americans and faith in the adored Führer and their readiness to continue fighting to the death.[143]

The participation of these adolescents in murderous acts against those they considered to be enemies of the regime should not, therefore, surprise us. They believed wholeheartedly in what they were doing. The enthusiasm and youthful ardor that accompanied their actions[144] should not overshadow the importance of their intuitive-emotional political faith. They took part in the escorting and murder of Jewish prisoners during the death marches from camps on the Hungarian border to Mauthausen. They also participated in brutal manhunts for prisoners who escaped from the camp in the months before the liberation.[145] Testimonies on the massacre at Celle indicate that Karl Genthe, commander of the Hitlerjugend unit at Celle, murdered with his own hands more than 20 prisoners caught wandering in the forest after the bombing of the train.[146] During the evacuation of the transport from Rottleberode, Hitlerjugend members were among the killers of prisoners who tried to escape or were wounded during the attack.[147] A number of 16- and 17-year-olds took an active part in the hunt for escaped prisoners in the Jävenitz forest[148] and in villages near Gardelegen.[149] Like some of the Volkssturm, they also escorted groups of prisoners on their final journey from the cavalry school to the barn.[150] Did some of them play a part in the final bloodbath? The question remains unanswered.

Various auxiliary forces were recruited in order to help erase the traces of the murders. On April 14 at 4 a.m., about 15 members of the local firefighters unit at Gardelegen were roused from their sleep. They arrived at the barn at about 5:30, where 50 local farmers, who belonged to the Volkssturm, were already busily digging burial trenches for the victims. At about 8:30 a.m., this group left the barn and were replaced by other Volkssturm men from Gardelegen. The firefighters joined their fellow townsmen in the effort to bury the 1,000 corpses that lay in the barn and around it. The chore was not completed. After several hours, the townspeople left the scene of the crime for fear that the Americans would catch them redhanded.[151]

One characteristic of the murders during the death marches period was the heterogeneity of the groups of murderers (Heterogenität de Tätergruppen). Among them were SS soldiers, army units, Volkssturm, police, Hitlerjugend, and ordinary civilians. Even select groups of prisoners, usually of German origin, were attached to the murder units in the event that additional manpower was needed. Although the murderers came from units and frameworks with no previous operational connections between them, from systems that functioned separately without command or systemic coordination, they succeeded in cooperating without difficulty when it came to murder. It was a collaboration of random, available forces that worked together ad hoc in order to carry out missions whose importance all of them acknowledged. Each component in the puzzle was responsible for only one part of the process: planning, transferring, escorting, guarding, supplying auxiliary aids such as carts, fuel or ammunition, committing the murders, burying corpses, and obliterating traces.[152]

The retreat into the borders of the disintegrating old Reich and the threat of conquest to which more and more Germans were exposed created total systemic disarray among organizations and frameworks that had been completely separate under the Third Reich. Their ability to collaborate in the killings stemmed, among other things, from the fact that each of the groups had accumulated considerable previous experience of such activity. During the death march period, all of these elements—the camp-SS, the Wehrmacht soldiers on the eastern front, or the various party zealots—had, as never before, common interests with the populace. The civilians were fearful and anxious with regard to the future, and were fed on stories of atrocities on the part of the approaching enemy. This situation fostered an outbreak of killings by ordinary citizens, with the backing, support, and guidance of more experienced killers. These activities, as noted earlier, were often referred to as "shooting zebras" (Zebra-Schießen) or "rabbit hunting" (Hasenjagd), which naturally facilitated the depersonalization of the victims in the eyes of their killers.[153]

During this period a special place was allotted as well to the monstrous and threatening image of the Jewish foe. There is no way of explaining the murderous incidents during the death marches in Austria without taking into account the fact that the murderers were well aware that the prisoners they were guarding were Jews. Volkssturm unit CO Ludwig Krenn, a fervent Nazi and implementer of the massacre at the Präbichl Pass, called them "dogs and pigs." Those who joined him were not necessarily individuals whose membership of the Volkssturm transformed them into potential perpetrators of genocide in the spirit of Nazi ideology. They were, after all, a fairly typical Volkssturm unit: middle-aged men, including farmers, workers, traders, and representatives of all the other occupations of a provincial town.[154]

It is not impossible that, for the random civilian-murderers who liquidated random escaping prisoners, it was more convenient to treat their victims as Jews, since, to a large extent, the pulling of the trigger was a self-evident move in such cases. For example, on April 9, 1945, an escaping French prisoner was caught in the small town of Langewiesen in Thuringia. He was apprehended by several soldiers and brought to the town hall, where he was placed under the guard of an older local policeman, Rudolf Kur., aged 55. Kur. and the others knew nothing about the prisoners, but one of them said: "You are a Jew. You'll be executed" *(Du bist ein Jude. Du wirst erschossen).*[155]

Thus the "Jew" became the representative of the collective identity of escaping enemies, who were endangering the local population close to home. Dangerous criminals, Red pigs from the East, rapists of women and children, Jews—all were melded together into a demonic existential threat that had to be extirpated as quickly as possible. From the viewpoint of the traditional murderers, there was nothing new in this, but in the final months of the war this ideological-genocidal virus broke free and infected wide sections of German civilian society.

Conclusion

Nazi genocide was first set in motion in fall 1939 after the invasion of Po-land.[1] It gained momentum when the extermination of Jews began in the German-occupied areas of the Soviet Union in summer 1941 and the deci-sion was taken to begin the Final Solution, and it continued until the last days of the Third Reich. Up to 1944 the Jews were the main, though not the sole, victims. In addition to the millions of Jews murdered in 1941–1944, millions of Soviet POWs were liquidated, Gypsies were slaughtered in Ser-bia and Rumania or sent to Auschwitz, Poles were murdered or deported to perish in the camps, and prisoners classified according to various diverse criteria were worked to death in the Nazi concentration camps. When the evacuation of the concentration camps began in early 1945, its victims were prisoners who were led on death marches from the camps in Poland into German territory. However, the killings on death marches should be ap-praised in their unique context: the twilight days of the regime, the era of the final breakdown after the military defeat.

Rudolph Rummel has calculated that more than 169 million human be-ings perished between 1900 and 1987 as a result of genocidal activity insti-gated and perpetrated by governments or by agencies acting at their behest.[2] His statistical calculations do not take into account the genocide of the 1990s in Rwanda, the civil war in the Balkans (e.g., the massacre at Srebrenica), or the twenty-first-century-massacre at Darfur in western Sudan.[3] Data on these cases of genocide, collated by the sociologist Helen Fein, one of the most important contemporary researchers into the subject, reveal that more than 1 million human beings fell victim to these massacres, mainly members of the Tutsi people, slaughtered in Rwanda, and victims of the killings that began in Darfur in 2003.[4] Most of the known cases of genocide in the twentieth century resulted from decisions taken by a regime that set the apparatus in motion and implicated its citizens, with varying degrees of responsibility and identification, in mass murder.

The Nazi state caused the deaths of close to 21 million human beings in its 12 years of existence; some 6 million of them were victims of the "final solution of the Jewish question."[5] The victims of Nazi genocide perished because of political decisions taken by the senior echelons of the Reich, which were implemented by diverse apparatuses and agents of the state, distinct from one another, and which were either established specifically for this purpose or adapted to this task in certain periods and in certain places. However, in the final chaotic period of the large-scale evacuations, the murder apparatuses and those in charge of them no longer functioned as they had in the past. Hence the need arises to scrutinize and evaluate the connection between the death march period and the extermination of the Jews and other kinds of genocide perpetrated by the Nazis, and to ask whether the death marches can be regarded as an example of genocide in modern times.

Chaos, Genocide, and Ideology

The killings of concentration camp prisoners in the last phase of the war occurred amid a situation in which confusion and disorder were rife and supervisory apparatuses and chains of command were disintegrating in all spheres of life in Germany. However, to define this situation as chaos and, as a consequence, to regard the final murders perpetrated by the regime as the product of this chaos[6] calls for a more precise explanation of the phenomenon.

As a rule, the term "chaos" relates to physical or mathematical systems, and its investigation entails examination of the conditions that create total imbalance and disintegration. Human society is also characterized, figuratively, by the existence of nonlinear nonequilibrium systems, and hence its unpredictability. This is because of the complex social processes generated by the emergence of uncontrolled hysteria, extreme mob reactions, the impact of value and cultural circumstances on human response, and the like. The shattering of the natural continuity of the social order, which can occur in the wake of an extraordinary, sudden, and traumatic crisis, elicits unanticipated collective behavior within a society. Panic-stricken reactions, transition of the masses to bloody conflict, the rise of extremist social movements, and the eruption of violence are common phenomena in such situations.[7]

That Germany was in a chaotic state in the last few months of the year was indisputable. The orderly continuity that enables social stability and a reasonable prospect for the future was breaking down. Its collapse led to disrupted communications and even disconnection between those who gave the orders and those who executed them; internal power struggles; a total loss of confidence; the inability of Hitler and the senior command to function; the rise in the power of extremists, such as Bormann and Goebbels; and severance of connections between vast occupied territories in the West and East and the heads of the regime.

All these phenomena created an irreparable rift between the populace and its rulers, and eroded that public confidence in the stability of the regime and its ability to guarantee continuity that had endured for years despite all the difficulties and crises Germany had faced, in particular since 1943.

Destruction of social and political continuity, leading to severe violence, had occurred in various places in Europe during the war. For example, in July 1941 in eastern Poland, in the weeks of transition between Soviet rule and German occupation, the Jews fell victim to the violence and savagery of their Polish neighbors. This phenomenon cannot, of course, be explained solely by the fact that it was a time of political calamity and of transition between the end of one era and the noncommencement of another. These lethal incidents were rooted deep in the relations between Jews and Poles in those regions, the mobilizing force of anti-Semitism, the role played by the Church, the impact of years of Soviet rule, the economic situation, and the fact that a new active political factor was instigating attacks on Jews, as Andrej Żbikowski shows in his research.[8] During the 1944 German retreat from the Ukrainian-Polish border with its numerous ethnic groups, there were incidents of violence against the rural Polish population and massacres, in the form of ethnic cleansing by an Ukrainian nationalist organization. They too had deep-rooted reasons, based on past relations between the two people and the national aspirations of the Ukrainians toward the end of the war.[9] In August 1944, when the Vichy regime was collapsing in France, a mini-civil war raged in the south of the country, in the course of which a number of Jews were liquidated by anti-Semitic Vichy supporters.[10] This phenomenon was identified by the philosopher Tzvetan Todorov as the tragic chapter in the history of the liberation.[11]

Is there a common denominator between these breakdown situations marked by an eruption of violence against ethic or national groups, and what occurred in Germany during the death marches? These phenomena cannot be explained solely by the fact that they occurred during the breakdown of a regime when individuals and the populace as a whole had lost their faith in continuity and order. All these situations occurred shortly before the vacuum was filled by a new force, which did not necessarily share the views of the forces that had taken the law into their own hands during the transition period. It is well known that the collapse of regimes in the heat of war has often been exploited in order to conduct a reckoning with hated minorities and with traditional enemies, to seize the assets of the victims, or to establish facts that will be taken into account when the new political order is instituted. Some of the features of this psychosocial and political reality did in fact exist in Germany in the few months before its capitulation.

However, theories that cite the chaos of war's end, the days of the *Götterdämmerung* (twilight of the gods) and other apocalyptic explanations of the collapse of the Third Reich, cannot fully elucidate individual reactions within the German population. Most Germans reacted to the situation by sinking into a state of apathy and huddling within the confines of the family and the community, awaiting the end of the war anxiously and with dull resignation. In others the situation evoked violent conduct and political fanaticism.[12] The murder of the camp prisoners occurred in a period of transition to a new era, which seemed vague and ominous. But, unlike massacres that happened elsewhere in Europe in transition periods between a collapsing regime and its successor, these massacres were totally devoid of political objectives and hence cannot be categorized as attempts at ethnic cleansing of a national territory. It is also difficult to regard them as manifestations of a desire for revenge against a traditional national enemy who had abetted past acts of injustice perpetrated, as it were, under the auspices of the overthrown regime. At the same time, the desire for vengeance against helpless individuals identified with the enemies of the nation, compounded by frustration at the imminent debacle undoubtedly played a part in the motivation of the various groups of killers.

Is it feasible to claim that the terror and extermination apparatus of the concentration camps supplied the practical and ideological infrastructure for the mass liquidation of prisoners during the death marches? To state, as Katrin Greiser does, that the concentration camp system continued to function in the last months of the war, even if in partial or illusory fashion, is problematic. The system did, in fact, succeed in providing the infrastructure that facilitated the conveyance of hundreds of thousands of prisoners from place to place in the last six months of the war, mainly from the hundreds of labor camps in Poland, which were emptied of prisoners in January–February 1945. Yet, the functioning of the camp system cannot be measured by its technical ability to transport prisoners almost up to the last day of the war, whether by rail or on foot, or by the hasty preparation of prisoners for evacuation, as was the case in a number of places.[13] As we have seen, the directives received were usually muddled and were constantly being modified; senior commanders evaded implementation; nobody knew what precisely Himmler or Pohl wanted, and above all—what was to be done with the prisoners. Moreover, the fact that the murders committed in the camps before the evacuation spilled outside the fence perimeters, and continued to occur when the prisoners were no longer under detention, cannot necessarily explain the functioning or nonfunctioning of the system. These murders had different motives and were perpetrated by different people.

The murder of the camp prisoners in the last months of the war is not necessarily part of the functionalist history of the concentration camps. In order to understand what occurred in the final months of Nazi genocide, one needs to examine its history and development until then and the attitude of German society toward it. The moment the prisoners left the camps, the spatial dimension of the murders changed, as did the circumstances and the reasons for their liquidation. Despite the scope of the evacuation phenomenon throughout the realm of the Nazi concentration camps, and the endless repetition of incidents of massacre, the question of motive remains significant and disturbing. We are dealing here with a totally different question from that underlying the killings inside the camps. Why did the men in charge decide to transport hundreds of thousands of prisoners along the retreat routes of the Third Reich, with no apparent advantage or clear purpose in view? Why did so many groups and individuals take part in their liquidation? Even if we take into account the vast dimensions of the Nazis' murderous lunacy, the death marches are still an inexplicable chapter in the annals of the genocide they perpetrated.

The question of motive was almost never broached by the numerous military investigators and legal experts who spent many years preparing the files for interrogation of war criminals suspected of murdering prisoners during the death marches. One of the few who tried to understand this phenomenon in depth was Baron Claud Schuster, the British interrogator of the Austrian Gauleiter, Siegfried Uiberreither. Schuster, attempting to uncover the underlying strategy of the evacuation phenomenon, asked Uiberreither to explain the objective of the evacuation of thousands of Jews to Mauthausen in order, according to Himmler's directive to Uiberreither, to detain them under reasonable conditions and provide them with nourishing food. In any case, the Red Army was about to liberate these prisoners within a few days. In other words, Schuster tried to solve one of the central questions of the death march period: why did this tale of horror unfold in the first place?

> *Uiberreither:* That is something that surprised us too. It did not surprise us so much that he (Himmler] gave the order that the Hungarian Jews were to be saved, because they were really good workers and we had quite good experience with them. However, it did surprise us that Himmler

expressly stated, twice, that they should receive good food and be well taken care of.

Schuster: I know, but I can't understand what the object of it was at all, because they were bound to be caught by the Red Army sooner or later.

Uiberreither: That was in no way clear because Mauthausen was not in a zone where the Red Army was; Mauthausen was actually in the American zone.

Schuster: I don't know why anyone wanted to keep 7,000 Hungarian Jews, as if they were a kind of curiosity, at Mauthausen. What good would they do anybody? [*sic*]

Uiberreither: It wasn't only they, it really concerned all manpower. And even prisoners of war. As I said before, the prisoners of war were very glad to turn around and march toward the West, because they did not care to fall into the hands of the Russian advancing army. Even East workers, on their own initiative, marched toward the West, because they were afraid of retaliation.

Schuster: I can understand that, but you were short of food, weren't you?

Uiberreither: Yes, it was terrible at that time. We did not receive any supplies at all; we had bombing attacks, and we lost 36,000 men in one air attack over Graz.[14]

Uiberreither's comments help to some degree to explain what the men who conducted the evacuations understood. Himmler wanted these Hungarian Jews in Mauthausen in order to prepare a large reserve of Jews who would serve as his lifeline at the last moment. The local Gauleiters, when not imbued with excessive motivation to kill the prisoners, considered them excellent laborers and thought it would be a pity to hand them over to the Russians, since the general trend was to avoid the Soviet-occupied areas and to prefer capture by the Western Allies. Moreover, it was extremely difficult to feed and house thousands of prisoners or foreign laborers in combat areas that were suffering from bombardments, in addition to the numerous German and Austrian citizens who were also in need of help. It was therefore in their systemic and social interest to move the columns of prisoners along. When it was no longer possible to drive them forward, into the hands of the next Kreisleiter or the officials of the next town, they were liquidated by the Volkssturm, the gendarmerie, the army, or the police—that is, local elements, and frequently local civilians in their home territory.

As the fighting grew fiercer, the German populace became increasingly confused, fearful, and frustrated, and these emotions were accompanied by manifestations of anger and violence toward individuals and groups identified as alien to the society. From 1941 on, each year was worse than the preceding year, bringing with it greater suffering, death and injury, and despair. As the frustration burgeoned and the fear of imminent catastrophe grew, the persecution of the "other" intensified. For example, in a number of places in Germany there was increased hostility toward homosexuals, and the number of arrests rose during the last years of the war. The untrammeled violence of the death marches was also a reflection of that atmosphere. Up to 1944 many prisoners were confined in camps in Poland or the Baltic countries, in regions without large German populations. When the camps in the East were evacuated, hundreds of thousands of prisoners were swept into the heart of Germany, into the living space of civilians who for years had been coping with the hardships of total war, painful loss, bombings, physical destruction, economic deprivation, and harsh internal terror. The escorts of the transports from Poland to Germany in winter 1945 must have thought to themselves from time to time that the fewer of these "human material" reached the homeland, the better.

The Nazi regime perpetrated countless acts of slaughter of political character. One type of murder was directed against the internal political foes of the regime. The first such massacre took place in 1934, when Hitler liquidated the party opposition on the "night of the long knives." Another such event was the execution of thousands suspected of complicity in the assassination plot against Hitler in summer 1944. Political massacres were also perpetrated against civilian populations throughout Europe. One of the most notorious occurred in the Czech village of Lidice on June 9–10, 1942, in retaliation for the assassination of Reinhard Heydrich, head of the RSHA. Heydrich was shot on May 27, 1942, by Czech partisans who had been trained in Britain and dropped by parachute into the Protectorate.[15] He died of his wounds a week later in a hospital in Prague. In reprisal, Liditz/Lidice, known for its hostility toward the German authorities, was selected as the target of collective punishment. All the men aged 16–60 were assembled in a barn and murdered. The women were sent to Ravensbrück, most of the children were murdered, and others were distributed among German families. All the houses were blown up, and the village was wiped off the face of the earth.[16]

Toward the end of the war, while the Germans were retreating in central and western Europe, a number of massacres were perpetrated against civilians. In April 1945, when the Germans withdrew from the Protectorate, Wehrmacht troops massacred Czech civilians. One such incident occurred at the end of April close to the town of Olomouc/Olmütz in eastern Moravia. The massacre, the culmination of a move that had begun in January, claimed 26 Czech civilian victims, who were suspected of partisan activity.[17] A similar massacre was carried out by a unit of Waffen-SS in the French village of Oradour-sur-Glane on June 10, 1944. There, 642 men, women, and children were slaughtered in one day in an act of reprisal against the French Resistance.[18] At the end of September and the beginning of October 1944 an SS unit massacred hundreds of villagers, including 211 children, in the Italian town of Marzabotto, some 12 miles (20 kilometers) south of Bologna, and several adjacent villages. Antifascist partisan activity had been on the increase in the region since 1943, and the local militia had clashed with German forces several times.[19]

All the victims of these events were civilians: they were singled out because they were identified with elements opposed to the regime that supported guerrilla action, and their liquidation was part of the oppressive policy wielded against enemies and underground fighters. Such acts of political massacre occur when a totalitarian regime is fighting for its life and begins to wage an uncompromising struggle against individuals and organizations that threaten its existence or against civilian populations identified with its enemies. The motivation for the murder is essentially political, and the victims are not exclusively political enemies but also civilians belonging to national or ethnic groups labeled as enemies, which are stamped with this collective identity. Hence, it is difficult to classify such murders as genocide.

How then can we characterize the murder of concentration camp prisoners during the death march period?

The definition of cases of mass murder, deportation, slavery, torture, rape, severe violence, and abuse of helpless populations as manifestations of genocide has been accepted by public opinion and the media, particularly since the genocide in Rwanda and the murders and ethnic cleansing in the Balkans in the mid-1990s. On the other hand, the reliance of international bodies and international law on the 1948 United Nations Convention on the Prevention and Punishment of the Crime of Genocide has led to avoidance of definition of clear cases of genocide as such, if only in order to preclude the need to put a stop to them and take punitive action. Thus, for example, the U.S. administration avoided defining the massacre of the Tutsi in Rwanda in 1994 as genocide so as not to become involved in halting it.[20] Similarly, in its February 2005 report, the UN commission that investigated the murders in Darfur carefully refrained from describing the situation as genocide and determined that "acts of mass atrocity were carried out on a wide scale and the perpetrators have not been punished to this day." This circumvention was helpful to the regime in Khartoum in its propaganda campaign against the pressure to bring the perpetrators to justice.[21]

That caution is required in defining such acts of mass atrocity as genocide is self-evident. Human beings murdered for political reasons by a country that employs terror, writes Helen Fein, are not necessarily victims of geno-cide aimed at whole or partial liquidation of a "real group." The victims of political murder, even when it is mass murder, are not necessarily part of such a real group, namely, an ethnic, racial, or national group. Sometimes they be-long to arbitrarily created imaginary or imagined categories that are labeled as "the enemies of the nation," "wreckers," "subversives," and so on.[22] Fran-çois Furet wrote in his 1996 correspondence with Ernst Nolte, which re-volved around the question of the relativism of Nazi crimes in comparison to those of communism, that Nazi genocide was different and distinct from all other forms of evil. The reason was that this industry of death set its sights on men, women, and children because of the fact that they had been born as such, and hence was totally dissociated from any interpretation that takes into account the struggle for power. Anti-Semitic terror forfeited all its con-nections to the political domain in which it was created.[23] The camp prisoners who were slaughtered in the thousands during the death marches were not a "real group," because they did not belong to a single ethnic, racial, or national group. Nor were they targeted as victims because they were born as such without political contexts. There is, therefore, an a priori problem entailed in defining their liquidation as a clear case of genocidal massacre.

David Scheffer, a legal expert from Northwestern University, Chicago, who served as the Clinton administration's ambassador-at-large for War Crimes Issues, pointed out the problematic nature of the UN Convention and the hiatuses in its definition of acts of mass murder. He proposed that geno-cide, ethnic cleansing, and mass murder be included in a wide category that he denoted "mass atrocity crimes." In his view, the courts should be allowed to determine whether the perpetrated crimes are defined as genocide, war crimes, crimes of aggression, or crimes against humanity, all of which vari-ous international treaties defined as cases calling for punishment.[24] Can we conceive of a tribunal trying Thiele, Jepsen, Dörr (two of whom, as we know, were in fact indicted), or any mass murderer who instigated a mas-sacre during the evacuations, and deciding that their crime did not come under the definition of complicity in genocide? It is a fact, however, that tribunals that convicted the death march murderers preferred not to deal with the issue of definition.

To what extent does Scheffer's proposal offer a solution to the question of characterizing the death march murders? As noted, the camp prisoners were not an ethnic or a racial group according to the UN Convention, and their liquidation would appear to be closer to politicide. In other words, it could certainly be included within the wide definition that Scheffer proposed. But even characterization of these killings as political murders like those perpe-trated in France, in the Protectorate, or in northern Italy is not applicable here. The murderers did not classify the prisoners as political enemies who were to be eliminated because they were fighting against the regime and endangering it, or sheltering others who fought it.

It seems that a fundamental requirement for understanding the phenomenon of the killings on death marches is examination of the various points of connection as well as the differences between this wave of murder and the killings perpetrated up to late 1944. The death march period differed from the past in this respect, mainly because of the identity of the victims. Although the vast camp population was composed of a melange of ethnic, national, and racial groups, it was nevertheless perceived as a collective with uniform features and conduct. The common denominator of this collective was, first and foremost, the demonic and essentially fantastic threat it posed to the murderers. The rhetoric that accompanied the preparations for and the perpetration of several massacres during the death marches indicates the level of fear, the sense of urgency, and the existential need to exterminate this enemy. These emotions were much stronger than those involved in the genocidal liquidation of an exclusively political enemy.[25] But in contrast to the genocide of earlier years, when an entire nation or collective or part of it are targeted for mass extermination, the intention of the killers on the death marches was not to murder the target group in entirety—namely, all the prisoners—but only some of them as dictated by changing interests and circumstances.

There remains the issue of the relation between the death march murders and the Holocaust, that is, the "final solution of the Jewish question." Was the ethnic or racial identity of the victims the guiding ideology of the murders? Daniel Goldhagen claimed that the motive for the killings during the death marches was fanatic and murderous anti-Semitism, and hence the linkage of this period to the Final Solution:

> These German guards . . . these ordinary Germans, knew that they were continuing the work that had been to a great extent already accomplished in the camp system and in other institutions of killing: to exterminate the Jewish people.[26]

The hypothesis that the death marches period was the final, conclusive link in the final solution of the Jewish question has been shared by other scholars in the past.[27]

It is my own belief that the genocide perpetrated by the Nazis was guided, in its final stages, by a different lethal ideology from that of the past. Throughout its existence, this genocide was perpetrated within an ideological framework that adopted diverse attitudes toward different groups of victims. It is true that the murderous ideology at the heart of the Nazi weltanschauung was anti-Semitism, but it was compounded by racial stances that shaped genocidal activity marked by other characteristics, sometimes similar to and sometimes different from the extermination of the Jews— targeted against Gypsies, Poles, Soviet POWs, and other victims. The deadly ideological consensus lasted into 1945, but the image of the victim had now changed. It was no longer exclusively the Jewish enemy (the main racial enemy) or other racial enemies (Gypsies, Poles) or defilers of the race and political foes (Soviet POWs, the mentally deficient, homosexuals, and various unfortunates). Killing was now a nihilistic act, committed locally and devoid of a guiding hand. It was backed by a certain consensus, but the identity and singularity of the victims was vague and undefined, apart from their broad and relatively illusory identity as a dangerous and inferior group that did not deserve to live. In this respect, the murderous activity continued to display the basic ideological features that had directed it in previous years, but in the last years of the war a new interpretation of the traditional malignant ideology was born.

As I have tried to show, in many cases of massacre of camp prisoners, the Jews were a dominant group among the victims, but certainly not the only one. The killers made no attempt to distinguish between Jews and non-Jews when pulling the trigger. In Gardelegen, not more than one-third of the victims were Jews.[28] In Celle as well, there were few Jewish victims among the prisoners from the stranded train because there had been almost no Jews in the camps from where they came. This was also true of the Lüneburg affair, where, for the same reason again, there were few Jewish victims. There were, of course, cases in which the prisoners who were slaughtered mercilessly on the death marches were of clearly Jewish origin, for example, on the Austrian death march, but one cannot establish with certainty that they were liquidated because they were Jewish.

It was the combination of military, political, economic, and ideological circumstances with local decisions that decided the fate of the prisoners, and not necessarily their national or racial identity. Under these circumstances, there was a striking distinction between the concentration camp prisoners and the tens of thousands of British and American POWs who marched with them along the evacuation routes. Despite the rigorous conditions on the marches and the fact that many among them fell victim, the fate of these POWs was entirely different. They were not massacred, and most survived to return home after the war.[29] They were not the targets of Nazi genocide.

Since it is universally accepted that the ideological aspect of the murders committed on death marches cannot be disregarded, I believe that there is no escape from the conclusion that this was a unique case of genocidal massacre, which is related in several ways to the previous years of extermination and the Holocaust. As a rule, the group singled out for such massacre was identified by common criteria such as race, ethnic origin, nationality, or religion. In many cases, genocidal killing occurs against a lengthy historical background of hostility between communities within the same state framework.[30] It is characterized as an act of murder that is not necessarily part of the continual process of genocide (although it can certainly be part of it),[31] but as slaughter perpetrated against a specific group, and it has the character of a pogrom or deadly riots of a racial nature.[32] The killings and massacres of concentration camp prisoners on death marches were not racial or ethnic by nature; they were perpetrated against a specific group identified and characterized by a range of collective features that legitimized the conversion of each of its members into a potential victim. This was an essentially virtual group that, by the will of the murderers, was transformed into a real group that was to be liquidated, in accordance with an ideological consensus. It is the existence of a murderous ideology shared by such wide sectors of society and the countless repetitions of the phenomenon that establishes the connection between the death marches and the other cases of Nazi genocide. But just as genocide against the Jews differed from that perpetrated against other nations and races, so genocidal massacre of the concentration camp prisoners differed from other murders.

In the months in which the Nazis perpetrated the genocide as a continual genocidal massacre, the extermination process was totally decentralized. In the final analysis, the decision to press the trigger during the death marches was taken by the killer who was marching alongside the prisoners. It was he who determined whether the time and conditions were ripe for the deed, he who decided on the moment when it would be carried out. The killings were not the outcome of spontaneous or impulsive reactions, but stemmed from deliberate calculations of advantage, efficiency, timing, and local conditions. They were by no means violent eruptions of emotion on the part of an inflamed rabble, fired by xenophobia or fanatic anti-Semitism. It seems that never before in the years of Nazi genocide had so many individuals been empowered to decide, at their own discretion, whether or not to kill. This was in total contrast to the way in which the killings were supervised, managed, and bureaucratically directed, albeit often in tenuous, haphazard, and unfocused fashion, up to summer 1944.

The psychological milieu in which the conditions for murder were created was influenced mainly by the identity of the victims. They were singled out for killing not because of the deeds they had committed but because of what they were capable of committing according to the fixed beliefs of wide sectors of German society. The camp inmates or, in other cases, the foreign laborers who escaped from their work crews caused no real harm to the civilian population. By the time they fell victim to SS guards, Luftwaffe and Wehrmacht men, or the Volkssturm, they were generally defenseless, exhausted, and helpless. The killings were the continuation of the familiar process of liquidating enemies, and to leave them alive ran counter to what had been self-evident for some time.[33]

Because it was not always possible to lead them to a place where they could be imprisoned again and worked to death, the liquidation of this demonic threat was the accepted, and above all familiar, response. In this respect, the familiar Nazi genocidal process continued, but because of its timing, the circle of brutality was expanded to include individuals who had not previously been involved.

What is unique about this phenomenon in the final months of killing is the emergence of a new community of murderers, "local liquidating communities," whose members were veteran killers (SS guards) who had brought the prisoners from the camps in the East, and others who joined in only when their hometowns, communities, and families were directly affected: Volkssturm, police, local party functionaries, Hitlerjugend members, and other civilians.

From Murderers to Nazis

It is difficult to sketch a single representative profile of the murderers who participated in the liquidation of prisoners during the death marches. It should be recalled that we are dealing with thousands if not tens of thousands of killers, most of whom did not organize the massacres and did not commit more than one murder or press the trigger more than a few times. In this respect, they cannot be categorized as mass killers like the experts of the death industry. They differ from the traditional groups of murderers who perpetrated Nazi genocide: the death camp commandants and their lackeys, the Einsatzgruppen and other murder units that operated in eastern Europe, or the bureaucratic experts in genocide for whom liquidation of the enemies of the race and the nation was their specialization and main objective. The killers on the death marches differed from them.

Christopher Browning tried to clarify the question of the transformation of a group of recruited individuals into a gang of murderers by studying the Order Police Reserve Battalion 101 of Hamburg, which conducted killings of Jews in Lublin district in 1942.[34] However, the cruel conduct of the death march killers differed from that of soldiers in remote combat areas. The death march killers were operating in 1945, when the outcome of the war had essentially been decided, and their crimes were not committed in the East, where the apocalyptic racial struggle was being waged. The numerous massacres of prisoners occurred on German and Austrian soil, in the streets and fields of civilian settlements, in the presence of local residents and often with their assistance. It encompassed wide social circles, including the remnants of fighting units that had fallen apart as a result of the military debacle, quasi-military units, and random collections of civilians; it was the outcome of total upheaval in a society that had lost control of its life and had been engulfed in a threatening black vacuum without a guiding hand.

Close perusal of the directives sent out by the authorities, by Himmler or his spokesmen, reveals that the massacre of the concentration camp prisoners was not the proposed default. The reverse was true; in contrast to the situation during the peak years of genocide, when the directives were clear even if issued in diverse forms, the orders issued by the authorities during the death marches were ambiguous and sometimes at odds with accepted policy. This was the case for all those who heard Himmler referring to the transfer of Jews to Mauthausen, and this could also be understood from his inconsistent instructions in the first months of the evacuations. That is, not only did the final chapter of genocide unfold without explicit official instructions, but it was frequently opposed to the spirit of the orders. It should be pointed out at once that Himmler, Pohl, and the Gauleiters involved never prohibited murder, but neither did they insist on it as explicit policy. As a consequence, individuals serving the murder machine were left without the cover of a state authority and were deprived of the accepted protective shield of obedience, namely, the obligation to carry out orders. It will be recalled that on innumerable occasions, a single murderer was obliged to decide for himself whether to kill. After the war, however, these killers charged their superiors in the hierarchy with responsibility for the deeds, or often simply pinned the blame on the conditions in the evacuation convoys.

The guards and escorts of the columns of prisoners who found themselves in a situation where they were expected to pull the trigger reacted in diverse ways, for which there are various explanations. The multiplicity of such situations created the diversity in response. In the evacuation columns, no guard was forced to press the trigger when a prisoner collapsed, but there was always another guard who would do the job in his stead. Many of the guards refrained from firing the death shot and left the coup de grâce to their colleagues. Nobody ordered the seven middle-aged guards at Stary Jaromierz to massacre Jewish women. Other guards and escorts did not take part. Yet, according to Jepsen's testimony, not a single guard refused to take part in the last massacre of prisoners at Lüneburg. None of the Volkssturm men who murdered prisoners in the Gardelegen area truly believed that, less than a day before the Americans were due to arrive, Thiele or one of his men could charge him or conduct a reckoning with him if he refused the order. What, therefore, motivated these killers?

The various motives that Browning attributes to the unit he studied, whose members murdered Jews in Poland, are not necessarily relevant in the case of the death marches. For example, there was almost no group pressure on the individual murderers at the end of the war that could coerce them into taking part. Was it a case of conformism, such as played a part in homogeneous combat units, where the men were under pressure or received directives from an authority believed to be in the know? Even fear of the powers that be loses its impact when it is not clear who represents that power or whether it exists at all. There definitely existed, however, conformism of another kind, based on a specific local shared interest or on a sense of fraternity such as was nonexistent in the murder units in earlier periods of extermination. It was the brotherhood of the basic social unit, a brotherhood of community or close family interests.

The uniformity of action in implementation of murder by men with no binding connection between them, who had not trained or worked together, and came from different political, personal backgrounds and age groups, is a source of amazement. Hundreds of murderers, mainly from the Volkssturm and the local police, as well as party activists and ordinary civilians, did not hesitate to take part in murder or to abet it, not because they were afraid to be considered shirkers who left the dirty work to others, cowards lacking in "manly" values, as may have been the case in the murder units in Poland and the Soviet Union.[35] They acted because they could not evade responsibility for the fate of their community and abandon their loved ones to a real and immediate danger. Their uniformity of action was, in practice, dictated by the genocidal mentality that had prevailed for some time in their society.

Eric Markusen and Damir Mirkovic proposed separating the "bystanders" who witness genocide into two distinct groups. Members of the first group witness the evolution of the genocide but do not take part directly or actively. Most of them remain indifferent to the sight of the victims' suffering. Some may pity the victims but fear to make any move dangerous to themselves.[36] Included in this category are tens of thousands of German civilians who witnessed the acts of murder being perpetrated on their very doorstep. After the war, many of them provided detailed descriptions of incidents in which prisoners were shot and killed by guards or other murderers who made no effort to conceal their actions. This conduct was particularly striking in places such as Celle or Lüneburg, where there were outbursts of mass slaughter, but it also occurred in small towns and rural areas, as in the case of the evacuations of Buchenwald and its subcamps. In quite a few cases, young children witnessed the killings without turning a hair. But it is impossible to explain the existence of this "murderous voyeurism,"[37] this equanimity, without taking into account the state of German society in 1945 and its attitude toward the camp inmates. The apathy and general anticipation of the end of the years of suffering, of Nazi terror, and of incessant enemy bombing raids, was compounded by the negative image of these prisoners and the absence of any humane emotions where they were concerned. Their liquidation was another of the phenomena of violence and death to which so many Germans were exposed at the time, and in this case toward human beings who evoked no sympathy in them.[38]

Yet one cannot comprehend the eruptions of lethal brutality during the death march period without considering the passive participation of a wide social stratum of people who, as a rule, did not sully their hands with such tasks, but did not merely witness the atrocities from the sidelines. This was the second group of bystanders, whom Markusen and Mirkovic call "accomplices." This sector of the population supported those who did the dirty work, exerted influence, and provided the social framework and the legitimization. It consisted of civilians who sanctioned the development of the genocidal mentality that caused individuals to become involved in mass killings. From within this group emerged all those who assisted in the murderous tasks, the "second circle," those who did not pull the triggers but without whom the murderers could not have done what they did.[39]

In the final months of the war, wide sectors of German society were infected with the virus of extreme violence. The "education for murder" *(Erziehung zum Mord),* as the historian Konrad Kwiet calls it, was a protracted process. The wider the circle of violence and murder, the more Germans were exposed to brutal and murderous action, and the more individuals played an active part. They served in combat units that fought in the East, guarded concentration and labor camps, liquidated partisans and civilians in the occupied territories, dispatched the trains conveying Jews throughout Europe to the death camps, or murdered other Jews in the Ukraine. The tens of thousands of Germans who were exposed to such actions carried them out often without explicit orders but as a result of local initiative, approved and supported by the decision makers. The Nazi "national community" *(Volksgemeinschaft)* developed with time into the "Greater German Reich" *(Großgermanische Reich),* which aspired to build a new order in Europe in which there was no room for nations defined as enemies of the people and the Reich *(Volks-und Reichsfeinde).* This development encompassed and extended the apparatus of terror, oppression, and murder.[40] In the final stages of the war, the Reich retreated into its old borders, which were being rapidly invaded by the threatening enemy. The urge to be rid of the "East," which was infiltrating the heart of the nation, was no longer of political or ideological significance. What was at stake now was not the future of the Reich, but the survival of hearth and home.

The thousands of killers of prisoners on the death marches were not necessarily anti-Semites or proponents of some orderly racial ideology. Like many others in German society, they were undoubtedly exposed to political indoctrination and an incessant flood of anti-Semitic and racial slogans and propaganda. However, it is questionable whether this propaganda juggernaut in fact had a strong and effective impact on the vast range of individuals who took part in acts of slaughter. Most had not served in the extermination machine in the years when it was operating at full force. Yet, the propaganda effort expanded and was internalized in the war years in one way or another by social and public networks, whose culture of action found room for the ideology it preached. The killers were the product of a society that for 12 years had promoted a certain ethos, which transformed many of them into Nazis, though they might not define themselves as such. The combination of "Nazi" beliefs with the circumstances that prevailed toward the end of the war turned a considerable number of them into murderers. They regarded the prisoners as instrumental objects, and their attitude toward those objects was entirely opportunistic. As long as the transportation of prisoners to the destination camps answered their needs and served as insurance that they would be deployed far from the front line, they continued to do their jobs. But the moment the prisoners became a liability, as often occurred, they did not hesitate to butcher them mercilessly. Actions that were ostensibly driven by zealous ideological motivation were in fact frequently fueled by solely opportunistic considerations.[41] These considerations took into account the prospects and dangers of evacuation, fear of falling captive, and the desire to shield the family against danger and violence. That being said, the murders could not have occurred without the close connection of the murderers to the social infrastructure that supported its perpetration.

In a biographical study of the Nazi murderers, Michael Mann concluded that the assorted murderers should be considered "true Nazis," though not necessarily in the sense that they adopted a uniform ideology. This particular genocide was not committed by a group of individuals with a single value system. However, all the people classified in the early 1930s as true Nazis, ordinary Nazis, ordinary policemen, ordinary Germans, and ordinary people were involved in the barbarous collective project. This involvement came about because of social processes, cultural interactions, and the shared experience of all those who participated. The senior echelons of Nazi functionaries were more dedicated Nazis than those who served under them. Obedience was followed by further obedience, which soon became routine, and the most experienced individuals in each echelon became quasi-instigators after the first or second action. In every institutional system in Germany that was implicated in genocide there existed a subculture of individual operators who supported Nazi ideology as they understood it, and interpreted the orders and instructions transmitted to them accordingly. Moreover, the professional ethos that developed in those institutions—of physicians, jurists, and policemen—generated a subculture in which Nazi ideology could find its place. This murderous ideology evolved gradually because of the impact of the unique subculture on the institution or organization.[42]

Without dehumanization of the enemy and the "other," the murderers could not have committed their crimes. Countless examples indicate the way in which the murderers treated their victims. The killers of the Jewish women at Stary Jaromierz regarded their victims as "pieces" *(Stücke);* Alfred Jepsen, who was responsible for the murder of hundreds of prisoners at Lüneburg claimed that they were "half dead" in any case. When the killers set out on manhunts, their prey were given the folklorist-macabre identity of zebras or rabbits. The metaphor that recurred in the testimony of survivors was that the guards treated them like rabid dogs that must be destroyed.

It is harder to explain the psychological metamorphosis that occurred the moment a column guard, a middle-aged Volkssturm recruit, or an anonymous village policeman turned into a violent killer. The first component of the explanation must be the power of the ideology that shaped the collective to which the individual belonged, namely, the clearly defined category of "us" threatened by "them." The fact that this ideology focused on the political and military context precipitated the psychological process required for activating the violence. The use of symbols, myths, and slogans with ethnic, racial, or national emphases intensified already existing fears evoked by the political and military situation in Germany at the time. But the energizing power of ideology alone is not enough. In order to transform a random group of individuals into murderers, a certain social dynamic must occur. In order for this violence to erupt and consolidate and ripen into massacre, the ideology must be interwoven with other factors.[43]

The collective image of the victims is of supreme importance for elucidating the phenomenon of murder. The foreignness of the victim provides the basis for the sense of threat and danger that leads to murder. This is, of course, the perspective of the persecutors, which shapes the terminology that determines who is to be a victim.[44] The definitive and collective identification of victims is based on "us" against "them," which, as is well known, is the main formative element of the conditions for murder. The typical group traditionally identified more than any other with victimization, is, of course, the Jews, but in Nazi Germany various groups were identified as "other," for political, ethnic, social, and, above all, racial reasons. This "other" should also be sought in the massacres of the death marches period, and in particular those killings in which ordinary civilians took part.

The concentration camp prisoners had been the typical "other" from the early days of the Nazi regime. In the first few years, when the regime was gaining popularity and the detainees were mainly communists and opponents, the camps were perceived as a legitimate means of defending the recuperating Reich against its enemies. Over time, these detainees came to be seen as a threatening, violent, lawless, and dangerous group. From mid-1942, when the "mob" from the East began to reach the camps, these installations became time bombs sited only a stone's throw from the homes of law-abiding citizens. From the second half of 1943, when the numerous subcamps became part of the scenery for German civilians, the danger appeared even greater.[45]

Although, from the outset, the concentration camp inmates were the first victims of Nazi violence, they were never earmarked for total extermination as an ethnic, political, or racial group. In 1944 they were liquidated in their thousands by the selective murder method of slave labor, but then too there remained a narrow outlet of rescue based on their labor skills and physical hardiness. Once they set out from the camp on the death marches, this outlet narrowed even further. Their collective identification as the enemy, the "alien," or the "other" was now perceived as even more menacing because they were no longer confined behind barbed wire fences, but could escape at any opportunity. Some of the killers continued to regard them as Jews, others as communists, and elsewhere they were described as criminals, rapists of women and children, and sometimes all of these together.

Total anonymity prevailed between the murderers and their victims. Only rarely could the survivors of the death marches identify by name the killers of their comrades. The survivors of the Gardelegen massacre, who were interrogated by the Americans, could not name any of the murderers. As almost always occurs when massacres are perpetrated during genocide, the victims are identified as an abstract collective identity. This is a situation in which a group of helpless human beings is murdered by another group of human beings who hold power, and whose own safety is not endangered. In other words, this activity, which occurs within a defined and restricted framework of time and place where an active element confronts a totally passive element, ends only with the liquidation of the last of the victims or when the murderous rage of the perpetrators dies down, or when they are interrupted by a more powerful element.[46] Countless incidents in the last chapter of Nazi genocide ended in one of these situations: either the last of the prisoners had been killed, or the killers preferred to flee rather than kill, or the liberating forces were too close at hand.

The diversity of the incidents and the fact that the murderers belonged to such a variety of groups and organizations attest to the heterogeneity of this group of killers. Among them were loyal Nazis, opportunists who were trying to steer a safe course in a hazardous situation, some who only wanted to reach home safely before the Third Reich disappeared, and ordinary civilians who were caught up in a situation such as they had never imagined. They did not decide a priori to become Nazis, but they became such by participating in the act of murder. They adopted the pattern of Nazi racial savagery the moment they decided to act in the spirit of Nazism.[47]

The incidents of murder and massacre toward the end of the war did not occur spontaneously, even if they sometimes appear to have done so. The murderers functioned in various ways. First among these were the organizers who planned the act and guided its execution. They included convoy commanders, local party functionaries, police and SS officers, and even mayors of towns and villages that the prisoners passed. But rarely were such men as Brauny, Friedrichs, or Thiele, not to mention camp commandants, encountered among those who aimed the rifles or the Panzerfäuste or among the men who burned down barns where the victims were trapped. Generally speaking, the organizers represented a wider interest, such as the ruling authority, and provided the required legitimization of the deed. It was they who instilled superstitious fear of the victims and their deeds and encouraged the perpetrators. It was also they who were identified with the regime's ideology. They did not always openly instigate the perpetrations, but their message was clear: the danger must be removed.

The implementers of the murders did not necessarily share the motives of the organizers. Their readiness to carry out orders often stemmed from their own particular circumstances. They always had a personal, direct connection to the event, and some personal interest in liquidating the victims. They were almost always of widely ranging ages, sometimes very young and even adolescent.[48] Their motivation veered between two extremes: one was immediate gain, namely, ridding themselves of an obstacle that was delaying and hampering them and endangering their escape plans; the other was belief that the act was of supreme importance for the future of their families, communities, or nation. They were not serial killers, impelled by psychosis or pathological motives. They also lacked the compensation motivation, although one cannot ignore the possibility that their motives were fueled by rage at the military defeat, the tales of atrocities perpetrated by the Red Army against civilians, and the U.S. bombings. In any event, a certain utilitarian motive undoubtedly played a part.

As we know, there were extensive utilitarian aspects to Nazi genocide; one of these was economic. The seizing of the assets of the victims, in particular the murdered Jews, directly affected the standard of living of all Germans. Looting the treasures of the occupied countries was a routine procedure. The arms industry in Germany in the last years of the war was propelled by the slave labor of hundreds of thousand of camp inmates and other forced laborers. The killing did not bestow material advantages or personal status and prestige on the murderers within their closed units. Their utilitarianism was of a different type: it was related to their desire to escape the combat areas as fast as possible, to avoid being taken captive in the Red Army, to obliterate the evidence, and to liquidate those witnesses who could point the finger of blame at them after the war. A particularly strong and existentially expedient motive was the desire to defend their homes and families as the war neared its end and the era of uncertainty began.

Against the background of the numerous atrocities, the conduct of certain guards who treated the prisoners with relative decency is noteworthy. Survivors testified that these guards did not abuse the prisoners, did not murder them, sought food for them in the villages they passed, and were not blatantly hostile even when it was clear to them that their prisoners were Jews. "The SS man of our group was not yet the greatest enemy of Israel. So far the weak who had to be taken in carts . . . he somehow . . . he rented us carts. That means he requisitioned carts there and they were transported . . . with horses," recalled a prisoner who was evacuated from a Dachau subcamp in April 1945. This guard even released the group of prisoners after several days when they were passing through Czech territory.[49] A considerable number of Polish, Czech, and German citizens handed out water and food to prisoners who passed through their hometowns and villages or were aboard trains halted at local stations. In many cases this involved risky confrontation with the guards. Quite a few prisoners survived thanks to the shelter they received from the civilian population before the liberating armies arrived.[50] And particularly impressive in their moral force were rescue operations such as that at Burgstall.

The Victims: No Way Out

Although in most cases, the imminence of the evacuation was sensed in the air before it was launched, and partial preparations began in some camps, the event was, generally speaking, sudden and traumatic for the prisoners. This was particularly true for prisoners evacuated in winter 1945 from Auschwitz and its subcamps. Many of them later related that everything happened suddenly, without preparation, so that they were unable to anticipate what lay ahead; their routine was completely disrupted.

Attempts to dodge the evacuation occurred everywhere, particularly during the spring 1945 evacuations, but few prisoners succeeded in hiding or
escaping. When camps were evacuated in stages, prisoners tried to avoid
leaving with the first groups. This was particularly evident in the case of
Jewish prisoners who regarded any change in the status quo as an ominous
indication that they were about to be liquidated. In several camps in Germany, in particular Buchenwald and Dachau, groups of prisoners made an
organized attempt in April 1945 to delay and resist the evacuation. There
was an organized underground movement in these camps, whose dominant
members were communist prisoners. Such attempts could only be made in
places where several specific conditions existed, especially an active underground organization. But the most important and effective one was the imminent arrival of the liberating forces that had already cut off the evacuation routes. In this situation, the camp command and guard often decided
that to abandon the camp without harming the prisoners and make a rapid
escape was a far superior alternative to captivity.[51]

Additional conditions that could help or jeopardize the chance of rescue
were related to the evaluations made during the evacuation and the march.
The camp, its horrors and routine of death notwithstanding, offered a stable reality. Day-to-day survival depended on many factors, one of which
was the daily routine. The wake-up call in the barracks, the head count,
watery coffee, labor, soup, another head count, sleep—all these provided
the prisoners with a framework within which they could try to stabilize
their efforts to survive. The unplanned evacuation shattered this routine and
confronted the prisoners with unexpected, drastic, and frequent changes,
which undermined their ability to survive, both physically and emotionally.
Their prospects of survival were naturally also influenced by their guards'
readiness to shoot, by exhaustion, hunger, and debilitation, and often also
by their belief that death was inevitable and did not depend on their own
actions. The never-ending trek through the snow along the retreat routes
from Poland westward, undertaken after months of oppression in the
camps, and their lack of conviction that it was possible to live through this
chaos, caused a considerable number of them to give up the struggle, as one
of the survivors explained in 1946:

> That was something that one is not able to tell. A man full of his senses in
> whom everything is still functioning, he is feeble and can't run any more, he
> stands by himself under a tree, his eyes shining like, like reflectors. And he waits
> for the moment when the whole formation will have passed by till the hind-
> most guards will arrive with the block leader, also an SS man, who will shoot
> him. Can you imagine what this is? A man with his full mental abilities, who

knows what is going on and he waits for death. And so every 3, 10 meters one saw somebody standing under a tree, or sitting down and such a man would be shot and thrown into the ditch.[52]

The main enigma for the prisoners, and especially the Jews, during the death marches period was why they were being allowed to live and why their captors were troubling to drag them from place to place instead of liquidating them. They could not have known, of course, of the various directives about the evacuation, the attempt to preserve a vital workforce for as long as possible, or Himmler's manipulations at that time. For the Jews evacuated from Auschwitz or other labor camps, this question was of particular significance. They knew only too well of the fate their families and community had suffered, and now suddenly they were being taken out and transferred to Germany or Austria. None of them believed that the objective of the evacuation was to keep them alive so that they could continue to labor in the service of the German war machine. They were convinced that they had not been exterminated before leaving the camp because the murderers had not had enough time to act since the enemy forces were too close, or for some other technical reason.

The decision to try to escape the column of marchers was almost always taken without prior planning and was a split-second choice. It seems that, at least in the first stage of the evacuation, prisoners who were still capable of walking began to realize after a few days that their strength was draining away. They were aware that if they wanted to escape their inevitable fate, which was to wait under a tree for the guard at the end of the column to catch up with them, they must do so before that moment arrived. These thoughts overwhelmed them, and they usually made the move when the conditions were right: during an aerial bombardment of the train that impelled the prisoners and their guards to flee in search of shelter; when they sensed that the guards were no longer focused on their task and had become lax; or when they hoped that the local population would agree to shelter them from their persecutors. However, many who decided to escape were driven by despair and acted after summoning up the remnants of their survival instinct.

The escape itself did not guarantee survival. In most cases the guards shot the escapees and sometimes even conducted a hunt for them. Generally speaking, the routes of the death marches were crowded with retreating army units, police and SS forces, Volkssturm companies, and various unorganized armed groups. There were always some among them who regarded the escaped prisoners as a danger to be eradicated mercilessly whenever encountered. The prisoner fleeing for his life, particularly if he was Jewish, Russian, or Polish, had to find a hiding place in Germany, sometimes for days or weeks, until the liberating forces arrived. Not all of them succeeded in holding fast through those few days, and often fell into a state of apathy, despair, and hopelessness after escaping, due to starvation, debilitation, and a fear of persecution that impelled them to hide like hunted animals from any civilian or man in uniform they spotted. For all these reasons, the escapees sometimes gave themselves up to any local authority in the hope that their luck would hold and they would not be liquidated immediately.

The decision to escape also stemmed from the conviction that it would be possible to melt into the local society. The death march period, in contrast to the past, was characterized by new patterns of encounter between the outside society and the victims, particularly where the Jews were concerned. In the years when the killings were conducted with full force, Jews who sought shelter among the local population encountered rejection, motivated by anti-Semitism, indifference, and fear of German reprisals. Those who decided to hide had to accept the fact that they would live like hunted animals, moving from place to place, exposed to blackmail and informers, without knowing how long this hazardous situation would last. They had one advantage, however: they were almost always operating within their natural surroundings. They were familiar with the towns where they lived and the surrounding areas, and in smaller settlements, they were acquainted with their non-Jewish neighbors. Many were fluent in the language of the country: Polish, Ukrainian, Russian, and, of course, French or Dutch. It is obvious that Polish or Russian prisoners could find hiding places in areas settled by Poles more easily than could Jews. This was also true of underground fighters or soldiers from the armies that fought the Germans, who could always hope for the aid of civilians hostile to the foreign occupier. But, as we know, none of this guaranteed rescue.

During the evacuations, many Jewish and non-Jewish prisoners were interned in unfamiliar surroundings within a population whose language they did not speak. From the moment the evacuation columns left Poland, few of the prisoners could establish contact with the population around them. Sometimes they had no idea where they were. An illuminating example of this insurmountable obstacle was the case of the Jewish prisoners from Greece who were incarcerated in Gęsiówka camp. They did not try to escape during the death march, although they passed a number of towns and villages where they could have sought shelter and even though it was clear that the Germans were in full retreat. One of the prisoners explained after the war:

Where would you escape to? Do you know where to? Escape? Who thought about escaping? You don't know where you are. You don't know Poland,

don't know Poland or Germany. Maybe it's between Poland and Germany . . .
don't know the language, don't know anything. And it's better to be together . . .
where exactly should I be?[53]

Nevertheless, the death marches and evacuations offered a slim prospect
of rescue. Once they were out of the camps, circumstances arose that facilitated escape and concealment. The prisoners soon realized that their guards
were tense, confused, and anxious at the prospect of being stranded with
their charges and falling captive. The aimless wandering, and the desire to
arrive as soon as possible at a camp or railway station where the prisoners
could be loaded onto freight cars, was one of the main threats to the marchers' lives. As the trek lengthened and opportunities were blocked, it seemed
increasingly likely that at some moment the guards would decide to liquidate them. The ability to survive the evacuation was naturally affected by
many factors: the physical condition of the prisoners before departure, the
length of the death route, the food the prisoners managed to find, their personal equipment, whether they were evacuated on foot or by rail, and so on.
But there were other highly significant factors originating in the internal
relations in the prison society.

What often sealed a prisoner's fate was the fact that he did or did not
belong to an intimate supportive group in the weeks of the evacuation. The
lone prisoner was forced to tackle the difficulties by himself, which reduced
the chances for survival. Fellow political associates, fellow nationals, people
from one's hometown, relatives or friends acquired in the camp—all these
improved the individual's prospects. However, the confusion and disorder
that accompanied departure from the camp often shattered these frameworks. Prisoners who had lived or worked side by side and had established
a supportive social framework ended up marching alone in a long column
of prisoners, most of whom they had never seen before. In this situation,
anyone who succeeded in remaining with a group of friends had a better
chance of surviving. Members of political movements, for example, who
had been in the camp together succeeded in establishing support groups
during the marches. This was particularly important for Jewish prisoners.

However, survival was not, in the final analysis, determined by the heroic
struggle for life that the prisoners waged, but mainly by the decision or ability of the murderers to slaughter them. The genocidal killings of those months
extracted a terribly bloody price. Hundreds of thousands of camp prisoners
died in the months before the liberation, sometimes only a few hours before
it occurred. The precise number of victims can never be determined. The last
stage of Nazi genocide was marked by the creation of countless murder sites
where columns of prisoners stopped. These columns split up again and

again in a mutational process that divided the mass of victims incessantly into smaller and smaller groups until the murderers had completed their work. In certain cases, almost all the prisoners were liquidated; in others, most of the evacuees succeeded in exploiting a local situation and survived. Quite a few of those who lived to see the day of liberation did not survive for long afterward because of their desperate physical condition.

The graves of these nameless victims are strewn along the paths, forests, and villages of Germany and Austria. In the last stage of Nazi genocide, the burial sites of its victims spilled beyond the traditional territorial borders, such as the crematoria in Polish death camps, the burial trenches in Lithuania and Byelorussia, and the snow-covered POW camps in the Ukraine; they were now dug on the very doorstep of the society that had produced the perpetrators from its midst.

Notes
Bibliography
Acknowledgments
Index

Notes

Abbreviations

AGD	Archiv KZ-Gedenkstätte Dachau, Dachau
AGF	Archiv KZ-Gedenkstätte Flossenbürg, Flossenbürg
AGM	Archiv KZ-Gedenkstätte Mittelbau-Dora, Nordhausen
AGN	Archiv KZ-Gedenkstätte Neuengamme, Neuengamme
AMS	Archiwum Muzeum Stutthof, Stutthof
AN	Archives Nationales, Paris
APMAB	Archiwum Państwowego Museum Auschwitz-Birkenau, Auschwitz
BstU	Bundesbeauftragte für die Unterlagen des Staatssicherheits-dienstes der ehemaligen DDR, Berlin
DÖW	Dokumentationsarchiv des österreichischen Widerstandes, Vienna
FO	Foreign Office
IHTP-CNRS	Institut d'histoire du temps présent–Centre National de la Reserche Scientifique, Paris
IMT	*Trials of the Major War Criminals before the International Military Tribunal, Nuremberg, 14 November 1945–1 October 1946*, Nuremberg, 1947 (New York: William S. Hein & Co., 1997)
ITS	International Tracing Services Archives
LKA Magdeburg	Report of the Criminal Section of the Upper Saxony Police in Magdeburg
MA	Moreshet Archive, Givat Chaviva, Israel
MGS Gardelegen	Staatsarchiv Gardelegen, Staatmueseum, Gardelegen
NARA	National Archives and Records Administration, College Park, MD

NdsH	Niedersächsisches Hauptstaatsarchiv Hannover, Hannover
NIOD	Netherlands Institute voor Oorlogsdocumentie, Amsterdam
OHP	Oral History Project
ÖSA	Österreichisches Staatsarchiv/Archiv der Republik, Vienna
PMGR	Państwowe Muzeum Groß-Rosen, Wałbrzych
SLA	Staatsanwaltschaft beim Landesgericht Aschaffenburg
SLD	Staatsanwaltschaft beim Landgericht Duisburg
SLK	Staatsanwaltschaft beim Landesgericht Köln
SLM	Staatsanwaltschaft beim Landesgericht München II
SLS	Staatsanwaltschaft beim Landesgericht Stendal
SMA	Sowjetische Militäradministration
StaB	Staatsarchiv Bremen, Bremen
THW	Thüringisches Hauptstaatsarchiv, Weimar
TNA	The National Archives of the United Kingdom, Kew
USHMMA	United States Holocaust Memorial Museum Archives, Washington, DC
VB	*Völkische Beobachter*
VfZ	*Vierteljahreshefte für Zeitgeschichte*
WO	War Office
YVA	Yad Vashem Archives, Jerusalem
ZStL	Zentrale Stelle der Landesjustizverwaltungen, Ludwigsburg

Introduction

1. Yehuda Bauer, "The Death Marches, January–May 1945," in Michael R. Marrus, ed., *The Nazi Holocaust,* vol. IX, *The End of the Holocaust* (Westport, CT: Meckler, 1989), pp. 503–505.
2. See Laurel Leff, *Buried by the Times: The Holocaust and America's Most Important Newspaper* (New York: Cambridge University Press, 2005), pp. 294–307.
3. Arieh J. Kochavi, *Confronting Captivity: Britain and the United States and Their POWs in Nazi Germany* (Chapel Hill: University of North Carolina Press, 2005), pp. 212–221.
4. Evacuation, Refugees and Displaced Persons in Germany, February 10, 1945, Supreme Headquarters Allied Expeditions Force, National Archives and Records Administration (hereafter NARA), RG-338 (1st Army), box 187, file 383.6, pp. 1–2; British Foreign Office Report, January 26, 1945, The National Archives of United Kingdom (hereafter TNA), FO 371/4676.
5. *Davar,* February 23, March 14, April 9, 1945; *Haaretz,* February 14, March 22, April 12, 1945; *Hatzofeh,* February 5, 14, 19, March 20, April 9, 10, 18, 1945.
6. Michael R. Marrus, *The Nuremberg War Crimes Trial, 1945–46: A Documentary History* (Boston: Bedford Books, 1997), pp. 206–207.
7. Irena Malá and Ludmila Kubátová, *Pochody Smrti* (Prague: Nakladatelství politické literatury, 1965).
8. Zygmunt Zonik, *Anus belli: Ewakuacja i wyzwolenie hitlerowskich obozów koncentracyjnch* (Warsaw: Państwowe Wydawnictwo Naukowe, 1988).
9. Andrzej Strzelecki, *The Evacuation, Dismantling and Liberation of KL Auschwitz* (Auschwitz: Auschwitz-Birkenau State Museum, 2001); Joachim Neander, "Das

Konzentrationslager 'Mittelbau' in der Endphase der NS-Dikatatur" (PhD diss., University of Bremen, 1996); Simone Erpel, *Zwischen Vernichtung und Befreiung: Das Frauen-Konzentrationslager Ravensbrück in der letzten Kriegsphase* (Berlin: Metropol, 2005).

10. Ulrich Herbert, Karin Orth, and Christoph Dieckmann, eds., *Die nationalsozialistischen Konzentrationslager: Entwicklung und Struktur,* vols. I and II (Göttingen: Wallstein Verlag, 1998); Wolfgang Benz and Barbara Distel, eds., *Der Ort des Terrors: Geschichte der nationalsozialistischen Konzentrationslager,* vol. I (Munich: C. H. Beck, 2005).

11. Daniel Jonah Goldhagen, *Hitler's Willing Executioners: Ordinary Germans and the Holocaust* (New York: Knopf, 1996), chaps. 13 and 14.

12. Ariel Horvitz, "Mitsad HaMavet shel Yehudey Chelm VeHrubieszów LeEver Nahar Bug BeDetsember 1939" [The death march of the Jews of Chełm and Hrubieszów toward the River Bug in December 1939], *Yalkut Moreshet* 68 (October 1999): 52–68; Goldhagen, *Hitler's Willing Executioners,* p. 569, note 3.

13. See Leah Prais, "Plitim BeMirkam HaKhayim HaYehudim BaIr Varsha Uba-Getto September 1939–July 1942" [Refugees in the fabric of Jewish life in the city of Warsaw and the ghetto, September 1939–July 1942] (PhD diss., Hebrew University, Jerusalem, 2006).

14. Karel C. Berkhoff, "The 'Russian' Prisoners of War in Nazi-Ruled Ukraine as Victims of Genocidal Massacre," *Holocaust and Genocide Studies* 15:1 (2001): 1–32.

15. Karin Orth, *Das System der nationalsozialistischen Konzentrationslager: Eine politische Organisationsgeschichte* (Hamburg: Hamburger Edition, 1999), pp. 270ff.

16. Wolfgang Sofsky, *The Order of Terror: The Concentration Camp* (Princeton, NJ: Princeton University Press, 1997), p. 43; Falk Pingel, *Häftlinge unter SS-Herrschaft: Widerstand, Selbstbehauptung und Vernichtung im Konzentrationslager* (Hamburg: Hoffman und Campe, 1978), p. 230.

17. Bauer, "The Death Marches," p. 494.

1. The Concentration Camps, 1933–1944

1. Eugen Kogon, *The Theory and Practice of Hell: The German Concentration Camps and the System behind Them* (London: Secker & Warburg, 1950), p. 30.

2. Dagmar Barnouw, *Germany 1945: Views of War and Violence* (Bloomington: Indiana University Press, 1996).

3. Nikolaus Wachsmann, "Looking into the Abyss: Historians and the Nazi Concentration Camps," *European History Quarterly* 36:2 (2006): 247.

4. Benedikt Kautsky, *Teufel und Verdammte: Erfahrungen und Erkenntnisse aus sieben Jahren in deutschen Konzentrationslagern* (Zurich: Büchergilde Gutenberg, 1946).

5. Erwin Gostner, *1000 Tage im KZ: Ein Erlebnisbericht aus den Konzentrationslagern Dachau, Mauthausen, Gusen* (Mannheim: W. Burger, 1946).

6. David Rousset, *L'univers concentrationnaire* (Paris: Pavois, 1946).

7. Israel Gutman, *Anashim VaEfer: Sefer Oshvits-Birkenau* [People and ashes: The book of Auschwitz-Birkenau] (Merhavyah: Sifriyat Poalim, 1957).

8. Hannah Arendt, "The Concentration Camps," *Partisan Review* 15:7 (1948): 743–763.

9. Ulrich Herbert, Karin Orth, and Christoph Dieckmann, "Die nationalsozialistischen Konzentrationslager: Geschichte, Erinnerung, Forschung," in Herbert, Orth, and Dieckmann, *Die nationalsozialistischen Konzentrationslager,* vol. I, p. 23.

10. The English-language edition appeared in 1997: see Sofsky, *The Order of Terror.*

11. Ibid., p. 14.

12. Ibid., pp. 16–27.

13. Sofsky defined it as a system on the social border *(an der Grenze des Sozialen)* because it was dynamic and variable, and adapted its functioning and internal social structure to the needs of oppression and murder relevant to time and place. Wolfgang Sofsky, "An der Grenze des Sozialen: Perspektiven der KZ-Forschung," in Herbert, Orth, and Dieckmann, *Die nationalsozialistischen Konzentrationslager,* vol. II, pp. 1141–1169.

14. Johannes Tuchel, "Organisationsgeschichte der 'frühen' Konzentrationslager," in Benz and Distel, *Der Ort des Terrors,* vol. I, pp. 43–57.

15. Benz and Distel, *Der Ort des Terrors,* vol. II, pp. 17–230.

16. Orth, *Das System,* pp. 23–26.

17. On the early days of the gulags, see Anne Appelbaum, *Goulag: A History* (New York: Doubleday, 2003), pp. 41–57; Oleg V. Khlevniuk, *The History of the Gulag: From Collectivization to the Great Terror* (New Haven, CT: Yale University Press, 2004), pp. 9–53.

18. Tuchel, "Organisationsgeschichte," p. 44; Wachsmann, "Looking into the Abyss," p. 251.

19. Charles W. Syndor Jr., *Soldiers of Destruction: The SS Death's Head Division, 1933–1945* (Princeton, NJ: Princeton University Press, 1990), pp. 4–7; Johannes Tuchel, ed., *Die Inspektion der Konzentrationslager 1938–1945: Das System des Terrors, eine Dokumentation* (Berlin: Hentrich, 1994), p. 32.

20. Stanislav Zámečník, "Dachau-Stammlager," in Benz and Distel, *Der Ort des Terrors,* vol. II, pp. 233–374; Orth, *Das System,* pp. 27–28.

21. Johannes Tuchel, "Planung und Realität des Systems der Konzentrationslager 1934–1938," in Herbert, Orth, and Dieckmann, *Die nationalsozialistischen Konzentrationslager,* vol. I, p. 44; Martin Broszat, "The Concentration Camps 1933–45," in Helmut Krausnick, Hans Buchheim, Martin Broszat, and Hans-Adolf Jacobsen, eds., *Anatomy of the SS State* (New York: Walker & Co., 1965), pp. 399–504.

22. "Disziplinar- und Strafordung für das Gefangenlager," October 1, 1933, in *Trials of the Major War Criminals before the International Military Tribunal, Nuremberg, 14 November 1945–1 October 1946, Nuremberg, 1947* (hereafter IMT), PS-778 (New York: William S. Hein & Co., 1997).

23. Rudolf Höß, *Kommandant in Auschwitz: Autobiographische Aufzeichnungen von Rudolf Höß* (Stuttgart: Deutsche Verlags-Anstalt, 1958), pp. 55–56; Karin Orth, *Die Konzentrationslager-SS: Sozialstrukturelle Analysen und Biographische Studien* (Göttingen: Wallstein Verlag, 2000), pp. 105–107.

24. Syndor, *Soldiers of Destruction,* p. 18.

25. Jörg Balcke, *Verantwortungsentlastung durch Organisation: Die "Inspektion der Konzentrationslager" und der KZ-Terror* (Tübingen: Edition Diskord, 2001), pp. 52–58.

26. In June 1935 only 11 people worked in the IKL. In 1939, with the expansion of the camp system and the new functions added, the number rose to more than 100. Balcke, *Verantwortungsentlastung*, pp. 31, 35; Orth, *Das System*, p. 39.

27. Orth, *Das System*, p. 32.

28. Nikolaus Wachsmann, *Hitler's Prison: Legal Terror in Nazi Germany* (New Haven, CT: Yale University Press, 2004), p. 112.

29. Orth, *Das System*, pp. 40, 44; Aleksander Lasik, "Organizational Structure of Auschwitz Concentration Camp," in Wacław Długoborski and Franciszek Piper, eds., *Auschwitz 1940–1945*, vol. I (Auschwitz: Auschwitz-Birkenau State Museum, 2000), pp. 170–171; Sofsky, *The Order of Terror*, p. 106.

30. Wachsmann, *Hitler's Prison*, pp. 118–149.

31. Ibid., pp. 184–188, 394–395.

32. Broszat, "The Concentration Camps," p. 450.

33. Klaus Drobisch, "Oranienburg—eines der ersten nationalsozialistischen Konzentrationslager," in Günter Morsch, ed., *Konzentrationslager Oranienburg, Stiftung Brandenburgische Gedenkstätten*, vol. III (Oranienburg: Edition Hentrich, 1994), pp. 13–22.

34. *Sachsenhausen: Dokumente, Aussagen, Forschungsergebnisse und Erlebnisberichte über das ehemalige Konzentrationslager Sachsenhausen*, vol. IV (Berlin Ost: Deutscher Verlag der Wissenschaften, 1982), pp. 20–21.

35. Günter Morsch, "Oranienburg-Sachsenhausen, Sachsenhausen-Oranienburg," in Herbert, Orth, and Dieckmann, *Die nationalsozialistischen Konzentrationslager*, vol. I, p. 120; Höß, *Kommandant in Auschwitz*, pp. 68–69.

36. Jeffrey Herf, "Reactionary Modernism: Reconciliations of Technics and Unreason in Weimar Germany and the Third Reich" (PhD diss., Brandeis University, 1980), pp. 236–240.

37. Michael Thad Allen, *The Business of Genocide: The SS, Slave Labor, and the Concentration Camps* (Chapel Hill: University of North Carolina Press, 2002), p. 32.

38. Leo Volk to Heinz-Karl Fanslau, July 13, 1944, IMT (Pohl trial), NO-1016. Emphasis in the original.

39. Jan Erik Schulte, *Zwangsarbeit und Vernichtung: Das Wirtschaftsimperium der SS: Oswald Pohl und das SS-Wirtschafts-Verwaltungshauptamt 1933–1945* (Paderborn: Ferdinand Schöningh, 2001), pp. 32–45. On Pohl's path to the heights of the SS economic command, see also Herman Kaienburg, *Die Wirtschaft der SS* (Berlin: Metropol, 2003), pp. 106–108.

40. Kaienberg, *Die Wirtschaft*, pp. 134–137; Allen, *The Business of Genocide*, p. 59; Hermann Kaienburg, *"Vernichtung durh Arbeit": Der Fall Neuengamme* (Bonn: J. H. W. Dietz, 1991), pp. 53–55; Albert Speer, *Inside the Third Reich: Memoirs by Albert Speer* (New York: Macmillan, 1970), pp. 151–160; Paul B. Jaskot, *The Architecture of Oppression: The SS, Forced Labor and the Nazi Monumental Building Economy* (London: Routledge, 2000), pp. 21, 61.

41. Franciszek Piper, *Auschwitz Prisoner Labor* (Auschwitz: Auschwitz-Birkenau State Museum, 2002), p. 35; Kaienburg, *Die Wirtschaft*, pp. 455–461; Schulte, *Zwangsarbeit*, pp. 103–105.

42. Allen, *The Business of Genocide,* pp. 42–43.

43. Karin Orth, "Experten des Terrors: Die Konzentrationslager-SS und die Shoah," in Gerhard Paul, ed., *Die Täter der Shoah: Fanatische Nationalsozialisten oder ganz normale Deutsche?* (Göttingen: Wallstein Verlag, 2002), pp. 95–96.

44. Sofsky, *The Order of Terror,* p. 103.

45. Ibid., p. 36; Kaienburg, *Vernichtung durch Arbeit,* p. 60.

46. Orth, *Das System,* p. 51.

47. Stutthof was established as a detention and imprisonment camp, and was under the jurisdiction of the Danzig SD until early 1942. Then it became part of the concentration camp system and came under the jurisdiction of the WVHA. Broszat, "The Concentration Camps," p. 476.

48. Ibid., pp. 460–461; Balcke, *Verantwortungsentlastung,* pp. 32–33.

49. On the new demographic planning of eastern Europe after the occupation of Poland, see Götz Aly and Susanne Heim, *Architects of Annihilation: Auschwitz and the Logic of Destruction* (London: Weidenfeld & Nicolson, 2002), pp. 73–114; Christopher R. Browning, *The Origins of the Final Solution, The Evaluation of Nazi Jewish Policy, September 1939–March 1942* (Lincoln: University of Nebraska Press, 2004), pp. 43–54.

50. Allen, *The Business of Genocide,* pp. 97–99; Debórah Dwork and Robert J. Van Pelt, *Auschwitz, 1270 to the Present* (New York: W. W. Norton, 1996), pp. 127ff.

51. Almost no Jews were sent to concentration camps in those months. They were murdered or violently deported to the Generalgouvernement from their homes in the areas annexed to the Reich; see Browning, *The Origins of the Final Solution,* pp. 28–35. On German terror in Poland in the first months of fighting and occupation, see Alexander B. Rossino, *Hitler Strikes Poland: Blitzkrieg, Ideology, and Atrocity* (Lawrence: University Press of Kansas, 2003), pp. 58ff.

52. Franciszek Piper, "The Origins of the Camp," in Wacław Długoborski and Franciszek Piper, eds., *Auschwitz 1940–1945,* vol. I (Auschwitz: Auschwitz-Birkenau State Museum, 2000), pp. 48–51.

53. Mirosław Gliński, "Organizacja obozu koncentracnyjnego Stutthof (1 Września 1939–9 Maja 1945)," *Stutthof Zeszyty Muzeum* 3 (1979): 65–70; Orth, *Das System,* pp. 69–72. Few Jews were sent to Stutthof in its first few months. Danuta Drywa, *Zagłada Żydów w obozie koncentracyjnym Stutthof 1939–1945* (Gdańsk: Muzeum Stutthof w Sztutowie, 2001), pp. 28–29.

54. Richard Glücks to Heinrich Himmler, February 21, 1940, IMT (Pohl trial), NO-034.

55. Rolf-Dieter Müller, *Hitler's Ostkrieg und die deutsche Siedlungspolitik* (Frankfurt am Main: Fischer, 1991), pp. 83–93, 139.

56. Piper, *Auschwitz Prisoner Labor,* table 3, pp. 64–65; Kaienburg, *Vernichtung durch Arbeit,* p. 229, note 9.

57. Orth, *Das System,* pp. 97–106.

58. Georg Lorner to Heinrich Himmler, September 14, 1940, IMT, NO-369; Allen, *The Business of Genocide,* pp. 117–121; Schulte, *Zwangsarbeit,* pp. 382–396.

59. Report of Waldemar Hoven, July 15, 1941, IMT (Pohl trial), NO-2367.

60. Ibid.

61. Allen, *The Business of Genocide,* p. 121; Orth, *Die Konzentrationslager-SS,* pp. 189–191. Koch and his wife gained notoriety for their extreme brutality toward prisoners in Buchenwald after his appointment as commandant in 1937. Despite all the reports about Koch's conduct, Himmler and Glücks refrained from deposing him until early 1942. *Justiz und NS-Verbrechen,* vol. VIII (Amsterdam: Amsterdam University Press, 1972), pp. 40–41; *Buchenwald: Mahnung und Verpflichtung—Dokumente und Berichte* (Berlin Ost: Deutscher Verlag der Wissenschaft, 1983), pp. 82ff.

62. Henry Friedlander, *The Origins of Nazi Genocide: From Euthanasia to the Final Solution* (Chapel Hill: University of North Carolina Press, 1995), pp. 142, 147–148.

63. Allen, *The Business of Genocide,* pp. 124–126; Robert Jay Lifton, *The Nazi Doctors: Medical Killing and the Psychology of Genocide* (New York: Basic Books, 1986), pp. 137–144. On the central role of the euthanasia team and the camp physicians in the 14f13 murders, see Peter Chroust, "Selected Letters of Doctor Friedrich Mennecke," in Götz Aly, Peter Chroust, and Christian Pross, *Cleansing the Fatherland: Nazi Medicine and Racial Hygiene* (Baltimore: Johns Hopkins University Press, 1994), pp. 238–295; Friedlander, *The Origins of Nazi Genocide,* pp. 144–150.

64. Friedrich Mennecke to his wife, November 26, 1941, in Chroust, "Selected Letters of Doctor Friedrich Mennecke," p. 254.

65. Isabell Sprenger, *Groß-Rosen: Ein Konzentrationslager in Schlesien* (Cologne: Böhlau Verlag, 1996), p. 217; Allen, *The Business of Genocide,* pp. 125–126.

66. Arthur Liebehenschel to concentration camp commandants, December 10, 1941, IMT (Pohl trial), PS-1151.

67. Richard Glücks to concentration camp commandants, April 27, 1943, IMT, PS-1933.

68. Oswald Pohl to Heinrich Himmler, January 19, 1942, IMT (Pohl trial), NO-495; Schulte, *Zwangsarbeit,* pp. 197–208; Kaienburg, *Die Wirtschaft,* pp. 403–409.

69. Piper, *Auschwitz Prisoner Labor,* pp. 36–37.

70. Karel C. Berkhoff, *Harvest of Despair: Life and Death in Ukraine under Nazi Rule* (Cambridge, MA: Belknap Press of Harvard University Press, 2004), pp. 253–268; Wendy Lower, *Nazi Empire-Building and the Holocaust in Ukraine* (Chapel Hill: University of North Carolina Press, 2005), pp. 122–126; Ulrich Herbert, "Labour and Extermination: Economic Interests and the Primacy of *Weltanschauung* in National Socialism," *Past and Present* 138 (1993): 167.

71. Testimony of Oswald Pohl, Pohl trial: Yad Vashem Archives (hereafter YVA), N4/Proc/E, box 223, pp. 1338–1340.

72. Berkhoff, "The 'Russian' Prisoners of War," pp. 1–32.

73. Pavel Polian, "La violence contre les prisoniers de guerre soviétiques dans le IIIᵉ Reich et en USSR," in Stéphane Audoin-Rouzeau, Annette Becker, Christian Ingrao, and Henry Rousso, eds., *La Violence de guerre 1914–1945* (Brussels: Éditions Complexe, IHTP-CNRS, 2002), p. 121.

74. Heinrich Himmler to Richard Glücks, January 26, 1942, IMT (Pohl trial), NO-500.

75. Christian Gerlach, "The Wannsee Conference, the Fate of German Jews, and Hitler's Decision in Principle to Exterminate All European Jews," in Omer Bartov, ed., *The Holocaust: Origins, Implementations, Aftermath* (London: Routledge, 2000), pp. 111–119.
76. Oswald Pohl to Heinrich Himmler, April 30, 1942, IMT (Pohl trial), R-129.
77. Schulte, *Zwangsarbeit,* pp. 206–207; Alexander Lasik, "The Auschwitz SS Garrison," in Długoborski and Piper, *Auschwitz 1940–1945* vol. I, p. 299. On manpower problems and ways of recruiting workers for the concentration camps, see Gudrun Schwartz, "SS-Aufseherinnen in nationalsozialistischen Konzentrationslagern (1933–1945)," *Dachauer Hefte* 10 (November 1994): 32–49.
78. Oswald Pohl, September 30, 1943, IMT (Pohl trial), PS-1469.
79. Oswald Pohl to Heinrich Himmler, IMT (Pohl trial), PS-1469.
80. Oswald Pohl to concentration camp commandants, April 31, 1942, IMT (Pohl trial), R-129.
81. Orth, *Die Konzentrationslager-SS,* pp. 213–214; Allen, *The Business of Genocide,* pp. 177–179.
82. Oswald Pohl to Heinrich Himmler, September 11, 1942, IMT, NI-15392.
83. From minutes of discussion of heads of the Committee for Planning the War Economy with Hitler, September 21–22, 1942, IMT, R-124.
84. Rainer Fröbe, "Hans Kammler: Technokrat der Vernichtung," in Ronald Smelser and Enrico Syring, eds., *Die SS: Elite unter dem Totenkopf. 30 Lebensläufe* (Paderborn: Ferdinand Schöningh, 2000), pp. 306–310.
85. Deposition of Gerhard Maurer, July 3, 1947, IMT (Pohl trial), Defense Exhibit 15; deposition of Gerhard Maurer, May 22, 1947, IMT (Pohl trial), Defense Exhibit 2; Orth, *Das System,* pp. 162–165; Schulte, *Zwangsarbeit,* pp. 205–207; Allen, *The Business of Genocide,* pp. 183–187.
86. Testimony of Oswald Pohl, Pohl trial, minutes, YVA, N4/Proc/E, box 223, p. 1498; deposition of Gerhard Maurer, May 22, 1947, Defense Exhibit 2.
87. Circular from Albert Speer, October 7, 1944, IMT, NI-638; testimony of Karl Sommler, Maurer's deputy in D-11 and Acting Head from January 1945, Pohl trial, minutes, YVA, N4/Proc/E, box 226, pp. 3689–3691.
88. Danuta Czech, *Auschwitz Chronicle, 1939–1945* (New York: Henry Holt & Co., 1990), pp. 261–262.
89. Herbert, "Labour and Extermination," p. 173.
90. Richard Glücks to physicians and commandants of concentration camps, December 21, 1942, in Reimund Schnabel, *Macht ohne Moral: Eine Dokumentation über die SS* (Frankfurt am Main: Rödeberg Verlag, 1957), p. 223.
91. Sofsky, *The Order of Terror,* pp. 36, 43.
92. Piper, *Auschwitz Prisoner Labor,* p. 49.
93. Ibid., pp. 41, 49; Schulte, *Zwangsarbeit,* p. 402; Sofsky, *The Order of Terror,* p. 36.
94. Piper, *Auschwitz Prisoner Labor,* p. 225; Orth, *Das System,* p. 237.
95. About 15 percent of the prisoners were employed in camp maintenance and various service tasks, and 20 to 25 percent were considered unfit for work. The rest were divided among the SS industrial concerns, the large building projects, and the private firms that produced for the armaments industry: report of D-II on employment of prisoners in camps from 1942 to 1944, February 24, 1944, IMT, NO-576; Herbert, *Labour and Extermination,* p. 164.

96. Speer, *Inside the Third Reich*, pp. 280–291.
97. Ian Kershaw, *Hitler 1936–1945: Nemesis* (New York: W. W. Norton, 2000), pp. 620–623.
98. Report by Oswald Pohl on the number of prisoners employed in the military aviation industry and accompanying projects, February 21, 1944; Heinrich Himmler to Hermann Goering, March 7, 1944, IMT, PS-1584 (111).
99. Testimony of Oswald Pohl, Pohl trial, minutes, p. 1352.
100. Jens-Christian Wagner, "Noch einmal: Arbeit und Vernichtung. Häftlingseinsatz im KL Mittelbau-Dora 1943–1945," in Norbert Frei, Sybille Steinbacher, and Bernd C. Wagner, eds., *Ausbeutung, Vernichtung, Öffentlichkeit: Neue Studien zur nationalsozialistischen Lagerpolitik* (Munich: Institut für Zeitgeschichte, K. G. Sauer, 2000), p. 11.
101. Albert Speer, *The Slave State: Heinrich Himmler's Masterplan for SS Supremacy* (London: Weidenfeld & Nicolson, 1981), p. 208.
102. André Sellier, *A History of the Dora Camp* (Chicago: Ivan R. Dee, 2003), pp. 45–46; Jens-Christian Wagner, *Produktion des Todes: Das KZ Mittelbau-Dora* (Göttingen: Wallstein Verlag, 2001), pp. 184–187, 647 (table 5); Allen, *The Business of Genocide,* pp. 213–216.
103. Wagner, *Produktion des Todes,* pp. 189–190.
104. On working conditions in the tunnels, see Wagner, *Production des Todes,* pp. 362–367.
105. Testimony of Josef Urbany, January 6, 1947, National Archives and Records Administration (hereafter NARA), M-1079, reel 2, target 3.
106. Testimony of Yudke Wasserman, June 2, 1947, NARA, M-1079, reel 2, target 1.
107. Testimony of Mordechai Rothschild, December 24, 2001, YVA, 03/1102.
108. Wagner, "Noch einmal," p. 12.
109. Wachsmann, *Looking into the Abyss,* pp. 263–264.
110. Testimony of Edwin Katzen-Ellenbogen, March 1, 1947, IMT, NO-2326; Fröbe, "Hans Kammler," p. 317.
111. Report of Reich Ministry of Justice on a meeting concerning the transfer to the SS of prisoners classified as antisocial in October 1942, IMT (The Justice Case), PS-662; letter of Otto Thierack to Martin Bormann, October 13, 1942, IMT (The Justice Case), NG-558; Nikolaus Wachsmann, "'Annihilation through Labor': The Killing of State Prisoners in the Third Reich," *Journal of Modern History* 71:3 (1999): 630–636.
112. Richard Glücks to concentration camp commandants, May 7, 1944, IMT (Pohl trial), NO-1558.
113. This was the situation, for example, in dozens of forced labor camps for Jews in Lublin district in 1940–1941. See David Silberklang, "HaShoah BeMakhoz Lublin" [The Holocaust in Lublin District], (PhD diss., The Hebrew University of Jerusalem, 2003), p. 92; Dieter Pohl, "Die großen Zwangsarbeitslager der SS und Polizeiführer für Juden im Generalgouvernement 1942–1945," in Herbert, Orth, and Dieckmann, *Die nationalsozialistischen Konzentrationslager,* vol. I, pp. 415–438; Wolf Gruner, *Jewish Forced Labor under the Nazis: Economic Needs and Racial Aims, 1938–1944* (New York: Cambridge University Press, 2006), pp. 230–275; Józef

Marszałek, *Obozy Pracy w Generalnym Gubernatorstwie w latach 1939–1945* (Lublin: Państwowe Muzeum na Majdanku 1998); Speer, *The Slave State,* pp. 328–329.

114. Bradley F. Smith and Agnes F. Peterson, eds., *Heinrich Himmler Geheimreden 1933 bis 1945* (Frankfurt on Main: Propyläen Verlag, 1974), p. 203.

115. Czech, *Auschwitz Chronicle,* pp. 632, 641, 642, 643, 647, 648, 655, 665, 666, 673.

116. Christian Gerlach and Götz Aly, *Das letzte Kapitel* (Stuttgart: Deutsche Verlags-Anstalt, 2002), p. 441.

117. Czech, *Auschwitz Chronicle,* pp. 627, 654, 664, 687; Serge Klarsfeld, *Le Calendrier de la Persécution des Juifs en France 1940–1944* (Paris: S. Klarsfeld, 1993), p. 1124; Gerlach and Aly, *Das letzte Kapitel,* p. 275.

118. Gliński, "Organizacja obozu," p. 114; Sprenger, *Groß-Rosen,* pp. 134–135.

119. *Unterteilung in Altersstufen im Konzentrationslager Weimar-Buchenwald,* December 30, 1944, YVA, JM/3864, p. 59; Hans Stein, "Funktionswandel des Konzentrationslagers Buchenwald im Spiegel der Lagerstatistiken," in Herbert, Orth, and Dieckmann, *Die nationalsozialistischen Konzentrationslager,* vol. I, p. 184.

120. Gerhard Maurer to Buchenwald command, December 16, 1944, YVA, JM/10.031, reel 2, target 2.

121. Testimony of Oswald Pohl, Pohl trial, minutes, p. 1433.

122. Zofia Leszczyńska, "Transporty więźniów chorych i kalek przeniesonych z obozu konczentracyjnego Dachau na Majdanek 7 stycnia 1944 roku," *Zeszyty Majdanka* 10 (1980): 136; Leszczyńska, "Transporty więźniów do obozu koncentrancyjnym Majdanku," *Zeszyty Majdanka* 4 (1969): 203–208.

123. Eberhard Kolb, *Bergen Belsen: Geschichte des "Aufenthaltslagers" 1943–1945* (Hanover: Verlag für Literatur und Zeitgeschehen, 1962), pp. 104–112; Alexandra-Eileen Wenke, *Zwischen Menschenhandel und "Endlöung": Das Konzentrationslager Bergen-Belsen* (Paderborn: Ferdinand Schöningh, 2000), pp. 338–351.

2. The Circumstances of Evacuation

1. Ruth Bettina Birn, *Die Höheren SS-und Polizeiführer: Himmlers Vertreter im Reich und in den besetzen Gebieten* (Düsseldorf: Droste Verlag, 1986), pp. 162–166, 168–185. For brief biographies of members of this special group of officers, see pp. 330–349.

2. Silberklang, "HaShoah BeMakhoz Lublin," pp. 133–137; Bogdan Musial, *Deutsche Zivilverwaltung und Judenverfolgung im Generalgouvernement: Eine Fallstudie zum Distrik Lublin 1939–1945* (Wiesbaden: Harrassowitz, 1999), pp. 201–208; Joseph Poprzeczny, *Odilo Globocnik: Hitler's Man in the East* (Jefferson, NC: McFarland & Co., 2004), pp. 144ff.; Allen, *The Business of Genocide,* pp. 135–139.

3. Dieter Pohl, *Nationalsozialistische Judenverfolgung in Ostgalizien 1941–1944* (Munich: R. Oldenbourg, 1997), pp. 83–93. Katzmann wrote a detailed report in June 1943 on "the solution of the Jewish problem in Galicia": Friedrich

Katzmann, *Lösung der Judenfrage im Distrikt Galizien* (Warsaw: Instytut Pamięci Narodowej, 2001).

4. *The Reports of Jürgen Stroop Concerning the Uprising in the Ghetto of Warsaw and the Liquidation of the Jewish Residential Area* (Warsaw: Jewish Historical Institute, 1958).

5. Himmler to senior SS officers, June 21, 1944, IMT, PS-3683; see also Kolb, *Bergen Belsen,* pp. 299–307.

6. Daniel Blatman, "The Death Marches, January–May 1945: Who Was Responsible for What?" *Yad Vashem Studies* 28 (2000): 155–161.

7. Neander, "Das Konzentrationslager 'Mittelbau,' " pp. 91–92.

8. Testimony of Rudolf Höß, April 15, 1946, IMT, vol. XI, p. 407.

9. Deposition of Gerhard Mauser, July 3, 1947, IMT (Pohl trial), Defense Exhibit 15.

10. Testimony of Wilhelm Burger, minutes of the Polish Military Mission for Investigation of War Crimes in Europe, October 9, 1947, YVA, JM/3936, Akt. 2220, p. 1.

11. Testimony of Oswald Pohl, Pohl trial, minutes, YVA, N4/Proc/E, box 223, pp. 1341–1342.

12. Oswald Pohl to Heinrich Himmler, April 5, 1944, IMT (Pohl trial), NO-021.

13. Ibid.

14. Piotr Weiser, "Transport z Majdanku do Groß-Rosen 6 kweitnia 1944 roku," *Zeszyty Majdanka* 27 (2003): 246.

15. Heinrich Himmler to Oswald Pohl, May 9, 1944, IMT (Pohl trial), NO-021.

16. Zofia Leszczyńska and Edward Dziadosz, "Ewakuacja obozy i wyzwolenie," in Tadeusz Mencla, ed., *Majdanek 1941–1944* (Lublin: Wydawnictwo Lubelskie, 1991), p. 399.

17. Strzelecki, *The Evacuation,* pp. 29–32.

18. Oswald Pohl to Heinrich Himmler, May 9, 1944, IMT (Pohl trial), NO-021; Martin Gilbert, *Auschwitz and the Allies: How the Allies Responded to the News of Hitler's Final Solution* (London: Michael Joseph/Rainbird, 1981), p. 307.

19. Gunther Kimmel, "Zum Beispiel: Tötungsverbrechen in nationalsozialistischen Konzentrationslagern," in Adalbert Röückel, ed., *NS-Prozesse: Nach 25 Jahren Straverfolgung: Möglichkeiten-Grenzen-Ergebnisse* (Karlsruhe: Verlag C. F. Müller, 1971), pp. 116–120.

20. Strzelecki, *The Evacuation,* p. 30; Sprenger, *Groß-Rosen,* pp. 292–293.

21. The prosecution at Nuremberg assumed that WB stood for Westbund—namely, the Western Allies. Bierkamp emphasized that leaving prisoners alive should not be permitted even if they were about to be liberated by the Western powers. IMT, vol. III, pp. 572–573.

22. Walter Bierkamp to Thiel, July 21, 1944, IMT, O-053.

23. See Felicja Karay, *Death Comes in Yellow: Skarżysko-Kamienna Slave Labor Camp* (Amsterdam: Harwood Academic Publishers, 1996), pp. 224–228; Christopher R. Browning, *Collected Memories: Holocaust History and Postwar Testimony* (Madison: University of Wisconsin Press, 2003), pp. 60, 74–76.

24. Gerhard L. Weinberg, *A World at Arms: A Global History of World War II,* new ed. (New York: Cambridge University Press, 2005), pp. 674–675.

25. Krystyna Marczewska and Władysław Ważniewski, "Obóz koncentracyjny na Majdanku w świetle akt Delegatura Rządu RP na Kraj," *Zeszyty Majdanka* 20 (1999): 216–218. The Delegatura reports mention a transport of 500 prisoners taken to Oranienburg and transports sent to the labor camp at Treblinka and to Gusen in Austria. Prisoners evacuated from Majdanek did not reach those camps.

26. Landsgericht Düsseldorf Urteil Hackmann u.a XV11 1/75S (Majdanek trial) YVA, P.26/166 (1), p. 73.

27. Ludwik Christians, *Piekło XX Wieku: Zbrodnia, hart ducha i miłosierdzie* (Warsaw: Katolockie Towarzystwo Wydawnicze "Rodzia Polska," 1946), pp. 178–186; Leszczyńska and Dziadosz, "Ewakuacja obuzo i wyzwolenie," pp. 400–402; Weiser, "Transport z Majdanku," pp. 245–259.

28. See route of this evacuation: *Death Marches (Marches de la Mort), Routes and Distances*, UNRRA (Central Tracing Bureau), May 26, 1946, vol. II, YVA, 018/276, p. 23 (hereafter *Death Marches*, UNRRA/Arolsen II).

29. Leszczyńska and Dziadosz, "Ewakuacja obuzo i wyzwolenie," pp. 404–405.

30. Strzelecki, *The Evacuation*, pp. 78–82.

31. Czech, *Auschwitz Chronicle*, p. 695.

32. In August 1944, when the systematic evacuation of the camp prisoners to other camps began, there were 130,000 prisoners in Auschwitz. At the start of the final evacuation in January 1945 they numbered 60,000; see Strzelecki, *The Evacuation*, pp. 82–83.

33. Oswald Pohl to Heinrich Himmler, April 5, 1944. IMT (Pohl trial), NO-020(a).

34. Alfred Streim, "Konzentrationslager auf dem Gebiet der Sowjetunion," *Dachauer Hefte* 5 (November 1989): 174–176; Yitzhak Arad, *Toldot HaShoah: Berit HaMoatsot VehaShtakhim HaMesupakhim* [The history of the Holocaust: The Soviet Union and the annexed territories], vol. II (Jerusalem: Yad Vashem, 2004), pp. 581–582; M. Dworzecki, *Makhanot HaYehudim BeEstonyah 1942–1944* [The Jewish camps in Estonia, 1942–1944] (Jerusalem: Yad Vashem, 1970), pp. 64–68, 72–84.

35. Leib Garfunkel, *Kovna HaYehudit BeKhurbanah* [The destruction of Jewish Kovno] (Jerusalem: Yad Vashem, 1959), pp. 191–192.

36. Yaakov Werwovski, "Die Likwidatsye fun Kovner Geto" [The liquidation of Kovno ghetto], August 15, 1945, YVA, M-11/114.

37. "Kovner Geto," testimony of Chaya Pikalzhik, July 14, 1947, M-1/E 1275; testimony of Mordechai Zuckerman, July 20, 2000, YVA, 03/11932.

38. Testimony of Adi Rabon (Porotzky), May 26, 1998, YVA, 03/10776.

39. Testimony of Raya Reichman, May 28, 1945, YVA, M-49E/216; testimony of Dov Zanotzky, January 7, 2002, YVA, 03/12087; testimony of Mina Shafir, May 1, 2003, YVA, 03/12254.

40. Testimony of Esther Harari, October 20, 1995, YVA, 03/9169; testimony of Rivka Politansky, October 29, 2002, YVA, 03/12201; testimony of Moshe Metzkewicz, September 13, 1999, YVA, 03/11942.

41. Testimony of Moshe Polansky, January 7, 1997, YVA, 03/9953.

42. Werwovski, "Die Likwidatsye fun Kovner Geto."

43. Yosef Gar, *Umkum fun der yiddisher Kovne* [The annihilation of Jewish Kovno] (Munich: Farband fun litwishe yidden in der amerikaner zone in Daytshland, 1948).

44. Christoph Dieckmann, "Das Ghetto und das Konzentrationslager in Kaunas 1941–1944," in Herbert, Orth, and Dieckmann, *Die nationalsozialistischen Konzentrationslager,* vol. I, p. 458; Streim, *Konzentrationslager,* p. 183; Edith Raim, *Die Dachauer KZ-Außenkommandos Kaufering und Mühldorf: Rüstungs-bauten und Zwangsarbeit im letzen Kriegsjahr 1944/45* (Landsberg: Martin Neu-meyer, 1992), pp. 178–179; Gliński, "Organizacja obozu," p. 114; Drywa, *Zagłada żydów,* p. 380.

45. Arad, *Toldot HaShoah,* vol. II, pp. 577–580; Andrew Ezergailis, *The Holocaust in Latvia, 1941–1944* (Riga: Historical Institute of Latvia and the United States Holocaust Memorial Museum, 1996), p. 263; Josef Katz, *One Who Came Back: The Diary of a Jewish Survivor* (New York: Herzl Press, 1973), pp. 140, 149.

46. Testimony of Luba Melekh, July 4, 1995, YVA, 03/8574; testimony of Abraham Shupungin, November 13, 1992, U.S. Holocaust Memorial Museum Archives (hereafter USHMMA), RG-50.120#148.

47. Testimony of Agnes Kreizler, January 15, 1958, YVA, 03/792.1

48. Testimony of Yaakov Efrat, December 1991, YVA 02/851; Abraham Shupungin, "The Terrors of Dundaga," in Gertrude Schneider, ed., *The Unfinished Road: Jewish Survivors of Latvia Look Back* (New York: Praeger, 1991), p. 159; Katz, *One Who Came Back,* p. 163.

49. Ezergailis, *The Holocaust in Latvia,* pp. 368–369.

50. Testimony of Abraham Shupungin, November 13, 1991, USHMMA, RG-50.120#148.

51. Ibid.

52. Adam Rutkowski, "Le camp de concentration pour Juifs á Varsovie (19 Juillet 1943–5 août 1944)," *Le Monde Juif* 119 (1985): 90.

53. Edward Kossoy, "The Gęsiówka Story: A Little Known Page of Jewish Fighting History," *Yad Vashem Studies* 32 (2004): 327–330.

54. Memoirs of Oscar Paserman, 1945, YVA, M-49E/2919.

55. Rutkowski, "Le camp de concentration pour Juifs," p. 94.

56. Testimony of Yaakov Levi, March 1988, YVA, 03/4536; testimony of Yosef Shi-bak, August 21, 1996, YVA, 03/10154; testimony of Shabtai Hanuka, July 15, 1991, YVA, 03/6433; Max Mannheimer, *Yoman Meukhar, Theresienstadt, Auschwitz, Varsha, Dachau* [A late diary, Theresienstadt, Auschwitz, Warsaw, Dachau] (Tel Aviv: Moreshet VeSifriyat Poalim, 1987), p. 60.

57. Edward Kossoy, "Gęsiówka (KZ Warschau)," *Zeszyty Historyczne* 110 (1994): 66.

58. Memoirs of Oscar Paserman, 1945; Rutkowski, "Le camp de concentration pour Juifs," pp. 91–92.

59. Testimony of Yehiel Daniel, May 30, 1995, YVA, 03/9991.

60. Testimony of Azriel Glick, July 5, 1996, YVA, 03/9327; Mannheimer, *Yoman Meukhar,* p. 62.

61. Testimony of Yosef Shibak, August 21, 1996; testimony of Yehiel Daniel, May 30, 1995; testimony of Yosef Rosenfeld, October 12, 1997, YVA, 03/10464.

62. Testimony of Shabtai Hanuka, July 15, 1991; testimony of Yaakov Sides, June 1986, YVA 03/6209.

63. Kossoy, "The Gęsiówka Story," pp. 329–330.

64. Ibid.; Rutkowski, "Le camp de concentration pour Juifs," p. 97.

65. Testimony of Yaakov Sides, June 1986.

66. Testimony of Yaakov Levi, March 1988.

67. Testimony of Pinkhas Greenburg, July 2, 1995, YVA, 03/8492; memoirs of James Bachner, YVA, 033/4255.

68. Testimony of Yosef Shibak, August 21, 1996; see also testimony of Zalman-Moshe Yavnelovitz, June 21, 1996, YVA, 03/9324; memoirs of James Bachner; Mannheimer, *Yoman Meukhar*, p. 67.

69. Testimony of Pinkhas Greenburg, July 2, 1995.

70. Memoirs of Noé Vilner, July 28, 1952, YVA, 033/131, p. 8.

71. Testimony of Yosef Shibak, August 21, 1996; testimony of Yosef Rosenfeld, October 12, 1997.

72. Testimony of Herman Kremer, July 21, 1945, YVA, 015E/530. See also Mannheimer, *Yoman Meukhar*, p. 68.

73. Kossoy, "The Gęsiówka Story," pp. 330–331.

74. Yehuda Deutsch, *Bor, Sakhar Avadim BeMilkhemet HaOlam HaShniya* [Bor, slave labor in the Second World War] (Netanya, Israel: Rachel Publishing House, 1998), p. 77.

75. Testimony of Kariel Gardosh, May 7, 1993, USHMMA, RG-50.120#0046.

76. Randolph L. Braham, *The Hungarian Labor Service System 1939–1945* (New York: Columbia University Press, 1977), p. 55; Deutsch, *Bor*, pp. 80–83.

77. Testimony of Willi Potesman, May 17, 1988, YVA, 03/4552.

78. Nathan Eck, "The March of Death from Serbia to Hungary (September 1944) and the Slaughter of Csrevenka," *Yad Vashem Studies* 2 (1958): 275–279. In November 1957, 680 corpses were removed from the mass grave in Csrevenka and reburied in the neighboring Jewish cemetery; see Deutsch, *Bor*, p. 130, note 41.

79. Testimony of Kariel Gardosh, May 7, 1993; Braham, *The Hungarian Labor Service*, p. 58; Zvi Erez, "Jews for Copper: Jewish-Hungarian Labor Service Companies in Bor," *Yad Vashem Studies* 28 (2000): 276–278.

80. Testimony of Shlomo Atzmon, December 16, 1997, YVA, 03/10560; Deutsch, *Bor*, pp. 97–104; Erez, "Jews for Copper," pp. 280–283.

81. Testimony of Kariel Gardosh, May 7, 1993.

82. Robert Steegman, *Struthof: Le KL-Natzweiler et ses Kommandos: Une rébule-use concentrationnaire des deux côtés du Rhin, 1941–1945* (Strasbourg: Nuée Bleue, 2005), pp. 44, 66; see also attached maps, pp. 288ff.

83. Deposition of Yosef Kramer, Natzweiler-Struthof commandant until May 1944, July 23, 1945; report on prisoner mortality at Natzweiler-Struthof, June 1–30, 1944, USHMMA, RG-04.030M, reel 1.

84. Steegman, *Struthof*, pp. 159–160.

85. Appendix to report of Natzweiler-Struthof commandant on the camp system and the prisoners, September 30, 1944, USHMMA, RG-04.030M, reel 1.

86. The prisoners who arrived from Dachau were sent to Barbe and Dautmergen. Ibid.

87. Déclaration de 5 Déportes revenant de Natzweiler-Neckargerach, Archives Nationales, Paris (hereafter AN), 72 AJ 318.

88. *Death Marches,* UNRRA/Arolsen II, p. 21.

89. Déposition d-un ancien détenu luxembourgois, July 10, 1946, AN, 72 AJ 377.

90. Eliezer Schwartz, "Yehudim KeOvdey Kefiya BaTaasiya HaBitchonit BeShitchey HaReich: HaMikre Shel Thil VeKochendorf (1944–1945)" [Jewish forced labor in the German armaments industry: A case study of Thil and Kochendorf (1944–1945)], *Dapim, Studies on the Holocaust* 23 (2009): 55–57.

91. Déposition de deux civils allemands enregistré par le Service américain des tombes militaires à Schwabisch Hall, February 24, 1946, AN, 72 AJ 377.

92. Steegmann, *Struthof,* pp. 166–167.

93. Déclaration de Hamlin Lucien de Talstein, déclaration de Lorenz Stach, témoignage de Christian Bouyer, September 25, 1952, témoignage de Louis Kaizer, May 12, 1957, AN, 72 AJ 338–340.

94. On the history of the camp, see Gedenksättte Schwäbisch-Hessental, http://www.kz-hessental.de/Ge_fr.htm (accessed May 15, 2007).

95. Schwarz, "Yehudim KeOvdey Kefiya," p. 67.

96. Gedenksättte Schwäbisch-Hessental, http://www.kz-hessental.de/Ge_fr.html (accessed March 20, 2009).

97. Claude Thomarat, *Rapport d'activité* (semaines du 19–24 janvier et du 25 janvier au 1er février 1947), February 3, 1947, AN, 72 AJ 325–326, pp. 2–4.

98. Ibid., p. 5.

3. Waves of Violence and Acts of Annihilation

1. Heinz Guderian, *Panzer Leader* (Costa Mesa, CA: The Noontide Press, 1988), p. 382.

2. Omer Bartov, *Hitler's Army: Soldiers, Nazis and War in the Third Reich* (New York: Oxford University Press, 1991), pp. 100–101; Kershaw, *Hitler 1936–1945,* p. 751; Marlis G. Steinert, *Hitler's War and the Germans* (Athens: Ohio University Press, 1977), p. 299; Hugh Trevor-Roper, ed., *Final Entries, 1945: The Diaries of Joseph Goebbels* (New York: G. P. Putnam's Sons, 1978), February 28, March 8, 1945, pp. 4–5, 80, 82.

3. Speer, *Inside the Third Reich,* pp. 421–423; Joachim Fest, *Hitler* (New York: Harcourt Brace Jovanovich, 1974), pp. 724–725.

4. Guderian, *Panzer Leader,* pp. 404–414.

5. Trevor-Roper, *Final Entries,* February 28, 1945, pp. 11–12.

6. "Sowjetische Außenmongolei," Völkische Beobachter (hereafter VB), January 5, 1945.

7. Johannes Steinhoff, Peter Pechel, and Dennis Showalter, eds., *Voices from the Third Reich: An Oral History* (New York: Da Capo Press, 1994), p. 420.

8. Testimony of Tadeusz Marchaj, May 18, 1998, USHMMA, 1998.A.0151.

9. Steinhoff, Pechel, and Showalter, *Voices from the Third Reich,* p. 418.

10. Ibid., p. 420.

11. "Evacuation, Refugees and Displaced Persons in Germany," February 10, 1945, Supreme Headquarters Allied Expeditions Force, NARA, RG-338 (1st Army), box 187, file 383.6, pp. 1–2.

12. British Foreign Office Report, January 26, 1945, TNA, FO 371/46764.
13. Testimony of Esther Konsens, July 1988, YVA, 03/5145.
14. Description of refugee columns that set out from Königsberg in late January 1945, in Kershaw, *Hitler 1936–1945*, p. 762.
15. Testimony of Esther Harari, October 20, 1995, YVA, 03/9169.
16. Catherine Merridale, *Ivan's War: Life and Death in the Red Army, 1939–1945* (New York: Metropolitan Books, 2006), pp. 307–311.
17. Trevor-Roper, *Final Entries*, March 1, 1945, pp. 16–17.
18. "Der bolschewistische Blutskampf, Sowjetische Grausamkeiten im deutschen Osten," VB, February 9, 1945.
19. "Das bolschewistische Grauen," VB, March 4, 1945.
20. Norman M. Naimark, *The Russians in Germany: A History of the Soviet Zone of Occupation, 1945–1949* (Cambridge, MA: Harvard University Press, 1995), pp. 76–77.
21. Ibid., p. 107; Merridale, *Ivan's War*, p. 305.
22. Naimark, *The Russians in Germany*, pp. 72–73.
23. Barbara Johr, "Die Ereignisse in Zahle," in Helke Sander and Barbara Johr, eds., *BeFreier und Befreite: Krieg, Vergewaltigung, Kinder* (Munich: Verlag Antje Kunstmann, 1992), pp. 48, 54–55.
24. Anonymous, *A Woman in Berlin: Eight Weeks in the Conquered City* (New York: Metropolitan Books, 2005), p. 63.
25. Atina Grossman, "A Question of Silence: The Rape of German Women by Occupation Soldiers," *October* 72 (Spring 1995): 55–61; Stuart Liebman and Annette Michelson, "After the Fall: Women in the House of the Hangmen," *October* 72 (Spring 1995): 9; Erich Kuby, *The Russians in Berlin, 1945* (New York: Hill & Wang, 1968), pp. 285–288.
26. Johr, "Die Ereignisse in Zahl," pp. 48, 54–55, 58.
27. Gertrud Koch, "Blood, Sperm, and Tears," *October* 72 (Spring 1995): 33.
28. Merridale, *Ivan's War*, pp. 306, 315–316, 318.
29. This was how the Volkische Beobachter denoted the Red Army troops in East Germany. "Das bolschewistische Grauen," VB, March 4, 1945.
30. Order of Fritz Bracht, December 21, 1944, in Strzelecki, *The Evacuation*, pp. 275–279.
31. Weinberg, *A World at Arms*, pp. 800–801.
32. Testimony of Advocate Kurt Schmidt-Klevenow, who worked at WVHA, Pohl trial, minutes, YVA, box 224, Na/Proc/E, p. 2057. Rudolf Höß put it like this: *"(das) kein gesunder Häftling in einem Lager seines Bereiches Zuruckbleibe"* [that no healthy prisoner remain behind without reporting in any camp]. See Strzelecki, *The Evacuation*, p. 38.
33. Testimony of Hans Schurtz, Höß trial, Archiwum Państwowego Muzeum Auschwitz-Birkenau (hereafter APMAB), Hd/16a, pp. 114–115.
34. Oswald Pohl to the concentration camps in Ostland, January 19, 1945, IMT, NO-2130; testimony of Josef Vogt, Head of Dept. A-IV at WVHA, Pohl trial, minutes, YVA, N4/Proc/E box 225, p. 2855.
35. Testimony of Oswald Pohl, WVHA, Pohl trial, minutes, YVA, N4/Proc/E box 223, p. 1343.

36. Zonik, *Anus Belli,* p. 47.
37. Strzelecki, *The Evacuation,* pp. 121–128.
38. Hans-Peter Messerschmidt, "Bericht über meine KZ-Zeit 1943–1945" [Report on my days in the camp, 1943–1945], June 1945, YVA, 033/1692, pp. 37–38.
39. Strafverfahren gegen Helmrich Heilmann, Josef Kierspel, and Johann Mirbeth, Staatsarchiv Bremen (hereafter StaB), 3 Js 1263/50, vol. XIV, pp. 2942–2944.
40. Testimony of Erwin Forelli, September 19, 1995, USHMMA, RG-50.106#18; memoirs of Hanoch Green, January 1987, YVA, 033/2387, p. 75.
41. Testimony of Henia Frydman, August 7, 1946, David Boder Collection, http://voices.iit.edu/interview.html (accessed February 21, 2010) (hereafter Boder Collection).
42. Testimony of Georg Kaldore, August 31, 1946, Boder Collection.
43. Primo Levi, *If This Is a Man/The Truce* (London: Abacus, 1979), p. 163.
44. Témoignage de Samuel Steinberg, AN, 72 AJ 318–321; Strzelecki, *The Evacuation,* p. 211.
45. Jerzy Fudziński, "Marsz śmierci," APMAB, IZ-27/11, p. 3.
46. Strzelecki, *The Evacuation,* pp. 135–136.
47. Rudolf Höß, *Death Dealer: The Memoirs of the SS Komandant at Auschwitz,* ed. Steven Paskuly (New York: Da Capo Press, 1996), pp. 234–235.
48. Testimony of Hans Schurtz, Höß trial, pp. 114–115.
49. Bella Guterman, *A Narrow Bridge to Life: Jewish Forced Labor and Survival in the Gross-Rosen Camp System, 1940–1945* (New York: Berghagan Books, 2008), pp. 192–193.
50. Testimony of David Wolff, May 8, 1989, YVA, 03/5418.
51. Testimony of Zvi Barlev (Henryk Bleicher), Moreshet Archive (hereafter MA), A.860.
52. Jan Delowicz, *Śladem krwi* (Katowice: Towarzystwo Opieki nad Oświęcimiem, 1995), p. 14.
53. Memoirs of Katerina (Bloch) Feuer, USHMMA, RG-02.209, p. 3.
54. Memoirs of Avram Koren, USHMMA, RG-02.191, p. 100.
55. Testimony of Anna Heilman, August 10, 1994, USHMMA, RG-50.030#258.
56. Philip Müller, *Eyewitness Auschwitz: Three Years in the Gas Chambers* (New York: Stein & Day, 1979), p. 166; Maurice Cling, *Vous qui entrez ici . . . Un enfant à Auschwitz* (Paris: Graphin, 1999), p. 146.
57. "A gruss fun a geheynem," memoirs of Adam Hacohen, YVA, 033/758, p. 31.
58. Testimony of Jeurgen Bassfreund, September 20, 1946, Boder Collection.
59. Testimony of Adolf Heisler, August 27, 1946, Boder Collection.
60. Dr. Haffner (Der Generalstaatsanwalt Kattowitz) an den Herrn Reichsminister der Justiz in Berlin, February 1, 1945, APMAB, D-RF-3/RSHA/160, pp. 45–46.
61. Höß, *Kommandant in Auschwitz,* pp. 140–142.
62. Testimony of Alexander Gertner, August 26, 1946, Boder Collection.
63. Memoirs of Avraham Baruch, January 1965, YVA, 033/1397, p. 31.
64. Beny Wirtzberg, *MiGai HaHariga LeShaar HaGai* [From the valley of death to the valley gateway] (Ramat Gan: Massada, 1967), pp. 72–73.
65. Testimony of Hadassa Marcus, September 13, 1946, Boder Collection.
66. Testimony of Simcha Appelbaum, March 25, 1988, YVA, 03/4561.

67. "A gruss fun a geheynem," p. 32.
68. Testimony of Juergen Bassfreund, September 20, 1946.
69. *Death Marches*, UNRRA/Arolsen II, pp. 9–9a.
70. Delowicz, *Śladem krwi*, p. 23. The report of the Polish legal commission of investigation that examined the mass graves at Leszczyny in late September 1945 noted that 292 corpses of prisoners were found. See Gmina Leszczyny pow. Rybnik, September 29, 1945, USHMMA, RG-15.019M, reel 12, no. 247.
71. See appended map of mass graves uncovered after the war in Delowicz, *Śladem krwi* (appendix).
72. Testimony of Yitzhak Peri, April 25, 1994, YVA, 03/9952.
73. Kwestionariusz o egzekucjach masowych i grobach masowych: Marklowiec, Orzepowice, Wodzisław Śląski, Rybnik, September 29, 1945, USHMMA, RG-15.019M, reel 12, nos. 250, 252, 258, 263.
74. Fudziński, "Marsz śmierci," p. 15.
75. Testimony of Kazimierz Grajewski, May 25, 1970, APMAB, Oświadczenia 81, p. 18.
76. Protokół—oględzin sądowo-lekarskich zwłok ludzkich znalazionych w dole z wapnem niedałeko ruin cegielni w Srarym Bieruniu [*sic*], APMAB, Mat./593–586a, November 3, 1945—June 6, 1946, pp. 8, 12, 16–18.
77. Protokoł—Komisja Lekarsko-Sądowaj odbytej w Kałkowie, November 11, 1947, APMAB, IZ-27/1, p. 17; Ciag Dalszy, March 28, 1946, APMAB, Mat./587–599, pp. 23–28.
78. Fudziński, "Marsz śmierci," pp. 5–7; testimony of Yitzhak Peri, April 25, 1994.
79. Testimony of Rupin Popek, December 11, 1989, APMAB, Oświadczenia 120, pp. 45–46.
80. Häftlinge aus KL. Auschwitz, Miedźana, January 19, 1945, APMAB, Mat./593–596a, p. 44; Gendarmerieposten Wrazlau, January 25, 1945; Gendarmerieposten Dobschikau, January 25, 1945, APMAB, IZ-26/2, pp. 3, 6.
81. Testimony of Gabriel and Suzanna Konieczny, testimony of Emilia Kulas, and testimony of Pavel Niezgoda, 1956, APMAB, IZ-27/11, pp. 52–55; testimony of David Stein, November 24, 1988, YVA, 033/1508, pp. 34–35.
82. Testimony of Jan Bieg, May 25, 1975, APMAB, Oświadczenia 81, p. 12; testimony of Kazimierz Grajewski, May 25, 1970, p. 19.
83. Testimony of Katerina Lubina, May 24, 1975, APMAB, Oświadczenia 81, p. 31.
84. Strafverfahren gegen Hans Stefan Olejak, Ewald Pansegrau, Staatsanwaltschaft beim Landesgericht Aschaffenburg (hereafter SLA), KS 201 Js 19730/76, pp. 17, 47.
85. Ibid., p. 46.
86. Testimony of Yitzhak Grabowsky, July 8, 1993, YVA, 03/7001.
87. Pfutze was commandant of Jaworzno from its establishment in summer 1943 until the evacuation on January 17, 1945. He died in Norway in 1945. Strafverfahren gegen Hans Stefan Olejak, Ewald Pansegrau, p. 22.
88. Ibid., p. 51.
89. Deposition of SS officer Franz-Xavier Krause. See Czech, *Auschwitz Chronicle*, p. 793.
90. Strafverfahren gegen Hans Stefan Olejak, Ewald Pansegrau, pp. 46–47, 52.

91. Ibid., pp. 369–371.
92. Ibid., pp. 5–7.
93. Ibid., pp. 48–49.
94. Ibid., pp. 49–50.
95. For example, the prisoners from the Gliwice subcamps: testimony of Marvin Mermelstein, November 13, 1969, USMHHA, 04/341, p. 7.
96. Testimony of Zeev Burger, February 20, 2002, YVA, 03/11411.
97. Memoirs of Jules Fainzang, USMHHA, 2000.18.
98. Survivors of the death march from Blechhammer to Groß-Rosen estimated that more than 1,500 prisoners perished en route. Testimony of Zeev Burger, February 20, 2002.
99. Testimony of Yitzhak Canetti, April 17, 1990, YVA, 03/5799; testimony of Avraham Hollander, March 14, 1990, YVA, 03/5711.
100. Rapport de Wolf Ernest, April 15, 1945, AN, 72 AJ 318–321, pp. 4–5.
101. Testimony of Yitzhak Salomon, July 20, 1995, USHMMA, RG-50.120#213.
102. Testimony of Shalom Herzberg, May 30, 1993, USHMMA, RG-50.120#64.
103. Testimony of Yitzhak Salomon, July 20, 1995.
104. Rapport de Wolf Ernest, April 15, 1945, p. 6.
105. Franciszek Piper, "Das Nebenlager Blechhammer," *Hefte von Auschwitz* 12 (1971): 37–39; Czech, *Auschwitz Chronicle,* p. 795.
106. Rapport de Wolf Ernest, April 15, 1945, p. 7.
107. Testimony of Yitzhak Canetti, April 17, 1990.
108. Rapport de Wolf Ernest, April 15, 1945, p. 7.
109. Irena Strzelecka and Tadeusz Szymański, "Podobozy Tschechowitz-Bomben-suchkommando i Tschechowitz-Vacuum," *Zeszyty Oświęcimskie* 18 (1983): 206–207; testimony of Erwin Habel, September 27, 1975, Zentrale Stelle der Landesjustizverwaltungen (hereafter ZStL), 402 AR-Z 158/78, vol. I.
110. Testimony of Erwin Habel, September 27, 1975; testimony of Stanislav Latanik, March 3, 1976; summary of investigation of Tschechowitz camp, ZStL, 402 AR-Z 158/78, vol. I; Strzelecka and Szymański, "Podobozy," pp. 218–222.
111. Summary of investigation of Tschechowitz camp.
112. Deposition of Franz Deschauer, YVA, JM/3934, Akt. 1684, pp. 14–15.
113. Trial of Heinrich Niemeyer: prosecutor's statement and accompanying evidence, August 18, 1977, YVA, 04/394. p. 25.
114. Strafverfahren gegen Helmrich Heilmann, Josef Kierspel, Johann Mirbeth, pp. 2944–2945.
115. Testimony of Yitzhak Grabowsky, July 8, 1993.
116. Neander, *Konzentrationslager Mittelbau,* p. 100.
117. On the evacuation route from Auschwitz to Mauthausen, see *Death Marches,* UNRRA/Arolsen II, p. 42.
118. On the evacuation route from Auschwitz to Buchenwald, see ibid., p. 8.
119. For details of the route the prisoners marched from the main camp and subcamps and an estimate of the number murdered during the death march from Auschwitz in the first stage, see Strzelecki, "The Liquidation of the Camp," in Dtugborski and piper, *Auschwitz 1940–1945,* vol. V, pp. 31–33. For a map of

the main evacuation routes from Auschwitz, see Strzelecki, *The Evacuation*, p. 47. For the number of prisoners who arrived from the various camps, see Strzelecki, "The Liquidation of the Camp," Appendix XVIII, p. 322.

120. Alfred Konieczny, "Ewakuacja obozu koncentracyjnego Groß-Rosen w 1945r.," *Acta Universitatis Wratislaviensis: Studia nad Faszyzmem i Zbrodniami Hitlerowskimi* (1975): 165.

121. Guterman, *A Narrow Bridge*, p. 358; Sprenger, *Groß-Rosen*, pp. 169–170.

122. Memoirs of Marcel Dolmaire (written in 1945) about his time in Groß-Rosen after the evacuation from Blechhammer, in the memoirs of Jules Fainzang.

123. Memoirs of Avraham Baruch, January 1965, pp. 34–35.

124. Testimony of Avraham Kimmelmann, August 27, 1946, Boder Collection; testimony of Charles Levin, February 14, 1989, USHMMA, RG-50.002#037; memoirs of Avram Stone, April 1983, USHMMA, RG-02.002#25; memoirs of Avram Korn, USHMMA, RG-02.191; testimony of Avraham Nagari, in Shmuel Rafael, ed., *BeNetivey Sheol: Yehudey Yavan BaShoah, Pirkey Edut* [Along the paths of hell: The Jews of Greece in the Holocaust, testimonies] (Tel Aviv: Institute for Study of Saloniki Jewry and the Association of Greek Death Camp Survivors in Israel, 1988), p. 361.

125. Testimony of Zeev Burger, February 20, 2002.

126. "A gruss fun a geheynem," p. 38.

127. Simon Klein to his brothers, March 12, 1946, USHMMA, RG-10.129.

128. Sprenger, *Groß-Rosen*, p. 293.

129. Guterman, *A Narrow Bridge*, p. 360.

130. Konieczny, "Ewakuacja obozu," p. 168; Sprenger, *Groß-Rosen*, p. 294.

131. Dorota Sula, *Arbeitslager Riese: Filia KL Groß-Rosen* (Wałbrzych: Muzeum Groß-Rosen, 2003), pp. 22–24.

132. Guterman, *A Narrow Bridge*, pp. 378–382; Sula, *Arbeitslager Riese*, pp. 115–118.

133. Guterman, *A Narrow Bridge*, p. 384.

134. Testimony of Indrich Fantl, July 1, 1969, Panstwowe Muzeum, Groß-Rosen (hereafter PMGR), 5903/DP.

135. Testimony of Josef D., May 2, 1945, PMGR, 8020/10/DP; testimony of Josef Y., May 29, 1945, PMGR, 8020/13/DP.

136. Testimony of Amanda Heinrich, May 27, 1945, PMGR, 8020/11/DP.

137. Report on examination of a mass grave uncovered in the Trutnov area, August 30–September 11, 1945, PMGR, 6500/19a/DP.

138. Testimony of Paweł Fantel, June 25, 1969, PMGR, 5903/54/DP; testimony of Jan Alač, October 1, 1971, PMGR, 5903/57/DP; testimony of Tomas Jurek, December 6, 1968, PMGR, 8020/14/DP.

139. Testimony of Josef Konejlem, May 30, 1945, PMGR, 8020/16/DP.

140. Guterman, *A Narrow Bridge*, p. 384.

141. Alfred Konieczny, "Transporty więźniów KL Groß-Rosen do innych obozów koncentracyjnych w latcah 1941–1945," *Acta Universitatis Wratislavienis: Studia nad Faszyzmem i Zbrodniami Hitlerowskimi*(1986): 291.

142. Statement of claim at trial of Johannes Hassebroek, YVA, TR-10/716, pp. 26–28, 58–59.

143. Testimony of Czesław Leśniak, June 14, 1971 and June 1986, PMGR, 99/DP, 2249/DP; testimony of Piotr Pławski, December 12, 1975, PMGR, 111/DP.

144. Testimony of Stanisław Frankowski, March 22, 1971, PMGR, 88/DP; testimony of Władisław Torliński, March 11 and June 2, 1971, PMGR, 88/DP.

145. Testimony of Władisław Torliński, March 11 and June 2, 1971.

146. Strafsache gegen Walter Knop, August 16, 1978, Staatsanwaltschaft beim Landesgericht Köln (hereafter SLK), 40–31/74, pp. 4–7, 9–13.

147. Ibid., pp. 27–28.

148. Ibid., pp. 28–29, 31, 35.

149. Ibid., p. 27.

150. Strafverfahren gegen Erich Assmann, Staatsanwaltschaft beim Landesgericht München II (hereafter SLM), 119 b KS 10/71, pp. 11–13, 16–17.

151. Testimony of Juergen Bassfreund, September 20, 1946.

152. Testimony of Alexander Gertner, August 26, 1946.

153. Mieczysław Mołdawa, *Groß Rosen: Obóz koncentracyjny na Śląsku* (Warsaw: Wydawnictwo Ministerstwa Obrony Narodowej, 1980), p. 28. For a detailed list of the transports from Groß-Rosen to German camps in January–April 1945, see Sprenger, *Groß-Rosen,* pp. 353–359.

154. Testimony of Fani Herschkovicz, July 3, 1945, Bernard Robinson Collection, testimony recorded in Budapest for the Jewish Agency for Palestine (hereafter Budapest testimonies); testimony of Shoshana Reich, March 21, 1963, Dörr trial: exhibits, vol. III, *Staatsanwaltschaft beim Landesgericht Hof,* ZStL, 410 AR 1750/61 2 Js 1325/62, p. 62 (hereafter Dörr trial).

155. Guterman, *A Narrow Bridge,* p. 318; Goldhagen, *Hitler's Willing Executioners,* pp. 332–335.

156. Testimony of Zissele Heidt, May 16, 1945, Dörr trial: exhibits, vol. I, p. 90.

157. Testimony of Bella Krausz, July 18, 1945, Budapest testimonies.

158. Report of Polish commission for investigation of Nazi crimes in Zielona Góra, November 28, 1968, USHMMA, 2000.311.

159. Ibid. After the war another three corpses of women murdered at Stary Jaromiez were found. All 41 corpses were transferred for burial to Kargowa.

160. Deposition of Florjan Drzymała, December 20, 1967, USHMMA, 2000.311.

161. Testimony of Florjan Drzymała, August 4, 1999, USHMMA, 2000.311.

162. Testimony of Monika Fröhlich, December 11, 1967, USHMMA, 2000.311.

163. Deposition of Francziszek Kluj, November 15, 1967; deposition of Jadwiga Kaczmarek, November 7, 1967, USHMMA, 2000.311.

164. Grünberg was the German name of Zielona Góra. File of the investigation of the labor camp for Jewish women at Zielona Góra, PMGR, 234/DP.

165. Report on the manpower quota at Grünberg, November 13, 1944, PMGR, 234/DP.

166. Bella Guterman, ed., *BaLev Baara HaShalhevet: Yomana Shel Fela Szeps, Makhane HaAvoda Grinberg* [A flame burned in her heart: The diary of Fela Szeps, Grunberg labor camp] (Jerusalem: Yad Vashem, 2002), p. 40; testimony of Nina Heller, February 28, 1963, Dörr trial: exhibits, vol. III, p. 34; testimony of Libka Lauber, March 4, 1963, Dörr trial: exhibits, vol. III, p. 43.

167. Goldhagen, *Hitler's Willing Executioners,* p. 334.

168. Testimony of Bella Krausz, July 18, 1945, Budapest testimonies; testimony of Nina Heller, February 28, 1963.
169. Gudrun Schwartz, *Die nationalsozialistischen Lager* (Frankfurt am Main: Fischer, 1996), p. 195.
170. Testimony of Anna Chorzychow, report on manpower quota of Grünberg camp, November 13, 1944, PMGR, 234/DP; report about Grünberg camp of the commission for investigation of Nazi crimes at Zielona Góra, April 22, 1971, PMGR, 234/DP, pp. 6–7.
171. Testimony of Rachel Bustan, MA, A.227; testimony of Julan Komova, July 5, 1945, Budapest testimonies.
172. Testimony of Sári Grunberger, August 22, 1945, Budapest testimonies.
173. Testimony of Margit Feldman, January 30, 1990, USMHHA, RG-50.002#03; testimony of Julan Friedman, July 13, 1945, Budapest testimonies.
174. Testimony of Manya Junger, July 22, 1945, Budapest testimonies.
175. *The Reichmanns of Bielitz: Our European Background,* memoirs of Emilia Robinson (Reichmann) (Los Angeles, 1992), p. 37.
176. Testimony of Golda Ickovitz, August 6, 1945, Budapest testimonies.
177. Testimony of Hanna Kotlicki, March 3, 1963, Dörr trial: exhibits, vol. III, p. 20.
178. Testimony of Halina Klein, July 23, 1987, USHMMA, RG-50.002#87.
179. Testimony of Minna Singer, May 14, 1945, Dörr trial: exhibits, vol. II, p. 84.
180. Testimony of Zissele Heidt, May 16, 1945, pp. 90–91; testimony of Hanna Kotlicki, March 3, 1963, p. 20; testimony of Libka Lauber, March 4, 1963, p. 43; testimony of Masha Jurkowska, March 31, 1963, Dörr trial: exhibits, vol. III, pp. 71–72; testimony of Miriam Freitag, September 4, 1963, Dörr trial: exhibits, vol. III, pp. 112–113.
181. Testimony of Halina Klein, July 23, 1987.
182. Goldhagen, *Hitler's Willing Executioners,* p. 334.
183. Krzysztof Dunin-Wąsowicz, *Obóz koncentracyjny Stutthof* (Gdańsk: Wydawnictwo Morskie, 1970), pp. 34–42; Gliński, "Organizacja obozu," pp. 54–65; *Stutthof: Hitlerowski obóz koncentracyjny* (Warsaw: Wydawnictwo Interpress, 1988), pp. 116–119.
184. Drywa, *Zagłada Żydów,* pp. 83–92. For details of the transports that brought Jewish prisoners to Stutthof in 1944, see Drywa, "Ruch transportów," pp. 29–30.
185. Testimony of Oswald Pohl, Pohl trial: Minutes YVA, N4/Proc/E, Box 223, p. 1343; deposition of Paul Werner Hoppe, August 24, 1946, Archiwum Muzeum Stutthof (hereafter AMS), Z-V-49.
186. Testimony of Esther Harari, October 20, 1995.
187. Drywa, *Zagłada Żydów,* pp. 128–132; *Justiz und NS-Verbrechen,* vol. XIV (Amsterdam: Amsterdam University Press, 1972), pp. 192–194.
188. Circular issued by Fritz Katzmann, January 8, 1945, USHMMA, RG-04.058M, reel 211.
189. Janina Grabowska, *Marsz śmierci: Ewakuacja piesza więźniów KL Stutthof i jego podobozów, 25 Stycznia–3 Maja 1945* (Gdańsk: Muzeum Stutthof w Sztutowie, 1992), p. 13; Gliński, "Organizacja obozu," p. 183.

190. Gliński, "Organizacja obozu," p. 184.

191. Deposition of Paul Werner Hoppe, August 24, 1946, AMS, A-Z-49.

192. Einsatzbefehl No. 3, January 25, 1945, USHMMA, RG-04.058M, reel 209.

193. Report on number of prisoners in Stutthof and subcamps, January 24, 1945, USHMMA, RG-04.058M, reel 223.

194. Ablaufplan, January 25, 1945, USHMMA, RG-04.058M, reel 209.

195. Grabowska, *Marsz śmierci,* pp. 15–16.

196. Deposition of Paul Werner Hoppe, August 24, 1946; Marek Orski, *The Last Days of Stutthof* (Gdańsk: Muzeum Stutthof w Sztutowie, 1995), p. 70.

197. The last remaining prisoners in the camp, about 4,500, were evacuated by sea between April 25 and 27, 1945. Reports on number of prisoners in Stutthof, January 30–April 23, 1945, USHMMA, RG-04.058M, reel 223; Elżbieta Grot, *Rejs Śmierci: Ewakuacja morska więźniów KL Stutthof 1945* (Gdańsk: Muzeum Stutthof w Sztutowie, 1993), p. 22.

198. Drywa, *Zagłada Żydów,* p. 282.

199. Ralys Sruoga, *Forest of the Gods: Memoirs* (Vilnius: Vaga, 1996), pp. 281, 290–291.

200. Testimonies of Guta Lev, July 29, 1968; Bernard Bugun, November 12, 1969; Henrik Libera, November 12, 1969; and Bronislav Gurlej, September 1, 1970, ZStL, 407 AR-Z, 44/7, vol. I.

201. Testimonies of Blanka Szabo, October 26/27, 1961; Leslie Keller, December 10, 1968; and Sara Alter, September 19, 1972, ZStL, 407 AR-Z 51/69, vol. II.

202. Summary of the conclusions of the investigation regarding Hopeehill, September 25, 1972, ZStL, 407 AR-Z, 182/72, vol. I.

203. Summary of conclusions of investigation of Krzemieniewo, November 17, 1972, ZStL, 407, AR-Z 242/72, vol. I.

204. Testimony of Minna Loyfgreben (Michalovsky), MA, A.229.

205. Memoirs of Leah Rozin-Straussman, April 11, 1999, USHMMA, 2000.149.

206. Testimony of Rochel Blackman-Slivka, June 15, 1990, USHMMA, RG-50.030# 216; testimony of Ruth Kenet, August 7, 1984, USHMMA, RG-50.155#03; memoirs of Sonia Heyd-Green, 1992, USHMMA, RG-02.112#01.

207. Testimonies of Fani Englrad, December 29, 1969; Hela Yisrael, July 30, 1968; Raya Abramoff, December 10, 1968; Glicka Tosch, April 6, 1969; and Trude Schloss, October 29, 1969, ZStL, 407 AR-Z 174/72, vol. I.

208. Testimony of Rivka Politansky, October 29, 2002, YVA, 03/12210.

209. Nowe groby więźniów Stutthofu, Pręgowo, November 18, 1947, AMS, Z-V-23; on the evacuation route, see Grabowska, *Marsz śmierci,* pp. 26–27.

210. Ermittlungsverfahren wegen der Ermordung von Juden in Palmnicken/Ostpreußen im Jahre 1945, August 14, 1961, YVA (Kurt Friedrichs Case), TR-10/1327, p. 446 (hereafter Friedrichs trial); report on number of prisoners at Stutthof and subcamps, January 24, 1945, USHMMA, RG-04.058M, reel 223.

211. Testimony of Dina Herzberg, January 10, 1961, YVA, 03/2279; testimony of Bluma Lonitzky, December 22, 1963, in Reinhard Henkys, "Ein Todesmarsch in Ostpreußen," *Dachauer Hefte* 20 (October 2004): 8; testimony of Dora

Houptman, in Shmuel Krakowski, ed., "Massacre of Jewish Prisoners on the Samland Peninsula—Documents," *Yad Vashem Studies* 24 (1994): 365.

212. Testimony of Frieda Kleinman, March 31, 1964, YVA, 03/2348.
213. *Abschlussbericht,* May 27, 1964, Friedrichs trial, p. 1082.
214. Local residents remembered that at the end of January 1945 the temperature dropped to –20°C. Testimony of Elisabet Michaelis, November 14, 1961, Friedrichs trial, p. 526.
215. Testimony of Esther Friedman, December 30, 1963, in Henkys, "Ein Todesmarsch," p. 9.
216. Testimony of Dora Hauptman, in Krakowski, "Massacre of Jewish Prisoners," p. 290; testimony of Frieda Kleinman, March 31, 1964.
217. Ermittlungsverfahren wegen der Ermordung von Juden, Friedrichs trial, p. 446; testimony of Anton Baumeister, Friedrichs trial, p. 265; testimony of Rudolf Johan Folger, January 14, 1961, Friedrichs trial, p. 227.
218. Report by the Head of the Political Directorate Section, 3rd Byelorussian Front, February 8, 1945, in Krakowski, "Massacre of Jewish Prisoners," p. 367.
219. Report of an Investigation Committee of the Red Army on mass graves discovered in a German area, April 17, 1945, in Krakowski, "Massacre of Jewish Prisoners," pp. 369–370.
220. *Abschlussbericht,* May 27, 1964, Friedrichs trial, p. 1082.
221. Testimonies of Emil Gelgau, Heinz Pipereit, and Emil Stahlbaum, May 24–25, 1945, in Krakowski, "Massacre of Jewish Prisoners," pp. 378–381.
222. Testimony of Eckerhard Heil, November 17, 1961, Friedrichs trial, pp. 501–502; testimony of Bruno Schröder, November 27, 1961, Friedrichs trial, p. 537.
223. Henkys, "Ein Todesmarsch," p. 10.
224. Testimony of Anton Baumeister, Friedrichs trial, p. 270.
225. Ermittlungsverfahren wegen der Ermordung von Juden, Friedrichs trial, p. 446; testimony of Elfriede Lison, October 17, 1960, Friedrichs trial, p. 115.
226. Testimony of Adolf Wittke, November 11, 1960, Friedrichs trial, p. 158; testimony of Maria Theodora Arms, May 5, 1961, Friedrichs trial, p. 281; testimony of Christa Weber, May 13, 1961, Friedrichs trial, p. 327.
227. Residents of Palmnicken were convinced that 5,000 Jews were brought there. Testimony of Anna Polleit, September 24, 1960, Friedrichs trial, pp. 40–41.
228. Testimony of Franz Horch, May 6, 1961, Friedrichs trial, p. 291.
229. Testimony of Paul Schilling, November 12, 1960, Friedrichs trial, p. 166.
230. Testimony of Gertrude Kohnke, May 8, 1961, Friedrichs trial, p. 303; testimony of Paul Adolf Schultz, August 29, 1961, Friedrichs trial, p. 342.
231. Testimony of Adolf Wittke, Friedrichs trial, p. 160; testimony of Oskar Laatsch, January 26, 1961, Friedrichs trial, p. 203; testimony of Rudolf Johan Folger, Friedrichs trial, p. 230; testimony of Helene Ziggert, Friedrichs trial, p. 547.
232. Testimony of Frieda Kleinman, March 31, 1964.
233. Testimony of Adolf Wittke; testimony of Rudolf Johan Folger, Friedrichs trial, pp. 159–160, 230.
234. Testimony of Franz Suhr, May 11, 1961, Friedrichs trial, p. 320; testimony of Gunther Bolgen, June 1, 1962, Friedrichs trial, pp. 600–601.

235. Testimony of Martin Bergau, in Krakowski, "Massacre of Jewish Prisoners," p. 281; testimony of Anton Baumeister, Friedrichs trial, p. 269.
236. Testimony of Augusta Hömke, September 15, 1961, Friedrichs trial, p. 414.
237. Henkys, "Ein Todesmarsch," pp. 14–15.
238. Minutes of interrogation of Kurt Friedrichs, June 23, 1961, Friedrichs trial, pp. 367–370.
239. Abschlussbericht, May 27, 1964, Friedrichs trial, p. 1083; Mord im Strafarbeitslager Palmnicken, May 29, 1967, Friedrichs trial, p. 1213; testimony of Frieda Kleinman, November 5, 1946, YVA 03/2348.
240. Henkys, "Ein Todesmarsch," p. 16.
241. Mord im Strafarbeitslager Palmnicken, May 29, 1967, Friedrichs trial, p. 1213.
242. Testimony of Frieda Kleinman, March 31, 1964.
243. Testimony of Celina Manielewicz, November 7, 1958, YVA, 03/1108.
244. Testimony of Frieda Kleinman, November 5, 1946. In the testimony she gave some 20 years later, the description of the murders is slightly different.
245. Testimony of Heinz Pipereit, May 25, 1945, in Krakowski, "Massacre of Jewish Prisoners," p. 380.
246. "On the Atrocities of the Germans against Soviet Citizens in the Township of Kraxtepellen," Head of the Political Directorate Section of the 2nd Army of the Guards, in Krakowski, "Massacre of Jewish Prisoners," pp. 317–372.
247. Testimony of Celina Manielewicz, November 7, 1958; testimony of Frieda Kleinman, March 31, 1964; testimony of Berta Pulwer, February 23, 1962, Friedrichs trial, p. 251; Henkys, "Ein Todesmarsch," p. 18.
248. Abschlussbericht, May 27, 1964, p. 1083; Mord in Strafarbeitslager Palmnicken, May 29, 1967, Friedrichs trial, p. 1213.
249. Orth, Das System, p. 286.

4. Administrative Chaos and the Last Order

1. Testimony of Rudolf Höß, April 15, 1946, IMT, vol. XI, p. 407.
2. Deposition of Rudolf Höß, March 20, 1946, in Orth, Das System, p. 296.
3. Justiz und NS-Verbrechen, vol. XVIII (Amsterdam: Amsterdam University Press, 1978), p. 295.
4. Deposition of Anton Kaindl, July 19, 1946, IMT, NO-1203; Justiz und NS-Verbrechen, vol. XVI (Amsterdam: Amsterdam University Press, 1976), p. 678; interrogation of Anton Kaindl, December 17, 1946, USHMMA, RG-06.025#26, N-19092, vol. I, file 1460, p. 4; Georg Wolff, "Kalendarium der Geschichte des KZ Sachsenhausen-Strafvefolgung," Sachsenhausen 3 (1987): 36.
5. Orth, Das System, p. 297.
6. Franciszek Piper, "The Methods of Mass Murder," in Długoborski and Piper, Auschwitz 1940–1945, vol. III, p. 177.
7. Deposition of Johann Schwarthuber, August 15, 1946, Ravensbrück trial, TNA, WO, 235/309; Germaine Tillion, Ravensbrück (Paris: Seuil, 1988), p. 246; Bernhard Strebel, Das KZ Ravensbrück: Geschichte eines Lagerkomplexes (Paderborn: Ferdinand Schöningh, 2003), p. 569.
8. Nelly Gorce, Journal de Ravensbrück (Arles: Actes Sud, 1995), pp. 103–104.

9. Bernhard Strebel, "Ravensbrück—das zentrale Frauenkonzentrationslager," in Herbert, Orth, and Dieckmann, *Die nationalsozialistischen Konzentrationslager,* vol. I, p. 240.

10. After the war Heißmeyer denied having given an order to evacuate any of the camps under his jurisdiction (Ravensbrück and Sachsenhausen) and was not convicted of having given the order: deposition of August Heißssmeyer, October 22, 1969, ZStL, 406 Ar-Z, 52/67, vol. I.

11. Depositions of Fritz Suhren, December 31, 1945, and July 22, 1946, Ravensbrück trial, TNA, WO 235/310, and deposition of April 1946, IMT, NO-3648; Delia Müller and Madlen Lepschies, *Tage der Angst und der Hoffnung: Erinnerungen an die Todesmarsche aus dem Frauen-Konzentrationslager Ende April 1945* (Berlin: Impressum, 2001), p. 19.

12. Depositions of Dr. Parzifal Triete, May 5, 1945, August 14, 1945, and October 3, 1946, Ravensbrück trial, TNA, WO 235/309.

13. Depositions of Johann Schwarzhuber, August 15 and 30, 1946, Ravensbrück trial, TNA, WO 235/309.

14. Suhren gave a much lower estimate. In his opinion, in the final months no more than 1,500 prisoners were liquidated (deposition of Fritz Suhren, December 30, 1945, IMT, NO-3647). Schwarzhuber referred to 2,300–2,400 (deposition of Johann Schwarzhuber, August 30, 1946, Ravensbrück trial). On the number of prisoners murdered in the camp in the final months, see Erpel, *Zwischen Vernichtung und Befreiung,* p. 75; Strebel, *Das KZ Ravensbrück,* pp. 485–486; Orth, *Das System,* p. 291.

15. Testimony of Dr. Adolf Winkelmann, January 22, 1947, Ravensbrück trial, TNA, WO 235/303, p. 311.

16. Bernard Strebel, "Das Mannerlager im KZ Ravensbrück 1941–1945," *Dachauer Hefte* 14 (1998): 167.

17. Deposition of Johann Schwarzhuber, August 30, 1946, Ravensbrück trial. On extermination in the gas chamber at Ravensbrück in 1945, see Strebel, *Das KZ Ravensbrück,* pp. 476–486.

18. Deposition of Dr. Parzifal Triete, May 5, 1945, Ravensbrück trial.

19. Depositions of Lotte Sontag, August 17, 1947, and Marta-Elizabet Ruthenberg, December 18, 1947, Ravensbrück trial, TNA, WO, 235/516A; Lucia Schmidt-Fels, *Deportation nach Ravensbrück* (Essen: Plöger, 2004), pp. 109–110; Gorce, *Journal de Ravensbrück,* pp. 107, 111.

20. Summary of the findings of the investigation in the trial of three women guards at Uckermark, Ravensbrück trial, the Deputy Judge Advocate General, British Army of the Rhine, May 18, 1948, TNA, WO 235/516A.

21. Deposition of Ruth Closius-Neudeck, December 2, 1947, Ravensbrück trial, TNA, WO 235/516A.

22. Deposition of Dr. Alfred Winkelmann, November 4, 1946, Ravensbrück trial, TNA, WO, 235/310.

23. Deposition of Johann Schwarzhuber, August 15, 1946, Ravensbrück trial.

24. Deposition of Fritz Suhren, December 30, 1945, Ravensbrück trial. After the war, no proof was found that it was Heißssmeyer who gave the order.

25. Deposition of Johann Schwarzhuber, August 15, 1946, Ravensbrück trial.

26. Strebel, *Das KZ Ravensbrück,* p. 477.

27. Deposition of Ruth Closius-Neudeck, December 2, 1947, Ravensbrück trial.

28. *Justiz und NS-Verbrechen,* vol. XVIII, pp. 299–306.

29. Orth, *Das System,* p. 299.

30. Stanislav Zámečník, *C'était ça, Dachau 1933–1945* (Paris: Fondation internationale de Dachau, 2003), pp. 408–409; Michael W. Perry, ed., *Dachau Liberated: The Official Report by the U.S. Seventh Army* (Seattle, WA: Inkling Books, 2000), p. 94.

31. Edgar Kupfer-Koberwitz, *Dachauer Tagebücher: Die Aufzeichnungen des Häftlings 24814* (Munich: Kindler, 1997), pp. 416–419.

32. Zámečník, "Dachau-Stammlager," p. 266.

33. Toni Siegert, "Das Konzentrationslager Flossenbürg: Ein Lager für sogenannte Asoziale und Kriminelle," in Martin Broszat and Elke Fröhlich, eds., *Bayern in der NS-Zeit,* vol. II (Munich: R. Oldenbourg, 1979), pp. 476–477.

34. Hans Maršálek, *The History of Mauthausen Concentration Camp: Documentation* (Linz: Gutenberg-Werbering, 1995), pp. 198–199.

35. Hans Maršálek, *Die Vergasungsaktionen im Konzentrationslager Mauthausen: Dokumentation* (Vienna: Steinde-Druck, 1988, pp. 13–15; Michel Fabréguet, *Mauthausen: Camp de concentration national-socialiste en Autriche rattachée (1938–1945)* (Paris: Champion, 1999), pp. 490–498.

36. David W. Pike, *Mauthausen: L'enfer nazi en Autriche* (Toulouse: Privat, 2004), p. 231.

37. Kaienburg, *Vernichtung durch Arbeit,* pp. 381–382.

38. "A gruss fun a geheynem," pp. 43–44.

39. *Buchenwald Concentration Camp 1937–1945: A Guide to the Permanent Historical Exhibition* (Göttingen: Wallstein Verlag, 2004), p. 224; Kogon, *The Theory and Practice of Hell,* p. 250.

40. On the development of Bergen-Belsen in 1943–1945, see Wenke, *Zwischen Menschenhandel,* pp. 94ff.; Kolb, *Bergen Belsen,* pp. 44ff.

41. Wagner, *Produktion des Todes,* p. 89.

42. Wenke, *Zwischen Menschenhandel,* pp. 338–347; Joanne Reilly, *Belsen: The Liberation of a Concentration Camp* (London: Routledge, 1998), pp. 15–17.

43. Deposition of Josef Kramer, July 23, 1945, USHMMA, RG-04.03M, reel 1.

44. Report of Josef Kramer to Richard Glücks, March 1, 1945, TNA, WO 309/17, in Raymond Phillips, ed., *The Trial of Josef Kramer and Forty-Four Others (The Bergen Trial)* (London: William Hodge & Co., 1949), pp. 164–166.

45. Wenke, *Zwischen Menschenhandel,* p. 362; Reilly, *Belsen,* p. 17.

46. Kolb, *Bergen Belsen,* pp. 9–10.

47. Rezsö Kasztner, *Der Bericht des jüdischen Rettungskomitees aus Budapest 1942–1945* (Budapest: Waad HaEzna VeHaazala, 1946), pp. 173–174.

48. Hanna Levi Hess, "Raav-terror-typhus-rakav-mavet" [Hunger-terror-typhus-rot-death], in Mordekhay Tsanin, ed., *Kakh Zeh Hayah: Dapei Edut shel She'erit HaPleita Yotsei Bergen Belsen* [This is how it was: Testimonies of survivors of Bergen-Belsen] (Tel Aviv: Organization of Survivors from the British Zone, 1987), pp. 144–145.

49. Karl Sommer met with Pohl several times in March–April 1945 and received instructions from him on these matters. Pohl trial, testimony of Karl Sommer, YVA, N4/Proc/E, box 226, p. 3694.

50. Testimony of Oswald Pohl, Pohl trial, minutes, YVA, N4/Proc/E, box 223, p. 1407.
51. Deposition of Rudolf Höß, March 14, 1946, TNA, WO 309/217.
52. Felix Kersten, *The Kersten Memoirs, 1940–1945* (New York: Macmillan, 1957), pp. 279–282.
53. Kasztner, *Der Bericht,* p. 172. In another deposition, from March 8, 1946, Becher claimed that by October 1944 he had in his possession written orders from Himmler to halt the extermination of the Jews. IMT, PS-3672.
54. Steven Koblik, *The Stones Cry Out* (New York: Holocaust Library, 1988), pp. 117ff.; Yehuda Bauer, *Jews for Sale? Nazi-Jewish Negotiations, 1933–1945* (New Haven, CT: Yale University Press, 1994), pp. 246–250; Orth, *Das System,* pp. 301–305.
55. Kersten, *The Kersten Memoirs,* p. 277; Walter Schellenberg, *The Labyrinth: Memoirs of Walter Schellenberg* (New York: Harper & Brothers, 1956), p. 380.
56. Neander, *Konzentrationslager Mittelbau,* pp. 117, 127.
57. Wagner, *Produktion des Todes,* pp. 274–277; Joachim Neander, *"Hat in Europa kein annäherndes Beispiel": Mittelbau-Dora—ein KZ für Hitlers Krieg* (Berlin: Metropol, 2000), p. 137.
58. Trevor-Roper, *Final Entries,* March 27 and 30, 1945, pp. 249, 279.
59. Neander, *Konzentrationslager Mittelbau,* p. 269.
60. Neander, *"Hat in Europa,"* p. 160.
61. Speer, *Inside the Third Reich,* pp. 455–456.
62. Sellier, *History of the Dora Camp,* p. 284.
63. Count Folke Bernadotte, *The Curtain Falls: A Unique Eyewitness Story of the Last Days of the Third Reich as Seen by a Neutral Observer inside Germany* (New York: Knopf, 1945), pp. 52, 86–91.
64. Neander, *"Hat in Europa,"* p. 142.
65. Wagner, *Produktion des Todes,* p. 271.
66. Testimony of Aharon Betsa, January 16, 1992, YVA, 03/6704.
67. Memoirs of Joe Gelber, USHMMA, RG-02.153.
68. Testimony of Pierre Auchabie, in Sellier, *A History of the Dora Camp,* p. 281.
69. Jens-Christian Wagner, "Gesteuertes Sterben: Die Boelke-Kaserne als zentrales Siechenlager KZ Mittelbau," *Dachauer Hefte* 20 (October 2004): 130–132.
70. Wagner, "Gesteuertes Sterben," pp. 285–286; Neander, *Konzentrationslager Mittelbau,* pp. 284–288.
71. Memoirs of Joe Gelber.
72. Peter Kuhlbrodt, ed., *Schicksalsjahr 1945: Inferno Nordhausen: Chronik, Dokumente, Erlebnisberichte,* Schriftenreihe "Heimatgeschichtliche Forschungen des Stadtarchivs Nordhausen/Harz," no. 6 (Nordhausen: Archivder Stadt, 1995), pp. 23–24; Wagner, *Produktion des Todes,* pp. 280–281; Neander, *"Hat in Europa,"* p. 153.
73. René Morel, *Les Derniers Supplices ou Mémoire d'apocalypse* (Oyonnax, France: Solypac, 1998), p. 12.
74. Yves Béon, *Planet Dora: A Memoir of the Holocaust and the Birth of the Space Age* (Boulder, CO: Westview Press, 1997), pp. 197–198, 202–203.

75. Joachim Neander, *Die Letzten von Dora in Gebiet Osterode: Zur Geschichte eines KZ-Evakuierungsmarsches im April 1945* (Nordhausen: Schriftenreihe der KZ-Gedenkstätte Mittelbau-Dora, 1994), pp. 10–16.

76. On the evacuation routes from Nordhausen to Bergen-Belsen, see *Death Marches,* UNRRA/Arolsen II, p. 31.

77. Neander gives a wide and detailed description of the evacuation routes of prisoners from the Mittelbau-Dora complex, the number of evacuees, and the destinations of the transports. See Neander, *"Hat in Europa,"* pp. 164–200.

78. Wagner, "Gesteuertes Sterben," p. 136.

79. Memoirs of James Livesay, USHMMA, RG-09.033; memoirs of William Bracey, USHMMA, RG-09.037.

80. Hans-Peter Messerschmidt, "Bericht über meine KZ-Zeit 1943–1945," June 1945, YVA, 033/1692, p. 45.

81. Reports on prisoner movements at Buchenwald, March 29, April 3, and April 8, 1945, Thüringisches Hauptstaatsarchiv, Weimar (hereafter THW), Buchenwald 4/7/1.

82. NARA, RG-153 (Buchenwald case), box 243, folder 1, p. 7; David A. Hackett, ed., *The Buchenwald Report* (Boulder, CO: Westview Press, 1995), p. 316; Zonik, *Anus belli,* pp. 29–30.

83. Deposition of Hermann Pister, July 2, 1945, IMT, NO-254.

84. Interrogation of Hermann Pister, NARA, RG-153, box 252, p. 14.

85. Ibid., pp. 8–9; deposition of Hermann Pister, July 2, 1945.

86. 12th Army Headquarters Report, April 24, 1945, NARA, RG-226, box 1, folder 6, pp. 3–4; interrogation of Hermann Pister, pp. 8–9; Katrin Greiser, "Die Auflösung des Lagerkomplexes Buchenwald und die Todesmärsche der Außenlager im Rheinland und in Westfalen im März und April 1945," in Jan Erik Schulte, ed., *Konzentrationslager im Rheinland und in Westfalen 1933–1945* (Paderborn: Ferdinand Schöningh, 2005), p. 285.

87. Vojtěch Blodig, "Die letzte Phase der Entwicklung des Ghettos Theresienstadt," in Miroslav Kárný, ed., *Theresienstadt in der "Endlösung der Judenfrage"* (Prague: Panorama, 1992), pp. 267–278; Marek Poloncarz, "Die Evakuierungstransporte nach Theresienstadt (April–Mai 1945)," *Theresienstädter Studien und Dokumente* (1999): 246–248; Hans Günter Adler, *Theresienstadt 1941–1945: Das Antlitz einer Zwangsgemeinschaft* (Tübingen: J. C. B. Mohr, 1960), p. 701.

88. For example, in those weeks, due to Kasztner's intervention, Hungarian Jews in labor camps in Vienna were transferred to Theresienstadt. Eleonore Lappin, "Der Weg ungarischer Juden nach Theresienstadt," *Theresienstädter Studien und Dokumente* (1996): 66–70.

89. OSS Report, August 8, 1945, NARA, RG-153, box 245, folder 5, p. 21; *Vorläufiges Verzeichnis der Konzentrationslager und deren Außenkommandos sowie anderen Haftstätten unter dem Reichsführer-SS, in Deutschland und Deutschen besetzten Gebieten (1933–1945)* (Arolsen, Germany: Comité international de la Croix-Rouge, 1969), pp. 46–47; Hackett, *The Buchenwald Report,* p. 307.

90. Testimonies of Viktor Abend and Bernard Lauber, Pohl trial, minutes, YVA, N4/Proc/E, box 221, pp. 261–264, 291–294; OSS Report, August 8, 1945, p. 21;

Christine Schäfer, "Evakuierungstransporte des KZ Buchenwald und seiner Außenkommandos," *Buchenwaldhefte* 16 (1983): pp. 27–28; Hackett, *The Buchenwald Report*, p. 99.

91. Letter of Al Sommer Jr. to his parents, April 8, 1945, USHMMA, RG-09.056.

92. Letter from Fred Diamond to his family, April 13, 1945, USHMMA, RG-04.055; letter of Joseph Cohen to his wife, May 9, 1945, USHMMA, 1998.A.004; interview with Claude Hipp, August 15, 1991, USHMMA, RG-50/16618; interview with George Chassy, April 9, 1992, USHMMA, RG-50/166#06.

93. Testimony of Anna Kovitzka, September 26, 1946, Boder Collection.

94. Simcha Bunem Unsdorfer, *The Yellow Star* (Jerusalem: Feldheim Publishers, 1983), pp. 177–188.

95. Isaac Leo Kram, "Liberation in Buchenwald," in Gertrude Schneider, ed., *Muted Voices: Jewish Survivors from Latvia Remember* (New York: Philosophical Library, 1987), pp. 245, 247.

96. Poloncarz, "Die Evakuierungstransporte," p. 248.

97. Greiser, "Die Auflösung," pp. 286–287.

98. Interrogation of Josias Waldeck-Pyrmont, NARA, RG-153, box 252, pp. 18–19.

99. Interrogation of Hermann Pister (Part 2), NARA, RG-153, box 252, p. 6; deposition of Hermann Pister, July 2, 1945; Greiser, "Die Auflösung," p. 289.

100. Deposition of Hermann Pister, July 2, 1945.

101. Pister to Office D, April 6, 1945, THW, Buchenwald 48–27; Glücks to Buchenwald command, April 7, 1945, THW, Buchenwald 48–27; Tuchel, *Die Inspektion*, pp. 214–215.

102. Deposition of Hermann Pister, July 2, 1945.

103. "Transportbefehl," Weimar-Buchenwald, April 7, 1945, NARA, RG-153 box 251, folder 2.

104. Interrogation of Josias Waldeck-Pyrmont, pp. 18–19.

105. Interrogation of Dr. Gerard Scheidlausky, March 11, 1947, NARA, RG-153, box 252, folder 1.

106. Reference is to a small group of less than 200 prisoners with special status. Among them was Leon Blum, French premier in the 1930s. Testimony of Walter Schellenberg, IMT, vol. IV, pp. 381–382.

107. Testimony of Ernst Kaltenbrunner, IMT, vol. IV, p. 299.

108. Peter R. Black, *Ernst Kaltenbrunner, Ideological Soldier of the Third Reich* (Princeton, NJ: Princeton University Press, 1984), p. 248.

109. This was also the view of Pohl, Pohl trial, minutes, box 223, p. 1409.

110. Only a limited number of officials were left in the unit, and some subdepartments were not manned. Tuchel, *Die Inspektion*, p. 210.

111. Greiser, "Die Auflösung," p. 291.

112. Testimony of Bernard Wahrsager, September 19, 1946, Boder Collection.

113. Testimony of Efraim Langsner, July 9, 1996, YVA, 03/10137.

114. Testimony of Bernard Wahrsager, September 19, 1946.

115. 12th Army Headquarters Report, April 24, 1945, pp. 3–4; Katrin Greiser, *Thüringen 1945—Todesmärsche aus Buchenwald, Überblick, Namen, Orte* (Weimar: Stiftung Gedenkstätten Buchenwald und Mittelbau-Dora, 2001), p. 10.

116. Testimony of Moshe Feldman, August 8, 1998, YVA, 03/11342.

117. Memoirs of Mordechai Shadmi, YVA, 033/1349; testimony of Moshe Eisner, November 28, 1996, YVA 03/10107.

118. On the evacuation routes from Buchenwald to Flossenbürg, see *Death Marches*, UNRRA/Arolsen II, pp. 11–12; Greiser, *Thüringen 1945*, pp. 10–11; François Bertrand, *Notre devoir de mémoire: Convoi de la mort Buchenwald à Dachau du 7 au 28 avril 1945* (Pau-Bizanos: Héraclés, 2000).

119. Memoirs of Mieczesław Makowski, USHMMA, RG-02.075#01.

120. Schafer, *Die Evakuierungstransporte,* pp. 53, 65. See details on the death march routes of the Buchenwald subcamp prisoners and estimates of the number murdered along the way in Greiser, *Thüringen 1945,* pp. 33–69.

121. Kogon, *The Theory and Practice,* p. 270; Emil Carlebach, *Tote auf Urlaub: Kommunist in Deutschland, Dachau und Buchenwald 1937–1945* (Bonn: Pahl-Rugenstein Verlag, 1995), pp. 85–91; *Buchenwald: Mahnung und Verpflichtung,* pp. 315–325, 409–411.

122. Karin Hartewig, "Wolf unter Wölfen? Die prekäre Macht der kommunistischen Kapos im Konzentrationslager Buchenwald," in *Abgeleitete Macht: Funktionshäftlinge zwischen Widerstand und Kollaboration* (Bremen: Edition Temmen, 1998), p. 117.

123. Jens Schley, *Nachbar Buchenwald: Die Stadt Weimar und ihr Konzentrationslager 1937–1945* (Cologne: Böhlau Verlag, 1999), pp. 109–110, 121.

124. Témoignage de M. Chambon, October 1960, AN, 72 AJ 323 (Buchenwald no. 24/II).

125. Kogon, *The Theory and Practice of Hell,* pp. 278–279.

126. Schulte, *Zwangsarbeit,* pp. 427–428.

127. Kasztner, *Der Bericht,* p. 177.

128. Testimony of Oswald Pohl, Pohl trial, minutes, box 223, pp. 1341–1342.

129. Schley, *Nachbar Buchenwald,* pp. 124–126.

130. Stanislav Zámečník, "'Kein Häftling darf lebend in die Hände des Feindes fallen': Zur Existenz des Himmler-Befehls vom 14/18 April 1945," *Dachauer Hefte* 1 (December 1985): 219–231; Orth, *Das System,* p. 311.

131. "Die Übergabe kommt nicht in Frage. Das Lager ist sofort zu evakuieren. Kein Häftling darf lebendig in die Hände des Feindes kommen. Die Häftlinge in Buchenwald haben sich gegen die Zivilbevölkerung benommen. (-) Himmler." See text of Himmler's order in Zámečník, "Kein Häftling," p. 219.

132. Zámečník, "Kein Häftling," pp. 219–224.

133. Ibid., pp. 220–222; Kupfer-Koberwitz, *Dachauer Tagebücher,* p. 455.

5. Murder Is Rampant

1. Interrogation of Georg-Henning Bassewitz-Behr, February 12, 1946, TNA, WO 309/408, p. 2.

2. Ibid.

3. Ibid.

4. Report on the condition of prisoners at Neuengamme, March 29, 1945, Neuengamme trial, TNA, WO 235/167.

5. Deposition of Max Pauly, March 30, 1946, Neuengamme trial, TNA, WO 309/408.

6. Herbert Obenaus, "Die Räumung der hannoverschen Konzentrationslager im April 1945," in Rainer Fröbe, Claus Füllberg-Stolberg, Christoph Gutman, Rolf Keller, Herbert Obenaus, and Hans Hermann Schröder, eds., *Konzentrationslager in Hannover: KZ-Arbeit und Rüstungsindustrie in der Spätphase des Zweiten Weltkriegs,* vol. II (Hildsheim: Verlag August Lax, 1985), pp. 497–502.

7. Comité de Coordination pour la Recherche et la Transfer des Corps, Göttingen, Ministré des Anciens Combattants et Victimes de Guerre, January 21, 1951, AN, 72 AJ 342, p. 4.

8. Deposition of Gustav Alfred Jepsen, February 4, 1946, trial of Gustav Alfred Jepsen, Joachim Friedrich Freitag, and Otto Müller, TNA, WO 235/229, p. 74; testimony of Rene Bauemer, October 13, 1951, AN, 72 AJ 331–332; *Kriegsverbrechen in Lüneburg: Das Massengrab im Tiergarten* (Lüneburg: Geschichtswerkstatt Lüneburg e.V, 2000), p. 12.

9. Deposition of Ilse Bähr, February 14, 1946, trial of Jepsen, Freitag, and Müller.

10. Deposition of Gustav Alfred Jepsen, February 4, 1946, trial of Jepsen, Freitag, and Müller, pp. 74–75; *Kriegsverbrechen in Lüneburg,* p. 13.

11. Deposition of Gustav Alfred Jepsen, February 4, 1946, trial of Jepsen, Freitag, and Müller, pp. 75–76.

12. Ibid., p. 76.

13. Comité de Coordination, January 21, 1951, p. 2.

14. Testimony of Gustav Alfred Jepsen, August 16, 1946, trial of Jepsen, Freitag, and Müller, p. 240.

15. *Kriegsverbrechen in Lüneburg,* pp. 28–30; testimony of Harold le Drullenec, Archiv KZ-Gedenkstätte Neuengamme (hereafter AGN), HSN/13-7-5-5.

16. Deposition of Gustav Alfred Jepsen, February 4, 1946, trial of Jepsen, Freitag, and Müller, p. 76.

17. Ibid., p. 77; testimony of Rene Bauemer, October 13, 1951; testimony of Harold le Drullenec, AGN, 13–7–5–5.

18. Deposition of Otto Müller, December 10, 1945, trial of Jepsen, Freitag, and Müller, p. 80.

19. Testimony of Gustav Alfred Jepsen, August 17, 1946, trial of Jepsen, Freitag, and Müller, p. 238.

20. Testimony of Gustav Alfred Jepsen, August 18, 1946, trial of Jepsen, Freitag, and Müller, p. 248.

21. Müller admitted in his postwar deposition that he talked to an SS man about the prisoners but did not mention the initiative to execute them. Ibid., p. 81.

22. *Kriegsverbrechen in Lüneburg,* pp. 38–40.

23. Deposition of Gustav Alfred Jepsen, February 4, 1946, trial of Jepsen, Freitag, and Müller.

24. Testimony of Gustav Alfred Jepsen, August 18, 1946, trial of Jepsen, Freitag, and Müller, p. 248.

25. Summary of investigation in matter of Jepsen, Freitag, and Müller, November 26, 1946, TNA, WO 235/229.

26. Testimony of Gustav Alfred Jepsen, August 18, 1946, trial of Jepsen, Freitag, and Müller, p. 249.

27. Ibid.

28. Deposition of Gustav Alfred Jepsen, February 4, 1946, trial of Jepsen, Freitag, and Müller, pp. 77–78.

29. Comité de Coordination, January 21, 1951, p. 4.

30. Lecture of Imo de Vries on the massacre at Lüneburg, June 8, 1999, AGN, XXXIV–A.

31. *Kriegsverbrechen in Lüneburg,* pp. 50–53.

32. Ibid., p. 45.

33. Testimony of Gustav Alfred Jepsen, August 18, 1946, trial of Jepsen, Freitag, and Müller, p. 249.

34. Summing up by prosecutor, trial of Jepsen, Freitag, and Müller, August 23, 1946, TNA, WO 235/226, pp. 346–347.

35. Ibid., p. 340.

36. Deposition of Anton Thumann, September 6 and 9, 1945, TNA, WO 309/64; testimony of Vladimir Timcenko, TNA, WO 309/64.

37. Testimony of Max Pauly, IMT, NO-1210; deposition of Pauly, March 30, 1946, TNA, WO 309/408.

38. On the evacuation routes of Neuengamme prisoners to Bergen-Belsen, see *Death Marches,* UNRRA/Arolsen II, p. 29.

39. On the evacuation routes from Neuengamme and its subcamps, see Katharina Hertz-Eichenrode, ed., *Ein KZ wird geräumt: Häftlinge zwischen Vernichtung und Befreiung: Die Auflösung des KZ Neuengamme und seiner Außenlager durch die SS im Frühjar 1945,* vol. II (Bremen: Edition Temmen, 2000).

40. Report on the evacuation of Neuengamme, TNA, WO 311/440; deposition of Max Pauly, March 30, 1945; Detlev Garber, "Das KZ-Neuengamme," in Ulrike Jureit and Karin Orth, eds., *Überlebensgeschichte: Gespräche mit Überlebenden des KZ-Neuengamme* (Hamburg: Dölling und Galitz, 1994), pp. 33–34.

41. Deposition of Karl Otto-Kurt Kaufmann, March 12, 1946, TNA, WO 309/408.

42. Deposition of Walter Abraham, May 23, 1946, and of Kurt Rickert, May 17, 1946, TNA, WO 309/408; Ulrich Bauche, Heinz Brüdigen, Ludwig Eiber, and Wolfgang Wiedey, eds., *Arbeit und Vernichtung: Das Konzentrationslager Neuengamme 1938–1945* (Hamburg: VSA-Verlag, 1986), pp. 242–243; Hertz-Eichenrode, *Ein KZ wird geräumt,* vol. I, pp. 52–55, 235ff.

43. Depositions of Kurt Emil Grafenhorst and Friedrich Ziemann, June 16, 1948, TNA, WO 309/408.

44. Garber, "Das KZ-Neuengamme," p. 34; Bauche et al., *Arbeit und Vernichtung,* p. 243.

45. Interrogation of Anton Kaindl, December 20, 1946, USHMMA, RG-06.025#26, N-19092, tom. 2, p. 77; Barbara Kühle, "Die Todesmärsche der Häftlinge des KZ Sachsenhausen," *Sachsenhausen* 1 (1987): 9.

46. Interrogation of Anton Kaindl, December 20, 1946, tom. 2, p. 77; Wolff, "Kalendarium," p. 36.

47. Wolff, "Kalendarium," pp. 36–37.

48. Andreas Weigelt, "Jüdischer Häftlingseinsatz für das SS-Führungshauptamt: Der SS-Truppenübungsplatz 'Kurmark' und das KZ-Nebenlager 'Arbeitslager Lieberose' in Jamlitz 1944–45," in Winfried Meyer and Klaus Neitmann, eds.,

Zwangsarbeit während der NS-Zeit in Berlin und Brandenbur (Potsdam: Verlag fur Berlin-Brandenberg, 2001), p. 185.

49. Andreas Weigelt, "'Komm, geh mit! Wir gehn zum Judenerschießen . . .': Massenmord bei der Auflösung des KZ-Außenlagers Lieberose im Februar 1945," *Dachauer Hefte* 20 (October 2004): 180.

50. Report on the evacuation of Sachsenhausen and subcamps, undated, TNA, WO 311/412.

51. Weigelt, "Komm, geh mit!" pp. 181–182.

52. Ibid., p. 184.

53. Report on the evacuation of Sachsenhausen and subcamps, undated.

54. Weigelt, "Jüdischer Häftlingseinsatz," p. 188; Kühle, *Die Todesmärsche,* pp. 16–17.

55. Deposition of August Heißmeyer, October 22, 1969, ZStL AR-Z 52/67, vol. I.

56. "Am 18 April 1945 bekam ich vom Inspekteur der Konzentrationslager, Glücks, den Befehl, die in Sachsenhausen und in seinen Zweiglagern verbliebenen Häftlinge auf Schleppkähnen ins Meer zu fahren und dort zu versenken." Protokoll über die Vernehmung, Anton Kaindl, December 20, 1946, USHMMA, RG-06.025#26, N-19092, tom. 2, p. 82.

57. Antje Zeiger, "Die Todesmärsche," in *Befreiung Sachsenhausen 1945* (Berlin: Edition Hentrich, 1996), pp. 69–70.

58. Report on evacuation of Sachsenhausen and subcamps, undated.

59. Paul Martin Neurath, *The Society of Terror: Inside the Dachau and Buchenwald Concentration Camps* (Boulder, CO: Paradigm Publishers, 2005), pp. 59–60; Sofsky, *The Order of Terror,* p. 141.

60. Interrogation of Anton Kaindl, December 20, 1946, tom. 1, p. 39.

61. Wolff, "Kalendarium," p. 37; Kühle, *Die Todesmärsche,* pp. 23–30.

62. Simone Erpel, "Machtverhältnisse im Zerfall: Todesmärsche der Häftlinge des Frauen–Konzentrationslagers Ravensbrück im April 1945," in Jörg Hillmann and John Zimmermann, eds., *Kriegsende 1945 in Deutschland* (Munich: R. Oldenbourg, 2002), p. 187.

63. Erpel, *Zwischen Vernichtung und Befreiung,* pp. 148–151.

64. Bauer, *Jews for Sale?* p. 246.

65. Erpel, *Zwischen Vernichtung und Befreiung,* p. 160.

66. Testimony of Dr. Adolf Winkelmann, January 22, 1947, Ravensbrück trial, TNA, WO 235/307, p. 313.

67. One of these camps was Neustadt-Glewe, with 4,200 women prisoners: Agnes Weiss-Balazs, *"Zusammen-Zusammen": Von Nordsiebenbürgen durch Auschwitz-Birkenau und Ravensbrück bis Neustadt-Glewe und Wittstock 1923–1945* (Konstanz, Germany: Hartung-Gorre, 2005), pp. 42–43; Müller and Lepschies, *Tage der Angst,* p. 22.

68. Testimony of Karol Stern-Steinhardt, June 3, 1906, USHMMA, RG-50.030#368.

69. Testimony of Fritz Suhren, July 22, 1946, Ravensbrück trial, TNA, WO 235/310.

70. Testimony of Leah Kravi, May 1, 1995, YVA, 03/9778; testimony of Klara Weiss, January 6, 2003, YVA, 03/12382.

71. Testimony of Irena Pall (Greenfeld), October 7, 1996, YVA, 03/10133.

72. Deposition of Franz Suhren, July 22, 1946, Ravensbrück trial, TNA, WO, 235/310.

73. Gorce, *Journal de Ravensbrück*, p. 167.
74. Testimony of Dr. Adolf Winkelmann, January 22, 1947, Ravensbrück trial, p. 313.
75. Ibid., p. 315.
76. Ibid., p. 314; Müller and Lepschies, *Tage der Angst*, p. 48; [Redaktion, Kurt Buck . . . et al.], *Kriegsende und Befreiung* (Bremen: Edition Temmen, 1995), pp. 143–144.
77. Testimony of Dr. Adolf Winkelmann, January 23, 1947, Ravensbrück trial, p. 329.
78. Erpel, "Machtverhältnisse," pp. 192–193.
79. Testimony of Dr. Adolf Winkelmann, January 23, 1947, Ravensbrück trial, p. 329; Orth, *Das System*, p. 330.
80. Erpel, *Zwischen Vernichtung und Befreiung*, pp. 172–174.
81. For a detailed description of the evacuation routes of the Ravensbrück women prisoners, see Müller and Lepschies, *Tage der Angst*, pp. 43–122.
82. Témoignage de Jean de Malherbe, March 10, 1953, AN, 72 AJ 334–336.
83. Kurt Redmer, *Vergeßt dieses Verbrechen nicht! Der Todesmarsch KZ Sachsenhausen-Schwerin 1945* (Rostock, Germany: Ingo Koch Verlag, 2000), p. 31.
84. Wolff, "Kalendarium," p. 39.
85. Testimony of Paula Turczinski, in Müller and Lepschies, *Tage der Angst*, p. 74; *Sachsenhausen: Dokumente*, p. 123.
86. Redmer, *Vergeßt dieses Verbrechen nicht!* p. 29.
87. Kühle, *Die Todesmärsche*, p. 32; Redmer, *Vergeßt dieses Verbrechen nicht!* p. 29.
88. Testimony of Simcha Appelbaum, March 25, 1988, YVA, 03/4561.
89. Zeiger, "Die Todesmärsche," p. 67.
90. Redmer, *Vergeßt dieses Verbrechen nicht!* pp. 39–54; Kühle, *Die Todesmärsche*, pp. 35–36.
91. Wolff, "Kalendarium," p. 39.
92. Memoirs of Wilhelm-Konrad Laros, USHMMA, RG-32.011#01.
93. Toni Siegert, *30000 Tote mahnen! Die Geschichte des Konzentrationslagers Flossenbürg und seiner 100 Außenlager von 1938 bis 1945* (Weiden: Verlag der Taubald'schen Buchhandlung, 1984), p. 62.
94. Isabel Alcoff and Mark Stern, *Shema, Secret of My Survival: Memoirs of Mark Stern* (1993), p. 58; Orth, *Das System*, pp. 314–315.
95. *Report about Flossenbürg*, April 30, 1945, NARA M-1204, roll 1, pp. 14–15; Gie van den Berghe, ed., *Au camp de Flossenbürg (1945): Témoignage de Léon Calembert* (Brussels: Commission Royal d'Histoire, 1995), p. 31.
96. Peter Heigl, *Konzentrationslager Flossenbürg in Geschichte und Gegenwart* (Regensburg: Mittelbayerische Druckerei- und Verlags-Gesellschaft, 1989), p. 18.
97. Siegert, *30000 Tote mahnen!* p. 62.
98. Heigl, *Konzentrationslager Flossenbürg*, p. 27.
99. Two hundred Flossenbürg prisoners began to work in the Messerschmidt works in February 1943. By the end of 1944 there were 8,000, and in February 1945 there were 11,000. Siegert, *30000 Tote mahnen!* pp. 450–451.

100. Benno Fischer, "Death March, April 14, 1945–April 24, 1945" (June 1945), USHMMA, RG-02.039, pp. 2, 9–10.

101. Testimony of Alfred Bertfuter, May 25, 1945, NARA, M-1024, roll 1.

102. Heigel, *Konzentrationslager Flossenbürg,* pp. 31–32; Siegert, *30000 Tote mahnen!* pp. 62–63; memoirs of David Gerst, August 1950, USHMMA, RG-02.093, p. 376; Jakub Breitowicz, "Durch die Holle zum Leben!" YVA, 033/1642, p. 111.

103. Identification Results, the Evacuation of C. C. Flossenbürg, International Tracing Service Archives (hereafter ITS), 5.4.1950, KZ-Gedenkstatte Flossenbürg (hereafter AGF).

104. Kasztner, *Der Bericht,* p. 178.

105. Heigl, *Konzentrationslager Flossenbürg,* p. 57; Siegert, *30000 Tote mahnen!* p. 65.

106. Memoirs of David Gerst, August 1950, pp. 374–373; Fischer, "Death March," pp. 12–13; Alcoff and Stern, *Shema,* pp. 59–60.

107. Memoirs of David Gerst, August 1950, pp. 375–376; Fischer, "Death March," p. 16.

108. Railway Transport Flossenbürg—Schwarzenfeld, ITS, 26.4.1950, AGF.

109. Ibid.

110. For example, http://de.wikipedia.org/wiki/Schwarzenfeld (accessed April 14, 2007).

111. Fischer, "Death March," pp. 24–25; interview with Keiman Eisenberg, July 31, 1946, USHMMA, RG-50.472#0010; testimony of Morris Kesterberg, May 29, 1945, NARA, M-1024, roll 1; Jakub Breitowicz, "Durch die Hölle zum Leben!" p. 113; Heigl, *Konzentrationslager Flossenbürg,* pp. 32–33.

112. Testimony of Morris Kestenberg, May 29, 1945.

113. Testimony of Max Hasender, May 30, 1945, NARA, M-1024, roll 1.

114. Testimony of Alfred Bertfuter, May 25, 1945.

115. Ibid.; memoirs of David Gerst, August 1950, pp. 380, 387; Fischer, "Death March," pp. 21–23.

116. Ibid., pp. 27–29; testimony of Alfred Bertfuter, May 25, 1945.

117. Memoirs of Mordechai Shadmi, YVA, 033/1349.

118. Interview with Kalman Eisenberg, July 31, 1946, Boder Collection.

119. During the evacuation of Regensburg there were also 800 prisoners there who had arrived from Flossenbürg several weeks before the final evacuation; see *Death Marches,* UNRRA/Arolsen I, March 19, 1946, AN, 72 AJ 372, p. 14.

120. Interview with David Kempinski, March 9, 1987, USHMMA, RG-50.002#11.

121. Déclaration de Frenand Trayer, May 20, 1950, AN 72 AJ 327.

122. Siegert, *30000 Tote mahnen!* pp. 66–68; Heigl, *Konzentrationslager Flossenbürg,* pp. 40–43.

123. Dörr trial: exhibits, vol. I, p. 169.

124. Dörr trial: verdict, p. 30. According to the indictment against Dörr and several guards, 579 Jewish women set out on this death march; see Dörr trial: indictment, p. 171.

125. Dörr trial: indictment, exhibits, vol. I, pp. 181–182.

126. Ibid., pp. 182–183.

127. Dörr trial: verdict, p. 9.

128. Testimony of Charlotte Stumer, May 13, 1945, Dörr trial: exhibits, vol. I, pp. 70–71; testimony of Herta Haase-Breitmann, May 13, 1945, Dörr trial: exhibits, vol. I, p. 75.
129. Notes of Helmbrechts camp guards, Dörr trial: exhibits, vol. I, p. 142–143.
130. Dörr trial: verdict, pp. 23–24.
131. Testimony of Anni Keller, May 10, 1945, Dörr trial: exhibits, vol. I, p. 53.
132. Dörr trial: verdict, pp. 10–12; testimony of Margareta Rycerz, January 27, 1965, Dörr trial: exhibits, vol. II, pp. 400–401.
133. Testimony of Golda Itzkowitz, August 6, 1945, Budapest testimonies.
134. Dörr trial: verdict, pp. 25–26; testimony of Hanna Kotlitzki, March 3, 1963, Dörr trial, exhibits, vol. III, p. 21.
135. Testimony of Max Reimann, November 16, 1962, Dörr trial: exhibits, vol. II, p. 386.
136. Dörr trial: exhibits, vol. II, p. 160.
137. Testimony of Max Reimann, November 16, 1962, p. 387.
138. Dörr trial: verdict, pp. 28–29; testimony of Max Reimann, November 16, 1962.
139. Dörr trial: verdict, p. 29.
140. Ibid., pp. 28–30.
141. Ibid., p. 29.
142. Ibid., p. 31.
143. Ibid.
144. Ibid., p. 33. The murdered prisoners were buried later by the local farmers who discovered the corpses.
145. Testimony of Minna Singer, May 14, 1945, Dörr trial: exhibits, vol. I, p. 82.
146. Testimony of Charlotte Stumer, May 13, 1945, pp. 71–72; testimony of Herta Haase-Breitmann, May 13, 1945, p. 78.
147. Dörr trial: verdict, p. 38.
148. Ibid., p. 78.
149. Ibid., p. 36.
150. Ibid., p. 37.
151. Ibid., p. 40.
152. Ibid., pp. 36–37.
153. Ibid., p. 77.
154. Ibid., p. 43.
155. Ibid., p. 39.
156. Ibid., p. 55.
157. Ibid., p. 40.
158. "Es war ihm aber gleichgültig, wenn einzelne Angehörige seiner Wachmannschaft Häftlingeeigenmächtig töteten." Ibid., p. 43.
159. Ibid., p. 41. The tribunal assumed that the guards were still bound to obey the explicit orders of SS officers. Consequently, Dörr, had he so wished, could have prevented the murder of the sick and exhausted. It is unlikely that this was the case in the chaos that prevailed in the evacuation columns at the time.
160. Ibid., p. 78.
161. Ibid., pp. 48–49.

162. Testimony of Max Reiman, November 16, 1962, p. 389.

163. Dörr trial: verdict, p. 49.

164. Ibid., pp. 49–50.

165. Ibid., pp. 50–51.

166. Ibid., p. 51.

167. Testimony of Livia Rottenstein, September 10, 1963, Dörr trial: exhibits, vol. III, p. 120; testimony of Nina Heller, February 28, 1963, Dörr trial: exhibits, vol. III, pp. 34–35; testimony of Bela Krausz, July 18, 1945, Budapest testimonies; *Jewish Women Prisoners Who Arrived in FAL Zwodau*, February 26, 1945, Bernard Robinson Collection.

168. Testimony of Emilia Menkes, October 15, 1945, Budapest testimonies.

169. Testimony of Herta Haase-Breitmann, May 13, 1945, p. 76.

170. Dörr trial: verdict, p. 53; testimony of Charlotte Stumer, May 13, 1945, p. 71.

171. Dörr trial: verdict, pp. 53–54.

172. Testimony of Herta Haase-Breitmann, May 13, 1945, p. 77.

173. Dörr trial: verdict, pp. 54–55.

174. Ibid., pp. 56, 77.

175. Ibid., p. 57; *The Reichmanns of Bielitz*, p. 39; Gerda Weissmann Klein, *All But My Life* (New York: Hill & Wang, 1957), p. 206.

176. Dörr trial: verdict, p. 58.

177. Ibid., p. 78.

178. Ibid., p. 60.

179. *The Reichmanns of Bielitz*, p. 39.

180. Dörr trial: verdict, p. 60.

181. Testimony of Mina Singer, May 14, 1945, p. 82.

182. Dörr trial: verdict, p. 62.

183. Ibid., pp. 63, 78.

184. Testimony of Anni Keller, May 10, 1945, p. 54.

185. Dörr trial: verdict, pp. 64–66.

186. Ibid., pp. 68, 78.

187. Ibid., p. 67.

188. Ibid.

189. Ibid., p. 78.

190. Ibid., pp. 69–70; testimony of Charlotte Stumer, May 13, 1945, p. 71; testimony of Mina Singer, May 14, 1945, p. 81. She estimated that about 140 sick prisoners reached Volary.

191. Dörr trial: verdict, p. 71.

192. Dörr trial: indictment, exhibits, vol. I, p. 179; testimony of Luba Federman, May 16, 1945, Dörr trial: exhibits, vol. I, p. 87.

193. Dörr trial: verdict, pp. 72–74.

194. Testimony of Luba Federman, May 16, 1945, p. 87.

195. Dörr trial: verdict, pp. 74–75.

196. Testimony of Lieutenant-Colonel Enos G. Walker, May 8, 1945, Dörr trial, exhibits, vol. I, p. 31; testimony of Captain Walter H. Watson, May 9, 1945, Dörr trial: exhibits, vol. I, p. 42.

197. Testimony of Aron S. Kahn, May 9, 1945, Dörr trial: exhibits, vol. I, p. 47.

198. Dörr trial: exhibits, vol. I, p. 180; Dörr trial: verdict, pp. 77–79.
199. Goldhagen, *Hitler's Willing Executioners,* pp. 348, 354.
200. Dörr trial: verdict, pp. 25–26.
201. Ibid., p. 95.
202. Testimony of Charlotte Stumer, May 13, 1945, p. 77.
203. Testimony of Herta Haase-Breitmann, May 13, 1945, p. 77.
204. "Was ich als Truppenführer auf dem Marsch zu tun habe." Testimony of Max Reimann, November 16, 1962, p. 386.
205. Ibid., pp. 387–388.
206. Dörr trial: verdict, pp. 40–41; Dorr trial, exhibits, vol. I, p. 161.
207. Dörr trial: verdict, p. 42.
208. Testimony of Margareta Rycerz, January 27, 1965, p. 404.
209. Dörr trial: verdict, p. 81.
210. Ibid., p. 84.

6. Dead Men Marching

1. This, in any event, was the assumption of the Nuremberg tribunal. Black, *Ernst Kaltenbrunner,* pp. 251–252.
2. Interrogation of Berthus Gerdes, November 20, 1945, IMT, PS-3462; Zámečník, *C'était ça, Dachau,* pp. 415–416.
3. Testimony of Friedrich von Eberstein, August 5, 1946, IMT, vol. XI, p. 408.
4. Testimony of Rudolf Höß, April 15, 1946, IMT, vol. XI, p. 408.
5. Weiß was commandant of Dachau from September 1942 to November 1943. He was then sent to Majdanek, where he served until April 1944, close to the camp's evacuation date. On returning to Dachau he was placed in charge of establishing the infrastructure of the special camps at Mühldorf in addition to his task at Dachau, but he was no longer stationed in the main camp: see testimony of Martin-Gottfried Weiß, YVA, JM/10.047, reel 2, target 5, pp. 109–112.
6. Zámečník, *C'était ça, Dachau,* p. 417.
7. Interrogation of Ernst Kaltenbrunner, April 11 and 12, 1946, IMT, vol. XI, pp. 285, 299–300.
8. Birn, *Die Höheren SS,* p. 146.
9. IMT, vol. XI, p. 299.
10. Ibid.
11. Deposition of Hermann Pister, July 2, 1945, IMT, NO-255.
12. Supreme Headquarters Allied Expeditionary Force (SHAEF) Report, March 16, 1945, TNA, WO 219/1567.
13. Stephen G. Fritz, *Endkampf: Soldiers, Civilians and the Death of the Third Reich* (Lexington: University Press of Kentucky, 2004).
14. Kupfer-Koberwitz, *Dachauer Tagebucher,* p. 427.
15. Zámečník, *C'était ça, Dachau,* pp. 417–418; Arthur Haulot, *Mauthausen Dachau* (Brussels: LeCri/Vander, 1985), p. 71.
16. Raim, *Die Dachauer KZ-Außenkommandos,* p. 272.
17. Stand vom 25 IV 1945, Archiv KZ-Gedenkstätte Dachau (hereafter AGD), no. 1667.

18. Témonignage de Jean Ache, April 27, 1953, AN, 72 AJ 318–321, p. 8.
19. Amicale des Anciens de Dachau, *Allach Kommando de Dachau* (Paris: France-Empire, 1986), pp. 150–153.
20. Adler, *Theresienstadt 1941–1945*, p. 202; Paul Berben, *Dachau 1933–45: The Official History* (London: Norfolk Press, 1975), p. 222.
21. Testimony of M. Treyger, AGD, no. 15321, pp. 1–2.
22. Testimony of Moshe Polansky, January 7, 1997, YVA, 03/9953.
23. Testimony of Adi Rabon (Porotzki), May 26, 1998, YVA, 03/10776; testimony of Shmuel Weiner, MA, A.1359.
24. Raim, *Die Dachauer KZ-Außenkommandos,* pp. 240–243.
25. Ibid., pp. 244–246.
26. An Informal Report on a Jewish Concentration Camp—Kaufering Camp #4 Subsidiary of Dachau, April 29, 1945, USHMMA, 2004.103.1.
27. Benjamin Kujawski, *Łódź Ghetto, Auschwitz-Birkenau, Dachau-Kaufering-Landsberg.* Memoirs of Holocaust Survivors in Canada, no. 23. (Montreal: Montreal Institute for Genocide and Human Rights Studies, 2002); interview with Fred Bechner, April 23, 1990, USHMMA, RG-50.120#0136; interview with Shlomo Shafir, 1991, USHMMA, RG-50.030#0012.
28. Testimony of Avraham Fein, May 18, 2000, YVA, 03/11624.
29. Testimony of Moshe Polansky, January 7, 1997.
30. Testimony of Moshe Matzkevitz, September 13, 1999, YVA, 03/11942.
31. Raim, *Die Dachauer KZ-Außenkommandos,* p. 274.
32. Testimony of Mendel Schuster, YVA, JM/10.052, reel 1, target 6, pp. 61–62.
33. Testimony of Herman Ellert, YVA, JM/10.052, reel 1, target 8.
34. Testimony of Yakob Globus, YVA, JM/10.052, reel 1, target 8, p. 131; testimony of David Idelson, YVA, JM/10.055, reel 2, target 1.
35. Testimony of Shmuel Hershkowitz, YVA, JM/10.052, reel 1, target 7, pp. 215–216; testimony of Aron Koren, YVA, JM/10.052, reel 1, target 7, pp. 170–171.
36. Testimony of Herman Ellert.
37. Testimony of Richard Zarnitz, July 2, 1945, YVA, JM/10.059, reel 6, target 2.
38. Raim, *Die Dachauer KZ-Außenkommandos,* p. 275.
39. Günther Kimmel, "Das Konzentrationslager Dachau: Eine Studie zu den nationalsozialistischen Gewaltverbrechen," in Martin Broszat and Elke Föhlrich, eds., *Bayern in der NS-Zeit*, vol. II (Munich: R. Oldenbourg, 1979), p. 409; Zámečník, *C'était ça, Dachau*, p. 421.
40. Interview with Fred Bechner, April 23, 1990.
41. Interview with David Kempinsky, March 9, 1987, USHMMA, RG-50.002#11.
42. Barbara Distel, "Öffentliches Sterben: Vom Umgang der Öffentlichen mit den Todesmärschen," *Dachauer Hefte* 20 (October 2004): 39; Kupfer-Koberwitz, *Dachauer Tagebücher,* p. 433; Zámečník, *C'était ça, Dachau,* pp. 422–423.
43. Testimony of Teresa Weigl, YVA, JM/10.047, reel 2, target 5.
44. The corpses of these prisoners were collected by local residents and buried in a mass grave. Testimony of Moritzo Sappl, YVA, JM/10.047, reel 2, target 5, p. 809.
45. Kimmel, "Das Konzentrationslager Dachau," p. 410; Zámečník, *C'était ça, Dachau,* pp. 423–425.

46. Deposition of Fritz Degelow, NARA, M-1174, roll 4; testimony of Adi Rabon (Porotzky), May 26, 1998; testimony of Avraham Fein, May 18, 2000.

47. Joseph Freeman, *The Road to Hell: Recollection of the Nazi Death March* (St. Paul, MN: Paragon House, 1998), pp. 57–58.

48. Testimony of Fred Bechner, April 23, 1990.

49. Testimony of Shamshiya Spivak, December 26, 1991, USHMMA, RG-50.120#152.

50. Ibid.

51. Solly Ganor, "Death March," in Wolfgang Benz and Barbara Distel, eds., *Dachau and the Nazi Terror 1933–1945,* vol. I, *Testimonies and Memoirs* (Dachau: Verlag Dachauer Hefte, 2002), p. 209.

52. Zámečník, *C'était ça, Dachau,* p. 425.

53. Gerd Vanselow, *KZ Hersbruck: Größtes Außenlager von Flossenbürg* (Bohn: Karl Pfeiffer Buchendruckerei und Verlag, 1983), pp. 39, 55–56.

54. Testimony of Morris Jacobs, USHMMA, RG-10.244.

55. Vanselow, *KZ Hersbruck,* pp. 56–57.

56. Vittore Bocchetta, *Jene fünf verdammten Jahre: Aus Verona in die Konzentrationslager Flossenbürg und Hersbruck* (Lage, Germany: Verlag Hans Jacobs, 2003), pp. 174–175.

57. Barbara Distel, "29 April 1945: The Liberation of the Concentration Camp at Dachau," in Wolfgang Benz and Barbara Distel, eds., *Dachau and the Nazi Terror 1933–1945, vol. II, Studies and Reports* (Dachau: Verlag Dachauer Hefte, 2002), p. 12.

58. Kupfer-Koberwitz, *Dachauer Tagebucher,* p. 434.

59. Interview with John Komski, June 7, 1990, USHMMA, RG-50.030#0115.

60. For a description and daily details of this death march from Buchenwald to Dachau, see Bertrand, *Notre devoir de memoire,* pp. 76–77.

61. Indictment: Buchenwald trial, November 15, 1947, NARA, RG-153, box 243, folder 1, p. 32; interrogation of Hans-Erich Merbach, NARA, RG-153, box 252, pp. 2–4.

62. Bertrand, *Notre devoir de memoire,* p. 79.

63. Ibid., pp. 112, 114.

64. Indictment: Buchenwald trial, November 15, 1947, pp. 93–95; interrogation of Johann Kick, NARA, M-1174, roll 1; Zámečník, *C'était ça, Dachau,* pp. 427–429

65. François Bertrand, "Der Todeszug nach Dachau," *Dachauer Hefte* 15 (November 1999): 37. An American officer who testified at the Dachau trial reckoned that the number of dead removed from the train near the camp was more than 700: http://www.scrapbookpages.com/DachauScrapbook/DachauLiberation/DeathTrain2.html (accessed July 1, 2007).

66. Letter from William Cowling to his parents, April 28, 1945, in Bertrand, *Notre devoir de memoire,* p. 139.

67. Zámečník, *C'était ça, Dachau,* pp. 426–429.

68. Deposition of Kurt Becher, March 8, 1946, IMT, PS-3762.

69. Deposition of Walter Schmutzler, August 14, 1947, NARA, RG-153, box 14, Clemency, vol. 3.

70. Deposition of Franz Ziereis as recorded by Hans Maršálek, May 22, 1945, IMT, PS-3870.
71. Benyamin Eckstein, *Mauthausen, Makhaneh Rikuz VeKhilayon* [Mauthausen, concentration and extermination camp] (Jerusalem: Yad Vashem, 1984), p. 265; deposition of Walter Schmutzler, May 18, 1946, NARA, RG-153, box 14, exhibits, vol. 3; Maršálek, *The History of Mauthausen*, p. 293.
72. David W. Pike, *Spaniards in the Holocaust: Mauthausen, the Horror on the Danube* (London: Routledge, 2000), pp. 192–193.
73. Testimony of Alfonse Pollak, May 18, 1945, Dokumentationsarchiv des österreichischen Widerstandes (hereafter DÖW), 20000/P359, p. 9.
74. Deposition of Franz Ziereis as recorded by Hans Maršálek, May 22, 1945.
75. Testimony of Mauricy Lampe, January 25, 1946, IMT, vol. VI, p. 188. According to other sources the number murdered in the liquidation of the sick from Sachsenhausen was between 200 and 300. Most were Poles and Russians. See Maršálek, *The History of Mauthausen*, p. 245.
76. Another transport from Sachsenhausen arrived on February 26, and included 1,451 prisoners. See Maršálek, *The History of Mauthausen*, p. 121.
77. Testimony of Kalman Eisenberg, July 31, 1946, Boder Collection.
78. Maršálek, *The History of Mauthausen*, pp. 122, 127.
79. Stanisław Dobosiewicz, *Mauthausen/Gusen, Obóz zagłady* (Warsaw: Wydawnictwo Ministerstrwa Obrony Narodowej, 1977), p. 371.
80. Maršálek, *The History of Mauthausen*, p. 74.
81. Ekstein, *Mauthausen*, pp. 291–292, 309.
82. Testimony of Gedalia Pollak, October 20, 1995, YVA, 03/8581.
83. Maršálek, *The History of Mauthausen*, p. 78.
84. Strafverfahren gegen Karl Bruno Blach, Dominik Gleba, Staatsanwaltschaft beim Landsgericht Duisburg (hereafter SLD), IX KS 130 (24), JS 28/72, p. 16.
85. Ibid., p. 24.
86. Memoirs of Rolf Busch-Waldeck, DÖW, No. 1459, pp. 87–89.
87. Ibid., p. 90.
88. Deposition of Walter Schmutzler, May 18, 1946.
89. Deposition of Otto Schrader, July 10, 1946, NARA, RG-153, box 14, exhibits, vol. 3.
90. Strafverfahren gegen Karl Bruno Blach, Dominik Gleba, p. 52.
91. Bertrand Perz, "Der Todesmarsch von Wiener Neudorf nach Mauthausen: Eine Dokumentation," in *Dokumentationsarchiv des österreichischen Widerstands, Jahrbuch 1988* (Vienna: Österreichischer Bundesverlag, 1988), p. 118.
92. Memoirs of Rolf Busch-Waldeck, DÖW, No. 1459, p. 106.
93. Ibid., p. 117.
94. Questionnaire pour la Commission d'Histoire de la Déportation, Robin Henri, AN, 72 AJ 329 (Mauthausen A no. 2II).
95. Perz, "Der Todesmarsch," p. 118. As in other cases the precise number of prisoners murdered cannot be established. Survivors of the death march reported that about 500 perished. Testimony of Roger Nedellac, NARA, RG-153, box 14, exhibits, vol. 3; memoirs of Stanley Kanai, USHMMA, RG-02.180.
96. Strafverfahren gegen Karl Bruno Blach, Dominik Gleba, pp. 43–46.

97. Ibid., pp. 57–61.
98. Eleonore Lappin, "The Death Marches of Hungarian Jews through Austria in the Spring of 1945," *Yad Vashem Studies* 28 (2000): 211.
99. Randolph L. Braham, *The Politics of Genocide: The Holocaust in Hungary*, vol. II (New York: Rosenthal Institute for Holocaust Studies, 1994), pp. 963–969; Eleonore Lappin, "Die Todesmärsche ungarischer Jüdinnen und Juden aus Ungarn nach Mauthausen im zeitgeschichtlichen Kontext," in Heimo Halbrainer and Christian Ehetreiber, eds., *Todesmarsch Eisenstraße 1945: Terror, Handlungsspielräume, Einnerung: Menschliches Handeln unter Zwangsbedingungen* (Graz, Austria: Cilo, 2005), p. 59.
100. Deposition of Dieter Wisliceny, January 3, 1946, http://www.ess.uwe.ac.uk/ genocide/wisliceny.htm (accessed February 21, 2010).
101. Aly and Gerlach, *Das letzte Kapitel*, pp. 360–361; interrogation of Siegfried Uiberreither, March 5, 1946, DÖW, 12.697, p. 8.
102. Kasztner, *Der Bericht*, pp. 119–120.
103. Deposition of Dieter Wisliceny, January 3, 1946; cable of Edmund Veesenmayer to German Foreign Ministry, November 21, 1944, in Randolph L. Braham, ed., *The Destruction of Hungarian Jewry: A Documentary Account*, vol. II (New York: World Federation of Hungarian Jews, 1963), pp. 532–533; Szabolcs Szita, "Die Todesmärsche der Budapester Juden im November 1944 nach Hegyeshalom-Nickelsdorf," *Zeitgeschichte* 3–4 (1995): 136.
104. Szabolcs Szita, "The Forced Labor of Hungarian Jews at the Fortification of the Western Border Regions of Hungary, 1944–45," in Randolph L. Braham, ed., *Studies on the Holocaust in Hungary* (New York: Social Science Monographs, 1990), p. 176.
105. Lappin, "The Death Marches," pp. 212–213; Szita, "The Forced Labor of Hungarian Jews," p. 179.
106. Interrogation of Siegfried Uiberreither, March 5, 1946, pp. 13–14.
107. Interrogation of Baldur von Schirach, May 24, 1946, IMT, vol. XIV, p. 440.
108. Interrogation of Siegfried Uiberreither, March 5, 1946, pp. 6–7, 9, 11, 17–18.
109. Rudolf Höß was responsible for intake of the Hungarian Jewish laborers and their dispatch to worksites in Germany and the labor camps along the Austrian-Hungarian border. However, the Office D unit was not involved in evacuating Jews from the labor camps in spring 1945. See Eleonore Lappin, "Ungarisch-jüdische Zwangsarbeiter in Österreich 1944/45," in Martha Keil and Eleonore Lappin, eds., *Studien zur Geschichte der Juden in Österreich* (Bodenheim, Germany: Philo, 1997), p. 148.
110. Lappin, "The Death Marches," p. 216.
111. Ibid., pp. 213–215.
112. Ronald Rogowski, "The Gauleiter and the Social Origins of Fascism," *Comparative Studies in Society and History* 19:4 (1977): 402.
113. Kershaw, *Hitler 1936–1945*, p. 515.
114. Jeremy Noakes, "'Viceroys of the Reich'? Gauleiters 1925–45," in Anthony McElligott and Tim Kirk, eds., *Working toward the Führer: Essays in Honour of Sir Ian Kershaw* (Manchester: Manchester University Press, 2003), pp. 142–144.

115. David K. Yelton, *Hitler's Volkssturm: The Nazi Militia and the Fall of Germany 1944–1945* (Lawrence: University Press of Kansas, 2002), p. 7; Burton Wright, "Army of Despair: The German Volkssturm 1944–1945" (PhD diss., Florida State University, 1982), p. 26.

116. Yelton, *Hitler's Volkssturm,* p. 21.

117. Ibid., p. 30.

118. Klaus Mammach, *Der Volkssturm: Das letzte Aufgebot 1944/45* (Cologne: Pahl-Rugenstein, 1981), p. 105.

119. Yelton, *Hitler's Volkssturm,* p. 27.

120. Dienstanweisung (No.) 24, March 22, 1945, Österreichisches Staatsarchiv/Archiv der Republik (hereafter ÖSA), 54.370-18/70.

121. Deposition of Paul Schmidt, June 29, 1964, ÖSA, 54.370-18/70.

122. Ibid.

123. Deposition of Paul Schmidt, October 17, 1945, ÖSA, 54.370-18/70.

124. Deposition of Kurt Nussbaumer, May 5, 1946, ÖSA, 54.370-18/70.

125. Deposition of Anton Unger, September 7, 1945, Aktenvermerk vom 17 April 1964, ÖSA 54.370-18/70.

126. Deposition of Paul Schmidt, June 29, 1964.

127. Deposition of Josef Dex, July 1, 1964, ÖSA, 54.370-18/70.

128. Ermittlungsverfahren gegen Eduard Meissl, Staatsanwaltschaft beim Landsgericht Stuttgart, 26.5.1964, ÖSA, 54.370-18/70, pp. 2, 4; deposition of Anton Unger, December 3, 1945, ÖSA, 54.370-18/70.

129. Interrogation of Siegfried Uiberreither, March 5, 1946, pp. 10, 12.

130. In "The Death Marches" (p. 218), Eleanore Lappin argues that Nazi leaders interpreted the murder of Jews as the inevitable outcome of "difficulties in transportation and communication," whereas in actual fact the murders were perpetrated on the basis of clear and explicit orders. These orders were not always given by the senior command and in most cases stemmed from the local command.

131. Since June 1943 Rutte had been provisional chief of the district (Kreis) of Feldbach; Klöch was one of its eight subdistricts. See deposition of Anton Rutte, May 25, 1946, TNA, WO, 310/144.

132. Deposition of Anton Oswald, June 14, 1946, TNA, WO, 310/144.

133. Investigation of the massacre at Rechnitz, ÖSA, 97.094-2/48.

134. Testimony of Anna Koineg, March 24, 1966, ÖSA, 54.297-18/70.

135. Report on the inquiry into the massacre at Jennersdorf, March 4, 1965, ÖSA, 54.297-18/70.

136. Testimony of Johann Petanovits, May 17, 1966, and testimony of Franz Wolf, May 18, 1966, ÖSA, 54.297-18/70.

137. Indictment against Karl Amlinger, Wilhelm Mohr, and Frantz Paul, May 30, 1968, ÖSA, 54.987-18/68, p. 22.

138. Ibid., pp. 32–33.

139. Testimony of Anna Koineg, March 24, 1966, indictment against Karl Amlinger, Wilhelm Mohr, and Frantz Paul, May 30, 1968, p. 33.

140. Testimony of Wilhelm Mohr, April 19, 1966, ÖSA, 54.297-18/70.

141. Testimony of Frantz Paul, April 7, 1966, ÖSA, 54.297-18/70.

142. Indictment against Karl Amlinger, Wilhelm Mohr, and Frantz Paul, May 30, 1968, p. 3.

143. Testimony of Theresa Neubauer, March 29, 1966, ÖSA, 54.297-18/70: testimony of Anna Koineg, March 24, 1966.

144. Testimony of Karl Großner, March 20, 1967, testimony of Johann Hauer, July 12, 1967, and reports on inquiry into the massacre of Jewish prisoners at Balf, April 1, 1968, and July 16, 1970, ZStL, 502 AR-Z 108/67.

145. Testimony of Adolf Blechner, November 21, 1969, ZStL, 502 AR-Z 108/67.

146. Testimony of Anna Ament, January 9, 1968, ZStL, 502 AR-Z 108/67.

147. Report on massacre during evacuation of labor camps in Gau of Styria, Graz Criminal Police, July 5, 1945, TNA, WO 310/155.

148. Ibid.

149. Werner Anzenberger, Heimo Halbrainer, and Hans Jürgen Rabko, *Zwischen den Fronten: Die Region Eisenerz von 1938–1945* (Leoben, Austria: Institut für Strukturforschung und Erwachsenenbildung, 2000), pp. 60–67; Lappin, "Die Todesmärsche," pp. 72–78.

150. Narrative of Eisenerz trial, February 9, 1946, TNA, FO 1020/2034, part 1; Aussage des Hauptmanns Ernst Bilke, 23.3.1946, TNA, FO, 1020/2059.

151. Deposition of Adolf Schumann, August 21, 1945, TNA, FO 1020/2056, p. 3.

152. Josef Junwanschitz to Denes Trajan, February 18, 1946, TNA, FO 1020/2034.

153. Deposition of Hans Bircks, January 5, 1946, TNA, FO 1020/2056, p. 1; deposition of Heinrich Thaller, January 23, 1946, TNA, FO 1020/2056, p. 1.

154. Fahndungsanzeige, Ludwig Krenn, Polizeidienstelle Eisenerz, 22.1.1946, TNA, FO 1020/2034.

155. Liste über Angehörige des Volkssturms Eibenery, Kompanie Krenn, Polizeidienstelle Eisenerz, January 19, 1946, TNA, FO 1020/2034.

156. Deposition of Anna Feda, January 28, 1946, TNA, FO 1020/2056.

157. Christandl was personally acquainted with Krenn. See deposition of Otto Christandl, January 31, 1946, TNA, FO 1020/2056; Ludwig Krenn also admitted that he knew Christandl well and was in direct contact with him during the establishment of the Volkssturm unit. See deposition of Ludwig Krenn, January 27, 1946, TNA, FO 1020/2056, p. 2.

158. Krenn shifted responsibility for issuance of all orders regarding the transports to Schumann and claimed that he also received orders from Eberl. See deposition of Ludwig Krenn, January 27, 1946, pp. 1–2.

159. Deposition of Fritz Wolf, January 31, 1946, TNA, FO 1020/2056, p. 1.

160. Deposition of Josef Sassman, August 1945, TNA, FO 1020/2056.

161. Eisenerz War Crime—General Narrative, February 8, 1946, TNA, FO 1020/2034, p. 1.

162. Deposition of six members of Krenn's Volkssturm unit, January 21, 1946, TNA, WO 1020/2056.

163. Eisenerz War Crime—General Narrative, February 8, 1946, p. 2.

164. Deposition of Ludwig Krenn, January 27, 1946, p. 1.

165. Deposition of Josef Sassman, August 1945.

166. Deposition of Adolf Schumann, August 21, 1945, p. 4.

167. Ibid.

168. Testimony of Zoltan Diamant, August 10, 1945, TNA, WO 310/143.
169. Testimony of Hedwig Lauber, April 20, 1946, YVA, 033/920.
170. Narrative of Eisenerz trial, February 9, 1946.
171. Report on massacre during evacuation of labor camps in Gau of Styria, Graz Criminal Police, July 5, 1945; deposition of Adolf Schumann, August 21, 1945, p. 4.
172. Dossier of investigation against Franz Puchner, Joseph Egger, Friedrich Winkler, and Karl Leitenmüller, August 1945, TNA, WO 310/155.
173. Ibid.
174. Deposition of Stefan Knaus, August 27, 1945, TNA, WO 310/143.
175. Report on massacres, Legal Department of GHQ, British Troops, Austria, October 8, 1946, TNA, WO 309/1927.
176. Report on war crimes, Special Investigation Branch, British Troops, Austria, September 9, 1945, TNA, WO 310/155.
177. Eleonore Lappin, "Todesmärsche im Reichsgau Oberdonau," in Siegfried Haider and Gerhart Marckhgott, eds., Oberösterreichische Gedenkstätten für KZ-Opfer (Linz: Kulturland Oberöstreich, 2001), pp. 83–89.
178. KZ-Lager Hinterberg bei Peggau, DÖW, 13.0Z8.
179. Testimony of Yosef Mermelstein, April 29, 1969, and testimony of Yosef Schweitzer, December 3, 1946, DÖW, 12.588.
180. Die Staatsanwaltschaft Wien erhebt gegen Alfred Waidmann, November 23, 1949, DÖW, 12.597.
181. Deposition of Wolfgang Lassmann, December 16, 1945, DÖW, 12.588.
182. Summary of criminal inquiry against Josef Entenfellner, Gustav Tamm, Karl Hahn, Franz Heger, and Johann Tabor concerning the murder of Jewish prisoners at Engeray, December 12, 1945, DÖW, 12.588, p. 6; indictment against Peter Acher, July 29, 1954, DÖW, 20.699.
183. Die Staatsanwaltschaft Wien erhebt gegen Alfred Waidmann, November 23, 1949.
184. Claudia Kuretsidis-Haider, "Justizakten als historische Quelle am Beispiel der 'Engerau-Prozesse,'" in Rudolf G. Ardelt and Christian Gerbel, eds., Österreichischer Zeitgeschichtetag 1995 (Innsbruck: StudienVerlag, 1996), p. 338.
185. Deposition of Rudolf Kronbergen, October 22, 1945, and deposition of Eduard Niklas, October 23, 1945, DÖW, 19.867; Lappin, "The Death Marches," p. 172 (note 48).
186. Kuretsidis-Haider, "Justizakten also historische Quelle," p. 340.
187. Lappin, "The Death Marches," p. 226.
188. Testimony of Y. Jelinek and A. Weiß, July 13, 1945, YVA, 015.E/434.
189. Interview with Mordechai Weiß, June 20, 1993, USHMMA, RG-50.120#0168.
190. Testimony of Alex Markovitz, March 31, 1964, ÖSA, 54.367-18/71.
191. Lappin, "The Death Marches," pp. 239–240. In the report of the Committee for Jewish History in Budapest, the number of victims of the death marches of Hungarian Jews through Austria was estimated at 21,800. Bericht des Geschaftsfuhrers vom 15 September 1948, YVA, 015E/1701.
192. Deposition of Karl Hobitsch, December 6, 1945, TNA, FO 1020/2056.

193. Christopher R. Browning, *Ordinary Men: Reserve Police Battalion 101 and the Final Solution in Poland* (New York: HarperCollins, 1992), pp. 65–68.

194. Dossier of investigation against Franz Puchner, Josef Egger, Friedrich Winkler, and Karl Leitenmüller, July 1945, TNA, WO 310/155.

195. Lappin, "The Death Marches," pp. 235–237; Günter Burczik, "'Nur net dran rührn!' Auf den Spuren der Todesmärsche ungarischer Juden durch Österreich nach Mauthausen im April 1945," in Martha Keil and Eleonore Lappin, eds., *Studien zur Geschichte der Juden in Österreich* (Bodenheim: Philo, 1997), p. 175.

196. Report on the number of sick prisoners at Mauthausen, March 25, 1945, USHMMA, RG-17.002M, reel 2, H/03/04.

197. Maršálek, *The History of Mauthausen,* p. 290.

198. Interview with Avraham Kafiza, March 24, 1994, USHMMA, RG-50.120#0192; interview with Daniel Hanoch, November 3, 1995, USHMMA, RG-50.120#0226.

199. Questionnaire pour la Commission d'Histoire de la Déportation, Robin Henri, AN, 72 AJ 329 (Mauthausen A, no. 2II).

200. Sinai Adler, *BeGay Tzalmavet* [In the valley of death] (Jerusalem: Yad Vashem, 1979), p. 55.

201. Testimony of Josef Szalant, July 13, 1945, YVA, 015.E/2376.

202. Interview with Mordechai Weiß, June 20, 1993.

203. Testimony of Israel Gutman, YVA, TR-3/1650; testimony of Asher Arad, September 16, 1994, YVA, 03/7869; testimony of Dov Staub, April 11, 1999, YVA, 03/11151; testimony of Nathan Ginzberg, February 21, 1995, YVA, 03/8842; testimony of Mordechai Eldar, August 7, 2001, YVA 03/11995; interview with Avraham Kafiza, March 24, 1994; interview with Daniel Hanoch, November 3, 1995.

204. Peter Kammerstätter, *Der Todesmärsch ungarischer Juden von Mauthausen nach Gunskirchen im April 1945: Eine Materialsammlung nach 25 Jahren,* DÖW, 12.854, p. 111.

205. Eckstein, *Mauthausen,* pp. 273–277.

206. Mauthausen trial: summary by prosecution, February 27, 1947, NARA, RG-153m box 6, review vol. 1, p. 73.

207. For details of places where prisoners were murdered during the death march from Mauthausen to Gunskirchen and the mass graves uncovered, see Kammerstätter, *Der Todesmarsch ungarischer Juden.*

208. Ibid., p. 51; Adler, *BeGay Tzalmavet,* p. 67; Eckstein, *Mauthausen,* p. 277.

209. Interview with Mordechai Weiß, June 20, 1993; testimony of Haim Tzvi Lavon, YVA, 03/4567; testimony of Mordechai Adler, August 7, 2001, YVA, 03/11995.

210. Testimony of David Sarid, May 20–28, 2005, YVA, 03/12091.

211. Ibid.

212. Testimony of Dov Staub, April 11, 1999.

213. Testimony of David Sarid, May 20–28, 2005.

214. Avraham Kokhavi, "Naar HaMakhanot" [Boy of the camps], *Yalkut Moreshet* 4 (July 1965): 19.

215. Interview with Mordechai Weiß, June 20, 1993.
216. Interview with Daniel Hanoch, November 3, 1995; testimony of Philip Markovitz, June 30, 1998, YVA, 03/10647; testimony of Yaakov Sarid, November 6, 2005, YVA, 03/12599.
217. Testimony of Haim Tzvi Lavon, YVA, 03/4567.
218. Testimony of Peretz Mor (Zultowski), MA, A.261.
219. Memoirs of David Ichelson, USHMMA, RG-09.006#01.
220. Report of Cameron Coffman to Headquarters 3rd Army, May 4, 1945, USHMMA, RG-09.024; see also *The Seventy-First Came . . . to Gunskirchen Lager,* USHMMA, RG-19.038, folder 4.
221. U.S. Army report on Gunskirchen, May 16, 1945, IMT, PS-2176 (85).
222. Eckstein, *Mauthausen,* p. 282. By Eckstein's estimate (pp. 325–326), in the month or so between the concentration of Jewish prisoners in the tent camp at Mauthausen and the liberation of Gunskirchen on May 5 more than 16,000 Jews perished. This figure appears exaggerated since he estimated that 20,000 (and not 15,000) prisoners were transferred to Gunskirchen, and he does not take into account the unknown number of prisoners who left the camp before the Americans arrived.
223. Adler, *BeGay Tzalmavet,* p. 58.
224. Memoirs of David Ichelson.

7. A Society in Collapse

1. Max Seydewitz, *Civil Life in Wartime Germany: The Story of the Home Front* (New York: Viking Press, 1945), pp. 45, 47; Wolframe Wette, "Zur Psychologischen Mobilmachung der deutschen Bevölkerung 1933–1939," in Wolfgang Michalka, ed., *Der Zweite Weltkrieg: Analysen-Grundzüge-Forschungsbilanz* (Munich: Piper, 1989), pp. 218–221; Steinert, *Hitler's War and the Germans,* pp. 41–42; Detlev J. K. Peukert, *Inside Nazi Germany: Conformity, Opposition, and Racism in Everyday Life* (New Haven, CT: Yale University Press, 1987), p. 67.
2. William L. Shirer, *Berlin Diary: The Journal of a Foreign Correspondent* (New York: Knopf, 1941), pp. 191–192.
3. Victor Klemperer, *I Shall Bear Witness: The Diaries of Victor Klemperer 1933–41* (London: Weidenfeld & Nicolson, 1998), p. 295.
4. Ian Kershaw, *The "Hitler Myth": Image and Reality in the Third Reich* (Oxford: Oxford University Press, 1989), pp. 151–168.
5. Steinert, *Hitler's War,* p. 68.
6. Shirer, *Berlin Diary,* p. 404.
7. Steinhoff, Pechel, and Showalter, *Voices from the Third Reich,* p. 78.
8. Aly and Heim, *Architects of Annihilation,* pp. 130–159.
9. See Browning, *The Origins of the Final Solution,* pp. 36ff.; Czesław Madajczyk, *Politika III Rzeszy w okupowanej Polsce,* vol. I (Warsaw: Państwowe Wydawnictwo Naukowe, 1970), pp. 234–287.
10. Shirer, *Berlin Diary,* p. 462.
11. Norbert Frei, "Der totale Krieg und die Deutschen," in Norbert Frei and Hermann Kling, eds., *Der nationalsozialistische Krieg* (Frankfurt am Main: Campus, 1990), p. 285.

12. Ian Kershaw, *Popular Opinion and Political Dissent in the Third Reich: Bavaria 1933–1945* (Oxford: Oxford University Press, 1983), p. 281.

13. George L. Mosse, *Nazi Culture: Intellectual, Cultural, and Social Life in the Third Reich* (Madison: University of Wisconsin Press, 1966), pp. 263ff.

14. Geoff Eley, "Ordinary Germans, Nazism, and Judeocide," in Geoff Eley, ed., *The "Goldhagen Effect": History, Memory, Nazism—Facing the German Past* (Ann Arbor: University of Michigan Press, 2000), p. 11.

15. Jeffrey Herf, *The Jewish Enemy: Nazi Propaganda during World War II and the Holocaust* (Cambridge, MA: Belknap Press of Harvard University Press, 2006), pp. 192–196.

16. For the full text of Goebbels's speech on February 18, 1943, see Irving Fetscher, *Joseph Goebbels im Berliner Sportpalast 1943: "Wollt ihr den totalen Krieg?"* (Hamburg: Europäische Verlagsanstalt, 1998), pp. 63–98; see also Günter Moltmann, "Goebbels' Speech on Total War, February 18, 1943," in Hajo Holborn, ed., *Republic to Reich: The Making of Nazi Revolution* (New York: Pantheon Books, 1973), pp. 319–322; Peter Longerich, "Joseph Goebbels und der totale Krieg: Eine unbekannte Denkschrift des Propagandaministers vom 18. Juli 1944," *Vierteljahreshefte für Zeitgeschichte* (hereafter VfZ) 35:2 (1987): 299–314.

17. The military man who expounded this theory was the Italian general Giulio Douhet, who published his book in 1921. His views influenced theories of aerial warfare in Britain and the United States during World War II. Giulio Douhet, *The Command of the Air* (New York: Arno Press, 1972).

18. Robert H. Whealey, *Hitler and Spain: The Nazi Role in the Spanish Civil War* (Lexington: University Press of Kentucky, 1989), pp. 103–105; Helene Graham, *The Spanish Republic at War 1936–1939* (Cambridge: Cambridge University Press, 2002), p. 308.

19. Erich Ludendorff, *Der totale Krieg* (Munich: Ludendorff Verlag, 1935).

20. On Ludendorff's theory of total war and its impact on Goebbels, see Fetscher, *Joseph Goebbels im Berliner Sportpalast*, pp. 46–61.

21. Ludolf Herbst, *Der totale Krieg und die Ordnung der Wirtschaft: Die Kriegswirtschaft in Spannungsfeld von Politik, Ideologie und Propaganda 1939–1945* (Stuttgart: Deutsche Verlags-Anstalt, 1982), p. 173.

22. Fetscher, *Joseph Goebbels in Berliner Sportpalast*, pp. 23–30.

23. Rudolf Semmler, *Goebbels, the Man Next to Hitler* (London: Westhouse, 1947), pp. 62–63.

24. Moltmann, "Goebbels' Speech," p. 305.

25. Elke Fröhlich, ed., *Die Tagebücher von Joseph Goebbels* (Munich: K. G. Sauer, 1993–1996), II/6, December 29, 1942, pp. 517–520; Moltmann, "Goebbels' Speech," p. 307; Eleanor Hancock, *The National Socialist Leadership and Total War, 1941–1945* (New York: St. Martin's Press, 1991), pp. 63–69; Speer, *Inside the Third Reich*, p. 267.

26. Herbst, *Der totale Krieg*, p. 200.

27. Moltmann, "Goebbels' Speech," p. 309; Fröhlich, *Tagebücher*, II/7, January 30, 1943, pp. 224–225.

28. Fröhlich, *Tagebücher*, II/7, February 8, 1943, pp. 285–290.

29. Moltmann, "Goebbels' Speech," pp. 310–311.

30. Kershaw, *Hitler, 1936–1945,* pp. 561–563, 568–573.
31. Pauline Elkes, "Assessing the 'Other Germany': The Political Warfare Executive on Public Opinion and Resistance in Germany, 1943–1945," in McElligott and Kirk, *Working toward the Führer,* pp. 226–229; Döte Winkler, "Frauenarbeit versus Frauenidologie: Probleme der weiblichen Erwerbstätigkeit in Deutschland 1930–1945," *Archiv für Socialgeschichte* 17 (1977): 116–120.
32. Timothy W. Mason, *Social Politics in the Third Reich: The Working Class and the "National Community"* (Providence, RI: Berg, 1993), pp. 28–32.
33. Goebbels viciously criticized several leaders of the Reich and the Nazi Party, particularly Frick and Göring, for failing to do anything except enjoy themselves at vacation areas and spas for a considerable part of the year. He also voiced implied criticism of Hitler and wrote in his diary that the Führer was not taking a firm enough stand and was irresolute in taking important decisions. *Fröhlich, Tagebücher,* II/7, March 2, 1943, p. 45; II/8, April 12, 1943, p. 98; and II/8, June 24, 1943, p. 521.
34. Herbst, *Der totale Krieg,* p. 187.
35. Frei, "Der totale Krieg," pp. 293–294.
36. Victor Klemperer, *I Will Bear Witness: A Diary of the Nazi Years 1942–1945.* (New York: Random House, 1999), p. 202.
37. Kershaw, *Hitler, 1936–1945,* pp. 575–577.
38. Peter Longerich, *Politik der Vernichtung: Eine Gesamtdarstellung der nationalsozialistischen Judenverfolgung* (Munich: Piper, 1998), p. 537.
39. Weinberg, *A World at Arms,* pp. 591–630. Speer described the terrible suffering of the population and the local Nazi leadership in Hamburg after the bombardment and Hitler's disregard of all the appeals that he visit there in order to raise the morale of the inhabitants. See Speer, *Inside the Third Reich,* pp. 283–284.
40. Fröhlich, *Tagebücher,* II/12, June 22, 1944, p. 521.
41. Longerich, "Joseph Goebbels und der totale Krieg," pp. 305–314.
42. Fröhlich, *Tagebücher,* II/13, July 23, 1944, pp. 135–136; Longerich, "Joseph Goebbels und der totale Krieg," pp. 304–305.
43. The literature on the anti-Nazi and anti-Hitler resistance movement and the July 20, 1944, plot is extensive and diverse. See, for example, Kershaw, *Hitler, 1936–1945,* pp. 655–684; Jürgen Schmädeke and Peter Steinbach, eds., *Der Widerstand gegen den Nationalsozialismus: Die deutsche Gesellschaft und der Widerstand gegen Hitler* (Munich: Piper, 1985); Theodore S. Hamerow, *On the Road to the Wolf's Lair: Ethics and Resistance in Nazi Germany* (Cambridge, MA: Belknap Press of Harvard University Press, 1997); Joachim Fest, *Plotting Hitler's Death: The Story of German Resistance* (New York: Metropolitan Books, 1994).
44. Fröhlich, *Tagebücher,* II/13, July 24, 1944, pp. 154–157, and July 27, 1944, 1995, p. 173; Herbst, *Der Totale Krieg,* p. 343; Longerich, "Joseph Goebbels und der totale Krieg," pp. 291–292.
45. Herf, *The Jewish Enemy,* pp. 250–251.
46. Seydewitz, *Civil Life,* pp. 275–279; Hancock, *National Socialist Leadership,* pp. 147–171.
47. Norbert Frei, *National Socialist Rule in Germany: The Führer State 1933–1945* (Oxford: Blackwell, 1993), pp. 138 (note 28), 214.

48. Steinert, *Hitler's War,* pp. 269–272.
49. Klemperer, *I Will Bear Witness,* p. 334.
50. Rüdiger Overmans, *Deutsche militärische Verluste im Zweiten Weltkrieg* (Munich: R. Oldenbourg, 1999), p. 239.
51. Klaus-Dietmar Henke, "Deutschland—Zweierlei Kriegsende," in Ulrich Herbert and Axel Schildt, eds., *Kriegsende in Europa: Vom Beginn des deutschen Machtzerfalls bis zur Stabilisierung der Nachkriegsordnung 1944–1948* (Essen: Klartext Verlag, 1998), p. 339.
52. Steinert, *Hitler's War,* p. 285.
53. Kershaw, *Popular Opinion,* pp. 310–311.
54. Christoph Kleßmann, "Untergänge—Übergänge: Gesellschaftsgeschichtliche Brüche und Kontinuitätslinien vor und nach 1945," in Christoph Kleßmann, ed., *Nicht nur Hitlers Krieg: Der Zweite Weltkrieg und die Deutschen* (Düsseldorf: Droste Velag, 1989), p. 85.
55. Hans Mommsen, "The Dissolution of the Third Reich: Crisis Management and Collapse, 1943–1945," *Bulletin of the German Historical Institute* 27 (Fall 2000): 9–23, http://www.ghi-dc.org/bulletin27f00/b27mommsenframe.html (accessed February 18, 2010).
56. Robert Gellately, *Backing Hitler: Consent and Coercion in Nazi Germany* (New York: Oxford University Press, 2001), pp. 230–231.
57. Fritz, *Endkampf,* p. 29; Michael Burleigh, *The Third Reich: A New History* (New York: Hill & Wang, 2000), p. 787.
58. Robert Gellately, *The Gestapo and German Society: Enforcing Racial Policy, 1933–1945* (Oxford: Clarendon Press, 1990), pp. 246–247.
59. Burleigh, *The Third Reich,* p. 783.
60. Klaus-Dietmar Henke, *Die amerikanische Besatzung Deutschlands* (Munich: R. Olenbourg, 1995), p. 87.
61. Kleßmann, *Untergänge—Übergänge,* pp. 342–343.
62. Testimony of Anna Braun, September 20, 1946, Boder Collection.
63. Ulrich Herbert, *Hitler's Foreign Workers: Enforced Foreign Labor in Germany under the Third Reich* (Cambridge: Cambridge University Press, 1997), pp. 359–365, 462.
64. Gabriele Lutfi, *KZ der Gestapo: Arbeitserziehungslager im Dritten Reich* (Stuttgart: Deutsche Velags-Anstalt, 2000), pp. 11–18.
65. "Aus Gründen der Sicherheit der kämpfenden Truppe wie zum Schutz der Zivilbevölkerung." Ibid., pp. 294–295.
66. Ibid., p. 294.
67. Ibid., pp. 295, 304.
68. Deposition of Adolf Wilhelm Methfessel, May 28, 1947, *Report of Commission for Investigation of War Crimes—the Gestapo in Hanover,* November 20, 1947, TNA, WO 309/313.
69. Herbert, *Hitler's Foreign Workers,* pp. 371–372; Lutfi, *KZ der Gestapo,* pp. 293, 305.
70. *Justiz und NS-Verbrechen,* vol. XVII (Amsterdam: Amsterdam University Press, 1977), pp. 283–284.
71. Ibid., p. 287.

72. Herbert, *Hitler's Foreign Workers,* pp. 375–376; *Justiz und NS-Verbrechen,* vol. XVII, pp. 288–290.

73. Mijndert Bertram, *April 1945: Der Luftangriff auf Celle und das Schicksal der KZ-Häftlinge aus Drütte* (Celle: Schriftenreihe des Stadtarchivs Celle und des Bomann-Museums, 1989), p. 9.

74. Gerd Wysocki, *Das KZ-Drütte bei den Hermann-Göring-Werke in Waterstend-Salizgitter, Oktober 1942 bis April 1945* (Salzgitter, Germany Arbeitskreis Stadtgeschichte, 1986), p. 29.

75. Testimony of Otto Klunder, August 30, 1965, AGN, Ng.2.8.472.

76. Deposition of French prisoner (no name), July 29, 1947, AGN, Ng.8.2.16; Jerzy Giergielewicz, *Endstation Neuengamme, Außenlager Drütte: Der Weg eines 17-jährigen aus Warschau durch vier Konzentrationslager* (Bremen: Edition Temmen, 2002), p. 77.

77. Hertz-Eichenrode, *Ein KZ wird geräumt,* vol. II, pp. 100–105.

78. Report on murder of concentration camp prisoners in Celle, April 16, 1946, TNA, WO 309/90.

79. Testimony of Wilhelm Sommer, June 9, 1989; interview with Bodo Grote, November 18, 1988; and interview with Inge Grothe, October 24, 1988, AGN (Mijndert Bertram interviews).

80. Bertram, *April 1945,* pp. 11–14.

81. Interview with Wassili Lukenovitz Krotjuk, August 10, 1993, AGN, Oral History Project (hereafter OHP), 2.8.1539; testimony of Hans Bluhm, AGN, 13-7-5-2.

82. Testimony of Hans Bluhm; Giergielewicz, *Endstation Neuengamme,* p. 78.

83. Testimony of Otto Klonder, August 30, 1965, AGN, 2.8.472; testimony of Janek Friedman (undated), AGN, 13-7-5-2; interview with Wassili Lukenovitz Krotjuk, August 10, 1993; Bertram, *April 1945,* p. 14.

84. Interview with Wilhelm Sommer, June 8, 1989; interview with Inge Grothe, October 24, 1988; interview with Bodo Grote, November 18, 1988; Bertram, *April 1945,* p. 14.

85. Deposition of Eberhard Streland, June 4, 1946, TNA, WO 309/374.

86. Testimony of Otto Klonder, August 30, 1965; interview with Bodo Grote, November 18, 1988.

87. Testimony of Otto Klonder, August 30, 1965.

88. Interview with Wassili Lukenovitz Krotjuk, August 10, 1993.

89. Bertram, *April 1945,* pp. 16–17; interview with Wilhelm Sommer, June 8, 1989.

90. Report on murder of concentration camp prisoners in Celle, April 16, 1946.

91. "Und dann haben Sie irgendwie ekant, daß das Juden sein könnten?" Testimony of Wilhelm Sommer, June 9, 1989.

92. Interview with Bodo Grote, November 18, 1988.

93. Interview with Boris Fyoderovitz Dudoladow, August 4, 1994, AGN, OHP, 2.8.–1513.

94. Bertram, *April 1945,* p. 18; Report on the murder of concentration camp prisoners in Celle, April 16, 1946.

95. Giergielewicz, *Endstation Neuengamme,* p. 95 (note 30).

96. In several cases, local citizens who wanted to aid the prisoners encountered hostile and violent reactions on the part of the units searching for prisoners: inter-

view with Wilhelm Sommer, June 8, 1989; interview with Gerhard Poerteners, November 14, 1988, AGN (Mijndert Bertram interviews); interview with Andre Berniot, AGN, OHP, 2.8–1503; testimony of Otto Klonder, August 30, 1965.

97. Bertram, *April 1945*, pp. 17–18; Report on the murder of concentration camp prisoners in Celle, April 16, 1946.

98. "Männer und Frauen in Hannover-Stadt und Land!" *Hannoversche Zeitung,* March 30, 1945.

99. "Achtet auf entwichene KZ-Häftlinge!" *Lüneburger Zeitung,* April 11, 1945.

8. Marched toward Gardelegen

1. In view of the pockets of stubborn resistance that the U.S. forces encountered in various towns in Germany and their subsequent losses, it was decided not to enter urban settlements before their total capitulation. If the town resisted it was shelled, or the U.S. Air Force was summoned to bomb the site until it surrendered. This threat was frequently the main cause for the cessation of hostilities; see Yelton, *Hitler's Volkssturm,* p. 147.

2. See the Web site of the 102nd Infantry Division; http://www.102ndinfantrydivi sion.homestead.com/Gardelegen.html (accessed September 27, 2005), and *With the 102nd Infantry Division through Germany,* a booklet published by Captain Allen Mick in September 1945, NARA, RG-407, box 14449, file 3102-0.

3. On the history of Gardelegen, see http://www.gardelegen.info/uk/geschichte _staatgeschichte.html (accessed April 20, 2009).

4. On the history of the Jewish community in the Altmark and Gardelegen, see Ernst Block, *"Wir waren eine glückliche Familie . . .": Zur Geschichte und den Schicksalen der Juden in Salzwedel/Altmark* (Salzwedel: Museum des Altmarkkreises Salzwedel, 1998); Gisela Bung and Rupert Kaiser, *Schicksale Jüdischer Familien aus Gardelegen* (Gardelegen: Schriftenreihe des Stadtmuseums Gardelegen, 1995).

5. On the battle route of the Division, see http://www.102ndinfantrydivision.home stead.com/history.html (accessed September 29, 2005). In all, 1,077 men of the Division were killed in battle in Europe and 3,668 were wounded. The Division took 147,358 German prisoners. After Action Report, April 1–April 30, 1945, May 7, 1945, NARA, RG-407, box 14452, file 3102-0-3.

6. Description of the battles in the Gardelegen area as detailed in the records of the 405th Regiment, NARA RG-407, box 14494, file 3102-Inf (405)-0.1.

7. G-3 Journal, April 14, 1945, 19.16, NARA, RG-407, box 14471, file 3102-3-2.

8. G-3 Journal, April 15, 1945, 20.15, NARA, RG-407, box 14471, file 3102-3-2.

9. First testimony of Edward Antoniak, undated (should be April 15, 1945), NARA, RG-407, box 14494, file 3102-Inf (405)-0-3.

10. Testimony of Alex Weiss, January 4, 1994, USHMMA, Acc. 1995.A.82.

11. Letter of anonymous soldier from 405th Regiment to his mother, April 19, 1945, USHMMA, Acc.1994.A.0252.

12. Wagner, *Production des Todt,* pp. 259–260.

13. Sellier, *A History of the Dora Camp,* pp. 222–223.

14. Schlußvermerk: Kontzentrationslager Dora/Mittelbau–Nebenlager Rotteleberode/Harz–Unterkommando Stempeda, Ludwigsburg, September 28, 1972,

ZStL, IV-429 AR-Z 192/72, vol. I, p. 1; Karl Gropengießer and Volker Decker, "Zusammenfassender Bericht über die Erfüllung des Forschungsauftrages zur Feststellung des Leidensweges der ehemaligen Häftlinge des KZ-Lagers Rottelberode," Archiv KZ-Gedenkstätte Mittelbau-Dora (hereafter AGM), E 3/A-96, pp. 1–3.

15. Testimony of Leonid Karzinkin, July 23, 1971, ZStL, IV-429 AR-Z 192/72, vol. II; interrogation of Walter Ulbricht, May 13, 1947, NARA, M-1079, roll 11, target 6.

16. Testimony of Walter Ulbricht, June 5, 1974, ZStL, IV-429 AR-Z 192/72, vol. II.

17. Report on number of prisoners at Mittelbau-Dora, November 1, 1944, NARA, M-1079, roll 2, target 6.

18. Several prisoners noted that in 1945 there were about 1,800 inmates at Rottleberode, but the prisoners who arrived in that period were not recorded in the camp files. However, when the camp was evacuated in April 1945, more than 1,600 prisoners were not evacuated, including those from Stempeda. On the number of prisoners at Rottleberode, see Thilo Ziegler, "Konzentrationslager im Kreis Sangerhausen," *Spengler-Museum Sangerhausen, Beiträge zur Heimatforschung*, 4 (1975): 25–27.

19. Gropengießer und Decker, "Zusamenfassender Bericht," p. 3. For data on the number of prisoners at Rottleberode in its first months, see ZStL, IV-429 AR-Z 192/72, vol. I, deposition of Hubert Hagen, who was the "Lagerältester" at Rottleberode, May 2, 1967.

20. Testimony of Yaakov Wajnberg, November 5, 1974, ZStL, IV-429 AR-Z 192/72, vol. 2.

21. Testimony of Stanisław Stepien, October 28, 1972, and testimony of Antony Szczepański, December 13, 1972, ZStL, IV-429 AR-Z 192/72, vol. 2.

22. Testimony of Walter Ulbricht, June 5, 1974; interrogation of Erhard Brauny, May 19, 1947, NARA, M-1079, roll 12, target 1.

23. Testimony of Bernhard Vorm-Brocke, May 15, 1970, ZStL, IV-429 AR-Z, vol. I; Willy Mirbach, *"Damit du es später deinem Sohn einmal erzählen kannst . . ."*: *Der autobiographische Bericht eines Luftwaffensoldaten aus dem KZ Mittelbau (August 1944–Juli 1945)* (Geldern, Germany: Verlag des Historischen Vereins für Geldern und Umgegend, 1997), pp. 95–96.

24. Schlußvermerk: Konzentrationslager Dora/Mittelbau, ZStL, IV-429 AR-Z 192/72, vol. I, pp. 4–5.

25. Deposition of Hubert Hagen, May 2, 1967.

26. Testimony of Walter Ulbricht, June 5, 1974. The prisoner Roman Drung referred to Ulbricht as the central authority in the camp. Testimony of Drung, August 18, 1945, NARA, M-1079, roll 6, target 8.

27. The prisoner Ludwig Brandt mentioned another German kapo in the camp named Fritz Gläsel. Testimony of Brandt, September 18, 1974, ZStL, IV-429 AR-Z, 192/72, vol. II. Another German Gypsy kapo was Hermann Ebender, against whom an indictment was prepared in 1984 on a charge of abusing prisoners. ZStL, IV-429 AR-Z 192/72, vol. III.

28. Diana Gring, ". . . Immer zwischen zwei Feuern: Der kommunistische Funktionshäftling Karl Semmler," in Annett Leo and Peter Reif-Spirek, eds., *Helden, Täter*

und Verräter: Studien zum DDR-Antifaschismus (Berlin: Metropol, 1999), pp. 112–113; testimony of Jan Paterek, November 11, 1972, ZStL, IV-429 AR-Z 192/72, vol. II.

29. On the complex function and status of these prisoners in the camps, see Hermann Kaienburg, "Freundschaft? Kameradschaft? . . . Wie kann denn das möglich sein? Solidarität, Widerstand und die Rolle der 'roten Kapos' in Neuengamme," in *Abgeleitete Macht: Funktionshäftlinge zwischen Widerstand und Kollaboration* (Bremen: Edition Temmen, 1998), pp. 18–50.

30. Sofsky, *The Order of Terror,* p. 145.

31. Testimony of Romuald Bąk, September 25, 1947, Strafsache gegen Rudolf Jordan, Gerhard Thiele, Staatsanwaltschafft beim Landesgericht Stendal (hereafter SLS), 21Js 87295/91, vol. I.

32. Testimony of Baruch Seidel, August 15, 1947, NARA, M-1079, roll 6, target 7.

33. Thilo Ziegler, *Das Außenlager Rottelberode,* November 8, 1966, and testimony of Kazimierz Cacek, October 25, 1972, ZStL, IV-429 AR-Z 192/72, vol. I; and indictment against Hermann Ebender, February 16, 1984, ZStL, IV-429 AR-Z 192/72, vol. III.

34. Deposition of Walter Ulbricht, October 23, 1947, NARA, M-1079, roll 12, target 2; interrogation of Walter Ulbricht, May 13, 1947; testimony of Franciszek Dzierzandowski, September 20, 1974, ZStL, IV-429 AR-Z 192/72, vol. II.

35. Wagner, *Produktion des Todes,* p. 405.

36. Kurt Pelny, *Das ehemalige KZ "Mittelbau-Dora,"* AGM, 50.1.7.1.3, pp. 16–18.

37. Testimony of Mojsek Lipowitz, May 1947, YVA, JM/10/031, roll 2, target 2; Wagner, *Produktion des Todes,* pp. 405–406.

38. Wagner, *Produktion des Todes,* pp. 406–409; Pelny, *Das ehemalige KZ "Mittelbau-Dora."*

39. Indictment against Hermann Ebender, February 16, 1984, p. 10; testimony of Yaakov Plat, February 20, 1948, YVA, M-1/E 2241; testimony of Yehuda Jedlinski, February 18, 1976, YVA, TR-11/629.1; testimony of Shlomo Schigelski, February 15, 1976, YVA, TR-11/629.1; testimony of Romuald Bąk, September 25, 1947, vol. I; Ziegler, "Konzentrationslager im Kreis Sangerhausen," pp. 22, 29.

40. Indictment against Hermann Ebender, February 16, 1984, p. 11.

41. Testimony of Yehuda Jedlinski, September 15, 1997, YVA, 03/10350; deposition of Walter Ulbricht, October 23, 1947.

42. Testimony of Yaakov Palt, March 26, 1966, YVA, 03/3032.

43. From the indictment against Hermann Ebender, February 16, 1984, p. 11; testimony of Haim Kleiner, March 2, 1976, YVA, TR-11/629.1.

44. Testimony of Barch Seidel, August 15, 1947, NARA, M-1079, roll 6, target 7; testimony of Haim Kleiner, March 2, 1976, YVA, TR-11/629.1.

45. Testimonies of Yehuda Jedlinski, February 18, 1976; Shlomo Schigalski, February 15, 1976; Avraham Seylis and Isaak Berkenstaff, February 27, 1976, YVA, TR-11/629.1.

46. Testimony of Hubert Ubner, August 8, 1963, AGM, E 3/A-96.

47. Indictment against Hermann Ebender, February 16, 1984.

48. Testimonies of Moshe Jacubowicz, March 25, 1976; Wolf Lass, March 17, 1976; and Haim Kleiner, March 2, 1976.

49. Testimony of Yaakov Palt, March 26, 1966; testimony of Yosef Feigenbaum, May 11, 1976, YVA, TR-11/629.1.
50. Clarence Lusane, *Hitler's Black Victims: The Historical Experience of Afro-Germans, European Blacks, Africans, and African Americans in the Nazi Era* (New York: Routledge, 2003), pp. 238–241.
51. Testimonies of Pesach Bornstein, March 21, 1976; Yisrael Baum, April 3, 1973; and Yehuda Jedlinski, February 18, 1976.
52. Testimony of Romuald Bąk, September 25, 1947, vol. I; interrogation of Walter Ulbricht, May 13, 1947.
53. Deposition of Walter Ulbricht, October 23, 1947; testimony of Haim Kleiner, March 2, 1976.
54. Testimony of Avraham Shilis, February 27, 1976, YVA, TR-11/629.1; testimony of Baruch Seidel, August 15, 1947.
55. Testimony of Avraham Shilis and testimony of Aryeh Rand, June 9, 1976, YVA, TR-11/629.1; testimony of Menahem Wajnrav, November 1968, YVA, 03/3343.
56. According to data from Mittelbau-Dora HQ, between August 1943, when the camp was established, and March 1944, some 600 prisoners perished. See Wagner, *Produktion des Todt,* pp. 189–190. In its final months, from January 21, 1945, to March 1945, according to SS reports, 3,571 prisoners died there. NARA, M-1079, roll 11, target 6.
57. Indictment against Hermann Ebender, February 16, 1984, p. 14.
58. Jewish prisoners testified that on some days at Stempeda between 5 and 10 prisoners died. Testimony of Avraham Shilis, February 27, 1976; testimony of Baruch Seidel, August 15, 1947.
59. Testimony of Menahem Wajnrav, November 1968, YVA, 03/3343; testimony of Shlomo Schigalski, February 15, 1976.
60. The figures on the number of prisoners at Rottleberode at the end of March 1945 are not clear-cut. According to several testimonies there were 1,699 prisoners there at the time. Testimony of Romuald Bąk, September 25, 1947, vol. I. In any event, at the time of the evacuation there were between 1,400 and 1,500 prisoners, including those at Stempeda.
61. Testimony of Romuald Bąk; September 25, 1947, vol. I; testimony of Andrzei Fankenberg, April 21, 1945, Nederlands Instituut voor Oorlogsdocumentie (hereafter NIOD), 250K Mittelbau/Dora, karton 13a; testimony of Karl Semmler, Massenmord an antifaschistischen Widerstandskämpfern in einer Feldscheune bei Gardelegen im Frühjahr 1945, Der Staatsanwalt des Bezirkes Magdeburg, February 12, 1960, Bundesbeauftragte für die Unterlagen des Staatssicherheitsdienstes der ehemaligen DDR (hereafter BstU), ZM1625 Bd.34, Akte 116–122, p. 4. Semmler testified several times about his years in concentration camps and the Gardelegen affair, and there are often discrepancies between the various versions.
62. Mirbach, *"Damit du es später,"* pp. 153–155.
63. Deposition of Erhard Brauny, October 24, 1947, NARA, M-1079, roll 12, target 2.
64. Sellier, *A History of the Dora Camp,* p. 147; Wagner, *Produktion des Todt,* pp. 234–235.
65. Testimony of Walter Ulbricht, October 6, 1989, SLS, 21Js 87295/91, vol. IV.

66. Interrogation of Erhard Brauny, December 3, 1947, NARA, M-1079, roll 10, target 3.
67. Testimony of Leonid Karzinkin, July 23, 1971. The prisoners' versions of the division into groups during the evacuation from Rottleberode are not identical. Karzinkin refers to three groups of 340 prisoners each, Ulbricht refers to about 10 groups of 200 each, and Bąk says there were groups of 100 prisoners. It seems that the prisoners were divided into groups and afterward into blocs, according to the division between the two evacuation commanders, Brauny and Lamp.
68. Karl Semmlers Erinnerungsbericht, AGM, 50.1.7.1/.11, p. 6; Joachim Neander, *Gardelegen 1945: Das Ende der Häftlingstransporte aus dem Konzentrationslager "Mittelbau"* (Magdeburg: Landeszentrale für politische Bildung Sachsen-Anhalt, 1998), p. 12.
69. Testimony of Romuald Bąk, September 25, 1947, SLS, 27Js 87295/91, special vol. IV; interrogation of Friedrich Teply, May 20, 1947, NARA, M-1079, roll 11, target 6; Neander, *Gardelegen 1945*, pp. 12–23; Kathrin Veigel, "Gardelegen 13/14. April 1945: Rekontruktion eines NS-Verbrechens" (MA thesis, Technical University of Berlin, 2001), pp. 63–64.
70. Testimony of Walter Ulbricht, May 13, 1947.
71. Testimony and interrogation of Walter Ulbricht, May 13 and October 23, 1947; and his testimony of October 6, 1969, SLS, 21Js 87295/91, vol. IV.
72. Testimony of Erhard Brauny, October 27, 1947, NARA, M-1079, roll 12, target 2; Neander, *Gardelegen 1945*, p. 13.
73. Interrogation of Friedrich Teply, May 20, 1947; testimony of Baruch Seidel, August 15, 1947. Seidel says that the prisoners received no additional food after the ration they were given on leaving Rottleberode.
74. Interrogation of Erhard Brauny, May 19, 1947; testimony of Wilhelm Hack, May 22, 1947, NARA, M-1079, roll 5, target 1; Veigel, "Gardelegen 13/14. April 1945," p. 64.
75. Interrogation of Erhard Brauny, December 3, 1947.
76. Sellier, *A History of the Dora Camp*, pp. 208–209.
77. Veigel, "Gardelegen 13/14. April 1945," p. 65; Morel, *Les Derniers Supplices*, p. 15.
78. Neander, *Gardelegen 1945*, p. 13.
79. Testimony of Adolf-August Pinnenkämper, April 30, 1945, NIOD, carton 13a; U.S. Army, Report of Investigation of Massacres of Political Prisoners at Gardelegen, Germany (Summary of facts), May 23, 1945, p. 9, NIOD, carton 13a-II; Karel Margry, "The Gardelegen Massacre," *After the Battle* 111 (2000): 6.
80. Interrogation of Friedrich Teply, May 20, 1947.
81. Interrogation of Erhard Brauny, December 3, 1947.
82. Testimony of Romuald Bąk, September 25, 1947, special vol. IV.
83. Ibid.
84. Interrogation of Erhard Brauny, May 19, 1947.
85. Margry, "The Gardelegen Massacre," p. 6; Neander, *Gardelegen 1945*, p. 14.
86. Neander, *Gardelegen 1945*, p. 14.
87. Karl Semmlers Erinnerungsbericht, p. 14; Neander, *Gardelegen 1945*, p. 15.
88. Neander, *"Hat in Europa,"* pp. 187–200.

89. Massenmord an antifaschistischen Widerstandskämpfern, p. 5.
90. Deposition of Fritz Hesse, commander of the gendarmerie unit at Obisfelde in 1945, February 18, 1961, SLS, 21Js 87295/91, vol. I; Karl Semmlers Erinnerungsbericht, p. 14; Margry, "The Gardelegen Massacre," p. 7.
91. Veigel, "Gardelegen 13/14. April 1945," p. 66.
92. Karl Semmlers Erinnerungsbericht, p. 12.
93. Testimony of Baruch Seidel, August 15, 1947.
94. Karl Semmlers Erinnerungsbericht, pp. 15–16.
95. Testimony of Hermann Lamp, November 27, 1974, ZStL, IV 429 AR-Z 192/71, vol. II; Neander, *"Hat in Europa,"* p. 191; Mirbach, *"Damit du es später,"* pp. 162–164.
96. Karola Fings, *Krieg, Gesellschaft und KZ: Himmlers SS-Baubrigaden* (Paderborn: Ferdinand Schöningh, 2005), pp. 34–44.
97. Allen, *The Business of Genocide,* p. 153; Schulte, *Zwangsarbeit,* pp. 345–346; Kaienburg, *Die Wirtschaft der SS,* pp. 395–396.
98. Neander, *"Hat in Europa,"* pp. 199–200; Wagner, *Produktion des Todt,* pp. 245–248; Sellier, *The History of Dora Camp,* pp. 187–190; Fings, *Krieg, Gesellschaft und KZ,* p. 23.
99. Veigel, "Gardelegen 13/14. April 1945," p. 71.
100. Neander, *Gardelegen 1945,* pp. 18, 21; Neander, *"Hat in Europa,"* pp. 199–200; Fings, *Krieg, Gesellschaft und KZ,* pp. 274–275.
101. Neander, *Gardelegen 1945,* p. 18.
102. Interrogation of Otto-Georg Brinkman, June 30, 1947, NARA, M-1079, roll 13, target 2.
103. Fings, *Krieg, Gesellschaft und KZ,* pp. 273–274.
104. Aimé Bonifas, *Prisoner 20801* (Wilmington, DE: Cedar Press, 1983), pp. 56–57.
105. Testimony of Jüger Georges, April 13, 1968, *Staatsarchiv Gardelegen,* Stadtmuseum (hereafter MGS Gardelegen), 410; Neander, *Gardelegen 1945,* p. 23.
106. Testimony of Georg Pieper, May 2, 1945, NIOD, carton 13a.
107. Interview with Lucien Colonel, May 23, 1997. I am grateful to Diana Gring for placing at my disposal a collection of interviews she conducted with survivors of and witnesses to the massacre at Gardelegen (hereafter Gring interviews); testimony of Georg Pieper, May 2, 1945.
108. Neander, *Gardelegen 1945,* p. 24; Margry, "The Gardelegen Massacre," p. 4.
109. Bonifas, *Prisoner 20801,* p. 57.
110. Testimony of Georg Pieper, May 2, 1945; testimony of Jüger Georges, April 13, 1968.
111. Manfred Uschner, "Bombennacht in Magdeburg," in Christine Krauss and Daniel Küchenmeister, eds., *Das Jahr 1945: Brüche und Kontinuitäten* (Berlin: Dietz Verlag, 1995), pp. 167–169.
112. Neander, *Gardelegen 1945,* p. 24.
113. Margry, "The Gardelegen Massacre," p. 4.
114. Deposition of Paul Mass, November 1, 1950, Strafsache gegen Wilhelm Genth, Paul Mass, Niedersächsisches Hauptstaatsarchiv Hannover (hereafter NdsH), 721 97/99 No. 26/1, p. 2
115. Die Verhältnisse im KL Hannover-Stöcken, April 10, 1963, NdsH, 721 97/99 No. 26/3, p. 5.

116. Außenkommando Stöcken, AGN, Ng. 8.2.7; Herbert Obenaus, "Konzentrationslager und Rüstungswirtschaft: Der Einsatz von KZ-Häftlingen in den Industriebetrieben Hannovers," in Ludwig Eiber, ed., *Verfolgung—Ausbeutung—Vernichtung: Die Lebens- und Arbeitsbedingungen in deutschen Konzentrationslagern 1933–1945* (Hanover: Fackelträger, 1985), pp. 163–172; Veigel, "Gardelegen 13/14. April 1945," p. 42.

117. Deposition of Kurt Klebeck, February 7, 1951, NdsH, 721 97/99 No. 26/1, p. 1.

118. "Kein Häftling lebend in die Hände der Alliierten fallen dürfe." Deposition of Paul Mass, November 1, 1950, p. 4.

119. Deposition of Wilhelm Gant, March 3, 1961, NdsH, 721 97/99 No. 26/2, p. 2.

120. Testimony of Roger Maria, July 16, 1947, SLS, 21Js 87295/91, special vol. IV; testimony of Goncourt-Mateu Lambert, April 22, 1945, NIOD, carton 13a.

121. Testimony of Władysław Waleszyński, AGN, OHP, 1117; testimony of Stanisław Majewicz, September 18, 1985, SLS, 21Js 87295/91, vol. VI; Obenaus, "Konzentrationslager und Rüstungswirtschaft," p. 173.

122. Das KL Hannover-Stöcken, Staatsanwaltschaft bei dem Landesgericht Hannover, 2 Js 622/49, January 28, 1963, NdsH, 721 97/99 No. 26/3, pp. 7–8.

123. Die Verhältnisse im KL Hannover-Stöcken, April 10, 1963, p. 8.

124. Testimony of René Baumer, October 13, 1951, AN, 72 AJ 320, dossier A.1 no. 7; testimony of Erhard Groellman, February 27, 1951, NdsH, 721 97/99 No. 26/1; Veigel, "Gardelegen 13/14. April 1945," pp. 44–45.

125. Deposition of Paul Mass, November 1, 1950, p. 5.

126. Testimony of Kurt Klebeck, February 7, 1951, p. 2.

127. Deposition of Kurt Klebeck, November 10, 1947, NdsH, 721 97/99 No. 26/4, No. 37A.

128. Deposition of Roger Maria, July 17, 1947, NdsH, 721 97/99 No. 26/4, p. 2.

129. Veigel, "Gardelegen 13/14. April 1945," p. 46; testimony of Stanisław Majewicz, September 18, 1985; testimony of Stanisław Waleszyński, 1117.

130. Testimony of Wilhelm Fentzling, April 25, 1945, NIOD, carton 13a.

131. AGN, Außenkommando Stöcken, Ng. 8.2.7.

132. Margry, "The Gardelegen Massacre," p. 8; testimony of Wilhelm Fentzling, December 10, 1946, MGS Gardelegen, 410. According to the prisoners' testimony, the Stöcken train reached Mieste while the train carrying Brauny's transport was already standing there. Fentzling testified in 1945 that the train reached Mieste at 6 p.m., and in a later testimony, in 1946, that it was at 4 p.m. on April 9.

133. Testimony of Fritz Pössel, in *Tage im April: Ein Lesebuch* (Gardelegen: Schriftenreihe des Stadtmusueums, 1995), p. 9.

134. Karl Semmlers Erinnerungsbericht, p. 23.

135. Testimony of Stanisław Majewicz, September 18, 1985; interview with Roger Maria, November 25, 1991, AGN OHP, 2.8–1555; U.S. Army, Report of Investigation, May 23, 1945, p. 9.

136. Deposition of Erhard Brauny, October 24, 1947, NARA, M-1079, roll 12, target 2.

137. Karl Semmlers Erinnerungsbericht, pp. 16, 19; Neander, *Gardelegen 1945*, p. 27.

138. Karl Semmlers Erinnerungsbericht, pp. 17–18.
139. Interrogation of Erhard Brauny, May 19, 1947.
140. Testimony of Baruch Seidel, August 15, 1947.
141. Deposition of Franz Unverdorben, April 28, 1945, SLS, 21Js 87295/91, special issue I; testimony of Romuald Bąk, September 25, 1947, vol. I; testimony of Wilhelm Fentzling, December 10, 1946; Margry, "The Gardelegen Massacre," p. 8.
142. Deposition of Adolf Krüger, May 21, 1945, NIOD, carton 13a.
143. U.S. Army, Report of Investigation, May 23, 1945, p. 18.
144. Testimony of Bruno Schachel, official of the district administration in Gardelegen, April 25, 1945, NIOD, carton 13a.
145. Testimony of Karl Lepa, acting mayor of Gardelegen, December 5, 1963, SLS, 21Js 87295/91, vol. III; Margry, "The Gardelegen Massacre," p. 8.
146. Deposition of Albert Borges, November 24, 1961, SLS, 21Js 87295/91, vol. II.
147. Testimony of Romuald Bąk, September 25, 1947, special vol. IV; Massenmord an antifaschistischen Widerstandskämpfern, p. 8; Karl Semmlers Erinnerungsbericht, p. 21.
148. Testimony of Wilhelm Fentzling, December 10, 1946.
149. Testimony of Adolf Krüger, May 21, 1945, NIOD, carton 13a.
150. Testimony of Bruno Schachel, April 25, 1945.
151. Deposition of Erich-August Rudolf Gotthard, November 26, 1961, SLS, 21Js 87295/91, vol. II.
152. Testimony of Hermann Schulze, in *Tage im April,* p. 15.
153. Testimony of Karl Lepa, December 5, 1963; interrogation of Erhard Brauny, May 19, 1947.
154. Interrogation of Erhard Brauny, May 20, 1947, NARA, M-1079, roll 12, target 1.
155. Deposition of Rudolf Ringstmeyer, February 15, 1961, SLS, 21Js 87295/91, vol. I.
156. See Avraham Margaliot and Yehoyakim Cochavi, eds., *Toldot HaShoah: Germania* [Annals of the Holocaust: Germany], vol. I (Jerusalem: Yad Vashem, 1998), pp. 264–265.
157. Bung and Kaiser, *Schicksale jüdischer Familien aus Gardelegen,* pp. 58, 62.
158. Testimony of Karl Lepa, December 5, 1963; deposition of Rudolf Ringstmeyer, February 15, 1961.
159. Testimony of Adolf-August Pinnenkämper, April 30, 1945; testimony of Baruch Seidel, August 15, 1947; Margry, "The Gardelegen Massacre," p. 8.
160. Veigel, "Gardelegen 13/14. April 1945," p. 77.
161. Testimony of Romuald Bąk, September 9, 1947, NARA, M-1079, roll 7, target 5. Bąk himself was unable to reconstruct precisely what he heard or understood from the kapo. In his testimony at the U.S. tribunal in the Mittelbau-Dora trial, he said that the prisoners were to have remained in the freight cars. In his testimony several weeks later before the Polish Military Committee for Investigation of German War Crimes, he said that they understood that the sick were to be liquidated: testimony of Romuald Bąk, September 25, 1947, special vol. IV.
162. Interrogation of Friedrich Teply, May 20, 1947.

163. Testimony of Wilhelm Fentzling, April 25, 1945; deposition of Adolf Krüger, May 21, 1945, NIOD, carton 13a.

164. Deposition of Adolf Kruger, May 21, 1945; testimony of Wilhelm Fentzling, December 10, 1946.

165. 102nd Infantry Div. G-2 Periodical Report #163, April 19, 1945, PW Interrogation Report, NIOD, carton 13a.

166. U.S. Army, Report of Investigation, May 23, 1945, p. 10.

167. Deposition of Adolf Krüger, May 21, 1945; testimony of Vassily Mitofanovic Mamoshuk, August 9, 1968, SLS, 21Js 87295/91, special issue I.

168. This was the phrase used by Rudolf Ringstmeyer in his deposition of February 5, 1961.

169. Testimony of Gonkheer-Mathieu Lambert, April 22, 1945; Massenmord an antifaschistischen Widerstandskämpfern, p. 9.

170. Testimony of Baruch Seidel, August 15, 1947; testimony of Aurel Szobel, April 20, 1945, NIOD, carton 13a; Morel, Les Derniers Supplices, p. 31.

171. Testimony of Romuald Bąk, September 9, 1947.

172. Testimony of Adolf-August Pinnenkämper, April 30, 1945.

173. Karl Semmler Erinnerungsbericht, p. 29.

174. Interrogation of Rudolf Kuhn, April 30, 1945, NIOD, carton 13a.

175. Testimony of Fritz Edling, in Tage im April, p. 27.

176. Testimony of Eugeniusz Ściwiarski, April 24, 1945, NIOD, carton 13a.

177. Deposition of Erhard Brauny, October 24, 1947; testimony of Edward Antoniak, June 28, 1969, ZstL, VI 302 AR 507/70, vol. V.

178. Testimony of Romuald Bąk, September 25, 1947, special vol. IV.

179. Testimony of Romuald Bąk, in Tage im April, p. 14.

180. Deposition of Franz Unverdorben, April 28, 1945, SLS, 27Js 87295/91, special issue I; testimony of Romuald Bąk, September 9, 1947; testimony of Baruch Seidel, August 15, 1947.

181. Testimony of Pyotrov Dimitry, May 6, 1945, NIOD, carton 13a.

182. Testimony of Romuald Bąk; September 9, 1947; testimony of D. Defo de Nord, April 23, 1945, NIOD, carton 13a.

183. Testimony of Baruch Seidel, August 15, 1947.

184. Testimony of Wilhelm Berlin, May 12, 1945, NIOD, carton 13a; testimony of Walter Neubaur, in Tage im April, p. 19.

185. Testimony of Walter Neubaur, in Tage im April, p. 19.

186. Testimony of Henryk Kostrzewa, May 11, 1945, NIOD, carton 13a.

187. Testimony of Henryk Kostrzewa, May 11, 1945; testimony of Jan Fromkanwiak, May 11, 1945, NIOD, carton 13a.

188. Testimony of Ewald Wendel, in Tage im April, pp. 19–20.

189. 102nd Infantry Div. G-2 Periodical Report #168, April 19, 1945, Consolidated PW Interrogation Report, NIOD, carton 13a.

190. Report of Investigation by Kenneth Russ of the Estedt massacre, May 14, 1945, NIOD, carton 13a.

191. Testimony of Wilhelm Berlin, May 12, 1945; testimony of Walter Neubauer, in Tage im April, p. 20.

192. Ludwig Lewin, Erlebnisbericht, Gardelegen, May 8, 1969, MGS Gardelegen, 523.

193. Testimony of Walter Neubauer, in *Tage im April,* p. 17; Margry, "The Gardelegen Massacre," p. 11.
194. Testimony of Pyotrov Dimitry, May 6, 1945.
195. Testimony of Stanisław Majewicz, September 18, 1985.
196. Interview with Roger Maria, November 25, 1991.
197. Testimony of Hermann Krischok, in *Tage im April,* p. 18.
198. Testimony of Yevgeny Ivanovitch Katev, April 25, 1945, NIOD, carton 13a; testimony of Stanisław Majewicz, September 18, 1985.
199. Deposition of Roger Maria, July 17, 1947, p. 2.
200. Testimony of Stanisław Waleszyński, April 25, 1945, NIOD, carton 13a.
201. Testimony of Andrzei Fankenberg, April 21, 1945.
202. Testimony of Wilhelm Fentzling, April 25, 1945; testimony of Leonid Maistro, April 25, 1945, NIOD, carton 13a; testimony of Yevgeny Ivanovitch Katev, February 15, 1971, SLS, 27Js 87295/91, special issue I. Fentzling is the only witness who speaks of about 60 corpses of prisoners who died or were murdered, but it is not clear from his testimony if he was referring only to the column of sick prisoners evacuated on wagons.
203. Diana Gring, *Die Todesmärsche und das Massaker von Gardelegen: NS-Verbrechen in der Endphase des Zweiten Weltkriegs* (Gardelegen: Stadtmuseum Gardelegen, 1993), p. 40.
204. Ibid.
205. Testimony of Hermann Pranden, December 10, 1963, SLS, 21Js 87295/91, vol. III; Neander, *Gardelegen 1945,* p. 25.
206. Testimony of Georg Pieper, May 2, 1945; testimony of Jüger Georges, April 13, 1968; interview with Lucien Colonel, May 23, 1997, Gring interviews.
207. Neander, *Gardelegen 1945,* pp. 25–26.
208. Bericht über Ausgrabungen in Dolle und Umgebung, March 31, 1949, AGM, 50.1.7.1, no. 2, p. 1.
209. Margry, "The Gardelegen Massacre," p. 4.
210. Testimony of Hermann Madowicz, May 5, 1945, NIOD, carton 13a.
211. Testimony of Kurt Weigert, in *Tage im April,* p. 23. The prisoners were often referred to by the local Germans as "zebras" because of their striped uniforms.
212. Testimony of G., in *Tage im April,* p. 24.
213. Testimonies of Jonas Bieneck, Fritz Kallweit, and Ulrich Freitag, April 28, 1945, NIOD, carton 13a.
214. Captain Luther E. Gowder to Headquarters Ninth U.S. Army JA Section, War Crimes Section, May 13, 1945, NIOD, carton 13a.
215. *DDR-Justiz und NS-Verbrechen,* vol. IV (Amsterdam: Amsterdam University Press, 2004), p. 260.
216. Gring, *Die Todesmärsche und das Massaker von Gardelegen,* p. 40.
217. Interrogation of Rudolf Kempe, May 9, 1945, NIOD, carton 13a.
218. Testimony of Erich Mattis, May 9, 1945, NIOD, carton 13a.

9. The Burning Barn

1. U.S. Army, Report of Investigation, May 23, 1945, p. 11.
2. Margry, "The Gardelegen Massacre," p. 3.

3. Deposition of Karl Lepa, December 5, 1963, SLS, 21Js 87295/91, vol. III.
4. Deposition of Rudolf Ringstmeyer, February 15, 1961, SLS, 21Js 87295/91, vol. I; Margry, "The Gardelegen Massacre," p. 12.
5. Interrogation of Josef-Rudolf Kuhn, May 6, 1950, BstU, RHE-West 33/3.
6. Deposition of Friedrich Hilmer von Sherr-Thoss, May 27, 1971, SLS, 21Js 87295/91, vol. V; deposition of Josef-Rudolf Kuhn, April 30, 1945, NIOD, carton 13a.
7. Interrogation of Josef-Rudolf Kuhn, May 6, 1950; interrogation of Josef-Rudolf Kuhn, August 16, 1946, SLS, 27Js 87295/91, special issue I.
8. Deposition of Josef-Rudolf Kuhn, April 30, 1945.
9. Interrogation of Josef-Rudolf Kuhn, August 16, 1946.
10. Deposition of Josef-Rudolf Kuhn, November 27, 1961, SLS, 21Js 87295/91, vol. II.
11. Interrogation of Josef-Rudolf Kuhn, May 6, 1950.
12. Interrogation of Walter Miltz, May 13, 1950, BstU, RHE-West 33/3; deposition of Walter Miltz, March 3, 1963, SLS, 21Js 87295/91, vol. I.
13. Deposition of Walter Miltz, March 3, 1963.
14. Testimony of Romuald Bąk, September 30, 1946, SLS, 27Js 87295/91, special issue IV.
15. Testimony of Josef Pamuta, April 23, 1945, NIOD, carton 13a; testimony of Piotrov Dmitry, May 6, 1945, NIOD, carton 13a.
16. Karl Semmlers Erinnerungsbericht, AGM, 50.1.7.1/11, pp. 30–31; testimony of Adolf-August Pinnenkämper, April 30, 1945, NIOD, carton 13a; *Tage im April,* p. 3.
17. Testimony of Andrezj Fankenberg, April 21, 1945, NIOD, carton 13a.
18. Deposition of Josef-Rudolf Kuhn, April 30, 1945.
19. Deposition of Walter Miltz, March 3, 1963; deposition of Josef-Rudolf Kuhn, April 30, 1945.
20. Interrogation of Josef-Rudolf Kuhn, August 16, 1946.
21. Interrogation of Erhard Brauny, May 20, 1947, NARA, M-1079, roll 12, target 1.
22. Deposition of Erhard Brauny, October 24, 1947, NARA, M-1079, roll 12, target 2.
23. Interrogation of Friedrich Teply, November 21, 1947, NARA, M-1079, roll 9, target 12.
24. Interrogation of Erhard Brauny, May 20, 1947.
25. Deposition of Erhard Brauny, October 24, 1947.
26. Interrogation of Friedrich Teply, April 28, 1947, NARA, M-1079, roll 11, target 6.
27. Ibid.
28. List of suspects of involvement in the murder of prisoners at Gardelegen prepared by Red Army interrogators in 1946, Ministerium der Justiz, Hauptkommission zur Untersuchung der Hitlerverbrechen in Polen, to Stellvertreter des Generalstaatsanwalts der Deutschen Demokratischen Republik, Warsaw, April 10, 1975, BStU, RHE-West 33/4.
29. Deposition of Hans Debrodt, May 10, 1945, NIOD, carton 13a.
30. Summary of findings of the investigation of the Gardelegen affair, Staatsanwaltschaft Göttingen, 43/4 Js 1184/63, October 5, 1990, SLS, 21Js 87295/91, vol. VI, p. 5; deposition of Josef-Rudolf Kuhn, November 27, 1961.

31. Report on investigation concerning Gerhard Thiele, Baverisches Landeskriminalamt, November 29, 1961, SLS, 21Js 87295/91, vol. I; deposition of Josef-Rudolf Kuhn, November 27, 1961.
32. Deposition of Hans Debrodt, May 10, 1945, NIOD, carton 13a.
33. Interrogation of Friedrich Teply, May 20, 1947, NARA, M-1079, roll 11, target 6.
34. Interrogation of Arno Brake, August 6, 1946, SLS, 27Js 87295/91, special issue I; deposition of Wilhelm Becker, April 26, 1945, NIOD, carton 13a.
35. Deposition of Hermann Holtz, May 10, 1945, NIOD, carton 13a.
36. Deposition of Hans Debrodt, May 10, 1945.
37. Ibid.
38. Deposition of Rudolf Ringstmeyer, November 21, 1961, SLS, 21Js 87295/91, vol. II.
39. Deposition of Hans Debrodt, May 10, 1945.
40. Interrogation of Josef-Rudolf Kuhn, August 16, 1946.
41. Deposition of Josef-Rudolf Kuhn, May 9, 1945, NIOD, carton 13a.
42. Deposition of Walter Miltz, November 22, 1961, SLS, 21Js 87295/91, vol. II.
43. Deposition of Gisela Schulze, May 3, 1945, NIOD, carton 13a.
44. Deposition of Hermann Holtz, May 10, 1945.
45. Deposition of Hans Debrodt, May 10, 1945.
46. Deposition of Fritz Rose, May 22, 1945; deposition of Friedrich Erlich, April 27, 1945, NIOD, carton 13a.
47. Deposition of Wilhelm Becker, April 30, 1945, NIOD, carton 13a.
48. Interrogation of Gustav Palis, July 30, 1946, BstU, RHE-West 33/1.
49. Deposition of Fritz Rose, May 22, 1945.
50. Deposition of Wilhelm Becker, November 11, 1963, SLS, 21Js 87295/91, vol. II.
51. Interrogation of Wilhelm Becker, April 26, 1945.
52. Interrogation of Wilhelm Biermann, June 30, 1946, BStU, RHE-West 33/1.
53. Interrogation of Arno Brake, August 6, 1946.
54. Becker denied any connection to this affair and told his U.S. interrogators in 1945 that he had no idea as to the identity of the Volkssturm men who murdered the prisoners: deposition of Wilhelm Becker, April 30, 1945.
55. Wilhelm Hausmann admitted that he was in the group that caught the two prisoners and that Becker too was there. Deposition of Wilhelm Hausmann, May 3, 1945, NIOD, carton 13a.
56. Willi Niebel was also a resident of Kloster-Beuendorf. Deposition of Willi Niebel, May 3, 1945, NIOD, carton 13a. Hausmann too lived in the village.
57. Deposition of Wilhelm Becker, April 30, 1945.
58. Deposition of Hermann Holtz, May 10, 1945.
59. Interrogation of Gustav Palis, July 30, 1946.
60. Interrogation of Josef-Rudolf Kuhn, May 6, 1950.
61. Deposition of Friedrich Lotz, March 7, 1961, SLS, 21Js 87295/91, vol. I.
62. Deposition of Josef-Rudolf Kuhn, April 30, 1945.
63. Interrogation of Kazimierz Drygalski, June 30, 1946, BStU, RHE-West 33/1.
64. Testimony of Adolf August, September 29, 1971, SLS, 21Js 87295/91, vol. VII.
65. Testimony of Andrzej Fankenberg, April 21, 1945.
66. Testimony of Karl Semmler, April 21, 1945, NIOD, carton 13a.

67. Testimony of Ludwig Juchocki, April 22, 1945, NIOD, carton 13a.

68. Testimony of Kazimierz Tygalski (should be Drygalski), April 30, 1945, NIOD, carton 13a; testimony of Kazimierz Drygalski, December 11, 1945, NIOD, carton 13a.

69. Karl Semmlers Erinnerungsbericht, p. 32; testimony of Josef Śrowieczki, April 23, 1945, NIOD, carton 13a; Lewin, *Erlebnisbericht*, MGS Gardelegen, 523.

70. When the groups of prisoners left Mieste, several kapos were given Volkssturm armbands and several also received pistols. Testimony of Adolf-August Pinnenkämper, April 30, 1945.

71. Interrogation of Friedrich Teply, May 27, 1947, NARA, M-1079, roll 11, target 6.

72. Interrogation of Friedrich Teply, November 21, 1947; interrogation of Friedrich Teply, May 27, 1947.

73. Interrogation of Josef-Rudolf Kuhn, May 16, 1950.

74. Interrogation of Kazimierz Drygalski, September 25, 1945, NIOD, carton 13a.

75. Deposition of Friedrich Hilmer, May 27, 1971, SLS, 21Js 87295/91, vol. IV.

76. Deposition of Josef-Rudolf Kuhn, May 9, 1945.

77. Testimony of Adolf-August Pinnenkämper, April 30, 1945.

78. Testimony of Franz Weiser, April 30, 1945; testimony of Kazimierz Tygalski (Drygalski), April 30, 1945.

79. Interrogation of Kazimierz Drygalski, September 25, 1945; testimony of Ludwig Juchocki, April 22, 1945; testimony of Adolf-August Pinnenkämper, April 30, 1945; interrogation of Friedrich Teply, May 20, 1947.

80. Deposition of Josef-Rudolf Kuhn, May 9, 1945; interrogation of Josef-Rudolf Kuhn, August 16, 1946.

81. Kuhn, who received the telephone call, was not convinced that it was Thiele himself, and it is possible that this time as well it was Debrodt. Interrogation of Josef-Rudolf Kuhn, August 16, 1946.

82. Interrogation of Friedrich Teply, May 20, 1947.

83. Interrogation of Friedrich Teply, November 21, 1947.

84. Interrogation of Josef-Rudolf Kuhn, May 6, 1950.

85. Margry, "The Gardelegen Massacre," p. 13.

86. Interrogation of Josef-Rudolf Kuhn, August 16, 1946; Margry, "The Gardelegen Massacre."

87. Testimony of Bondy Geza, April 20, 1945, NIOD, carton 13a; Karl Semmlers Erinnerungsbericht, p. 33.

88. Testimony of Adolf-August Pinnenkämper, April 30, 1945; interrogation of Friedrich Teply, May 20, 1947, NARA, M-1079, roll 11, target 6.

89. Testimony of Karl Semmler, March 16, 1961, SLS, 21Js 87295/91, vol. I.

90. Testimony of Evgeny Ivanovic Katev, February 15, 1971, SLS, 27Js 87295/91, special issue I.

91. Testimony of Romuald Bąk, September 25, 1947, SLS, 27Js 87295/91, special issue IV.

92. Karl Semmlers Erinnerungsbericht, p. 32; testimony of Włodzimierz Woźny, April 22, 1945, NIOD, carton 13a.

93. Testimony of Josef Pamuta, April 23, 1945; testimony of Kazimierz Tygalsky (Drygalski), April 30, 1945.

94. Testimony of Adolf-August Pinnenkämper, April 30, 1945.
95. Testimony of Kazimierz Tygalski (Drygalski), April 30, 1945.
96. Interrogation of Friedrich Teply, May 20, 1947.
97. Testimony of Stanisław Majewicz, September 18, 1985, SLS, 21Js 87295/91, vol. IV.
98. Testimony of Leonid Pimonovic Maystrov, April 11, 1971, SLS, 27Js 87295/91, special issue I.
99. Testimony of Stanisław Majevitz, September 18, 1985.
100. Deposition of Adolf-August Pinnenkämper, April 30, 1945.
101. Testimony of Evgeny Ivanovic Katev, April 25, 1945, NIOD, carton 13a.
102. Testimony of Adolf-August Pinnenkämper, April 30, 1945; testimony of Leonid Piminovic Maystrov, April 25, 1945, NIOD, carton 13a.
103. Interrogation of Friedrich Teply, May 20, 1947.
104. Testimony of Edward Antoniak, June 28, 1968, ZstL, VI 302 AR 507/70, vol. I; interrogation of Kazimierz Drygalski, July 30, 1946, BStU, RHE-West 33/1.
105. Karl Semmlers Erinnerungsbericht, p. 34; testimony of Witold Mondzelewski, April 20, 1945, NIOD, carton 13a.
106. Testimony of Stanisław Majewicz, September 18, 1985; testimony of D. Depo de Nord, April 23, 1945, NIOD, carton 13a.
107. Interrogation of Friedrich Teply, May 20, 1947.
108. Testimony of Stanisław Majewicz, September 18, 1985; testimony of Witold Mondzelewski, April 20, 1945.
109. Testimony of Romuald Bąk, September 9, 1947, NARA, M-1079, roll 7, target 5.
110. Testimony of Bondy Gaza, April 20, 1945, NIOD, carton 13a; testimony of Witold Mondzelewski, April 20, 1945.
111. Testimony of Georges Crétin, November 15, 1945, AN, F/9/5590.
112. Testimony of Romuald Bąk, September 9, 1947.
113. Testimony of Leonid Pimonovic Maystrov, April 11, 1971.
114. Testimony of Romuald Bąk, September 9, 1947.
115. Testimony of Adolf-August Pinnenkämper, April 30, 1945.
116. Karl Semmlers Erinnerungsbericht, p. 35.
117. Interrogation of Friedrich Teply, May 20, 1947.
118. Testimony of Edward Antoniak, April 22, 1945, NIOD, carton 13a.
119. Testimony of Romuald Bąk, September 9, 1947.
120. Karl Semmlers Erinnerungsbericht, p. 35; deposition of Kazimierz Drygalski, December 11, 1945.
121. Testimony of Adolf-August Pinnenkämper, April 30, 1945.
122. Testimony of Leon Mawice, MGS Gardalegen, 495; deposition of Erich August Adolf Gotthard, November 26, 1961, SLS, 21Js 87295/91, vol. II.
123. Deposition of Kazimierz Drygalski, December 11, 1945. "Evacuation Marches," Review of Recommendations, April 15, 1948, NARA, M-1079, roll 12, target 3, p. 26; Karl Semmlers Erinnerungsbericht, p. 36.
124. Testimony of Evgeny Ivanovic Katev, April 25, 1945, and his testimony of February 15, 1971.
125. Testimony of Romuald Bąk, September 9, 1947.

126. Testimony of Vassily Mitofanovic Mamoshuk, August 9, 1968, SLS, 27Js 87295/91, special issue I.
127. Testimony of Evgeny Ivanovic Katev, April 25, 1945.
128. Testimony of Szobel Aurel, April 20, 1945, NIOD, carton 13a.
129. Zygmunt Kozanecki, "Gardelegen," *Biuletyn Głównej Komisji badania zbrodni Hitlerowskich w Polsce* 29 (1979): 204–205.
130. Testimony of Mieczesław Kołodzjeski, April 24, 1945, NIOD, carton 13a.
131. Testimony of Włodzimierz Wosńy, April 22, 1945, NIOD, carton 13a.
132. Karl Semmlers Erinnerungsbericht, p. 36. In the various versions of his testimony after the war Semmler counted himself among the survivors of the massacre. However, he was one of the prisoners who became a guard and not one of the survivors.
133. Testimony of Menachem Wajnraw, November 1968, YVA 03/3343; testimony of Baruch Seidel, August 15, 1947, NARA, M-1079, roll 6, target 7; testimony of Georges Crétin, November 15, 1945; Morel, *Les Derniers Supplices,* pp. 32–33.
134. Testimony of Adolf-August Pinnenkämper, April 30, 1945.
135. Deposition of Kazimierz Drygalski, December 11, 1945; testimony of Ludwig Juchocki, April 22, 1945; testimony of Adolf-August Pinnenkämper, April 30, 1945.
136. Deposition of Hans Debrodt, May 10, 1945.
137. Deposition of Karl Lepa, May 10, 1945.
138. Deposition of Hans Debrodt, May 10, 1945.
139. Deposition of Paul Schrinkau, April 30, 1945, NIOD, carton 13a.
140. Deposition of August Bomm, April 30, 1945, NIOD, carton 13a.
141. Deposition of Hermann Holtz, May 10, 1945.
142. Deposition of Gustav Palis, April 28, 1945, NIOD, carton 13a.
143. Interrogation of Gustav Palis, July 30, 1946. König admitted that he tried to kill the wounded prisoner, and when he failed his weapon was confiscated. Deposition of Franz König, May 11, 1945, NIOD, carton 13a.
144. Deposition of Gustav Palis, April 28, 1945.
145. Deposition of Hermann Holtz, May 10, 1945.
146. Testimony of Georges Crétin, November 15, 1945.
147. Deposition of Hermann Holtz, May 10, 1945.
148. Ibid.
149. Deposition of Hans Debrodt, May 10, 1945.
150. Testimony of Georges Crétin, November 15, 1945.
151. Deposition of Hermann Holtz, May 10, 1945.

10. After the Flames

1. Testimony of Emmy Möhring, January 24, 1948, MGS Gardelegen, 492.
2. Minutes of the commission of inquiry of the Sowjetische Militäradministration (hereafter SMA) on the Burgstall affair, February 1947, MGS Gardelegen, 492.
3. Bericht über Ausgrabungen in Dolle und Umgebung, March 31, 1949, AGM, 50.1.7.1/2.
4. Interview with Lucien Colonel, May 27, 1997, Gring interviews.

5. Testimony of Emmy Möhring, January 24, 1948, MGS Gardelegen, 492; testimony of August Schulze, January 22, 1948, MGS Gardelegen, 492.
6. Testimony of Hermann Pett, October 10, 1945, MGS Gardelengen, 492.
7. Testimony of Andreas Lahse, January 22, 1948, MGS Gardelengen, 492.
8. Interview with Lucien Colonel, May 23, 1997, Gring interviews.
9. Testimony of Ursula Stachetski, October 10, 1945, MGS Gardelengen, 492.
10. Minutes of the SMA commission of inquiry, February 14, 1947, Gring interviews.
11. Testimony of Ursula Stachetski, October 10, 1945.
12. Neander, *Gardelegen 1945,* p. 26; Margry, "The Gardelegen Massacre," p. 6; Viegel, "Gardelegen 13/14. April 1945," p. 75.
13. Interview with Lucien Colonel, May 23, 1997, Gring interviews.
14. Testimony of Hermann Manecke, January 22, 1948, MGS Gardelegen, 492.
15. Deposition of Captain Edward Beale concerning examination of the barn and the massacre, May 14, 1945, NIOD, carton 13a-II.
16. "Nazi Boys Burn 700 'Slaves,'" *New York Times,* April 17, 1945.
17. "Americans Seize Murderer of 1000," *New York Times,* April 19, 1945; "Germans Must Bury 1,100 Burned Alive," *New York Times,* April 20, 1945.
18. "1000 Burned, Shot in Barn before Germans Flee," *Stars and Stripes,* April 20, 1945; "Sickened Nazis Made to Dig up Burned Bodies," *New York Herald Tribune,* April 22, 1945; "Mass Slaughterer Caught," *Washington Post,* April 19, 1945.
19. *Life* magazine, May 7, 1945, pp. 34–35.
20. Rolf Seubert, "A Country That Feels No Guilt or Shame: Das Ende des 'Dritten Reichs' im US-Magazin 'Life,'" *Diagonal, Zeitschrift der Universität-Gesamthochschule-Siegen* 2 (1996): 96–99.
21. Interview with Herbert Ehle, February 25, 1997, Gring interviews.
22. Testimony of August Blumenthal, MGS Gardelegen, 415; Civilian Population, Headquarters 102nd Infantry Division, Military Government, April 30, 1945, NARA, RG-407, box 14452, file 3102-0-3.
23. Margry, "The Gardelegen Massacre," p. 21.
24. After Action Report, G-1 Operations, May 8, 1945, NARA, RG-407, box 14452, file 3102-0-3.
25. U.S. Army, Report of Investigation of Massacres of Political Prisoners at Gardelegen, Germany, May 23, 1945, p. 18.
26. Gring, *Die Todesmärsche und das Massaker von Gardelegen,* p. 40.
27. Testimony of Yehuda Jedlinski, November 17, 1997, YVA, 03/10350.
28. Speech of Colonel Lynch at the inauguration of the cemetery at Gardelegen, April 25, 1945, NARA, RG-407, box 14452, file 3102-0-3.
29. http://www.scrapbookpages.com/Gardelegen/index.html (accessed July 19, 2006).
30. The summarizing report of the HQ command responsible for establishing the Gardelegen cemetery states that a certain number of corpses had been identified by their metal discs (i.e., were captured soldiers). Colonel Geo. A. Carlson, Graves Registration Office, to Headquarters 1st Platoon 3046, 102nd Infantry Division, April 25, 1945, AN, F/9/5590.
31. Reports on interment of prisoners murdered at Jävenitz and Estedt, May 13 and 14, 1945, NIOD, carton 13a.

32. Testimony of Edward Antoniak, April 22, 1945, NIOD, carton 13a; Margry, "The Gardelegen Massacre," p. 25.
33. Civilian Population, Headquarters 102nd Infantry Division, Military Government, April 30, 1945.
34. Confirmation of handover of the Gardelegen investigation file to the Soviet authorities, July 25, 1946, NIOD, carton 13a; Robert Sales to Colonel S. V. Phifer, August 7, 1945, NIOD, carton 13a.
35. Testimony of Hans Spilner, December 7, 1963, ZstL, IV 429 AR-Z 62/62, vol. V.
36. Interview with Dieter Rieke, April 7, 1997, Gring interviews.
37. Margry, "The Gardelegen Massacre," p. 26.
38. Naimark, *The Russians in Germany,* pp. 376–378; Jefrey Herf, *Divided Memory: The Nazi Past in the Two Germanys* (Cambridge, MA: Harvard University Press, 1997), pp. 72–73.
39. Olaf Groehler, "Integration und Ausgrenzung von NS-Opfern: Zur Anerkennungs- und Entschädigungsdebatte in der Sowjetischen Besatzungszone Deutschlands 1945 bis 1949," in Jürgen Kocka, ed., *Historische DDR-Forschung: Aufsätze und Studien* (Berlin: Akademia Verlag, 1993), pp. 106–108.
40. Jürgen Danyel, Olaf Groehler, and Mario Kessler, "Antifaschismus und Verdrängung: Zum Umgang mit der NS-Vergangenheit in der DDR," in Jürgen Kocka and Martin Sabrow, eds., *Die DDR als Geschichte: Fragen-Hypothesen-Perspektiven* (Berlin: Akademia Verlag, 1994), pp. 148–149.
41. Mary Fulbrook, *German National Identity after the Holocaust* (Cambridge: Polity Press, 1999), p. 57.
42. Herf, *Divided Memory,* pp. 95, 164.
43. Jochen Spielman, "Denkmal in Bewegung—Der Wandel von Gestalt, Widmung und Funktion von Denkmalen in ehemaligen Konzentrations-und Vernichtungslagern 1945–1991—Ein Überblick," in Thomas Lutz, Wulff E. Brebeck, and Nicolas Hepp, eds., *Über-Lebens-Mittel: Kunst aus Konzentrationslagern und in Gedenkstätten für Opfer des Nationalsozialismus* (Marburg: Jonas Verlag, 1992), pp. 108–109; Manfred Overesch, *Buchenwald und die DDR, oder Suche nach Selbstlegitimation* (Göttingen: Vandenhoeck und Ruprecht, 1995), pp. 14–15; Fulbrook, *German National Identity,* p. 30.
44. On the Gardelegen memorial site, see http://www.scrapbookpages.com/Gardelegen/Memorial/Site.html (accessed July 21, 2006).
45. Monika Zorn, ed., *Hitlers zweimal getötete Opfer: Westdeutsche Endlösung des Antifaschismus auf dem Gebiet der DDR* (Freiburg: Ahriman Verlag, 1994), p. 113.
46. Konzentrationslager "Mittelbau-Dora"—Zwanzig Monate Produktionsstätte des Todes, AGM, 50.1.7.1 no. 10.
47. Margry, "The Gardelegen Massacre," p. 26.
48. Anna Dora Miethe, ed., *Gedenkstätten: Arbeiterbewegung, Antifaschistischer Widerstand, Aufbau des Sozialismus* (Leipzig: Urania Verlag, 1974), p. 237; Zorn, *Hitlers zweimal getötete Opfer,* p. 113.
49. "Globke-Opfer wurden geehrt: Nationaler Gedenkweg im Bezirk Magdeburg," *Magdeburger Volksstimme,* July 12, 1963, in Zorn, *Hitlers zweimal,* pp. 113–115; Miethe, *Gedenkstätten,* pp. 237–239.

50. Konzentrationslager "Mittelbau-Dora"—Zwanzig Monate Produktionsstätte des Todes, pp. 6–7.

51. "Massenmord an antifaschistischen Widerstandskämpfern in einer Feldscheune bei Gardelegen im Frühjahr 1945," Der Staatsanwalt des Bezirkes Magdeburg, February 12, 1960, BstU, ZM 1625, Bd. 34, Akte 116–122.

52. Rudolph Becker, Heinz Schenk, and Lies Wolf, *Ihr Opfer bleibt unvergessen! Zur Geschichte des Mahn- und Gedenkweges Gardelegen* (Gardelegen: Kreisleitung Gardelegen der Sozialistischen Einheitspartei Deutschlands, 1984), p. 13.

53. Ibid., p. 20.

54. Testimony of Ludwig Lewin, March 30, 1961, SLS, 21Js 87295/91, vol. I; Lewin, Erlebnisbericht, MGS Gardelegen, 523.

55. Gring, ". . . Immer zwischen zwei Feuern," pp. 112–113; testimony of Jan Paterek, November 11, 1972, ZstL, IV 429 AR-Z 192/72, vol. II.

56. Gring, ". . . Immer zwischen zwei Feuern," pp. 114–115.

57. Ibid., p. 114; "Massenmord an antifaschistischen Widerstandskämpfern in einer Feldscheune bei Gardelegen im Frühjahr 1945."

58. Testimony of Kazimierz Morus, April 22, 1945, NIOD, carton 13a.

59. Testimony of Karl Semmler, April 21, 1945, NIOD, carton 13a.

60. Karl Semmlers Erinnerungsbericht, AGM, 50.1.7.1 no. 11, pp. 16–19, 22–23, 25.

61. Gring, ". . . Immer zwischen zwei Feuern," pp. 122–125.

62. Herbert Becker, "Dokumentationsreihe zum faschistischen Verbrechen am 13. April in Gardelegen, part I: Der KZ-Staat Deutschland bricht zusammen," *Volksstimme* (Gardelegener Kreisanzeiger), March 15, 1995.

63. Becker, "'Dokumentationsreihe,' Part V: 12. April 1945: Die Morde in den Straßen von Gardelegen," *Volksstimme* (Gardelegener Kreisanzeiger), April 5, 1995.

64. Becker, "'Dokumentationsreihe,' Part VII: Erschießung von 500 Häftlingen in Burgstall wurde verhindert," *Volksstimme* (Gardelegener Kreisanzeiger), April 10, 1995.

65. Becker, "'Dokumentationsreihe,' Part VIII: Der Thiele-Befehl: Alle sind zu erschießen," *Volksstimme* (Gardelegener Kreisanzeiger), April 11, 1945; Becker, "'Dokumentationsreihe,' Part IX: Aussonderung beim Zählappell," April 12, 1995.

66. Neander, *Gardelegen 1945*, p. 33.

67. Herbert Becker, "Das rätselhafte Verbrechen," *General-Anzeiger,* April 15, 1998.

68. Herbert Becker, "Der rätselhafte Friedhof in Gardelegen," *Altmark-Blätter,* February 5, 2000.

69. Colonel Geo. A. Carlson, Graves Registration Office, to Headquarters 1st Platoon 3046, 102nd Infantry Division, April 25, 1945.

70. Indication sur les décédes a Gardelegen, August 13, 1945, NA, F/9/5590.

71. Margry, "The Gardelegen Massacre," p. 26.

72. Conversation with Annette Bernstein, Deputy Director, Municipal Museum and Archive at Gardelegen, October 4, 2002.

73. ". . . dass dort nicht nur Antifaschisten und Juden ums Leben gekommen sind, unter den Opfer haben sich wohl auch ein paar kleine Kriminelle befunden." "Zunehmend aggressivere Töne," *Altmark-Blätter,* February 11, 2000.

74. Margry, "The Gardelegen Massacre," p. 27.
75. "Keine 'Ende der Geschichte' für Gardelegen?" in Neander, *Gardelegen 1945*, pp. 36–40.
76. Günther Wieland, "Die Ahndung von NS-Verbrechen in Ostedeutschland 1945–1990," in *DDR-Justiz und NS-Verbrechen*, vol. I (Amsterdam: Amsterdam University Press, 2002), pp. 34–35.
77. Personal details of suspects of participation in the Gardelegen murders, U.S. Army data, SLS, 21Js 87295/91, vol. IV; ZstL, IV 429 AR-Z 62/69, vol. V.
78. Der Staatsanwalt des Bezirkes Magdeburg, Mageburg, an die Oberste Staatsanwaltschaft der Deutschen Demokratischen Republik, June 12, 1961, BstU, RHE-West 33/3.
79. Interrogation of Arno Brake, August 6, 1946, SLS, 27Js 87295/91, special issue I.
80. Interrogation of Hermann Kohle/Mohle, August 8, 1946, SLS, 27Js 87295/91, special issue I.
81. Erster Stellvertreter des Generalstaatsanwaltes der Union Sozialistischer Sowjetrepubliken, Moskau, an den Stellvertreter des Generalstaatsanwaltes der Deutschen Demokratischen Republik, Berlin, February 5, 1971, BStU, RHE 22/71 SU.
82. Testimony of Szobel Aurel, April 20, 1945, NIOD, carton 13a; interrogation of Adolf Pinnenkämper, July 30, 1946, SLS, 27Js 87295/91, special issue I.
83. Testimony of Edward Antoniak, April 22, 1945; interrogation of Kazimierz Drygalski, August 12, 1946, SLS, 27Js 87295/91, special issue I.
84. For the summary of the trial, see http://www.archive.gov/research/captured-german-records/microfilm/m1079.pdf) (accessed July 25, 2006).
85. Margry, "The Gardelegen Massacre," p. 26.
86. Erster Stellvertreter des Generalstaatsanwaltes der Union Sozialistischer Sowjetrepubliken, Moskau, ander Stellvertreter des Generalstaatsanwaltes der Deutschen Demokratischen Republik, Berlin, February 5, 1971.
87. Peter Erler, "Zur Tätigkeit der sowjetischen Militärtribunale in Deutschland," in Peter Reif-Spirek and Bodo Ritscher, eds., *Speziallager in der SBZ: Gedenkstätten mit "doppelter Vergangenheit"* (Berlin: Ch. Links, 1999), pp. 209–211; Wieland, "Die Ahndung von NS-Verbrechen," pp. 35–40.
88. Der Staatsanwalt des Bezirkes Magdeburg, Magdeburg, an die Oberste Staatsanwaltschaft der Deutschen Demokratischen Republik, June 12, 1961.
89. Erster Stellvertreter des Generalstaatsanwaltes der Union Sozialistischer Sowjetrepubliken, Moskau, an den Stellvertreter des Generalstaatsanwaltes der Deutschen Demokratischen Republik, Berlin, February 5, 1971.
90. Office of the Judge Advocate, U.S. Army Headquarters in Europe, July 25, 1960, SLS, 21Js 87295/91, vol. I.
91. Interrogation of Hans Debrodt, May 10, 1945, NIOD, carton 13a.
92. Deposition of Rosemaria Thiele (Kaufmann), September 29, 1961, SLS, 21Js 87295/91, vol. I.
93. Der Generalstaatsanwalt der Deutschen Demokratischen Republik, Quelinburg, November 27, 1971, SLS, 21Js 87295/91, vol. IV.
94. "Identification of Prisoner," Thiele Gerhardt, Headquarters Seventh Army, War Crimes Branch, SLS, 21Js 87295/91, vol. I; Diana Gring, "Von Antworten und

offenen Fragen—Das Ende der jahrzehntelangen Suche nach dem NS-Täter Gerhard Thiele," in *Abgeleitete Macht: Funktionshäftlinge zwischen Widerstand und Kollaboration* (Bremen: Edition Temmen, 1998), p. 143.

95. Report of the Criminal Section (LKA) of the Upper Saxony police in Magdeburg on the Gerhard Thiele affair, September 29, 1997, SLS, 27Js 87295/91, Vol. X (hereafter LKA Magdeburg), p. 5.

96. Diana Gring, "Eine Täterbiographie mit Lücken: Skizzen zum Leben des NSDAP-Kreisleiters Gerhard Thiele (1909–1994) und die Ermittlungsarbeit in Ost und Westdeutschland seit 1945," Seminar zum KZ Mittelbau-Dora in der Gedenkstätte Mittelbau-Dora, Nordhausen, October 28–November 1, 2002 (unpublished presentation).

97. Ibid.

98. Thiele and his partner were together from 1953. Interrogation of Margaret-Gertrude Glandien, September 3, 1997, LKA Magdeburg, pp. 3–4.

99. Gring, "Eine Täterbiographie mit Lücken."

100. Der Staatsanwalt Magdeburg an die Oberste Staatanswaltschaft der Deutschen Demokratischen Republik, November 13, 1961, SLS, 27Js 87295/91, vol. VII.

101. Simon Wiesenthal to Willi Dresden, Ludwigsburg, October 3, 1990, SLS, 27Js 87295/91, vol. VII.

102. "DDR erpreßte Naziverbrecher," interview mit Simon Wiesenthal, *Berliner Kurier am Sonntag,* March 15, 1992.

103. Gring, "Eine Täterbiographie mit Lücken."

104. Interview with Bernard Daenekes, April 7, 1997, Gring interviews.

105. Gring, "Eine Täterbiographie mit Lücken."

106. Der Staatsanwalt des Bezirkes Magdeburg an den Kreisleiter der Sozialistischen Einheitspartei Deutschland, Ideologische Kommission, Gardelegen, August 30, 1963, SLS, 27Js 87295/91, vol. VII.

11. The Murderers

1. Raul Hilberg, "Gehorsam oder Initiative? Zur arbeitsteiligen Täterschaft im Nationalsozialismus," *Frankfurter Lern- und Dokumentationszentrum des Holocaust,* Materialien No. 3, October 1991; Raul Hilberg, *Perpetrators, Victims, Bystanders: The Jewish Catastrophe 1933–1945* (New York: HarperCollins, 1992), pp. 20–26.

2. Gerhard Paul, "Von Psychopathen, Technokraten des Terrors und 'ganz gewöhnlichen Deutschen': Die Täter der Shoa im Spiegel der Forschung," in Gerhard Paul, ed., *Die Täter der Shoah: Fanatische Nationalsozialisten oder ganz normale Deutsche?* (Göttingen: Wallestein Verlag, 2002), p. 15.

3. Thomas Sandkühler, "Die Täter des Holocaust: Neuere Überlegungen und Kontroversen," in Karl H. Paul, ed., *Wehrmacht und Vernichtungspolitk: Militär im nationalsozialistischen System* (Göttingen: Vandenhoeck und Ruprecht, 1999), p. 58.

4. On this, see Browning, *Ordinary Men,* pp. 159–189.

5. Orth, "Experten des Terrors," pp. 94–95.

6. For example, Rudolf Höß, (born in 1900), Josef Kramer (1906), Martin-Gottfried Weiß (1905), Hans Loritz (1895), and Karl-Otto Koch (1896).

7. Orth, *Die Konzentrationslager-SS,* pp. 115–120, 225–233.

8. Orth, "Experten des Terrors," pp. 99, 102.

9. Sofsky, *The Order of Terror,* pp. 106–108; Orth, *Die Konzentrationslager-SS,* p. 335.

10. Heinz Boberach, "Die Überführung von Soldaten des Heeres und der Luftwaffe in die SS-Totenkopfverbände zur Bewachung von Konzentrationslagern 1944," *Millitärgeschichte Mitteilungen* 2 (1983): 185–190; Sofsky, *the Order of Terror,* p. 102.

11. Mirbach, *"Damit du es später,"* pp. 26–27, 260–263.

12. Interrogation of Friedrich Teply, April 28, 1945, NARA, M-1079, roll 11, target 6.

13. Deposition of Otto Schrader, May 16, 1947, NARA, RG-153, box 14, exhibits, vol. 3.

14. Deposition of Franz Unverdorben, April 28, 1945, SLS, 27Js 87295/91, special issue I; interrogations of Franz Unverdorben, July 31 and September 25, 1946, BStU, RHE-West 33/1.

15. Dörr trial: indictment, exhibits, vol. I, pp. 183, 187.

16. Testimony of Max Reimann, November 15, 1962, Dörr trial: exhibits, vol. II, pp. 381–382.

17. Wilhelm Genth, Gebührnis-Karte NdsH, 721 97/99 No. 02 0310; deposition of Wilhelm Genth, May 19, 1961, NdsH, 721 97/99 No. 26/2, p. 1.

18. Ibid., p. 2.

19. Ibid., pp. 3–15; deposition of Wilhelm Genth, March 3, 1963, NdsH, 721 97/99 No. 26/2, pp. 2–3; deposition of Wilhelm Genth, July 20, 1961, NdsH, 721 97/99 No. 26/2, p. 2.

20. Die Verhältnisse im KL Hanover-Stöcken, April 10, 1963, NdsH, 721 97/99 No. 26/3, p. 9.

21. Das KL Hanover-Stöcken, Staatsanwaltschaft bei dem Landesgericht Hanover, 2 Js 622/49, January 28, 1963, NdsH, 721 97/99 No. 26/3, p. 16.

22. Deposition of Wilhelm Genth, July 20, 1961, p. 2.

23. Mirbach, *"Damit du es später,"* pp. 28–35.

24. Ibid., pp. 55, 95.

25. Christopher Browning, "German Killers: Behavior in the Light of New Evidence," in *Nazi Policy, Jewish Workers, German Killers* (Cambridge: Cambridge University Press, 2000), p. 143.

26. Deposition of Florjan Drzymała, December 20, 1967, USHMMA 2000.311.

27. Interview with Florjan Drzymała, August 4, 1999, USHMMA 2000.311.

28. Deposition of Jan Wojcienchowski, December 11, 1967, deposition of Franczyszek Kluj, November 15, 1967, and report of commission of inquiry into Nazi crimes at Zielona Góra, November 28, 1968, USHMMA 2000.311.

29. *Justiz und NS-Verbrechen,* vol. VII (Amsterdam: Amsterdam University Press, 1972), p. 440; vol. XXXIV (Amsterdam: Amsterdam University Press, 2005), p. 694.

30. *Justiz und NS-Verbrechen,* vol. VII, p. 441. *Note:* Here and elsewhere in the chapter, surnames were sometimes abbreviated to protect the privacy of the individuals involved.

31. Browning, "German Killers," p. 147.

32. Jürgen Matthäus, "What about the 'Ordinary Men'? The German Order Police and the Holocaust in the Occupied Soviet Union," *Holocaust and Genocide Studies* 10:2 (1996): 141–145.

33. *DDR-Justiz und NS-Verbrechen,* vol. VI (Amsterdam: Amsterdam University Press, 2004), pp. 624–625.

34. Interrogation of Friedrich Teply, April 28, 1947, NARA, M-1079, roll 11, target 6; interrogation of Josef Fuchsloch, May 7, 1947, NARA, M-1079, roll 11, target 6; Mirbach, *"Damit du es später,"* p. 95.

35. Testimony of Wilhelm Hack, May 22, 1947, NARA, M-1079, roll 5, target 1.

36. Interrogation of Franz Unverdorben, September 25, 1946.

37. Mauthausen trial: prosecution's summary, NARA, RG-153, box 6, review, vol. 1, pp. 24, 50–51.

38. Interrogation of Oskar-Georg Helvig, July 10, 1947, NARA, M-1079, roll 11, target 6.

39. Report on Gustav Alfred Jepsen, November 12, 1945, trial of Jepsen, Freitag, and Müller, TNA WO 235/229; *Kriegsverbrechen in Lüneburg,* p. 13.

40. Buchenwald trial: indictment, November 15, 1947, NARA, RG-153, box 243, folder 1, p. 93; interrogation of Erhard Brauny, May 19, 1947, NARA, M-1079, roll 11, target 7; biographical details on Erhard Brauny, NARA, M-1079, roll 13, target 2. Brauny was given a life sentence and died in jail in Landsberg on June 16, 1950.

41. Testimony of Romuald Bąk, September 30, 1946, SLS, 21Js 87295/91, special issue, vol. I; interrogation of Walter Ulbricht, May 13, 1947, NARA, M-1079, roll 11, target 6; deposition of Walter Ulbricht, October 23, 1947, NARA, M-1079, roll 12, target 2; testimony of Haim Kleiner, March 2, 1976, YVA, TR-11/629.

42. Interrogation of Hans Erich Merbach, NARA, RG-153, box 252, Buchenwald trial: exhibits.

43. Deposition of Alfred Jepsen, February 4, 1946, TNA, WO 235/229, p. 78.

44. Dörr trial: exhibits, vol. I, p. 186; testimony of Max Reimann, November 16, 1962, Dörr trial: exhibits, vol. II, p. 395.

45. Buchenwald trial: indictment, November 15, 1947, p. 89.

46. Interrogation of Josef Wurst, May 25, 1945, NARA, M-1204, roll 11.

47. Herbert C. Kelman, "Violence without Moral Restraint: Reflection on the Dehumanization of Victims and Victimizers," *Journal of Social Issues* 29:4 (1973): 39–40.

48. Mirbach, *"Damit du es später,"* pp. 262–263. Mirbach was imprisoned for a short period in a British prison camp but was released in July 1945. He lectured extensively after the war on his time in the Mittelbau-Dora camps. Deposition of Otto Schrader, July 10, 1946, NARA, RG-153, box 6, exhibits, vol. 3.

49. Josef Wurst claimed that he was given the order to murder several prisoners during the evacuation from Flossenbürg and that the transport CO threatened that if he did not do so, he too would be executed. This claim was reiterated by a number of Nazi murderers after the war. Interrogation of Josef Wurst, May 25, 1945.

50. Indictment against Karl Amlinger, Wilhelm Mohr, and Franz Paul, May 30, 1968, ÖSA, 54.987–18/68.

51. 102nd Infantry Division, G-2 Periodical Report #163, April 14, 1945, NIOD, carton 13a.
52. Description of the battles in the Gardelegen area as detailed in the records of the 405th Regiment, NARA, RG-407, box 14494, file 3102-Inf (405)-0-1.
53. "Consolidated PW Interrogation Report: Col. von Einem," 102nd Infantry Division G-2 Periodical Report #164, April 15, 1945, NIOD, carton 13a.
54. Omer Bartov, "The Missing Years. German Workers, German Soldiers," in David F. Crew, ed., *Nazism and German Society 1933–1945* (London: Routledge, 1994), p. 50.
55. Stephen F. Fritz, *Frontsoldaten: The German Soldier in World War II* (Lexington: University Press of Kentucky, 1995), pp. 201–207; Bartov, *Hitler's Army*, pp. 106–178.
56. Thomas Kühne, *Kameradschaft: Die Soldaten des nationalsozialistischen Kriegs und das 20. Jahrhundert* (Göttingen: Vandenhoeck und Ruprecht, 2006), pp. 202–205.
57. Ute Frevert, *A Nation in Barracks: Modern Germany, Military Conscription and Civil Society* (Oxford: Berg, 2004), pp. 258–259.
58. "Wem gehört der Eiffelturm? Die Amerikanner beschlagnahmen Europas höchstes Bauwerk," *Der Führer*, Karlsruhe, no. 228, October 28/29, 1944; "Plan des Juden Morgenthau: Roosevelt wünscht völlige Vernichtung Deutschlands," *Rheinisch-Bergische Zeitung*, no. 21, January 25, 1945. Henry Morganthau Jr. was the U.S. Secretary of the Treasury during the administration of Franklin D. Roosevelt. In 1944 he proposed a plan for postwar Germany calling for the country to be partitioned into separate independent states and stripped of all heavy industry. He was a satanic symbol in Nazi propaganda and was considered the most dangerous threat to the German people.
59. Henke, *Die amerikanische Besetzung Deutschlands*, pp. 87–91.
60. Trevor-Roper, *Final Entries*, March 2 and 8, 1945, pp. 21, 75.
61. John Zimmermann, "Die Kämpfe gegen die Westalliierten 1945—Ein Kampf bis zum Ende oder Kreierung einer Legende?" in Jörg Hillmann and John Zimmermann, eds., *Kriegsende 1945 in Deutschland* (Munich: R. Oldenbourg, 2002), pp. 117–119.
62. "Consolidated PW Interrogation Report: Col. von Einem." 102nd Infantry Division, G-2 Periodical Report #164, April 15, 1945.
63. Deposition of Friedrich Hilmer von Sherr-Thoss, May 27, 1971, SLS, 21Js 87295/91, vol. IV; deposition of Rudolf Kuhn, April 30, 1945, NIOD, carton 13a; interrogation of Rudolf Kuhn, May 6, 1950, BStU, RHE-West 33/3; interrogation of Rudolf Kuhn, August 16, 1946, SLS, 27Js 87295/91, special issue I.
64. Interrogation of Rudolf Kuhn, August 16, 1946.
65. Interrogation of Rudolf Kuhn, May 6, 1950.
66. Deposition of Walter Miltz, March 3, 1963, SLS, 21Js 87295/91, vol. I.
67. Interrogation of Walter Miltz, May 13, 1950, BStU, RHE-West 33/3.
68. 102nd Infantry Division, G-2 Periodical Report #163, April 14, 1945.
69. Interrogation of Karl Strewe, January 29, 1981, and interrogation of Heinz Klaus, August 13, 1981, SLS, 21Js 87295/91, vol. V.
70. Interrogation of Max Barella, October 24, 1958, SLS, 21Js 87295/91, vol. I.

71. Testimony of Adolf-August Pinnenkämper, April 30, 1945, NIOD, carton 13a; testimony of Leonid Maistro, April 25, 1945, NIOD, carton 13a; interrogation of Friedrich Teply, May 20, 1947, NARA, M-1079, roll 11, target 6.

72. Testimony of Willi Baum, November 23, 1961, SLS, 21Js 87295/91, vol. II; summary of facts in the affair of the massacre at Gut Pollwitz, January 17, 1961, SLS, 21Js 87295/91, vol. I.

73. 102nd Infantry Division, G-2 Periodical Report #168, April 19, 1945, Consolidated PW Interrogation Report, NIOD, carton 13a.

74. Fritz, *Endkampf*, pp. 40–44.

75. Testimony of Albert Borges, November 24, 1961, SLS, 21Js 87295/91, vol. I.

76. Testimony of Fritz-Karl Miltz, October 7, 1958, SLS, 21Js 87295/91, vol. I.

77. Testimony of Ulrich Rutger, December 2, 1970, SLS, 27Js 87295/91, special issue II.

78. Testimony of Ernst Wetzel, February 19, 1958, SLS, 21Js 87295/91, special issue II.

79. Greiser, *Die Todesmärsche von Buchenwald*, pp. 130–131.

80. Ibid., pp. 131–132.

81. Celle massacre trial, http://www.celle-im-nationalsozialismus.de/Texte/Presse_Treibjagd.html (accessed April 4, 2007).

82. Report on the murder of concentration camp prisoners at Celle, April 16, 1946, TNA, WO 309/90.

83. Rogowski, "The Gauleiter and the Social Origins," p. 402.

84. Deposition of Rudolf Karl Jordan, July 14, 1958, SLS, 27Js 87295/91, vol. I.

85. Report of investigation on Rudolf Jordan, January 24, 1961, SLS, 27Js 87295/91, vol. I; Rudolf Jordan, *Erlebt und Erlitten: Weg eines Gauleiters von München bis Moskau* (Freising: Duffel Verlag, 1971), p. 262.

86. Summary of findings of investigation into the Gardelegen affair, October 5, 1990, Staatsanwaltschaft Göttingen, 43/4 Js 1184/63, SLS, 21Js 87295/91, vol. VI, p. 12.

87. Richard Overy, *The Dictators: Hitler's Germany, Stalin's Russia* (New York: W. W. Norton, 2004), p. 146.

88. Carl-Wilhelm Reibel, *Das Fundament der Diktatur: Die NSDAP-Ortsgruppen 1932–1935* (Paderborn: Ferdinand Schöningh, 2002), p. 328.

89. Barbara Fait, "Die Kreisleitung der NSDAP—nach 1945," in Martin Broszat, Klaus-Dietmar Henke, and Hans Woller, eds., *Von Stalingrad zur Währungsreform: Zur Sozialgeschichte des Umbruchs in Deutschland* (Munich: R. Oldenbourg, 1989), pp. 221–222.

90. Wolfgang Stelbrink, *Die Kreisleiter der NSDAP in Westfalen und Lippe: Versuch einer Kollektivbiographie mit biographischem Anhang* (Münster: Nordrhein-Westfälisches Staatsarchiv, 2003), pp. 62–66.

91. Claudia Roth, *Parteikreis und Kreisleiter der NSDAP unter besonderer Berücksichtigung Bayerns* (Munich: C. H. Beck, 1997), p. 179.

92. Wolfgang Stelbrink, "Die Kreisleiter der NSDAP in den beiden westfälischen Parteigauen," in Michael Ruck and Kal Heinrich Pohl, eds., *Regionen im Nationalsozialismus* (Bielefeld: Verlag für Regionalgeschichte, 2003), pp. 164–170; Fait, "Die Kreisleitung der NSDAP," pp. 223–225.

93. Report of the Criminal Section (LKA) of the Upper Saxony police in Magdeburg on the Gerhard Thiele affair, September 29, 1997, SLS, 27Js 87295/91, vol. X, (hereafter LKA Magdeburg).

94. Testimony of Rudolf Kuhn, April 30, 1945; testimony of Hugo Beckert, April 29, 1945, NIOD, carton 13a.

95. Interrogation of Erhard Brauny, May 19, 1947.

96. Report of the Criminal Section of the Upper Saxony police on the Gerhard Thiele affair, September 29, 1997, LKA Magdeburg.

97. Dienstanweisung (No.) 24, March 22, 1945, ÖSA, 54.370-18/70.

98. The Narrative of Eisenerz trial, February 9, 1946, TNA, FO 1020/2034, Part 1, Aussage des Hauptmanns Ernst Bilke, March 23, 1946, TNA, FO 1020/2059.

99. Staatsanwaltschaft Wien erhebt Anklage gegen Alfred Waidmann, November 23, 1949, DÖW, 12.597.

100. Deposition of Paul Schmidt, October 17, 1945, ÖSA, 54.370–18/70.

101. Deposition of Anton Oswald, June 14, 1946, TNA, WO, 310/144.

102. Report on murder of concentration camp prisoners at Celle, April 16, 1946, TNA, WO 309/90.

103. DDR-Justiz und NS-Verbrechen, vol. VII (Amsterdam: Amsterdam University Press, 2005), pp. 186–189.

104. Paul, "Von Psychopathen, Technokraten des Terrors," p. 61.

105. On this see Reibel, Das Fundament der Diktatur, p. 378.

106. Yelton, Hitler's Volkssturm, pp. 33–34.

107. Franz W. Seidler, "Deutscher Volkssturm": Das letzte Aufgebot 1944/1945 (Munich: Bechtermünz Verlag, 1999), pp. 298–302; Yelton, Hitler's Volkssturm, p. 118.

108. Yelton, Hitler's Volkssturm, pp. 146–147.

109. Deposition of Hans Debrodt, May 10, 1945, NIOD, carton 13a.

110. Gordon J. Horwitz, In the Shadow of Death: Living Outside the Gates of Mauthausen (London: I. B. Tauris, 1991), pp. 42, 52–53.

111. Sybille Steinbacher, Dachau—Die Stadt und das Konzentrationslager in der NS-Zeit: Die Untersuchung einer Nachbarschaft (Frankfurt am Main: Peter Lang, 1993), pp. 144–145; Schley, Nachbar Buchenwald, pp. 110, 121.

112. DDR-Justiz und NS-Verbrechen, vol. III (Amsterdam: Amsterdam University Press, 2003), pp. 65–67.

113. DDR-Justiz und NS-Verbrechen, vol. IV (Amsterdam: Amsterdam University Press, 2004), pp. 17–20.

114. Greiser, Die Totesmärsche von Buchenwald, pp. 111–122.

115. The United States Army Air Forces in World War II, "Combat Chronology of the US Army Air Forces, March 1945," http://www.usaaf.net/chron/45/mar45 .htm (accessed July 11, 2006).

116. Waltraut Juretzky-Waschek, Als "Künstlerin" in der russischen Kommandantur: Eine 18 jährige erlebt das Kriegsende und die ersten Nachkriegsjahre in Gardelegen (Oschersleben: Dr. Ziethen Verlag, 1998), pp. 8–9.

117. Testimony of Rudolf Ringstmeyer, February 15, 1961, SLS, 21Js 87295/91, vol. I.

118. Civilian Population, Headquarters 102nd Infantry Division, Military Government, April 30, 1945, NARA, RG-407, box 14452, file 3102-0-3.

119. Testimony of Annalisa Hennig, December 4, 1961, SLS, 21Js 87295/91, vol. III.
120. Testimony of Otto Künnemann, NIOD, carton 13a.
121. Interrogation of Wilhelm Biermann, June 30, 1946, BStU, RHE-West 33/1.
122. Gordon W. Allport and Leo Postman, *The Psychology of Rumor* (New York: Henry Holt & Co., 1947), pp. 3–9.
123. Interrogation of Richard-Rudolf Bischof, November 25, 1961, SLS, 21Js 87295/91, vol. II; interrogation of Erich August Rudolf Gotthard, November 26, 1961, SLS, 21Js 87295/91, vol. II.
124. Allport and Postman, *The Psychology of Rumor,* p. 33.
125. Ibid., pp. 193–194.
126. Deposition of Hermann Holtz, May 10, 1945, NIOD, carton 13a.
127. Interrogation of Wilhelm Becker, April 26, 1945; testimony of Willi Niebel, May 3, 1945; and testimony of Wilhelm Haushahn, May 3, 1945, NIOD, carton 13a.
128. Testimony of Karl Lepa, May 10, 1945, NIOD, carton 13a.
129. Interrogation of Richard-Rudolf Bischof, November 25, 1961.
130. Interrogation of Erich-August Rudolf Gotthard, November 26, 1961.
131. Testimony of Friedrich-Wilhelm Ernst, November 26, 1961; report of investigation of Gerhard Thiele, Bayerisches Landeskriminalamt, November 29, 1961, SLS, 21Js 87295/91, vol. II.
132. *DDR-Justiz und NS-Verbrechen,* vol. IV, pp. 259–260.
133. Celle massacre trial, http://www.celle-im-nationalsozialismus.de/Texte/Presse _Treibjagd.html (accessed April 4, 2007).
134. *DDR-Justiz und NS-Verbrechen,* vol. V (Amsterdam: Amsterdam University Press, 2004), pp. 730–731.
135. Horwitz, *In the Shadow of Death,* pp. 127–136.
136. *DDR-Justiz und NS-Verbrechen,* vol. VIII (Amsterdam: Amsterdam University Press, 2006), pp. 512–514.
137. Deposition of Anton Oswald, June 14, 1946.
138. Paul, "Von Psychopathen, Technokraten des Terrors," p. 61.
139. Hans J. Wolfgang Koch, *The Hitler Youth: Origins and Development 1922–1945* (New York: Cooper Square Press, 2000), pp. 243–247.
140. Gerhard Rempel, *Hitler's Children: The Hitler Youth and the SS* (Chapel Hill: University of North Carolina Press, 1989), p. 231.
141. Hans Holzträger, *In a Raging Inferno: Combat Units of the Hitler Youth 1944–45* (Solihull, England: Helion & Co., 2000), pp. 31–37.
142. Klaus Granzow, *Tagebuch eines Hitlerjungen* (Bremen: Carl Schünemann, 1965), pp. 172–175.
143. Fritz, *Endkampf,* pp. 7, 202–205.
144. Testimony of Kurt Weigart, in *Tage im April,* p. 23.
145. Holzträger, *In a Raging Inferno,* pp. 124–125; Horwitz, *In the Shadow of Death,* p. 134.
146. Report on the massacre of concentration camp prisoners at Celle, April 16, 1946.
147. Testimony of Romuald Bąk, September 25, 1947, SLS, 27Js 87295/91, special vol. IV.

148. Testimony of Herman Madrowicz, May 5, 1945; testimonies of Joannes Biencak, Fritz Klolwit, and Ulrich Freitag, April 28, 1945, NIOD, carton 13a; Captain Luther E. Gowder to Headquarters Ninth U.S. Army JA Section, War Crimes Section, May 13, 1945, NIOD, carton 13a; Gring, *Die Todensmärsche und das Massaker von Gardelegen,* p. 40.

149. Testimony of Yehuda Jadlinski, September 15, 1997, YVA, 03/10350; testimony of Shlomo Schcigelski, February 15, 1976, YVA, TR-11/629.1.

150. Testimony of Menahem Wajnrev, November 1968, YVA, 03/3343.

151. Testimony of Paul Scherinkau, April 30, 1945, NIOD, carton 13a.

152. Diana Gring, "Das Massaker von Gardelegen," *Dachauer Hefte* 20 (October 2004), pp. 118–119.

153. Fabréguet, "Entwicklung und Veränderung," p. 210.

154. Deposition of Anna Feda, January 28, 1946, TNA, FO 1020/2056; Liste über Angehörige des Volkssturmes Eibenery, Kompanie Krenn, Polizeidienstelle Eisenerz, January 19, 1946, TNA, FO 1020/2034.

155. *DDR-Justiz und NS-Verbrechen,* vol. VI, pp. 208–209.

Conclusion

1. Rossino, *Hitler Strikes Poland,* pp. 88–143.

2. Rudolph J. Rummel, *Death by Government* (New Brunswick, NJ: Transaction Publishers, 1994), pp. 1–42.

3. The most detailed and accurate document on the circumstances and events regarding the Srebrenica massacre is the report of the commission of inquiry of the Netherlands Institute for War Documentation (NIOD), published in 2002: http://www.srebrenica.nl (accessed September 30, 2005). See also David Rohde, *Endgame: The Betrayal and the Fall of Srebrenica, Europe's Worst Massacre since World War II* (New York: Farrar, Straus & Giroux, 1997); Jan Willem Honig and Norbert Both, *Srebrenica: Record of a War Crime* (London: Penguin Books, 1996). On the genocide in Rwanda and its origins, see Shaharyar M. Khan, *The Shallow Graves of Rwanda* (London: I. B. Tauris, 2000); Howard Adelman and Astri Suhrke, eds., *The Path of a Genocide: The Rwanda Crisis from Uganda to Zaire* (New Brunswick, NJ: Transaction Publishers, 1999); Ben Kierman, *Blood and Soil: A World History of Genocide and Extermination from Sparta to Darfur* (New Haven, CT: Yale University Press, 2007), pp. 554–568. On the historical background, the beginning of the massacre, and the ethnic cleansing in Darfur, see House of Commons Report: Conflict in Darfur, Research Paper 04/51, House of Commons Library, June 23, 2004, http://www.parliament.uk/commons/lib/research/rp2004/rp04-051/pdf (accessed September 30, 2005).

4. Helen Fein, *Human Rights and Wrongs: Slavery, Terror, Genocide* (Boulder, CO: Paradigm Publishers, 2007), p. 128.

5. Rummel, *Death by Government,* pp. 111–122.

6. See Bauer, "The Death Marches," p. 496.

7. Renate Mayntz, "Chaos in Society: Reflections on the Impact of Chaos Theory on Sociology," in Celso Grebogi and James A. Yorke, eds., *The Impact of*

Chaos on Science and Society (Tokyo: United Nations University Press, 1997), pp. 299–300.

8. Jan Tomasz Gross, *Neighbors: The Destruction of the Jewish Community in Jedwabne, Poland* (Princeton, NJ: Princeton University Press, 2001); Andrej Żbikowski, *U genezy Jedwabnego: Żydzi na Kresach Północno-Wschodnich II Rzeczypospolitej, wrzesień 1939–lipiec 1941* (Warsaw: Żydowski Instytut Historyczny, 2006).

9. Berkhoff, *Harvest of Despair,* pp. 285–300; Alexander V. Prusin, "Revolution and Ethnic Cleansing in Western Ukraine: The OUN-UPA Assault against Polish Settlements in Volhynia and Eastern Galicia, 1943–1944," in Steven Béla Várdy and T. Hunt Tooly, eds., *Ethnic Cleansing in Twentieth-Century Europe* (New York: Social Science Monographs, 2003), pp. 517–535; Timothy Snyder, "The Causes of Ukrainian-Polish Ethnic Cleansing, 1943," *Past and Present* 79 (May 2003): 197–234.

10. Renée Poznanski, *Jews in France during World War II* (Hanover, NH: University Press of New England, 2001), pp. 445–446.

11. Tzvetan Todorov, *Une tragédie française: Été 1944: scènes de guerre civile* (Paris: Seuil, 1994).

12. Doris L. Bergen, "Death Throes and Killing Frenzies: A Response to Hans Mommsen's 'The Dissolution of the Third Reich: Crisis Management and Collapse, 1943–1945,'" *Bulletin of the German Historical Institute* 27 (2000): 25–37, http://www.ghi-dc.org/publications/ghipubs/bu/027/b27bergenframe.html (accessed February 18, 2010).

13. Greiser, *Die Todesmärsche von Buchenwald,* pp. 31, 136–139.

14. Interrogation of Siegfried Uiberreither, March 5, 1946, DÖW, 12.6Z7, pp. 19–20.

15. On the assassination of Heydrich, see Callum MacDonald, *The Killing of SS Obergruppenführer Reinhard Heydrich* (New York: The Free Press, 1989).

16. For reports on the Lidice massacre and testimony of women survivors, see Uwe Nauman, ed., *Lidice: Ein Böhmisches Dorf* (Frankfurt am Main: Röderbeg-Verlag, 1983); MacDonald, *The Killing of Heydrich,* pp. 184–187.

17. *DDR-Justiz und NS-Verbrechen,* vol. III, pp. 699–700.

18. Sarah Farmer, *Martyred Village: Commemorating the 1944 Massacre at Oradour-sur-Glane* (Berkeley: University of California Press, 1999); Robin Mackness, *Massacre at Oradur* (New York: Random House, 1988).

19. Christian S. Ortner, *Marzabotto: The Crimes of Walter Reder—SS-Sturmbannführer* (Vienna: Dokumentationsarchiv des österreichischen Widerstandes, 1986), pp. 11–18; Joachim Staron, *Fosse Ardeatine und Marzabotto: Deutsche Kriegsverbrechen und Resistenza* (Paderborn: Ferdinand Schöningh, 2002), pp. 84–87, 101.

20. Samantha Power, *"A Problem from Hell": America and the Age of Genocide* (New York: HarperCollins, 2002), pp. 358–364.

21. Gareth Evans, "Crimes against Humanity: Overcoming Indifference," *Journal of Genocide Research* 8:3 (2006): 330.

22. Fein, *Human Rights and Wrongs,* p. 132.

23. François Furet and Ernst Nolte, *Fascism and Communism* (Lincoln: University of Nebraska Press, 2001), p. 66.

24. Evans, "Crimes against Humanity," p. 331.
25. Jacques Sémelin, "Toward a Vocabulary of Massacre and Genocide," *Journal of Genocide Research* 5:2 (2003): 197.
26. Goldhagen, *Hitler's Willing Executioners*, p. 371.
27. Livia Rotkirchen, "The 'Final Solution' in Its Last Stages," *Yad Vashem Studies* 8 (1970): 7–29; Shmuel Krakowski, "The Death Marches in the Period of the Evacuation of the Camps," in Michael R, Marrus, ed., *The Nazi Holocaust,* vol. IX: *The End of the Holocaust* (Westport, CT: Meckler, 1989), pp. 476–490.
28. On this, see Dieter Pohl, "Die Holocaust-Forschung und Goldhagens Thesen," VfZ 1 (1997): 35.
29. Aryeh Kochavi denotes the evacuations of prison camps "forced marches." See Kochavi, *Confronting Captivity,* p. 221.
30. Brenda K. Uekert, *Rivers of Blood: A Comparative Study of Government Massacres* (Westport, CT: Praeger, 1995), pp. 167–173.
31. For example, the massacre of Armenians in Constantinople in 1895 can be considered part of the Armenian genocide of 1915–1916. See Vahakan N. Dadrian, *The History of the Armenian Genocide: Ethnic Conflict from the Balkans to Anatolia to the Caucasus* (Providence, RI: Berghahn Books, 1995), pp. 121ff.; James J. Reid, "Total War, the Annihilation Ethic, and the Armenian Genocide, 1870–1918," in Richard G. Hovannisia, ed., *The Armenian Genocide: History, Politics, Ethics* (New York: St. Martin's Press, 1992), pp. 21–52.
32. Helen Fein, *Genocide: A Sociological Perspective* (London: Sage Publications, 1993), pp. 18–19, 88; Eric Markusen and David Kopf, *The Holocaust and Strategic Bombing: Genocide and Total War in the 20th Century* (Boulder, CO: Westview Press, 1995), p. 63.
33. Kelman, "Violence without Moral Restraint," pp. 32–33.
34. Browning, *Ordinary Men,* pp. 147–189.
35. Ibid., pp. 184–185.
36. Eric Markusen and Damir Mirkovic, "Understanding Genocidal Killing in Former Yugoslavia: Preliminary Observations," in Craig Summers and Eric Markusen, eds., *Collective Violence: Harmful Behavior in Groups and Governments* (Lanham, MD: Rowman & Littlefield, 1999), pp. 41–42.
37. Sönke Zankel, "Voyeurismus und Sadismus, Todesmärsche als 'Varinte' des deutschen KZ-Systems," *Frankfurter Allgemeine Zeitung,* January 27, 2009, p. 8.
38. Greiser, *Die Todesmärsche von Buchenwald,* pp. 260–269.
39. Markusen and Mirkovic, "Understanding Genocidal Killing," pp. 41–42.
40. Konrad Kwiet, "Erziehung zum Mord—Zwei Beispiele zur Kontinuität der deutschen 'Endlösung der Judenfrage,'" in Michael Grüner, Rüdiger Hachtmann, and Heinz-Gerhard Haupt, eds., *Geschichte und Emannzipation: Festschrift für Reinhard Rürup* (Frankfurt am Main: Campus, 1999), pp. 436–438.
41. Bergen, "Death Throes and Killing Frenzies," p. 37.
42. Michael Mann, "Were the Perpetrators of Genocide 'Ordinary Men' or 'Real Nazis'? Results from Fifteen Hundred Biographies," *Holocaust and Genocide Studies* 14:3 (2000): 331–366.
43. Jacques Sémelin, *Purifier et détruire: Usages politiques des massacres et génocides* (Paris: Seuil, 2005), pp. 288–289.

44. Leo Kuper, *Genocide: Its Political Use in the Twentieth Century* (Middlesex, England: Penguin Books, 1981), p. 41.
45. Greiser, *Die Todesmärsche von Buchenwald,* pp. 258–259.
46. Mark Levene, "Introduction," in Mark Levene and Penny Roberts, eds., *The Massacre in History* (New York: Berghahn Books, 1999), pp. 5–6.
47. On this, see Zygmunt Bauman, *Modernity and the Holocaust* (Cambridge: Polity Press, 1989), pp. 152–153.
48. Jacques Sémelin, "In Consideration of Massacres," *Journal of Genocide Research* 3:3 (2001): 384–385.
49. Testimony of Pinchas Rosenfeld, September 19, 1946, Boder Collection.
50. Bauer, "The Death Marches," pp. 499–500; Greiser, *Die Todesmärsche von Buchenwald,* pp. 217–225.
51. Greiser, *Die Todesmärsche,* pp. 217–225.
52. Testimony of Avraham Kimmelman, August 27, 1946, Boder Collection.
53. Testimony of Yehiel Daniel, May 30, 1995, YVA, 03/9991.

Bibliography

Primary Sources

ARCHIVES

Archiv KZ-Gedenkstätte Dachau (AGD), Dachau
  Reports
  Testimonies

Archiv KZ-Gedenkstätte Flossenbürg (AGF), Flossenbürg
  International Tracing Service Archives: The Evacuation of C.C. Flossenbürg

Archiv KZ-Gedenkstätte Mittelbau-Dora (AGM), Nordhausen
  Testimonies

Archiv KZ-Gedenkstätte Neuengamme (AGN), Neuengamme
  Collection of interviews, Mijndert Bertram
  Oral History Project
  Testimonies

Archives Nationales (AN), Paris
  Military affairs (Gardelegen)—F9/5590
  Testimonies and reports (Comité d'histoire de la seconde guerre mondiale)—72
    AJ 318, 320, 321, 323, 325–326, 327, 329, 331–332, 334–336, 338–340, 342,
    372, 377

Archiwum Muzeum Stutthof (AMS), Stutthof
  Z–V: 23, 49

Archiwum Państwowego Muzeum Auschwitz-Birkenau (APMAB), Auschwitz
  D-RF-3/RSHA
  IZ-26/2, 27/1, 27/11

Materiały/ 593–596a, 597–599
Owiadczenia 81, 120
Proces Hößa/ 16a

Bernard Robinson Collection
Death Marches: Bergen-Belsen, Grünberg, Helmbrechts, Schlesiersee, Zwodau

Bundesbeauftragte für die Unterlagen des Staatssicherheitsdienstes der ehemaligen
DDR (BstU), Berlin
ZM 1625 Bd. 34—Der Staatsanwalt des Bezirkes Magdeburg

Collection of Interviews, Diana Gring (The Gardelegen Massacre)
Lucien Colonel, Bernhard Daenekas, Herbert Ehle, Fritz und Ursula Matthies,
Gerhard Pagels, Dieter Rieke

Dokumentationsarchiv des österreichischen Widerstandes (DÖW), Vienna
12.588
12.597
12.854
19.867
20.699
12.6Z7
13.0Z8
No. 1459
20.000/P359

Moreshet Archive (MA), Givat Chaviva, Israel
Collection of testimonies: A: 227, 229, 261, 860, 1359

National Archives and Records Administration (NARA), College Park,
Maryland
M-1079—Dora-Nordhausen Case
M-1174—Dachau Case
M-1204—Flossenbürg Case
RG-153—Buchenwald Case; Mauthausen Case
RG-226—U.S. 12th Army Headquarters
RG-338—1st Army
RG-407—102nd Infantry Division

The National Archives of the United Kingdom (TNA), Kew
Foreign Office—FO
War Office—WO

Nederlands Instituut voor Oorlogsdocumentie (NIOD), Amsterdam
Sammlung 250K Mittelbau/Dora
Carton 13a
Carton 13a-II

Niedersächsisches Hauptstaatsarchiv Hannover (NdsH), Hannover
Strafverfahren gegen Wilhelm Genth, Paul Mass, 721 97/99 Nr. 26/1, 2, 3, 4

Österreichisches Staatsarchiv/Archiv der Republik (ÖSA), Vienna
 54.297–18/70
 54.987–18/68
 97.094–2/48

Państwowe Muzeum Gross-Rosen (PMGR), Wałbrzych
 DP: 88, 91, 97, 99, 111, 234, 2249, 5903, 5903/54, 5903/57, 6500/19a, 8020/10,
   8020/11, 8020/13, 8020/14, 8020/16

Staatsanwaltschaft beim Landesgericht Aschaffenburg (SLA)
 Strafverfahren gegen Hans Stefan Olejak, Ewald Pansegrau, KS 201 Js 19730/76

Staatsanwaltschaft beim Landesgericht Duisburg (SLD)
 Strafverfahren gegen Karl Bruno Blach, Dominik Gleba, IX KS 130 (24) Js 28/72

Staatsanwaltschaft beim Landesgericht Köln (SLK)
 Strafsache gegen Walter Karl Heinrich Knop, 40–31/74

Staatsanwaltschaft beim Landesgericht München II (SLM)
 Strafverfahren gegen Erich Assmann, 119 b KS 10/71

Staatsanwaltschaft beim Landesgericht Stendal (SLS)
 Strafsache gegen Rudolf Jordan, Gerhard Thiele, 21Js 87295/91, vols. I, II, III,
   IV, VI
 Strafsache gegen Rudolf Jordan, Gerhard Thiele, 27Js 87295/91, vol. VII
   Sonderband IV
   Sonderheft I

Staatsarchiv Bremen (StaB), Bremen
 Strafverfahren gegen Helmrich Heilmann, Josef Kierspel, Johann Mirbeth, 3 Js
   1263/50

Staatsarchiv Gardelegen, Staatmuseum (MGS), Gardelegen
 Ludwig Lewin, *Erlebnisbericht,* No. 523
 Testimonies: No. 410, 492

Thüringisches Hauptstaatsarchiv (THW), Weimar
 KZ Buchenwald

United States Holocaust Memorial Museum Archives (USHMMA), Washington, DC
 Acc—1994.A.0252, 1995.A.82, 1998.A.0151, 2000.18, 2000.149, 2000.311,
   2004.103.1
 RG-02.002#25
 RG-02.039
 RG-02.075#01
 RG-02.093
 RG-02.112#01
 RG-02.153
 RG-02.180
 RG-02.191
 RG-02.209

RG-04.030M
RG-04.055
RG-04.058M
RG-06.025#26
RG-09.006#01
RG-09.024
RG-09.033
RG-09.037
RG-09.056
RG-10.244
RG-15.019M
RG-17.002M
RG-19.038
RG-32.011#01
RG-50.002#03, 11, 037, 087
RG-50.030#012, 115, 192, 216, 226, 258, 368
RG-50.106#18
RG-50.120#046, 136, 148, 152, 168
RG-50.155#03
RG-50.166#06, 18
RG-50.472#0010

Yad Vashem Archives (YVA), Jerusalem
  Adolf Eichmann trial: TR-3/1650
  The Bureau for Investigation of Nazi Crimes, Israeli Police: TR-11/629.1
  Collection of Testimonies, Hungary: 015E/ 434, 530, 1701, 2376
  Collection of Testimonies, Jewish historical commission of the American occupation zone, Munich: M-1/E 1275
  Diaries and Testimonies: 033/ 758, 920, 1317, 1349, 1397, 1508, 1642, 1692, 2387, 4255
  Heiner Lichtenstein Collection: P-26/166(1)
  Johannes Hassebroek trial: TR-10/716
  Kurt Friedrichs trial: TR-10/1327 (Bd. I, II)
  Microfilms: JM/ 3864, 3934, 3936, 10.031, 10.047, 10.052, 10.055, 10.059
  Oswald Pohl trial: TR-2 Na/Proc/E
  Testimonies, the Jewish Historical Institute, Warsaw: M-49/E 216, 2919
  Testimonies, Wiener Library (London): 02/851
  The Underground Archives of the Białystok Ghetto (Marsik-Tenenbaum Collection): M-11/114
  War crime testimonies: 04/ 341, 394
  Yad Vashem Collection of Testimonies: 03/792.1, 1108, 2279, 2348, 3343, 4536, 4552, 4561, 4567, 5145, 5418, 5799, 6209, 7001, 7869, 8492, 8574, 8842, 9169, 9327, 9952, 9953, 9978, 9991, 10137, 10154, 10464, 10560, 10647, 10776, 11020, 11151, 11342, 11411, 11624, 11932, 11942, 11995, 12087, 12091, 12201, 12254, 12382, 12599
  Yitzhak Stone Collection: 018/276

Zentrale Stelle der Landesjustizverwaltungen (ZStL), Ludwigsburg
  302 AR 507/70
  410 AR 1750/61
  402 AR-Z 158/78
  406 AR-Z 52/67
  407 AR-Z 44/73
  407 AR-Z 51/69
  407 AR-Z 174/72
  407 AR-Z 182/72
  407 AR-Z 242/72
  429 AR-Z 192/72
  502 AR-Z 108/67

Press

American Newspapers
  Life magazine, *New York Herald Tribune, New York Times, Stars and Stripes, Washington Post*

Contemporary German Newspapers
  Berliner Kurier, Frankfurter Allgemeine Zeitung

Gardelegen Local Newspapers, 1995–2000
  Altmark-Blätter, General-Anzeiger, Volksstimme

German Newspapers, 1945
  Der Führer (Karlsruhe), *Hannoversche Zeitung, Lüneburger Zeitung, Rheinisch-Bergische Zeitung, Völkische Beobachter*

Hebrew Newspapers, 1945
  Davar, Haaretz, HaTsofe

Documentary Collections

Bauche, Ulrich, Heinz Brüdigen, Ludwig Eiber, and Wolfgang Wiedey, eds. *Arbeit und Vernichtung: Das Konzentrationslager Neuengamme 1938–1945.* Hamburg: VSA-Verlag, 1986.

Braham, Randolph L., ed. *The Destruction of Hungarian Jewry: A Documentary Account,* vol. II. New York: World Federation of Hungarian Jews, 1963.

Buchenwald: Mahnung und Verpflichtung—Dokumente und Berichte. Berlin Ost: Deutscher Verlag der Wissenschaft, 1983.

Buchenwald Concentration Camp 1937–1945: A Guide to the Permanent Historical Exhibition. Göttingen: Wallstein Verlag, 2004.

Czech, Danuta. *Auschwitz Chronicle, 1939–1945.* New York: Henry Holt & Co., 1990.

DDR-Justiz und NS-Verbrechen, vols. III–VIII. Amsterdam: Amsterdam University Press, 2003–2006.

Hackett, David A., ed. *The Buchenwald Report.* Boulder, CO: Westview Press, 1995.

Hertz-Eichenrode, K., ed. *Ein KZ wird geräumt: Häftlinge zwischen Vernichtung und Befreiung—Die Auflösung des KZ Neuengamme und seiner Außenlager durch die SS im Frühjahr 1945.* 2 vols. Bremen: Edition Temmen, 2000.

Holzträger, Hans. *In a Raging Inferno: Combat Units of the Hitler Youth 1944–45.* Solihull, England: Helion & Co., 2000.

Justiz und NS-Verbrechen, vols. VII, VIII, XIV, XVI, XVII, XVIII, XXXIV. Amsterdam: Amsterdam University Press, 1972–2005.

Kasztner, Rezsö. *Der Bericht des jüdischen Rettungskomitees aus Budapest 1942–1945.* Budapest: Waad Haezna VeHaazala, 1946.

Katzmann, Friedrich. *Lösung der Judenfrage im Distrikt Galizien.* Warsaw: Instytut Pamięci Narodowej, 2001.

Klarsfeld, Serge. *Le Calendrier de la Persécution des Juifs en France 1940–1944.* Paris: S. Klarsfeld, 1993.

Krakowski, Shmuel, ed. "Massacre of Jewish Prisoners on the Samland Penisula—Documents." *Yad Vashem Studies* 24 (1994): 349–387.

Marrus, Michael R. *The Nuremberg War Crimes Trial, 1945–46: A Documentary History,* Boston: Bedford Books, 1997.

Naumann, Uwe, ed. *Lidice: Ein Böhmisches Dorf.* Frankfurt am Main: Röderberg-Verlag, 1983.

Perry, Michael W., ed. *Dachau Liberated: The Official Report by the U.S. Seventh Army,* Seattle, WA: Inkling Books, 2000.

Perz, Bertrand. "Der Todesmarsch von Wiener Neudorf nach Mauthausen: Eine Dokumentation." In *Dokumentationsarchiv des österreichischen Widerstandes, Jahrbuch 1988,* pp. 117–137. Vienna: Österreichischer Bundesverlag, 1988.

Phillips, Raymond, ed. *The Trial of Josef Kramer and Forty-Four Others (The Bergen Trial).* London: William Hodge & Co., 1949.

[Redaktion, Kurt Buck . . . et al.]. *Kriegsende und Befreiung.* Bremen: Edition Temmen, 1995.

Redmer, Kurt. *Vergeßt dieses Verbrechen nicht! Der Todesmarsch KZ Sachsenhausen-Schwerin 1945.* Rostock, Germany: Ingo Koch Verlag, 2000.

The Reports of Jürgen Stroop Concerning the Uprising in the Ghetto of Warsaw and the Liquidation of the Jewish Residential Area. Warsaw: Jewish Historical Institute, 1958.

Sachsenhausen: Dokumente, Aussagen, Forschungsergebnisse und Erlebnisberichte über das ehemalige Konzentrationslager Sachsenhausen, vol. IV. Berlin Ost: Deutscher Verlag der Wissenschaften, 1982.

Schnabel, Reimund. *Macht ohne Moral: Eine Dokumentation über die SS.* Frankfurt am Main: Röderberg Verlag, 1957.

Smith, Bradley F., and Agnes F. Peterson, eds. *Heinrich Himmlers Geheimreden 1933 bis 1945.* Frankfurt am Main: Propyläen Verlag, 1974.

Trials of the Major War Criminals before the International Military Tribunal, Nuremberg, 14 November 1945–1 October 1946, Nuremberg 1947. New York: William S. Hein & Co., 1995–1997.

Trials of War Criminals before the Nuremberg Military Tribunals, vol. III (The Justice Case), vol. V (Pohl Trial). Washington, DC: U.S. Government Printing Office, 1953.

Tuchel, Johannes, ed. *Die Inspektion der Konzentrationslager 1938–1945: Das System des Terrors,* eine Dokumentation. Berlin: Hentrich, 1994.

Vorläufiges Verzeichnis der Konzentrationslager und deren Außenkommandos sowie anderer Haftstätten unter der Reichsführer-SS, in Deutschland und von Deutschland besetzten Gebieten (1933–1945). Arolsen, Germany: Comité international de la Croix-Rouge, 1969.

Diaries, Memoirs, Personal Accounts

Adler, Sinai. *BeGay Tzalmavet* [In the valley of death]. Jerusalem: Yad Vashem, 1979.

Alcoff, Isabel, and Mark Stern. *Shema, Secret of My Survival: Memoirs of Mark Stern.* 1993.

Amicale des Anciens de Dachau. *Allach Kommando de Dachau.* Paris: France-Empire, 1986.

Anonymous. *A Woman in Berlin: Eight Weeks in the Conquered City.* New York: Metropolitan Books, 2005.

Béon, Yves. *Planet Dora: A Memoir of the Holocaust and the Birth of the Space Age.* Boulder, CO: Westview Press, 1997.

Berghe, Gie van den, ed. *Au camp de Flossenbürg (1945): Témoignage de Léon Calembert.* Brussels: Commission Royal d'Histoire, 1995.

Bernadotte, Folcke, Count. *The Curtain Falls: A Unique Eyewitness Story of the Last Days of the Third Reich as Seen by a Neutral Observer inside Germany.* New York: Knopf, 1945.

Bertrand, François. "Der Todeszug nach Dachau." *Dachauer Hefte* 19 (November 1999): 17–37.

———. *Notre devoir de mémoire: Convoi de la mort Buchenwald à Dachau du 7 au 28 avril 1945.* Pau-Bizanos: Héraclés, 2000.

Bocchetta, Vittore. *Jene fünf verdammten Jahre: Aus Verona in die Konzentrationslager Flossenbürg und Hersbruck.* Lage, Germany: Verlag Hans Jacobs, 2003.

Bonifas, Aimé. *Prisoner 20801.* Wilmington, DE: Cedar Press, 1983.

Broszat, Martin, ed. *Kommandant in Auschwitz: Autobiographische Aufzeichnungen von Rudolf Höß.* Stuttgart: Deutsch Verlags-Anstalt, 1958.

Carlebach, Emil. *Tote auf Urlaub: Kommunist in Deutschland, Dachau und Buchenwald 1937–1945.* Bonn: Pahl-Rugenstein Verlag, 1995.

Christians, Ludwik. *Piekło XX Wieku: Zbrodnia, hart ducha i miłosierdzie.* Warsaw: Katolockie Towarzystwo Wydawnicze "Rodzina Polska," 1946.

Cling, Maurice. *Vous qui entrez ici . . . : Un enfant à Auschwitz.* Paris: Graphin, 1999.

Eck, Nathan. "The March of Death from Serbia to Hungary (September 1944) and the Slaughter of Cservenka." *Yad Vashem Studies* 2 (1958): 255–294.

Freeman, Joseph. *The Road to Hell: Recollection of the Nazi Death March.* St. Paul, MN: Paragon House, 1998.

Fröhlich, Elke, ed. *Die Tagebücher von Joseph Goebbels,* vols. VI, VII, VIII, XII, XIII. Munich: K. G. Sauer, 1993–1996.

Ganor, Solly. "Death March." In Wolfgang Benz and Barbara Distel, eds., *Dachau and the Nazi Terror 1933–1945,* vol. I, *Testimonies and Memoirs,* pp. 204–215. Dachau: Verlag Dachauer Hefte, 2002.

Gar, Yosef. *Umkum fun der yiddisher Kovne*. [The annihilation of Jewish Kovno]. Munich: Farband fun litwishe yidden in der amerikaner zone in Daytshland, 1948.

Garfunkel, Leib. *Kovna HaYehudit BeKhurbanah* [The destruction of Jewish Kovno]. Jerusalem: Yad Vashem, 1959.

Giergielewicz, Jerzy. *Endstation Neuengamme, Außenlager Drütte: Der Weg eines 17-jährigen aus Warschau durch vier Konzentrationslager*. Bremen: Edition Temmen, 2002.

Gorce, Nelly. *Journal de RavEnsbrück*. Arles: Actes Sud, 1995.

Gostner, Erwin. *1000 Tage im KZ: Ein Erlebnisbericht aus den Konzentrationslagern Dachau, Mauthausen, Gusen*. Mannheim: W. Burger, 1946.

Granzow, Klaus. *Tagebuch eines Hitlerjungen*. Bremen: Carl Schünemann, 1965.

Guderian, Heinz. *Panzer Leader*. Costa Mesa, CA: The Noontide Press, 1988.

Guterman, Bella, ed. *BaLev Baara HaShalhevet: Yomana Shel Fela Szeps, Makhane HaAvoda Grinberg* [A flame burned in her heart: The diary of Fela Szeps, Grinberg labor camp]. Jerusalem: Yad Vashem, 2002.

Gutman, Israel. *Anashim VaEfer: Sefer Oshvits-Birkenau* [People and ashes: The book of Auschwitz-Birkenau]. Merḥavyah: Sifriyat Poalim, 1957.

Haulot, Arthur. *Mauthausen Dachau*. Brussels: Le Cri/Vander, 1985.

Hess, Hanna Levi. "Raav-terror-typhus-rakav-mavet" [Hunger-terror-typhus-rotdeath]. In Mordekhay Tsanin, ed., *Kakh Zeh Hayah: Dapei Edut shel She'erit HaPleita Yotsei Bergen Belsen* [This is how it was: Testimonies of survivors of Bergen-Belsen]. Tel Aviv: Organization of Survivors from the British Zone, 1987.

Höß, Rudolf. *Death Dealer: The Memoirs of the SS Komandant at Auschwitz Rudolph Höß*. Steven Paskuly, ed. New York: Da Capo Press, 1996.

———. *Kommandant in Auschwitz: Autobiographische Aufzeichnungen von Rudolf Höß*. Stuttgart: Deutsche Verlags-Anstalt, 1958.

Jordan, Rudolf. *Erlebt und Erlitten: Weg eines Gauleiters von München bis Moskau*. Freising: Druffel Verlag, 1971.

Juretzky-Waschek, Waltraut. *Als "Künstlerin" in der russischen Kommandantur: Eine 18 jährige erlebt das Kriegsende und die ersten Nachkriegsjahre in Gardelegen*. Oschersleben: Dr. Ziethen Verlag, 1998.

Katz, Josef. *One Who Came Back. The Diary of a Jewish Survivor*. New York: Herzl Press, 1973.

Kautsky, Benedikt. *Teufel und Verdammte: Erfahrungen und Erkenntnisse aus sieben Jahren in deutschen Konzentrationslagern*. Zurich: Büchergilde Gutenberg, 1946.

Kersten, Felix. *The Kersten Memoirs, 1940–1945*. New York: Macmillan, 1957.

Klein, Gerda Weissmann. *All But My Life*. New York: Hill & Wang, 1957.

Klemperer, Victor. *I Shall Bear Witness: The Diaries of Victor Klemperer 1933–41*. London: Weidenfeld & Nicolson, 1998.

———. *I Will Bear Witness, A Diary of the Nazi Years 1942–1945*. New York: Random House, 1999.

Kogon, Eugen. *The Theory and Practice of Hell: The German Concentration Camps and the System behind Them*. London: Secker & Warburg, 1950.

Kokhavi, Avraham. "Naar HaMakhanot" [Boy of the camps]. *Yalkut Moreshet* 4 (July 1965): 7–20.

Kram, Isaac Leo. "Liberation in Buchenwald." In Gertrude Schneider, ed., *Muted Voices: Jewish Survivors from Latvia Remember*. New York: Philosophical Library, 1987.

Kuhlbrodt, Peter, ed. *Schicksalsjahr 1945: Inferno Nordhausen: Chronik, Dokumente, Erlebnisberichte*. Schriftenreihe "Heimatgeschichtliche Forschungen des Stadtarchivs Nordhausen/Harz," no. 6. Nordhausen: Archiv der Stadt, 1995.

Kujawski, Benjamin. *Łódź Ghetto, Auschwitz-Birkenau, Dachau-Kaufering-Landsberg*, Memoirs of Holocaust Survivors in Canada, no. 23. Montreal: Montreal Institute for Genocide and Human Rights Studies, 2002.

Kupfer-Koberwitz, Edgar. *Dachauer Tagebücher: Die Aufzeichnungen des Häftlings 24814*. Munich: Kindler, 1997.

Levi, Primo. *If This Is a Man/The Truce*. London: Abacus, 1979.

Mannheimer, Max. *Yoman Meukhar, Theresienstadt, Auschwitz, Varscha, Dachau* [A late diary, Theresienstadt, Auschwitz, Warsaw, Dachau]. Tel Aviv: Moreshet VeSifriyat Poalim, 1987.

Mirbach, Willy. *"Damit du es später deinem Sohn einmal erzählen kannst . . .": Der autobiographische Bericht eines Luftwaffensoldaten aus dem KZ Mittelbau (August 1944–Juli 1945)*. Geldern, Germany: Verlag des Historischen Vereins für Geldern und Umgegend, 1997.

Morel, René. *Les Derniers Supplices ou Mémoire d'apocalypse*. Oyonnax, France: Solypac, 1998.

Müller, Philip. *Eyewitness Auschwitz: Three Years in the Gas Chambers*. New York: Stein & Day, 1979.

Rafael, Shmuel, ed. *BeNetivey Sheol: Yehudey Yavan BaShoah, Pirkey Edut* [Along the paths of hell: The Jews of Greece in the Holocaust, testimonies]. Tel Aviv: Institute for Study of Saloniki Jewry and the Association of Greek Death Camp Survivors in Israel, 1988.

The Reichmanns of Bielitz: Our European Background. Memoirs of Linilia Robinson (Reichmann). Los Angeles, 1992.

Rousset, David. *L'univers concentrationaire*. Paris: Pavois, 1946.

Schellenberg, Walter. *The Labyrinth: Memoirs of Walter Schellenberg*. New York: Harper & Brothers, 1956.

Schmidt-Fels, Lucia. *Deportation nach Ravensbrück*. Essen: Plöger, 2004.

Schneider, Gertrude, ed. *Muted Voices: Jewish Survivors from Latvia Remember*. New York: Philosophical Library, 1987.

Shirer, William L. *Berlin Diary: The Journal of a Foreign Correspondent*. New York: Knopf, 1941.

Shupungin, Abraham. "The Terrors of Dundaga." In Gertrude Schneider, ed., *The Unfinished Road: Jewish Survivors of Latvia Look Back*, pp. 151–165. New York: Praeger, 1991.

Speer, Albert. *Inside the Third Reich: Memoirs by Albert Speer*. New York: Macmillan, 1970.

Sruoga, Ralys. *Forest of the Gods: Memoirs*. Vilnius: Vaga, 1996.

Steinhoff, Johannes, Peter Pechel, and Dennis Showalter, eds. *Voices from the Third Reich: An Oral History*. New York: Da Capo Press, 1994.

Tage im April: Ein Lesebuch. Gardelegon; Schriftenreihe des Stadtmusueums, 1995.

Trevor-Roper, Hugh, ed. *Final Entries, 1945: The Diaries of Joseph Goebbels.* New York: G. P. Putnam's Sons, 1978.

Tsanin, Mordekhay, ed. *Kakh Zeh Hayah: Dapei Edut shel She'erit HaPleita Yotsei Bergen Belsen* [This is how it was: Testimonies of survivors of Bergen-Belsen]. Tel Aviv: Organization of Survivors from the British Zone, 1987.

Unsdorfer, Simcha Bunem. *The Yellow Star.* Jerusalem: Feldheim Publishers, 1983.

Uschner, Manfred. "Bombennacht in Magdeburg." In Christine Krauss and Daniel Küchenmeister, eds., *Das Jahr 1945: Brüche und Kontinuitäten,* pp. 167–177. Berlin: Dietz Verlag, 1995.

Weiss-Balazs, Agnes. *"Zusammen-Zusammen": Von Nordsiebenbürgen durch Auschwitz-Birkenau und Ravensbrück bis Neustadt-Glewe und Wittstock 1923–1945.* Konstanz, Germany: Hartung-Gorre, 2005.

Wirtzberg, Beny. *MiGai HaHariga LeShaar HaGai* [From the valley of death to the valley gateway]. Ramat Gan: Massada, 1967.

Wysocki, Gerd. *Das KZ-Drütte bei den Hermann-Göring-Werken in Watenstedt-Salzgitter, Oktober 1942 bis April 1945.* Salzgitter, Germany: Arbeitskreis Stadtgeschichte, 1986.

Secondary Sources

Adelman, Howard, and Astri Suhrke, eds. *The Path of a Genocide: The Rwanda Crisis from Uganda to Zaire.* New Brunswick, NJ: Transaction Publishers, 1999.

Adler, Hans Günter. *Theresienstadt 1941–1945: Das Antlitz einer Zwangsgemeinschaft.* Tübingen: J. C. B. Mohr, 1960.

Allen, Michael Thad. *The Business of Genocide: The SS, Slave Labor, and the Concentration Camps.* Chapel Hill: University of North Carolina Press, 2002.

Allport, Gordon W., and Leo Postman. *The Psychology of Rumor.* New York: Henry Holt & Co., 1947.

Aly, Götz, and Susanne Heim. *Architects of Annihilation: Auschwitz and the Logic of Destruction.* London: Weidenfeld & Nicolson, 2002.

Anzenberger, Werner, Heimo Halbrainer, and Hans Jürgen Rabko. *Zwischen den Fronten: Die Region Eisenerz von 1938–1945.* Leoben, Austria: Institut für Strukturforschung und Erwachsenenbildung, 2000.

Appelbaum, Anne. *Goulag: A History.* New York: Doubleday, 2003.

Arad, Yitzhak. *Toldot HaShoah: Berit HaMoatsot VehaShtakhim HaMesupakhim* [The history of the Holocaust: The Soviet Union and the annexed territories], vol. II. Jerusalem: Yad Vashem, 2004.

Arendt, Hannah. "The Concentration Camps." *Partisan Review* 15:7 (1948): 743–763.

Balcke, Jörg. *Verantwortungsentlastung durch Organisation: Die "Inspektion der Konzentrationslager" und der KZ-Terror.* Tübingen: Edition Diskord, 2001.

Barnouw, Dagmar. *Germany 1945: Views of War and Violence.* Bloomington: Indiana University Press, 1996.

Bartov, Omer. *Hitler's Army: Soldiers, Nazis and War in the Third Reich.* New York: Oxford University Press, 1991.

———. "The Missing Years: German Workers, German Soldiers." In David F. Crew, ed., *Nazism and German Society 1933–1945,* pp. 41–66. London: Routledge, 1994.

Bauer, Yehuda. "The Death Marches, January–May 1945." In Michael R. Marrus, ed., *The Nazi Holocaust*, vol. IX, *The End of the Holocaust*, pp. 491–511. Westport, CT: Meckler, 1989.

———. *Jews for Sale? Nazi-Jewish Negotiations, 1933–1945*. New Haven, CT: Yale University Press, 1994.

Bauman, Zygmunt. *Modernity and the Holocaust*. Cambridge: Polity Press, 1989.

Becker, Rudolph, Heinz Schenk, and Lies Wolf. *Ihr Opfer bleibt unvergessen! Zur Geschichte des Mahn- und Gedenkweges Gardelegen*. Gardelegen: Kreisleitung Gardelegen der Sozialistischen Einheitspartei Deutschlands, 1984.

Benz, Wolfgang, and Barbara Distel, eds. *Der Ort des Terrors: Geschichte der nationalsozialistischen Konzentrationslager*, vol. I. Munich: C. H. Beck, 2005.

Berben, Paul. *Dachau 1933–45: The Official History*. London: Norfolk Press, 1975.

Bergen, Doris L. "Death Throes and Killing Frenzies: A Response to Hans Mommsen's 'The Dissolution of the Third Reich: Crisis Management and Collapse, 1943–1945,'" *Bulletin of the German Historical Institute* 27 (2000): 25–37, http://www.ghi-dc.org/publications/ghipubs/bu/027/b27bergenframe.html (accessed February 18, 2010).

Berkhoff, Karel C. *Harvest of Despair: Life and Death in Ukraine under Nazi Rule*. Cambridge, MA: Belknap Press of Harvard University Press, 2004.

———. "The 'Russian' Prisoners of War in Nazi-Ruled Ukraine as Victims of Genocidal Massacre." *Holocaust and Genocide Studies* 15:1 (2001): 1–32.

Bertram, Mijndert. *April 1945: Der Luftangriff auf Celle und das Schicksal der KZ-Häftlinge aus Drütte*. Celle: Schriftenreihe des Stadtarchivs Celle und des Bomann-Museums, 1989.

Birn, Ruth Bettina. *Die Höheren SS-und Polizeiführer: Himmlers Vertreter im Reich und in den besetzten Gebieten*. Düsseldorf: Droste Verlag, 1986.

Black, Peter R. *Ernst Kaltenbrunner, Ideological Soldier of the Third Reich*. Princeton, NJ: Princeton University Press, 1984.

Blatman, Daniel. "The Death Marches, January–May 1945: Who Was Responsible for What?" *Yad Vashem Studies* 28 (2000): 155–201.

———. "Die Todesmärsche—Entscheidungsträger, Mörder und Opfer." In Ulrich Herbert, Karin Orth, and Christoph Dieckmann, eds., *Die nationalsozialistischen Konzentrationslager: Entwicklung und Struktur*, vol. II, pp. 1063–1092. Göttingen: Wallstein Verlag, 1998.

———. "Rückzug, Evakuierung und Todesmärsche 1944–1945." In Wolfgang Benz and Barbara Distel, eds., *Der Ort des Terrors: Geschichte der nationalsozialistischen Konzentrationslager*, vol. I, pp. 296–312, Munich: C. H. Beck, 2005.

Block, Ernst. "*Wir waren eine glückliche Familie . . .*": Zur Geschichte und den Schicksalen der Juden in Salzwedel/Altmark*. Salzwedel: Museum des Altmarkkreises Salzwedel, 1998.

Blodig, Vojtěch. "Die letzte Phase der Entwicklung des Ghettos Theresienstadt." In Miroslav Kárný, ed., *Theresienstadt in der "Endlösung der Judenfrage,"* pp. 267–278. Prague: Panorama, 1992.

Boberach, Heinz. "Die Überführung von Soldaten des Heeres und der Luftwaffe in die SS-Totenkopfverbände zur Bewachung von Konzentrationslagern 1944." *Militärgeschichtliche Mitteilungen* 2 (1983): 185–190.

Braham, Randolph L. *The Hungarian Labor Service System 1939–1945.* New York: Columbia University Press, 1977.

———. *The Politics of Genocide: The Holocaust in Hungary,* vol. II. New York: Rosenthal Institute for Holocaust Studies, 1994.

Broszat, Martin. "The Concentration Camps 1933–45." In Helmut Krausnick, Hans Buchheim, Martin Broszat, and Hans-Adolf Jacobsen, eds., *Anatomy of the SS State,* pp. 399–504. New York: Walker & Co., 1965.

Browning, Christopher R. *Collected Memories: Holocaust History and Postwar Testimony.* Madison: University of Wisconsin Press, 2003.

———. "German Killers: Behavior in the Light of New Evidence." In *Nazi Policy, Jewish Workers, German Killers,* pp. 143–169. Cambridge: Cambridge University Press, 2000.

———. *Ordinary Men: Reserve Police Battalion 101 and the Final Solution in Poland.* New York: HarperCollins, 1992.

———. *The Origins of the Final Solution: The Evaluation of Nazi Jewish Policy, September 1939–March 1942.* Lincoln: University of Nebraska Press, 2004.

Bung, Gisela, and Rupert Kaiser. *Schicksale Jüdischer Familien aus Gardelegen.* Gardelegen: Schriftenreihe des Stadtmuseums Gardelegen, 1995.

Burczik, Günter. "'Nur net dran rührn!' Auf den Spuren der Todesmärsche ungarischer Juden durch Österreich nach Mauthausen im April 1945." In Martha Keil, and Eleonore Lappin, eds., *Studien zur Geschichte der Juden in Österreich,* pp. 169–204. Bodenheim: Philo, 1997.

Burleigh, Michael. *The Third Reich: A New History.* New York: Hill Wang, 2000.

Chroust, Peter. "Selected Letters of Doctor Friedrich Mennecke." In Götz Aly, Peter Chroust, and Christian Pross, *Cleansing the Fatherland: Nazi Medicine and Racial Hygiene,* pp. 238–295. Baltimore: Johns Hopkins University Press, 1994.

Dadrian, Vahakan N. *The History of the Armenian Genocide: Ethnic Conflict from the Balkans to Anatolia to the Caucasus.* Providence, RI: Berghahn Books, 1995.

Danyel, Jürgen, Olaf Groehler, and Mario Kessler. "Antifaschismus und Verdrängung: Zum Umgang mit der NS-Vergangenheit in der DDR." In Jürgen Kocka and Martin Sabrow, eds., *Die DDR als Geschichte: Fragen-Hypothesen-Perspektiven,* pp. 148–152. Berlin: Akademie Verlag, 1994.

Delowicz, Jan. *Śladem krwi.* Katowice: Towarzystwo Opieki nad Oświęcimiem, 1995.

Deutsch, Yehuda. *Bor, Sakhar Avadim BeMilkhemet HaOlam HaShniyah* [Bor, slave labor in the Second World War]. Netanya, Israel: Rachel Publishing House, 1998.

Dieckmann, Christoph. "Das Ghetto und das Konzentrationslager in Kaunas 1941–1944." In Ulrich Herbert, Karin Orth, and Christoph Dieckmann, eds., *Die nationalsozialistischen Konzentrationslager: Entwicklung und Struktur,* vol. I, pp. 439–471. Göttingen: Wallstein Verlag, 1998.

Distel, Barbara. "Öffentliches Sterben: Vom Umgang der Öffentlichen mit den Todesmärschen." *Dachauer Hefte* 20 (October 2004): 39–46.

———. "29 April 1945: The Liberation of the Concentration Camp at Dachau." In Wolfgang Benz and Barbara Distel, eds., *Dachau and the Nazi Terror 1933–1945,* vol. II, *Studies and Reports,* pp. 9–17. Dachau: Verlag Dachauer Hefte, 2002.

Dobosiewicz, Stanisław. *Mauthausen/Gusen, Obóz zagłady.* Warsaw: Wydawnictwo Ministerstwa Obrony Narodowej, 1977.

Dorobisch, Klaus. "Oranienburg—eines der ersten nationalsozialistischen Konzentrationslager." In Günter Morsch, ed., *Konzentrationslager Oranienburg, Stiftung Brandenburgische Gedenkstätten,* vol. III, pp. 13–22. Oranienburg: Edition Hentrich, 1994.

Douhet, Giulio. *The Command of the Air,* New York: Arno Press, 1972.

Drywa, Danuta. "Ruch transportów między KL Stutthof a innymi obozami." *Stutthof Zeszyty Muzeum* 9 (1990): 7–31.

———. *Zagłada Żydów w obozie koncentracyjnym Stutthof 1939–1945.* Gdańsk: Muzeum Stutthof w Sztutowie, 2001.

Dunin-Wąsowicz, Krzysztof. *Obóz koncentracyjny Stutthof.* Gdańsk: Wydawnictwo Morskie, 1970.

Dwork, Debórah, and Robert J. Van Pelt. *Auschwitz. 1270 to the Present.* New York: W. W. Norton, 1996.

Dworzecki, M. *Makhanot HaYehudim BeEstonyah 1942–1944* [The Jewish camps in Estonia, 1942–1944]. Jerusalem: Yad Vashem, 1970.

Eckstein, Benjamin. *Mauthausen, Makhaneh Rikuz VeKhilayon* [Mauthausen, concentration and extermination camp]. Jerusalem: Yad Vashem, 1984.

Eley, Geoff. "Ordinary Germans, Nazism, and Judeocide." In Geoff Eley, ed., *The "Goldhagen Effect": History, Memory, Nazism—Facing the German Past,* pp. 1–31. Ann Arbor: University of Michigan Press, 2000.

Elkes, Pauline. "Assessing the 'Other Germany': The Political Warfare Executive on Public Opinion and Resistance in Germany, 1943–1945." In Anthony McElligott and Tim Kirk, eds., *Working toward the Führer: Essays in Honour of Sir Ian Kershaw,* pp. 243–286. Manchester: Manchester University Press, 2003.

Erez, Zvi. "Jews for Copper: Jewish Hungarian Labor Service Companies in Bor." *Yad Vashem Studies* 28 (2000): 243–286.

Erler, Peter. "Zur Tätigkeit der sowjetischen Militärtribunale in Deutschland." In Peter Reif-Spirek and Bodo Ritscher, eds., *Speziallager in der SBZ: Gedenkstätten mit "doppelter Vergangenheit,"* pp. 204–221. Berlin: Ch. Links, 1999.

Erpel, Simone. "Machtverhältnisse im Zerfall: Todesmärsche der Häftlinge des Frauen–Konzentrationslagers Ravensbrück im April 1945." In Jörg Hillmann and John Zimmermann, eds., *Kriegsende 1945 in Deutschland,* pp. 179–202. Munich: R. Oldenbourg, 2002.

———. *Zwischen Vernichtung und Befreiung: Das Frauen-Konzentrationslager Ravensbrück in der letzen Kriegsphase.* Berlin: Metropol, 2005.

Evans, Gareth. "Crimes against Humanity: Overcoming Indifference." *Journal of Genocide Research* 8:3 (2006): 325–339.

Ezergailis, Andrew. *The Holocaust in Latvia, 1941–1944.* Riga: Historical Institute of Latvia and the United States Holocaust Memorial Museum, 1996.

Fabréguet, Michel. "Entwicklung und Veränderung der Funktionen des Konzentrationslagers Mauthausen 1938–1945." In Ulrich Hebert, Karin Orth, and Christoph Dieckmann, eds., *Die nationalsozialistischen Konzentrationslager: Entwicklung und Struktur,* vol. I, pp. 193–214. Göttingen: Wallstein Verlag, 1998.

———. *Mauthausen: Camp de concentration national-socialiste en Autriche rattachée (1938–1945).* Paris: Champion, 1999.

Fait, Barbara. "Die Kreisleitung der NSDAP—nach 1945." In Martin Broszat, Klaus-Dieter Henke, and Hans Woller, eds., *Von Stalingrad zur Währungsreform: Zur*

Sozialgeschichte des Umbruchs in Deutschland, pp. 214–299. Munich: R. Oldenbourg, 1989.

Farmer, Sarah. *Martyred Village: Commemorating the 1944 Massacre at Oradour-sur-Glane.* Berkeley: University of California Press, 1999.

Fein, Helen. *Genocide: A Sociological Perspective.* London: Sage Publications, 1993.

———. *Human Rights and Wrongs: Slavery, Terror, Genocide.* Boulder, CO: Paradigm Publishers, 2007.

Fest, Joachim. *Hitler.* New York: Harcourt Brace Jovanovich, 1974.

———. *Plotting Hitler's Death: The Story of German Resistance.* New York: Metropolitan Books, 1994.

Fetscher, Irving. *Joseph Goebbels im Berliner Sportpalast 1943: "Wollt Ihr den totalen Krieg?"* Hamburg: Europäische Verlagsanstalt, 1998.

Fings, Karola. *Krieg, Gesellschaft und KZ: Himmlers SS-Baubrigaden.* Paderborn: Ferdinand Schöningh, 2005.

Frei, Norbert. "Der totale Krieg und die Deutschen." In Norbert Frei and Hermann Kling, eds., *Der nationalsozialistische Krieg,* pp. 283–301. Frankfurt am Main: Campus, 1990.

———. *National Socialist Rule in Germany: The Führer State 1933–1945.* Oxford: Blackwell, 1993.

Frevert, Ute. *A Nation in Barracks: Modern Germany, Military Conscription and Civil Society.* Oxford: Berg, 2004.

Friedlander, Henry. *The Origins of Nazi Genocide: From Euthanasia to the Final Solution.* Chapel Hill: University of North Carolina Press, 1995.

Fritz, Stephen G. *Endkampf: Soldiers, Civilians, and the Death of the Third Reich.* Lexington: University Press of Kentucky, 2004.

———. *Frontsoldaten: The German Soldier in World War II.* Lexington: University Press of Kentucky, 1995.

Fröbe, Rainer. "Hans Kammler: Technokrat der Vernichtung." In Ronald Smelser and Enrico Syring, eds., *Die SS: Elite unter dem Totenkopf. 30 Lebensläufe,* pp. 305–319. Paderborn: Ferdinand Schöningh, 2000.

Fulbrook, Mary. *German National Identity after the Holocaust.* Cambridge: Polity Press, 1999.

Furet, François, and Ernst Nolte. *Fascism and Communism.* Lincoln: University of Nebraska Press, 2001.

Garber, Detlev. "Das KZ-Neuengamme." In Ulrike Jureit and Karin Orth, eds., *Überlebensgeschichte: Gespräche mit Überlebenden des KZ Neuengamme,* pp. 16–43. Hamburg: Dölling und Galitz, 1994.

Gellately, Robert. *Backing Hitler: Consent and Coercion in Nazi Germany.* New York: Oxford University Press, 2001.

———. *The Gestapo and German Society: Enforcing Racial Policy, 1933–1945.* Oxford: Clarendon Press, 1990.

Gerlach, Christian. "The Wannsee Conference, the Fate of German Jews, and Hitler's Decision in Principle to Exterminate All European Jews." In Omer Bartov, ed., *The Holocaust: Origins, Implementations, Aftermath,* pp. 108–161. London: Routledge, 2000.

Gerlach, Christian, and Aly Götz. *Das letzte Kapitel.* Stuttgart: Deutsche Verlags-Anstalt, 2002.

Gilbert, Martin. *Auschwitz and the Allies: How the Allies Responded to the News of Hitler's Final Solution.* London: Michael Joseph/Rainbird, 1981.

Gliński, Mirosław. "Organizacja obozu koncentracnyjnego Stutthof (1 Września 1939–9 Maja 1945)." *Stutthof Zeszyty Muzeum* 3 (1979): 5–225.

Goldhagen, Daniel Jonah. *Hitler's Willing Executioners: Ordinary Germans and the Holocaust.* New York: Knopf, 1996.

Grabowska, Janina. *Marsz śmierci: Ewakuacja piesza więźniów KL Stutthof i jego podobozów, 25 Stycznia–3 Maja 1945.* Gdańsk: Muzeum Stutthof w Sztutowie, 1992.

Graham, Helen. *The Spanish Republic at War 1936–1939.* Cambridge: Cambridge University Press, 2002.

Greiser, Katrin. "Die Auflösung des Lagerkomplexes Buchenwald und die Todesmärsche der Außenlager im Rheinland und in Westfalen im März und April 1945." In Jan Erik Schulte, ed., *Konzentrationslager im Rheinland und in Westfalen 1933–1945,* pp. 281–299. Paderborn: Ferdinand Schöningh, 2005.

———. *Die Todesmärsche von Buchenwald: Räumung, Befreiung und Spuren der Erinnerung.* Göttingen: Wallestein Verlag, 2008.

———. *Thüringen 1945—Todesmärsche aus Buchenwald, Überblick. Namen, Orte.* Weimar: Stiftung Gedenkstätten Buchenwald und Mittelbau-Dora, 2001.

Gring, Diana. "Das Massaker von Gardelegen." *Dachauer Hefte* 20 (October 2004): 112–126.

———. *Die Todesmärsche und das Massaker von Gardelegen: NS-Verbrechen in der Endphase des Zweiten Weltkriegs.* Gardelegen: Stadtmuseum Gardelegen, 1993.

———. "Eine Täterbiographie mit Lücken: Skizzen zum Leben des NSDAP-Kreisleiters Gerhard Thiele (1909–1994) und die Ermittlungsarbeit in Ost und Westdeutschland seit 1945." Seminar zum KZ Mittelbau-Dora in der Gedenkstätte Mittelbau-Dora, Nordhausen, October 10–November 1, 2002 (unpublished presentation).

———. ". . . Immer zwischen zwei Feuern: Der kommunistische Funktionshäftling Karl Semmler." In Anette Leo and Peter Reif-Spierk, eds., *Helden, Täter und Verräter: Studien zum DDR-Antifaschismus,* pp. 109–125. Berlin: Metropol, 1999.

———. "Von Antworten und offenen Fragen—Das Ende der jahrzehntelangen Suche nach dem NS-Täter Gerhard Thiele." In *Abgeleitete Macht: Funktionshäftlinge zwischen Widerstand und Kollaboration,* pp. 142–145. Bremen: Edition Temmen, 1998.

Groehler, Olaf. "Integration und Ausgrenzung von NS-Opfern: Zur Anerkennungs- und Entschädigungsdebatte in der Sowjetischen Besatzungszone Deutschlands 1945 bis 1949." In Jürgen Kocka, ed., *Historische DDR-Forschung: Aufsätze und Studien,* pp. 105–127. Berlin: Akademie Verlag, 1993.

Gross, Jan Tomasz. *Neighbors: The Destruction of the Jewish Community in Jedwabne, Poland.* Princeton, NJ: Princeton University Press, 2001.

Grossman, Atina. "A Question of Silence: The Rape of German Women by Occupation Soldiers." *October* 72 (Spring 1995): 43–63.

Grot, Elżbieta. *Rejs Śmierci: Ewakuacja morska więźniów KL Stutthof 1945.* Gdańsk: Muzeum Stutthow w Sztutowie, 1993.

Gruner, Wolf. *Jewish Forced Labor under the Nazis: Economic Needs and Racial Aims, 1938–1944.* New York: Cambridge University Press, 2006.

Guterman, Bella. *A Narrow Bridge to Life: Jewish Forced Labor and Survival in the Gross-Rosen Camp System, 1940–1945.* New York: Berghahn Books, 2008.

Hamerow, Theodore S. *On the Road to the Wolf's Lair: Ethics and Resistance in Nazi Germany.* Cambridge, MA: Belknap Press of Harvard University Press, 1997.

Hancock, Eleanor. *The National Socialist Leadership and Total War, 1941–1945.* New York: St. Martin's Press, 1991.

Hartewig, Karin. "Wolf unter Wölfen? Die prekäre Macht der kommunistischen Kapos im Konzentrationslager Buchenwald." In *Abgeleitete Macht: Funktionshäftlinge zwischen Widerstand und Kollaboration,* pp. 117–122. Bremen: Edition Temmen, 1998.

Heigl, Peter. *Konzentrationslager Flossenbürg in Geschichte und Gegenwart.* Regensburg: Mittelbayerische Druckerei- und Verlags-Gesellschaft, 1989.

Henke, Klaus-Dietmar. "Deutschland—Zweierlei Kriegsende." In Ulrich Herbert and Axel Schildt, eds., *Kriegsende in Europa: Vom Beginn des deutschen Machtzerfalls bis zur Stabilisierung der Nachkriegsordnung 1944–1948,* pp. 337–354. Essen: Klartext Verlag, 1998.

———. *Die amerikanische Besetzung Deutschlands.* Munich: R. Oldenbourg, 1995.

Henkys, Reinhard. "Ein Todesmarsch in Ostpreußen." *Dachauer Hefte* 20 (December 2004): 3–21.

Herbert, Ulrich. *Hitler's Foreign Workers: Enforced Foreign Labor in Germany under the Third Reich.* Cambridge: Cambridge University Press, 1997.

———. "Labour and Extermination: Economic Interests and the Primacy of *Weltanschauung* in National Socialism." *Past and Present* 138 (1993): 144–195.

Herbert, Ulrich, Karin Orth, and Christoph Dieckmann, eds. *Die nationalsozialistischen Konzentrationslager: Entwicklung und Struktur.* 2 vols. Göttingen: Wallstein Verlag, 1998.

Herbert, Ulrich, Karin Orth, and Christoph Dieckmann. "Die nationalsozialistischen Konzentrationslager: Geschichte, Erinnerung, Forschung." In Ulrich Herbert, Karin Orth, and Christoph Dieckmann, eds., *Die nationalsozialistischen Konzentrationslager: Entwicklung und Struktur,* vol. I, pp. 17–40. Göttingen: Wallstein Verlag, 1998.

Herbst, Ludolf. *Der totale Krieg und die Ordnung der Wirtschaft: Die Kriegswirtschaft im Spannungsfeld von Politik, Ideologie und Propaganda 1939–1945.* Stuttgart: Deutsche Verlags-Anstalt, 1982.

Herf, Jeffrey. *Divided Memory: The Nazi Past in the Two Germanys.* Cambridge, MA: Harvard University Press, 1997.

———. *The Jewish Enemy: Nazi Propaganda during World War II and the Holocaust.* Cambridge, MA: Belknap Press of Harvard University Press, 2006.

———. "Reactionary Modernism: Reconciliations of Technics and Unreason in Weimar Germany and the Third Reich." PhD diss. Brandeis University, 1980.

Hertz-Eichenrode, Katharina, ed. *Ein KZ wird geräumt: Häftlinge zwichen Vernichtung und Befreiung: Die Auflösung des KZ Neuengamme und seiner Außenlager durch die SS in Frühjahr 1945.* 2 vols. Bremen: Edition Temmen, 2000.

Hilberg, Raul. "Gehorsam oder Initiative? Zur arbeitsteiligen Täterschaft im Nationalsozialismus." *Frankfurter Lern- und Dokumentationszentrum des Holocaust,* Materialien no. 3, October 1991.

———. *Perpetrators, Victims, Bystanders: The Jewish Catastrophe 1933–1945*. New York: HarperCollins, 1992.

Honig, Jan Willem, and Norbert Both. *Srebrenica: Record of a War Crime*. London: Penguin Books, 1996.

Horvitz, Ariel. "Mitsad HaMavet shel Yehudey Chelm VeHrubieszów LeEver Nahar Bug BeDetsember 1939" [The death march of the Jews of Chelm and Hrubieszów toward the River Bug in December 1939], *Yalkut Moreshet* 68 (October 1999): 52–68.

Horwitz, Gordon J. *In the Shadow of Death: Living Outside the Gates of Mauthausen*. London: I. B. Tauris, 1991.

Jaskot, Paul B. *The Architecture of Oppression. The SS, Forced Labor and the Nazi Monumental Building Economy*. London: Routledge, 2000.

Johr, Barbara. "Die Ereignisse in Zahle." In Helke Sander and Barbara Johr, eds., *BeFreier und Befreite: Krieg, Vergewaltigung, Kinder,* pp. 46, 73. Munich: Verlag Antje Kunstmann, 1992.

Kaienburg, Hermann. *Die Wirtschaft der SS*. Berlin: Metropol, 2003.

———. "Freundschaft? Kamaradschaft? . . . Wie kann denn das möglich sein? Solidarität, Widerstand und die Rolle der 'roten Kapos' in Neuengamme." In *Abgeleitete Macht: Funktionshäftlinge zwischen Widerstand und Kollaboration,* pp. 18–50. Bremen: Edition Temmen, 1998.

———. *"Vernichtung durch Arbeit": Der Fall Neuengamme*. Bonn: J. H. W. Dietz, 1991.

Karay, Felicja. *Death Comes in Yellow: Skarżysko-Kamienna Slave Labor Camp*. Amsterdam: Harwood Academic Publishers, 1996.

Kelman, Herbert C. "Violence without Moral Restraint: Reflection on the Dehumanization of Victims and Victimizers." *Journal of Social Issues* 29:4 (1973): 25–61.

Kershaw, Ian. *The 'Hitler Myth": Image and Reality in the Third Reich*. Oxford: Oxford University Press, 1989.

———. *Hitler 1936–1945: Nemesis*. New York: W. W. Norton, 2000.

———. *Popular Opinion and Political Dissent in the Third Reich: Bavaria 1933–1945*. Oxford: Oxford University Press, 1983.

Khan, Shaharyar M. *The Shallow Graves of Rwanda*. London: I. B. Tauris, 2000.

Khlevniuk, Oleg V. *The History of the Gulag: From Collectivization to the Great Terror*. New Haven, CT: Yale University Press, 2004.

Kiernan, Ben. *Blood and Soil: A World History of Genocide and Extermination from Sparta to Darfur*. New Haven, CT: Yale University Press, 2007.

Kimmel, Günther. "Das Konzentrationslager Dachau: Eine Studie zu den nationalsozialistischen Gewaltverbrechen." In Martin Broszat and Elke Fröhlich, eds., *Bayern in der NS-Zeit,* vol. II, pp. 349–413. Munich: R. Oldenbourg, 1979.

———. "Zum Beispiel: Tötungsverbrechen in nationalsozialistischen Konzentrationslagern." In Adalbert Rückel, ed., *NS-Prozesse: Nach 25 Jahren Strafverfolgung: Möglichkeiten-Grenzen-Ergebnisse,* pp. 65–106. Karlsruhe: Verlag C. F. Müller, 1971.

Kleßmann, Christoph. "Untergänge—Übergänge: Gesellschaftsgeschichtliche Brüche und Kontinuitätslinien vor und nach 1945." In Christoph Kleßmann, ed., *Nicht nur Hitlers Krieg: Der Zweite Weltkrieg und die Deutschen,* pp. 83–97. Düsseldorf: Droste Verlag, 1989.

Koblik, Steven. *The Stones Cry Out.* New York: Holocaust Library, 1988.

Koch, Gertrud. "Blood, Sperm, and Tears." *October* 72 (Spring 1995): 27–41.

Koch, Hans J. Wolfgang. *The Hitler Youth: Origins and Development 1922–1945.* New York: Cooper Square Press, 2000.

Kochavi, Arieh J. *Confronting Captivity: Britain and the United States and Their POWs in Nazi Germany.* Chapel Hill: University of North Carolina Press, 2005.

Kolb, Eberhard. *Bergen Belsen: Geschichte des "Aufenthaltslagers" 1943–1945.* Hanover: Verlag für Literatur und Zeitgeschehen, 1962.

Konieczny, Alfred. "Ewakuacja obozu koncentracyjnego Groß-Rosen w 1945r." *Acta Universitatis Wratislaviensis: Studia nad Faszyzmem i Zbrodniami Hitlerowskimi* (1975): 163–189.

———. "Transporty więźniów KL Groß-Rosen do innych obozów koncentracyjnych w latach 1941–1945." *Acta Universitatis Wratislavienis: Studia nad Faszyzmem i Zbrodniami Hitlerowskimi* (1986): 269–292.

Kossoy, Edward. "Gęsiówka (KZ Warschau)." *Zeszyty Historyczne* 110 (1994): 62–73.

———. "The Gęsiówka Story: A Little Known Page of Jewish Fighting History." *Yad Vashem Studies* 32 (2004): 323–350.

Kozanecki, Zygmunt. "Gardelegen." *Biuletyn Głównej Komisji badania zbrodni Hitlerowskich w Polsce* 29 (1979): 198–210.

Krakowski, Shmuel. "The Death Marches in the Period of the Evacuation of the Camps." In Michael R. Marrus, ed., *The Nazi Holocaust,* vol. IX: *The End of the Holocaust,* pp. 476–490. Westport, CT: Meckler, 1989.

Kriegsverbrechen in Lüneburg. Das Massengrab im Tiergarten. Lüneburg: Geschichtswerkstatt Lüneburg e.V., 2000.

Kuby, Erich. *The Russians in Berlin, 1945.* New York: Hill & Wang, 1968.

Kühle, Barbara. "Die Todesmärsche der Häftlinge des KZ Sachsenhausen." *Sachsenhausen* 1 (1987): 5–52.

Kühne, Thomas. *Kameradschaft: Die Soldaten des nationalsozialistischen Kriegs und das 20. Jahrhundert.* Göttingen: Vandenhoeck and Ruprecht, 2006.

Kuper, Leo. *Genocide: Its Political Use in the Twentieth Century.* Middlesex, England: Penguin Books, 1981.

Kuretsidis-Haider, Claudia. "Justizakten als historische Quelle am Beispiel der 'Engerau-Prozesse.'" In Rudolf G. Ardelt and Christian Gerbel, eds., *Österreichischer Zeitgeschichtetag 1995,* pp. 337–343. Innsbruck: StudienVerlag, 1996.

Kwiet, Konrad. "Erziehung zum Mord—Zwei Beispiele zur Kontinuität der deutschen 'Endlösung der Judenfrage.'" In Michael Grüner, Rüdiger Hachtmann, and Heinz-Gerhard Haupt, eds., *Geschichte und Emanzipation: Festschrift für Reinhard Rürup,* pp. 435–457. Frankfurt am Main: Campus, 1999.

Lappin, Eleonore. "The Death Marches of Hungarian Jews through Austria in the Spring of 1945." *Yad Vashem Studies* 28 (2000): 203–242.

———. "Der Weg ungarischer Juden nach Theresienstadt." *Theresienstädter Studien und Dokumente* (1996): 52–81.

———. "Dic Todesmärsche ungarischer Jüdinnen und Juden aus Ungarn nach Mauthausen im zeitgeschichtlichen Kontext." In Heimo Halbrainer and Christian

Ehetreiber, eds., *Todesmarsch Eisenstraße 1945: Terror, Handlungsspielräume, Erinnerung: Menschliches Handeln unter Zwangsbedingungen*, pp. 59–94. Graz, Austria: Clio, 2005.

———. "Todesmärsche im Reichsgau Oberdonau." In Sigfried Haider and Gerhart Marckhgott, eds., *Oberösterreichische Gedenkstätten für KZ-Opfer*, pp. 77–91. Linz: Kulturland Oberöstreich, 2001.

———. "Ungarisch-jüdische Zwangsarbeiter in Österreich 1944/45." In Martha Keil and Eleonore Lappin, eds., *Studien zur Geschichte der Juden in Österreich*, pp. 141–168. Bodenheim, Germany: Philo, 1997.

Lasik, Alexander. "The Auschwitz SS Garrison." In Wacław Długoborski and Franciszek Piper, eds., *Auschwitz 1940–1945*, vol. I, pp. 281–337. Auschwitz: Auschwitz-Birkenau State Museum, 2000.

———. "Organizational Structure of Auschwitz Concentration Camp." In Wacław Długoborski and Franciszek Piper, eds., *Auschwitz 1940–1945*, vol. I, pp. 145–280. Auschwitz: Auschwitz-Birkenau State Museum, 2000.

Leff, Laurel. *Buried by the Times: The Holocaust and America's Most Important Newspaper*. New York: Cambridge University Press, 2005.

Leszczyńska, Zofia. "Transporty więźniów chorych i kalek przeniesonych z obozu konczentracyjnego Dachau na Majdanek 7 stycnia 1944 roku." *Zeszyty Majdanka* 10 (1980): 135–183.

———. "Transporty więźniów do obozu koncentrancyjnym Majdanku." *Zeszyty Majdanka* 4 (1969): 174–232.

Leszczyńska, Zofia, and Edward Dziadosz. "Ewakuacja obozy i wyzwolenie." In T. Mencla, ed., *Majdanek 1941–1944*, pp. 399–404. Lublin: Wydawnictwo Lubelskie, 1991.

Levene, Mark. "Introduction." In Mark Levene and Penny Roberts, eds., *The Massacre in History*, pp. 1–38. New York: Berghahn Books, 1999.

Liebman, Stuart, and Annette Michelson. "After the Fall: Women in the House of the Hangmen." *October* 72 (Spring 1995): 5–14.

Lifton, Robert Jay. *The Nazi Doctors. Medical Killing and the Psychology of Genocide*. New York: Basic Books, 1986.

Longerich, Peter. "Joseph Goebbels und der totale Krieg: Eine unbekannte Denkschrift des Propagandaministers vom 18. Juli 1944." *Vierteljahreshefte für Zeitgeschichte* 35:2 (1987): 299–314.

———. *Politik der Vernichtung: Eine Gesamtdarstellung der nationalsozialistischen Judenverfolgung*. Munich: Piper, 1998.

Lower, Wendy. *Nazi Empire-Building and the Holocaust in Ukraine*. Chapel Hill: University of North Carolina Press, 2005.

Ludendorff, Erich. *Der totale Krieg*. Munich: Ludendorff Verlag, 1935.

Lusane, Clarence. *Hitler's Black Victims: The Historical Experience of Afro-Germans, European Blacks, Africans, and African Americans in the Nazi Era*. New York: Routledge, 2003.

Lutfi, Gabriele. *KZ der Gestapo: Arbeitserziehungslager im Dritten Reich*. Stuttgart: Deutsche Verlags-Anstalt, 2000.

MacDonald, Callum. *The Killing of SS Obergruppenführer Reinhard Heydrich*. New York: The Free Press, 1989.

Mackness, Robin. *Massacre at Oradur*. New York: Random House, 1988.

Madajczyk, Czesław. *Politika III Rzeszy w okupowanej Polsce,* vol. I. Warsaw: Państwowe Wydawnictwo Naukowe, 1970.

Malá, Irena, and Ludmila Kubátová. *Pochody Smrti.* Prague: Nakladatelství politické literatury, 1965.

Mammach, Klaus. *Der Volkssturm: Das letzte Aufgebot 1944/45.* Cologne: Pahl-Rugenstein, 1981.

Mann, Michael. "Were the Perpetrators of Genocide 'Ordinary Men' or 'Real Nazis'? Results from Fifteen Hundred Biographies." *Holocaust and Genocide Studies* 14:3 (2000): 331–366.

Marczewska, Krystyna, and Władysław Ważniewski. "Obóz koncentracyjny na Majdanku w świetle akt Delegatura Rządu RP na Kraj." *Zeszyty Majdanka* 20 (1999): 139–226.

Margaliot, Avraham, and Yehoyakim Cochavi, eds. *Toldot HaShoah: Germania* [Annals of the Holocaust: Germany], vol. I. Jerusalem: Yad Vashem, 1998.

Margry, Karel. "The Gardelegen Massacre." *After the Battle* 111 (2000): 3–27.

Markusen, Eric, and David Kopf. *The Holocaust and Strategic Bombing: Genocide and Total War in the 20th Century.* Boulder, CO: Westview Press, 1995.

Markusen, Eric, and Damir Mirkovic. "Understanding Genocidal Killing in Former Yugoslavia: Preliminary Observations." In Craig Summers and Eric Markusen, eds., *Collective Violence: Harmful Behavior in Groups and Governments,* pp. 35–67. Lanham, MD: Rowman & Littlefield, 1999.

Maršálek, Hans. *Die Vergasungsaktionen im Konzentrationslager Mauthausen: Dokumentation.* Vienna: Steinde-Druck, 1988.

———. *The History of Mauthausen Concentration Camp: Documentation.* Linz: Gutenberg-Werbering, 1995.

Marszałek, Józef. *Obozy Pracy w Generalnym Gubernatorstwie w latach 1939–1945.* Lublin: Państwowe Muzeum na Majdanku, 1998.

Mason, Timothy W. *Social Politics in the Third Reich: The Working Class and the "National Community."* Providence, RI: Berg, 1993.

Matthäus, Jürgen. "What about the 'Ordinary Men'? The German Order Police and the Holocaust in the Occupied Soviet Union." *Holocaust and Genocide Studies* 10:2 (1996): 134–150.

Mayntz, Renate. "Chaos in Society: Reflections on the Impact of Chaos Theory on Sociology." In Celso Grebogi and James A. Yorke, eds., *The Impact of Chaos on Science and Society,* pp. 298–323. Tokyo: United Nations University Press, 1997.

Merridale, Catherine. *Ivan's War: Life and Death in the Red Army, 1939–1945.* New York: Metropolitan Books, 2006.

Miethe, Anna Dora, ed. *Gedenkstätten: Arbeiterbewegung, Antifaschistischer Widerstand, Aufbau des Sozialismus.* Leipzig: Urania Verlag, 1974.

Mołdawa, Mieczysław. *Groß Rosen: Obóz koncentracyjny na Śląsku.* Warsaw: Wydawnictwo Ministerstwa Obrony Narodowej, 1980.

Moltmann, Günter. "Goebbels' Speech on Total War, February 18, 1943." In Hajo Holborn, ed., *Republic to Reich: The Making of Nazi Revolution,* pp. 298–342. New York: Pantheon Books, 1973.

Mommsen, Hans. "The Dissolution of the Third Reich: Crisis Management and Collapse, 1943–1945." *Bulletin of the German Historical Institute* 27 (2000): 9–23, http://www.ghi-dc.org/bulletin27f00/b27mommsenframe.html (accessed February 18, 2010).

Morsch, Günter. "Oranienburg-Sachsenhausen, Sachsenhausen-Oranienburg." In Ulrich Herbert, Karin Orth, and Christoph Dieckmann, eds., *Die nationalsozialistischen Konzentrationslager. Entwicklung und Struktur,* vol. I, pp. 101–134. Göttingen: Wallstein Verlag, 1998.

Mosse, George L. *Nazi Culture: Intellectual, Cultural, and Social Life in the Third Reich.* Madison: University of Wisconsin Press, 1966.

Müller, Delia, and Madlen Lepschies. *Tage der Angst und der Hoffnung: Erinnerungen an die Todesmärsche aus dem Frauen-Konzentrationslager Ravensbrück Ende April 1945.* Berlin: Impressum, 2001.

Müller, Rolf-Dieter. *Hitler's Ostkrieg und die deutsche Siedlungspolitik.* Frankfurt am Main: Fischer, 1991.

Musial, Bogdan. *Deutsche Zivilverwaltung und Judenverfolgung im Generalgouvernement: Eine Fallstudie zum Distrikt Lublin 1939–1945.* Wiesbaden: Harrassowitz, 1999.

Naimark, Norman M. *The Russians in Germany: A History of the Soviet Zone of Occupation, 1945–1949.* Cambridge, MA: Belknap Press of Harvard University Press, 1995.

Neander, Joachim. "Das Konzentrationslager 'Mittelbau' in der Endphase der NS-Dikatatur." PhD diss., University of Bremen, 1996.

———. *Die Letzten von Dora im Gebiet Osterode: Zur Geschichte eines KZ-Evakuierungsmarsches im April 1945.* Nordhausen: Schriftenreihe der KZ-Gedenkstätte Mittelbau-Dora, 1994.

———. *Gardelegen 1945: Das Ende der Häftlingstransporte aus dem Konzentrationslager "Mittelbau."* Magdeburg: Landeszentrale für politische Bildung Sachsen-Anhalt, 1998.

———. *"Hat in Europa kein annäherndes Beispiel": Mittelbau-Dora—ein KZ für Hitlers Krieg.* Berlin: Metropol, 2000.

Neurath, Paul Martin. *The Society of Terror: Inside the Dachau and Buchenwald Concentration Camps.* Boulder, CO: Paradigm Publishers, 2005.

Noakes, Jeremy. "'Viceroys of the Reich?' Gauleiters 1925–45." In Anthony McElligott and Tim Kirk, eds., *Working toward the Führer: Essays in Honour of Sir Ian Kershaw,* pp. 118–152. Manchester: Manchester University Press, 2003.

Obenaus, Herbert. "Die Räumung der hannoverschen Konzentrationslager im April 1945." In Rainer Fröbe, Claus Füllberg-Stolberg, Christoph Gutman, Rolf Keller, Herbert Obenaus, and Hans Hermann Schröder, eds., *Konzentrationslager in Hannover: KZ-Arbeit und Rüstungsindustrie in der Spätphase des Zweiten Weltkriegs,* vol. II, pp. 493–544. Hildesheim: Verlag August Lax, 1985.

———. "Konzentrationslager und Rüstungswirtschaft: Der Einsatz von KZ-Häftlingen in den Industriebetrieben Hannovers." In Ludwig Eiber, ed., *Verfolgung—Ausbeutung—Vernichtung: Die Lebens- und Arbeitsbedingungen in deutschen Konzentrationslagern 1933–1945,* pp. 160–183. Hanover: Fackelträger, 1985.

Orski, Marek. *The Last Days of Stutthof.* Gdańsk: Muzeum Stutthof w Sztutowie, 1995.

Orth, Karin. *Das System der nationalsozialistischen Konzentrationslager: Eine politische Organisationsgeschichte.* Hamburg: Hamburger Edition, 1999.

———. *Die Konzentrationslager-SS: Sozialstrukturelle Analysen und Biographische Studien.* Göttingen: Wallstein Verlag, 2000.

———. "Experten des Terrors: Die Konzentrationslager-SS und die Shoah." In Gerhard Paul, ed., *Die Täter der Shoah: Fanatische Nationalsozialisten oder ganz normale Deutsche?* pp. 93–108. Göttingen: Wallstein Verlag, 2002.

Ortner, Christian S. *Marzabotto: The Crimes of Walter Reder—SS-Sturmbannführer.* Vienna: Dokumentationsarchiv des österreichischen Widerstandes, 1986.

Overesch, Manfred. *Buchenwald und die DDR, oder Suche nach Selbstlegitimation.* Göttingen: Vandenhoeck and Ruprecht, 1995.

Overmans, Rüdiger. *Deutsche militärische Verluste im Zweiten Weltkrieg.* Munich: R. Oldenbourg, 1999.

Overy, Richard. *The Dictators: Hitler's Germany, Stalin's Russia.* New York: W. W. Norton, 2004.

Paul, Gerhard. "Von Psychopathen, Technokraten des Terrors und 'ganz gewöhnlichen Deutschen': Die Täter der Shoa im Spiegel der Forschung." In Gerhard Paul, ed., *Die Täter der Shoah: Fanatische Nationalsozialisten oder ganz normale Deutsche?* pp. 13–90. Göttingen: Wallstein Verlag, 2002.

Peukert, Detlev J. K. *Inside Nazi Germany: Conformity, Opposition, and Racism in Everyday Life.* New Haven, CT: Yale University Press, 1987.

Pike, David W. *Mauthausen: L'enfer nazi en Autriche.* Toulouse: Privat, 2004.

———. *Spaniards in the Holocaust: Mauthausen, the Horror on the Danube.* London: Routledge, 2000.

Pingel, Falk. *Häftlinge unter SS-Herrschaft: Widerstand, Selbstbehauptung und Vernichtung im Konzentrationslager.* Hamburg: Hoffman und Campe, 1978.

Piper, Franciszek. *Auschwitz Prisoner Labor.* Auschwitz: Auschwitz-Birkenau State Museum, 2002.

———. "Das Nebenlager Blechhammer." *Hefte von Auschwitz* 12 (1971): 19–39.

———. "The Methods of Mass Murder." In Wacław Długoborski and Franciszek Piper, eds., *Auschwitz 1940–1945,* vol. III, pp. 63–204. Auschwitz: Auschwitz-Birkenau State Museum, 2000.

———. "The Origins of the Camp." In Wacław Długoborski and Franciszek Piper, eds., *Auschwitz 1940–1945,* vol. I. pp. 39–62. Auschwitz: Auschwitz-Birkenau State Museum, 2000.

Pohl, Dieter. "Die großen Zwangsarbeitslager der SS und Polizeiführer für Juden im Generalgouvernement 1942–1945." In Ulrich Herbert, Karin Orth, and Christoph Dieckmann, eds., *Die nationalsozialistischen Konzentrationslager: Entwicklung und Struktur,* vol. I, pp. 415–438. Göttingen: Wallstein Verlag, 1998.

———. "Die Holocaust-Forschung und Goldhagens Thesen." *Vierteljahreshefte für Zeitgeschichte* 1 (1997): 1–48.

———. *Nationalsozialistische Judenverfolgung in Ostgalizien 1941–1944.* Munich: R. Oldenbourg, 1997.

Polian, Pavel. "La violence contre les prisoniers de guerre soviétiques dans le IIIe Reich et en USSR." In Stéphane Audoin-Rouzeau, Annette Becker, Christain Ingrao, and Henry Rousso, eds., *La Violence de guerre 1914–1945,* pp. 117–131. Brussels: Éditions Complexe, IHTP-CNRS, 2002.

Poloncarz, Marek. "Die Evakuierungstransporte nach Theresienstadt (April–Mai 1945)." *Theresienstädter Studien und Dokumente* (1999): 242–262.

Poprzeczny, Joseph. *Odilio Globocnik: Hitler's Man in the East.* Jefferson, NC: Mc-Farland & Co., 2004.

Power, Samantha. *"A Problem from Hell": America and the Age of Genocide.* New York: HarperCollins, 2002.

Poznanski, Renée. *Jews in France during World War II.* Hanover, NH: University Press of New England, 2001.

Prais, Lea. "Plitim BeMirkam HaKhayim HaYehudim BaIr Varsha *UbaGetto* September 1939–July 1942" [Refugees in the fabric of Jewish life in the city of Warsaw and the ghetto, September 1939–July 1942]. PhD diss., The Hebrew University of Jerusalem, 2006.

Prusin, Alexander V. "Revolution and Ethnic Cleansing in Western Ukraine: The OUN-UPA Assault against Polish Settlements in Volhynia and Eastern Galicia, 1943–1944." In Steven Béla Várdy and T. Hunt Tooly, eds., *Ethnic Cleansing in Twentieth-Century Europe,* pp. 517–535. New York: Social Science Monographs, 2003.

Raim, Edith. *Die Dachauer KZ-Außenkommandos Kaufering und Mühldorf: Rüstungsbauten und Zwangsarbeit im letzen Kriegsjahr 1944/45.* Landsberg: Martin Neumeyer, 1992.

Reibel, Carl-Wilhelm. *Das Fundament der Diktatur: Die NSDAP-Ortsgruppen 1932–1935,* Paderborn: Ferdinand Schöningh, 2002.

Reid, James J. "Total War, the Annihilation Ethic, and the Armenian Genocide, 1870–1918." In Richard G. Hovannisian, ed., *The Armenian Genocide: History, Politics, Ethics,* pp. 21–42. New York: St. Martin's Press, 1992.

Reilly, Joanne. *Belsen: The Liberation of a Concentration Camp.* London: Routledge, 1998.

Rempel, Gerhard. *Hitler's Children: The Hitler's Youth and the SS.* Chapel Hill: University of North Carolina Press, 1989.

Rogowski, Ronald. "The Gauleiter and the Social Origins of Fascism." *Comparative Studies in Society and History* 19:4 (1977): 399–430.

Rohde, David. *Endgame: The Betrayal and the Fall of Srebrenica, Europe's Worst Massacre since World War II.* New York: Farrar, Straus & Giroux, 1997.

Rossino, Alexander B. *Hitler Strikes Poland: Blitzkrieg, Ideology, and Atrocity.* Lawrence: University Press of Kansas, 2003.

Roth, Claudia. *Parteikreis und Kreisleiter der NSDAP unter besonderer Berücksichtigung Bayerns.* Munich: C. H. Beck, 1997.

Rotkirchen, Livia. "The 'Final Solution' in Its Last Stages." *Yad Vashem Studies* 8 (1970): 7–29.

Rummel, Rudolph J. *Death by Government.* New Brunswick, NJ: Transaction Publishers, 1994.

Rutkowski, Adam. "Le camp de concentration pour Juifs á Varsovie (19 juillet 1943–5 août 1944)." *Le Monde Juif* 119 (1985): 87–114.

Sandkühler, Thomas. "Die Täter des Holocaust: Neuere Überlegungen und Kontroversen." In Karl H. Paul, ed., *Wehrmacht und Vernichtungspolitk: Miltiär im nationalsozialistischen System,* pp. 39–65. Göttingen: Vandenhoeck und Ruprecht, 1999.

Schäfer, Christine. "Evakuierungstransporte des KZ Buchenwald und seiner Außenkommandos." *Buchenwaldhefte* 16 (1983): 7–95.

Schley, Jens. *Nachbar Buchenwald: Die Stadt Weimar und ihr Konzentrationslager 1937–1945*. Cologne: Böhlau Verlag, 1999.

Schmädeke, Jürgen, and Peter Steinbach, eds. *Der Widerstand gegen den National-sozialismus: Die deutsche Gesellschaft und der Widerstand gegen Hitler*. Munich: R. Piper, 1985.

Schulte, Jan Erik. *Zwangsarbeit und Vernichtung: Das Wirtschaftsimperium der SS: Oswald Pohl und das SS-Wirtschafts-Verwaltungshauptamt 1933–1945*. Pader-born: Ferdinand Schöningh, 2001.

Schwartz, Eliezer. "Yehudim KeOvdey Kefiya BaTaasiya HaBitchonit BeShitchey HaReich: HaMikre Shel Thil VeKochendorf (1944–1945)." [Jewish forced labor in the German Armaments industry: A case study of Thil and Kochendorf (1944–1945)]. *Dapim, Studies on the Holocaust* 23 (2009): 47–80.

Schwartz, Gudrun. *Die nationalsozialistischen Lager*. Frankfurt am Main: Fischer, 1996.

———. "SS-Aufseherinnen in nationalsozialistischen Konzentrationslagern (1933–1945)." *Dachauer Hefte* 10 (November 1994): 32–49.

Seidler, Franz W. *"Deutscher Volkssturm" Das letzte Aufgebeot 1944/1945*. Mu-nich: Bechtermünz Verlag, 1999.

Sellier, André. *A History of the Dora Camp*. Chicago: Ivan R. Dee, 2003.

Sémelin, Jacques. "In Consideration of Massacres." *Journal of Genocide Research* 3:3 (2001): 377–389.

———. *Purifier et détruire: Usages politiques des massacres et génocides*. Paris: Seuil, 2005.

———. "Toward a Vocabulary of Massacre and Genocide." *Journal of Genocide Research* 5:2 (2003): 377–389.

Semmler, Rudolf. *Goebbels, the Man Next to Hitler*. London: Westhouse, 1947.

Seubert, Rolf. "A Country That Feels No Guilt or Shame. Das Ende des 'Dritten Reichs' im US-Magazin 'Life.'" *Diagonal, Zeitschrift der Universität-Gesamthochschule-Siegen* 2 (1996): 85–103.

Seydewitz, Max. *Civil Life in Wartime Germany: The Story of the Home Front*. New York: Viking Press, 1945.

Siegert, Toni. "Das Konzentrationslager Flossenbürg: Ein Lager für sogenannte Aso-ziale und Kriminelle." In Martin Broszat and Elke Fröhlich, eds., *Bayern in der NS-Zeit*, vol. II, pp. 429–492. Munich: R. Oldenbourg, 1979.

———. *30000 Tote mahnen! Die Geschichte des Konzentrationslagers Flossenbürg und seiner 100 Außenlager von 1938 bis 1945*. Weiden: Verlag der Taubald'schen Buchhandlung, 1984.

Silberklang, David. "HaShoah BeMakhoz Lublin" [The Holocaust in Lublin dis-trict]. PhD diss., The Hebrew University of Jerusalem, 2003.

Snyder, Timothy. "The Causes of Ukrainian-Polish Ethnic Cleansing, 1943." *Past and Present* 79 (May 2003): 197–234.

Sofsky, Wolfgang. "An der Grenze des Sozialen: Perspektiven der KZ-Forschung." In Ulrich Herbert, Karin Orth, and Christoph Dieckamnn, eds., *Die nationalsozialis-tischen Konzentrationslager: Entwicklung und Struktur*, vol. II, pp. 1141–1169. Göttingen: Wallstein Verlag, 1998.

———. *The Order of Terror: The Concentration Camp*. Princeton, NJ: Princeton University Press, 1997.

Speer, Albert. *The Slave State: Heinrich Himmler's Masterplan for SS Supremacy.* London: Weidenfeld & Nicolson, 1981.

Spielman, Jochen. "Denkmal in Bewegung—Der Wandel von Gestalt, Widmung und Funktion von Denkmalen in ehemaligen Konzentrations-und Vernichtungslagern 1945–1991—Ein Überblick." In Thomas Lutz, Wulff E. Brebeck, and Nicolas Hepp, eds., *Über-Lebens-Mittel: Kunst aus Konzentrationslagern und in Gedenkstätten für Opfer des Nationalsozialismus,* pp. 103–130. Marburg: Jonas Verlag, 1992.

Sprenger, Isabell. *Groß-Rosen: Ein Konzentrationslager in Schlesien.* Cologne: Böhlau Verlag, 1996.

Staron, Joachim. *Fosse Ardeatine und Marzabotto: Deutsche Kriegsverbrechen und Resistenza.* Paderborn: Ferdinand Schöningh, 2002.

Steegmann, Robert. *Struthof: Le KL-Natzweiler et ses Kommandos: Une nébuleuse concentrationnaire des deux côtés du Rhin, 1941–1945.* Strasburg: Nuée Bleue, 2005.

Stein, Hans. "Funktionswandel des Konzentrationslagers Buchenwald im Spiegel der Lagerstatistiken." In Ulrich Herbert, Karin Orth, and Christoph Dieckmann, eds., *Die nationalsozialistischen Konzentrationslager: Entwicklung und Struktur,* vol. I, pp. 167–192. Göttingen: Wallstein Verlag, 1998.

Steinbacher, Sybille. *Dachau—Die Stadt und das Konzentrationslager in der NS-Zeit: Die Untersuchung einer Nachbarschaft.* Frankfurt am Main: Peter Lang, 1993.

Steinert, Marlis G. *Hitler's War and the Germans.* Athens: Ohio University Press, 1977.

Stelbrink, Wolfgang. "Die Kreisleiter der NSDAP in den beiden westfälischen Parteigauen." In Michael Ruck and Karl Heinrich Pohl, eds., *Regionen im Nationalsozialismus,* pp. 157–187. Bielefeld: Verlag für Regionalgeschichte, 2003.

———. *Die Kreisleiter der NSDAP in Westfalen und Lippe: Versuch einer Kollektivbiographie mit biographischem Anhang.* Münster: Nordrhein-Westfälisches Staatarchiv, 2003.

Strebel, Bernhard. *Das KZ Ravensbrück: Geschichte eines Lagerkomplexes.* Paderborn: Ferdinand Schöningh, 2003.

———. "Das Männerlager im KZ Ravensbrück 1941–1945." *Dachauer Hefte* 14 (1998): 141–174.

———. "Ravensbrück—das zentrale Frauenkonzentrationslager." In Ulrich Herbert, Karin Orth, and Christoph Dieckmann, eds., *Die nationalsozialistischen Konzentrationslager: Entwicklung und Struktur,* vol. I, pp. 215–258. Göttingen: Wallstein Verlag, 1998.

Streim, Alfred. "Konzentrationslager auf dem Gebiet der Sowjetunion." *Dachauer Hefte* 5 (November 1989): 174–187.

Strzelecka, Irena, and Tadeusz Szymański. "Podobozy Tschechowitz-Bombensuchkommando i Tschechowitz-Vacuum." *Zeszyty Oświęcimskie* 18 (1983): 187–222.

Strzelecki, Andrzej. *The Evacuation, Dismantling and Liberation of KL Auschwitz.* Auschwitz. Auschwitz-Birkenau State Museum, 2001.

———. "The Liquidation of the Camp." In Wacław Długoborski and Franciszek Piper, eds., *Auschwitz 1940–1945,* vol. V, pp. 9–85. Auschwitz: Auschwitz-Birkenau State Museum, 2000.

Stutthof: Hitlerowski obóz koncentracyjny. Warsaw: Wydawnictwo Interpress, 1988.

Sula, Dorota. *Arbeitslager Riese: Filia KL Groß-Rosen.* Wałbrzych: Muzeum Groß-Rosen, 2003.

Syndor, Charles W., Jr. *Soldiers of Destruction: The SS Death's Head Division, 1933–1945.* Princeton, NJ: Princeton University Press, 1990.

Szita, Szabolcs. "Die Todesmärsche der Budapester Juden im November 1944 nach Hegyeshalom-Nickelsdorf." *Zeitgeschichte* 3–4 (1995): 124–137.

———. "The Forced Labor of Hungarian Jews at the Fortification of the Western Border Regions of Hungary, 1944–45." In Randolph L. Braham, ed., *Studies on the Holocaust in Hungary,* pp. 175–193. New York: Social Science Monographs, 1990.

Tillion, Germaine. *Ravensbrück.* Paris: Seuil, 1988.

Todorov, Tzvetan. *Une tragédie française: Été 1944: scènes de guerre civile.* Paris: Seuil, 1994.

Tuchel, Johannes. "Organisationsgeschichte der 'frühen' Konzentrationslager." In Wolfgang Benz and Barbara Distel, eds., *Der Ort des Terrors: Geschichte der nationalsozialistischen Konzentrationslager,* vol. I, pp. 43–57. Munich: C. H. Beck, 2005.

———. "Planung und Realität des Systems der Konzentrationslager 1934–1938." In Ulrich Herbert, Katrin Orth, and Christoph Dieckmann, eds., *Die nationalsozialistischen Konzentrationslager: Entwicklung und Struktur,* vol. I, pp. 43–59. Göttingen: Wallstein Verlag, 1998.

Uekert, Brenda K. *Rivers of Blood: A Comparative Study of Government Massacres.* Westport, CT: Praeger, 1995.

Vanselow, Gerd. *KZ Hersbruck: Größtes Außenlager von Flossenbürg.* Bonn: Karl Pfeiffer Buchdruckerei und Verlag, 1983.

Veigel, Kathrin. "Gardelegen 13/14. April 1945: Rekonstruktion eines NS-Verbrechens." MA thesis, Technical University of Berlin, 2001.

Wachsmann, Nikolaus. "'Annihilation through Labor': The Killing of State Prisoners in the Third Reich." *Journal of Modern History* 71:3 (1999): 624–659.

———. *Hitler's Prison: Legal Terror in Nazi Germany.* New Haven, CT: Yale University Press, 2004.

———. "Looking into the Abyss: Historians and the Nazi Concentration Camps." *European History Quarterly* 36:2 (2006): 247–278.

Wagner, Jens-Christian. "Gesteuertes Sterben: Die Boelcke-Kaserne als zentrales Siechenlager des KZ Mittelbau." *Dachauer Hefte* 20 (October 2004): 127–138.

———. "Noch einmal: Arbeit und Vernichtung. Häftlingseinsatz im KL Mittelbau-Dora 1943–1945." In Norbert Frei, Sybille Steinbacher, and Bernd C. Wagner, eds., *Ausbeutung, Vernichtung, Öffentlichkeit: Neue Studien zur nationalsozialistischen Lagerpolitik,* pp. 11–41. Munich: Institut für Zeitgeschichte, K. G. Sauer, 2000.

———. *Produktion des Todes: Das KZ Mittelbau-Dora.* Göttingen: Wallstein Verlag, 2001.

Weigelt, Andreas. "Jüdischer Häftlingseinsatz für das SS-Führungshauptamt: Der SS-Truppenübungsplatz 'Kurmark' und das KZ-Nebenlager 'Arbeitslager Lieberose' in Jamlitz 1944–45." In Winfried Meyer and Klaus Neitmann, eds., *Zwang-sarbeit während der NS-Zeit in Berlin und Brandenburg,* pp. 177–189. Potsdam: Verlag für Berlin-Brandenburg, 2001.

———. "'Komm, geh mit! Wir gehn zum Judenerschießen . . .': Massenmord bei der Auflösung des KZ-Außenlagers Lieberose im Februar 1945." *Dachauer Hefte* 20 (December 2004): 179–193.

Weinberg, Gerhard L. *A World at Arms: A Global History of World War II,* new ed. New York: Cambridge University Press, 2005.

Weiser, Piotr. "Transport z Majdanku do Gross-Rosen 6 kwietnia 1944 roku." *Zeszyty Majdanka* 27 (2003): 241–304.

Wenke, Alexandra-Eileen. *Zwischen Menschenhandel und "Endlöung": Das Konzen-trationslager Bergen-Belsen.* Paderborn: Ferdinand Schöningh, 2000.

Wette, Wolframe. "Zur Psychologischen Mobilmachung der deutschen Bevölkerung 1933–1939." In Wolfgang Michalka, ed., *Der Zweite Weltkrieg: Analysen-Grundzüge-Forschungsbilanz,* pp. 205–223. Munich: Piper, 1989.

Whealey, Robert H. *Hitler and Spain: The Nazi Role in the Spanish Civil War.* Lex-ington: University Press of Kentucky, 1989.

Wieland, Günther. "Die Ahndung von NS-Verbrechen in Ostdeutschland 1945–1990." In *DDR-Justiz und NS-Verbrechen,* vol. I, pp. 13–99. Amsterdam: Amster-dam University Press, 2002.

Winkler, Döte. "Frauenarbeit versus Frauenideologie: Probleme der weiblichen Erw-erbstätigkeit in Deutschland 1930–1945." *Archiv für Sozialgeschichte* 17 (1977): 99–126.

Wolff, Georg. "Kalendarium der Geschichte des KZ Sachsenhausen-Strafverfolgung." *Sachsenhausen* 3 (1987): 5–71.

Wright, Burton. "Army of Despair: The German Volkssturm 1944–1945." PhD diss., Florida State University, 1982.

Yelton, David K. *Hitler's Volkssturm: The Nazi Militia and the Fall of Germany 1944–1945.* Lawrence: University Press of Kansas, 2002.

Zámečnik, Stanislav. *C'était ça, Dachau 1933–1945.* Paris: Fondation internationale de Dachau, 2003.

———. "Dachau-Stammlager." In Wolfgang Benz and Barbara Distel, eds., *Der Ort des Terrors: Geschichte der nationalsozialistischen Konzentrationslager,* vol. II, pp. 233–374. Munich: C. H. Beck, 2005.

———. "'Kein Häftling darf lebend in die Hände des Feindes fallen': Zur Existenz des Himmler-Befehls vom 14/18 April 1945." *Dachauer Hefte* 1 (December 1985): 219–231.

Żbikowski, Andrej. *U genezy Jedwabnego: Żydzi na Kresach Północno-Wschodnich II Rzeczypospolitej, wrzesień 1939—lipiec 1941.* Warsaw: Żydowski Instytut Historyczny, 2006.

Zeiger, Antje. "Die Todesmärsche." In *Befreiung Sachsenhausen 1945,* pp. 64–72. Berlin: Edition Hentrich, 1996.

Ziegler, Thilo. "Konzentrationslager im Kreis Sangerhausen." *Spengler-Museum Sangerhausen, Beiträge zur Heimatforschung* 4 (1975): 21–32.

Zimmermann, John. "Die Kämpfe gegen die Westalliierten 1945—Ein Kampf bis zum Ende oder Kreierung einer Legende?" In Jörg Hillmann and John Zimmermann, eds., *Kriegsende 1945 in Deutschland,* pp. 115–133. Munich: R. Oldenbourg, 2002.

Zonik, Zygmunt. *Anus belli: Ewakuacja i wyzwolenie hitlerowskich obozów koncentracyjnch.* Warsaw: Państwowe Wydawnictwo Naukowe, 1988.

Zorn, Monika, ed. *Hitlers zweimal getötete Opfer: Westdeutsche Endlösung des Antifaschismus auf dem Gebiet der DDR.* Freiburg: Ahriman Verlag, 1994.

Internet Sites

The Buchenwald-Dachau death train. http://www.scrapbookpages.com/Dachau Scrapbook/DachauLiberation/DeathTrain2.html.

The Celle massacre trial. http://www.celle-im-nationalsozialismus.de/Texte/Presse _Treibjagd.html.

David Boder collection of testimonies, 1946. http://voices.iit.edu/.

Deposition of Dieter Wisliceny. http://www.ess.uwe.ac.uk/genocide/Wisliceny.html.

The Dora-Nordhausen trial (Arthur-Kurt Andrae). http://www.archives.gov/research/ captured-german-records/microfilm/m1019.pdf.

The Gardelegen massacre. http://www.scrapbookpages.com/Gardelegen/index.html.

Gardelegen memorial site. http://www.scrapbookpages.com/Gardelegen/Memorial Site01.html.

Hessental Camp. http://www.kz-hessental.de/Ge_fr.html.

History of Gardelegen. http://www.gardelegen.info/uk/geschichte_staatgeschichte .html.

History of Schwarzenfeld. http://de.wikipedia.org/wiki/Schwarzenfeld.

House of Commons Report on the massacre and ethnic cleansing in Darfur, Sudan. http://www.parliament.uk/commons/lib/research/rp2004/rp04–051/pdf.

The 102nd in combat in Germany, 1944–1945. http://www.102ndinfantrydivision .homestead.com/history.html.

102nd Infantry Division. http://www.102ndinfantrydivision.homestead.com/Gardele gen.html.

Report of commission of inquiry of the Netherlands Institute of War Documentation (NIOD), Amsterdam. http://www.srebrenica.nl.

The United States Army Air Forces in World War II. Chronology of operational activity. http://www.usaaf.net/chron/45/mar45.htm.

Acknowledgments

This book started out on its lengthy journey during a conversation with my teacher (and later close friend) Professor Yehuda Bauer. I had recently completed my doctorate and was taking my first steps as teacher and researcher at the Hebrew University, and naturally enough, our discussion revolved around the developments in Holocaust studies. Yehuda Bauer asked me about my plans, and when I replied that I had not yet formulated them he stood up, went over to a bookshelf, and took out a file bulging with photocopies of documents, articles, and handwritten notes, and said, "Take it, it's time someone started to work on the death marches. I've collected a little material, perhaps it will interest you."

Quite a few years have elapsed since then. Because of the need to settle into academic teaching, and other research occupations, my work on the death marches was consigned to periods when I was not teaching, and then not consecutively. The archival material piled up, and in 2002 I began to devote most of my free time to this study. That year I also received more than a thousand pages of the investigation into the massacre of concentration camp prisoners at Gardelegen. I realized then that, until that moment, I had not been clearly aware of the complexity of the historical issue I was studying.

Over the years I benefited from the assistance of many institutions and individuals. I took my first steps as a research fellow at the International Institute for Holocaust Research at Yad Vashem, a period of great import for the consolidation of the project. The Center for Advanced Holocaust Studies at the Holocaust Memorial Museum in Washington, D.C., placed research grants at my disposal in 1998 and 2006. The Center enabled me to work in archives and libraries, and the Holocaust Museum made it possible for me to devote an entire academic year to writing. The helpfulness, courtesy, and patience of the staff of the Museum library and archive were outstanding and unparalleled. I am grateful to all of them. I owe a special debt of gratitude to Paul Shapiro, director of the Center, who removed a considerable number of obstacles from my path; thanks to him the period I spent at the Center while writing was intensely rewarding. The semester I spent at the Skirball Department of Hebrew and Judaic Studies at New York University also enabled me to devote my time to research and writing.

The Israel Science Foundation placed at my disposal a three-year grant. It enabled me to carry out the complicated examination of archival material outside Israel at more than 20 archives in six European countries and in the United States. I could not have implemented this vast task without the dedicated and diligent aid of my research assistants: Mirjam Triendl (Austria); Marcus Gryglewski, Silke Struck, and Christa Schikkora (Germany); Jakub Petelewicz (Poland); and Barbara Lambauer (France). Anette Bernstein of the Gardelegen Museum opened the doors of the little municipal archive to me, a task that was by no means easy.

I am especially grateful to the scholar and script-writer Diana Gring, who studied the Gardelegen massacre in the 1990s and produced a documentary film on the affair. She placed at my disposal the collection of interviews she conducted and other documents she obtained. Yona Kovo of Yad Vashem made available to me various testimonies and documents that she collected while studying the death march of Jewish women from Helmbrechts. Two of my students at the Hebrew University were also of assistance: Shmuel Barnai in deciphering difficult handwriting in Russian and Leah Prais in locating and classifying important archival material at the Yad Vashem Archive. My thanks to all of them.

I conducted conversations and consultations with many friends and colleagues during my years of work on this book. Some of them enabled me to present my work at workshops and study days to researchers or advanced students in their universities or research institutes. These discussions made an inestimable contribution to the final crystallization of the book. Others read parts of the manuscript and offered valuable comments. In particular I would like to thank David Engel, Omer Bartov, Jan Tomasz Gross, Jürgen Mätthaus, Martin Dean, Annette Becker, Florent Brayard, Tony Judt, Ulrich Herbert, Peter Romjin, Henry Rousso, Michael Marrus, and Nechama Tec.

The dozens of staff members of archives and libraries without whom this study could never have been completed are too numerous to mention. I am deeply indebted to them for their goodwill and the vast assistance they extended to me and to my research assistants. Chaya Galai translated the complicated manuscript from Hebrew with impressive talent and skill, and Kathleen McDermott, senior editor at Harvard University Press, accompanied its publication with the utmost dedication and professionalism. My thanks to all of them. And, as always, while all these individuals have a share in the qualities of the final products, its flaws are mine alone.

My daughters, Naama and Nitzan, had only just emerged from adolescence when I began working on the study of the death marches, and by the time it was completed they were young women launched on independent lives. Nonetheless, their interest and support never waned. The moments of gratification, detachment, and joy, which were essential for me as I journeyed into the abyss of Nazi evil, were supplied throughout these years by all our grandchildren. Throughout the arduous voyage, my partner, Renée, not only supplied warmth and support but also pointed to the right direction at moments when it seemed that the road was blocked and impenetrable. Without her it would never have reached its end.

This book is dedicated to her.

Index